The Big Emerging Markets

1996 Outlook and Sourcebook

U.S. International Trade Administration
Ronald H. Brown, Secretary

≣BERNAN PRESS

Published by Bernan Press
in conjunction with
the National Technical Information Service

The Big Emerging Markets
1996 Outlook and Sourcebook

Bernan Press
4611-F Assembly Drive
Lanham, MD 20706-4391
(800) 865-3457
(301) 459-7666 (Outside North America)
e-mail: bems@kraus.com

ISBN 0-89059-053-2

Cover photo: Uniphoto, Inc.

Contents

The Americas

Tough policies and shrewd economic management have wrought an economic miracle over a mere four years. From an environment of 5,000 percent annual inflation and negative growth, Argentina has been transformed into a high-growth, low-inflation land of privatization and potential.

For years, the largest and most industrialized nation in Latin America has been known as the country of tomorrow, but under the guidance of current president and former finance minister Cardoso, tariffs and inflation have come down, with steady growth and further reform in the offing. Tomorrow may be here.

An excellent example of both the promise and peril of doing business in a Big Emerging Market, Mexico's future is brighter than ever in the post-NAFTA world. By sticking to its reform efforts and its engagement with trading partners despite a crisis, it revealed itself as a BEM determined to emerge.

Asia

Singapore, Indonesia, Thailand, Malaysia, the Philippines, Brunei and new-member Vietnam are the roaring, young Asian "Tigers" and "Tigers-to-Be" who will produce $1.1 trillion in GDP in less than a decade. Rapid growth, expanding purchasing power and falling import barriers make this region one of the most dynamic in the world.

Letter from the President

Dear Friends:

It has been almost two years since we announced the establishment of a new commercial strategy focusing on the overseas markets that hold the most promise for U.S. exports and investment over the long term. We selected 10 economies, designated them the Big Emerging Markets (BEMs), and designed a strategy aimed at encouraging commercial cooperation with the BEMs and helping U.S. firms seize the opportunities these markets offer. These 10 markets are expected to account for over 40 percent of total world imports and growth over the next 15 years.

Since that time, the BEMs Initiative has been instrumental in redefining our commercial relationships abroad, especially with these economies. The BEMs Initiative has become a cornerstone of our commercial and trade agenda.

The BEMs Initiative streamlines Administration resources to focus on the markets in which government involvement can truly make a difference for America's businesses and workers. Governments play a key role in deciding major contracts in the BEMs. If the U.S. government does not actively support U.S. businesses competing in these markets, we will lose contracts needlessly to our competitors who have the full support of their governments. That is why a critical component of the BEMs Initiative is our Administration-wide Advocacy Network, actively promoted through the Trade Promotion Coordinating Committee (TPCC). The highly successful trade missions of Secretary of Commerce Ronald H. Brown, Chairman of the TPCC, and other U.S. Cabinet Secretaries represents just one aspect of our aggressive advocacy efforts.

The BEMs Initiative is built on the premise that the private sector is the engine of economic growth, with government playing a supporting role. That is why a central aspect of our BEMs strategy focuses on developing strong private-public partnerships. We have already established Business Development Councils with five of the 10 BEMs, with plans to establish others.

A BEMs Internet Home Page will connect businesspeople in the U.S. with businesspeople in the BEMs, giving them access to trade information from the private sector, U.S. government and universities. This is truly a major step toward commercial integration worldwide.

This book lays out the Big Emerging Markets strategy. It contains information about the risks, challenges and obstacles that will be faced doing business in these economies and regions. It is designed as a practical guide to doing business in these dynamic markets.

I commend Secretary Brown for his efforts to help U.S. businesses seize opportunities in these markets, and for being such a strong advocate for U.S. business at home and abroad. Three years ago, I asked him to turn the Commerce Department into a powerhouse for U.S. business, and he has. As a result, countless jobs for American workers have been created. I urge him and his colleagues to continue their impressive work and to think boldly in developing the next, crucial phase of the BEMs Initiative.

In our expanding global economy, competition is fierce. I am determined that we fulfill our economic growth agenda at home, while meeting both our promise and our responsibilities as the world's economic leader.

William J. Clinton

Letter from the Secretary

Dear Friends:

I am pleased to introduce you to "The Big Emerging Markets." This book amply demonstrates why President Clinton has made trade a centerpiece of his foreign and domestic policy, and why the Big Emerging Markets (BEMs) are a key focus of our National Export Strategy.

The Clinton Administration has identified ten markets — the Chinese Economic Area (China, Hong Kong and Taiwan), India, ASEAN, South Korea, Mexico, Brazil, Argentina, South Africa, Poland and Turkey —in which opportunities for American businesses are particularly impressive. We have launched an aggressive effort to increase U.S. market share in these BEMs, to strengthen our relationships with them, and to improve cooperation between the U.S. and the BEMs on a wide range of issues related to our national interest.

Our success in these dynamic markets will largely determine the United States' position as the world's economic leader. Our ability to compete in these markets will assure that we have the economic strength and vitality essential to preserving our national security, and will further our ability to create high-wage, high-quality jobs for all Americans. The locus of world economic growth is shifting dramatically towards these markets of the future, and we as a nation must respond swiftly and aggressively if we hope to maintain our global competitiveness.

We are fortunate that we have the resources to compete — and to win. American workers are the most highly skilled and productive in the world, and American products are of the highest quality. Consequently, there is tremendous demand for American products and services in the BEMs — from large infrastructure projects in such sectors as power generation, transportation and telecommunications, to medical equipment, pollution control equipment, computer software, insurance and other financial services, and consumer goods.

Nevertheless, the task ahead is a daunting one. The traditions and demands of these markets may be unfamiliar to us. We may not have the ties of a common culture and language. We must navigate their government bureaucracies not only to win the initial contracts, but to receive the myriad permits, licenses and approvals necessary to bring the projects to fruition. Our competitors from other industrialized countries are frequently there on the ground ahead of us, and the playing field is often tilted in favor of domestic companies or those of competing nations.

That is why the U.S. Department of Commerce has a critical role to play in assisting U.S. businesses compete and win in the Big Emerging Markets. We serve as the partner and ally of American firms and American workers seeking to succeed in these markets — providing information, guidance, contacts and advocacy. Every one of the countries with which we are in fierce competition for these markets is providing similar — if not more aggressive — services to their own industries. If we do not match our competitors' efforts, we cede market share to them. If we do not actively support our companies, we do more than let them down. We handicap them. The U.S. government is a vital partner to U.S. industry as we seek to broaden our engagement in these markets.

There is no doubt that our efforts thus far have been effective. Through our National Export Strategy, we have leveraged a $250 million annual export promotion budget into at least $45 billion in overseas deals, with U.S. content of $20 billion supporting 300,000 jobs.

Still, this is just the beginning. To retain our competitive edge, to ensure that we remain the world's economic leader, we must increase our efforts and fight harder on behalf of U.S. business. This book makes a compelling case for why this effort is not only beneficial, but essential to the United States' economic strength and future. I hope you find it a useful guide.

Ronald H. Brown

Preface

Since the first days of our history Americans have been defined by and taken great pride in what we have called our "frontier spirit." Whether it was the spirit of native Americans building their nations on a vast, virgin continent or that of the first settlers from across the sea, that of the pioneers of the old West or those who took us to the moon, we have been made great by a sense of destiny, of vision, of elevating optimism and of good old-fashioned can-do ingenuity.

The first important wave of history which drove us to these frontiers was the Age of Exploration. Freedom and independence came with the Enlightenment. Greatness came as we led the world's Industrial Revolution. Now, we stand at the threshold of another age, one in which a seemingly endless succession of technological breakthroughs has made a global economy and a global society a transforming reality.

America's future greatness will depend in large part on our ability to rise to the challenges of this new age just as we did to those that came before. As in the past, what will lead us to success will be our sense of the possibilities offered by the new world and our commitment to realizing their promise. We enter this new time as the world's leader. To maintain that lead and fulfill the promise of delivering an even better America to our children, we must once again journey to a frontier consisting of places that once seemed exotic or forbidding. We will have to learn new skills, explore new ideas, adapt and work hard. In order for this new America to grow, we will all have to grow.

Economically, to grow we must turn to the markets that will grow fastest tomorrow. No longer is the American market alone sufficient to fuel the kind of growth we need to preserve opportunity for all of our people. At the same time, the development of a global economy is creating enormous new markets for many products and services in which America has a special edge, the kind of comparative advantages on which our new economy can be built.

The Clinton Administration has undertaken a study of the world's markets and our special strengths and has developed an initiative designed to carry us successfully to this new economic frontier. We call it the Big Emerging Markets Initiative. It focuses the resources of all the agencies of the U.S. government that have programs designed to stimulate U.S. exports on 10 of the markets that will be most important to our growth in the new world economy. It does not preclude a continuing focus on our traditional trading partners. It does not minimize the need to help American firms export successfully to all the world's emerging markets, large and small, as dictated by the needs of the businesses themselves. Rather, it acknowledges that we are in the midst of a period of great change, that new powers are emerging and that for the sake of all of our national interests we must focus our efforts on those countries. It notes that, in addition to offering an exciting new set of opportunities for American companies and workers, the Big Emerging Markets of tomorrow also pose a broad set of policy challenges. These range from market access and intellectual property protection on the trade policy side to human rights, workers' rights, the environment, non-proliferation and other important national security concerns.

The Big Emerging Markets Initiative recognizes that the changes that have given rise to this new approach are as sweeping and irreversible as they are fundamental. The rise of the global economy is as profound a transformation as has swept the globe since the Industrial Revolution. It corresponds to and is in important ways linked to the end of the Cold War and the consequent realignments of the world's power structure. America must find a new way in this world, a new way to preserve the American dream of a better future for our children and a new way to lead. It is our conviction that this new way will inevitably take us to these markets that once seemed so remote and with whom we often only had contact at times of conflict. It will not be an easy path. But we must proceed because we cannot turn back.

This book is conceived as something of a guidebook for American businesspeople as to what the Big Emerging Markets (BEMs) Initiative is about, what these markets offer in the eyes of the U.S. Commerce Department specialists and others in the government who are now studying them and, thanks to our directory at the back, who to contact in order to further explore this new frontier. The publication of the book is part of a major education program that is part of the BEMs Initiative. That education effort includes seminars and workshops across the country that have already attracted thousands of American business leaders and will continue throughout the year ahead. It includes expanding the information tools available via the global network of the U.S. Foreign & Commercial Service. It even includes the launch of an extensive BEMs Internet service available at http://www.stat-usa.gov/itabems.html.

Of course the BEMs Initiative is much more than information services; it also includes advisory programs, expanded human and other resources on the ground in these markets, greater interagency cooperation on financing U.S. exports to them, an active and unprecedented advocacy program that is heavily focused on the BEMs, new bilateral councils designed to deepen the relations between the U.S. public and private sectors and our counterparts in each of these markets, trade missions and many other components. These too are described in the book.

We recognize that there are many complications in preparing a book such as this. The pace of global change is rapid and nowhere is this felt more acutely than in the BEMs. Volatility is anticipated, and we have tried to make the chapters of this book on each market as evergreen as possible. Nonetheless, some elements of each may be overtaken by events, and it is important that all who are exploring opportunities in the BEMs take advantage of the full range of public and private sector information resources to check the current facts and status of each marketplace.

In many cases, information is still somewhat difficult to get out of all of these countries. The World Bank, the United Nations, and a variety of other public and private sources offer good statistics, and we have tried to use them in a way that is as comparable as possible market to market. There are some discrepencies, however, and in these cases we have simply relied on our judgment to use the most representative possible figures. All are sourced carefully to allow readers the opportunity to make their own judgments regarding each.

The Big Emerging Markets Initiative is only two years old. This is the first public study produced by the government on this program. We are still learning, and our views are evolving. It is clear, however, judging from the virtually universal positive reaction to the program from business leaders and others around the world that we are on the right track. The introduction of the book describes the current state of our thinking and the issues we intend to address in the future. It also makes it clear that we know we must continue. Exports have been perhaps the most important source of new jobs in the U.S. economy during the past decade. Exports and trade are only becoming more important. The Big Emerging Markets are where the big upside promise of tomorrow lies — by our conservative estimates representing perhaps a trillion dollar gain over 1990 export levels by the year 2010 from just these 10 markets. Perhaps that alone would be justification for exploring this new frontier. But, of course, for Americans the reason runs deeper, with roots in our history and an even clearer explanation that comes from considering our future.

David J. Rothkopf
Deputy Under Secretary of Commerce
for International Trade
Chairman, Big Emerging Markets Task Force

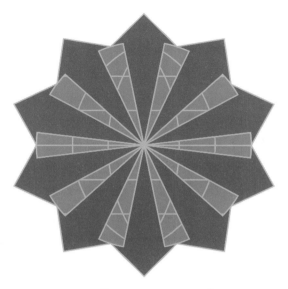

The Big Emerging Markets Initiative

Ronald H. Brown
Secretary of Commerce

Jeffrey E. Garten
Under Secretary of Commerce
for International Trade

David J. Rothkopf
Deputy Under Secretary of Commerce
for International Trade
Chairman, Big Emerging Markets
Task Force

Jen Sacks
Editor

Daniel Stafford
Production and Design Supervisor

Carola McGiffert
Project Coordinator

BEMs Book Country Team Leaders

Argentina and Brazil: Walter Bastian • *Mexico:* Regina Vargo • *ASEAN:* Robert S. LaRussa
CEA: Donald Forest • *India:* Richard Harding • *South Korea:* Susan Blackman
Poland: Franklin Vargo • *South Africa:* Sally Miller • *Turkey:* Charles Ludolph

Contributors

Alice Gray
Tom Witherspoon
Clyde W. Robinson, Jr.
Michael Whitener
Eddi Edwards
Suzanne Kamalieh

Country Teams

Chinese Economic Area
Donald Forest
Cheryl McQueen
Scott Goddin
Sheila Baker
Chris Cerone
Paul Kullman
Laurette Newsom
Laura McCall
Jamie Horsley
Craig Allen
Charles Martin
David Katz
Rosemary Gallant
Ira Kasoff
Matt Brady
Olevia Yim
Caroline Yuen
Victor Ho
Elanna Tam
Alan Turley
Bob Chu
Shirley Wang
Zhiqiang Huang

India
Kathleen Keim
John McPhee
Gary Bouck
Jacqueline Rhodes
Art Stern

ASEAN
Robert S. LaRussa
Herbert Cochran
Sarah E. Kemp
Lisabeth A. Sarin
Jean Kelly
Raphael Cung
Alice Simmons
Hong-Phong Pho
Carmine D'Aloisio
Michael Hand
Steven Craven
Carol Kim
Paul Scogna
August Maffry

Turkey
Eileen Hill
Boyce Fitzpatrick
James Wilson
Charles Ludolph

Poland
Franklin J. Vargo
Susanne Lotarski
Jay A. Burgess
Pamela Green
Lian Von Wantoch
Monika Michejda-Goodrich

Argentina
Randolph Mye

Mexico
Regina Vargo
Juliet Bender
Karen Chopra
Kevin Brennan
Reginald Biddle
Laurie Goldman
Toni Dick
Paul Dacher
Eric Fredell
Charles Winburn
Edgar Rojas
Frank Foster

Brazil
Walter Bastian
Laura Zeiger-Hatfield

South Korea
Linda Droker
Jeff Donius
William Golike
Dan Duvall
Robert Connan
Sam Kidder
Helen Lee

South Africa
Emily Solomon
Katie Moore
Dennis Goldenson
Sally Miller

Trade Advocacy

Basic Industries
Chad Breckenridge
John Mearman
Jay Smith
Catherine Vial
Mary Ann Slater
Randy Miller
Melissa Harrington
Raimundo Prat
Vincent Kamenicky
William Hurt
Stuart Keitz

Services Industries and Finance
Douglas Cleveland
Irene Finel-Honigman
John Shuman

Environmental Technologies Exports
Kristine Bretl
Denise Carpenter
Eric Fredell
Rizwan Khaliq
Mark O'Grady
Camille Richardson
Richard Sousane

Office of Trade and Economic Analysis
Ron Levin
Howard Schreier
John Jelacic

Textiles, Apparel and Consumer Goods Industries
William E. Dawson
Kim-Bang Nguyen
Les Simon
William Lofquist
Donald Hodgen
James Byron
Kevin Ellis
Rose Marie Bratland
John Harris
John Vanderwolf
Jonathan Freilich

Advocacy Center
T.S. Chung

Technology and Aerospace Industries
Sally Bath
Dorothea Blouin
Mark Cooper
Matt Edwards
Sean Iverson
Victoria Kader
Eric McDonald
Tim Miles
Judy Mussehl-Aziz
Robin Roark
Mary Smolenski
Clay Woods

The Big Emerging Markets:

These are emerging markets; they are constantly changing, occasionally unstable. But because of their enormous promise, they are a magnet for the world's most competitive companies from the U.S. and abroad.

Discovering the BEMs

During the first year of the Clinton Administration, a good deal of analysis was devoted to answering the questions, "Looking toward the next century, where will we find the engines of American growth? What markets hold the most promise? And what is the role of the U.S. government in helping to ensure that the country realizes that promise?" Although such questions seem rational enough, as far as Washington has been concerned in past years, they have rarely been pursued in the international economic arena, let alone answered. Nevertheless, the Clinton Administration broke with past patterns. It put an enormous amount of effort into looking over the immediate horizon and came up with some interesting —and powerful—conclusions.

We found, for example, that the markets in Europe and Japan will be growing much more slowly over the next two decades than a good deal of the rest of the world. Moreover, we discovered that, despite optimism about future prospects throughout East Asia and Latin America, the markets that will account for the overwhelming incremental growth in world imports can be narrowed down to fewer than a dozen, which we called "The Big Emerging Markets," or "BEMs." The BEMs are: in Asia—the Chinese Economic Area (China, Hong Kong and Taiwan), South Korea, the Association of Southeast Asian Nations (ASEAN), initially Indonesia, then expanded to include all the ASEAN economies, and India; in Africa—South Africa; in Europe—Poland and Turkey; and in Latin America—Mexico, Brazil and Argentina.

We also found that to be successful in these markets will require us to completely rethink our approach to trade. Because these are emerging markets, they are constantly changing, occasionally unstable. They do not have the established ties to the United States that our traditional partners have had. Relations with them are volatile. And, because of the enormous promise of these markets, they are a magnet for the world's most competitive companies from the U.S. and abroad.

In each, competition will be fierce. But, because many have important state sectors—and because virtually all are focusing heavily on infrastructure projects that demand involvement of local governments—U.S. companies will need the U.S. government at their side to win a fair hearing. What is more, because of the intensity of foreign competition and the capital demands on these economies, our competitors will be public-private partnerships in which foreign governments are providing concessionary financing and aggressive advocacy to support their companies' efforts. If we don't do the same, we will lose not only our chance to succeed in these markets but our chance to remain the world's economic leader into the next century.

The New Economic Frontier

BEMs in the Headlines

Earlier this year, every newspaper in America ran daily stories chronicling the state of American negotiations with Chinese officials concerning illegal trade in pirated compact discs and computer software. Why? Because the issue is central both to the future well-being of hundreds of thousands of American workers and to our prospects in a market of 1.2 billion consumers with a voracious appetite for the information products in which we are the world's leader.

When Mexico stumbled, the president reacted swiftly and decisively. Why? Because just as Mexico is already the third largest consumer of American exports and growing fast—up over 20 percent in 1994, the first full year of the North American Free Trade Agreement (NAFTA)—it promises even more for the future. In 1994, direct foreign investment in Mexico rose almost two-thirds over the year before. Whatever problems came at the end of the year, Mexico remains a market that is much richer in resources than it was 12 months before. And that means much for tomorrow: more jobs for us and our children. Mexico's growth enhances our growth. And just as its stability enhances our stability, so, too, would its instability undermine our own security. As we realize the promise of closer cooperation and more openness, we also accept that our destinies become more intertwined.

South Africa's historic political transition is an inspiration to nations around the world that aspire to democracy. Now, South Africa's public and private sectors are boldly confronting the imperatives of addressing mass poverty and catalyzing economic growth. Few governments in history have taken on such a challenge. Almost half of Africa's GDP is generated in South Africa, almost three-quarters of the GDP of southern Africa. The country's re-entry into the international community will benefit its African neighbors and attract more commercial activity to the African continent.

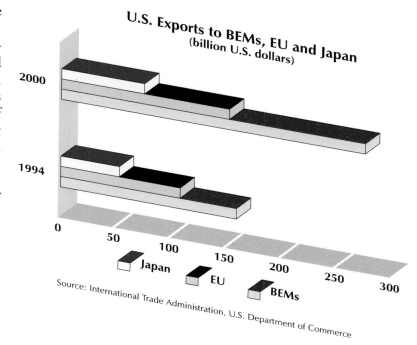

U.S. Exports to BEMs, EU and Japan
(billion U.S. dollars)

Source: International Trade Administration, U.S. Department of Commerce

As we realize the promise of closer cooperation and more openness, we also accept that our destinies become more intertwined.

Brazil, South America's largest and most populous country, has long been a beacon for international investors drawn by sheer potential. In fact, the old joke had it that "Brazil is the country of the future... and always will be." Not long ago, the country was wracked with the severe problems of hyperinflation and aching poverty. Then, last year, something more momentous was happening. True economic reform came to Brazil, first in the form of a new currency that was called the "real." At the same time, Brazil began playing a new influential role in the region, including becoming one of the undisputed leaders of the run-up to the "Summit of the Americas" by adopting a new outward-oriented posture and winning strong support from nations throughout the hemisphere. Brazil just might be the country of tomorrow... today.

Turkey has been the crossroads of the world since Alexander the Great. In recent years, an economic renaissance made the Istanbul stock market one of the most attractive in the world. Now, Turkey has entered a period of difficulties. But no matter how you look at it, Turkey will play a pivotal role in our future. For it is both the link and the buffer between Europe and the Middle East, between Europe and the southern tier of the former Soviet Union. It is at the border between the developed and developing worlds, on the front line in the dynamic exchanges that will define the nature of the next century.

What could be more remote to most Americans than the ASEAN nation of Indonesia, a string of 13,000 islands located on the opposite side of the world? Yet last November the President of the United States led a high-level U.S. delegation to the Asia Pacific Economic Cooperation (APEC) leaders' meeting and ministerial held in Jakarta, Indonesia's capital. Headlines about human rights problems surfaced at the time of the meeting, as did stories about workers' rights. The president did not shirk from addressing these issues. At the same time, however, he presented our strong desire to see change happen in the context of a new approach. He determined to base our relationship with Indonesia and countries like it on the enormous interests we share.

Moments before the president's major address in Jakarta, Secretary Brown presided over the signing of approximately $40 billion in deals between U.S. and Indonesian companies, including one energy deal worth $35 billion alone. In his speech, President Clinton spoke about Indonesian President Soeharto's leadership in getting the 18 nations of APEC to agree to free trade within the region by the year 2020, with free trade among the developed countries by 2010. The president recognized that we were drawn together. He identified the broad range of issues—political, social, environmental as well as economic— on which we were slowly achieving consensus, and acknowledged that the promise of closer ties and more open borders was driving us toward more progress.

Rethinking a BEM: Approaching ASEAN as a BEM

From the early stages of the initiative, we have viewed the BEMs as regional economic drivers instead of isolated markets. This was because of the great influence they had on surrounding economies. However, in the case of the Chinese Economic Area, the trade and investment flows of the three economies had become so interdependent that we decided to do as many businesses had done and view them as one regional Big Emerging Market. In other words, we sought to define the market in terms of economic rather than regional boundaries. In other cases, such as in the Southern Cone of South America, the BEMs of Argentina and Brazil were linking themselves economically to two non-BEMs through Mercosur. The resulting regional economic trading area created by this integration will obviously influence the trade and investment decisions of U.S. companies as they look to do business in South America, even though we decided not (yet) to designate the entire region as a BEM because of the relatively small size of the two other economies, Paraguay and Uruguay.

We initially viewed the relationship between Indonesia and the rest of Southeast Asia as that between BEM and surrounding region, naming Indonesia with its 190-million population and explosive growth as a BEM even though countries like Thailand and Malaysia already had established significant trading relationships with the U.S., and Singapore was an important hub for the entire Asian market.

But the more we looked at ASEAN, the more we recognized that both the countries of the region and the U.S. businesses investing there were already thinking regionally. The Association of Southeast Asian Nations had started as a geo-political entity in 1967, but the organization's raison d'etre over the past several years has been economic. In late 1994, ASEAN decided to accelerate implementation of the ASEAN Free Trade Area, a common-market style arrangement that would lower intra-regional tariffs to no more than 5 percent by the year 2008. ASEAN has also just expanded its membership, welcoming Vietnam to its association. The resulting regional economic market is one of the largest and most dynamic in the world. By some estimates, ASEAN will have a combined population of between 500-700 million by the year 2010 and a combined GDP of $1.1 trillion.

The U.S. government is also beginning to view ASEAN as a region for trade and economic purposes in addition to our traditional approach to the individual nations comprising it. The U.S.-ASEAN Alliance for Mutual Growth, with its focus on the creation of regional economic partnerships and regular multilateral meetings, acknowledges ASEAN as a cohesive economic entity.

But again, the U.S. government is only following the lead of the private sector, which is not only approaching ASEAN as a regional market, but also understands the strategic economic importance of ASEAN as a base for Asia-wide trading platforms. In many industries, individual country markets within ASEAN will not sustain major investment or trade by U.S. companies, especially with Japanese competition having established a strong foothold in sectors like autos and auto parts. Such factors make a regional strategy a necessity.

In infrastructure sectors such as power generation, telecommunications and transportation, countries such as Malaysia, Thailand and Indonesia are all undergoing similar, unprecedented development and privatization. In industries such as autos and auto parts, the traffic-clogged streets of Kuala Lumpur, Bangkok and Jakarta point to the rapid cross-regional growth in demand for cars, trucks, motorcycles and the parts from which they are made. In planning sectoral strategies and trade missions with the private sector, we were told time and again to adopt a regional approach to ASEAN trade.

Expanding the Indonesia BEM to include all of ASEAN has had a significant impact on our data and analyses of the BEMs. U.S. exports to ASEAN for 1993 were more than eight times greater than U.S. exports to Indonesia alone. U.S. exports to ASEAN for 1993 were $23.9 billion, second only to Mexico among the BEMs. For the years 1993 through 1998, both U.S. and world exports to ASEAN will exceed those to any other BEM economy, including China. ASEAN's GDP for 1994 was the third highest among the BEMs, after China and Brazil.

Taking a regional approach to ASEAN also increases several-fold the infrastructure opportunities available to U.S. companies. It has been estimated that Indonesia plans to spend $113 billion on three sectors—energy, telecommunications and transportation—over the next several years. Malaysia plans to spend at least $6.8 billion on power projects, $5 billion on aerospace and airport projects and $2 billion on telecommunication projects in the next five years, with an additional $10 billion on a variety of other infrastructure. Thailand plans to spend $60 billion to the year 2000, including more than $35 billion to meet its electric power needs. The Philippines has set a target of $20-30 billion in private sector infrastructure investment for the rest of the decade, and Singapore plans to spend $2.4 billion by 1997 to upgrade its telecommunications network.

Other evidence exists that ASEAN plans to expand its regional focus to areas that have not always represented a regional priority. ASEAN named 1995 the Year of the Environment, opening new possibilities not only for quality of life in the region, but for an industry that is on the cutting edge of U.S. technology. As ASEAN continues to expand into one of the world's most dynamic regional markets, so too will the opportunities for U.S. companies.

The BEMs will double their share of world imports, rising to 38 percent by 2010. No other category of market shows such dramatic growth potential.

The Economic Stakes

Our economic stakes in the BEMs are enormous. The 10 BEMs as a group are importing about as much merchandise from us as Japan and the European Union combined. In fact, during the period 1990-2010, the BEMs could account for at least $1 trillion in incremental U.S. export growth.

Our merchandise exports to the BEMs totaled $159 billion in 1994, approximately 30 percent of all our merchandise exports. We expect that the BEMs will double their share of world imports as well, rising to 38 percent by 2010 from 19 percent in 1994. No other category of market shows such dramatic growth potential. From Seoul to Bombay, plans call for well over $1 trillion of infrastructure projects in the next ten years—in energy exploration and generation, airports and air traffic control systems, phones and satellites, hospitals and health care services, auto and auto parts production, banking and insurance, and environmental clean-up. At least half that much is projected for Latin America. These mega-deals portend massive trade and investment opportunities for American companies.

The case for the magnitude and importance of these changes has been supported by many sources. The Organization for Economic Cooperation and Development (OECD) has estimated that if just three of the Asian BEM economies—China, India and Indonesia—grow by an average of 6 percent a year through the year 2010 (well within our projections), by that year approximately 700 million people in those countries will have an average income equivalent to that of Spain today. This is a group of people that is roughly equivalent in size to the population of the U.S., Japan and Europe added together. The World Bank, using its purchasing power parity evaluation of the size of economies, has estimated that whereas in 1992 only three of the world's 10 largest markets were BEMs, by 2020 six of the 10 will be BEMs.

Just as important, any survey of these Big Emerging Markets will reveal that these economies—all problems we may have with them aside—are far more open to imports than Japan and the Asian Tigers were when they themselves were at roughly the same place in their development. So, their rapid growth offers an immediate opportunity for us, and is likely to have a major immediate impact on global growth, integration and even the underlying dynamics of international relations.

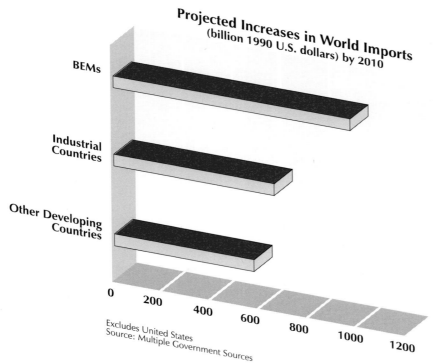

Projected Increases in World Imports
(billion 1990 U.S. dollars) by 2010

- BEMs
- Industrial Countries
- Other Developing Countries

0   200   400   600   800   1000   1200

Excludes United States
Source: Multiple Government Sources

To illustrate the importance of these changes from another perspective, we need look only to the fact that in the first three years of this decade America's exports to developing countries grew at an average of 12 percent a year, while those to our traditional trading partners crept forward at only 2 percent per year. In the words of *The Economist*, "For the first time developing economies were acting as a locomotive, helping to pull the rich world out of its recession of the early 1990s."

We certainly understand the limitations of long-term economic projections, and also the possibility that economic policies in certain BEMs could fail. Our outlook, in fact, is based on some critical assumptions, such as the belief that world trade will remain open and continue to expand, and that policy reforms initiated in the BEMs will continue. The BEMs list is, therefore, one which could evolve depending on trends. If the Russian economy really turns the corner, it could be added to the list. Some day, some markets might "graduate," having completed their emergence into the ranks of the world's developed economies. By the same token, it is also possible that a market that endured a prolonged setback might be taken off the list.

Nonetheless, the economies we have identified today as BEMs have certain characteristics that force us to pay attention. In Latin America, two BEMs—Mexico and Brazil—account for 61 percent of the Southern Hemisphere's GDP and 53 percent of its population. Two Asian BEM countries—China and India—account for 40 percent of the world's population. In Africa, one BEM—South Africa—accounts for 45 percent of the entire continent's GDP. Poland is Europe's fastest growing major economy, and Indonesia is the world's fourth most populous nation.

In this sense, the BEMs category is illustrative of a certain kind of market. They have large territories. They have big populations with massive future demands for infrastructure, like power generation and telecommunications, and for consumer goods, like computers and washing machines. They are economies which have undertaken significant economic policies that have already contributed to faster growth and expanding trade and investment with the rest of the world. They aspire to be technological leaders. They are markets whose economic growth would have enormous spillover in their respective geographical regions. They all have significant political influence in their backyards and beyond.

The Clinton Administration didn't discover the BEMs, of course. They have been emerging on the world scene for years, and quite a few big U.S. companies have been active in them for a long time. In fact, we noticed the BEMs precisely because some of the more farsighted American firms were moving into these markets already. But the U.S. government has only recently begun to focus on them the attention they deserve — not as foreign policy problems, which they have often been perceived as being, but as major and essential opportunities for future cooperation.

If just three of the Asian BEM economies — China, India and Indonesia — grow by an average of 6 percent a year through the year 2010 (well within our projections), by that year approximately 700 million people in those countries will have an average income equivalent to that of Spain today.

Thus there is a direct link between the BEMs focus as a tool for increasing our market share abroad and the American role in relationships of all types among all the nations of the world.

The Stakes Are Not Just U.S. Sales

While the underlying rationale for the BEMs strategy relies in great part on the opportunities for American exports, it would be a major mistake to look at the BEMs only through that lens. The fact is that every aspect of the world we live in will be heavily influenced by what the BEMs do or don't do. There is no scenario for containing nuclear proliferation without the cooperation of the Chinas, the Indias and the Brazils of the world. There is no hope for protecting the environment without the BEMs being on board. The future of trade liberalization, and the possibilities for meaningful monetary arrangements will both require the inclusion and cooperation of the BEMs. The international institutions on which we increasingly depend will be more and more influenced by BEMs policies and perspectives.

Thus there is a direct link between the BEMs focus as a tool for increasing our market share abroad and the American role in relationships of all types among the nations of the world. If we fail in our commercial battles for these markets, we also give up our most powerful tool for influencing them, growing closer to them and ensuring their future stability through prosperity.

The Role and Policies of the U.S. Government

There is an important role for our government to play in helping to stimulate our trade with each of the BEMs. The BEMs are unlike our more traditional trading partners, such as Great Britain or Germany. There are frequently severe barriers to entering these markets, including high tariffs, quotas and protectionist regulatory restrictions. Commercial systems, including full respect for intellectual property rights, smoothly functioning capital markets and open government procurement procedures, are often still developing or lacking altogether. In some of the BEMs, impartial legal systems are missing, too. And as noted earlier, the nature of the competition we face in these markets is dramatically different from what we have been used to.

In these markets, therefore, we can and should help American businesses in a variety of ways—from securing market access, to providing financing, to supporting U.S. companies seeking to win major projects on deals in which foreign governments are helping their firms or play an important decision-making role in awarding projects. In addition, good information on the BEMs is

BEMs' Share of Global GDP

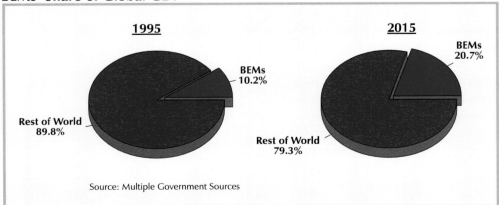

1995

BEMs 10.2%

Rest of World 89.8%

2015

BEMs 20.7%

Rest of World 79.3%

Source: Multiple Government Sources

often in short supply, and through our embassies and our Foreign Commercial Service, we can marshal and analyze much of what is available and provide it to our country's firms. Finally, we need to work with the governments and private sectors of the BEMs in order to assist them in developing the skills and the institutions to build open, modern capitalist systems. The approach must not be patronizing, but based on common goals of expanding trade in their markets and our own.

It is, of course, much easier to proclaim a policy than it is to implement it. In the past year, however, a great deal has already been accomplished.

Perhaps the most important achievement so far has been the evolution in the Executive Branch of an intense export consciousness. Since almost its first days in office, the Clinton Administration, under the auspices of the interagency Trade Promotion Coordinating Committee (TPCC), has worked hard to move export promotion out of the shadows of trade policy and into the limelight. Through the President's National Export Strategy—our nation's first—the Administration has launched a major interagency effort to coordinate federal government support on behalf of U.S. firms bidding for major contracts overseas; implemented a more flexible and aggressive approach to trade finance; liberalized unnecessary and outdated controls on computers and telecommunications exports; and established several U.S. Export Assistance Centers to provide American businesses with comprehensive export promotion and finance services from a single location. After two years, we are proud to say that we have a National Export Strategy that is in full force. (The TPCC will deliver its third annual Report to Congress on the National Export Strategy in late September 1995.)

Indeed, with these policies in place, and with more to come, we anticipate a major expansion of U.S. sales abroad, with exports alone reaching well over $1 trillion by the year 2000, supporting some six million additional jobs. These exports will also help reduce our chronic and growing trade deficit. (Exporters are advised that controls still exist to many of these destinations. For clarification of these policies, contact the export counseling division of the Bureau of Export Administration at (202) 482-4811.)

A focus on the BEMs is a crucial and pervasive part of this export push. It is not a substitute for continued efforts to open markets and promote American sales in Europe, Japan or Canada. Nor does it mean we will let up on commercial efforts to draw closer to Russia, the other newly independent states, or entire regions such as Latin America or Southeast Asia.

But a Big Emerging Markets strategy deserves special emphasis and requires an extraordinary effort because it represents a radical departure from traditional policies and because it is oriented way beyond the usual government policy time horizons. The focus of this strategy is more

Perhaps the most important achievement so far has been the evolution in the Executive Branch of an intense export consciousness. Export promotion has moved out of the shadows of trade policy and into the limelight.

U.S. Export Growth: Trajectory Has Sharply Increased (billion U.S. dollars)

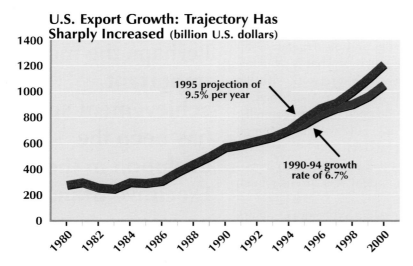

1400
1200
1000
800
600
400
200
0

1980 1982 1984 1986 1988 1990 1992 1994 1996 1998 2000

1995 projection of 9.5% per year

1990-94 growth rate of 6.7%

Source: International Trade Administration, U.S. Department of Commerce

intense and its implementation is more aggressive than any export strategy the American government has mounted.

Time, adequately trained people, and severe budgetary limitations make it impossible to do everything at once. We have, therefore, instituted several pilot projects. The idea is to experiment in individual BEMs with new policies and programs, with the ultimate intention of transferring what works from one location to another, with appropriate modifications for individual circumstances.

Country Strategies and Country Teams

For decades, agencies of the Executive Branch have been notorious for pursuing many different commercial approaches to a particular country with little or no coordination. Every Administration has tried to fix the problem. At last, we are making significant progress. A successful BEMs strategy requires fully coordinated export strategies toward the ten economies or regions.

Example: Indonesia

The ASEAN country of Indonesia was the first test case developed under the BEMs strategy. We selected it because it holds enormous importance to us in the most dynamic region of the world, and since virtually every one of our export promotion programs are operating in this country already.

We began with a far-reaching interagency study of U.S. commercial interests in Indonesia through the year 2000. The analysis examined how American firms had been doing over the last decade; it evaluated the efforts of U.S. agencies in working with them; and it took stock of how foreign competition had been performing. We noticed, for example, that although we had large Export-Import Bank, Overseas Private Investment Corporation (OPIC), and other programs in Indonesia, they were not well coordinated. Moreover, despite the amount of resources we were pouring into Indonesia, we were still losing market share to Japan, Europe and several other Asian countries.

The study zeroed in on those sectors and projects that held the most promise for U.S. firms, relating them as best as possible to the potential benefits to the American economy. On the basis of this examination, a subcabinet trip was made to discuss the findings with the American Embassy and the U.S. business community in Indonesia. Consultations were held with Indonesian government officials and local business leaders to see how they perceived the U.S. effort. An interagency task force then reconvened to formulate a strategic plan.

The strategy is now unfolding. It will take time to evaluate. But we have already begun to roll out similar efforts for Argentina, Turkey and Poland, and other BEMs economies.

Big questions remain, of course. It will be important to measure the success of what we do, but concrete results stemming directly from government action will not be easy to separate from the efforts of the competing firms themselves. At a time when the effectiveness of all U.S. government programs is rightfully under intense budgetary scrutiny, however, we must put a premium on assessing performance.

The fact is, the Administration's National Export Strategy is geared toward performance and the measurement of performance. In the old days, export promotion meant exhortations to "buy American." Today, export promotion zeros in on specific deals. With this new focus, we can better marshal our limited resources and measure the results in concrete terms to decide whether those resources are being used wisely. We can determine just how much was spent to achieve a particular aim.

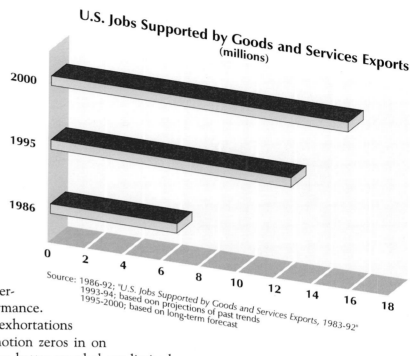

U.S. Jobs Supported by Goods and Services Exports (millions)

Source: 1986-92; "U.S. Jobs Supported by Goods and Services Exports, 1983-92"; 1993-94; based oon projections of past trends; 1995-2000; based on long-term forecast

Example: Brazil

In light of the new Cardoso Administration's commitment to pursue further economic reform and stabilization, the outlook for building a stronger U.S.-Brazil commercial partnership has never been more favorable. Although market access barriers—including government monopolies in such sectors as telecommunications, mining, petroleum and electrical energy and restrictive government procurement practices—continue to pose problems for U.S. firms in Brazil, we are determined to do everything we can to assist the U.S. private sector to reap the tremendous commercial opportunities that Brazil offers, while at the same time helping promote Brazil's economic development.

We are monitoring closely opportunities to participate in such projects as the Brazil-Bolivia natural gas pipeline; clean-up projects for the Tiete River, Guanabara Bay and Guaiba Bay; the Tiete-Parana Waterway project; and the Sao Paulo metro expansion.

The U.S. and the Brazilian governments recently co-signed terms of reference establishing a U.S.-Brazil Business Development Council (BDC). The BDC will aim to enhance public-private sector cooperation between the two countries. The first meeting of the BDC was held on

U.S. Trade Balance (billion U.S. dollars)

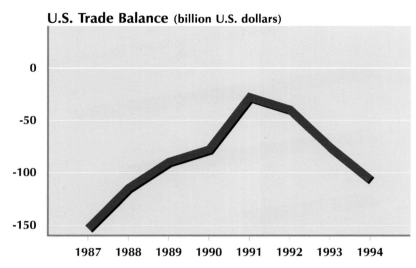

Source: International Trade Administration, U.S. Department of Commerce

June 29, 1995, just prior to the Hemispheric Trade and Commerce Forum in Denver, Colorado. A number of senior U.S. and Brazilian government officials participated, as well as some 25 private sector representatives from each country.

BIG EMERGING SECTORS

Part of every country strategy is a focus on selected industries in which U.S. exports have particularly good prospects. In our in-depth studies on Indonesia, China, Argentina and Brazil, and from additional research, we have formulated a vision of the areas where the BEMs imports are likely to be greatest.

Several clusters of industries are high on the list. They include:

- Information technology, including telecommunications, computers and software;

- Environmental technology, including pollution control equipment and consulting services;

- The transportation industry, including aviation, automotive trade, and the services and equipment needed to build modern rail systems and airports;

- Energy technology, especially for the soaring demand for electric power;

- Healthcare technology, including advanced medical equipment, pharmaceuticals, biotechnology and hospital management services;

- Financial services, including banking, insurance and the securities business.

As in the BEMs category itself, these Big Emerging Sectors are illustrative. We also have a great interest in advanced materials, in the chemical industry, and in industrial machinery, for example, all of which could be added to the initial list.

A sectoral strategy is not an "industrial policy." It does not involve subsidies. It does not rest on a notion of picking winners and losers, but rather it supports those industries where we know markets abroad are expanding, where the U.S. is already doing well, and where it could do much better with additional U.S. government help.

Bilateral Commercial Dialogues

It is important to remember that the BEMs are up-and-coming markets that are trying to modernize their commercial infrastructures very rapidly. No two are in an identical situation, but many need to strengthen their systems for protecting intellectual property rights; many need to make progress in opening their markets to foreign goods and services, both for imports and for foreign investment; and many need to build up a better regulatory framework for such industries as telecommunications and finance.

While the International Monetary Fund (IMF), the World Bank and other international institutions can provide assistance in these areas, stronger bilateral links between Washington and each of the BEMs are critical. America has a wealth of technical expertise and policy experience to impart. Moreover, we have a strong interest in the commercial links that can be developed through this kind of interaction. In the Cold War, ties between the U.S. and many of our friends in the world were developed through military exchanges and training programs. Now, and in the future, the most important links will not be men in uniform carrying weapons, but men and women in blue suits carrying laptops.

We have, therefore, set up special commercial forums with several of the BEMs under which a broad range of common concerns can be addressed. To date, these have been established in South Africa, Argentina, Brazil, India and China. All have a significant role in helping to build solid commercial institutions, but they are all structured in various ways, with somewhat different agendas. All have a sectoral industrial component—a focus on telecommunications, energy, financial services, etc.—so that commercial matters relating to the promotion of trade and investment have a particular "real world" focus. Some have heavy involvement of the U.S. and foreign private sectors.

> ## Highlights of ASEAN Strategy
>
> **Establishment of U.S. Commercial and Information Center in Jakarta.**
>
> **Coordination of financing for large projects among OPIC, Ex-Im Bank and TDA.**
>
> **Focus on opportunites in such sectors as power generation, automotive, aerospace, computers and information technology, and health care technologies.**
>
> **"Matchmaker" missions to ASEAN under aegis of U.S.-ASEAN Alliance for Mutual Growth.**

Example: The U.S.-China Joint Commission on Commerce and Trade

A good example of such a forum is the U.S.-China Joint Commission on Commerce and Trade (JCCT). The JCCT, which was established in 1983 and reinvigorated during the 1994 visit of China Trade Minister Wu Yi to Washington, D.C., provides an important venue for China and the U.S. to identify problems and seek long-term remedies outside the glare of heated trade negotiations. It serves as a mechanism to promote U.S. commercial interests in China and build stronger relations overall between the two governments. Through joint working level efforts, the JCCT focuses on expanding trade in priority sectors, such as information technology, energy and transportation, seeking resolution of exporter and investor problems, exchanging views on the evolution and role of commercial law, and offering technical assistance in the areas of IPR, environmental and other standards, management education and training and export control.

The ninth session of the JCCT will be held in Beijing during the fall of this year. The major focus will be on expanding the U.S. commercial presence in priority sectors and easing the way for U.S. firms regarding critical infrastructure projects. Other initiatives include: **(1)** opening of the U.S. Commercial Center in Shanghai; **(2)** also, in Shanghai, unveiling of the U.S.-China Management Education and Business Leadership Program, a bilateral management education and training initiative to be sponsored at Fudan University (in addition to the management curriculum, special topics will include IPR protection and environmental awareness); **(3)** establishment of a U.S.-China Business Development Council to enable U.S. companies and their enterprise counterparts to discuss commercial issues; **(4)** recognition of the State Planning Commission's growing involvement in the JCCT, including its role as Vice Chair; and **(5)** a focus on ways the many day-to-day challenges investors face can be addressed at the local level. Other highlights will include emphasis on finance, IPR training and environment in the context of the JCCT's sectoral working groups.

Example: Business Development Committees

Similar forums with other markets will have a much larger private sector component. Last year we formalized BDCs with South Africa and Argentina. In January of this year, we announced the U.S.-India Commercial Alliance. Just this spring, as noted earlier, we signed the terms of reference launching a BDC with Brazil. In June 1995, the first full, formal meetings of the Argentina, Brazil and India BDCs met in the U.S. These BDCs, which are joint business-government endeavors, are aimed at strengthening business ties and trade between the member countries, and will provide the private sectors in those countries with an avenue for rec-

---

1995 Strategy for Mexico: Key Elements

Attention to completing environmental and other infrastructure projects at border.

Assisting U.S. firms to participate in upcoming Mexican privatization.

Counseling U.S. firms on customs and other procedures for entering Mexican markets.

Possible expansion of U.S. Trade Center in Mexico City.

---

ommending government action that will stimulate more extensive commercial relationships.

Need to Consider Training Programs

In all of our commercial efforts, we have become aware that commercial policy means much more than trade or exports or financing. One of the major constraints facing many of the BEMs is the lack of trained people to manage modern enterprises, public or private. We believe that the U.S. has a lot to offer in this regard, through both our government and our private sector.

We recently followed up with officials in Shanghai on Secretary Brown's announcement last August of plans to develop a pilot training program in China. After extensive discussions, we reached agreement with Fudan University to train managers to meet the needs of China's transition to a market economy and to support the management needs of the growing numbers of Sino-American joint ventures.

In addition to providing management education training, we propose to make available information and undertake training on the broader issues associated with managing and sustaining economic growth and a healthy investment environment, such as market economics, financing, intellectual property rights and comparative legal systems. To carry out this program, we envision the creation of a Curriculum Development Center, a Management Training Institute, and a Distance Learning medium for disseminating curriculum information. We plan to seek the support of U.S. and Chinese academic institutions and private sector firms for resource assistance and their expertise and wisdom.

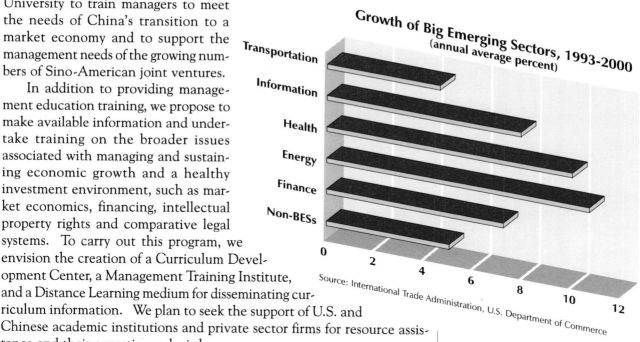

Growth of Big Emerging Sectors, 1993-2000 (annual average percent)

Source: International Trade Administration, U.S. Department of Commerce

We also want to take advantage of the phenomenal technology that the U.S. now possesses for imparting information—technology that is nowhere so advanced as it is here. Our corporate sector has all manner of training programs that can be beamed around the world via satellite, for example. We are in a position to have a global classroom for a global market.

The concept of expanded training, while providing many benefits to China, is not a purely altruistic venture by any means. Managers and technicians trained by Americans will likely be inclined to buy American goods and services. In addition, one of the major problems for U.S. firms in China is lack of Chinese personnel who have the requisite skills for modern-day work.

It would be misleading to say that we have all the answers—or even many of them — to this complicated issue. But this much we do know: in the 1950s, 60s and 70s, a good deal of our ties with key developing nations revolved around military training and exchanges. Now, and in the 21st century, the rules will be different. And just as our armed services brought more than military training, so will the links brought about by people-to-people contact in the commercial areas carry with them much broader benefits to both sides.

The value of training is never just to facilitate the exchange of products and services. It is about the exchange of ideas and ideals as well. It helps build bridges to span the political, economic and cultural gaps that separate "us" and "them."

Commercial Centers

In all the BEMs, we hope to create special commercial centers outside the American embassies. The idea is to elevate the commercial objectives of our foreign policy by enhancing U.S. trade promotion facilities and by making them more accessible to American and foreign business people.

Example: Sao Paulo, Brazil

The prototype is the new facility in Sao Paulo, Brazil, opened by Secretary Brown last summer. Located in the central commercial district, this four-story building makes available to business people from America and Brazil a comprehensive commercial library with the latest computerized databases on the two countries. It houses the U.S. and Foreign Commercial Service, and provides "one-stop" export advisory services. One floor is reserved for the exhibition of American products. There is an auditorium with simultaneous translation capability for company presentations. The center has become a magnet for more American trade fairs and missions, and for U.S. business-people needing help in penetrating the Brazilian market.

Examples: Jakarta, Shanghai

Last November, Secretary Brown opened another commercial center in Jakarta. We also plan to open a

Bilateral Commercial Forums	
Argentina	Business Development Council
ASEAN	U.S.-ASEAN Alliance for Mutual Growth
Brazil	Business Development Council
China	U.S.-China Joint Commission on Commerce and Trade
India	U.S.-India Commercial Alliance
South Africa	Business Development Council

center in Shanghai later this year. Down the road we are considering similar facilities for India.

Financing and Government Support for U.S. Firms

A major reason why the BEMs constitute such important markets for us is that some of the world's largest infrastructure projects will be mounted in these regions, with billions of dollars of potential sales for U.S. companies. In most instances the projects are awarded by governments, or are under heavy government influence. This means that the bidding process is highly political and that companies vying for contracts often receive help from their own governments, particularly in the area of long-term financing. Before 1993, Washington's support for American business had been episodic at best. President Clinton, Secretary Brown and others have instituted a radical change in this policy, mounting the most consistently aggressive effort on behalf of U.S. firms in memory.

The Commerce Department has set up a special Advocacy Center to track the largest projects around the world and to work closely with other agencies — State, Treasury, the Export-Import Bank, OPIC and the Trade and Development Agency (TDA), to name a few—to marshal all the muscle in the Administration when it comes to winning large contracts. The new policy can be called "aggressive defense." That is, we will never be the first to provide below-market-rate financing in violation of the OECD rules, but if we find other governments breaking those rules, we are willing to match the financing. In addition, we are mobilizing high-level Administration support for individual projects—via trips, phone calls and other contacts between Administration officials and their counterparts in the governments awarding the contracts.

We are turning up the heat as never before. But the issue is not just throwing money at specific deals. The International Trade Administration coordinates all the programs of the U.S. government aimed at increasing the competitiveness of U.S. companies via the Trade Promotion Coordinating Committee (TPCC). We can use information from the Commercial Service and the State Department to ensure that Exim, OPIC and TDA put the right financing package together. We can work with Treasury on multilateral

> **A major reason why the BEMs constitute such important markets for us is that some of the world's largest infrastructure projects will be mounted in these nations.**

Highlights of Brazil Commercial Center

- **During FY 1995, the Center has sponsored 7 Trade and Matchmaker missions.**

- **During FY 1995, the Center has held more than 30 other trade promotion events.**

- **Each month, 200 - 250 firms visit the Center.**

- **Each month, the Center receives 1,000 - 1,500 phone calls requesting advice.**

- **Each month, the Center receives approximately 1,800 faxes requesting advice.**

While we want the contracts — and the U.S. jobs they bring — we do not want to see a trade finance war in which governments are fighting to see who can deplete their treasuries the fastest.

institution financing issues or Defense or the Bureau of Export Administration regarding export licensing issues. In each case, the actions required will be different.

Example: Indonesia

In late 1991, Indonesia announced plans to do what others in Asia had failed to do — initiate an extensive private power program. To achieve this goal, the government decided to invite foreign companies to bid on the first privately-financed build-operate-transfer power plant in Paiton, East Java. The project, valued at over $2.6 billion, involved setting up a turnkey operation equal in generating capacity to over 37 percent of Java's current electrical supply.

Dozens of companies expressed interest, but in the end only two proposals were submitted. The first was from a U.S. company, International Electric Incorporated (IEI). The second was from an Indonesian consortium, Bimantara, which had partnered with Hopewell Group of Hong Kong. Hopewell, owned by the billionaire industrialist Gordon Wu, was a hands-down favorite given the depth of its experience building large power plants in Asia. However, within five weeks after submitting its joint proposal with Bimantara, Hopewell dropped out. Bimantara then approached IEI about partnering on the bid.

The Indonesian government, citing a need for more competition, called for a second round of proposals. A U.S.-led consortium of Mission Energy, General Electric and Mitsui responded. With two bids in hand, the Indonesian government opened negotiations with IEI. The negotiations, after six months of false starts, collapsed completely, paving the way for Mission Energy to negotiate in earnest for the Paiton Project.

Over the next twelve months, the U.S. government moved into action to support Mission Energy. The U.S. ambassador to Indonesia wrote letters of support on behalf of Mission Energy, and sent Washington monthly updates on how the Paiton Power Project talks were progressing. When it looked like the negotiations might stall, our ambassador arranged for the Indonesian Paiton Power Purchasing Negotiating Team to visit Washington in April 1993 to meet with select U.S. government officials at the Departments of Commerce, Energy and State, as well as the Export-Import Bank.

Secretary Brown, in bilateral meetings with key Indonesian government officials, also raised U.S. support for Mission Energy, and sent advocacy letters of support to key Indonesian ministers involved in the project on Mission's behalf. In early 1994, a small group from Commerce went to Indonesia and pushed the project with senior government officials in Jakarta. All of these efforts were undertaken to ensure that Mission had the support it needed. In fact, Mission needed to fight hard to keep its competitors at bay, for companies like Hopewell of Hong Kong and others were still hoping they would find a way to get back in.

In the end, the two-year long effort to support Mission Energy's bid paid off. Secretary Brown, during his November 1994 visit to Jakarta, witnessed the signing of the Paiton Power Purchase agreement between the Indonesian government and Mission Energy. According to Mission Energy's press release, the total value of U.S. goods and services is expected to exceed $500 million and the project is estimated to support 5,000 U.S. jobs. But, the effort didn't end with the press release. For almost six months thereafter the final details and negotiations for the financing

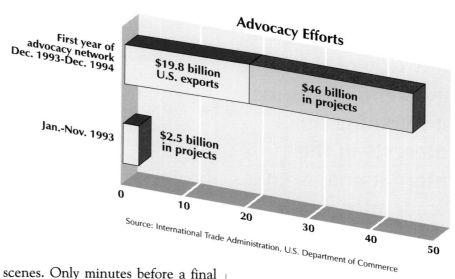

package were conducted behind the scenes. Only minutes before a final financing deadline did the U.S. government put together a package that met all the criteria and sealed the deal for good.

Example: China

A much broader advocacy effort was mounted in August 1994 in China when Secretary Brown led a Presidential Business Development Mission comprised of twenty-four CEOs to Beijing, Shanghai and Guangzhou. Brown met with the president of China, the premier, two vice premiers and several ministers. He pressed hard for contracts for American firms in specific projects. The ground had been well prepared by previous trips of former Treasury Secretary Bentsen and others, by several subcabinet trips, by around-the-clock efforts on the part of the Advocacy Center, and by close coordination between the entire Administration and the U.S. firms involved. Over $6 billion in sales contracts were announced while Brown was in China, and we are hopeful that a good deal more will come to fruition in the months ahead. We certainly will continue to push.

This is a tough game we are playing, and the stakes are high in many different ways. Millions of American jobs will hang on our successful advocacy in the future. We, therefore, must continue to press, and press hard. But, while we want the contracts—and the U.S. jobs they bring— we do not want to see a trade finance war in which governments are fighting to see who can deplete their treasuries the fastest. That's why we only respond to below-market financing from others. And our hope is to show that it doesn't pay to cheat on the OECD rules, because everyone will pay dearly. But we will not stand by and watch others capture markets by subsidizing.

The BEMs will be—indeed, they are already—the battleground on which these tensions will be played out.

Dealing with the BEMs requires a new way of thinking and acting in terms of pursuing our interests in the international arena. Academics would call it a "new paradigm" of foreign policy; more simply, we can call it a major shift in the way we see the world.

Global Marketing Network

The implementation of a BEMs strategy is conducted not just by the Washington agencies but also by representatives of all U.S. agencies overseas, including especially ambassadors and State Department teams. From the Commerce Department, 250 American men and women, plus 700 foreign employees of the U.S. and Foreign Commercial Service, are stationed in 73 offices around the U.S. and 130 markets abroad. This entire trade promotion network is now emphasizing the importance of BEMs to interested American firms. They are being armed with important data on the key economies, visits and trade missions.

The Commercial Service is a crucial link for the BEMs strategy but, as in other areas, budgets are badly stretched. In China, for example, only 10 U.S. professionals, working with 31 local men and women, are currently responsible for the entire country. So few people could hardly cover adequately the booming southern region alone. In Dalian, China, which is located in a province whose population is larger than most developed countries, we have only a single U.S. government representative.

In all of the BEMs combined, we have a mere 76 Commercial Service personnel. Some 60 positions around the world are now unfilled due to budgetary constraints, and the requirement for people is only escalating, particularly in the biggest and fastest growing markets. Training for our men and women abroad is also crucial. We are focusing now on upgrading their knowledge of trade financing, but more specialized skills regarding the Big Emerging Sectors, where technology is changing so rapidly, is also badly needed. But progress is being made. We have just now completed the intra-governmental process by which we can begin to upgrade our resources in China. Over a period of time, we intend to double our personnel on the ground in the world's largest market—and we will attempt to do the same in other BEMs.

But even as we grow, we will not be outpacing our competition. The U.S. spends less as a percentage of GDP on export promotion than any other developed nation. So, while we are getting smarter and working harder, it is still an uphill battle against better equipped and funded competition.

The domestic part of the commercial service network is undergoing major reorganization as we build a new system around some 15 Export Assistance Centers, which bring together, under one roof, all the Federal services and, where possible, state and local export facilities, too. It is an awesome undertaking. Providing export promotion services is often more difficult than many other governmental programs, because the global economic environment is changing so rapidly.

Other Issues

There are other difficult issues, too. In our bilateral commercial dialogues with the BEMs, we are combining a focus on immediate and longer-term trade issues—on market access today and on building the commercial infrastructure for tomorrow. At times, therefore, we have to manage the delicate balance of the threat that we may have to impose trade sanctions, for lack of market access or inadequate enforcement of intellectual property rights, with more cooperative discussions of, say, promoting investment in the automotive or computer industries. The tensions require governments on all sides to balance immediate problems and long-range opportunities. It's not always easy to do. Our efforts in the BEMs are also carefully coordinated with other Administration efforts, from our efforts to curb human rights abuses to our efforts regarding workers' rights and non-proliferation.

A final element of the BEMs strategy is to add a BEMs component to many of the Administration's more global initiatives. A good example is Vice President Gore's proposal for a global counterpart to the National Information Infrastructure (the "Information Superhighway"). Called the Global Information Infrastructure, the proposal calls for far-reaching telecommunications links among nations in the interests of expanded trade, investment and social development. Several of the BEMs could be prototype "off ramps" of the Global Highway. We are looking seriously at some possibilities in East Asia and in Latin America.

Lessons Learned from the BEMs Strategy

For more than a year now, we have been pursuing the BEMs-focused strategy just described. Over that period, our conviction has grown that this strategy is the right one. At the same time, the dimensions of the challenge we face have become clearer. Dealing with the BEMs requires a new way of thinking and acting in terms of pursuing our interests in the international arena. Academics would call it a "new paradigm" of foreign policy; more simply, we can call it a major shift in our view of the world.

Here are some lessons we have learned (or have had reinforced) from our BEMs strategy that will help guide and motivate our relations with the BEMs through the end of this century and beyond.

Lesson #1: Revising Our Notions of National Security

President Clinton came into office with the strong conviction that a strong economy at home was a prerequisite for our national security. Secretary of State

The U.S. spends less as a percentage of GDP on export promotion than any other developed nation. So, while we are getting smarter and working harder, it is still an uphill battle against better equipped and funded competition.

Worldwide Advocacy Project Opportunities by Industry

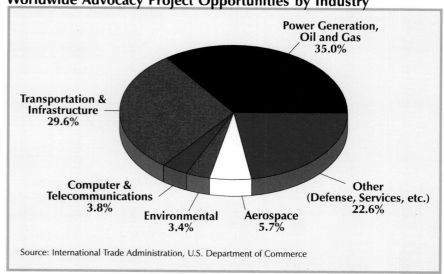

Power Generation, Oil and Gas 35.0%

Transportation & Infrastructure 29.6%

Computer & Telecommunications 3.8%

Environmental 3.4%

Aerospace 5.7%

Other (Defense, Services, etc.) 22.6%

Source: International Trade Administration, U.S. Department of Commerce

We must acknowledge that the BEMs, unlike Europe or Japan, are not mature markets. Their ups and downs will be bigger, their crises more frequent.

Warren Christopher admits that economic issues are at the top of our foreign policy agenda. Secretary of Commerce Ronald H. Brown talks about the fact that our economy and our destiny in the world are inextricably linked. It is safe to say that the Administration is singing from the same songbook.

Moreover, words are being translated into action. One sign is the overwhelming priority given to NAFTA, the General Agreement on Tariffs and Trade (GATT), trade negotiations with China and Japan, and expanding free trade throughout Latin America and throughout Asia. The establishment of a super-aggressive National Export Strategy and a highly organized approach to working with our private sector to win projects abroad is another sign.

It is in the BEMs, however, that commercial engagement and commercial diplomacy are being tested as never before. There are many reasons why this is the case, and why we will need to evolve an ever more sophisticated foreign economic policy to meet these challenges.

- The economic stakes, as mentioned, are enormous. Our exports and our jobs are dependent on gaining a larger market share in the BEMs. No U.S. firm will be a world class company without substantial involvement in the BEMs.

- The competition, often supported by other governments, is severe.

- The political leadership in the BEMs is preoccupied with achieving growth as a foundation of domestic stability. This is their number one goal, and unless we are able to relate to them and engage them on economic issues—from trade to banking reform, from building phone systems to training management— we will not have much influence on the other issues we care about, from human rights to arms sales.

- Most important of all, perhaps, is that without economic progress in the BEMs we could see a world of Bosnias— countries torn asunder, regional instability that not only spells tragedy for millions of people but spills over to the stage of world politics.

This is a clear and present danger for the next century: 800 million people unemployed or underemployed in the emerging markets, according to the U.N.; increasing nationalism; increasing frustration; people with little to lose by resorting to violence to improve their lot. Economic links to the BEMs not only benefit us; they provide hope and opportunity as an antidote to frustration and despair. It is not just market share that calls us to the BEMs—it is a desire for a more peaceful world.

Foreign Competition

The major European governments of the United Kingdom, France and Germany stand out most prominently for their efforts in attempting to expand their firms' commercial presence in the BEMs. The governments of Canada, Italy and Japan are almost as busy, while Australian, Taiwanese and Spanish officials push for their firms in these markets, but with a lower level of involvement. Although South Korean firms are aggressive, the government of South Korea, interestingly, does not have an active export promotion program to the other BEMs.

Paris, London and Bonn advocate for their firms in all of the BEMs, though the French and Germans have been focusing increased attention on the Asian BEMs. Tokyo has chosen to de-emphasize the South American BEMs, but is active among the rest. Taipei focuses its export promotion efforts almost exclusively on the Asian and Latin American BEMs, while Canberra puts its attention almost entirely on the Asian BEMs. Ottawa and Rome are involved in most, but not all, of the BEMs. Madrid remains selective in its focus, concentrating its resources in the South American BEMs and China.

U.S. rivals' export promotion efforts in the BEMs take a variety of forms. The most common methods our competitors use to help their firms increase market share are high-level visits, financing, trade missions, lobbying, trade shows and local advocacy. Their promotion activities are focused on key growth sectors in the BEMs, including power generation/energy, transportation, infrastructure, environment and telecommunications. Specific approaches vary:

UNITED KINGDOM: London uses high-level visits more frequently than any other rival. London calls on the prime minister, cabinet officials and the royal family to travel to almost all of the BEMs in pursuit of business opportunities. It is most interested in promoting sales in the power generation and transportation sectors.

GERMANY: Bonn makes frequent use of financing and high-level visits to promote sales, but the most striking German tactic is the extensive use of local German chambers of commerce and trade associations. Bonn advocates for sales in most of the five major areas listed above, with particular emphasis on infrastructure and machinery.

FRANCE: Paris uses lobbying — which takes the form of visits, letters, phone calls or other interventions — far more often than any other U.S. rival. The French promote exports in all of the major growth sectors, especially high-technology projects such as high-speed trains, nuclear power plants and telecommunications.

JAPAN: Tokyo is most likely to use some form of financing — aid, concessional financing or loans — to promote Japanese exports. For Tokyo, projects related to the environment and infrastructure loom largest.

ITALY: The Italians favor trade missions, financing and trade shows as export-supporting tactics. Rome focuses heavily on advocating for machinery and machine tools.

CANADA: Canada's favorite tactics are high-level visits, financing and trade missions.

AUSTRALIA: High-level visits, trade shows and trade missions are the hallmarks of Australia's promotion efforts. Australia's interests in these countries include telecommunications, information technology, financial services, aviation and mining.

TAIWAN: Taiwan also makes use of trade missions, as well as its high-level representatives' visits to regions of interest. Taiwan directs its export promotion efforts in the BEMs toward infrastructure, power plants and labor-intensive products, such as textiles, footwear and electronics.

SPAIN: Spain utilizes a mix of tactics ranging from preferential bilateral agreements to trade shows, trade missions, high-level visits and favorable financing programs. The country is particularly interested in promoting sales of agricultural products and military equipment in the BEMs.

The BEMs have improved their future by lessening their trade dependence on the U.S. and the West, and trading more with one another — a prudent diversification.

The ability of the U.S. to fashion and carry out the right kind of foreign economic policy will require far-reaching changes in the way we conduct international affairs. From the coordination of policies at home, including the central involvement of the "economic" agencies, to the revamping of embassies abroad; from the education of the Congress and public about the new world we face, to the kind of people who are recruited for the highest levels of our foreign policy establishment, change is required. President Clinton and his cabinet have made a superb start, but this revolution has just begun.

Lesson #2: Patience with Change and Instability

We must acknowledge that the BEMs, unlike Europe or Japan, are not mature markets. Their ups and downs will be bigger, their crises more frequent — as the Mexican peso crisis amply attests. But these are not reasons to second guess their importance or our strategy for dealing with them.

Look first to the fundamentals. In contrast to the newspaper headlines, the underlying momentum of the Big Emerging Markets is impressive. Less than two years ago, Brazil's annual inflation was approaching 2,500 percent per year; by the end of last year it had decelerated to under 2 percent per month. Two years ago, India's top tariff rates hit 110 percent; by 1995, the ceiling was cut by more than half. Not long ago, Indonesia was hostile to most foreign investors, but in the wake of deregulation and the removal of onerous restrictions, foreign investment in plants and factories grew to $4.1 billion in 1993. Since 1990, Argentina—once an example of a state-run, closed economy — has privatized virtually all its major companies, including its national energy company and its national airline. Poland, recovering from negative growth, is today one of the fastest expanding economies in Europe. And let's not forget how far Mexico has come. In 1990, it was running enormous budget deficits totalling 4 percent of its GDP. In 1994, Mexico had a balanced budget.

A lot has happened in just the last year in the world economy to bolster the long-term prospects of the Big Emerging Markets. NAFTA was established to provide a long-term framework for expanded trade and investment in North America—which has been and will be of great benefit to Mexico, as well as to the U.S. and Canada. An agreement was reached among all the democracies of the Western

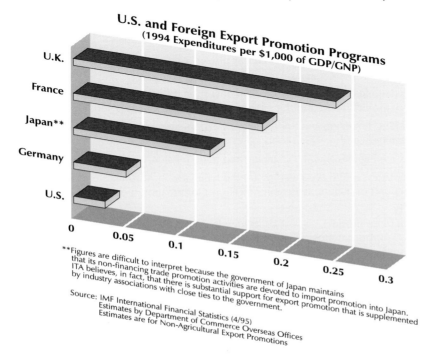

U.S. and Foreign Export Promotion Programs
(1994 Expenditures per $1,000 of GDP/GNP)

U.K.
France
Japan**
Germany
U.S.

0   0.05   0.1   0.15   0.2   0.25   0.3

**Figures are difficult to interpret because the government of Japan maintains that its non-financing trade promotion activities are devoted to import promotion into Japan. ITA believes, in fact, that there is substantial support for export promotion that is supplemented by industry associations with close ties to the government.

Source: IMF International Financial Statistics (4/95)
Estimates by Department of Commerce Overseas Offices
Estimates are for Non-Agricultural Export Promotions

Hemisphere to move towards free trade arrangements, including more openings for foreign investors, within a decade. The eighteen economies of the Asia-Pacific region also committed themselves to move in this direction, albeit over a longer period of time. The European Union is heading toward new trade arrangements with its East European neighbors, and with Turkey, too. The GATT treaty was concluded and a new World Trade Organization was set up which requires developing countries to adhere to all the rules—on lowering tariffs, reducing trade-blocking regulations, enforcing patent laws, treating foreign investors fairly—or face serious penalties.

Furthermore, the BEMs have improved their future by lessening their trade dependence on the U.S. and the West, and trading more with one another — a prudent diversification. Trade among the economies of East Asia is growing faster than it is between the U.S. and them. Trade among Latin American countries has more than tripled in the last decade.

Understandably, we are mesmerized by the ups and downs of financial markets, and by the latest trade battles. Nevertheless, fundamental advances in BEMs in education and technology constitute a more powerful trend. Look at the thousands of Indian engineers who are designing computer chips for America's leading firms, and beaming those designs overnight to California and Texas by satellite. Think about the high-tech industrial parks being erected in Indonesia. Consider the companies from Taiwan, South Korea, Brazil and India that are moving onto the world stage.

While some of our projections, such as those in Mexico, may have changed somewhat since our last comprehensive Big Emerging Markets analysis in late 1993, we don't expect major changes for the BEMs as a whole. Mexico may be down today, but many forecasters see growth next year. In any event, we surely underestimated the pro-business changes taking place in the gigantic markets of India and Brazil. Although we may have recurrent trade problems with Beijing, we have achieved some far-reaching agreements, including intellectual property rights agreements, and trade continues to expand dramatically.

Moreover, precisely because of the Mexican crisis, other Big Emerging Markets are becoming acutely conscious of greater scrutiny from financial markets. As a result, they are likely to move faster than ever to balance their budgets, sell off their bloated state-owned companies, reduce reliance on volatile short-term capital, attract long-term investors in manufacturing and services, improve their financial management systems (including disclosure of vital information for investors), and manage their currencies with heightened sensitivities to the world's capital markets which have become their lifelines. The result should be more stable economic growth, greater ability to attract private capital, and more trade for U.S. firms.

Trade among the economies of East Asia is growing faster than it is between the U.S. and them. Trade among Latin American countries has more than tripled in the last decade.

A strategy of broad engagement with the BEMs will not only open a wealth of commercial opportunities for U.S. business, but will encourage positive political and economic change in the BEMs.

Some of the signs are extremely encouraging. In the midst of major economic strains, Argentina reelected a government dedicated to open markets and continued liberalization. President Cardoso of Brazil continues to push far-reaching reforms despite strong counter pressures. India's government, rebuffed in local elections, refuses to backtrack on its promise to further open the economy.

If the BEMs fail to follow sound economic policies, the verdict of the capital markets will be rapid and powerful. This lesson was delivered harshly to Mexico and the rest of Latin America, which made the mistake of interpreting an abundance of capital as a permanent vote of confidence in their market reform and liberalization efforts. The figures tell the tale: in 1993, private capital flows to Latin America amounted to $75.6 billion; this year, the flows are expected to plummet to only $1.3 billion! These kinds of sanctions are far more severe—and more effective—than anything the IMF could dream of.

This leads us, however, to the analysis of foreign direct investment, which is much more indicative of the underlying strength of these markets than portfolio flows can be. Portfolio investment has a tendency to over-react in the short-term. Foreign direct investment is a different story. Not only do bricks and mortar investments stay put, but they are made on the basis of long-term trends and do not react so fast to business cycles or momentary concerns.

According to UN estimates, foreign direct investment flows to the world's developing economies grew from $31 billion in 1990 to $80 billion in 1993. All of the ten largest recipients of foreign direct investment in the period from 1988 to 1992 were from the Big Emerging Markets.

During the period 1989 to 1993, U.S. direct investment in the BEMs increased from $6.1 billion per year to $13.7 billion, an increase of 125 percent. This can be compared to a 55 percent increase in U.S. investment to all countries and a 23 percent increase to the G-7 countries.

No one is saying that there won't be more problems. On occasion reforms will stall, currencies will gyrate, and there will be political turmoil, too. Two steps forward, one step back will be the order of the day. We call the BEMs "emerging markets" because they have a long way to go. And, from the standpoint of the American government, we have a great interest in helping them to make the journey. The alternative is a world of vastly slower growth and increasing political chaos in which everyone, including ourselves, will be a loser.

As always, history offers valuable lessons. We need only recall the example of the most important Big Emerging Market of a century ago: a nation rich in resources and promise that lacked infrastructure, depended on foreign investment to finance its growth, experienced multiple stock market panics, and saw a traumatic political assassination. Even as its great resources of gold, oil, agriculture and manufacturing capacity were becoming known to the world, it was torn apart by civil war. That Big Emerging Market was, of course, the United States.

Lesson #3: Balancing Big Emerging Complications

If you look at how we have conducted our relations with the BEMs in the past, you will notice that for the most part they have been considered either peripheral to our core interests or that we have been obsessed with one issue. Put another way, we sat up and noticed these countries when they became problems. We tended to focus on only one difficulty connected with any of these places — illegal immigration or nuclear proliferation or human rights violations. We seldom considered them from any other angle.

All this is changing, of course, as we achieve more balance in the assessment of our national interest with these important economies.

Our economic calculations dictate that commercial goals should rise higher on the agenda than before. But we are not a purely mercantilist nation—should not be and won't be—and the other goals, political, humanitarian, environmental, etc., must be kept in full view, too.

No one would object to this formulation, but the implementation of a balanced policy is not easy to do, nor is it easily understood by broad segments of our citizens. The best example is China this past year.

First, there was the MFN debate. The Administration asserted that we want to expand commercial ties and pursue a vigorous human rights policy at the same time. Apart from the fact that the old link had taken us as far as it could, and apart from the fact that access to the China market was critical to U.S. jobs, the president also felt that commercial engagement would, over time, give us some influence in China. To this day, many critics want to see the picture in black and white terms: either the entire relationship is mortgaged to one issue or we do not adequately support that issue, they say.

Earlier this year, a similar argument took place over the simultaneous events of a trade showdown over intellectual property rights with China and a U.S. trade mission to Beijing led by Energy Secretary Hazel O'Leary. Critics moaned, "How could we do both?" The rationale, however, was clear. We want to trade more with China, first, because trade benefits us, and second, because of the broader importance of commercial engagement. The U.S. Trade Representative and Secretary O'Leary were doing the same thing—trying to open China's market, trying to get the U.S. inside this lucrative market. Since then the relationship has been buffeted by additional complications in the areas of human rights, nonproliferation, relations with Taiwan, commercial disputes, among others.

We should not underestimate the complexity of these kinds of issues. When Secretary Brown visited India, he talked about the human rights

> **Our economic calculations dictate that commercial goals should rise higher on the agenda than before. But other goals — political, humanitarian, environmental, etc. — must be kept in full view, too.**

For each of the major industrial countries, winning the big infrastructure contracts — the multibillion dollar awards — has become a national priority; for some, perhaps one of the highest priorities.

issues in Kashmir. When Commerce officials were in Brazil and Argentina in February, they brought up sensitive IPR issues even as they talked about new ways to expand ties.

The basic lesson is that engagement with the BEMs is an important end in itself, and engagement must be on all levels: commercial, political, macroeconomic and personal. In the vocabulary of the Clinton Administration, "engagement" is not an academic term, but rather represents a conscious decision to abandon single-issue policies for frequent dialogues on issues of bilateral and multilateral importance. The logic is clear: a strategy of broad engagement with the BEMs will not only open a wealth of commercial opportunities for U.S. business, but will encourage positive political and economic change in the BEMs.

Lesson #4: Cooperation and Competition with Traditional Allies
Dealing with the Big Emerging Markets is challenging America's relationships with its closest allies in Europe and Japan. If real progress is to be made in maintaining an open world economy, stable currencies, respect for human rights, containment of nuclear proliferation, protection of the environment and other important objectives, the BEMs will need to be central players and the U.S. will need a lot of help from London,

Recent Economic Reforms in the BEMs

INDIA
Eased foreign investment restrictions
Lowered income tax rates
Reduced tariffs
Made currency convertible

BRAZIL
Eliminated most nontariff trade barriers
Reduced tariffs
Reduced government economic regulation

POLAND
Eased foreign investment restrictions
Liberalized foreign exchange rules
Reformed social welfare system

SOUTH AFRICA
Adopted unified exchange rate
Reduced export subsidies
Reduced tariffs

TURKEY
Accelerated privatization program. Eased foreign investment restrictions
Reduced import charges/fees

ARGENTINA
Eliminated price controls
Privatized public sector companies. Reduced tariffs and import quotas

MEXICO
Privatized public sector companies
Liberalized financial sector regulation
Reduced trade barriers via NAFTA
Imposed strict government credit controls

SOUTH KOREA
Relaxed foreign exchange controls
Eased foreign investment restrictions
Downsized bureaucracy

CHINA
Introduced enterprise reform measures
Pledged IPR enforcement
Reduced tariffs

HONG KONG
Improved securities fraud enforcement
Centralized bank supervision
Created new telecom policy authority

BRUNEI
No duties on food products, building materials and most industrial machinery. Most goods imported under open general license.

MALAYSIA
Reducing tariffs on a wide variety of products. Strong IPR protection.

SINGAPORE
Strengthened patent protection laws. 96% of imports enter duty free.

VIETNAM
Liberalized foreign investment code.

PHILIPPINES
Simplified foreign investment rules & regulations. Reduced, restructured and simplified tariffs.

THAILAND
Reduced and simplified import tariffs. Reduced duties on manufactured goods. Liberalizing foreign investment.

INDONESIA
Eased foreign investment restrictions. Reduced tariffs for agricultural products. Reformed banking sector.

TAIWAN
Improved IPR protection
Liberalized insurance market
Simplified import licensing

Bonn and Tokyo in providing the incentives and the disciplines. But on the other hand, it would be foolish to underestimate the pressures among the allies to compete for the biggest markets in the world at a time when everyone is recognizing that exports equal jobs and growth.

These competitive pressures are now enormous. Much of it involves ruthless, but market-oriented, competition among firms of different nationalities. But it also includes government financing subsidies, heads-of-state involvement in commercial awards, use of foreign aid, and— on the part of many non-U.S. firms —illicit payments. For each of the major industrial countries, winning the big infrastructure contracts— the multibillion dollar awards—has become a national priority; for some, perhaps one of the highest priorities. (Why else would Chancellor Kohl or Prime Minister Major lead high-powered trade missions themselves?)

The stakes are too big to think that this intense competition will soon end. And, to the degree that this competition is among firms, acting in an open competitive arena, that's fine. But there is a strong case for the allies to think about a framework for keeping competition in which governments themselves participate within bounds. That would mean taking a look together at all the tools which are being used, and trying to develop some rules of the game in terms of financing (including foreign aid), illicit payments and other kinds of arrangements which are being used to win deals.

We also need more concerted allied policies when it comes to pressing for protection of intellectual property rights and human rights. There is a real danger that rifts over the BEMs could become one of the most divisive issues among the allies. In the first place, we don't have a clear-cut, common security threat to hold us together as we did during the Cold War. Add to that the primacy of jobs—and the chain of connections from BEMs to exports to jobs—and you can see why the BEMs will loom so large for us, Europe and Japan. It would be a mistake, moreover, to think of this potential divisiveness as being contained in economic and commercial channels. For France, Japan and others, there is almost no distinction now between their foreign policies and their commercial aims.

All this has to be seen against the potential threat of instability in the BEMs. Unless we find ways to work with our allies to draw these markets into the center of the international system, to extend to their people the opportunity to participate in the world marketplace, to dream of a better life, we ourselves will find ourselves in a new kind of Cold War... maybe not so cold. What will be the cost? What will be the judgment of history as to how we grasped—or failed to grasp—the end of the Cold War?

As carefully as we consider our options with the BEMs, we must carefully watch our relations with our traditional partners and study them for their implications in the BEMs.

Lesson #5: Mixing Bilateral and Multilateral Efforts

As the U.S. increases its engagement with the BEMs, a judicious mix of bilateral and multilateral approaches will be required. The context of these policies is as important as the policies themselves.

First, we have direct commercial instruments, as we have been discussing.

Second, we want to help create an environment in which the leadership of the BEMs have strong incentives to pursue and sustain politically difficult economic reforms.

On the bilateral end, as noted, we have established several new forums (e.g., the Joint Commission on Commerce and Trade (China), and Business Development Committees (Argentina, Brazil, South Africa, India)); we have established—or are working on establishing—special U.S. commercial centers in Brazil, China and Indonesia; and we are setting up special training programs.

With regard to multilateral institutions, we are less advanced. If the Mexican crisis did anything, however, it served as a call which said that the BEMs were not at the periphery of the world economy.

One challenge is to look again at institutions like the IMF to make sure that they are equipped as best as possible to handle the kind of volatility which stems from the central role that Wall Street now plays in international affairs. Another challenge is to ensure that international mechanisms are supportive of the expansion of an open world trading system, the only environment in which the BEMs will grow fast enough, and in which our interests and theirs are satisfied.

> **If we fail to be aggressive, if we lose these "markets of tomorrow" to our competitors, then we won't get the market share we deserve, we won't build the relationships we need, we won't create the jobs our children expect, and we won't ensure the market openness on which we will depend.**

In the last year much progress has been made on this multilateral trade front. The North American Free Trade Agreement (NAFTA), the General Agreement on Tariffs and Trade (GATT), the Asia-Pacific Economic Cooperation (APEC) meeting and the Summit of the Americas all pointed in the same direction of freer trade. APEC is potentially a very useful regional framework for the Asia-Pacific area, and we will need to have a sophisticated foreign economic policy to work effectively in this new context. Following from the Summit of the Americas in Miami, the Western Hemisphere is more united than ever within a regional framework, too.

At the base of this new emerging architecture for world trade must be a vision and a promise. The vision is one of increasing prosperity. The promise is that if countries and regions pursue sound economic policies, particularly those requiring courageous political discussion, then they participate in the vision.

The pivotal players in all this are not so much the industrialized countries, because the trading system was originally designed for them. The fault line is the role of the BEMs, whether the multilateral system works for them and, equally important, whether they perceive it that way.

It is a moving target, because even as the multilateral institutions are critical to the BEMs, they will need to change to meet the new world which is being shaped by the BEMs themselves.

Lesson #6: Notions of Broader Regional Markets

We talk about the BEMs mostly in terms of individual sovereign nations. And of course, the majority of them are. But the world that is emerging is more complicated, especially when commercial considerations are accorded increasing importance.

When we began identifying BEMs, we put China, Taiwan and Hong Kong together in what we called the "Chinese Economic Area." The reasoning was that trade among the three entities was growing too fast to track, and that U.S. companies themselves would be focused on the entire Chinese growth area. We may need to move in this same direction in thinking about a 21st century framework for several other BEMs. Mexico might be seen in the NAFTA context, Poland as linked to Hungary and the Czech Republic, and Argentina and Brazil to the new customs union called Mercosur. Already we have shifted from regarding Indonesia by itself as a BEM to considering the entire ASEAN region as belonging in this category (see accompanying box).

The challenge for our international policies towards the BEMs is not unlike the one we have faced in Europe for a long time: dealing on two levels at once, government-to-government, and Washington to whomever makes decisions for the broader trading framework. In Europe we had an overwhelming reason for making this effort: we wanted a strong European Community as insurance against the rise, once again, of destructive nationalism on the continent. With the BEMs, the issues are more commercial, but not entirely.

Lesson #7: Not Corporate Welfare But Business Necessity

The ultimate lesson from our BEMs strategy is our obligation to be much more aggressive in our advocacy and export promotion efforts in the BEMs. This obligation arises from the sky-high commercial stakes involved: the chance for U.S. companies to play a big role in responding to the huge demand for infrastructure building in the BEMs—roads, ports, airports, phone systems and electric power generation.

If we fail to be aggressive, if we lose these "markets of tomorrow" to our competitors, then we won't get the market share we deserve, we won't build the relationships we need, we won't create the jobs our children expect, and we won't ensure the market openness on which we will depend.

Advocacy and export promotion, of course, don't come free. But consider the returns: these services, as offered by the International Trade Administration, cost taxpayers just over $236 million a year. But in the last year, ITA-coordinated advocacy has played a key role in $45 billion in deals signed, with nearly $20 billion in U.S. export content. That is a profit margin with which any investor would be delighted.

Occasionally you hear this Administration's advocacy efforts criticized as "corporate welfare" or "industrial policy." That is a gross misreading of reality. All we are trying to do is ensure simple justice for U.S. firms as they compete for overseas business. We need to play by the rules of foreign markets if we are to succeed in those markets. In an ideal world, advocacy would not be necessary. But until global playing fields are truly level, and bidding processes are truly open and transparent, we cannot afford to keep our hands tied. We cannot, as some have suggested, unilaterally disarm in this competitive struggle and expect to be unhurt. We will lose exports, we will lose jobs, our standard of living will be hurt, and we will feel the pain for a long, long time.

The ASEAN Market

Member nations: Brunei, Indonesia, Malaysia, Philippines, Singapore, Thailand, Vietnam*

1994 combined population: 414.2 million

1994 combined GDP: US$ 473 billion

*** An ASEAN member as of July 28, 1995**

CONCLUSION

All too often, as a consequence of the heavy, time-intensive demands to respond to current concerns and crises, there is a temptation among policymakers to downplay or overlook both history and the long-term consequences of our actions. It is a struggle to do otherwise. But all of our best leaders have risen to the challenge and we must do so as well.

Perhaps this avoidance of considering the sweep of the past is natural in a country with only 200 years of history it can call its own. To consider the history of remote civilizations from which we had broken or with which we had little contact would have been—at times in our past— almost un-American. Besides, it didn't seem important to the average American in the first 200 years of our existence. The Holy Land, Greece, Rome, China, India and Africa were all oceans away, as distant as myth. Though we were born of the Age of Enlightenment, and though we sparked an era of democratic revolutions across Europe, triggered the collapse of mercantilism and imperial systems, and were transformed by the Industrial Revolution even as we were its best example—America's impact on and connections to other parts of the world were always more relevant in academic circles than they were to American workers, politicians or public opinion makers.

In this century, we find ourselves drawn inexorably into the world, integrated into its history. Wars did this as did satellites and 747s. So today, while it is possible to argue that the first 140 years of American history developed in many ways apart from that of the rest of the world, virtually no one can dispute that hence forward our histories shall be written together—America's, Europe's, Japan's and the history of the giants of tomorrow, the economies we call the Big Emerging Markets.

This is a straightforward but powerful concept. We must grasp it if we are to have any control at all over our own destiny. We must realize that our future—and that of our children—will be shaped by events, actions and actors in places our forefathers would have considered as otherworldly as the moon.

The post-Cold War era has posed many challenges for every government in the world. For the Clinton Administration, at the helm of the world's richest and most powerful country, these challenges have been recognized and viewed with great care and considerable thought. Our ability to rise to them will be the ultimate measure of our success.

Of all the defining aspects of this new era, the rise of the Big Emerging Markets stands as one of the most important. In facing it, we have been presented with new issues, new questions and bountiful new opportunities.

By viewing these new conditions in the light of history and by learning from our preliminary experiences, we have gone a long way toward developing the kind of new economic world view that will guide us in our policymaking for the foreseeable future. What was fuzzy at the outset, what was even opaque, is now becoming clearer. Surely, we have not discovered all the answers. But we understand the stakes.

Indeed, we face a stark choice. Either we rise to the challenge of these markets of tomorrow, answer the call of our businesses and workers to ensure that government is there, by their side, to do what is needed to succeed—or we step back, unilaterally disarm, and leave the markets of the 21st century to those who understand the stakes better than we do.

It is nothing less than a choice between continuing American economic leadership and prosperity or accepting our decline and a future as a second-class economic power.

It is a choice. And clearly, it is no choice at all.

Either we rise to the challenge of these markets of tomorrow — or we step back, unilaterally disarm and leave the markets of the 21st century to those who understand the stakes better than we do.

The Americas

Argentina: A

Population
34.1 Million

Population Growth Rate
1.2%

Gross Domestic Product
US$ 280 Billion

GDP Growth Rate
7.4%

Per Capita GDP
US$ 8,400

Inflation Rate
3.9%

Industrial Production, % Change
4.6%

1994. Source: U.S. Dept. of Commerce, ITA

Democracy and shrewd economic management have brought Argentina back from the brink, allowing it not only to experience again the kind of economic growth it saw back in the late 19th century, but, even more importantly, to triumph over recent crises. In the wake of the 1994 Mexico crisis, President Carlos Saul Menem's accomplishment in having— with the aid and guidance of his economy minister Domingo Cavallo —successfully reformed the country's economy means that Argentina should be able to overcome most obstacles on its path to prosperity. Already what Menem has done appears little less than a miracle.

When he took office six years ago, Menem's inheritance was an economy in disarray, still plagued by high inflation, a bloated public sector, and a tax regime suffering from evasion and an overly complicated set of tax regulations. The result was a weak fiscal structure, subject to deficits. Buenos Aires had financed these deficits by borrowing from the financial system, suspending payment to international creditors, and accumulating arrears with social security pensioners and suppliers.

In less than four years, through a series of fiscal and trade liberalization reforms, Menem has turned the economy around, restoring macroeconomic stability, cutting inflation—from nearly 5,000 percent to 3.9 percent in 1994—and spurring domestic growth—from minus 6.6 percent in 1989 to 7.4 percent in 1994, resulting in a cumulative growth of 34 percent from 1991-1994. While growth will be very low or negative in 1995, as a result of the Mexico situation, and the country currently shows signs of a recession, there is every reason to believe that, having taken and continued to take the hard steps, Menem has ensured that any downshift in Argentina's economic engine will be a temporary one.

Restoration of fiscal control, restructuring the public sector through privatizations, liberalization of the foreign trade regime, and strong efforts to attract foreign investment are hallmarks of this economic transformation. By the end of 1994, 215,000 public sector workers were fired or retired and over 500,000 transferred to privatized firms or provincial governments.

Interestingly, from the late 19th century onward, Argentina's economy experienced a period of considerable expansion, largely driven by strong world demand for its traditional exports—wool, grain and beef— resulting in an annual GDP growth of 4.6 percent. In 1916, its per capita income was $700 compared to Australia's $1,300, Canada's $1,000, and

Miracle Redux

the U.S.'s $1,800. But after peaking in the 1920s, the Argentine economy suffered a slow but sustained deterioration. Nevertheless, per capita income levels remain close to those of many industrialized countries, such as Greece and Spain. The key difference, of course, is the nature of the reforms behind today's re-emergence, which allow the government to make the kinds of hard decisions in the face of difficulties that give good reason to be optimistic about the economy in the long-term.

With its wealth of natural and human resources, Argentina has always possessed vast potential for economic development. Its large and fertile plains, known as the Pampas, are among the world's richest agricultural areas. Other basic resources have barely been developed, including potentially large mineral deposits in the western sections of the country and potential petroleum and gas deposits in various locations. The country is energy self-sufficient.

The manufacturing and processing industries are well-developed to produce a wide variety of products, but in many cases have been, until recently, highly protected. Argentina's 34 million inhabitants have, over the years, enjoyed a high standard of health and education services, comparing favorably with many industrialized countries. With an adult population 96 percent literate, the Argentine labor force of 13 million is considered a highly skilled one.

A Painful Prologue

Unfortunately, more than 50 years of recurring bouts of inflation (exacerbated by volatile commodity prices) and inadequate economic policies including excessive government intervention, distorting trade policies, chronic public sector deficits, and recurrent bouts of high inflation— paved the way to Argentina's severe and steady economic decline. By the mid-1980s, per capita income was falling at an annual rate of 1.7 percent. In 1982, Argentina suffered a major political and military debacle with the invasion of the Falklands/Malvinas Islands.

Virtually simultaneously, the international debt crisis, provoked by the Mexican financial meltdown, hit Argentina. The country entered a period of hyperinflation and stagnant economic activity—in fact, the GDP registered a minus 4.4 percent growth rate in 1985. Even as Argentina made tremendous progress in rebuilding

The magnitude of Argentina's economic crisis in 1989 makes its turnaround in less than four years under President Menem that much more impressive.

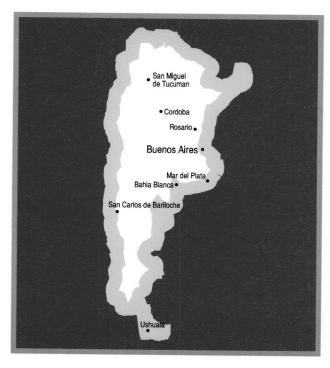

Rate of Inflation through 2010 (percent)

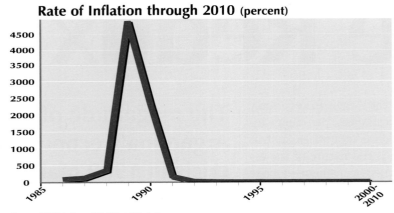

4500
4000
3500
3000
2500
2000
1500
1000
500
0

1985   1990   1995   2000-2010

Source: DRI/McGraw Hill, World Markets
Executive Overview, second quarter 1995

political institutions and democratic process-es, the economy began to spin out of control. Political reform was not adequately accom-panied by sound economic policies. Economy ministers were frustrated by the lack of sup-port for repeated stabilization programs. Sizeable fiscal deficits, financed largely through foreign borrowing, saddled the Ar-gentine economy with an unsustainable burden.

Four unsuccessful stabilization and trade liberalization programs between 1983 and 1989 failed to sufficiently address public sec-tor deficits or to implement fiscal and credit restraints to achieve a lasting reduction of inflation. When the 1985 Plan Primavera failed — the plan initiated before President Menem came to power — hyperinflation, a crisis in the financial system and recession followed. The magnitude of Argentina's economic crisis in 1989 makes its turnaround in less than four years that much more impressive. Popular support for Menem's economic policies was reconfirmed on May 14, 1995, when he was re-elected for a second term of four years.

President Menem's free-market reforms have led to only moderate export growth, while imports grew considerably, financed by substantial foreign capital inflows. Since 1992, Argentina has attracted more than $25 billion in foreign capital in the form of portfolio investment, import financing and direct investment, according to the International Mone-tary Fund (IMF). Direct investment flows increased substantially as a result of the privatizations and a series of investment treaties with Europe and the U.S. The Bilateral Investment Treaty with the U.S. providing interna-tional arbitration for settling investment disputes and national treatment came into force on October 20, 1994.

President Menem recognized the urgent need to take drastic mea-sures to restore confidence in the economy. His administration focused on restructuring the public sector and on emergency measures to stabilize the economy. These measures included laws to reduce the role of govern-ment in the economy and to liberalize the foreign trade and investment regimes, as well as steps to eliminate the financial causes of inflation.

Since the introduction of these early economic policy measures, the Menem Administration has consistently moved toward fully opening its economy to market forces. Slippage in policy implementation, particular-ly in dealing with the fiscal problem, has required continuous adjustments in macroeconomic policy, but always in the direction of stopping infla-tion, stabilizing the financial markets and generally liberalizing the economy.

Simultaneously, the government reduced its role in the economy by selling or closing state-owned enterprises, removing or reducing regulatory impediments in the market (including elimination of virtually all price controls), revamping the tax system and reducing the size of public sector employment. Successful privatization of some railroads, the telephone company, energy companies and the national airline are clear indicators of the seriousness of the Menem government in encouraging domestic and foreign private participation in promoting Argentine economic competitiveness.

Senior policy officials understand that for reforms to be successful, there is a need for growth in net investment. To this end, the administration has set out to establish legal and regulatory environments that will increase transparency, consistency and stability in order to attract domestic as well as foreign investors. They also recognize the need to maintain a vigilant eye on macroeconomic policies. Argentina reacted decisively to the spillover from the Mexico pesos crisis, known as the "tequila effect." The government raised taxes and cut expenditures even in the midst of a presidential campaign, and even though such actions were sure to have a negative effect on economic growth in the short term.

BIG EMERGING SECTORS

Argentina enjoys a strategically desirable location, providing access to the Southern Cone regional market. It has, in the past five years, been transformed into a market with substantial potential for growth within the larger Mercosur market composed of Brazil, Uruguay and Paraguay. If the Mercosur countries expand and improve their open market economic policies, this emerging market of 200 million people with an aggregate GDP of $1 trillion will offer the U.S. an increasingly dynamic market.

Following a stagnant 1995, industry and service sectors are expected to grow in Argentina on average about 5 percent annually through 1998. The automotive and ancillary sectors will show consistent expansion, provided the Mercosur integration process continues without major problems. Financial service sectors—pension funds and insurance—will yield the most positive results. However, a constraint to growth could be the failure of the agriculture export sector to boost productivity and restructure to promote penetration into international markets.

President Menem cut inflation from nearly 5,000 percent to 4 percent in 1994 and spurred domestic growth from -6.6 percent in 1989 to 7.4 percent in 1994.

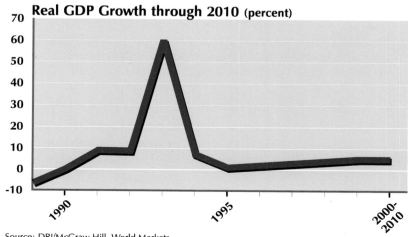

Real GDP Growth through 2010 (percent)

Source: DRI/McGraw Hill, World Markets
Executive Overview, second quarter 1995

Industry and service sectors are expected to grow in Argentina on average about 5 percent annually through 2010.

Individual industries that require substantial modernization—chemical, agriculture machinery and some capital goods—will have to make adjustments within the next two years, if they expect to survive. Already some bankruptcies have occurred in the chemical industry.

In trying to assess opportunities for U.S. business from 1995-2010, it is important to note that although Argentina's large-scale national level privatizations will be complete by the end of 1995, additional privatizations will occur at the provincial level and the process of upgrading infrastructure and services still will be underway. Argentina, therefore, should be an attractive market for U.S. exporters of heavy machinery, construction, mining and telecommunications equipment.

The Impact of Mexico's Peso Crisis

The Mexican financial crisis which began in December 1994 led investors in Argentina to voice concern about the dependence of the Argentine economy on capital inflows to sustain the fixed exchange rate regime. This policy has brought Argentine inflation rates down to a sustainable 3-4 percent while stimulating economic growth. The economy has grown by 30 percent since 1990. Although growth is expected to be negligible or negative in 1995 due to the aftershocks of the Mexico crisis, the economy should grow an average of 4 percent each year thereafter for the remainder of the decade.

One of the more inefficient sectors of the Argentine economy is the banking system, which has come under increasing pressure as capital inflows have weakened, causing a liquidity constraint in the Argentine economy. The banking sector was already undergoing a restructuring prior to the Mexican crisis. The crisis has accelerated the process; 30 banks have been consolidated or merged and a few insolvent banks have been liquidated. Also, the Treasury (not the central bank) has offered to provide discounts to overcome liquidity shortages. In addition, the Treasury will obtain guarantees for rediscounts, including the bank owners' personal assets. This response is necessary to avoid a liquidity problem for the private sector. Already new bank credits are hard to obtain and interest costs have risen rapidly.

Environmental Technology

The Argentine market for environmental technology (envirotech) goods and services is worth $160 million (as of 1993). However, the country will need over $10 billion' worth of investment in water projects alone.

Annual growth in the Argentine pollution control equipment market has averaged 5 percent through 1994. Market growth is expected to continue at least at the level of GDP growth but may grow faster in the coming years. U.S. firms supply approximately 15 percent of Argentina's envirotech market.

From an exporter's perspective, Argentina's diversified industrial and agricultural base provides a ready market for a wide array of envirotech goods and services. Also significant are recent and anticipated moves toward trade liberalization. In addition, a growing environmental awareness is catalyzing demand for envirotech goods and services. The World Bank and Inter-American Development Bank are providing approximately $700 million in project financing for Argentina's environmental sector over the next two to five years.

In addition to public water and sewage treatment and cleanup activities, many larger manufacturing industries are excellent potential clients for U.S. envirotech firms. Chemicals, leather, plastics, metal-working and food processing industries should be the leading generators of demand for envirotech goods and services in the next few years. These industries are concentrated in the Buenos Aires metropolitan area and, to a lesser extent, in the provincial cities of Cordoba, Rosario, Mendoza and Tucuman.

Service is an important factor for the Argentines. In-country contact and prompt service is essential. The privatization of water services, in particular, requires a significant in-country commitment on the part of the U.S. firm. Cost competitiveness is potentially a more important selling point than technological superiority. More advanced technologies are accepted to the extent that they are economical.

Healthcare Technology

The pledge of the government of Argentina (GOA) to budget a 270 percent increase in funds for the healthcare industry between 1993 and 1995 served to increase demand for health technology products and services. The GOA has also begun to transfer most of the government-controlled healthcare facilities to municipal and provincial authorities.

The Argentine market for medical devices reached $384 million in 1994. Imports from the U.S. totalled $155 million, nearly 45 percent of the total import market of $266 million. Also, since the GOA lifted the ban on the importation of used and refurbished healthcare products in June 1994, U.S. companies have captured 70 percent of the total import market of $30 million.

Argentina is currently the third largest pharmaceutical market in Latin America, after Brazil and Mexico. The value of the Argentine market for pharmaceuticals was estimated at $3.2 billion in 1993.

Over the past two decades, the Argentine healthcare sector deteriorated as funding for health services decreased. While healthcare services are available in the richest provinces, they are inadequate in the poor provinces of the north and northwest. Many wealthy Argentine patients go to the U.S. for medical treatment. In 1992, it was reported that cross-border sales of U.S. healthcare services for Argentina reached $55 million.

But beginning in mid-1993, the GOA took aggressive strides toward remodeling the healthcare industry. A massive inflow of capital has followed, stemming primarily from private interests as facilities are forced into competition. The new competitive structure has begun to replace the stagnant healthcare organization that was characteristic of the sector for the past two decades.

Argentina is currently the third largest pharmaceutical market in Latin America, after Brazil and Mexico.

Information Technology

Although direct sales are frequently undertaken with end-users, U.S. companies are advised to establish a direct presence in the market to strengthen contacts in this rapidly changing market. This presence may be a licensing agreement with local manufacturers or a designated sales representative to promote sales and provide follow-up service.

Electronic Components and Test Equipment

Argentina is a small market for U.S. exports of electronic components and test equipment, but one that has experienced vigorous growth since 1990. Among component products, best prospects for exports include: assembled printed circuit boards, tubes, antenna products, bare printed circuit boards, and connectors. These products enjoyed the strongest growth among electronic component exports to Argentina in 1993. U.S. export statistics suggest that Argentina's domestic market is growing rapidly. The combined estimate for U.S. exports of electronic components in 1994 is $88 million, approximately 2.5 times the 1993 level. U.S. exports of electronic test equipment to Argentina reached an estimated $25 million in 1994, roughly double the 1993 level.

Despite rapid growth, the Argentine market for electronic components will remain small during the next five years compared to other countries. At present, Argentina is not a major world center for electronics assembly. Growth in U.S. exports of electronic components to Argentina will reflect growth in the telecommunications and computer product segments, as Argentina's imports of such equipment spur imports of associated parts and installation equipment. The presence in Argentina of major original equipment manufacturers (OEMs) such as Motorola, GTE and AT&T may provide a key customer base for U.S. component companies.

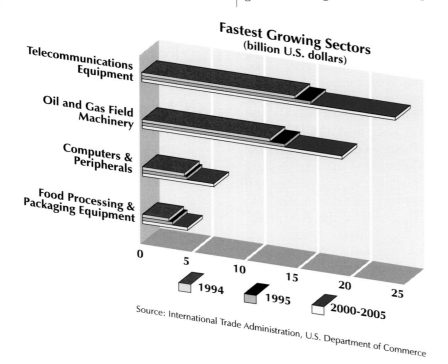

Fastest Growing Sectors
(billion U.S. dollars)

Telecommunications Equipment

Oil and Gas Field Machinery

Computers & Peripherals

Food Processing & Packaging Equipment

0   5   10   15   20   25

1994   1995   2000-2005

Source: International Trade Administration, U.S. Department of Commerce

Computer Equipment and Software

Argentina's $900 million combined computer and software market is the 24th largest in the world and the third largest in Latin America. Sales are expected to grow at a 15 percent average rate over the next several years.

Market trends mirror those in the U.S. with software, networking and communications-related products selling faster than computer systems and peripherals. Software sales now represent about 16 percent of the total market. The downsizing efforts of Argentine companies to reduce costs and increase productivity drives the demand for local and wide area network technologies. Consequently, purchases of personal computers and workstations are growing at twice the rate of large mainframe and midrange computers and represent about 75 percent of the hardware market, up from 50 percent in 1990.

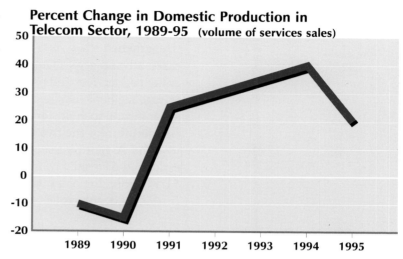

Percent Change in Domestic Production in Telecom Sector, 1989-95 (volume of services sales)

Source: INDEC (Argentina)

Government purchasing in the past has comprised up to 40 percent of Argentina's computer market, but because of restrictions on public spending, demand now comes mostly from large and medium-size companies, as well as professional and self-employed individuals. The consumer, home and education markets that are now taking off in the U.S. are still undeveloped. These market segments are very price sensitive and are unlikely to be significant in the foreseeable future because of Argentina's low personal income levels.

There are around 30 large corporations in Argentina ("large" means employing over 1,000 people), 1,000 medium-sized firms (annual sales over $5 million) and over 200,000 small companies. The large corporations, traditional mainframe users, are seeking to utilize local area networks and client-server architectures as they downsize to become more competitive. Mid-range and small firms are facing increasing competition from imports and are also seeking to cut costs through automation.

The largest user sectors are financial institutions (including approximately 150 banks), public utilities and heavy industry. Privatization will drive sales in electricity generation, petroleum production, telecommunications services, natural gas distribution, railroads, hospitals and airports.

Telecommunications Equipment and Services

Since the 1990 privatization of ENTEL, Argentina's state-owned telecommunications operator, the telecommunications sector has been characterized by rapidly expanding coverage, improved services and increased competition. ENTEL was split into two regional operators, Telecom (North) and Telefonica (South), each with five-year monopolies for basic services. Telecom, owned by France Telecom and STET (Italy), and Telefonica, owned by Telefonica de Espana (Spain), are aggressively deploying new networks in preparation for upcoming competition. Strong government support for competition in the sector has begun to reverse

Argentina's $900 million combined computer and software market is the 24th largest in the world and the third largest in Latin America. Sales should grow at a 15 percent average rate over the next several years.

the uneven regulatory practices that had dampened U.S. commercial enthusiasm for this otherwise expanding market. U.S. companies have strengthened their supplier position in the past two years and have also taken advantage of regulatory openings for private competition in paging, enhanced services and private networks. The February 1994 award of both private regional cellular concessions to a GTE/AT&T consortium provides a significant toehold for U.S. companies in what is seen as the first real competition for the two European-owned network operators.

The Argentine telecommunications equipment market was worth an estimated $1.7 billion in 1993, up 15 percent from a 1992 market size of $1.5 billion. Imports traditionally supply around 35 percent of the market. In 1993 U.S. companies exported $193.2 million worth of telecommunications equipment, a 50 percent increase over 1992 exports of $128.3 million.

In the near term, the key buyers of telecommunications equipment are the two monopoly operators Telecom and Telefonica. Each regional operator also must increase its network to 1.5 million lines. Efforts to upgrade, digitize and expand the existing network will provide solid opportunities for U.S. equipment suppliers.

Wireless services and equipment also offer good opportunities for U.S. equipment and service suppliers. Argentina is currently negotiating spectrum allocation with two U.S. personal communications services (PCS) companies. Demand for PCS equipment and handsets is expected to grow rapidly once these licenses are granted. Demand for cellular handsets and equipment will also increase dramatically with the competitive award of two regional licenses to the GTE/AT&T consortium. The consortium is expected to invest over $700 million to deploy the network and will have a two year monopoly.

Development of Regulatory Activity

Although a well-defined regulatory framework was legally in place after the privatization of telecommunications, regulatory practice did not conform to the framework. Charged with regulatory responsibilities in November 1990, the Comision Nacional de Telecomunicaciones (CNT) did little until the end of 1991. No clear regulatory processes were developed, and a backlog of decisions began to pile up. Experienced staff were lacking, as were resources to hire additional staff or even pay existing staff on a regular basis.

The outcome of these regulatory and staffing gaps was that the development of new telecommunications services proceeded slowly. This was due in part to CNT's failure to formulate standards and processes for issuing licenses, making most of these services uneconomical. Meanwhile, a number of radio operators and telephone cooperatives, faced with little or no regulation, started operations without licenses. Consumers also suffered from CNT's inability to effectively address service complaints.

Since mid-1993—almost three years after the beginning of the reform process—CNT has improved its performance, in particular with respect to the concerns of consumers. A team of outside consultants, working with CNT, made progress in developing strategies and procedures. Moreover, after some early difficulties in the selection process, CNT's top staff (6 directors) are now in place. The selection was made by an independent private recruitment company after a rigorous screening of 125 professionals, and its five nominees were retained as directors, including the president. The last director was proposed by the provinces.

Progress in Argentina's telecommunications sector has been significant, and privatization has been able to move ahead in spite of the delays in implementing regulatory changes.

Infrastructure

Argentina has been Latin America's pioneer in transportation infrastructure privatization. Most privati- zation decisions have already been made. The country's rail and transit systems were privatized in the 1990-1994 period. Most of its port facilities are in the final phases. A contractor was selected for the Buenos Aires port in early 1994.

While feasibility studies are under way for several ambitious projects, e.g., a bridge across the Rio de la Plata; the Hydrovia Paraguay-Parana, an 1,800-mile waterway linking five South American nations; and a Trans-Andean Railway, these projects may not be implemented before the end of the century.

In addition to the professional experience and technical excellence of the U.S. civil engineering industry, Argentine investors are interested in the extensive experience U.S. firms have obtained in operating transportation systems, particularly railroads, at a profit.

Key determinates of sales, in order of importance, are financing/investment terms, price, quality/technical specifications and government advocacy. U.S. engineers and manufacturers are quite competitive in price, quality and technology.

Aerospace

In 1993, the U.S. exported $220 million of aerospace products to Argentina, 70 percent in the form of complete aircraft.

Argentina has the second largest air transport network in Latin America. Argentina's major airlines—Aerolineas Argentinas, LADE, LAER, LAPA, and TANSE—have been plagued with financial losses. There are 350 authorized airports in Argentina, of which 14 are international airports that serve regular and general air traffic, and seven are for general international air traffic exclusively. Privatization of airports is in the planning stages.

Argentina presents growing opportunities to U.S. aerospace exporters. The total market size for aircraft in Argentina was estimated to be $234 million in 1994, and is projected to be $286 million in 1995. U.S. aerospace suppliers have an excellent reputation for price, quality and after-sales service of their products. Standardization of equipment is a key factor in maintaining the U.S. position in the Argentine market. Some of the best prospects for the Argentine market are aircraft parts and components, air traffic control systems and navigation aids.

> **Argentina has been Latin America's pioneer in transportation infrastructure privatization. Most privatization decisions have already been made.**

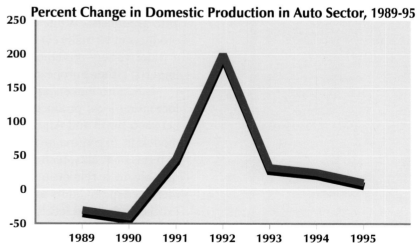

Percent Change in Domestic Production in Auto Sector, 1989-95

Source: INDEC (Argentina)

Transportation

Motor Vehicles and Parts

Argentina has the third largest motor vehicle market in Latin America, after Brazil and Mexico. New motor vehicle sales in Argentina accelerated to 405,000 units in 1993, up from 336,000 in 1992, and 167,000 in 1991. Through July 1994, sales jumped another 60 percent over the same period for 1993. Twenty percent of total vehicle sales are commercial vehicles.

New vehicle demand in Argentina has grown significantly in the last three years, primarily in response to the economic recovery and deregulation.

New vehicle demand in Argentina has grown significantly in the last three years, primarily in response to the Argentine government's 1991 economic recovery and deregulation plan. Although Argentina's automotive industry remains its most protected, Mercosur allows for duty-free trade of 20,000 vehicles per year with Brazil. Also, the quota for private purchasers of imported vehicles was increased in 1994 by 60 percent to 7,900 units. Current Argentine economic growth rates suggest a total vehicle market of 600,000 units in 2000, and 870,000 units in 2010. The automotive parts market should expand by five percent annually from 1995 to 2000. U.S. automotive parts exports to Argentina in 1994 were valued at $300 million. The U.S. export share of this market is expected to grow from 16 percent in 1994 to 20.5 percent in 2000.

Demand for imported automobiles is growing at a sustained rate, despite import quotas and other government protection enjoyed by local auto producers. While the Argentine public has had access to imported products in virtually every field, it is still looking forward to free access for a wider variety of vehicles. Argentines who can afford new cars prefer imports, either European or American.

U.S. auto makers are responding to increased Argentine demand by increasing local production and by taking advantage of duty free trade between Brazil and Argentina. GM, Ford and Chrysler will soon produce models in Argentina nearly identical to those made in the U.S. or Europe in terms of quality, technology and style. Therefore, they will be less vulnerable to a relaxation of import quotas. Although Argentina has increased quota limits somewhat in the past year, demand for imports still exceeds permitted levels. The growing market can still absorb higher imports even as local production increases. Thus, should the government decide to relax quotas further, local U.S.-owned interests are unlikely to be jeopardized.

Given the existing import quotas, U.S. auto makers with local manufacturing operations will obviously find it easier to sell their U.S.-made vehicles in Argentina than those who do not manufacture in Argentina. The best opportunities are in the sale of small vans, convertibles, and moderately priced sedans and station wagons.

Financial Services

Argentina has a large financial sector that provides a wide variety of services through the banking system, securities and commodities markets, and insurance providers. The financial system is primarily controlled and supervised by the Central Bank of the Argentine Republic (BCRA)—an agency that is legally required to operate independently of the executive branch.

Privatization of the social security system—the bill was passed in 1994 and the pension administrators opened for business in July 1994—is helping to boost long-term domestic savings, revitalize local capital markets and reduce dependence on foreign capital inflows to fund domestic investment.

Banking

Argentina's financial system includes both publicly-owned and privately-owned banks that operate as commercial, investment or mortgage banks. Various nonbanking institutions, such as finance companies and savings and loans institutions, also provide financial services.

Assets of the banking sector—which consists of approximately 150 banks—are highly concentrated: the five largest banks had total assets of $29 billion at year-end 1993, or 35 percent of all assets. Public sector banks dominate the system—the top three banks are state-owned and control $22 billion in assets. Moreover, government banks have an effective monopoly on public sector deposits. Argentine private banks tend to be relatively small.

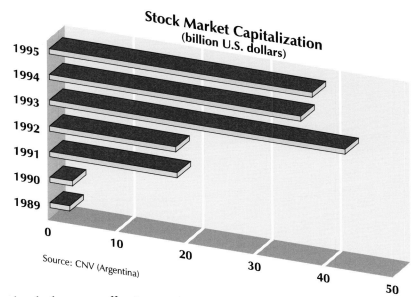

Stock Market Capitalization
(billion U.S. dollars)

Source: CNV (Argentina)

Foreign banks account for over 16 percent of the bank deposits in Argentina. Although U.S.-based banks generally have wholesale operations, only two of the U.S. banks licensed in the Argentine market remain active in retail banking (Citibank and First National Bank of Boston). Eight licensed banks are either branches or wholly-owned subsidiaries of U.S. institutions. At year-end 1993, these eight banks operated 77 branches in Argentina and held $2.7 billion in deposits (approximately 7 percent of total deposits).

The Central Bank has removed the legal distinction between domestic and foreign banks. In early 1994, the Central Bank introduced reforms that eliminated legal constraints on the establishment, acquisition and branching of foreign banks. Lending limits are based on the local capital of bank branches rather than the consolidated capital of the parent company. Consequently, local operating costs increase, and there may be limits on the range of operations that foreign bank branches can conduct.

Securities Markets

Argentine capital markets are relatively small compared to the nation's extensive banking activities. Corporate fund raising consists mainly of borrowing from banks. Moreover, the local bond market is dominated by public sector securities. There is a small, locally-based mutual fund market and an incipient private sector pension fund market.

The country's principal stock market—the Bolsa de Comercio—is located in Buenos Aires. Five provincial cities have minor stock markets. Argentina also has an over-the-counter securities market—the Mercado Abierto Electronico (MAE). Capital market participants are regulated by the National Securities Commission (Comision Nacional de Valores or CNV), as well as MAE and stock exchange regulatory mechanisms.

The stock market was relatively inactive until 1991, with a daily trading volume of about $4 million as the norm. The success of the Argentine economic stabilization program and the subsequent interest of international investors propelled the market to new heights. Average daily trading volumes reached a record $630 million in August 1994. Market capitalization has also grown rapidly, rising from just over $5 billion in March 1991 to $44 billion at year-end 1993.

There is no legal discrimination between foreign and domestic firms in Argentine securities markets. Foreign-owned securities firms are allowed to underwrite equity and fixed income securities instruments. They may also broker and trade both domestic and foreign securities. Moreover, foreign securities firms can engage in mutual funds activities directly and may conduct pension fund activities through a separately licensed company. Residents of Argentina have free access to offshore securities instruments.

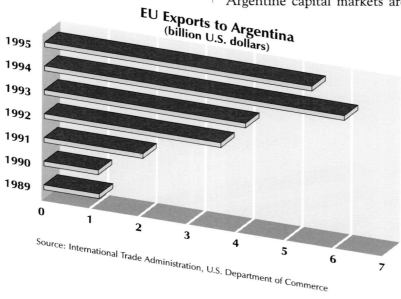

EU Exports to Argentina
(billion U.S. dollars)

Source: International Trade Administration, U.S. Department of Commerce

ALADI Exports to Argentina
(billion U.S. dollars)

Source: International Trade Administration, U.S. Department of Commerce

Argentina is a fertile market for securitization. New mutual funds are being created to hold asset-backed securities that will be issued by Argentine banks and backed by various assets including automobile and credit card loans or mortgages. Until 1993, mutual funds were limited to holding stocks or public bonds. Some U.S. mutual funds are also active in the Argentine market, and six U.S. firms have shares in pension fund management companies.

The market was propelled to new heights by the stabilization program's success; from a norm of $4 million, average daily trading volumes reached a record $630 million in August 1994.

Private rating agencies have opened offices and are working to support the CNV in its efforts to obtain better accounting standards and other mechanisms to improve information available to the investing public. The rating agencies have begun to publish information that has greater reliability.

Insurance

In recent years, the insurance sector has been radically deregulated. In 1989, 40 percent of the reinsurance market was opened to the private sector. Moreover, an industry-wide deregulation program was launched in 1992. It was decided to open the entire reinsurance market to the private sector. Foreign entry was permitted with equalized treatment for foreign and domestic insurers, and the product/price control regime was substantially dismantled.

These recent industry reforms, coupled with low inflation and economic stability, have brought substantial improvements to the insurance sector. Controls over the reinsurance business have been largely removed. In 1991-1994, Argentina received nearly $250 million in foreign investment in local insurance companies. Insurance premiums also grew from $1.3 billion in 1989 to over $4 billion in 1994. Despite significant new entry, the sector has been consolidating. While 230 companies existed in 1989, there were 180 in 1994, of which only 160 were operational.

Energy

The Argentine government has made great strides in its privatization of the non-nuclear electric power sector since 1991. Approximately 80 percent of Argentina's electrical infrastructure now belongs to the private sector.

This privatization supports Argentina's long-term goal of becoming a net exporter of energy to neighboring countries, such as Uruguay, Paraguay and Chile. The Overseas Development Agency estimates that, by the year 2010, Argentina will add approximately 8,000 MW to its current electrical generation capacity of 17,800 MW. This alone represents a $12 billion market.

The government has successfully instituted a market-based system, which allows easy market entry for power generation companies and regulated entry for the distribution and transmission sector. The planning process for the privatization of the nuclear power industry is underway and should be completed by early 1996. U.S. firms have been very successful at winning privatization projects in the Argentine electric energy sector.

As a result of the privatization, a substantial wholesale power market has emerged, including for self-generators and cogenerators to sell to the national or local utility grid.

Electricity pricing is based on marginal costs within a competitive market. While wholesale prices are intended to reflect fair market value based on short-run marginal costs of the system, prices at the retail level are regulated through the RPI-X calculation used by the United Kingdom at the time of its privatization. This system is geared to reward efficiency.

U.S. Exports to Argentina (billion U.S. dollars)

Source: International Trade Administration, U.S. Department of Commerce

Hydroelectric

Hydroelectric stations account for approximately 40 percent of the country's power generation. Argentina emphasized hydroelectric power generation because operating costs are low and it is non-polluting. The country has unused hydroelectric potential and reliable hydroelectric infrastructure. Planned hydroelectric projects that could be put in place by private sector investments include: Chapeton (3,000 MW), Corpus Christi (6,900 MW) and Pati (3,300 MW) on the Parana River; Roncador (2,800 MW) and Garabi (1,800 MW) on the Uruguay River; and Itati-Itacora (1,700 MW) on the Limay River.

Nuclear

The government is planning to sell 70 percent of a package composed of three nuclear plants (Atucha I and II, and Embalse) and a pumping station to private investors. The government would retain 20 percent of the shares and the remaining 10 percent would be sold to employees. The bid will be auctioned to a group of pre-selected bidders, based on their technical qualifications and on their ability to obtain insurance against a nuclear accident.

As a result of cost overruns, the completion of the Atucha II nuclear power plant has been postponed to 1997; approximately $350 million is needed to finish the plant.

MARKET ACCESS

Tariffs and Import Barriers

Argentina indicated in 1991 that it will no longer avail itself of the balance of payments escape provisions in the General Agreement on Tariffs and Trade (GATT)/World Trade Organization (WTO) agreements. This means that Argentina will no longer use quantitative measures to resolve balance of payments problems.

With the policy changes introduced since the middle of 1989, the GOA has removed all but a few non-tariff barriers and specific duties, reduced the average tariff and the tariff range dramatically, simplified document requirements substantially, and opened the trade registry to all potential exporters and importers.

Government Procurement Practices

There are no legal obstacles to foreign participation in Argentine government contracts.

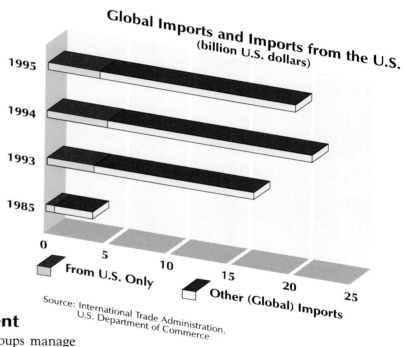

Global Imports and Imports from the U.S.
(billion U.S. dollars)

1995
1994
1993
1985

0   5   10   15   20   25

From U.S. Only   Other (Global) Imports

Source: International Trade Administration, U.S. Department of Commerce

Openness to Foreign Investment

Approximately 25 major holding company groups manage about 50 percent of Argentina's economic wealth. Privatizations have increased their economic power through their purchases of major state assets sold in the last two years. Their financial strength and access to domestic debt instruments facilitated the holding company groups' participation in key privatizations (communications, electricity and natural gas systems).

The companies that are owned by these groups include the largest private banks, significant shares of the natural monopolies recently privatized, urban property, manufacturing facilities in many key industries, and large service companies. Comparable to the Japanese "keiretsu," they could conceivably come to dominate the Argentine business sector and use this power to engineer a similar development strategy as Japan. This is not likely to happen for many years, but their existing influence over economic policy could provide the necessary threshold.

The transfer of know-how and technology through joint ventures is allowing the Argentine economy to modernize. Foreign firms joined these groups to provide their technical know-how and operating experience.

There are no legal obstacles to foreign participation in government contracts.

Joint ventures appear to be a particularly useful form of foreign participation, and U.S. companies have been active in using this approach. But it requires caution and "due diligence."

Terms and conditions established by the Argentine government for privatizations virtually mandated the presence of qualified foreign firms. Without local partners familiar with the political, cultural and social pitfalls, foreign participation would have been limited.

In general, joint ventures appear to be a particularly useful form of foreign participation, and U.S. companies have been active in using this approach. Such an approach requires caution and appropriate "due diligence." The selection of a joint venture partner can be a difficult task, because financial and other information is generally not available in a form that can be easily verified through independent sources.

The stock of U.S. foreign direct investment in 1994 was about $5.5 billion, nearly $3.3 billion more than in 1990. U.S. direct investment is largely concentrated in manufacturing, banking and petroleum. The U.S. ranks first among the sources of foreign direct investment. In addition, U.S. portfolio investment appears to be about $2-3 billion. Major privatizations that occurred in 1993 promoted greater U.S. investor participation, particularly in the power generation, transport and the oil and gas sectors.

Special Considerations

Intellectual Property Rights

The Menem Administration has sought to fulfill a 1989 commitment to the U.S. to enact modern patent legislation. In April 1995, the Menem Administration vetoed portions of recently enacted patent legislation which were inconsistent with Argentina's obligations under the WTO's Trade Related Aspects of Intellectual Property (TRIPs) Agreement and Argentina's commitment to the U.S.

As of May 30, 1995, the Congress of Argentina had voted to override President Menem's partial veto of the patent legislation. The Menem Administration has expressed its commitment to reforming the patent system. It is unclear what, if any, compromise the administration will be able to achieve. Some of the major points of contention include a five-year transition period for pharmaceuticals protection (currently, Argentina does not provide patent protection for pharmaceutical products), overly broad compulsory licensing provisions and no prohibition of parallel imports. Additional issues that still need to be addressed include adequate protection of data submitted to regulatory agencies in the process of obtaining marketing approval and lack of adequate pipeline protection.

On April 29, 1995, before the vote to override President Menem's veto, the United States Trade Representative (USTR) moved Argentina from the Special 301 "priority watch list" to "watch list" in recognition of positive developments up to that point. At the same time, USTR scheduled an out-of-cycle review to closely monitor Congressional and administrative action with regard to the patent system. The review will have taken place by the end of July 1995.

THE COMPETITION

Regional proximity and historic ties have shaped Argentina's trading patterns. Regional trading partners are a consistent source of Argentine imports—holding a steady market share of 33 percent since 1988—and the European Union follows as Argentina's second major trading group partner. Trade with the U.S. has grown rapidly in recent years. Argentina's widening trade deficit has prompted Buenos Aires to backpedal on some trade reforms and impose various restrictions on imports of paper, textiles and clothing.

U.S. exports to Argentina have quadrupled since 1989, but still face stiff competition from regional trading partners, particularly Brazil and the EU. The U.S. now ranks as Argentina's second-largest trading partner after Brazil. In fact, Argentina's growing trade gap with the U.S. is driving its global trade deficit. Recent statistics indicate the U.S. will post a $3.2 billion trade surplus with Argentina in 1994.

U.S. exports to Argentina grew 20 percent in 1994 over 1993, totaling nearly $4.5 billion, while imports from Argentina grew 40 percent to $1.8 billion. During this period, exports of U.S. capital goods jumped 56 percent, manufactured goods rose 21 percent, and intermediate goods increased 12 percent.

Meanwhile, the Latin American Integration Association (ALADI) still ranks as Argentina's largest group of trading partners, holding a steady 35 percent market share in exports to Argentina. ALADI members include Bolivia, Brazil, Chile, Colombia, Ecuador, Mexico, Paraguay, Peru, Uruguay and Venezuela.

MERCOSUR: The Southern Cone Common Market

The Southern Cone Common Market (Mercosur) was formed in 1991. It is comprised of Argentina, Brazil, Paraguay and Uruguay. The group has a combined market of over 200 million people and accounts for roughly two-thirds of South America's GDP.

Mercosur was established by the Treaty of Asuncion. The treaty provided for the establishment of a common market among its member countries with free circulation of goods, services, capital and workers.

The Mercosur members signed an agreement in 1991 to implement a free trade agreement by January 1995. Mercosur concluded negotiations in August 1994 for a common external tariff (CET), which went into effect on January 1, 1995, and is applied to third-country trading partners. The CET is currently applicable to about 85 percent of the customs categories. The remaining categories will be subject to a CET tariff in stages between 1996 and 2006. The external tariff rate is to be no more than 20 percent for most imports, with a 35 percent duty on a limited number of goods to be reduced over a six-year period. Mercosur members are allowed exceptions lists of up to 300 items per country (except Paraguay, which is authorized 399 items) to the CET-negotiated tariff scheme.

This integration process will confront many challenges in the future. Individual sectors will be subject to competitive pressures and seek protection from the vagaries of the market. The recent spat between Argentina and Brazil over auto imports reflects the inevitable pressure on policy makers to seek unilateral solutions to problems. Other sector complaints will inevitably pressure officials to promote protectionist solutions. However, as additional sectors benefit from the integration, we expect to see increasing success for Mercosur.

U.S. Investment in Argentina (billion U.S. dollars)

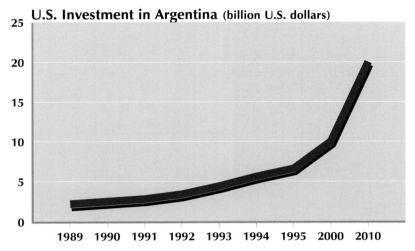

Source: INDEC (Argentina)

U.S. exports to Argentina have quadrupled since 1989, but still face stiff competition from regional trading partners, particularly Brazil and the EU.

When it comes to foreign investment, Italian and Spanish companies have a controlling interest in some key privatized sectors, including the two telephone companies and several natural gas companies.

In some major upcoming cross-border projects, U.S. companies appear strongly positioned to be important participants: the southern railroad connection to Chile, a natural gas pipeline to Uruguay, and the Colonia bridge integrating Southern Brazil, Uruguay and Argentina land transport systems.

Overall, the U.S. and EU countries are in a tight competition for market share in Argentina. U.S. firms selling in Argentina face strong competition from West European exports of power generating equipment, production machinery and metal-working machine tools, as well as Japanese exports of general industrial equipment.

Trade with the EU provides Argentina with about 25 percent of its total imports since 1988. Sales of EU goods to Argentina were up an estimated 24 percent in 1994, compared to 1993, totalling some $5.2 billion. Within the EU, France and Germany were estimated to have increased their share of EU exports to about 30 percent of total EU exports in 1994. Italy remains a major supplier as its soft long-term trade credits are utilized to modernize plant and equipment.

France

Paris uses a full range of tactics to aid domestic firms in Argentina, including government-to-government lobbying, financing and trade shows. Paris has lobbied intensively in Argentine government procurement contracts. French firms—often state-owned or controlled—provide free consultants to the Argentine government to evaluate bids as well as to write specifications that tip the scales in their favor. The French are extremely interested in water and sewage infrastructure and shopping malls.

Spain

Madrid relies on a mix of tactics to boost sales in Argentina, including a very favorable bilateral commercial agreement, trade shows, trade missions, highlevel visits and financing. A bilateral economic integration agreement between Spain and Argentina provides Spanish exporters with a roughly 20-percent cost advantage through elimination of Argentine surcharges and taxes on a variety of manufactured goods. Madrid focuses its attention on the full range of infrastructure activity.

United Kingdom

British officials are making a major effort to rebuild commercial links to Argentina that were severed in the 1982 Falklands conflict. London primarily relies on high-level visits. Secondary tactics for boosting sales are chamber of commerce activity, trade missions, trade shows and preferential financing.

Germany

Bonn relies primarily on its local chambers of commerce and industry associations in supporting domestic firms in Argentina. Germany also uses high-level visits to promote exports. Germany's export credit agencies are not active in Argentina.

Only two commercial officers are posted to the German Embassy in Buenos Aires, probably because almost all of Germany's export promotion activities in Argentina are handled through industry associations and chambers of commerce financially supported by Bonn. To generate future sales, German industry associations donate equipment for training and familiarizing potential Argentine customers' personnel.

Leading Sources of Imports/Destination of Exports

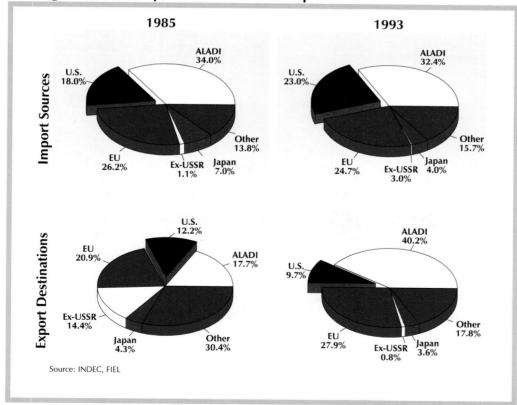

Source: INDEC, FIEL

Other Regional Trading Groups

Latin American Integration Association (ALADI)

Argentina is also a member of the Latin American Integration Association. ALADI membership encompasses Mexico and most of the countries of South America. ALADI was formed under the Montevideo Treaty of 1980. This treaty calls for the gradual integration of the Latin American economies. Its rules and regulations are oriented toward the promotion and regulation of reciprocal trade, economic complementarity (e.g., agreements in specific sectors in trade and production), and the development of economic cooperation and market expansion. There are a number of agreements under the ALADI, but the institution has lost much of its impetus with the advent of subregional and other trade arrangements.

Argentina-Chile Trade Agreement

Investment and trade between Argentina and Chile has soared as a result of a bilateral treaty signed two years ago—which froze trade barriers at 1991 levels. Between 1990-1994, two-way trade jumped 130 percent, with Argentina exporting primarily wheat, soy and sunflower products, and petroleum derivatives. Sales of Chilean goods to Argentina—including copper products, newspapers and other publications, transport vehicles, forest products, and processed foods—have been facilitated by the strength of the Argentine peso.

In 1994, Chile ranked fourth on the list of foreign investors in Argentine privatizations, with significant participation in the electricity and gas distribution business. Other sectors receiving Chilean direct investment include: heavy industry, brewing, publishing and insurance.

Italy

Rome depends heavily on a preferential commercial accord with Buenos Aires, as well as trade missions, to help its firms win contracts in Argentina. Italy has an economic integration agreement with Argentina that provides preferential tax treatment for most manufactured goods exported to Argentina. Italy is especially interested in the food industry.

Canada

Ottawa is increasingly more assertive in commercial relations with Argentina. Canada recently signed a nuclear cooperation agreement with Argentina that should help Canada's nuclear industry with technology transfer and sales to Argentina.

Taiwan

Taipei has a growing interest in Argentina and is using trade missions to encourage sales. Economic Minister Chiang and a 34-member trade mission held meetings with Argentine officials in August 1994 to discuss ways to promote economic cooperation. Taiwan has offered to help Argentina develop its small and medium-sized industries and to assist in training Argentine trade promoters.

Trade with the newly industrializing economies (NIES) of Asia, Taiwan, Indonesia, Hong Kong, South Korea, Singapore and Thailand is growing much faster than trade with Japan. These countries sold $1.8 billion worth of goods in 1993 achieving a 7 percent market share, a 40 percent jump in exports over 1992.

Japan

Tokyo is relatively inactive in Argentina with no cabinet level visits in 1994 nor any commercial representatives in the country. Nonetheless, Japan is trying to build relationships with organizations where industrial sales potential exists. A Japanese expert has been assigned to work in Argentina's National Institute of Industrial Technology (INTI), and Tokyo donated $800,000 in machine tools and other equipment to INTI.

The value of Japanese exports to Argentina has been growing since 1988, but its market share has remained fairly flat at less than 7 percent. The value of exports was $739 million in 1993, an increase of only about 3 percent over 1992. Manufactured goods accounted for nearly 98 percent of Japanese exports in 1993, but its market share in manufactures was only 5 percent.

— *Contributor: Randolph Mye*

Brazil: Is It

Population
162 Million

Population Growth Rate
1.93%

Gross Domestic Product
US$ 508 Billion

GDP Growth Rate
5.7%

Per Capita GDP
US$ 3,256

Inflation Rate
1,000% (Jan-June)
22.1% (July-Dec)

Industrial Production, % Change
16.7%

1994. Source: U.S. Dept. of Commerce, ITA

For years, the largest and most industrialized nation in Latin America has been known as the country of tomorrow. That moniker may soon be out of date. Under the guidance of former finance minister and current president Fernando Henrique Cardoso, this 10th largest economy in the world, once known for its high tariffs and even higher inflation, has entered a period of steady growth, the fruit of a newly-stable political and commercial environment. In combination with the upturn in its economy, Brazil's demonstrated preference for U.S. products, its geographic proximity and strong U.S. direct investment presence bode well for expanded sales of U.S. equipment and services in future years.

And President Cardoso is committed to deepening economic reform in Brazil, which will translate into even greater commercial opportunities for U.S. companies. A dynamic private sector and a wealth of natural resources furnish Brazil with commercial potential unparalleled by most markets worldwide. Brazil accounts for 36 percent of total Latin American/Caribbean exports and 23 percent of total Latin American/Caribbean imports.

Brazil represents the U.S.'s third largest market in the Western Hemisphere, after Canada and Mexico, and ranks as the U.S.'s fifteenth largest market in the world. Total U.S. exports to Brazil in 1994 were $8.1 billion (up from $6 billion in 1993). The U.S. is Brazil's chief supplier, with a 24 percent market share. The U.S. is also Brazil's leading investor; U.S. direct investment in Brazil is almost $19 billion, accounting for a third of total foreign investment in the country.

Under Cardoso's stewardship in 1993, Brazil introduced and implemented a truly effective economic stabilization program, known as the "Real Plan." This plan included a three-phased fiscal and monetary program designed to reduce inflation and establish market and economic stability. The centerpiece of this program was a new currency (the Real) which was introduced on July 1, 1994.

Political and economic uncertainty had contributed to runaway inflation which approached 2,500 percent in 1993. The outlook for political and economic stabilization has reduced inflation to 1-3 percent per month since August 1994.

As reforms were implemented and inflation was brought under control, the lackluster performance of the Brazilian economy in 1991 and 1992 gave way to an economy which grew by 5 percent and 5.7 percent in 1993 and 1994, respectively. The Real Plan, coupled with the new Brazilian Administration's commitment to furthering economic reform, has substantially elevated business confidence and augers well for the

Today At Last?

future of Brazil's economy. In spite of the Mexico crisis, economic forecasts indicate that continued growth of 3-5 percent is expected in 1995 and 1996 in Brazil.

Other key elements of the plan include balancing the budget, privatization and strict monetary controls. Monetary policy, however, is constrained by the need to maintain positive real interest rates to roll over domestic government debt and to prevent capital outflow. Fiscal equilibrium is what Brazil needs to achieve long-term stability in its economy. Unfortunately, provisions of the 1988 Constitution transfer revenues to the states and municipalities, in addition to mandating other expenditures. This effectively leaves the government with discretionary control over only about 10 percent of revenue collected.

Like a number of other Big Emerging Markets, Brazil has made significant advancements in the area of trade liberalization and economic reform. Tariff rates have been lowered and many non-tariff barriers eliminated. Since 1990, Brazil has lowered tariff rates from a ceiling of 105 percent to a current maximum of 20 percent, with few exceptions.

In 1994, Brazil's total foreign trade increased to almost $77 billion (up from $64.5 billion in 1993), with imports and exports climbing to $33.2 billion and $43.6 billion (compared to $25.7 billion and $38.8 billion, respectively, in 1993).

Brazil is blessed with a diversified industrial, agricultural and services base; a gross domestic product of approximately $508 billion; and a wealth of resources, both human and material. Brazil gets roughly 54 percent of its GDP from services, 35 percent from industry and about 11 percent from agriculture.

To enable the Brazilian government to put its fiscal house in order and ensure the long-term sustainability of its economy, most observers agree that Brazil should:

"For those who believed that Brazil would forever be the country of the future, I have a piece of bad news. The future has finally arrived."

*— Stephen Kanitz,
Brazil: The Emerging
Economic Boom,
1995-2005*

Real GDP Growth through 2010 (percent)

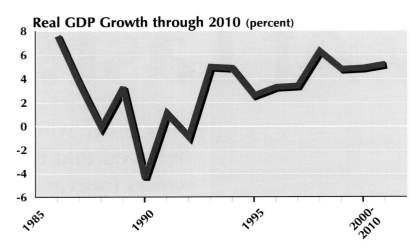

Source: DRI/McGraw Hill, *World Markets Executive Overview*, second quarter 1995

(1) continue to privatize state industries and liberalize investment policies; (2) reform taxes, social security and public administration; and (3)redistribute governmental functions (federal/state/municipal). Most of these reforms will require revisions in Brazil's 1988 Constitution. President Cardoso has indicated that constitutional reform is a priority for his administration and has already introduced constitutional amendments addressing investment liberalization and social security reform to the congress. President Cardoso is also advocating a comprehensive privatization program which includes targeting major parastatals, such as Electrobras (the state power holding company) and CVRD (the state mining conglomerate), for eventual sale.

BIG EMERGING SECTORS

Access to Brazilian markets in most sectors is generally good, and most markets are characterized by competition and participation by foreign firms through imports, local production and joint ventures. Some sectors of the economy, such as the telecommunications, petroleum and electrical energy sectors, are still dominated by the government, and opportunities to further expand trade and investment are restricted.

Healthcare Technology

Brazil is an excellent market for U.S. manufacturers of health technology products and services.

In the medical device sector, the products which should have the best long-term prospects in Brazil are medical imaging equipment, electro-diagnostic apparatus, and technologically advanced disposable medical products, and implants/prostheses. In the pharmaceutical sector, long-term prospects for over-the-counter (OTC) drugs and vitamins are excellent because of the high cost of private medical assistance and a growing trend toward home treatment.

Market opportunities for U.S. biotechnology products are also promising in the long term, particularly in technological innovations in agriculture which have the potential to increase crop yield and quality.

In the healthcare services sector, the best market opportunities include the following areas: (1) hospital management and consulting services; (2) training for allied healthcare personnel; (3) hospital renovation; and (4) health maintenance organizations.

The total market for medical devices reached $816 million in 1993 and is expected to grow 7 percent annually through 2000. Medical device imports from the U.S. totalled $180 million in 1993, representing 40 percent of the total import market of $450 million.

Brazil's $3.8 billion pharmaceutical market ranks among the top ten global markets for this industry and is expected to grow 8 percent per year through 2000. Brazil has over 400 drug-producing laboratories and 177 companies in the pharmaceutical sector. Although 80 percent of laboratories are Brazilian owned, they account for only 25 percent of the sales in the sector, and 300 of the laboratories account for less than 1 percent of sales in the domestic market.

In order to provide more efficient health-care, the Brazilian government has begun to reform the country's entire medical care delivery system. It has decentralized the system, giving more autonomy to states and cities in the planning and controlling of local healthcare programs. The Ministry of Health has also decentralized procurement practices, transferring the planning and decision making on hospital equipment needs to state health secretariats.

Brazil ranks as the third largest U.S. consumer of medical devices among the 10 BEMs. During 1989-1993, U.S. medical device exports to Brazil grew at an annual rate of 11.5 percent, reaching $136 million in 1993. U.S. exports of pharmaceuticals to Brazil last year totaled over $130 million, more than double the level of five years earlier.

Approximately 19,000 of Brazil's public hospitals require rehabilitation. The Brazilian government has created a committee to revamp the public healthcare sector by controlling fraudulent activity and ensuring adequate financial resources for the Health Ministry to reimburse its hospitals. These measures should increase the demand for private healthcare services, medical devices and pharmaceutical products.

Democracy and Development

According to Paulo Tarso Flecha de Lima, Brazil's Ambassador to the U.S., "The election of President Fernando Henrique Cardoso last October was a watershed in Brazilian political history. It marked the end of a decade-long process of democratic consolidation and opened up a new horizon for Brazil's future, a future in which a pluralistic and free society will be able to determine its hard-won destiny, building a brighter future for all its members."

He adds, "The old pattern of development followed until the 1980s is rapidly being replaced by a new model based on a competitive integration into the international economy and modernization through gains in productivity. Competitiveness in both internal and external markets is now the name of the game. There is a widespread consensus within Brazil that this is the only solution through which we can resume our historical rates of growth."

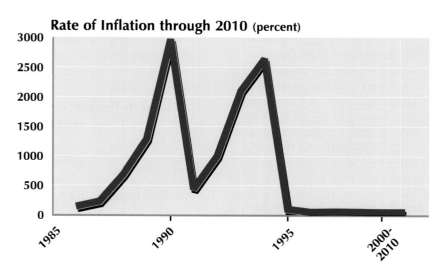

Rate of Inflation through 2010 (percent)

Source: DRI/McGraw-Hill, *World Markets Executive Overview*, second quarter 1995

The Pace of Privatization

The Brazilian government initiated an ambitious privatization program in 1990 and has successfully sold off approximately 33 state companies, which has brought in approximately $11.8 billion in revenues. However, by 1994, the privatization program had lost much of its earlier momentum and the planned sale of part of the electricity sector was halted, while a number of planned auctions of financially troubled or non-competitive state-owned companies were delayed in response to lukewarm investor interest and low price offers. Only three companies (in mining, fertilizer and aeronautics) and minority shares in petrochemicals/rubber firms were sold in 1994.

The first privatization of the Cardoso Administration, which took place July 11, 1995, was of Escelsa (the state electric company of Espirito Santo). Only a few others, largely holdovers from last year, are planned for this year. These include several petrochemical companies, Light electricity company of Rio de Janeiro and a few state banks. The Cardoso Administration has announced intentions to privatize major parastatals, such as Companhia Vale Do Rio Doce (CVRD; the state mining conglomerate), and parts of Telebras (the state tele-communications holding company), but they are unlikely to be sold this year. President Cardoso also plans to issue special decrees which would allow foreign participation in the privatizations of state-owned banks.

The Brazilian market is very receptive to U.S. health technology products because of their technological advancement and quality, which is considered to be the best in the world by the healthcare sector in Brazil. However, U.S. health technology exporters face some impediments in Brazil. Financial uncertainty and lack of intellectual property rights protection can deter U.S. companies from realizing their full export and investment potential in Brazil. Losses due to patent piracy in pharmaceuticals and other specialty chemicals are estimated by industry sources at $125 million per year.

Overall, though, improvements in Brazil's public healthcare sector, coupled with its trade liberalization measures, should improve the prospects for U.S. technology firms in the Brazilian market.

Environmental Technology

The Brazilian market for environmental technologies (envirotech) goods and services had an estimated value of over $1 billion in 1993. However, a number of sources, including the National Department of Sanitation and Environmental Equipment (DESAM), estimate that total investments needed to equip Brazil with necessary pollution control equipment and services amounts to over $19 billion.

The Brazilian market's size alone makes it worth consideration; its population is the largest in Latin America. Additionally, Brazil's diversified industrial and agricultural base has proved a ready market for a wide array of envirotech goods and services. Also significant are recent and anticipated moves toward trade liberalization. Brazilian tariffs affecting pollution control equipment have been lowered from 25 to 20 percent while non-tariff barriers have, in large part, been eliminated. Finally, a growing environmental awareness, including stricter fines for non-compliance with environmental standards, is catalyzing demand for envirotech goods and services.

Annual growth in the Brazilian pollution control equipment market has averaged 6 percent through 1994, but that rate is likely to increase significantly in the coming years.

Growth Projections for U.S. Exports of Medical Devices and Pharmaceuticals to Brazil

	1989-1993	1993 Total Exports	1993-2000	2000 Total Exports
Medical Devices	11.5%	$136M	7%	$218M
Pharmaceuticals	19.5%	$131M	8%	$224M

Source: International Trade Administration, U.S. Department of Commerce

Although import restrictions and duties have limited imports of envirotech goods and services to 10-15 percent of the Brazilian market, U.S. firms are the leading suppliers of that import market, with an estimated market share of 25 percent.

Service is an important factor for the Brazilians. In-country contacts and prompt service is essential. Partnering is an excellent means of providing adequate customer service. Local firms are looking for foreign firms to ally with in order to obtain new technology and know-how to deal with environmental problems in Brazil. Teaming with a strong Brazilian partner can provide U.S. firms with access to product end-users and project opportunities. As in Argentina, cost competitiveness is potentially a more important selling point than technological superiority.

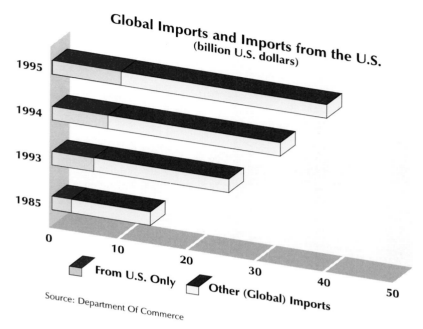

Global Imports and Imports from the U.S. (billion U.S. dollars)

From U.S. Only   Other (Global) Imports

Source: Department Of Commerce

In addition to public water and sewage treatment and clean-up activities, many larger manufacturing industries are excellent potential clients for U.S. envirotech firms. Exporting industries are concerned with compliance issues, as well as stricter fines being enforced by state governments. The petrochemical, steel, food, beverage, fertilizer, alcohol and sugar industries have been targeted as significant potential customers for liquid industrial waste treatment equipment. Major buyers for solid waste treatment equipment include the plastic, footwear, rubber, petrochemical and chemical sectors. The cement, paper and chemical industries are the largest air polluters and thus the largest consumers of industrial air pollution control technologies.

The three largest Brazilian environmental recovery projects are essentially projects for industrial and domestic sewage collecting and treatment: the Tiete River Basin Cleanup in Sao Paulo ($2.6 billion), the Guanabara Bay Cleanup in Rio de Janeiro ($793 million), and the Guaiba River Cleanup in Porto Alegre ($1.5 billion). Other Brazilian states, such as Bahia, Pernambuco, Parana and Santa Catarina are also commencing bidding processes for the construction of sewage treatment facilities and the installation and

Doing Business the Brazilian Way

A U.S. business person is encouraged to learn as much about the Brazilian economic, political and commercial environment as possible before doing business in Brazil. This would not only enable the business person to better understand relevant issues about doing business in Brazil, but also allow him/her to demonstrate familiarity with Brazilian culture and current issues.

Compared to the U.S., the pace of negotiations is slower and is based much more on personal contact. Letters and telephone calls are seldom used to close important business deals. A continuous and personal working relationship is valued.

Many Brazilians who speak English may wish to conduct business in Portuguese. The non-Portuguese speaking U.S. executive may need an interpreter on more than 50 percent of business calls. Correspondence and product literature should be in Portuguese.

Major Cleanup Projects

Guanabara Bay Cleanup: the elimination of pollution in the Guanabara Bay Basis, with nearly 4,000 sq km of land and 35 rivers, affecting a population of 8.6 million people and 6,000 industrial plants.
Total cost: $793 million.
Opportunities: sewage collection and treatment; potable water supply; solid waste collection and disposal; canal and river drainage; industrial pollution control; environmental monitoring and education; and digital mapping and municipal institutional development.

Guaiba River Cleanup: covers approximately 30 percent of the state of Rio Grande do Sul in southern Brazil, an area comprising 176 jurisdictions and a population of around 6 million people. Includes sanitation works, environmental auditing services, the creation of parks, and other environmental recovery programs.
Total cost: $1.5 billion
Opportunities: sewage treatment, wastewater treatment stations, interceptors, trunk sewers, industrial pollution control, dredging work, and environmental consulting services.

Tiete River Cleanup: Phase 1—construction and expansion of five conventional (activated sludge) sewage treatment stations and the installation of interceptors and sewage collectors. Phase 2—construction of 600 km of main collectors and 115 km of interceptors. In addition, private companies will have to make significant investments in pre-treatment processes by the end of 1995.
Total cost: $2.6 billion
Opportunities: sewage treatment, wastewater treatment stations, trunk sewers, industrial pollution control and dredging work, and construction of a thermal-energy-from-garbage facility.

expansion of collecting networks. Funding for a significant portion of these projects is being provided by the Inter-American Development Bank and the World Bank.

Transportation

Motor Vehicles

Brazil surpassed Mexico and Italy in 1993 to become the 10th largest car producer in the world. After a decade of consistent sales and production levels, Brazil set records for both in 1993. Motor vehicle sales reached 1.1 million units, up 43 percent from 1992's 740,000 units. Total 1993 motor vehicle production equalled 1.4 million units, a 30 percent increase over the 1992 level of 1.1 million units. Brazil is Latin America's largest automotive market.

Over the last ten years Brazil's market has supported sales averaging 750,000 units from typical production levels of 900,000 to one million units per year. (Most of the remaining vehicles are exported to Argentina.) Brazil's success in 1993 is due to a government decree which virtually eliminated the federal industrial products tax on small "popular models" such as the GM Corsa, Volkswagen Gol and Fiat Uno. The decree includes commitments by the automakers to pass on the entire tax reduction to consumers and to expand production and employment. These incentives apply only to specific locally-assembled vehicles meeting strict local content requirements.

Both General Motors and Ford maintain large vehicle assembly operations in Brazil, and Chrysler has announced that it may build a Dodge-based vehicle plant there within a few years. For several years Ford maintained a partnership with Volkswagen called Autolatina in both Brazil and Argentina. However, the companies decided to dissolve their arrangement because it was limiting their growth potential.

While U.S. auto exports to Brazil grew considerably durng the 1993-1994 period due to market opening policies and lower tariff rates, Brazil reversed its policies by raising tariff rates and instituting quotas on auto imports in March and June 1995, respectively.

In March 1995, Brazil raised import tariffs on imported automobiles to 70 percent, up from the previous 20 percent. Tariff rates were also raised on approximately 109 consumer durables and footwear, reflecting concerns regarding Brazil's mounting trade deficit. Brazil is expected to reduce the tariff rates on automobile imports to 30 percent in April 1996.

EU Exports to Brazil — by Sector, 1993

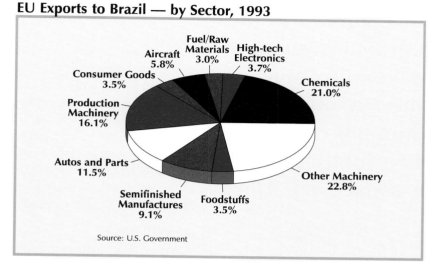

Aircraft 5.8%
Fuel/Raw Materials 3.0%
High-tech Electronics 3.7%
Consumer Goods 3.5%
Chemicals 21.0%
Production Machinery 16.1%
Autos and Parts 11.5%
Other Machinery 22.8%
Semifinished Manufactures 9.1%
Foodstuffs 3.5%

Source: U.S. Government

As for the new auto quota scheme instituted in June 1995, it is currently being reviewed for consistency with World Trade Organization (WTO) standards, and it is unclear how long Brazil plans to maintain this quota system. Prior to the imposition of the auto quotas and tariff rate increases, the prospects for expanded sales of imported vehicles looked promising. However, the implementation of the new measures will have a severe negative impact on U.S. auto exports, at least in the short term.

Automotive Parts

In 1994, the Brazilian automotive parts market totaled $9.7 billion; the market is expected to grow about 3 percent annually from 1994 to 2000. The U.S. export share of this market is also expected to grow from 3 percent in 1994 to 5 percent in 2000.

Brazil's current market-opening policy is to promote the sector in order to boost investment in manufacturing processes, training and research. However, trade sources have reported that some manufacturers are unable to invest and therefore achieve the necessary international quality and price standards. Thus, motor vehicle manufacturers are expected to increase purchases of automotive parts manufactured abroad. This condition represents a huge long-term trade opportunity for American automotive parts suppliers.

The amount of imported U.S. equipment is expected to increase an average of 10 percent per year during the next few years because of lower transportation costs (in comparison to Europe or Asia) and the relatively high acceptance level that American automotive parts have historically had among Brazilian customers.

Motor vehicle manufacturers are expected to increase purchases of automotive parts manufactured abroad. This condition represents a huge long-term opportunity.

The country has the largest air transport network in Latin America, offering a number of opportunities to U.S. aerospace exporters.

Another important element influencing sales of American automotive parts is that American products have been available in the Brazilian market since the birth of the Brazilian motor vehicle industry. U.S. industry's export potential is great as high-tech, high-quality U.S. automotive parts will be in high demand if the Brazilian market grows at its high estimated rate. In the long term, the U.S. competitive stance will improve in Brazil if demand for technologically advanced parts from automotive manufacturers increases and tariffs decrease.

The most important purchasing factors are price and quality. Nevertheless, Brazilian customers favor products that have already been successful in the international market. Products that have been standard approved and have good brand recognition are readily acceptable to buyers in Brazil.

Aerospace

For more than a quarter of a century, Brazil has been a strong market for U.S. aerospace products. The country has the largest air transport network in Latin America, offering a number of opportunities to U.S. aerospace exporters. The U.S. has a favorable balance of aerospace trade with Brazil. In 1993, the U.S. exported $627 million in aerospace products to Brazil, making the country the 17th largest market for U.S. aerospace products in the world. In 1993, the U.S. imported only $119 million in aerospace products from Brazil.

Brazil imports almost half of all its aircraft parts, the majority of which are supplied by the U.S. (followed by France and the United Kingdom). Import demand for aircraft and aircraft parts has increased to allow for upgrades on airline fleets and maintenance facilities. Brazil is a growing and prosperous market for U.S. and international airlines. Brazil's three major airline companies—Varig, Transbrasil and VASP—are all suffering from financial difficulties. Since 1986, the three airlines combined have lost $1.6 billion.

In Brazil's post-recession environment, U.S. commercial aircraft and aircraft parts manufacturers have good medium- and long-term market prospects, particularly in such subsectors as general aviation aircraft, with an estimated market of $320 million, and civilian helicopters with an estimated market of $265 million. Other encouraging prospects for the Brazilian market are: air traffic control systems, civilian aircraft parts, aircraft engines, civilian helicopters and general aviation aircraft.

Japan's Exports to Brazil — by Sector, 1993

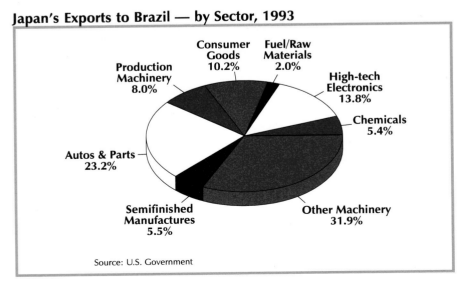

Consumer Goods 10.2%
Fuel/Raw Materials 2.0%
Production Machinery 8.0%
High-tech Electronics 13.8%
Chemicals 5.4%
Autos & Parts 23.2%
Semifinished Manufactures 5.5%
Other Machinery 31.9%

Source: U.S. Government

In another part of the sector, a U.S. consortium, led by the Raytheon Company, won a contract valued at $1.4 billion to provide a major surveillance system throughout the Amazon basin.

The government of Brazil has supported its aerospace industry by requiring offsets and the use of countertrade for government purchases of foreign aerospace equipment. Brazil is a member of GATT, but not a signatory to the Agreement on Trade in Civil Aircraft and, therefore, not required to eliminate tariffs on all civil aircraft and most of their parts.

Infrastructure

Brazil's transportation infrastructure expenditures from the present through the year 2000 could exceed $10 billion, if political and financial problems are resolved. The vast bulk of this would involve local labor and locally manufactured materials and equipment, however.

American engineers have been largely excluded from the Brazilian market in recent decades. Major U.S. transportation manufacturers have serviced the market, to the extent they have done so, through local manufacturing and licensing arrangements.

However, if the privatization plans of the Brazilian government are implemented effectively, the country could develop into a major transportation infrastructure market. Still, local engineers and manufacturers will enjoy substantial advantage in terms of the cost of mobilizing personnel, equipment and materials at job sites.

U.S. engineers and manufacturers will find their best prospects in the high-tech airport/navaids/communications/ground equipment sector. They will find only limited, niche-market opportunities in the more basic civil construction projects—roads, ports and mainline railroads—for which local firms will be competitive.

The key factors in making sales, in order of importance, are market access, financing and investment, price, quality and technical specifications, and government advocacy. The Eximbank's willingness-to-match program is designed to provide a level playing field for American companies, although the creditworthiness of Brazilian government agencies may limit Eximbank operations in that country.

If privatization plans are implemented effectively, the country could develop into a major transportation infrastructure market.

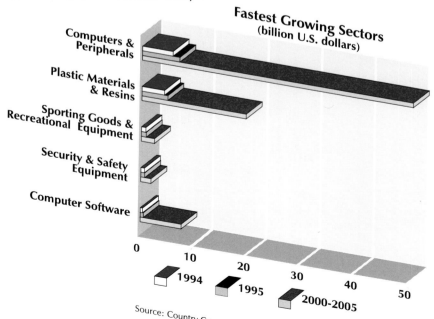

Fastest Growing Sectors
(billion U.S. dollars)

Computers & Peripherals

Plastic Materials & Resins

Sporting Goods & Recreational Equipment

Security & Safety Equipment

Computer Software

0   10   20   30   40   50

■ 1994   ■ 1995   ■ 2000-2005

Source: Country Commercial Guide, International Trade Administration

The continued development of the infotech industry is critical to Brazil's ability to compete in global markets — as well as to stay connected across a country with a land mass greater than the contiguous U.S.

Information Technology

Brazil is the largest market for information technology (IT) equipment, software and services in South America. With a population exceeding 150 million, longstanding repressed demand, and an underdeveloped infrastructure, the country has tremendous potential. Brazil's IT market exceeded $11 billion in 1993 and has grown at a 9-10 percent annual rate over the past several years. International Data Corporation projects IT market growth at 13 percent for the period 1992 to 1997. If economic stability and growth improve, the market should rise even faster over the rest of the decade.

The continued development of this industry is critical to Brazil's economic growth and its ability to compete in global markets, to educate its population, and to link remote communities across a country with a land mass greater than the contiguous U.S.

U.S. exports of IT equipment and components, totaling $985 million in 1993, have grown at an annual average rate of 13 percent since 1991. However, these numbers are understated because of the large number of products that enter the country illegally. IT services exports were estimated at $27 million in 1993.

Since the 1970s, the Brazilian government had targeted the IT sector for protection in order to create domestic manufacturing, technology and jobs. The futility of these "informatics policies," plus the continued pressure from domestic end-users and the U.S. government, forced Brazil to eliminate some of its market reserve regulations and to improve market access for foreign suppliers. This has allowed foreign multinationals, in particular, to increase their presence in the market. However, tax incentives and government procurement preferences are still used to promote local manufacturing.

Despite the elimination of market reserve barriers in 1992, many IT products still face high import fees. Import tariffs and taxes can add up to 90 percent to the price of some kinds of electronics equipment, although certain components and parts, such as microprocessors, have zero tariffs. It is this situation that is responsible for creating a market that is heavily supplied by contraband and gray market activities. In addition, certain IT products are still subject to domestic distribution and government procurement restrictions and registration requirements.

The protection of intellectual property rights (IPR) is another significant problem in Brazil. The Business Software Alliance has estimated that there was an 83 percent piracy rate in 1993 that resulted in $331 million in lost sales. This is over twice the rate in the U.S. and means that for every legal copy of software sold in Brazil, there were four illegal copies.

U.S. products have a reputation in Brazil for quality, durability and state-of-the-art technology that make them attractive to purchasers. This is an advantage to U.S. exporters; however, small firms and other users concerned mainly with price are increasingly attracted to less expensive products from aggressive Asian suppliers. This situation forces some U.S. suppliers to focus mainly on high-end market segments.

Telecommunications Equipment and Services

Brazil's telecommunications market has enormous potential. In order for the country to modernize its governmental and economic structures, it must upgrade its communications services: Brazil has a lower teledensity than other several emerging markets including India, China, Indonesia and Turkey. Teledensity in Brazil (the number of lines per 100 people) was 6.8 in 1993 with 10.3 million lines in service.

Most future investment in the information sector will be in the telecommunications arena, as Brazil develops its communications infrastructure. In August 1994, the Brazilian government announced a plan to spur investment through partnerships with Telebras (the national telecom company) subsidiaries. This scheme would permit foreign investment in communications projects that then could be leased by state-owned Telebras subsidiaries. Telebras expects to attract over $7 billion in new investment over the next five years through the partnership program.

Further liberalization of the telecommunications sector should create an enormous market for U.S. products and services. A constitutional amendment which would allow greater private sector participation in the telecommunications sector and eliminate Telebras's monopoly on basic telecom services, is currently under review by the Brazilian congress. U.S. companies are also encouraged by falling import tariffs on telecommunications products. The telecommunications investment plan announced in August 1994 should generate billions of dollars in investment and sales over the next 5-10 years. Liberalization of Brazil's telecommunications sector will also contribute to growth in computer

Major Information Technology Projects

Pro-Amazon Project: purchase by the federal police of surveillance and communications equipment to support intervention activities; prevent and eradicate illicit drug traffic; investigate and interdict smuggling, unauthorized mining and other illegal activities in the Amazon region.

Total cost: $248 million

Opportunities: supply of surveillance and communications equipment, helicopters, informatic products, police equipment, including arms and ammunition.

Telebras Pro-Rural Project: a turn-key project to purchase 1,000 small earth stations to link the rural Amazonia frontier area with the rest of the country via satellite. Telebras intends to use a network of small satellite dishes.

Total cost: $150-200 million

Opportunities: satellite communications equipment.

U.S. suppliers of petroleum equipment and services have a strong competitive position in terms of product quality and price. And Eximbank can be very helpful in providing financing — a crucial element in major purchases by Petrobras.

hardware, software and information services, as communications costs drop and technology is upgraded.

Energy

Oil & Gas Field Machinery

The total Brazilian market for petroleum equipment and services was about $2.85 billion in 1993, of which 47 percent or $1.35 billion was supplied by imports. This market includes exploration, drilling and production equipment and services for both onshore and offshore operations. It also includes specialized pipe-laying and subsea diving equipment.

According to U.S. Bureau of the Census data, U.S. exports of oil and gas field machinery to Brazil was $63 million in 1993 and $37 million in the first half of 1994. Petrobras, the government-owned oil monopoly, imports about 25 percent of its equipment purchases, up from 10 percent three years ago.

The Campos Basin oilfield complex coming on stream recently helped Petrobras reach a new oil production record. Campos Basin is considered the deepest offshore production system in the world. Over 60 percent of Brazil's current petroleum reserves lie in deepwater, i.e., in depths over 400 meters. This deepwater exploration and development requires advanced and specialized petroleum equipment and services of which the U.S. is a major supplier. Many future petroleum projects should provide major market opportunities for U.S. petroleum equipment suppliers and service companies.

The Brazilian constitution has not been amended to allow foreign companies to participate directly in petroleum exploration and production. However, Petrobras has discontinued its restrictive contract leasing practices and is now sourcing more of its equipment and services from foreign companies, including many U.S. petroleum equipment manufacturers and service companies. In addition, the Brazilian congress has demonstrated initial positive support for a Constitutional revision which would demonopolize the petroleum industry. Final approval of the legislation is expected in September, which would allow for greater foreign participation in the petroleum and natural gas sector.

As a state-owned entity, Petrobras procurement abides by the Brazilian public tenders law. Most major purchases of equipment and services are made through international tenders. For major projects, competition can be keen in terms of product quality, price and financing terms. U.S. suppliers of petroleum equipment and services have a strong competitive position in terms of product quality and price. And Eximbank can be very helpful in providing financing—a crucial element in major purchases by Petrobras.

Other projects being undertaken in the energy field include: the $1.6 billion Serra da Mesa Hydroelectric Project to generate 1,200 MW; the $200 million Co-generation Project/National Steel Company, a co-generation project to use energy released by gases generated by its large gas furnaces;

the $2.1 billion Brazil-Bolivia Gas Pipeline; and the $800 million Salobo Project to start copper-mining operations in the Amazon.

Financial Services

Brazil has a large and sophisticated financial sector that provides a wide range of services. Brazil's National Monetary Council (NMC)—whose membership includes the Ministers of Finance and Planning and the Central Bank President—establishes overall policies for the financial system. The nation's Central Bank has broad discretion to implement NMC policies, executes monetary and credit policy, and regulates banks and other financial institutions.

Banking

Brazil's banking sector includes some 238 banks operating 17,000 branches. It comprises both private-sector and government banks. All-service multiple banks—which dominate the market—provide commercial banking, broker-age and investment services. Brazil does not have a deposit insurance system. If the Central Bank decides to compensate depositors in the event of a bank failure, it will need appropriated funds from Congress to offset any shortfalls.

The Brazilian constitution prohibits new entry of foreign banks and imposes a freeze on increases in foreign participation in the owner-ship of existing Brazilian financial institutions. Foreign banks also face discriminatory capital standards. Despite these restrictions, U.S. banks are well represented in Brazil. By late December 1993, six U.S. banks were able to operate 119 branches in Brazil with total assets of $7.8 billion—a 48 percent asset increase from their 1989 position. Moreover, four other U.S. banks have substantial interests in Brazilian banks. In recent years, foreign banks have been able to expand into new areas by converting into multiple banks.

Brazilian banks profited from Brazil's high inflation and high real interest environment. They were able to earn high yields on non-interest bearing deposits and float. However, banks have been losing windfall profits after the recent success of anti-inflation measures. Many banks are under pressure to adjust to the new economic environment by cutting costs

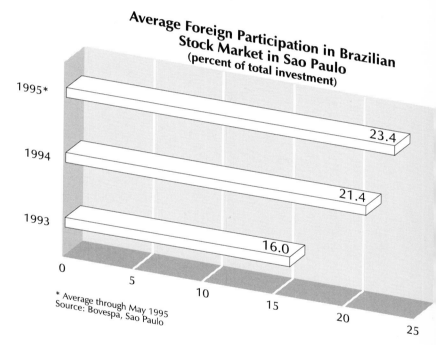

Average Foreign Participation in Brazilian Stock Market in Sao Paulo
(percent of total investment)

1995* — 23.4
1994 — 21.4
1993 — 16.0

* Average through May 1995
Source: Bovespa, Sao Paulo

Tariffs, 1988-94

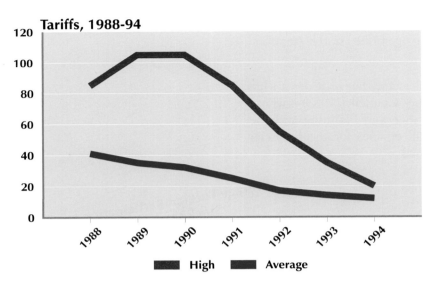

High   Average

Source: WEFA, Department of Commerce

and diversifying into new activities. State-owned banks, with high personnel costs and large bad-debt portfolios, are expected to face a more difficult adjustment process than private banks.

Securities Markets

Foreign and domestic multiple banks are the primary players in Brazil's securities markets (with 40 percent of trading volume), followed by large public and private pension funds and mutual funds. Although constitutional provisions prohibit new foreign securities and brokerage firms from entering the Brazilian market, foreign brokerage firms have entered Brazil's securities markets in recent years as minority partners in joint ventures with Brazilian companies.

Since 1991, the government has liberalized regulations to facilitate foreign portfolio investment in Brazil. Foreign participation in the Brazilian stock markets has increased sharply to $5.8 billion in 1993 from $386 million in 1991. However, relatively few corporations get funds through Brazilian exchanges — Brazilian firms have tended to go to international markets to raise capital on cheaper and more flexible terms. In the midst of high internal interest rates, U.S. securities/brokerage firms played a leading role in helping Brazilian borrowers gain access to foreign capital markets.

Insurance

Brazil is a large potential market for U.S. insurance providers. Relatively recent data illustrates this market potential—Brazil's 1991 premiums per capita of $28 and premiums/GDP ratio of 1.4 percent are low compared to other key Latin countries. The Brazilian market is currently served by about 105 companies and a government-controlled monopoly reinsurer.

A number of foreign insurers, including U.S. insurance providers, have ownership interests in Brazilian insurance companies. Nevertheless, access to and treatment in Brazil's insurance market is relatively restricted. Foreign insurers' participation is limited to 50 percent of the capital and about one-third of the voting stock of a Brazilian insurance company. However, in a move that could benefit U.S. and other foreign insurers, Brazil recently agreed to slowly open portions of its market to private reinsurers beginning in 1995.

Although Brazilian restrictions currently tend to limit commercial and investment opportunities for U.S. insurance and other financial services firms, the prospect of growth-oriented economic stabilization and global trade and investment liberalization could likely enhance future opportunities for U.S. companies in the Brazilian financial sector.

MARKET ACCESS

Tariffs and Import Barriers

Most of Brazil's import duties range from 0 to 20 percent; however, a few items are high as 70 percent. The average duty is approximately 14 percent. Duties are assessed on the c.i.f. (cost, insurance and freight) value of the import. Under the Uruguay Round of the General Agreement on Tariffs and Trade (GATT), Brazil agreed to bind tariffs on 100 percent of its industrial tariff lines (up from a pre-Uruguay Round level of 6 percent of tariff lines) at a ceiling of 35 percent, with subceiling bindings in certain sectors.

The internal Brazilian taxes of consequence to U.S. exporters are the Industrial Products Tax (Imposto Sobre Produtos Industrializados, or IPI) and the Merchandise Circulation Tax (Imposto Sobre Circulação de Mercadorias, or ICM).

The IPI is a federal tax levied on most domestic and imported manufactured products. The ICM is a state government value-added tax applicable to both imports and domestic products. Some sectors of the economy, such as construction services, mining, electrical energy, liquid and gaseous fuels, and locally produced machinery and equipment, are exempt from the ICM tax. For the most part, Brazilian exports are exempt.

In the first half of 1995, Brazil imposed quotas on auto imports and significantly raised import duties on more than 100 consumer durables, footwear and autos. Although deemed temporary measures to address Brazil's trade deficit, they have raised concerns that Brazil may be stepping back from its trade liberalization program.

Government Procurement Practices

Brazilian government procurement policies apply to purchases by government entities and by parastatal companies. Price is usually the determining factor in selecting suppliers, and most government procurements are opened to international competition either through direct bidding, consortia or imports. International bidding is allowed for most procurements with related international development bank funding.

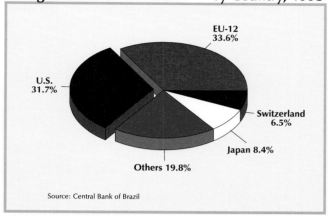

Foreign Investment in Brazil — by Country, 1993

EU-12 33.6%

U.S. 31.7%

Switzerland 6.5%

Japan 8.4%

Others 19.8%

Source: Central Bank of Brazil

Since 1990, Brazil has lowered tariff rates from a ceiling of 105 percent to a current maximum of 20 percent, with few exceptions.

However, government procurement of telecommunications and information processing (informatics) equipment and services is exempted from the general practice described above. Special requirements were established in 1993 and early 1994 allowing locally manufactured telecommunications and informatics products to receive preferential treatment in government procurement, and to be eligible for tax and other fiscal benefits based on meeting local content and other requirements.

In practice, it is difficult for foreign service firms to operate in the public sector in Brazil unless work is performed in association with a local firm. To be considered Brazilian, a firm must have majority Brazilian capital participation and decision making authority — "operational control." A Brazilian state enterprise is permitted to subcontract services to a foreign firm if domestic expertise is not available for the specific task. A foreign firm may only bid for government contracts to provide technical services when no qualified Brazilian firm exists.

In the case of international bidding to supply goods and services for specific government projects, successful bidders are required to have local representation, i.e., "legal presence," in Brazil. Since the open period for bidding is often as short as one month, it is highly advisable to have a permanent resident in Brazil able to act on tenders as soon as they are announced.

Major Transportation Infrastructure Projects

Tiete-Parana Valley Waterway: the area covered represents the largest consumer market in Latin America.
Total cost: $930 million
Opportunities: construction of highways; construction of railroads and supply of equipment; supply of signalling/monitoring equipment for the waterway; supply of barges, boats and related navigation equipment; Port of Santos and Paranagua remodeling. Also energy and environmental activity.

REDE Locomotive Rehabilitation: the rehabilitation and upgrading of a number of REDE Ferroviaria Federal S.A.'s diesel electric locomotives
Total cost: $400 million
Opportunities: railroad locomotive rebuild-kits.

Expansion of Sao Paulo City Mass Transportation: to expand the current subway line to implement an integrated urban transport system in Sao Paulo.
Total cost : $1.2 billion
Opportunities: construction of subway tunnels and underground stations, supply of ventilation and monitoring equipment, supply of signalling equipment for the railway network expansion.

Ferronorte S.A.: designed to satisfy the need for the transportation of grain production from the east-west region to southern ports of Brazil and to improve the intermodal transportation network in Amazonia.
Total cost: $1.2 billion
Opportunities: construction of railway line and supply of maintenance.

A U.S. supplier may find that including local purchases of Brazilian goods and services within its bid, or developing a significant subcontract association with a Brazilian firm, will improve the chances for success. Similarly, a financing proposal that includes credit for purchase of local goods and services for the same project will be more attractive than one that ignores local business.

The U.S. Embassy in Brazil advises U.S. exporters interested in supplying goods and services for Brazilian Government projects that advance descriptions of U.S. suppliers' capabilities can often be influential in gaining a sale. These early proposals can be effective even before the exact terms of an investment plan are defined or the design of a project's specifications is completed. Such a proposal should include financing, engineering and equipment presentations.

Openness to Foreign Investment

The 1988 Constitution restricts foreign investment in several sectors: petroleum and natural gas, telecommunications, mining, power generation, nuclear activities, fishing, internal transport, health care services, financial institutions, insurance and reinsurance, print and electronic media, construction and professional services. In the case of petroleum and telecommunications, state-owned monopolies dominate the market. In other sectors investment is restricted so that the majority of voting capital and the actual decision-making power is held by individuals domiciled and residing in Brazil.

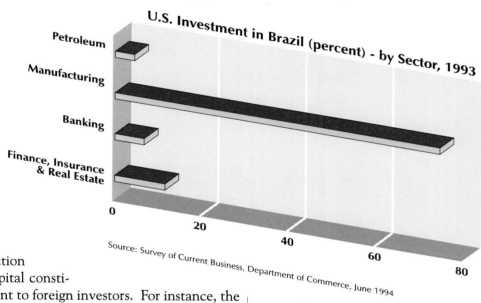

Source: Survey of Current Business, Department of Commerce, June 1994

Brazil's constitutional distinction between national and foreign capital constitutes a denial of national treatment to foreign investors. For instance, the constitution permits the Brazilian government to offer temporary protection and benefits to companies with national capital. It also requires preferential treatment for national companies in the procurement of goods and services by the government. Foreign companies can be excluded from certain bids and competitions. Another constitutional provision gives the state the right to intervene to protect a domestic industry's market share (establishing the principle of market reserve).

President Cardoso has introduced legislation to the Brazilian congress which, if approved, will significantly liberalize Brazil's investment regime. He proposed constitutional amendments which would eliminate the distinction between national and foreign capital and allow greater foreign participation in the telecommunications and petroleum and natural gas sectors.

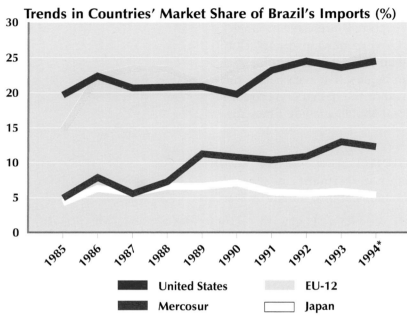

Trends in Countries' Market Share of Brazil's Imports (%)

United States

Mercosur

EU-12

Japan

Source: IMF   *Data from the first three quarters of 1994

Special Considerations

Intellectual Property Rights

Although Brazil is a signatory to the Paris, Berne and Universal Copyright conventions on intellectual property rights (IPR) protection and supports the GATT Trade Related Aspects of Intellectual Property (TRIPS) accord, current IPR protection remains inadequate and uncertain. Current regulations provide only limited or no protection for: (1) pharmaceuticals, (2) metallic admixtures and alloys or (3) substance, matter or products obtained by chemical means or processes. Other weaknesses include: onerous compulsory licensing provisions, stringent local working requirements explicit authority for parallel importation, weak enforcement provisions for trade secrets and poor copyright protection. Brazil has been placed on the U.S. government's Special 301 "priority watch list." However, Brazil has instituted some improvements in its IPR regime through the implementation of new rules protecting well-known trademarks. In addition, bills that would strengthen patent and copyright protection are currently under review in the Brazilian congress.

Rival governments want to diversify their export promotion efforts away from a heavy East Asia orientation and do not want to concede the Americas to the U.S.

THE COMPETITION

The governments of key U.S. economic rivals are redoubling their efforts to help their firms increase market share in Brazil. Widespread interest in emerging countries like Brazil is prompted in part by reductions in trade barriers, recent economic reforms and improving growth prospects. Moreover, rival governments want to diversify their export promotion efforts away from a heavy East Asia orientation and do not want to concede the rapidly growing Western Hemisphere market to the U.S.

The U.S. and the European Union have taken turns in the role of leading exporter to Brazil for much of the period since 1986, with U.S. exporters holding a narrow lead in total market share in 1993. The EU currently is in the lead in such products as general industrial equipment, metal-working machine tools and pharmaceuticals, and is challenging the U.S. lead in office machines. Japan's market share in Brazil has remained stagnant at about 6 percent since the mid-1980s.

France

Paris emphasizes government lobbying, favorable financing and the use of its embassies and consulates in Brazil to push for sales. The French often lobby the Brazilian Congress; in the recent Amazon Surveillance System (SIVAM) case, such lobbying led to subsequent Congressional speeches in support of French firms. Paris actively lobbied for Thomson during the SIVAM bidding in the summer of 1994, including sending Trade Minister Longuet to Brazil. In Brazil, 80 percent of the French mission is engaged in commercial activities, compared with roughly 10 percent for the U.S.

Germany

Bonn operates in Brazil primarily through the German Chamber of Commerce. The Germans use trade missions and trade shows as key tactics for targeting the Brazilian market. The German Chamber promotes trade shows by offering financial support and a variety of services, such as transportation and hotel reservations. The Chamber receives indirect subsidization from Bonn through tax benefits to fund such trade promotion activities. Bonn promotes an average of four official trade missions per year to Brazil.

Leading Sources of Imports/Destination of Exports

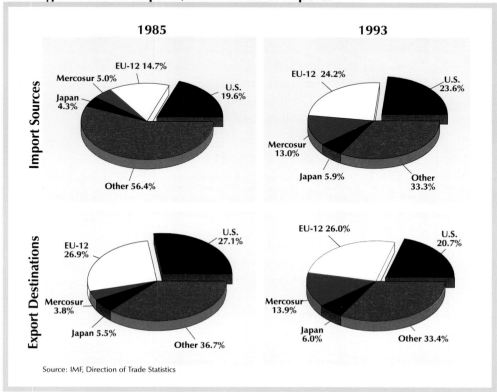

Source: IMF, Direction of Trade Statistics

United Kingdom

London considers Brazil a priority export market and relies primarily on high-level visits to promote exports. The British also look to preferential financing, Chamber of Commerce trade promotion activities and government lobbying as a means to boost sales.

London's Export Credit Guarantee Division (ECGD) restored coverage to Brazil in May 1994, and predicted it would guarantee about $160 million over the next two years, primarily for private infrastructure projects, and the government urged British exporters in July 1994 to take advantage of the ECGD's expanded overseas investment scheme to target Brazil.

Italy

The centerpiece of Rome's support for domestic firms in Brazil is a preferential commercial accord that has given Italian firms a significant competitive edge. Based on the accord, Brasilia recently awarded a telecommunications contract for cellular equipment to Italy without a competitive bid. Rome also makes use of trade missions as well as government lobbying in Brazil.

Canada

Ottawa's strategy in Brazil emphasizes high-level visits and trade shows. The Canadian Consulate organized pavilions in six major trade shows in Brazil in 1994.

Taiwan

Taipei uses governmental agreements and high-level visits to promote trade in Brazil. Taiwan has established a bilateral commission with the Brazilian National Confederation on Industry and is actively building relationships with Brazilian state and local governments.

Japan

Tokyo is relatively inactive in Brazil.

The Japan External Trade Organization (JETRO) has been doing little to support Japanese exports to Brazil; the last trade show JETRO participated in was in 1992. Nor has Tokyo sent official trade missions to Brazil in the last few years.

The Japanese Export-Import Bank has held back on extending credits to Brazil because of payments arrears and the lack of an IMF program. Tokyo, however, is willing to provide concessional loans and other support for environmental projects, as evidenced by its pledge of funding for the Guanabara and Tiete River projects in 1992.

European Union

In addition to the activities of individual European governments, the EU has embarked on an active program of trade promotion in Brazil through the establishment of trade centers. The EU is opening seven trade centers throughout Brazil and is providing up to $1.2 million for European-Brazilian joint venture feasibility studies.

The EU is working through the Rio de Janeiro State Federation of Industries to develop a computer-based link with Brazilian partners and potential customers and has promised to follow up with credits, financing and other assistance to European exporters.

EU Commission Vice-President Marin proposed in October, 1994, a framework agreement for enhanced cooperation between the EU and the Southern Cone Common Market (Mercosur) linking Argentina, Brazil, Paraguay and Uruguay.

— *Contributors: Walter Bastian, Laura Zeiger-Hatfield*

Mexico: Life

1994. Source: U.S. Dept. of Commerce, ITA

The Mexican market, with its recent turbulence, typifies both the promise and problems of doing business in a Big Emerging Market. For the past few years, Mexico has provided a fertile market for U.S. products. As nearly a decade of slow growth and austerity came to an end, Mexican consumers eagerly purchased American-made consumer goods to the tune of more than $5 billion in 1994. As it continued to modernize its infrastructure, Mexico also provided an excellent outlet for U.S. durable goods and industrial supplies, a market which has grown rapidly in the last few years. In late December 1994, however, the Mexican economy received a severe shock as the Mexican government was forced to devalue the peso.

The rapid depreciation of the peso ushered in a time of uncertainty in the financial markets and gave rise to concerns over the short-term prospects for U.S.-Mexican trade. Most economists and other experts maintain, however, that Mexico's long-term future remains bright. In their view, the path taken by the Mexican authorities has been the correct one; the devaluation was a necessary adjustment which will improve Mexico's ability to create a stable economic environment for sustainable growth.

The devaluation will improve the competitiveness of Mexican exports, cutting Mexico's burgeoning trade deficit. Moreover, since the current account will be more sustainable as a result, long term interest rates will begin to fall, easing credit to fuel domestic investment. Mexico's continued commitment to implementing the North American Free Trade Agreement (NAFTA) provisions will ensure that U.S. companies that manufacture goods in North America will continue to enjoy favorable access to the Mexican market.

U.S. firms looking to do business in Mexico will have to view the market strategically, looking to the long term. For although the lack of certainty in Mexico has created risks, it has also created opportunity.

In 1994 U.S. merchandise exports to the BEMs totaled $159 billion. Mexico accounted for nearly a third of that ($50.8 billion). In fact, U.S. exports to Mexico accounted for nearly 70 percent of Mexico's overall imports. The eleventh largest market in the world, Mexico was, in 1994, the third largest of the U.S.'s export markets.

Mexico's demonstrated preference for U.S. products and its geographic proximity bode well for expanded U.S. sales in future years. Without a doubt, the devaluation of the Mexican peso will affect U.S. exports over the short-term. However, NAFTA still gives U.S. exports an edge over

After NAFTA

European and Japanese goods on price. It is well to remember that during NAFTA's first year of implementation alone, U.S. exports to Mexico increased 22.3 percent.

The Fruits of a Crisis

In the wake of Mexico's financial storm, two key points must be made. As a result of the peso crisis, Mexico has enacted an economic program to restore business and consumer confidence and stabilize the economy. And despite the crisis, Mexico is continuing to liberalize its economy and to meet its NAFTA commitments.

On March 9, 1995, Mexico announced its revised economic program. Major elements of the package are reductions in government spending, tax and price increases, and strict control of credit. The new plan reinforces actions announced on January 3, 1995, which also included accelerated privatization and liberalization of key industries. The Mexican government estimates that the immediate impact of its economic plan in 1995 will be to cut the current account deficit from $28 billion to $2 billion. Real GNP growth is expected to decline, and 1995 inflation is projected at 42 percent.

The U.S. has organized an international financial support package with the participation of international financial institutions and other countries aimed at restoring confidence and containing the crisis. Participating alongside the U.S. are the International Monetary Fund (IMF), the central banks of major industrialized nations (via the Bank of International Settlements), the Bank of Canada, and a group of Latin American countries.

NAFTA was a critical factor in Mexico's outward-looking response to its financial problems. In sharp contrast to previous devaluations in which Mexico dramatically raised tariffs and imposed across-the-board licensing requirements, on January 1, 1995—with the peso crisis in full swing—Mexico quietly implemented the second round of scheduled NAFTA tariff cuts.

In 1994 U.S. exports to the BEMs totaled $159 billion. Mexico accounted for nearly a third of that — $50.8 billion.

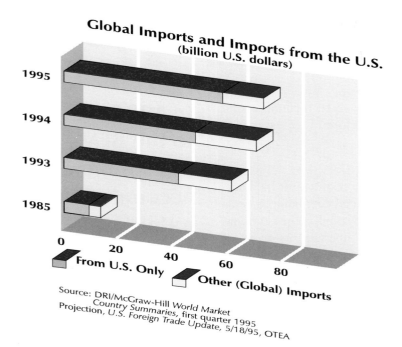

Global Imports and Imports from the U.S.
(billion U.S. dollars)

1995
1994
1993
1985

0   20   40   60   80

From U.S. Only

Other (Global) Imports

Source: DRI/McGraw-Hill World Market
Country Summaries, first quarter 1995
Projection, U.S. Foreign Trade Update, 5/18/95, OTEA

Even in the midst of the crisis, Mexico moved not to close its market as in 1982, but to open it further by accelerating its privatization efforts.

In addition, Mexico has continued to liberalize its economy and hasten the pace of its economic reform. Even in the midst of the crisis associated with the peso's devaluation, the Mexican government moved not to close its market as it did in 1982, but to open it further by accelerating its privatization efforts.

In a move to significantly reduce its current account deficit, Mexico plans to accelerate its privatization efforts in the areas of petrochemicals, ports, railroads and satellite communications. Not only are these the building blocks for a strong commercial infrastructure for the future, but they will also provide immediate export and investment opportunities for U.S. firms.

Significantly, Mexico is taking these actions in a manner consistent not only with its World Trade Organization (WTO) obligations, but with the obligations of NAFTA and similar free trade agreements with other Latin American partners. Thus, U.S. and Canadian companies trading goods produced in North America will continue to enjoy favored access to the Mexican market and certainty as to the rules of the game.

Still a Critical Market

Whether the Mexican economy adjusts rapidly or slowly to the peso's devaluation, however, certain facts about the Mexican market will continue to be true for U.S. exporters. First, Mexico is and will continue to be the U.S.'s third largest trading partner after Canada and Japan. In 1994, over $100 billion in merchandise crossed over the Mexican-U.S. border, dwarfing the U.K. in the number four position. Second, Mexico's consumers have shown a marked preference for U.S. goods as U.S. exports to Mexico accounted for almost three-quarters of Mexico's overall imports in 1994. Although the overall level of consumption in Mexico may fall in 1995, this strong preference is unlikely to change. Third, and most importantly, NAFTA has permanently changed the trade equation in favor of the U.S. over non-NAFTA suppliers. The liberalization of trade between the two countries has become entrenched and will likely be accelerated. This has important implications for U.S. exporters vis-a-vis their competition.

Over the past ten years, the Mexican government has made great strides to put the economy on the sound footing necessary for sustained growth. The export sector has been successfully diversified by shifting sharply away from a dependence on oil and toward a range of manufactured goods. In 1994, for instance, manufactured goods accounted for 81 percent of Mexico's exports, up from a mere 14 percent in 1982. The bulk of state enterprises including banks, telecommunications firms, and large industrial groups have been effectively privatized. Mexico's government has also managed to lighten the country's debt burden, lowering its debt service to export ratio from 57 percent in 1982 to 24 percent in 1994. Perhaps most importantly, Mexico has pursued a balanced budget since 1990, showing a fiscal surplus in 1992 and 1993. Although the peso crisis has thwarted the quick pace of economic growth, Mexico's past accomplishments should form a strong basis to help it through this economic crisis.

There is no doubt that NAFTA accomplished a tremendous amount in its first year. At the end of 1994, three-way trade among the U.S., Mexico and Canada stood at $350 billion, or about $1,000 of trade for each of NAFTA's 380 million consumers.

Two points stand out with regard to U.S.-Mexico trade. First, how incredibly dynamic the growth in trade was. Far surpassing expectations, one-fifth of all the trade between the U.S. and Mexico was "created" during NAFTA's first year.

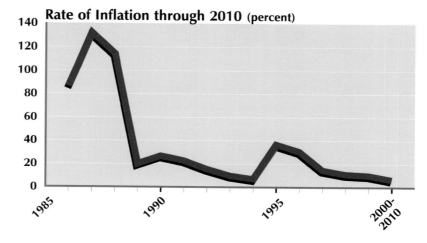

Source: DRI/McGraw Hill, *World Markets Executive Overview*, second quarter 1995

Examples of U.S. exports that surged as Mexican trade barriers came down include autos, semiconductors, machine tools and even apples.

The second notable characteristic is how well-balanced trade was. The U.S. and Mexico each realized roughly $10 billion in new export sales in each other's market, illustrating the reciprocal nature of the agreement. Reflecting this, the modest 1993 U.S. merchandise trade surplus with Mexico ($1.7 billion) barely budged in 1994 ($1.3 billion), despite the explosion in trade.

Manufactured goods exported to Mexico benefited both from strong Mexican demand as well as tariff reductions. Overall manufactured goods grew by 22.6 percent in 1994, accounting for roughly four-fifths of total U.S. exports to Mexico. The fastest growing exports in the manufactures sector were automobiles and capital goods such as machine tools. The value of U.S. auto exports exceeded half a billion dollars in 1994, representing 32,000 vehicles—a nearly nine-fold increase over the 3,800 shipped in 1993. Computer sales to Mexico expanded by 40.6 percent,

Leading Sources of Imports/Destination of Exports

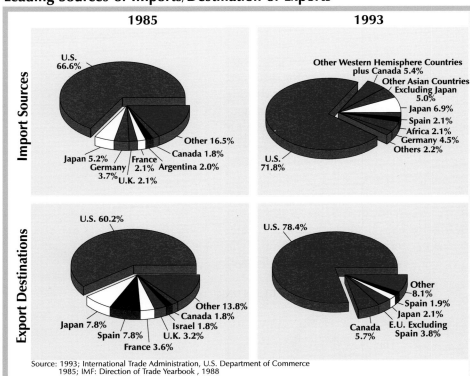

1985

1993

Import Sources

- U.S. 66.6%
- Other 16.5%
- Japan 5.2%
- Germany 3.7%
- France 2.1%
- U.K. 2.1%
- Argentina 2.0%
- Canada 1.8%

- Other Western Hemisphere Countries plus Canada 5.4%
- Other Asian Countries Excluding Japan 5.0%
- Japan 6.9%
- Spain 2.1%
- Africa 2.1%
- Germany 4.5%
- Others 2.2%
- U.S. 71.8%

Export Destinations

- U.S. 60.2%
- Japan 7.8%
- Spain 7.8%
- France 3.6%
- U.K. 3.2%
- Israel 1.8%
- Canada 1.8%
- Other 13.8%

- U.S. 78.4%
- Other 8.1%
- Spain 1.9%
- Japan 2.1%
- E.U. Excluding Spain 3.8%
- Canada 5.7%

Source: 1993; International Trade Administration, U.S. Department of Commerce
1985; IMF: Direction of Trade Yearbook , 1988

while exports of semiconductors surged by 88 percent. Oil drilling and mining equipment mushroomed by 30.6 percent, reaching a level of $674 million. Total export of capital goods to Mexico in 1994 amounted to $16 billion, a 24.6 percent increase over the previous year.

Those products which became duty-free under NAFTA grew especially rapidly, surging by 26 percent. Among other examples, diesel locomotive exports climbed from $4.9 million in 1993 to $40.8 million in 1994 after a 10 percent tariff was eliminated. Instant print film, the duty on which dropped from 15 percent to zero, saw a 3,000 percent increase in sales, from $236,000 in 1993 to close to $7 million in 1994.

NAFTA has greatly benefited Mexico's export sectors as well. In 1994 Mexico's overall exports to the U.S. grew 24 percent.

In 1995, the peso crisis and the resulting slower economic growth will temporarily dampen potential Mexican demand for U.S. exports, while U.S. demand for price-sensitive imports from Mexico will likely increase. But the U.S. economy should be able to handle this adjustment in stride until the Mexican market recovers in 1996.

In any case, without NAFTA, the boom in trade between the U.S. and Mexico would not have taken place in 1994, or not, at least, to the same degree. As helpful as NAFTA was in assisting U.S. exporters in an up market, NAFTA is critical in Mexico's current economic downturn. NAFTA's provisions and commitments offer greater certainty and protection in business transactions. In the wake of the current crisis, Mexico has thus far proven that it is willing to stay the course toward economic reform.

BIG EMERGING SECTORS

Trends such as ongoing NAFTA tariff reductions, privatization, modernization of industry and domestic demand indicate that Mexico's big emerging sectors are poised for solid growth in the next few years, despite the economic impact of the 1994 devaluation. Moreover, increasing growth and modernization in these sectors will help build productive capacity within Mexico.

Environmental Technology

Mexico's environmental problems are severe, and these needs should buoy demand for environmental technologies, though anticipated high rates of growth for 1995 have been lowered in the wake of the December 1994 peso devaluation and the ensuing financial turmoil it triggered.

While economic conditions are expected to lead to lower economic growth rates in 1995, the environmental business segment is expected to be one of the leading economic sectors. Although enforcement of environmental laws and regulations is a concern under the newly re-organized environmental ministry, growing public pressure and NAFTA obligations should ensure continued attention to this area.

Market opportunities in Mexico, particularly in 1995, will be available to firms that offer flexible solutions to specific environmental problems and that have access to relatively low-cost financing. Generally, the fastest growing markets are expected to be in water pollution control and solid and hazardous waste. Some estimates indicate that these two segments will grow at an average rate of 24 percent per year between 1994 and 1996, although those rates should drop modestly due to the peso devaluation.

The current need for environmental technologies in Mexico is immense. Demographic and industrial growth trends have placed extreme pressure on Mexico's ecological systems. These trends have exacerbated the deterioration of air, water and soil quality in most regions of the country. Mexico City hosts 50 percent of the country's total industrial production and special characteristics of the Mexico Valley airshed have exacerbated the problems associated with urban and industrial concentration in this area. Twenty of the country's 40 river basins receive 90 percent of Mexico's discharges, with only a small fraction treated effectively. And over 95 percent of

A Boom In Privatization

Mexico's ambitious privatization programs, initiated some eight years ago, have been revitalized. In the coming months and years, the following are expected to be included in the transfer to the private sector:

- 22 ocean ports through an Integral Port Administration (API) organization;
- 9 ocean port terminals and others in the future,
- 58 airports,
- 26,000 kilometers of railroad lines and intermodal yards,
- Up to 60 petrochemical plants,
- The development of natural gas urban distribution systems,
- The building of hundreds of miles of toll highways,
- The opening to competition of the domestic long distance telephone service - allowing domestic and/or international competition,
- The opening of international long distance telephone service—allowing domestic and/or international competition, and
- The development of the satellite system.

The privatization program was given priority after the December 1994 devaluation of the peso through the government of Mexico's (GOM) economic recovery program of January 1995. This move toward further privatization permits the GOM to conserve resources in sectors which private investors are willing to invest in and develop. Although many of the commercial activities mentioned above and the supporting equipment need to be modernized and/or repaired/upgraded, this opening will provide American firms with many business opportunities in the coming years. The process of upgrading the commercial activities mentioned above will require the purchase of services and equipment from a wide range of firms. Consequently, it is important for American companies to be partners/concessionaires in this program.

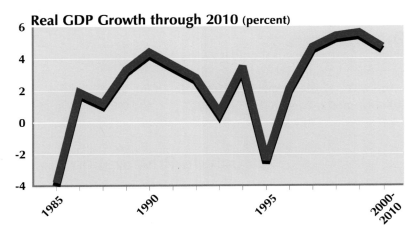

Real GDP Growth through 2010 (percent)

Source: DRI/McGraw Hill, *World Markets Executive Overview,* second quarter 1995

Mexico's solid and hazardous waste is dumped in unregistered, unsecured dump sites, affecting water and soil quality.

Demand for environmental technologies in Mexico should also be driven by potential cost savings and plant and equipment modernization, which will offer Mexico-based firms opportunities to become more efficient and to comply with environmental laws and regulations. The ongoing privatization of state-owned enterprises will increase the demand for site assessment and remediation services and will provide additional capital that can be used to invest in environmental projects.

Mexico's environmental ministry has been the largest consumer of environmental technologies and services. Recently reorganized and now named the Secretariat for Environment, Natural Resources and Fisheries, the ministry develops and enforces environmental regulations for the air, water and waste media and contracts for environmental impact assessments, risk assessments, drafting of standards and audits of industrial activity.

Petroleos Mexicanos (PEMEX), the state oil monopoly; CFE, the federal electricity commission; and CNA, the state water commission, are three of the other largest consumers of environmental technologies in Mexico. PEMEX is a large purchaser of remediation equipment, wastewater treatment equipment and services; CFE contracts for pollution abatement and emissions monitoring equipment and for services; and CNA, now part of the reorganized environmental ministry, procures goods and services in the water sector. Continuing privatizations, including the national railway and state-owned petrochemical plants, may also offer new opportunities for firms.

Real-Life Challenges

In May 1994, Joan Gardner, founder and president of Boston's three-year-old Applied Geographics, Inc., signed a $550,000 contract to design a computer program that would allow Mexico City to plan and implement critical upgrades to its antiquated water and sewage system. That contract comprised one third of the company's revenues in 1994.

One year later, Applied Geographics is negotiating a second consulting project in Mexico, this one to the tune of $1 million.

While the peso's devaluation initially caused Gardner serious concern, subsequent trips to Mexico have put many of her fears to rest. Says Gardner, "There is such a need [in Mexico] for infrastructure projects that they have to keep going. What I've noticed on my trips is that while the devaluation has caused a lot of personal crisis in Mexico, people are making the adjustment because they've been through the situation before."

In the wake of the peso devaluation and the added financial stress on industries in Mexico, concern has grown that enforcement of environmental laws and regulations would be a secondary priority. However, statements from the new environmental minister, Julia Carabias, have emphasized that enforcement will continue to be a high priority. Enforcement in 1995 may be most directly affected by budget cuts, which will likely prevent the anticipated hiring of new inspectors.

Pressure to improve enforcement will continue to come from the Mexican public and non-governmental organizations, growing media attention, and the NAFTA-inspired North American Commission on Environmental Cooperation.

The market for water pollution control equipment and services is currently the largest market segment and accounts for about 40 percent of the total environmental market. The private sector market for industrial wastewater treatment plants is expected to be the largest segment of this market, followed by government-funded municipal wastewater treatment and build-operate-transfer (BOT) projects for municipal wastewater treatment, respectively. In early 1995, the CNA, Mexico City, and the Federal District were moving forward with plans to procure wastewater treatment facilities, expected to be the world's largest, for the Valley of Mexico.

The solid and hazardous waste equipment and services market is expected to reach $402 million in 1996. The greatest demand in this segment is expected to come from states and municipalities, although private sector customers are growing as a result of governmental pressures for self-sufficiency. In hazardous waste, the largest customers are the private sector and government entities such as PEMEX. The Metropolitan Commission for Pollution Prevention and Control has undertaken a $250 million project to manage and treat hazardous waste in the Mexico Valley.

The air pollution control equipment and services market is expected to grow at more modest rates of 13 percent between 1994-1996, reaching about $456 million in 1996. Mexico City and the Federal District have been implementing an aggressive program to eliminate air emissions in the valley of Mexico and have a number of projects underway. The Federal District, drawing on World Bank funds, will require more than 350 gas stations to install vapor recovery systems

"Two days after NAFTA was signed, we received a telephone call saying that the contract that we had been working on for a year had been approved."

— *Joan Gardner, President, Applied Geographics*

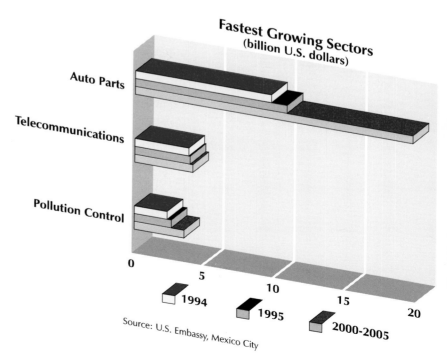

Source: U.S. Embassy, Mexico City

The 100 Cities Program

The 100 Cities program was launched by Mexico to promote migration away from the largest metropolitan areas. Participating cities are required to develop master plans that outline plans for wastewater treatment, solid waste management, the creation of nature reserves, and land use planning and regulation. The program is jointly funded by federal, state and city governments, private funds and international financing. A number of the participating cities have submitted municipal development plans, but only a few have begun implementation. The U.S. Embassy is working with Mexican officials to identify five target cities as primary opportunities for U.S. firms.

beginning in mid-1995. It is also conducting an emissions inventory and seeking to strengthen its air quality monitoring network.

Renewable energy is also expected to grow a modest 6.4 percent between 1995-1996. Some of the most important opportunities will be in windfarm development.

The remediation market is the least documented environmental market in Mexico. There are as yet no regulations or guidelines covering the remediation of contaminated sites and no inventory of such sites. The market for remediation, emergency spill response and tank cleaning services is expected to reach $78 million in 1996, with site remediation accounting for the largest share. But growth may be limited until appropriate legislation and regulations are in place. Continued privatization of state-owned industrial assets may boost demand for remediation work in the short term.

Information Technology

The information technology (IT) sector should show strong growth in Mexico, even after the devaluation of the peso. Moreover, Mexico's determination to privatize this sector will open new opportunities.

The Mexican government has generated a program to modernize the computing system in Mexico. There is also a telecommunications revolution underway that is aimed at transforming Mexico's telecommunications network into the largest, most comprehensive and modern in Latin America. These projects present an opportunity for U.S. electronic component and test equipment producers.

The best prospects for U.S. exports to Mexico are in: semiconductors, electrolytic capacitors, potentiometers, diodes, rectifiers, ceramic capacitors, polyester capacitors, tantalum capacitors, mica capacitors, resistances, connectors, switches, terminals and relays.

Electronic Components and Test Equipment

The Mexican market for electronic components and test equipment, used in the production of computers, telecommunications, consumer electronics and office machines, has experienced a healthy rate of growth since 1992 and is estimated to have grown at an annual rate of approximately 12 percent through 1994. While Mexico has opened its borders to imports and continues to lower its duties, Mexican firms which previously manufactured in this sector have found importing, distributing and, in some cases, assembling to be more profitable than local production, a situation ripe with benefits for U.S. manufacturers.

The total domestic market for electronic components and test equipment was $508 million in 1992, and the market is estimated to have grown 12 percent per year over the last two years. An estimated 95 percent of the electronic components presently used in Mexico's total domestic market are classified as imported.

U.S. exports of electronic components and test equipment to Mexico grew from $1.45 billion in 1989 to $1.94 billion in 1993. U.S. exports grew 48 percent in 1994, to $3.56 billion.

The U.S. was Mexico's largest supplier with 51 percent of the total import market in 1993. The Mexican market is highly receptive to U.S. electronic components and test equipment for both maquiladora and non-maquiladora industries. The key factors in the decision making of Mexican consumers of electronic components and test equipment are quality and support.

Computer Equipment and Software

Mexico's $1.9 billion computer equipment market is the second largest in Latin America and the 16th largest in the world. As in many countries, the computer industry is one of the most dynamic sectors of the Mexican economy with sales expected to grow at a 14 percent average rate over the next several years. Overall market trends mirror those in the U.S. with software, computer services, networking and communications-related products selling faster than computer systems and peripherals.

Driving the demand for information processing and communications technologies is the necessity for Mexican companies to become more internationally competitive as they face more competition at home. Consequently, purchases of personal computers and workstations, integral parts of modern computer networks, are growing at twice the rate of traditional mainframe and midrange computers and represent about 80 percent of the hardware market, up from 66 percent in 1991.

The environmental business segment is expected to be one of the leading economic sectors. The fastest growing markets will be in water pollution control and solid and hazardous waste.

Prospects are good for Mexico's computer market because of its trade-oriented economic policies and low computer penetration. (Mexico's computer industry represented only 0.7 percent of GDP in 1993, while the U.S. ratio exceeded 2 percent.) More open and competitive markets resulting from NAFTA will provide Mexican users access to a wider variety of computer applications, which will spur economic development in a number of industrial and service sectors. Mexico's need to upgrade its communications infrastructure will also create greater demand for computer and software products.

As the market becomes more competitive and sophisticated, opportunities will expand. The market is moving more toward open systems and standardized networking environments, and local computer prices

Market Share of Imports by Country: Electronic Comp., 1993

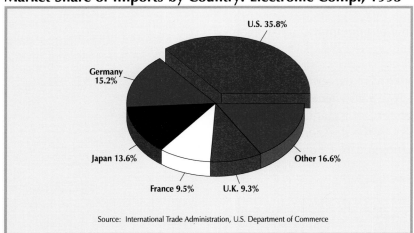

Germany 15.2%

U.S. 35.8%

Japan 13.6%

France 9.5%

U.K. 9.3%

Other 16.6%

Source: International Trade Administration, U.S. Department of Commerce

are falling as government restrictions expire, duties decline, and international prices drop. Today, most of the difference between real U.S. and Mexican computer prices is due to tariffs.

Although the Mexican computer hardware market is relatively small by global standards (about 2.3 percent the size of the U.S. market), it offers significant opportunities for U.S. suppliers. Mexico accounted for about 40 percent of U.S. computer equipment exports to Latin America in 1994 and was the seventh largest market for U.S. computer exports in the world. A significant portion of these goods is shipped to the maquiladora industry, which processes and re-exports products to the U.S. and other countries.

Over the last four years, the software market in Mexico grew at a compound annual rate of 25 percent, reaching revenues of $400 million by 1994. One reason for this strong growth is that the installed computer base in Mexico has been expanding at an average annual rate of 15 percent over the last three years.

U.S. firms supply 75 percent of Mexico's packaged software markets. The popularity of U.S. software is based on technological leadership, ease of use, high level of technical support and the widespread use of U.S.-brand computers. American software developers should benefit from technologies such as electronic data interchange and e-mail, which are now possible because the Mexican telecommunications infrastructure is being upgraded and expanded. Data communication applications hold opportunities because an increased number of companies are establishing computer networks to automate their operations. Other promising software applications include word processing, spreadsheets, databases and system utilities.

Driving the demand for information processing and communications technologies is the need for Mexican companies to boost their competitiveness at home.

Telecommunications Equipment and Services

The market for telecommunications equipment and services will experience slower growth as the benefits of NAFTA implementation and upcoming competition in long distance services are counteracted by the 1994 devaluation of the peso. Mexico's continued drive to modernize its commmunications infrastructure coupled with expected new competition in local, satellite and long distance services will spur future growth in the sector. Although the economic crisis has delayed some planned investment in 1995, Mexico will continue to be one of the largest and most important markets for U.S. telecommunications exports in the world.

The Secretariat of Communications and Transport (SCT) has continued to deregulate the telecommunications market since TELMEX was privatized in 1990. Current plans include ending the TELMEX monopoly on long distance services in mid-1996 (a tender will be released in August 1995 containing terms and conditions), increasing competition in local/rural services markets through wireless technologies, and privatizing the state-owned satellite services company, TELECOM. New concessions for broadcast and cable TV as well as for paging, trunking and radiotelephony are now being granted by the SCT.

Mexico exported $53 million more in telecommunications equipment in 1995 than in 1993 (hitting $303 million). Mexican imports rose from $2.5 billion in 1993 to more than an estimated $2.8 billion in 1995. Of that, imports from the U.S. are expected to reach $1.35 billion in 1995.

The best opportunities for telecommunications equipment manufacturers exist in switching equipment, cellular transmission equipment, paging equipment, fiber optic cable, multiplexers and microwave transmission equipment. NAFTA also stimulated development in the markets for value-added network services and intracorporate communications systems that were liberalized under the agreement. Service companies now have access rights to the public switched network for e-mail, voice mail and other enhanced services, as well as for very small aperture terminal (VSAT) and intracorporate microwave links.

The stampede to compete with TELMEX for long distance services in 1996-97 will require major investments in competing long distance service infrastructures. Competition will drive demand for billions of dollars of switching equipment, microwave transmission equipment and fiber optic cable. To date, eight major companies/consortia have announced plans to compete with TELMEX for long distance services when the market is deregulated in mid-1996.

Mexico's 1994 Computer Market

	Total Market	Projected Market Growth	U.S. Market Share	U.S. Exports	Annual Export Growth
Computer Equipment	$1.9 Billion	14%	67%	$1.8 Billion	21%
Software	$0.4 Billion	25%	77%	$0.34 Billion	25%

Source: International Data Corporation; U.S. Census Bureau

Mexico will continue to be one of the largest and most important markets for U.S. telecommunications exports in the world.

The market for cellular services in Mexico has tripled in the past four years, and there are now close to 500,000 cellular subscribers in Mexico. Ten companies hold concessions to provide cellular services in 145 cities across nine regions. The market for cellular equipment is expected to reach $130 million in 1995. It is projected to experience 15-20 percent growth in 1996 and 1997. U.S. companies also benefit from a reputation for quality products, lower transportation costs, compatibility of power standards, high name recognition and technological leadership.

Healthcare Technology

Despite its current economic crisis, Mexico's growing income, population and the recent NAFTA agreement will create attractive and lucrative opportunities for healthcare technology products and services. There is an increased demand for home care, intermediate care and hospital care services. Potential market areas also exist for hospital construction, medical training, management and consulting services, medical information services, computer software for clinical and administrative applications, hospital maintenance and other services.

In the medical device sector, products which have the best marketing prospects in Mexico are: respiration therapy equipment, electrocardiography equipment, ultrasound equipment, incubation equipment for newborns, electrosurgery equipment, cardiology and resuscitation equipment, surgical needles, intravenous catheters, x-ray equipment, and ophthalmological equipment and instruments. Medical disposable products are among the fastest growing market segments in Mexico. The best sales prospects in this segment are: syringes, adhesive tapes, band-aids, gauze and surgery threads.

In the immediate future, the devaluation of the peso and the slowdown of the economy will tend to moderate the previously fast-growing Mexican healthcare technology market. However, in the long term, the Zedillo Administration's plans to expand healthcare coverage under the Mexican Social Security Institute (IMSS), the country's largest healthcare provider, will almost certainly boost the demand for health technology products and services.

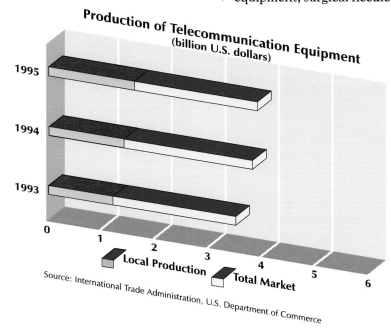

Production of Telecommunication Equipment
(billion U.S. dollars)

Source: International Trade Administration, U.S. Department of Commerce

Public sector expenditures were estimated to be $15.4 billion for 1994, an 8 percent increase over 1993, with private expenditures at $3.8 billion for 1994. The Mexican public healthcare sector is an important one because it provides 80 percent of the medical services to the country's fast-growing population of over 87 million. IMSS owns about 20 percent of Mexico's 3,000 healthcare facilities providing services to over 60 million Mexicans. Thus the Mexican government is an important buyer of healthcare products and services. In comparison, the private sector provides 20 percent of medical services, mainly to the wealthy population.

Under NAFTA, the Mexican healthcare system is transforming rapidly. In response to the growing demand for private healthcare services, the U.S. healthcare industry is investing heavily in healthcare projects. Many U.S. healthcare companies are engaged in hospital/health maintenance organization (HMO) activities in Mexico. Medium-sized cities in Mexico, which have few private hospitals, are being targeted by U.S. based companies.

Imports continue to be the most important source of supply for healthcare technology products in Mexico. Imports accounted for approximately 70 percent of the $620 million medical device market in 1993. The U.S. is the leading supplier of medical devices to this market, accounting for over 50 percent of total imports. The Mexican market is one of the 15 largest markets for U.S. medical devices. Unfortunately, third-country competitors have been undercutting U.S. prices, decreasing the U.S. share.

Currently, Mexican companies do not have the technology to produce advanced medical devices. They need foreign suppliers who can provide quality high-end medical devices with excellent after-sales service. One major complaint against U.S. medical device suppliers with sales representatives in Mexico is poor service and inadequate spare parts for repairs. Mexico lacks trained technicians to service highly advanced medical devices. If U.S. firms make extra efforts to improve after-sales service (and add better financing terms), it will help them maintain or increase their currently declining medical device market share in Mexico.

> ## "Ever since NAFTA was passed, we've been swamped with inquiries from Mexico about our products."
>
> — *Michael Muzzy, CFO,*
> *Bennett X-Ray Technologies*

What's Good For Mexico...

Bennett X-Ray Technologies of Copiague, NY, is one of the nation's leading manufacturers of radiographic and mammographic equipment. In 1993, Bennett realized sales of more than $2 million in high-technology exports to Mexico. Despite the devaluation, CEO Cal Kleinman is confident that Mexico still offers tremendous opportunity for Bennett products. Kleinman believes the company's early success in Mexico clearly illustrates the importance of NAFTA and Mexico's interest in obtaining state-of-the-art medical technology.

While Bennett reps project that 1995 sales to Mexico will be slower than the previous year's, they are confident that NAFTA will help the company maintain a distinct edge in the Mexican market. Under NAFTA, the 10-15 percent tariffs on Bennett's exports to Mexico have been eliminated, making the New York company's products that much more competitive than those of Japanese and German companies.

Chief Financial Officer Michael Muzzy says the peso devaluation has not hurt Bennett's exports to Mexico because its clients are primarily government agencies whose contracts are denominated in dollars. Says Muzzy regarding the Mexican economic reform package put into effect in early 1995, "If it's good for the Mexican economy in the long term, it's good for us."

Regardless of the current situation, Mexico will remain the most important growth market for U.S. vehicle exports during the next decade.

Pharmaceuticals

Mexico represents the second largest Latin American pharmaceutical market. U.S. companies have 50 percent of that market. The U.S. pharmaceutical industry is the world's leader in the research and development that produces new organic and inorganic compounds and drug precursors. The U.S. is also the largest market for finished pharmaceuticals. The most important developments in Mexico for the industry will not only be exports of finished drugs and precursors, but investments as well.

Mexico has implemented new patent protection rules, improved access to government contracts and eliminated licenses and investment restrictions. The largest export opportunities are heterocyclic compounds, normal blood sera, opacifying preparations, eye, ear and respiratory medicaments, cardiovascular drugs and measured retail dose medicaments.

Transportation

Motor Vehicles

Mexico is the second largest motor vehicle market in Latin America after Brazil. Twenty-nine percent of new vehicle sales are commercial vehicles. New light vehicle sales in Mexico totalled 597,000 in 1994, up 3.7 percent over 1993.

In view of the peso's recent devaluation, higher prices and interest rates in Mexico will significantly curtail overall vehicle sales in 1995. U.S. vehicle exports in 1995 are highly unlikely to reach 1994 figures but will remain higher than pre-NAFTA levels. In fact, sales in 1995 are expected to drop by at least 40 percent to 350,000 units. Vehicle sales should recover steadily through 2000 to reach 1994 levels; however, lost vehicle sales will average 200,000 units per year through this period compared to previous projections. In the long term, demand in Mexico will spur annual sales to one million units by 2000, and 1.5 million units by 2010.

Until 2004, companies must manufacture vehicles in Mexico in order to sell light vehicles in Mexico. General Motors, Chrysler and Ford combined have one-half of the Mexican light vehicle market; however, Volkswagen and Nissan control larger shares. Because of market-opening measures in NAFTA, U.S. exports of new passenger vehicles in 1994 increased nearly 1,000 percent over 1993. The U.S. import share of the Mexican market also increased tenfold to 5 percent in 1994.

**Market Share of Imports by Country:
Automotive Parts and Service Equipment, 1994***

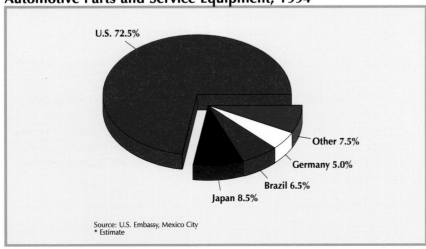

U.S. 72.5%

Other 7.5%

Germany 5.0%

Brazil 6.5%

Japan 8.5%

Source: U.S. Embassy, Mexico City
* Estimate

U.S. vehicle assemblers are well positioned to take advantage of the growing Mexican market. Although small cars will continue to hold the largest share of the Mexican market, mid-size passenger sedans, minivans, sport-utility vehicles and luxury cars will claim increasingly greater sales. Mexican quotas and tariffs for medium and heavy vehicles will end by 1999, allowing U.S. manufacturers of these vehicles barrier-free access to the Mexican market at that time.

Regardless of the current situation, Mexico will remain the most important growth market for U.S. vehicle exports during the next decade. NAFTA will eliminate all tariff and non-tariff barriers between the U.S., Canada and Mexico by 2004 for new light vehicles which meet the NAFTA rule of origin. As Mexican tariffs and import quotas on medium and heavy vehicles are reduced annually, U.S. truck and bus manufacturers will have increasingly greater access to the Mexican market; in 1999, all Mexican restrictions on U.S. exports of these vehicles will be lifted. U.S. new truck exports to Mexico in 1994 were up 30 percent from 1993.

Automotive Parts

The Mexican automotive parts market is becoming increasingly competitive as a result of the increased market access provided by NAFTA; it is probably the fastest growing market in the Western Hemisphere.

With all the major vehicle producers increasing their production capacity in Mexico (GM, Ford, Chrysler, Nissan and VW), and with new producers planning investment, (Honda, BMW), there are increased market opportunities for suppliers of both original equipment and aftermarket parts. However, the devaluation of the peso has caused vehicle assemblers to shut down some facilities on a temporary basis. Production of vehicles for the domestic market is down and the number of imported vehicles will probably decline. Parts suppliers to both U.S. and Mexican facilities will be affected.

Still, excellent opportunities exist for U.S. aftermarket suppliers in Mexico. With increased U.S. service and parts investment contemplated by firms such as Midas and Speedy Auto Glass, U.S. manufacturers already selling to these firms will have the competitive edge in the Mexican aftermarket.

In general, high-tech, high value-added parts are needed in Mexico. Coming out of the previous era of a high-level of government protection and intervention in the automotive sector (1962 through 1989), the Mexican parts industry is relatively inefficient. Capital equipment is typically less than state-of-the-art. Many Mexican parts producers have entered into joint ventures with foreign firms as a way to secure capital for modernization and expansion; many have gone out of business.

By most estimates, U.S. parts firms already have more than a 50 percent share of the Mexican parts market and at least a 65 percent share of the import market. The Mexican automotive parts market is estimated

Because of NAFTA, U.S. exports of passenger vehicles in 1994 rose nearly 1,000 percent over 1993. The U.S. import share of the Mexican market also increased ten-fold to 5 percent in 1994.

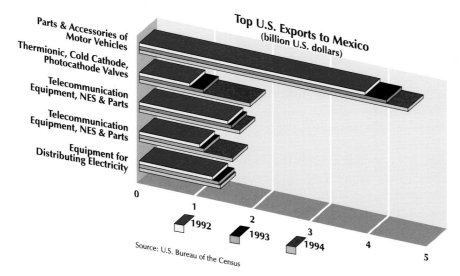

Top U.S. Exports to Mexico
(billion U.S. dollars)

Parts & Accessories of Motor Vehicles

Thermionic, Cold Cathode, Photocathode Valves

Telecommunication Equipment, NES & Parts

Telecommunication Equipment, NES & Parts

Equipment for Distributing Electricity

0   1   2   3   4   5

■ 1992   ■ 1993   ■ 1994

Source: U.S. Bureau of the Census

to be worth $13.4 billion for 1994 and should grow to $16.9 billion in 2000.

Aerospace

The U.S. has a very favorable balance of aerospace trade with Mexico. In 1993, the U.S. exported $554 million worth of aerospace products to Mexico, making the country the 19th largest market for U.S. aerospace products in the world. In 1993, the U.S. imported $86 million worth of aerospace products from Mexico.

Mexico holds great promise as an export market for U.S. aerospace products. The market size for aircraft and aircraft parts in 1993 was estimated to be over $767 million. Significant growth in the commercial aviation industry began with the privatization and liberalization of the Mexican airline industry several years ago. Mexican air carriers, although suffering from some financial problems, are replacing aircraft in response to new increased demand.

The aviation infrastructure of Mexico is expanding and modernizing to face the challenges and demands of the 21st century. These efforts should result in new acquisitions of airport equipment, aircraft and aircraft parts in the near future. The commercial aviation industry in Mexico is undergoing major restructuring, and purchases of new equipment are not expected to grow rapidly in the next two years. To date, most of the airlines in Mexico have purchased just the essential aircraft and equipment.

Mexico's ambitious privatization programs, initiated eight years ago, will soon include the transfer to the private sector of 58 airports and the decentralization of the airport system. Other airport projects include the building of Mexico City's second airport and construction of a new airport terminal building in Cancun.

Energy

The oil and gas industry, which generates 30 percent of Mexico's foreign exchange earnings, is the largest industry in the Mexican economy, ahead of manufacturing and tourism. Power generation, too, is booming; Mexico will need to nearly double its power generation capacity over the next 12 years.

However, despite the size and apparent promise of the Mexican energy sector, its state-controlled structure was left essentially intact during NAFTA negotiations and remains one of the most restricted sectors of the country's economy.

Still, some limited opportunities exist and many industry experts expect that Mexico will be forced to allow greater foreign investment in the future in order to facilitate continued economic growth. Within the hydrocarbon sector, the petrochemical subsector has been opened up somewhat. For example, Mexico has announced the privatization (with foreign participation allowed) of 61 secondary petrochemical plants. However, foreign involvement in the energy sectors which spark the greatest interest — most notably exploration and production of Mexico's extensive oil and gas reserves — remains a distant proposition at best.

Despite the generally unwelcoming image presented by PEMEX, industry experts expect that opportunities for foreign involvement in the Mexican gas sector are growing, particularly for relatively small, low-key projects. Of particular promise is the upgrade and expansion of Mexico's insufficient gas distribution system. Mexico has announced that it will allow private and foreign participation in the storage, distribution and transportation of natural gas; a law has already been approved.

Power generation, too, presents some limited opportunities for foreign participation. The CFE has earmarked several big power projects for foreign investment. However, while the CFE has legalized foreign participation in independent power projects, lingering political and statutory obstacles have dissuaded many U.S. investors from pursuing projects.

Chemical and Petrochemical Industry

The chemical industry is characterized by strong global competition, and Mexico offers several important and distinct advantages: the existence of huge hydrocarbon reserves that place the country among the world's principal producers; the Mexican government's promotion of increased chemical production, requiring large quantities of imports and investment; and heavy dependence on export markets for Mexican chemical and petrochemical products to bring in hard currency which has left a weakened domestic supply for Mexican production of more advanced products.

This will all change over the next few years as the government begins to focus on value-added products for export. During this period, U.S. chemical exports to Mexico should increase by double digits. At the same time U.S. industry is expected to make significant investment in Mexico estimated at $3-$4 billion over the next two to four years.

NAFTA and Information Technology (IT)

Because of NAFTA and the efforts of the previous Salinas Administration, most market restrictions in IT have been reduced or eliminated. In the important public sector market, NAFTA provides greater opportunities for U.S. suppliers by establishing non-discriminatory and transparent rules for competition. Liberalized investment rules, including the elimination of trade distorting performance requirements, make it easier and less risky for U.S. companies to participate from within Mexico and allow companies to make more rational business decisions regarding production strategies.

U.S. exporters continue to benefit from implementation of NAFTA, which immediately eliminated tariffs on 80 percent of U.S. telecommunications exports. American manufacturers have a competitive advantage over non-NAFTA suppliers given ad valorem duties for third countries that vary from 10 to 20 percent.

Under the NAFTA Telecommunications Services Annex, Mexico has agreed to streamline its testing and certification procedures for telecom equipment and to accept data from testing laboratories within North America. NAFTA also allows U.S. companies to bid on major tenders for telecommunications equipment and services by all Mexican federal and state-controlled agencies.

1994 marks a new record in U.S.-Mexican trade and the seventh consecutive year of increased trade. Between 1991 and 1994, total U.S. merchandise exports and chemical exports increased 52 and 69 percent, respectively.

U.S. chemical sector exports to Mexico increased by 29 percent in 1994 over 1993 levels. Organic chemicals and plastics account for over 60 percent of total chemical exports. If the period 1990-1994 may be taken as a gauge, chemical exports to Mexico increased at a compound annual rate of 16 percent.

The largest increases will occur in commodity organic chemicals and polymers. Even with the peso devaluation, exports will increase since export unit values will decrease, making commodity chemicals economically attractive.

Mexico's proximity to the U.S. offers a strategic advantage in the reduction of transport time and other costs related to trade. This advantage is particularly significant for the chemical industry in Mexico and the U.S. The chemical industry is energy intensive and energy dependent, using energy as a raw material (feedstock) and fuel. Organic chemicals, about 90 percent of the industry's output, require organic raw materials in the form of oil, gas and their derivatives.

The existence of an ample supply of crude oil to fully cover the needs of the Mexican chemical industry and the location of chemical facilities along the coast of the Gulf of Mexico are major strengths for the Mexican industry. The proximity of the Gulf facilities to Texas, the center of petrochemical production in the world's largest market, is both an advantage for Mexico and for the U.S. in the world market. Low-cost, value-added products from Texas can be exported to the world from efficient U.S. ports. Consequently, sectors in Mexico that have shown a particularly sharp rise in output are automotive, construction, electronics and agriculture, all major consumers of chemical products.

Virtually every modern industry is dependent on a vast array of chemical products made from organic inputs, e.g., coatings, sealants, plastics, composites, artificial fibers, synthetic rubber and pharmaceuticals. According to official forecasts, the Mexican domestic petrochemical market will grow at an annual average rate of 7 percent through 1998. By that year, internal demand for chemicals is estimated to reach 46 million tons per year, which can only be satisfied by imports, since domestic capacity is in the range of 31-33 million tons.

Market Share of Imports by Country: Electric Power Systems, 1993

U.S. 35.8%
Germany 15.2%
Japan 13.6%
France 9.5%
U.K. 9.3%
Other 16.6%

Source: International Trade Administration, U.S. Department of Commerce

Total U.S. merchandise exports to Mexico reached $50.8 billion in 1994, a 22.3 percent increase over 1993, while chemical exports reached nearly 9 percent of total exports, or $4.4 billion, a 28 percent increase for the same period.

1994 marks a new record in U.S.-Mexican trade and the seventh consecutive year of increased trade. Between 1991 and 1994, total U.S. merchandise exports and chemical exports increased 52 and 69 percent, respectively. Canada is the U.S. chemical industry's largest trading partner, Mexico the third largest. Exports to Mexico in 1995 will probably make Mexico the second largest with a combined total exceeding 27 percent of total chemical exports. Mexico is and will continue to be a growth market for U.S. chemical exports for the next three to five years.

Financial Services

Mexico has a large financial sector that provides a variety of services through the banking system, securities markets, insurance providers and other financial institutions. In recent years, Mexican authorities have implemented major market-oriented reforms in the financial system. The Mexican government is using NAFTA's financial services chapter as a means to open up the local financial sector to foreign investment. The adoption of financial sector liberalization measures provides greater opportunities to U.S. firms in the banking, insurance and securities markets.

Banking

Mexico's banking system has undergone, and continues to undergo, a significant transformation. In 1982, the country nationalized the banking system. In 1991 and 1992, Mexico's commercial banks were sold back to investors. This not only reversed the nationalization process, it also marked the end of a consolidation trend that had begun in the 1970s. In order to increase competition and improve the level of service, 14 new banks were licensed between June 1993 and March 1994, raising the total number of banks in Mexico to 34.

Despite the increase in the number of banking establishments, the system is still highly concentrated, with the three largest commercial banks holding, as of December 31, 1993, a total of 50 percent of all assets, 53 percent of all loans and 59 percent of commercial banking system capital.

Privatization and PEMEX

Dominating any discussion of the energy sector is the fact that selling or privatizing any part of PEMEX is considered politically impossible at present. After a recent press conference in New York at which a Pemex official noted that Pemex and CFE would consider allowing several billion dollars of foreign participation in limited energy sectors, the Mexican press erupted in negative reports accusing the Pemex "privatizers" of selling off the country's patrimony.

Mexican officials frequently assert that such privatization is prohibited by Article 27 of the country's constitution. While it is actually subsequent interpretations of it that ban foreign investment in the sector, popular support for retaining full control over the industry casts doubt on the extent to which any privatization effort can succeed. It is unlikely that foreign participation will, in the forseeable future, extend far beyond certain petrochemical operations and select pipeline projects.

The implementation of NAFTA marked the start of a process that, over time, should level the playing field for U.S. and Canadian investors in the Mexican banking industry. Through wholly-owned subsidiaries, U.S. and Canadian investors may engage in the full range of activities permitted their Mexican counterparts, with certain minor exceptions.

Developed in response to the peso crisis, Mexico early this year rushed legislation through its Congress which liberalized Mexican banking markets beyond NAFTA. The purpose of the changes is to strengthen the capitalization of banks and brokerages by permitting increased investment by foreign investors as well as Mexican industrials. This major market opportunity includes increasing the minority investment stakes of foreign banks up to 100 percent control of existing Mexican banks, making it easier for them to establish subsidiaries in Mexico and for Mexican industrial groups to buy banks.

Securities Markets

NAFTA has opened up Mexico's securities market to U.S. and Canadian firms. U.S. and Canadian securities firms, securities specialists and mutual fund management firms can now enter Mexico's market through wholly-owned subsidiaries. U.S.-owned subsidiaries will be allowed to engage in the full range of activities open to Mexican-owned securities firms under the same rules and regulations.

Foreign investment has become very important, amounting to nearly 27 percent of stock market capitalization and over 60 percent of holdings of government securities held outside the Central Bank as of April 1994. Foreign entities may invest freely in government debt securities. Moreover, foreign investors may acquire nonvoting shares in Mexican equities through mutual funds, trusts, offshore funds and American Depository Receipts.

Mexico has one securities exchange—the Bolsa Mexicana de Valores. The exchange has two sections, the main exchange and a market for smaller companies with lower capitalization. A section is being introduced for trading securities issued in overseas markets. The Bolsa trades stocks, warrants, fixed income securities issued by Mexican companies, government securities and a small volume of metals contracts.

U.S. Dollar Returns on the Mexican Stock Market
(annual percent change)

Categories (top to bottom): Stock Market Index, Mining Sector, Industrials, Construction, Commerce, Communications/Transportation, Utilities, Holding Companies

Axis: -60 -40 -20 0 20 40 60 80 100

Legend: 1993, 1994

Source: Mexican Stock Exchange, "Anuario Bursatil," 1994

As of August 1994, 28 brokerage houses were operating in Mexico. Although brokerage houses are most active in trading, the money market and foreign exchange desks at banks are also involved in buying and selling securities. The securities market is dominated by trading in money market operations.

Insurance

NAFTA provides greatly liberalized market access and investment opportunities for insurance companies throughout Mexico, the U.S. and Canada. U.S. and Canadian insurance companies will have the ability to establish and be more competitive in an expanding Mexican market. In recent years, insurance premiums in Mexico have experienced rapid growth; NAFTA will facilitate future growth trends.

Mexican firms and individuals are greatly underinsured, and additional coverage will be needed for foreign investment inflows developing under NAFTA. U.S. insurers are expected to provide important services, including new products, technical expertise and needed investment capital. By late 1994, the Mexican government had already announced that it would issue licenses to operate in Mexico to 12 foreign insurance companies.

Tourism

For Mexico, the U.S. is the number two international tourism market in terms of arrivals (over 11 million visitors in 1994) and the number four international tourism receipts- generating country (at over $5 billion annually). The most recent statistics on trade in tourism between Mexico and the U.S. indicate that in 1994 Mexican travel increased 17 percent to 11.5 million. Conversely, U.S. departures to Mexico in 1994 are estimated to have fallen 1 percent to 15.1 million.

Receipts garnered from Mexican tourism in the U.S. totaled $5.5 billion, while U.S. residents spent $5.7 billion in Mexico. Through 1998, Mexican arrivals will be somewhat hard to predict, given the current economic situation which calls for a major decline in travelers from Mexico in 1995, but are expected to increase slightly in 1997 and 1998 to reach 10.9 million.

Given the current circumstances, it is foreseeable that there would be a possible reduction of promotion budgets for tourism in both countries in the near future. In addition, domestic tourism in Mexico will probably react negatively to the recent devaluation and inflation. As stated earlier, it will also translate into sharp declines of outbound tourism to the U.S. Tourism expenditures would be likely to decrease noticeably—even though the impact at the U.S. border may be less pronounced, since it is an area so closely related to the U.S. economy.

Foreign investment has become very important; it amounted to nearly 27 percent of stock market capitalization and over 60 percent of government securities held outside the Central Bank, as of April 1994.

MARKET ACCESS

Many U.S. companies shy away from doing business in Mexico out of concerns about the difficulties of operating there. Potential U.S. exporters worry about everything from customs regulations to language differences, from ability to pay, to fear of fraud. As a Big Emerging Market, Mexico certainly presents more challenges to selling goods than does Canada or the U.S. The blizzard of paperwork required is just one example. Armed with the appropriate information, though, most U.S. exporters can find success in Mexico.

The North American Free Trade Agreement

On January 1, 1994, the U.S, Mexico and Canada implemented the North American Free Trade Agreement, a comprehensive trade agreement that will eliminate tariffs completely, and remove many of the non-tariff barriers, such as import licenses, that have helped to exclude the three countries' goods from each other's markets. Because of NAFTA, U.S. businesses have the advantage over most other competitors in Mexico. NAFTA grants the U.S. and Canada preferential access to the Mexican market by eliminating duties on all industrial products within 10 years. As of January 1, 1994, duties were eliminated on 50 percent of all U.S. and Canadian products sold in Mexico.

NAFTA eliminates non-tariff barriers, including almost all import license requirements; makes it easier for U.S. and Canadian companies to win Mexican government contracts; allows the U.S. and Canada to expand their provision of services in Mexico, notably important infrastructure services such as transportation, financial, telecommunication and engineering services; and protects the intellectual property rights of U.S. and Canadian companies in Mexico.

The best intellectual property provisions ever negotiated by the U.S. ensure that the U.S. competitive advantage in high technology is fully protected. NAFTA provides for guaranteed access to lucrative government procurement contracts in Canada and Mexico.

The true test of a trade agreement is not how it performs in good times, but under difficult circumstances. NAFTA was launched in a year in which all three North American economies were growing; in light of the peso crisis, 1995 will be a very different year. Yet a key objective of NAFTA for all its members was to "lock in" the economic reforms and trade liberalizations that had already taken place in North America. NAFTA has met this test very well.

Tariffs and Import Barriers

U.S. two-way trade with Mexico increased by over 22 percent in 1994. Bilateral trade in the first year of NAFTA was fairly balanced, with the U.S. registering a small surplus of $1.3 billion, virtually unchanged from 1993. This positive trade climate resulted largely from NAFTA's tariff provisions which provide preferential or duty-free entry for U.S. manufactured goods.

In real terms, since NAFTA implementation, half of all U.S. exports to Mexico have been eligible for zero Mexican tariffs. These include some of the most competitive U.S. products—semiconductors and computers, machine tools, aerospace equipment, telecommunications equipment, electronic equipment and medical devices. Those products which became duty-free under NAFTA grew especially rapidly in 1994, surging by 26 percent.

U.S. companies also benefited directly from NAFTA's phaseout of important non-tariff barriers. The gradual phaseout of the Mexican Auto Decree under NAFTA, for example, helped to quadruple U.S. exports of passenger cars and contributed toward a shift toward higher-valued units. In October 1994, for the first time in 50 years, Mexico approved the establishment of wholly owned major U.S. banks such as Chemical Bank, Bank of America, Chase Manhattan and NationsBank.

Elimination of tariff and non-tariff barriers represents the cornerstone of NAFTA and provides the majority of benefits for U.S. manufactured products. U.S. and Canadian companies enjoy unique benefits that put their products at a distinct competitive advantage compared with their counterparts from Asia and Europe. These advantages are even further magnified given the current economic climate in Mexico.

Government Procurement Practices

NAFTA covers procurement by federal government departments, agencies and enterprises. For departments and agencies, it applies to contracts of more than $50,000 for goods and services and over $6.5 million for construction contracts. For federal government enterprises, it applies to procurements of over $250,000 for goods and services and $8.0 million for construction projects.

Mexico initially preserves half of PEMEX and Federal Electricity Commission acquisitions for Mexican suppliers. This figure progressively falls 30 percent over a 10-year period. However, U.S. and Canadian firms will now be able to compete in all other sectors previously reserved for Mexicans (e.g., pharmaceuticals, telecommunications and construction services).

During NAFTA's first year of implementation alone, U.S. exports to Mexico increased 22.3 percent.

The U.S. currently dominates the Mexican market, but the Europeans and Japanese are looking at Mexico as a possible springboard to the NAFTA and South American markets.

Each parastatal or government agency is now responsible for reviewing the financial solvency, technical capability and moral character of its suppliers and contractors. Therefore, they may request registration by suppliers, even though this procedure is no longer mandated by law. Registration can usually take place at the time of bidding. While maintaining a representative or office is not a prerequisite to obtaining contracts, it can facilitate obtaining the information needed to prepare bid documents and support of after-sales service and parts supply.

Openness to Foreign Investment

Mexico has significantly liberalized its foreign investment regime over the last decade. In December 1993, the government passed a new foreign investment law and more liberal implementing regulations that replaced a restrictive 1973 statute. The new law is consistent with the foreign investment chapter of NAFTA and will legally open more areas of the economy (not restricted by the Constitution) to foreign ownership. It also provides national treatment for most foreign investment, eliminates most performance requirements for foreign investment projects, and liberalizes criteria for automatic approval of foreign investment proposals.

The NAFTA Investment Chapter provides that NAFTA investors will receive both national and Most Favored Nation (MFN) treatment in setting up operations or acquiring firms. Unless they have requested specific exceptions for certain types of industries, states and provinces must accord national treatment to investors from any NAFTA country.

Special Considerations
Intellectual Property Rights

NAFTA strengthens IPR protection in Mexico by providing for nondiscriminatory treatment of IPR matters, establishing certain minimum standards for protection of sound recordings, computer programs and proprietary data, and providing express protection for trade secrets and proprietary information. Mexico is a member of the major international organizations regulating the protection of intellectual property rights.

The Mexican government passed a new industrial property law (patents and trademarks) and an extensive revision of its copyright law, both effective in 1991. Product patent protection was extended to virtually all processes and products, including chemicals, alloys, pharmaceuticals, biotechnology and plant varieties. The term of patent protection was extended from 14 to 20 years from the date of filing. Trademarks are now granted for 10-year renewable periods. The enhanced copyright law provides protection for computer programs against unauthorized reproduction for a period of 50 years. Sanctions and penalties against infringements were increased, and damages now can be claimed regardless of the application of sanctions.

Extensive amendments to the patent and copyright laws were issued on August 2, 1994, and the new laws and their regulations entered into force in late 1994. The amendments were designed to eliminate defects in the existing laws and to bring Mexico's laws into conformity with its NAFTA commitments on IPR enforcement.

As a result of NAFTA, import duties on American software have been lifted. Although copyright protection has been strengthened, piracy remains a major threat. Estimates have placed the ratio of illegal to legal copies of software at five to one. The number of illegal copies has been decreasing over the last four years with the support of leading American software developers who have helped to launch an anti-piracy campaign.

Although raids by federal authorities led to the confiscation and destruction of hundreds of thousands of pirated audio and video cassettes in 1993 and early 1994, U.S. industry sources estimate that two out of every three audio tapes sold in Mexico still are pirated products (an annual loss of about $240 million). While these raids have affected street vendors, they have not produced indictments or prosecutions of large-scale pirates.

Cumulative Direct Foreign Investment in Mexico (billion U.S. dollars)

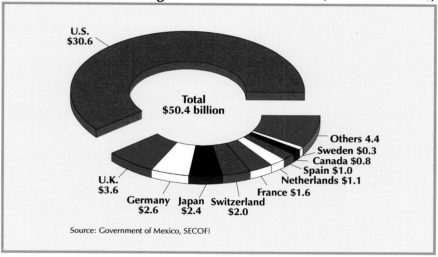

Source: Government of Mexico, SECOFI

In an effort to improve enforcement and put teeth into its IPR laws, the Mexican government formed an inter-secretarial commission in October 1993 to cut through the bureaucratic obstacles hindering effective action to date. The Mexican Attorney General's Office created a special investigative section to give priority attention to IPR enforcement. In addition, the government began a radio and television advertising campaign designed to raise public awareness of the destructive effects of IPR piracy on Mexico's own economic growth and development.

THE COMPETITION

The U.S. currently dominates the Mexican market, with U.S. exports 10 times larger than the next highest competitor. Nonetheless, several European countries—particularly Germany—as well as Japan regard Mexico as a growing market that can serve as their springboard to the NAFTA and South American markets.

Germany

Bonn has given high priority to expanding trade with Mexico, focusing especially on automotive vehicles and parts, environmental technologies, electric power systems and healthcare technology. German Economic Minister Rexrodt stated during his early 1994 trip to Mexico that Germany has given it priority status in its relations with Latin America. Trade shows and high-level visits are the hallmark of Germany's strategy in Mexico.

Economic Minister Rexrodt opened the TechnoGerman 1994 industrial trade show in Mexico—an event that is held every three or four years in an important trading partner country. Bonn paid for 23 firms from eastern Germany to participate; this was the largest single country exhibition ever in Mexico. Germany also places advisers in key Mexican ministries, such as transportation, as well as in the Mexican standards-making agency.

Canada

Ottawa has looked with more interest at Mexico recently. The country has paid special attention to the field of telecommunications. Canada relies primarily on trade shows and exhibits with active support from its embassy and consulates.

The Canadian embassy in Mexico City recently added a trade center director to its staff and opened a new center in Mexico City in July, 1994. Meanwhile, the Canadian consulate in Monterrey works closely with Nuevo Leon state organizations responsible for promoting foreign direct investment in Mexico.

Taiwan

Taipei is interested in expanding sales of its electronics and computer equipment to Mexico and is using high-level visits to boost opportunities. Premier Lien visited Mexico in June 1994 to expand economic ties, and Taiwan's China External Trade and Development Council and the Economic Ministry signed cooperation agreements with Mexico's National Bank of Foreign Trade late in 1993.

Japan

Tokyo is more active in Mexico than in the other Latin America BEMs, with tax credits and financing at the heart of its efforts. Tokyo has designated Mexico a strategic market, which enables Japanese companies to use sales and promotion expenses in Mexico as a tax credit against Japanese taxes.

So far the Japan Export-Import Bank (JEXIM)—through its environmental lending program—has committed $200 million in untied loans to Mexico for pollution control. It is also interested in increasing its exports of automotive vehicles and parts; information technology, electric power systems and healthcare technology products.

European Union

Brussels' attempts to help European firms expand exports to Mexico via programs designed to encourage investments and joint ventures. It has established a program to facilitate investment by European firms in targeted sectors in the Monterrey area, including plastics, auto parts, electric machinery and environmental equipment.

> — *Contributors: Regina Vargo, Juliet Bender, Karen Chopra, Kevin Brennan, Reginald Biddle, Laurie Goldman, Toni Dick, Paul Dacher, Eric Fredell, Charles Winburn, Edgar Rojas, Frank Foster*

Asia

ASEAN: Tigers

Economies
Brunei, Indonesia, Malaysia, The Philippines, Singapore, Thailand, Vietnam

Population
414.2 Million

Population Growth Rate
1.85%

Gross Domestic Product
US$ 473 Billion

GDP Growth Rate
7.6%

Per Capita GDP
US$ 1,346

Inflation Rate
6.2%

Industrial Production, % Change
8.6%

1994. Source: U.S. Dept. of Commerce, ITA
Figures exclude Vietnam, member as of 7/28/95

There are six countries whose combined GDP is likely to reach $1.1 trillion in little over a decade. And by that time, U.S. exports to the region where these countries are found will probably equal or exceed exports to China or Japan. These tigers and tigers-of-the-future are six of the countries of ASEAN — the Association of Southeast Asian Nations. And as ASEAN lowers past barriers to the flow of goods, services, funds and human resources, U.S. firms will find this developing region to be one of the largest, most attractive markets in Asia.

The ASEAN region—consisting of Brunei, Indonesia, Malaysia, the Philippines, Singapore, Thailand and, as of July 28, 1995, Vietnam—has become one of the most dynamic economic areas in the world. The reasons: rapid growth, expanding purchasing power and falling market access barriers. Most of the countries of the region are moving swiftly from economic structures that were based on agriculture and resource extraction to economies that are based primarily on manufacturing, distribution and services.

ASEAN's success as a driving force for the entire Asia-Pacific region comes from its rapidly growing market potential, its expanding programs for economic integration, joint ventures and trading, and ASEAN's potential to include new members such as Laos, Cambodia and Burma, which would also improve political stability in the region. Attention to the region has also come in the form of corresponding U.S. programs, such as the export promotion initiative called "Destination ASEAN," and the U.S.-ASEAN Alliance for Mutual Growth.

The Alliance for Mutual Growth is a multilateral trade initiative designed to strengthen commercial ties between the U.S. and ASEAN through practical business programs. Such programs include a series of Matchmakers missions, introducing U.S. companies to decision makers across ASEAN and to potential agents, distributors and ASEAN partners, as well as programs focusing on human resource development and technical training.

By the year 2010, the ASEAN market will have, by some estimates, a combined population of about 686 million. The combined GDP is projected to rise from about $440 billion to $1.1 trillion between 1993-2010. Indonesia and Thailand together will represent 60 percent of this total.

In fact, while initially Indonesia alone was looked at as a BEM, the degree of integration among the ASEAN countries and businesses operating there have led to the classification of the entire ASEAN region as a Big Emerging Market.

# of Tomorrow

In addition, ASEAN is both a market and a gateway to the Northeast Asia economies of Japan and China. Many ASEAN businesses are run by ethnic Chinese, working through family firms now developing into multinational corporations. ASEAN firms, especially firms from Thailand and Singapore, have invested heavily in China's export-based coastal industries. U.S. companies that form strategic relations with these firms will be positioned not only for business throughout the ASEAN region, but also for business with China. For example, the Charon Pokphand Group of Thailand (CP Group) is involved in about 50 ventures in China, including a motorcycle factory joint venture with Honda and a brewery joint venture with Heineken. CP Group also is the principal owner of Bangkok-based Telecom Asia, which includes NYNEX as a strategic partner. Many major projects involve strategic partnerships between U.S., Japanese and ASEAN firms, which could eventually lead to opportunities for U.S. companies in Japan.

Rapid growth, expanding purchasing power and falling market access barriers make the ASEAN region one of the most dynamic areas in the world.

BIG EMERGING SECTORS

As the economies of the ASEAN countries have grown, so have their infrastructure needs. For example, even the massive Paiton Power Project will not, by itself, meet Indonesia's long-term energy requirements—and such infrastructure bottlenecks exist across the ASEAN region. Each country is mapping out its own national plan, which includes spending huge sums to upgrade projects in telecommunications, energy and transportation infrastructure. Indonesia plans to spend $113 billion on these three sectors; Malaysia plans to spend at least $6.8 billion on power projects, $5 billion on aerospace and airport projects, and $2 billion on telecommunication projects in the next five years, with an additional $10 billion on a variety of other infrastructure projects.

Thailand plans to spend $60 billion to the year 2000, including more than $35 billion to meet its electric power needs, and the Philippines has set a target of $20-30 billion in private sector infrastructure investment for the rest of the decade. Even Singapore, which competes on a par with other highly developed financial centers such as Hong Kong, New York and Paris, plans to spend $2.4 billion by 1997 to upgrade its telecommunications network.

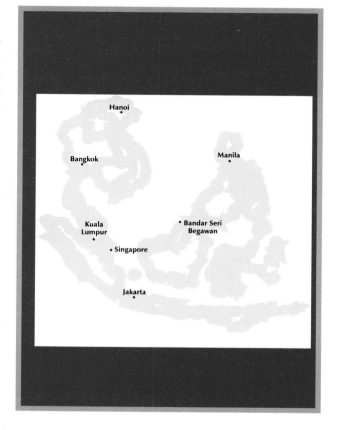

From Political Organization
To Integrated Market

The Association of Southeast Asian Nations was founded on August 8, 1967, with the signing of the Bangkok Declaration by Indonesia, Malaysia, the Philippines, Singapore and Thailand. In 1984, Brunei Darussalam joined. ASEAN's purpose is to strengthen regional cohesion and self-reliance, while emphasizing economic, social and cultural cooperation and development.

Although ASEAN has increasingly focused on economic issues, it initially concentrated on political questions. Established primarily to deal with regional political issues, during its early years ASEAN focused on coordinating policies to persuade Vietnam to withdraw from its invasion of Cambodia. When a Cambodian peace agreement was signed in October 1991, ASEAN began to address other security issues such as ownership of the Spratley Islands in the South China Sea, which are claimed by China, Vietnam, Taiwan, the Philippines, Malaysia and Brunei. The group's leaders also announced publicly and in a unified voice that they wanted the U.S. to remain in the region as a power, even though it had withdrawn from military bases in the Philippines.

ASEAN's emergence as an increasingly important U.S. partner over the past 17 years has been based on its contributions to regional stability and economic growth. The region has become peaceful and stable, with an atmosphere conducive to economic and social development. These positive regional developments and the demise of the Cold War have drawn the nations of ASEAN into a closer relationship with the U.S. ASEAN's increased relevance has contributed to productive and more predictable commercial relations in the region.

The result of this boom can be summed up in one word: opportunities. In the Philippines, for instance, the planned construction of new highways, state-of-the-art seaports and airports offer significant business potential for U.S. companies. Successful oil exploration projects also hold promise. The privatization and break-up of government monopolies throughout ASEAN, such as Malaysia's national electric power and telecommunications authorities, will further open doors for interested U.S. firms.

The region's rapid economic growth—averaging nearly 6 percent a year for the past five years—is projected to continue, as is the need and desire for U.S. goods and services—especially in high-technology infrastructure. U.S. exports to ASEAN grew by 100 percent between 1989 and 1994—from $16 billion to about $32 billion—and are expected to double again over the next five years if current trends continue.

Hundreds of U.S. firms, both large and small, are enjoying an export boom to ASEAN. The relative openness of the ASEAN economy, coupled with the need and desire by ASEAN companies for American goods and services, could make ASEAN the equal of the Chinese Economic Area as a market for U.S. exports by 1999. In the same period, U.S. exports to ASEAN could surpass those to Japan, which seem to be stuck at just under $50 billion per year.

The best opportunities for U.S. firms across the board in ASEAN are in telecommunications, electric power, environmental and information technologies. U.S. firms' advantages come from the technical strengths of their products and services, but equally from their ability to form partnerships with customers and suppliers and to manage complex projects for on-time, on-budget delivery.

Energy

Electric power generation is a key infrastructure requirement for economic growth, and is increasing at 10-15 percent a year throughout the ASEAN region, creating exciting opportunities for U.S. providers of equipment and controls, design/engineering services and, more recently, system developers and managers.

U.S. electric power developers will continue to participate in these growth markets as more ASEAN countries shift from the state enterprise monopoly electric utilities to independent power producers (IPP) such as Indonesia's Paiton project and to "co-generation" arrangements. Mission Energy is pursuing a co-generation project at a Caltex refinery in the Philippines, with electricity to be provided to the National Power Corp. and steam to be provided to Caltex. And U.S. energy conservation engineering/consulting firms will be able to participate in the market when regulations implementing demand-side management are implemented.

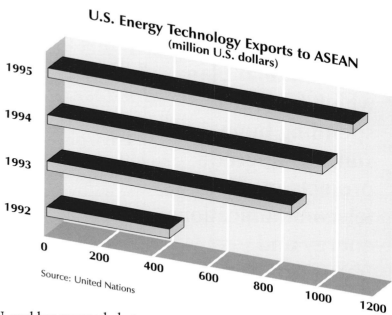

Privatization of electric power has been an important issue for all the governments of ASEAN, and has proceeded at different paces among these economies. Most ASEAN countries have established "state enterprises" that are the electric power utilities. Examples include EGAT in Thailand, PLN in Indonesia and TNB in Malaysia. Privatization would allow private sector firms to generate electricity for the national grid.

One of the sensitive issues involved in privatization involves corresponding reductions in employment at the state enterprises, where there are often relatively powerful labor organizations. Other issues include possible cost increases stemming from of the loss of low-cost government-backed loans, generous depreciation schedules, self-insurance for the state enterprises, and the shift in focus from providing electricity to develop the national economy to a focus on generating profits to attract investors. Privati-zation often requires changes in the existing rules to clarify the roles of the independent power producers and the existing utilities. For example, how should governments account for IPPs in overall power planning for a country, and how do they ensure that power supply meets power demand?

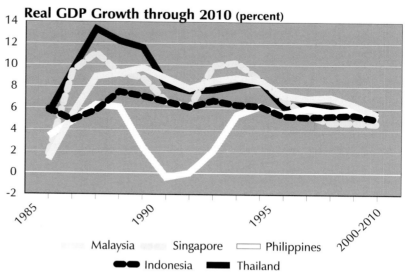

Each country is mapping out its own national plan, which includes spending huge sums to upgrade projects in telecommunications, energy and transportation infrastructure.

The process of privatization—or deregulation—of electric power in the U.S. was not an easy or simple one, and involved legislation, court cases, and considerable work by all parties involved to make it a success. There will undoubtedly be similar setbacks and delays as the electric power sector in ASEAN changes to allow more private sector participation. U.S. firms that are alert to opportunities and sensitive to the difficulties that deregulation can bring can benefit from the process.

Environmental Technology

The noise and fumes of rush hour in the capitals of Southeast Asia are striking reminders that ASEAN's tremendous economic growth has been accompanied by significant environmental problems. One illustration of this relationship is the private power sector. As the need to provide electricity across ASEAN grows, so does the number of coal-fired plants. Carbon dioxide emissions in East Asia per unit of GDP are three times the level in Latin America.

Growing concern over environmental damage, which adversely affects the quality of life in the ASEAN region, has resulted in increased government spending for environmental protection. In fact, the World Bank estimates that the ASEAN governments will increase their spending for environmental protection and improvement by 20-30 percent every year until the turn of the century.

To take advantage of these tremendous commercial opportunities, U.S. companies will have to overcome several challenges. First, there is a lack of trained personnel to enforce environmental regulations. Second, U.S. environmental companies interested in exporting to this region must be prepared to take the time to build the relationships that are necessary to do business in ASEAN. And third, in some cases there exists a lack of knowledge in ASEAN regarding the technologies available to address environmental problems.

As ASEAN governments address their environmental problems, they are realizing the cost savings associated with choosing "environmentally friendly" technology as a preventative measure. In 1990, $500 million was spent on medical costs and lost wages due to illness from environmental conditions. By 2010, according to some estimates, that number could exceed $4.5 billion.

A Changing Purpose

During the 1980s, the ASEAN organization increasingly addressed economic and commercial questions. Japan's rapid yen appreciation following the Plaza Accord in September 1985 led to massive Japanese foreign direct investment in Southeast Asia in the late 1980s, which launched ASEAN's economic take-off with several years of double-digit economic growth.

The tidal wave of direct investment from Japan was followed by investment from Taiwan and Hong Kong, as their currencies appreciated and labor became more expensive. U.S. and European investors soon joined this flood. Much of this investment came in the form of offshore production facilities that supplied markets in the industrialized democracies. For example, Thailand and Malaysia have become leading exporters of computer system components such as hard disk drives and memory semiconductors, as a result of investments by U.S. firms like Seagate and Motorola. They also export telephone sets, televisions, stereos and radios — all products of offshore production-base type investments.

Each country in ASEAN has enacted protective measures for its air, land and water, and created environmental ministries and specialized agencies to enforce legislation. Singapore is overhauling its environmental system; Thailand enacted the Environmental Act of 1992 and established a new environmental fund to focus on environmentally clean projects. Most importantly, ASEAN governments have adopted new approaches, which promote environmental protection in commercial opportunities. These include taxation and investment promotion incentives, programs to upgrade technologies, and lower tariffs on environmentally friendly products.

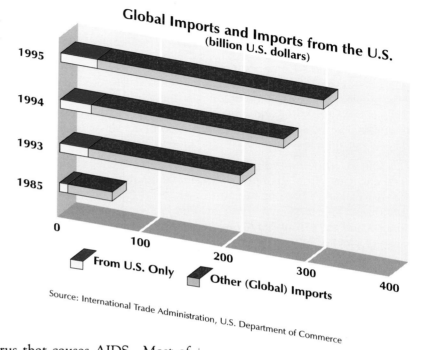

Global Imports and Imports from the U.S.
(billion U.S. dollars)

1995
1994
1993
1985

0   100   200   300   400

From U.S. Only   Other (Global) Imports

Source: International Trade Administration, U.S. Department of Commerce

Healthcare Technology

By the year 2000, one million people a year in Asia will have contracted HIV, the virus that causes AIDS. Most of these cases will be in the Southeast Asian region. Thailand already has the highest number of cases in the world—and it is growing by 1,200 each day. Limiting the outbreak of AIDS is just one of the many factors that drives ASEAN healthcare policies and spending—an estimated $9.8 billion in 1991—making ASEAN one of the world's fastest growing markets for healthcare technologies.

Rapid economic development and population expansion are also propelling growth in this sector. As incomes rise, people live longer, and the demand for healthcare increases. ASEAN's population will swell to approximately 500 million people by 2010.

ASEAN is the fastest growing market for U.S. exports of health technologies equipment and health care services. The medical equipment market size has more than doubled from 1991, to an estimated $920 million this year. Singapore alone accounts for 53 percent of this total. Thailand (28 percent) and Malaysia (15 percent) are the next largest buyers in the region. Southeast Asia, particularly Thailand, is building new facilities, upgrading existing ones and expanding the number of people who have access to health care, in order to combat the chronic shortage of hospitals and clinics, hospital beds, doctors, dentists and nurses.

From 1991-96, ASEAN will concentrate on purchases of electro-medical equipment, electro-magnetic diagnostic equipment, X-ray equipment and monitoring equipment. As for medical services, ASEAN needs specialized application software, facilities design, and facilities management.

U.S. exports to ASEAN grew by 100 percent between 1989 and 1994—from $16 billion to about $32 billion — and are expected to double again over the next five years, if current trends continue.

A Home Away From Home for Business

At the World Trade Center complex in Jakarta, there is now a "home-away-from-home" for U.S. businesses. The U.S. Commercial Center provides visiting U.S. companies with a world-class business facility, including meeting and office space, phones, faxes, computers, market research, translation services and export counseling by the U.S. and Foreign Commercial Service.

This shift in venue for the U.S. Commerce Department and two other federal agencies—from cramped, inaccessible quarters in the U.S. Embassy to Jakarta's bustling business district—symbolizes a more widespread understanding by both government and business that Indonesia and the rest of ASEAN had arrived as a Big Emerging Market.

ASEAN's domestic production of healthcare equipment primarily covers low-tech or low-cost commodity items such as tongue depressors or latex products. Also, most ASEAN countries cannot locally produce pharmaceuticals or high-tech equipment. This is why Malaysia does not levy duties on pharmaceuticals and why Singapore imposes relatively few import restrictions, even though the health sector is one the government seeks to develop.

Market receptivity for U.S. products is high in ASEAN—doctors throughout the region are familiar with U.S. standards and products, either through their studies or travel in the U.S. for training and conferences. Price and lack of adequate after-sales service, however, often preclude U.S. firms from gaining a higher share of the market. In 1993, the European Union and Japan had 32 percent and 25 percent market shares, respectively, compared to 20 percent for the U.S.

As the health technology industry matures and domestic production improves in ASEAN over the next decade, the region will evolve from a market for U.S. goods to an American competitor. Companies that enter this market within this decade can position themselves to expand sales to the rest of Asia in the next decade.

Meanwhile, each ASEAN government is looking to the private sector to ease the public burden for healthcare costs. Governments and the private sector have been working closely to improve healthcare facilities and systems. If current trends continue, ASEAN countries' expenditures will increase 10 percent each year—to build, expand and staff new facilities. In 1991 alone, Thailand spent $3.5 billion on the health industry—the highest in the region.

Transportation

There is no shortage of traffic in the booming capitals of Southeast Asia. While some of the resulting traffic problems reflect infrastructure bottlenecks—such as the stalled mass-transit effort in Bangkok—the automotive market has also increased rapidly in Southeast Asia as cars and motorcycles become more affordable for a growing middle class.

ASEAN - Fastest Growing Sectors
(million U.S. dollars)

Information Technologies
Energy Technologies
Aircraft/Parts
Automotive/Parts

0   50   100   150   200   250   300   350

1994   1995   1995-2010

Source: United Nations

Vehicle sales across ASEAN reached $4.8 billion in 1993, up from $2.8 billion just four years earlier. Almost seven million motor vehicles were registered in Malaysia in 1993, up 22 percent from three years earlier. Sales and production of motor vehicles in Indonesia have expanded 9 percent annually since 1989. Thailand is the world's third-largest pick-up truck market, and the small island nation of Singapore imported almost 300,000 vehicles in 1992.

Only a very small percentage of vehicles purchased in ASEAN are American models, and few of the auto parts were made in the U.S. Because they arrived early and in some cases shifted production from Japan to Southeast Asia, Japanese companies dominate both the auto and auto parts markets throughout Southeast Asia.

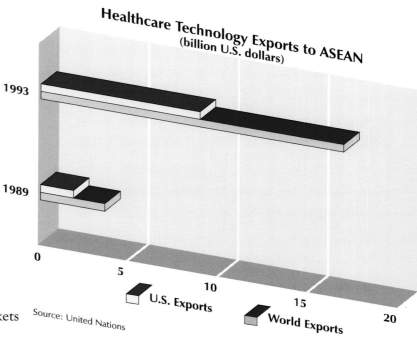

Healthcare Technology Exports to ASEAN (billion U.S. dollars)

Source: United Nations

□ U.S. Exports   ■ World Exports

But after a prolonged absence—General Motors pulled its operations out of Indonesia in the 1960s—the Big Three are returning to the region. General Motors signed a joint venture agreement with an Indonesian company in 1993, investing in a production facility outside of Jakarta that began producing Opel Vectra sedans the following year. Chrysler and Ford are also establishing a stronger foothold, with Chrysler importing Jeep Cherokee kits for assembly and sale in Thailand and Ford involved in both the auto and auto parts sectors.

U.S. auto parts companies are also looking to expand operations throughout the Asia-Pacific region, but they must make some difficult and strategic business decisions before following the Big Three auto makers they supply in North America. While the growth and opportunities in Southeast Asia are beyond question—by the turn of the century, more than one million vehicles a year will be produced in Thailand alone—breaking into the market at this late stage requires not just a commitment of time and resources, but also the desire to take on the Japanese in their own "backyard." In addition to Japanese competition, companies face high tariffs, taxes and a host of non-tariff barriers. Most individual countries in Southeast Asia are not large enough for single-market strategies, and Japanese keiretsu relationships close the door to many "outsiders."

Information Technology

Telecommunications Equipment and Services

The U.S. has 52 phone lines per 100 people. In contrast, ASEAN countries—with the exception of Singapore—have an average of 1.7 lines for every 100 people. ASEAN's newest member, Vietnam, has a telephone

1995 Best Prospects for Envirotech

- Waste water treatment technologies for industrial pollutants;
- Cleanup of contaminated river beds polluted with sludge and silts;
- Hazardous waste treatment, storage and disposal technologies;
- Monitoring and chemical analysis equipment related to water quality management;
- Air quality monitoring equipment;
- Motor vehicle exhaust testing equipment;
- Compact, centralized wastewater treatment systems for industrial and housing estates;
- Scrubbers and other air pollution technologies for controlling emissions, especially for power generation, cement, and steel sectors;
- Environmental data management systems;
- Training, particularly related to environmental management and environmental sampling/monitoring.

penetration rate of only 0.8 lines per 100 people. Double-digit growth rates of mobile phone subscribers reflect the pent-up demand for fixed phone lines across the region, as well as a fascination with the latest technologies. Singapore, for instance, has the highest penetration rate in the world for pagers: 26 per 100 people.

Privatization efforts by governments across ASEAN have jump-started the telecommunications industry, encouraging established companies to improve their services and systems, and enticing other companies into the market—often attracting foreign investment and foreign technology.

These opportunities do not, however, come without challenges. Some stem from the physical geography of the region. For example, both Indonesia and the Philippines are multi-island countries, which will require state-of-the-art satellite, wireless and extensive submarine cable systems. Government deregulation also has drawbacks—in the Philippines, deregulation has caused a flood of new companies in the industry—many more than the market can handle.

Even faced with challenges like these, ASEAN remains a booming market for the U.S. telecommunications industry. Each ASEAN nation is spending billions on developing its telecommunications infrastructure — buying satellites, switchers, voice and data transmissions systems, mobile telephone systems and a host of other telecommunications products. Thailand, for example, is expected to import $865 million worth of equipment and services in this year alone. In 1993, Singapore was the region's largest importer of telecommunications products, but U.S. exports to Singapore totaled only $128 million, or 17 percent of total telecommunications imports in the same year—not even making the U.S.'s top ten export market list. Exports from Japan accounted for 63 percent of total telecommunications imports.

Computer Equipment and Software

ASEAN offers a rich market for U.S. information technology firms, with opportunities especially in the financial, retail and manufacturing sectors. Singapore is the largest and most advanced market, with customers there about three to five years ahead of buyers in Malaysia, the second largest market. Thailand is the third-ranked market, in terms of size and development. Indonesia and the Philippines offer good opportunities for major system sales to government agencies that are working to lay an information technology foundation for future business growth. As the largest and most advanced market, Singapore is often considered the hub of the ASEAN information technology (IT) market. The largest buyer of IT products and services in Southeast Asia is probably the Singapore Government National Computer Board (NCB), which spends over $100 million a year on information technology.

Best sales prospects for new-to-market U.S. suppliers lie in new, more advanced high-technology products that can command a price premium. These include networking software and hardware accessories, hardware peripherals for multimedia systems, telecommunications products and other data communications-related products.

U.S. firms already have a major position in ASEAN markets for information technology—with annual exports of about $6.8 billion—and are working to expand this position. Hardware makers like Hewlett-Packard, Apple, IBM, Compaq, Digital Equipment (DEC) are well represented. DEC's first major sale in Thailand was a project with the Mid-western Stock Exchange to provide a computer system including software to manage trading on the Stock Exchange of Thailand. Supported by a U.S. Export-Import Bank loan, this initial $8 million sale quickly led to additional system sales in the financial sector. DEC then began to develop business in the manufacturing sector.

Aerospace

ASEAN has been the engine of growth for the world's aerospace industry. Modernization of existing airports and the planned construction of new facilities—such as in Kuala Lumpur and Bangkok— rank near the top of each ASEAN country's priority list of projects. Furthermore, the rapid expansion of the number of national carriers throughout the ASEAN region has fostered a range of diversified aerospace industries ranging from the design and manufacturing of components to the maintenance, modification and servicing of a variety of modern civil

> **Privatization efforts by governments across ASEAN have jump-started the telecommunications industry.**

Size of Telecommunications Market in ASEAN
(billion U.S. dollars)

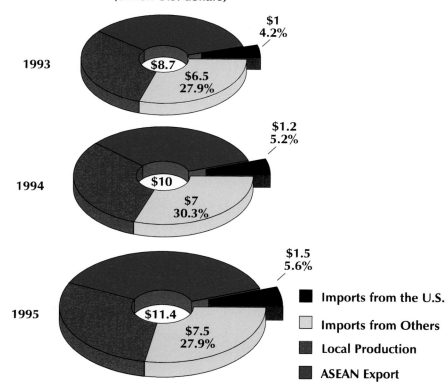

1993
$8.7
$6.5
27.9%
$1
4.2%

1994
$10
$7
30.3%
$1.2
5.2%

1995
$11.4
$7.5
27.9%
$1.5
5.6%

■ Imports from the U.S.
□ Imports from Others
■ Local Production
■ ASEAN Export

Source: *ITA Country Commercial Guide, 1994*

ASEAN has been the engine of growth for the world's aerospace industry. Airport building and modernizing rank near the top of each country's priority list of projects.

and military aircraft. Purchases by ASEAN countries of all types of aircraft— fixed wings as well as rotary—for commercial, private, military and utility purposes continue to outpace other regional markets. The biannual "Asian Aerospace" exhibition in Singapore has effectively replaced the Paris Airshow as the number one aviation and aerospace trade mart for Asian buyers.

Until the early 1980s, U.S. technology largely dominated the ASEAN aerospace market. U.S. manufactured jets were guided by U.S. air traffic control equipment, landing at local airports designed and built by U.S. architects and engineers with a range of American-made passenger and cargo service equipment. Today, U.S. technology faces not only fierce competition from traditional rivals but Southeast Asian companies as well. Well-financed European and Japanese consortia offer stiff competition for U.S. suppliers. In addition, government-supported domestic production of components and the de-

Strategies for U.S. Companies in ASEAN

Although U.S. goods and services are generally well regarded in ASEAN, many U.S. firms have a long way to go to develop a substantial presence in these markets. In some cases, the firms were doing business in Southeast Asia, but withdrew because of political concerns (or instability). In other cases, the market for a product or service is a relatively new development.

Japanese firms have dominated this region, in many cases through the kind of keiretsu manufacturer-supplier networks with which they control their home market. Although they will be playing catch-up, U.S. firms can build their business in ASEAN, if they follow these six guidelines:

1. Make a high-level corporate commitment to the ASEAN market;

2. Maintain a local presence and choose partners carefully;

3. Work as a team with business and government partners, especially for infrastructure sales;

4. Develop a quality product or service—modified for the ASEAN market. Make it timely and price it competitively;

5. Make technical and management training a key "sales feature"; and

6. Work with other firms to be a "global supplier."

velopment of low-end, home-grown niche technologies are challenging American firms for the first time. With sales opportunities in ASEAN for aerospace equipment and services over the next 10 years estimated to exceed hundreds of billions of dollars, U.S. companies will find it necessary to mount an aggressive effort—and sustain their efforts—if they are to win a share of this business.

MARKET ACCESS

Direct investment into ASEAN dropped sharply in the early 1990s as capital moved to take advantage of the opportunities opened up by the negotiation and implementation of the EC 92 Maastricht Treaty, the political and economic changes in Eastern Europe and the Newly Independent States, the North American Free Trade Agreement, and the special economic zones of China near Hong Kong.

The highly competitive global environment for investment caused ASEAN leaders to reassess their investment and economic development strategies. Led by Thailand, they decided in 1992 to establish an ASEAN Free Trade Area (AFTA), with tariffs on intra-regional trade no more than 5 percent by 2008. This regional approach marked a shift away from an export-led growth strategy that depended on American, Japanese and European markets for more than 52 percent of exports—as well as for economic growth through the "export multiplier."

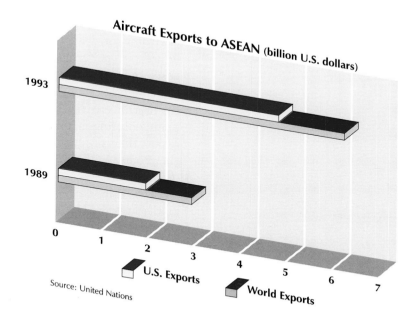

Source: United Nations

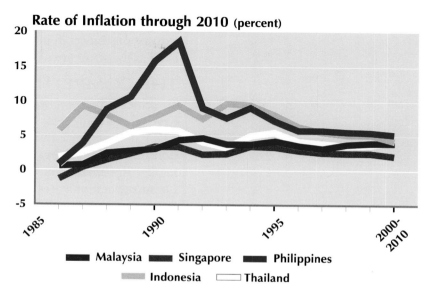

Source: DRI/McGraw-Hill, *World Markets Executive Overview,* second quarter 1995

The AFTA agreement will provide a more stable business planning environment, with lower, "bound" tariff levels and reduced local content/export performance requirements, all of which will decrease business costs, reduce uncertainty and create a larger, regional ASEAN market. Implementation of AFTA will allow U.S. companies to export more easily to the entire ASEAN market. U.S. companies with existing manufacturing facilities in any of the ASEAN countries will be able to export their products to the other countries at reduced tariffs, provided the products are subject to AFTA treatment and meet local content requirements.

U.S. firms can benefit from AFTA even without manufacturing facilities in ASEAN. For example, by working with an ASEAN joint venture partner to produce a product that has up to 60 percent U.S. content and not less than 40 percent ASEAN content, a business exporting products originating in the U.S. can qualify for AFTA's preferential tariffs.

Moreover, the ASEAN public and private sectors welcome U.S. firms as "strategic partners" in their vast infrastructure ventures not only for access to U.S. technology, but also for a U.S. corporate culture that depends on training technical and managerial employees. Two decades of deregulation in key sectors in the U.S., such as telecommunications, have given U.S. companies experience that proves invaluable to developers, bankers, owners and operators of infrastructure facilities in ASEAN.

Although political and government leaders are now permitting more private sector participation, U.S. firms should be aware that the pace proceeds at different speeds in different countries and in different sectors. It is therefore important to continue to work with existing customers in infrastructure sectors—usually state enterprises—even as the structure of the sector evolves.

THE COMPETITION

To achieve the promise offered by the ASEAN market, U.S. firms will have to overcome significant logistical obstacles, including distance and a lack of experience in an area of the world that values long-term relationships. Japanese and European competitors already have considerable market share based on historical presence and proximity to the region. Other key determinates include after-sales service and support, training, financing, agents and distributors on the ground, and a demonstrated commitment to the region. It is clear that the outcome will reward those who make the extra effort.

Moreover, while U.S. executives need a regional strategy to develop economies of scale, they must be aware of individual country differences. The ASEAN region has a great diversity of peoples and cultures, as well as differences in government and business structures. These differences mean that regional strategies, or timing, will have to be modified slightly to fit the particular national market.

— *Contributors: Robert S. LaRussa, Herbert Cochran, Sarah E. Kemp, Lisabeth A. Sarin, Jean Kelly, Raphael Cung, Alice Simmons, Hong-Phong Pho, Carmine D'Aloisio, Michael Hand, Steven Craven, Carol Kim, Paul Scogna, August Maffry*

Brunei Darussalam:

Geography
About the size of Delaware. Total area: 5,770 sq. km.

Population
300,000

Languages
Malay, English, Chinese, Iban and other indigenous dialects

Cultural Mix
70% Malay
18% Chinese
12% Other

GDP
US$ 2.5 Billion

GDP Growth Rate
1.0%

Per Capita GDP
US$ 9,000

Inflation
2.0%

1991-94. Source: CIA World Factbook

Brunei Darussalam, "Brunei, Abode of Peace," is an oil-rich Islamic sultanate on the northeastern edge of Borneo and one of the world's last absolute monarchies. The Sultan of Brunei is Prime Minister, Minister of Defense and Supreme Commander of the Armed Forces; his brothers are the Minister of Foreign Affairs and Minister of Finance. Brunei's parliament was dissolved in 1962. Formerly a British protectorate, Brunei became independent and joined ASEAN in 1984.

Despite repeated calls for "diversification," Brunei is overwhelmingly dependent on oil and natural gas, which represent 97 percent of Brunei's total exports and 56 percent of its gross domestic product. Another major source of revenue is overseas investments—Brunei has invested hundreds of millions of dollars in foreign assets, mostly in the United Kingdom, Singapore and the U.S.

Oil revenues provide a comfortable quality of life for Brunei's citizens, who pay no taxes, receive free education, free medical care and, sometimes, free housing. Brunei's government personnel are among the highest paid in the world, so virtually everyone aspires to work for the government. The private sector is small and tends to be dominated by ethnic Chinese.

With a population of about 300,000, Brunei's market is small. Notwithstanding all the benefits provided by the government, the average Bruneian's purchasing power and demand for consumer goods are limited. In fact, aside from their propensity to purchase cars (the car ownership rate is among the world's highest), many Bruneians lead a traditional life style. The Water Village (Kampong Ayer) in Bandar Seri Begawan, Brunei's capital, is still home to thousands of residents, despite efforts to provide them with more modern facilities.

BIG EMERGING SECTORS

Infrastructure projects offer opportunities for U.S. firms. Brunei has undertaken to renovate its international airport. A number of American companies have bid to supply a new radar system for the airport. Aircraft sales represent another major opportunity. Royal Brunei Airlines purchases or leases a number of Boeing aircraft. Brunei's military as well as the Sultan's personal air squadron also purchase numerous civilian and military aircraft.

Peaceful Abode

MARKET ACCESS

Brunei has few formal trade restrictions. Most goods are brought in under an open general license, although some—principally pharmaceuticals, poisons, used vehicles, gaming machines and some timber products—require specific import licenses. Customs duties are waived for most goods, unless considered luxury items. There are no duties on food products, building and construction materials, non-alcoholic beverages and most industrial machinery. Electrical appliances, photographic products, tires, motor vehicles and parts, furniture and timber face a 20 percent duty. Cosmetics and perfumes merit a 30 percent duty, and apparel and jewelry are subject to a 10 percent tariff. Tobacco and tobacco products are subject to a specific duty of B$6 per pound.

U.S. exporters typically approach this small, but rich, market through Singapore middlemen. This has worked in some cases, but there is a feeling in Brunei that Americans overlook the potential for direct sales. There is also a resentment of the insistence by many American suppliers of minimum purchases that are far too high for this tiny economy.

THE COMPETITION

Given their lengthy historical relationship with the British, Bruneian buyers will typically look first to the British suppliers with which they are most familiar. This is not overt discrimination, but a behavior pattern that has emerged after many years. There is no aversion to American products, but there is a severe lack of knowledge of what U.S. companies have to offer. Others, particularly the Japanese, have faced a similar lack of familiarity with their products and have been able to overcome it.

Despite repeated calls for "diversification," Brunei is overwhelmingly dependent on oil and natural gas.

Share of Brunei's Import Market for Aircraft, 1993

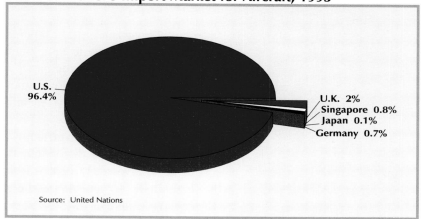

U.S. 96.4%

U.K. 2%
Singapore 0.8%
Japan 0.1%
Germany 0.7%

Source: United Nations

Indonesia:

Geography
An archipelago nation of 13,000 islands, stretching the equivalent breadth of the continental U.S. Total area: 1,919,440 sq. km.

Population
193 million

Languages
Bahasa Indonesia and regional languages. English widely spoken among the educated and the business community.

Religion
87% Moslem
9% Christian
2% Hindu
1% Buddhist

GDP
US$ 166.1 Billion

GDP Growth Rate
7.3%

Per Capita GDP
US$ 874

Inflation Rate
11%

1994. Source: U.S. Embassy, Indonesia

With its GDP growing at a robust rate of over 7 percent annually, this nation of 13,000 islands, with a population of 193 million people, is quickly joining the ranks of the fastest growing economies in the world—on a par with the four "tigers" of East Asia. For the last quarter century, it has demonstrated a long-term record of steady growth that has, over the last few years, blossomed into the impressive economic takeoff that can be witnessed today.

During this period, President Soeharto, whose current term ends in 1998, has ruled unchallenged with the support of the military. Under a "dual function" concept, military leaders play an active role in the social, political and economic life of the country, with active and retired senior officers holding key civilian government positions and parliamentary posts and serving as senior executives in leading corporations.

Traditionally agrarian-based, Indonesia's economy historically depended upon non-value-added exports of wood, rubber, spices, coffee and tea. Today, agriculture accounts for less than 20 percent of its gross domestic product. While oil and gas production continue to be important to its economy, their role is declining. Non-oil exports comprise over 70 percent of export earnings. Manufactured goods such as textiles and garments, chemicals, electronic equipment and even airplanes now make up 58 percent of its exports—compared with 28 percent only seven years ago.

The Indonesian government is working to make Indonesia an easy place to do business by streamlining its investment regulations and removing import license requirements. Economic and market reforms undertaken by the government have begun to pay big dividends over the past five years, with foreign and domestic private investment soaring. In 1993, investment approvals totaled $4.1 billion. In 1994, they topped $20 billion. In June 1994, the government removed restrictions on foreign ownership in a wide variety of industries to further encourage foreign investment. It also lowered tariffs on almost 700 items.

President Clinton's participation at last November's Asia-Pacific Economic Cooperation (APEC) leaders' meeting in Bogor, Indonesia, followed by a state visit, the signing of 15 contracts worth more than $40 billion, and the opening of the U.S. Commercial and Information Center in Jakarta — the first in Asia—further cemented the U.S. and Indonesia's already close commercial ties.

Island Dynamo

U.S. firms have reacted enthusiastically to this new economic environment by boosting their exports 113 percent—from $2.3 billion in 1989 to $4.9 billion in 1994. In addition, Indonesia is the largest recipient of U.S. Export-Import Bank loans.

Friction points in the bilateral political relationship between the U.S. and Indonesia in recent years have centered on human rights and workers' rights. The U.S. Congress cut off military assistance to Indonesia in response to a November 1991 incident in East Timor involving Indonesian security forces and Timorese demonstrators. Indonesia was the target of two 1992 petitions filed under the Generalized System of Preferences (GSP) legislation. The petitions argued that Indonesia did not meet recognized international norms for labor relations and imposed severe restraints on the rights of workers to organize. A formal GSP review was suspended in February 1994 without terminating legislated benefits.

Still, the fact remains that business opportunities for American firms in Indonesia are substantial and growing. Its large population and flourishing middle class provide a ready market for American consumer goods and services. Also, the government's plan to modernize its infrastructure, by pumping more than $113 billion into the aerospace, telecommunications and energy sectors, offers vast opportunities for U.S. business interests.

Once an agrarian society, today, agriculture accounts for less than 20 percent of Indonesia's GDP. Manufactured goods add up to 58 percent — from 28 percent seven years ago.

BIG EMERGING SECTORS

Energy

The Paiton project is a four-way partnership involving Mission Energy of California and General Electric, as well as Mitsui and the Indonesian company PT Batu Hitan Perkasa. This $2.2 billion power generation plant, the first large-scale privatization of power generation in Indonesia, represents 15 percent of Indonesia's current output, and will include a pair of 600 megawatt coal-fired plants on the north coast of Java and a massive coal unloading port on the Java Sea to service the power facility.

The project will require huge amounts of switching gear for the generating system; roads and other infrastructure will need to be built in the

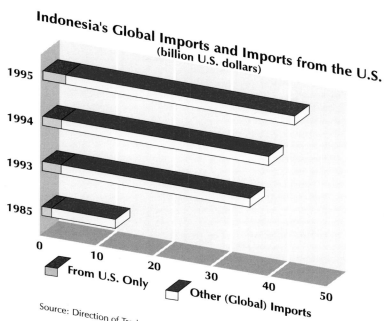

Indonesia's Global Imports and Imports from the U.S.
(billion U.S. dollars)

1995
1994
1993
1985

0   10   20   30   40   50

■ From U.S. Only   □ Other (Global) Imports

Source: Direction of Trade Statistics Yearbook, 1994 & 1992

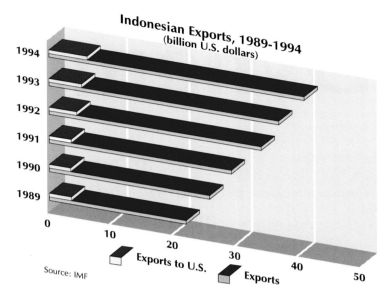

Indonesian Exports, 1989-1994
(billion U.S. dollars)

1994
1993
1992
1991
1990
1989

0   10   20   30   40   50

□ Exports to U.S.   ■ Exports

Source: IMF

vicinity of the plant, along with towers; and miles of transmission lines and wires will need to be installed.

Mission Energy, General Electri, and its partners have been treading on new ground here — for the first time most of the financing for such a huge project in Indonesia is coming from independent foreign sources—and the painstaking negotiating process showed it. It took the parties three years to reach a memorandum of agreement, including 200 days of direct negotiations.

This exceptional opportunity will translate into some $500 million in U.S. exports over the next six years, which will create thousands of U.S. jobs. Still to come will be Paiton III and a Paiton IV for the not-too-distant future. (The current project is Paiton II; Paiton I is already under construction.)

Indonesia plans to spend nearly $62 billion on electric power systems in the coming decade to increase capacity from about 13,500MW in 1994 to more than 41,000MW by 2004. Demand for electric power is expected to increase by nearly 12 percent per year over the next ten years.

Electric power has historically been produced and distributed by the state power company, Perusahaan Listrik Negara (PLN). But future plans will rely on privately owned power plants for 7,345MW over the next decade. U.S. companies should be aware that private power operators may submit unsolicited proposals for consideration by the government.

Share of Indonesia's Import Market for Energy Technology, 1993

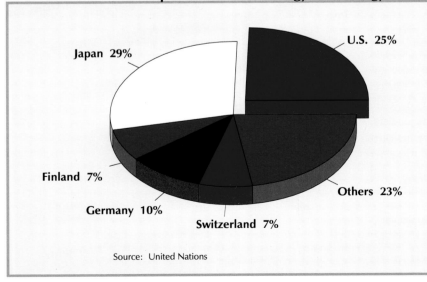

Japan 29%

U.S. 25%

Others 23%

Switzerland 7%

Germany 10%

Finland 7%

Source: United Nations

Environmental Technology

Concern for the environment is relatively new in Indonesia, but with the emergence of a large manufacturing sector and the recognition of the growing importance of tourism as a major employer and foreign exchange generator, Indonesia is seriously addressing the need to find a balance between protecting the environment while encouraging industry. The government is beginning to put real teeth into its penalties for violating environmental standards. Water quality remains a primary concern—more than half of the rivers on the island of Java are highly polluted. Manufacturing facilities with substantial out-flows of fluid wastes have become targets for investigation and enforcement.

Air quality is also an issue, given the country's reliance on coal-fired electric plants. Automotive emissions concerns will likely lead to calls for the imposition of new standards, the use of catalytic converters and the switch to unleaded gas. U.S. engineering expertise, state-of-the-art equipment and ability to design turnkey solutions for environmental problems will offer American firms substantial opportunities to help clean up and maintain Indonesia's environment.

U.S. companies have captured approximately 40 percent of the water pollution control market. U.S. environmental technology and products are generally perceived as superior but are often too sophisticated and expensive for Indonesia's needs.

Healthcare Technology

Because it has a limited budget for health services, the Indonesian government is concentrating its resources on the lower-income population and encourages the private sector to provide health services to middle- and upper-income individuals. Under this policy, the number of private hospitals increased by 27 percent, while government hospitals increased only by four percent. Currently, about one third of the country's 938 hospitals are privately owned.

One interesting trend in the Indonesian market is the development of "polyclinics"—a grouping of several local doctors to provide comprehensive medical services similar to health maintenance organizations (HMOs) in the U.S. To date, 1,000 "polyclinics" are in operation in Jakarta. These clinics prefer to use the latest technology—and are potential customers for U.S. products.

Private sector purchases account for nearly half of the total import market. U.S. companies are in direct competition with the Japanese, with Japan leading in high-tech equipment imports. In such a tight competitive market, relationships, service and price play key roles in closing a deal.

Transportation

Motor Vehicles and Parts

The Indonesian auto market has been characterized by a high degree of volatility in the 1990s—high tariffs and import taxes had a major impact on the market. Demand for automobiles sharply declined, which is attributable to the implementation of a tight monetary policy and an increase of the luxury tax in 1992. Since then, total sales and production have increased about 9 percent annually. Imports of vehicles and vehicle parts reached $1.4 billion in 1993. Overall market growth is expected to continue at roughly 9 percent annually through 1998.

With the emergence of a large manufacturing sector and the recognition of the growing importance of tourism, Indonesia is addressing the need to find a balance between protecting the environment while encouraging industry.

1995 Best Prospects in Indonesia

- Electric power systems
- Industrial chemicals
- Iron and steel
- Automotive parts
- Telecommunications equipment
- Plastic materials and resins
- Oil/gas field equipment and services
- Pulp and paper products
- Pumps, valves and compressors

Source: Country Commercial Guide 1994, U.S. Embassy

Success in Indonesia is often directly proportional to a firm's willingness to make a long-term commitment to the market.

The market is rebounding from the drastic drop in sales between 1991 and 1992, assisted in part by a 1993 deregulation package designed to encourage automotive assemblers to increase the local content in their vehicles. Although Japanese companies and joint ventures dominate the automotive and automotive component industry in Indonesia, the renewed commitment to ASEAN by General Motors could open doors for many U.S. component manufacturers. At the same time, supply relationships established in the U.S. between Japanese and U.S. companies could translate into supply relationships in Indonesia.

U.S. involvement in the components market is almost non-existent. Only a few U.S. brand automotive components, such as Champion sparkplugs, are produced locally under licensing agreements. Most auto components produced in Indonesia are based on Japanese technology and tend to be less technologically advanced. Interestingly, even though the majority of the automobiles assembled in Indonesia are of Japanese origin, private car owners favor purchasing U.S. and European components.

Information Technology

Telecommunications Equipment and Services

Indonesia's 13,000 islands stretch 3,300 miles east to west, and 1,300 miles north to south, posing a formidable telecommunication challenge. Microwave transmissions have bridged this distance and become the backbone of the Indonesian telecommunications system, serving as the long distance link within the islands. Cable networks are used for local transmissions within the cities, and satellite transmission for inter-island and international communications.

Like the rest of its ASEAN neighbors, Indonesia has big plans for its telecommunications industry—an estimated $10 billion worth of projects in the next five years. Central to the government's efforts is the installation of at least five million telephone lines—tripling the number of existing lines—and adding at least 600,000 cellular units. Of these new lines, two million have been set aside for open competition, and the remaining will be installed by PT Telekom, the state-owned telecommunications company. Mastel, the Indonesian Telecommunications Society, believes 13 million lines are needed to keep pace with the country's economic growth.

After years of government control, the Indonesian telecommunications market is finally being opened to private competition. Private sector companies are permitted to participate in basic domestic and international telecommunications services through management agreements, joint operating schemes or joint venture agreements with PT Telekom or Indosat, the country's primary provider of international telecommunications services. Private companies may offer non-basic services such as facsimiles and e-mail without the involvement of either PT Telekom or Indosat, but do require a license from the Ministry of Tourism, Posts and Telecommunications. The government recently introduced additional regulatory reforms, designed to enhance market opportunities for privately owned companies.

In order to accomplish its goals, Indonesia is expected to import a significant amount of telecommunications equipment—especially complete cellular phone systems, major central digital switch manufacturing and assembly systems, satellites, radio navigation equipment and transmission apparatus. U.S. telecommunications exports to Indonesia, growing at an average annual rate of 13.3 percent, have more than tripled from $20.3 million in 1989 to $73 million in 1993.

A number of U.S. companies are very active in the Indonesian market. AT&T operates a plant in Bekasi, which recently began delivering central office switching equipment, primarily assembling equipment from U.S. parts. Hughes Satellite provides all of the country's Palapa satellites, and recently won a contract to provide two new Palapa-C satellites. And Motorola continued its string of Asia-Pacific successes by winning a Ministry of Forestry radio communications contract. For these companies and others, success in Indonesia is often directly proportional to a firm's willingness to make a long-term commitment to the market.

Computer Equipment and Software

Indonesia claims fifth place after Singapore, Malaysia, Thailand and the Philippines as a market for information technologies in ASEAN. Twenty-five percent annual growth is predicted, although some experts expect growth to reach as high as 40 percent. Future growth in Indonesia depends largely on the ability of exporters to find good local distributors.

Despite the lack of effective protection for intellectual property, the computer software market in Indonesia is promising. With current growth at 12 percent per annum, industry experts estimate that the size of the software market share is approximately 20-30 percent of the total computer market. The Indonesian government, working with groups such as the U.S. Business Software Alliance and the Association of American Publishers, has taken strong action against counterfeiters: in November 1993, it conducted the largest raid in the world, confiscated software worth nearly $5 million, and arrested three individuals.

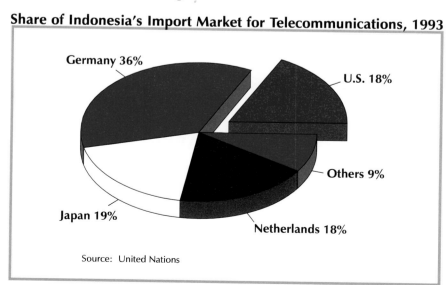

Share of Indonesia's Import Market for Telecommunications, 1993

Germany 36%

U.S. 18%

Others 9%

Netherlands 18%

Japan 19%

Source: United Nations

Share of Indonesia's Import Market for Aircraft, 1993

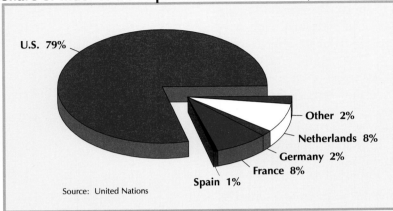

U.S. 79%

Other 2%

Netherlands 8%

Germany 2%

France 8%

Spain 1%

Source: United Nations

Although hardware still retains the biggest portion of the Indonesian computer market, software (both application and system software) will offer greater opportunities as the market develops further.

Aerospace

The very nature of Indonesia's geography makes it a natural market for the full range of aerospace products and services. Air travel is critical to linking this archipelago nation of 192.2 million people, both economically and politically.

At present, approximately 15 million passengers move through Indonesia's airports annually. By the year 2000, the Indonesian government expects more than 50 million passengers a year to use its airports.

A recently completed U.S. Trade and Development Agency (TDA)-funded study for Indonesia's Directorate General of Civil Aviation revealed the need for more than $11 billion in expenditures over the next 20 years for air transport infrastructure and new aircraft.

Responding to the Indonesian government's expressed policy to attract private sector investment in the development of new airports and the expansion of existing ones, TDA is proposing a grant to the Ministry of Communications with the hope of attracting several private U.S. consortia to develop these airports.

Government authorities also recognize that tourism could well become the largest industry if they provide an air transport system that can handle a substantial volume of visitors. Improved air transport will allow outlying areas to improve their standard of living by fostering infrastructure and community development programs and giving them better access to modern goods and services.

Of the 400-plus air strips in the country, only 26 can accommodate planes of a significant size (DC-9/B-737 and larger). Indonesia expects to establish nine new international gateway airports in the near future and is in the process of planning how to expand seven existing airports.

MARKET ACCESS

Tariffs and Import Barriers

The Indonesian government unveiled a major trade and investment deregulation package in May 1995. The package is a comprehensive commitment to lower tariff and non-tariff barriers on roughly two-thirds of all traded items. The average tariff has been slashed to 15 percent, and further phased tariff cuts will chop that average in half by 2003. With assurances of future tariff reductions, the package sends a strong signal to the private sector regarding the direction of Indonesian economic policy. By lowering the surrounding sea of tariff barriers, the package leaves the remaining islands of privilege and protection starkly exposed to public scrutiny and criticism. The government is now working on another deregulation package for agricultural products. Approximately 50 percent of potential duties and taxes are exempt, including capital goods for approved investments, imports used to produce exported goods, and imports exempted by the Ministry of Finance. Smuggling and under-invoicing also reduce the effective tariff rate.

Government Procurement Practices

Since many of the major companies in Indonesia are state-owned, the government of Indonesia is a major customer for a variety of products and services. These cover the full range of defense materials, items needed for infrastructure projects, research and development programs, and several of the pure industrial needs categorized under "Strategic Industries," which are under national government control. These industries include steel making, ship building, aircraft assembly, some electronics and communications manufacturing.

Generally, government procurement is largely financed through foreign donors, soft loans and some export credits. Each donor in turn imposes its own procurement requirements. The government of Indonesia recently enacted a new procurement law, but local groups and domestic products continue to be given preferences. Japan alone will provide $1.9 billion in donor credits in FY 1995/96.

While many of the items sold to the government can be negotiated directly, there is still reason to utilize the services of an agent or distributor, for the early stages of project development and for delivery, installation and service needs later. Most sales to the military, however, require that an agent is used.

Openness to Foreign Investment

The Foreign Capital Investment Law of 1967, with later amendments, provides the basic framework for foreign investment. The Capital Investment Coordinating Board (BKPM) plays a key role in promoting foreign investment and approving project applications. Investments in the oil and gas, mining, banking and insurance industries are handled by the relevant technical government departments. All other foreign investment must be approved by the BKPM, which also approves domestic investments when the owners seek investment incentives. BKPM aims to function as a one-stop investor service; however, investors should also work closely with relevant technical government departments and with regional and local authorities.

Government authorities recognize that tourism could well become the largest industry if they provide an air transport system that can handle a substantial volume of visitors.

Leading Sources of Imports/Destination of Exports

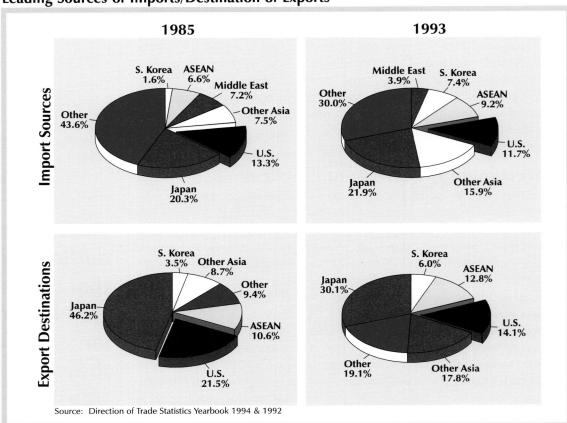

Source: Direction of Trade Statistics Yearbook 1994 & 1992

Since the early 1980s, the government has implemented a series of economic reforms to improve the investment climate and to encourage private sector activity. In June 1994, the government dropped initial equity requirements for most types of foreign investment and sharply reduced divestiture requirements. It has simplified procedures for obtaining foreign investment approvals and offered foreign investors incentives, including duty exemptions on capital equipment. The list of sectors closed to foreign investment is quite short, but the ban on direct foreign involvement in distribution continues to hinder trade, although the government has made some progress. Historically, only 100 percent domestically owned companies were allowed to participate in trading activities—defined as the import, export, distribution and sale of imported and domestic goods and services.

The government periodically updates its negative investment list and list of sectors reserved for small business. Most recently in June 1994, several previously restricted sectors were opened to foreign investment, including harbors, electricity generation, telecommunications, shipping, airlines, railways and water supply. Foreign investors may not invest in retail operations though they may post technical advisors to Indonesian companies which distribute their products at the retail level. Foreign investors may distribute their products at the wholesale level.

Special Considerations

Intellectual Property Rights

Intellectual property protection has improved significantly with the passage of copyright, patent and trademark legislation. Enforcement, however, still poses some problems. Indonesia is a member of the World Intellectual Property Organization. Indonesia's first patent law entered into effect on August 1, 1991. The patent law and accompanying regulations include product and process protection for both pharmaceuticals and chemicals. Implementing regulations clarified several questions regarding the law, but industry has identified other remaining areas of concern, including compulsory licensing provisions, a relatively short term of protection (14 years), and a provision which allows unauthorized importation of 50 specific products by third countries. The government of Indonesia is currently amending the 1989 Patent Act.

A new trademark act took effect in April 1993. The new law sets forth substantial civil and criminal penalties for trademark infringement, unfair competition and counterfeiting. Under the new law, trademark rights are determined on a first-to-file basis rather than on a first-use basis. The new law offers protection for service marks and collective marks as well as setting forth procedures for opposition prior to examination by the trademark office. It also includes well-known mark provisions.

Parliament enacted amendments to its copyright law in September 1987. The amended law affords protection to foreign works, expands the scope of coverage and raises the terms of protection for most categories of works to international standards.

There is no explicit trade secret protection legislation in effect in Indonesia. Indonesian law does not include specific protection for biotechnology or integrated circuits. Indonesia remains on the Special 301 "watch list," and will be subject to a Special 301 "out-of-cycle" review in December 1995 to ensure that steps are being taken against software and book piracy.

THE COMPETITION

Competition from other countries in Indonesia is brutal—especially from Japan and European Union countries such as France and Germany. These countries established themselves in the market years ago and have built up relationships with Indonesian business and government leaders— a key component of doing business there.

Intellectual property protection has improved significantly with the passage of copyright, patent and trademark legislation. Enforcement, however, still poses some problems.

Malaysia: High-

Geography
Slightly larger than New Mexico. Total area: 329,750 sq. km.

Population
19.5 million

Languages
Malay, English, Chinese, Tamil. English is the language of business.

Cultural Mix
59% Malay
32% Chinese
9% Indian

GDP
US$69.6 Billion

GDP Growth Rate
8.8%

Per Capita GDP
US $ 3,570

Inflation Rate
3.8%

1994. Source: U.S. Embassy, Malaysia

In less than four decades, Malaysia has transformed itself from a British colony dependent on rubber and palm oil production to one of East Asia's "mini dragons." No longer relying primarily on commodity exports, Malaysia is now a middle-income exporter of such manufactured products as electronics circuits, data processing machines, radio-phone reception equipment, videocassette machines and semiconductor devices. In fact, Malaysia is the world's third largest producer of semiconductor chips—due in part to the fact that the electronics products and components sector consists almost entirely of wholly-owned U.S. subsidiaries of Motorola, Texas Instruments, Intel, National Semiconductor, Harris, Seagate and Komag.

Like its Asian neighbors, Malaysia's economy is booming—its GDP growth rate averaged 8.7 percent between 1989 and 1993. As the economy grows, so does the consumer base and its purchasing power. Per capita GDP reached $3,500 per person in 1994.

Malaysia has been a growing market for U.S. exporters because of its increasing purchasing power and massive spending on infrastructure-building projects. U.S.-Malaysia trade totalled $16.6 billion in 1993 (a 31 percent increase over 1992's $12.7 billion) and $21 billion in 1994 (a 66 percent increase over 1992). Malaysia is the U.S.'s second largest trading partner in ASEAN, right behind Singapore.

Malaysia has been breaking up monopolies controlled by a variety of government-operated entities, such as the national electric power and telecommunications authorities, further opening doors for interested U.S. firms. The most promising sectors include electronic components, aircraft and parts, computers and software, oil and gas machinery, telecommunications and power generation.

As its economy and population grows, so does Malaysia's need for solid, up-to-date infrastructure. Malaysia plans to spend $60 billion to upgrade its infrastructure—including at least $6.8 billion dollars on power projects, $5 billion on aerospace and airport projects, and $2 billion on telecommunications projects—all in the next five years.

Goals like these translate into opportunities for U.S. companies. Currently, the two public works projects of most interest to U.S. companies include the new Kuala Lumpur international airport to be constructed in Sepang and the Bakun hydroelectric dam on the island of Borneo. The new international airport, which will cost $3.5 billion, is set to open in early 1998 before the start of the Commonwealth Games in Malaysia. The Bakun Hydroelectric Project, which will cost $5.6 billion, is sched-

Tech Performer

uled for completion by the year 2002. Even though the project will be financed by the private sector, the Malaysian government will play a key role in choosing contractors for construction.

The Malaysian government encourages international investment in almost all industry sectors. It has taken a proactive role in the development and industrialization of its economy—including developing a closer alliance between government and the private sector. The U.S. is currently the fourth largest investor in Malaysia, behind Japan, Singapore and Taiwan.

Malaysia is no longer a preferred site for labor-intensive, low-technology assembly operations. These days, it is Malaysia's growing economy, significant assets, skilled workforce, overall business environment, political stability and the established presence of most of the major multinational electronics firms that make Malaysia an attractive place to do business.

BIG EMERGING SECTORS

Energy

Malaysia's state-owned electric utility, Tenaga Nasional Berhad (TNB), is on track to increase generating capacity by 3,688MW between 1993 and 1997. An additional 4,070MW of generating capacity is to be provided by independent power producers, such as YTL and Sikap. YTL is building two combined cycle power stations with a combined capacity of 1,170MW.

One of Malaysia's most exciting ventures is a joint project with Indonesia to develop a $9.5 billion coal-fired power station and transmission system. Located in southern Sumatra, the 5,000MW plant will produce electricity for Indonesia and peninsular Malaysia and will be developed over the next 15 years.

Environmental Technology

According to a Malaysian Department of Environment study of 116 Malaysian rivers, only 27 percent were pollution-free. The rest were either "biologically dead or dying." In 1992, 53 percent of the

Malaysia is the U.S.'s second largest trading partner in ASEAN, right behind Singapore.

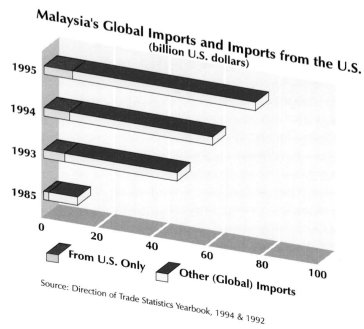

Malaysia's Global Imports and Imports from the U.S. (billion U.S. dollars)

From U.S. Only   Other (Global) Imports

Source: Direction of Trade Statistics Yearbook, 1994 & 1992

1995 Best Prospects in Malaysia

- Electronic components
- Telecommunications equipment
- Electric power systems
- Oil/gas field machinery
- Industrial chemicals
- Computers and peripherals
- Defense equipment
- Computer software
- Electronic industry production and test equipment
- Aircraft and parts

4,300 companies operating in Malaysia were identified as significant sources of water pollution. In 1988, Malaysia spent $45 million on solid waste management, and is expected to double that amount by 1995.

U.S. companies interested in the Malaysia market face stiff competition from all over ASEAN, as well as from Japan, Italy, Taiwan, the United Kingdom, China and Germany. Japan has the most aggressive program, providing soft loans and attractive financing. The Japanese have also sponsored seminars and studies on environmental topics, including the *Action Plan for a Beautiful and Clean Malaysia*, a study on municipal waste conducted for the Ministry of Housing and Local Government.

Healthcare Technology

The Malaysian healthcare technology market has been expanding rapidly in recent years—everything from domestic production of medical equipment to the building of new hospitals is fueling this growth. Spending on imports in the healthcare field increased from $733 million in 1991 to $960 million in 1994.

The Malaysian government is the principal provider of health services. Despite the $227 million increase in spending, the government is finding it difficult to keep up with the increasing demand for services and equipment, especially high-technology equipment such as magnetic resonance imaging machines, ultrasound equipment and diagnostic machinery. In recent years, the government has turned to the private sector to complement its efforts. As a result, the number of private hospitals and other healthcare facilities is growing.

Share of Malaysia's Import Market for Healthcare Equipment, 1993

Germany 15%
Japan 14%
U.S. 18%
Singapore 18%
Others 17%
U.K. 19%

Source: United Nations

Private hospitals are playing an increasing role in the healthcare industry, especially in major cities, where the demand for top-quality service is highest. Private hospitals are more likely to purchase higher priced items, such as high-tech equipment, because they have more resources.

The private sector is also driving the growth in the import market, especially for high-technology products such as respiratory equipment, dialyzers and diagnostic equipment. More than 93 percent of all medical equipment is sourced from other countries. U.S. products are renowned for their quality and performance, as well as their high price. In contrast, Japanese products are known for their quality, reasonable prices and excellent follow-up service.

Domestic production of medical supplies and equipment is growing along with the industry. Since Malaysia is a major producer of rubber products, it has a competitive edge for manufacturing latex products such as surgical gloves, syringes and catheters. Other low-technology products, like surgical blades and scissors, are produced in-country—95 percent of them for export. Some U.S. and European multinational corporations have set up operations in Malaysia's free trade zones to produce products for export—including Johnson & Johnson, Braun and Euromedical.

U.S. health equipment manufacturers will find a customer base in Malaysia that is receptive to U.S. technology and products, but wary of the lack of support services offered after a sale is completed. U.S. manufacturers of products such as surgical appliances, x-ray equipment, respiratory apparatus, electro-diagnostic equipment, and those offering medical software, insurance and other services are well-positioned to take advantage of the growing Malaysian market.

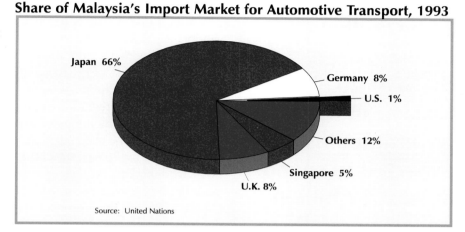

Share of Malaysia's Import Market for Automotive Transport, 1993

Japan 66%
Germany 8%
U.S. 1%
Others 12%
Singapore 5%
U.K. 8%

Source: United Nations

Transportation

Motor Vehicles and Parts

Compared to Indonesia, the Malaysian automotive industry is more developed, in part because of two government-initiated automotive companies —Proton and Perodua. Proton was created as part of Malaysia's efforts to create a profitable automotive industry. As would be expected, Proton receives preferential treatement from the government on duties and taxes. Despite this advantage, the cost of Proton's cars has risen steadily. In response, the government created Perodua, hoping to make a more affordable car for a larger segment of the population. Malaysia added one more automaker to its list in 1994—Prime Minister Mathatir signed a memorandum of understanding with the French government to import Citroen kits and eventually manufacture the components for those kits in Malaysia.

To be "fully industrialized" by the year 2020, the Malaysian government is expected to spend at least $2 billion dollars annually on telecommunications infrastructure.

When Proton began its operations nine years ago, only 17 outside vendors supplied 228 parts for the Proton Saga. As a result of Proton's vendor development program, by July 1994, 125 vendors supplied about 1,100 parts. Most of the existing parts manufacturers are tied to Japanese, Korean and European technology suppliers.

Buoyed by the record-breaking number of vehicles sold in 1994, the Malaysian Motor Traders Association is predicting a 20 percent growth in sales for 1995. The passenger car subsector saw the most growth in 1994 —accounting for 78 percent of the year's total sales. Proton models continue to dominate the market. Perodua, launched in August of 1994, made an impressive showing for only five months on the market—clinching third place in the passenger vehicle market.

Malaysia's new local content requirements—60 percent for most passenger vehicles—are set to take effect in 1996. These goals will be difficult for assemblers to achieve, and the cost of meeting these requirements will hinder the industry's efforts to be more internationally competitive. Importing components is likely to become an attractive option for the industry, as duties are reduced in accordance with the GATT Uruguay Round agreement.

In an effort to stimulate commercial vehicle production, some assemblers are being asked by the government to stop passenger vehicle assembly operations and shift to commercial vehicles. Companies agreeing to the shift could import more passenger vehicle kits, possibly at reduced import duties.

At the present time, there is very little U.S. involvement in the Malaysian automotive vehicle or components sectors.

Information Technology

Telecommunications Equipment and Services

As part of its efforts to be "fully industrialized" by the year 2020, the Malaysian government is expected to spend at least $2 billion annually on improving its telecommunications infrastructure.

Since 1987, Malaysia has been experimenting with deregulation and privatization measures in the telecommunications industry because both are fundamental to the creation of an "information superhighway." The results of this experiment speak for themselves: prior to privatization, there were barely one million telephone subscribers; by June 1993, there were 2.2 million. Industry analysts expect the number to reach 7.8 million by the year 2000, offering expansive opportunities for U.S. companies, provided they can position themselves with strategic partners, adapt to the prevailing financing practices and react to Malaysia's national development plans.

For example, in the cellular phone market alone, U.S. firms have enjoyed 43 percent of the market, due in part to the strategic relationship U.S. suppliers have with Mobikon, the nation's third cellular telephone system. Mobikon uses mostly U.S. equipment, and as Mobikan grows, sales of U.S. cellular telephones are expected to increase at a rate of 40 percent for the next three years.

In 1992, U.S. firms had only a small presence in the Malaysian telecommunications market, selling mostly hand-held mobile phones. Since then, the U.S. has made major inroads, including winning the contract for the GSM network, successfully partnering with Malaysian firms to provide new value-added services and launching MEASAT 1, Malaysia's first satellite. The Hughes International Corporation battled French and German competitors for three years before winning the contract to supply Malaysia with this first satellite. Through continued negotiations and persistence, the company was recently awarded the contract to supply Malaysia's second satellite, MEASAT 2. The value of these satellites is more than $150 million.

Malaysia's Most Promising Telecommunications Subsectors

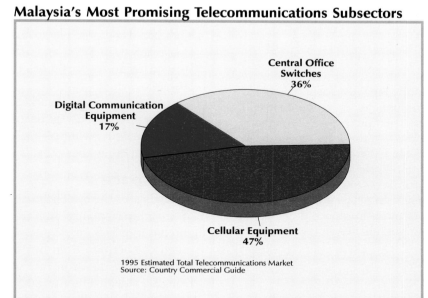

Central Office Switches 36%

Digital Communication Equipment 17%

Cellular Equipment 47%

1995 Estimated Total Telecommunications Market
Source: Country Commercial Guide

Computer Equipment and Software

Malaysia's information technology market, the second largest in ASEAN, has evolved into one which demands the latest sophisticated technology. U.S. companies are already active in the market. The maturity of the market is demonstrated by the fact that the government and major corporate buyers —the principal buyers in the early stage of market development —represent only 27 percent of the 1993 sales, while small- and medium-sized businesses accounted for about 50 percent, and personal computer users, 15 percent. Continued 8.7 plus percent annual growth in the economy has increased pressure for higher productivity in all sectors, driving demand for computer applications.

Out of the Past

"In the past, we were committed to the Japanese for supply of components as we were linked in joint venture projects with them. However, this is no longer the case as the Japanese are no longer competitive in terms of cost ... [The proposed switch to new components suppliers] is also in line with our move to reduce dependency on our Japanese foreign partner."

— *Ed Nazimi, New Straits Times,*
9 August 1994

To promote the development of information technology, Malaysia launched a National Electronic Data Interchange (EDI) Clearing Center, Dagang*Net, in 1993, and amended the Evidence Act and the Customs Act to remove obstacles to the validity of EDI transactions in business.

Malaysia is a good market for U.S. software suppliers. A 1987 copyright law provides substantial protection for computer software as a literary work. Malaysia's Ministry of Domestic Trade and Consumer Affairs has undertaken a number of raids to reduce software piracy.

Aerospace

Malaysia sees the establishment of an aircraft industry as an essential part of its plans to upgrade its infrastructure. Malaysia is a major purchaser of U.S.-made aircraft, both military and commercial. Despite tough competition from British and Russian suppliers, Malaysia recently purchased a squadron of F/A-18D fighter aircraft from McDonnell-Douglas, a deal valued at $600 million.

A new $3.5 billion international airport will be built at Sepang, south of Kuala Lumpur. When it opens in 1998, the airport will accommodate 25 million passengers annually. When all phases are completed in the early part of the next century, 100 million passengers will be served. Upgrades and improvements are also planned at airports in Johor Bharu; the current international airport at Subang, west of Kuala Lumpur; on the island resort of Penang; and at Sibu in the east Malaysian state of Sarawak. Malaysian Airlines, or "MAS," is undertaking a major expansion of its fleet and plans to purchase 72 new aircraft valued at $10.6 billion over the next five to ten years.

MARKET ACCESS

Tariffs and Import Barriers

Malaysia has few trade barriers. Import permits are generally not required. Import duties range from zero to 300 percent, but on most goods the duty is 10 percent. Also, Malaysia exacts a 10 percent sales tax on most imports, but imports of products not available locally and used for export production are exempt from both the duty and sales tax. U.S. semiconductor companies operating in Malaysia have benefited from this provision. Licensing requirements cover primarily arms, explosives, motor vehicles, controlled substances, some raw materials and agricultural products. Malaysia has agreed to substantial tariff reductions on a wide range of products to comply with GATT and World Trade Organization standards.

Malaysia has no foreign exchange restrictions that would impede trade or repatriation of profits. Local agents are required for sales to the government and are highly recommended for sales to the private sector.

Government Procurement Practices

Generally, two types of tenders are issued by the Malaysian government—local and international. Foreign contractors are not allowed to bid on local tenders, while on international tenders, there are no prohibitions on U.S. contractors to bid, and no licenses are required. Foreign contractors interested in participating in turnkey projects must be prequalified by the Implementation and Coordination Unit (ICU) of the Prime Minister's department before they can tender.

To perform construction in Malaysia, U.S. firms should have a local representative—which may be Malaysian or American. If a U.S. company wants to win construction projects, it will need to have a Malaysian partner. In general, local joint venture partners should have at least 30 percent equity in the partnership and play an active role in the implementation of the project.

As with other countries, contractors should use Malaysian products and services to the extent possible.

Openness to Foreign Investment

The Promotion of Investment Act of 1986 and the Industrial Coordination Act of 1974 specify investment guidelines. The Malaysian Industrial Development Authority (MIDA) screens proposals for a manufacturing license to determine whether or not they are consistent with the Industrial Master Plan (IMP) and government social policy. Approval depends on the size of the investment, whether or not it includes local equity participation, the type of financing required, the ability of existing and planned infrastructure to support the effort, and the existence of a local or foreign market for the output. MIDA applies the criteria in a non-discriminatory manner, except in rare instances when a domestic and a foreign firm propose identical projects. One-hundred percent foreign ownership in manufacturing is permitted only in certain instances.

Special Considerations

Intellectual Property Rights

Malaysia has one of the region's strongest regimes for protecting intellectual property rights (IPR). In fact, the Business Software Alliance gave Malaysia an award in 1992 for its vigilance against software piracy.

> **Malaysia has no foreign exchange restrictions that would impede trade or repatriation of profits.**

Leading Sources of Imports/Destination of Exports

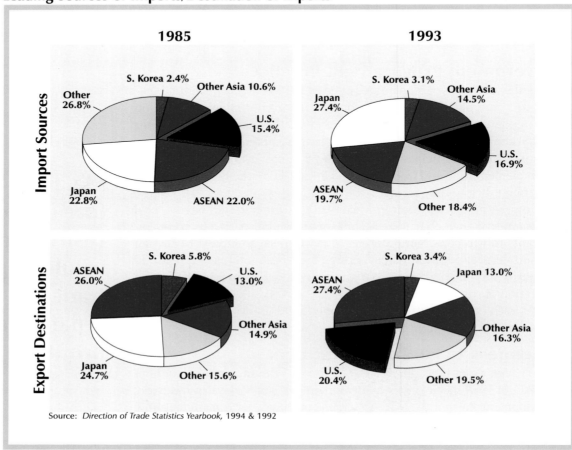

Source: *Direction of Trade Statistics Yearbook,* 1994 & 1992

IPR legislation includes the Trade Description Act of 1976, the Patent Act of 1983 and the Copyright Act of 1987, as amended in 1990. In addition, Malaysia has acceded to the Berne Convention for the Protection of Literary and Artistic Works and the Paris Convention for the Protection of Industrial Property, and is a member of the World Intellectual Property Organization (WIPO). The Copyright Act includes enforcement provisions allowing government officials to enter and search the premises of those suspected of infringement and to seize infringing copies and reproduction equipment.

Most patents registered in Malaysia are good for the relatively short period of 15 years. The duration can be extended under certain circumstances. Malaysia's patent law will need to be amended to meet the WTO TRIPS Agreement requirements. Processing time for trademark registration may be as long as 18 months. Copyright protection extends to computer software and lasts for life plus 50 years.

THE COMPETITION

In 1993, Malaysia imported $12.5 billion from Japan and more than $7.7 billion of goods and services from the U.S. Japanese firms have been more successful partly because they are more aggressive than their U.S. competitors in developing business relationships in Malaysia—positioning themselves well for upcoming opportunities.

Like the rest of ASEAN, heavy competition from other countries such as Japan and European Union members makes doing business—especially on large projects—difficult for many U.S. companies. U.S. firms who want to succeed in the Malaysian market would be best served by establishing themselves in the market and forming relationships with local companies.

Philippines:

Geography
An archipelago of more than 7,100 islands located approximately 500 miles off the southeast coast of Asia. Total area: 300,000 sq. km.

Population
67.1 million

Languages
Filipino, a language based on Tagalog, is one official language; English is the other.

Cultural Mix
91.5 Christian Malay
4.0% Muslim Malay
1.5% Chinese
3% Other

GDP
US$ 56.9 Billion

GDP Growth Rate
5.4%

Per Capita GDP
US$ 848

Inflation
9.1%

1994. Source: U.S. Embassy, Philippines

A few years ago, everyday life in Manila was a challenge. Executives suffered in their offices through frequent half-day power cuts — without air conditioning or fans to combat the heat. Factories were often idle, and the economy lagged behind the rest of its ASEAN neighbors.

When President Ramos was elected in 1992, he vowed to "turn on the power"—both figuratively and literally—and Filipinos have begun to respond to the challenge. Fast-track power station projects have restored electricity to the industrial centers of the Philippine islands, and more power plants are under construction. The government has set a goal of almost doubling the Philippines' power capacity—from 6,700MW in1992 to 11,200MW in 1998.

It may be a number of years before the Philippines infrastructure catches up with its ASEAN neighbors. Nevertheless, these infrastructure needs offer potential business for some U.S. firms, and the Philippines does appear to have turned the corner—and started to enjoy the economic growth its neighbors have experienced since the late 1980s. Part of the blame for the Philippines' previous lack of economic energy can be attributed to political uncertainty during the Marcos period, which started a downward spiral that has taken time to reverse. Add to this the political upheavals since the early 1980s—including a peaceful civilian-military, "people power" revolution in 1986, several coup attempts since then, and natural disasters including earthquakes, the eruption of Mt. Pinatubo, as well as the closing of U.S. bases at Clark and Subic Bay—and it is no wonder the Philippines has spent a long time recovering.

Under President Aquino, at least six coup attempts scared away many potential major investors. Since taking office in June 1992, President Ramos has largely restored democratic stability to the Philippines—negotiating settlements with Muslim, communist and military rebels—thus greatly reducing the once-frequent threats to the government.

After the restoration of political stability, the Philippine economy rebounded in 1992-93. Events such as the restructuring of the Central Bank (Bangko Sentral ng Pilipinas (BSP)), a stock market boom, deregulation in the telecommunications sector, the successful privatization of a number of large, state-owned firms, and the elimination of "brown-outs" renewed Filipinos' confidence in their economy—and piqued the interest of foreign investors. Real GDP expanded by 5.4 percent in 1994, with the assistance of import liberalization, tariff reform, foreign exchange liberalization and foreign investment liberalization. As reforms like these

Newly Powered

continue, the real GDP growth between 1995 and the end of the century should at least sustain that rate.

Aside from regular trading opportunities, infrastructure development in the Philippines over the next five years presents numerous opportunities for U.S. firms—especially in the power, transportation and telecommunications sectors. For example, Motorola, AT&T and Hughes recently secured contract financing for a variety of projects designed to upgrade and expand the telecommunications network across the Philippines. Government plans also include the construction of new highways, state-of-the-art seaports and airports.

Successful finds during gas exploration projects undertaken by Shell and Occidental Petroleum also offer opportunities. For other industries—such as power generation—the build-operate-transfer (BOT) laws now employed by the Philippines can open doors for U.S. companies with expertise in infrastructure development. The Philippine government relies heavily on private sector investments, both domestic and foreign, to achieve and sustain its higher economic growth path.

BIG EMERGING SECTORS

Energy

Fast-track power station projects restored sufficient electricity to the industrial centers of the Philippine islands - but this is only the beginning. More power plants are under construction, and even more are planned, with the goal of almost quadrupling the Philippines power capacity—from 6,700MW in 1992 to 25,000MW by 2005. In addition, the Philippine Energy Plan anticipates increasing Filipinos' access to electricity from 60 percent in 1992 to 96 percent by the year 2000.

Faced with long and persistent power outages in 1993, the Philippines turned to private sector solutions, mainly through BOT laws, and was effectively free of outages in 1994. An American energy company

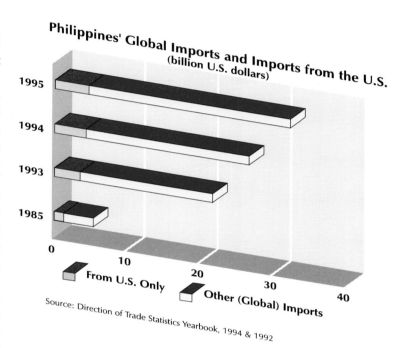

Philippines' Global Imports and Imports from the U.S. (billion U.S. dollars)

From U.S. Only

Other (Global) Imports

Source: Direction of Trade Statistics Yearbook, 1994 & 1992

When President Ramos was elected in 1992, he vowed to "turn on the power" — both figuratively and literally — and Filipinos have begun to respond to the challenge.

Share of Philippines' Import Market for Healthcare Technology, 1993

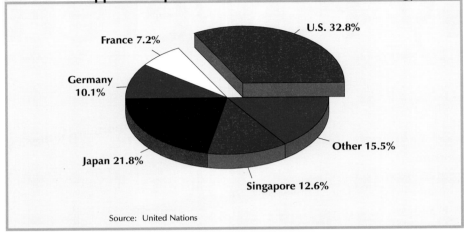

France 7.2%
U.S. 32.8%
Germany 10.1%
Japan 21.8%
Singapore 12.6%
Other 15.5%

Source: United Nations

recently said that the Philippines is now five years ahead of the rest of the world in using BOT for power projects.

As part of the move to privatize the power sector, the Manila Electric Company (MERALCO) is trying to get back into power generation. The firm is responsible for electricity distribution within a 9,000 square kilometer area centering on Manila, which has 20 percent of the nation's population, 50 percent of the industrial output and 56 percent of total energy sales. Three independent power firms are developing projects to supply power directly to MERALCO, bypassing the government-owned National Power Corporation (NPC).

U.S. suppliers have a solid reputation in the Philippines and are aggressively pursuing opportunities in private power development either through BOT, build-own-operate (BOO), or rehabilitate-own-lease (ROL) arrangements. Filipino electrical engineers are well-versed in U.S. technical standards, designs and concepts, and use the U.S. voltage system. Sales of U.S. products are now in second place and account for nearly 17 percent of the total import market, but U.S. firms are slowly losing ground because of competitors' more favorable pricing, delivery, payment terms and design flexibility. To gain share in the Philippine market, U.S. firms need to enter into agent/distributor agreements with local firms who will maintain technical sales staff that regularly visit NPC, MERALCO and other end-users.

Since taking office in 1992, President Ramos has largely restored democratic stability to the Philippines.

Environmental Technology

According to the Climate Institute, by the year 2070, Manila may be under a meter of water from rising sea levels. Fortunately, the Philippines' Department of Environment and Natural Resources (DENR) has established a national program to eliminate ozone depleting substance use by 1996, as well as an anti-pollution program that includes increasing penalties for polluting, imposing duties on imported engine sets.

Competition in the environmental sector in the Philippines is fierce, and many countries vie for market share. Germany, Japan and the U.S. are in close competition for the $16-million-and-growing water treatment market.

Healthcare Technology

The Philippines is expanding its public and private healthcare facilities. The private sector operates the majority of the nation's 1,748 hospitals. Even though the government runs 574 facilities, it offers 11,400 more beds than private hospitals. Private facilities are the principal consumers of high-tech equipment.

Health equipment imports by the Philippines—$44 million in 1993—are projected to grow 5.6 percent annually for the next two years. Spurred by the importance the government places on increasing the number and quality of medical facilities available to its rural population, the medical equipment market will offer sizable opportunities to U.S. companies.

A new trend in the Philippines healthcare industry is the health maintenance organization (HMO). HMOs allow private organizations to pool funds to obtain state-of-the-art medical equipment and supplies, such as CAT scans, magnetic resonance imaging (MRI) and ultrasound machines. Currently, 16 HMOs are operating in the country, serving an estimated 400,000 people. Because they have more resources for purchasing, HMOs represent another set of potential customers for U.S. companies.

Domestic production is limited to producing medical gloves, pumps, furniture, sterilizers and orthopedic appliances. Most of the medical equipment in both public and private hospitals is imported. U.S. products are preferred by Filipino doctors, because of the quality of U.S. goods. Also, many Filipino physicians were trained in the U.S. and are familiar with U.S. equipment and products.

Although it is one of the smallest health-care markets in ASEAN, the Philippines offers a diverse market for all levels of medical technology equipment. Familiarity with U.S. products will continue to give U.S. companies an edge, provided they can match the competition's after-sales service record.

Transportation

Manila's crowded streets can be distinquished from those of other Southeast Asian capitals by the colorful Jeepneys—van-like taxies adorned with special nicknames and home-made design. But as in the rest of ASEAN, recent years have seen an increase in the purchase of automobiles, a boost that is attributable to real economic growth and increasing public confidence in the economy. New vehicle sales, including passenger cars, utility

Share of Philippines' Import Market for Auto Transport, 1993

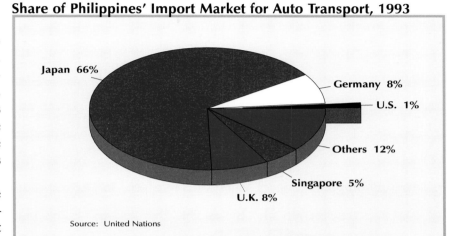

Japan 66%
Germany 8%
U.S. 1%
Others 12%
Singapore 5%
U.K. 8%

Source: United Nations

vehicles, trucks and buses are expected to double between 1994 and 1998. This growth trend is expected to continue at an average annual rate of 16 percent. The Philippine market mirrors the rest of ASEAN in another way—Japanese-made cars and trucks crowd the streets of metropolitan Manila.

The Philippine automotive industry is highly regulated and protected. To support Filipino companies, the Board of Investment allows joint ventures and partnerships only with existing auto parts manufacturers. Foreign investment is limited to 40 percent, and local content requirements range from 40-50 percent.

In addition to changes agreed to in the Uruguay Round of the GATT, the Philippine media and public criticism of the auto industry may be responsible for this "evolution." Initial efforts to change have been modest, and formidable market entry barriers still exist. One obstacle, the ad valorem tax, ranges from 15 to 100 percent on all vehicles, considerably raising the cost to the Filipino consumer.

Secretary of Trade and Industry Rizalino Navarro has indicated that the auto industry will be completely open by 1998—and there are signs that the Board of Investment is liberalizing the automotive market, in favor of component manufacturers over assemblers. However, no plan to reform has been put forth and revisions in the car development program have not been substantial enough to make the Philippine market more accessible. Further liberalization of the Philippine automotive market is necessary in order for U.S. manufacturers to compete in small and mid-size car production, where the greatest potential exists.

Share of Philippines' Import Market for Infotech, 1993

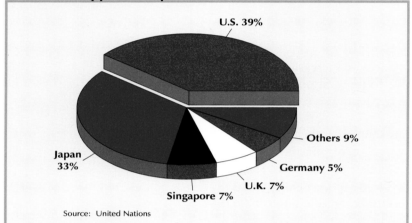

Source: United Nations

Information Technology

Telecommunications Equipment and Services

For years, requests for new telephone lines in the Philippines went unfulfilled. The dominant phone company, Philippine Long Distance Telephone Company (PLDT), had a backlog of 800,000 applications for new telephone lines in 1992. But in that same year, the government responded to the public's discontent with PLDT's service by issuing a decree opening up the industry. In response, PLDT stepped up its efforts to clear the backlog and initiated plans to add four million new lines by the end of the century, which would quadruple the number of lines installed in the last 65 years.

Telephone installation in both metropolitan Manila and other major cities is still not fast enough for some—stimulating demand for cellular telephones and pagers. The two largest cellular systems service providers, Piltel and Express Telecommunications Company, recorded an increase in subscriptions of 69 percent in 1992. In the same year, pager subscriptions increased 43 percent.

The huge increase in phone lines will increase demand on telephone line-dependent technology, such as fax machines. Industry experts expect demand for fax machines to increase at an average annual rate of 60 percent in the next three years. Also, these improvements in technology and the increasing volume of telephone line transmissions will stimulate the need for fiber optic cables and digital based network systems.

The move to privatize the telecommunications industry provides tremendous opportunities for U.S. companies. In the next three years, hundreds of telecommunications improvement projects will require at least $2 billion in government and private sector investment. Five hundred thousand of PLDT's planned installations will be established on a "build-manage-transfer" (BMT) basis. BMT is a system designed to encourage foreign companies to build and manage a project, then transfer ownership to a local partner.

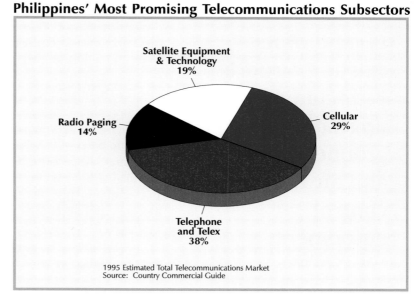

Philippines' Most Promising Telecommunications Subsectors

Satellite Equipment & Technology 19%

Cellular 29%

Radio Paging 14%

Telephone and Telex 38%

1995 Estimated Total Telecommunications Market
Source: Country Commercial Guide

U.S. companies are taking advantage of the myriad of opportunities in the Philippines market. AT&T, for example, recently secured financing for two projects, totalling $69 million, to expand Metro Manila's cellular network. Hughes will provide earth stations, satellites and other equipment for a very small aperture terminal (VSAT)-based telephone system—important technology for a nation composed of 7,100 islands — which will supply telephone service to rural areas via satellite.

Some telecommunications equipment—such as wires, cables and towers—can be sourced from the Philippine market, but most telecommunications equipment is imported, simply because it is not manufactured locally. Duty rates for telecommunications equipment, spare parts and accessories range from 10 to 40 percent, and a 10 percent value-added tax is also imposed.

Computer Equipment and Software

Smallest of the ASEAN country markets for information technology, the Philippine market is expected to grow at 21 percent annually over the next few years with intense government support. Government agencies

Like Indonesia, the Philippines is an expansive archipelago. The government is considering major improvements to several of its existing airports — including the upgrading of ground support and air traffic control equipment.

and state enterprises are major customers, an indication of the current status of the market.

All government units are required to develop information systems plans — five-year plans to use information technology to achieve agency missions. Two projects funded by the World Bank illustrate the plans: the Bureau of Internal Revenue is negotiating with suppliers on a $41 million Philippine Tax Computerization Project (part of which was won by the local distributor of Sun Microsystems), and the Bureau of Customs (BOC) aims to provide full computerized and electronic links between the BOC headquarters and all the ports in the Philippines. The internal revenue computerization project should dramatically increase tax collections, while the customs project—won by the American firm Unisys—will expedite trade document processing. The contracts included hardware, system software and relational database management systems, communications equipment, application software development, facilities management, and support and maintenance.

Philippine information technology distributors are shifting from hardware or software vendors to total solutions providers on open systems platform. Sales of U.S. software firms like Microsoft and Oracle are up by more than 20 percent. Systems suppliers, including IBM, Hewlett Packard, Digital Equipment, Sun Microsystems and Unisys report similar gains, and computer peripherals are expected to grow at 45 percent per year. Industry specialists forecast continued strong growth, especially for networking, client-server computing and peripherals.

The strongest business demands include retail, manufacturing and finance. Philippine business is also trying to lay another foundation for information technology: 383 firms, including more than 100 small and medium-sized firms, have joined to push for nationwide implementation of bar-coding technology.

Aerospace

Like Indonesia, the Philippines is an expansive archipelago with non-military airports operated by the government and private sector airports that are serviced by Philippine Airlines and other Filipino domestic carriers. With its political stability restored, the government is anticipating a boom in tourism.

The government is considering major improvements to several of its existing airports — including the upgrading of ground support and air traffic control equipment. Three new domestic airlines were recently given approval to begin operations and will need to acquire short-haul aircraft in the 30-50 passenger range. The government is also interested in attracting foreign firms to operate, with local partners, maintenance overhaul and repair facilities.

MARKET ACCESS
Tariffs and Import Barriers

There are some barriers that make market entry in the Philippines difficult, including quantitative restrictions on more than 100 agricultural and industrial items. Overall tariff rates are still relatively high at about 22 percent, and further reductions are planned. Customs valuations procedures are based on the "home consumption value" (HCV) rather than invoice value, which sometimes results in arbitrary and unreasonably high valuations of U.S. exports. The Philippines is moving to implement a transaction-based valuation system that will be introduced sometime within the next five years, but potential customs valuations problems remain.

An ongoing tariff reduction, restructuring and simplification program was completed by July 1, 1995, on schedule. It lowers the average nominal tariff to 20 percent, grouped into four tiers of 3, 10, 20 and 30 percent. Discussions are underway in the Philippine government on further tariff reductions to the year 2000.

About 208 products are exempt from the tariff reduction program and remain subject to 50 percent tariff — including many agricultural products and luxury consumer-oriented goods. The Philippines participated in the GATT Uruguay Round, but bound few items at existing tariff rates and made no commitments for further reductions.

Government Procurement Practices

The Philippine government is a large, direct importer of many essential products, including road building equipment and military and defense equipment. Government agencies pattern their regulations and procedures after those of the U.S.

Procurement regulations permit a foreign company to bid on government projects only if it maintains a registered branch office or a registered resident agent in the Philippines. The first step in obtaining government business is to be placed on the Bidder's Mailing List of the agency with which the applicant is interested in doing business.

In addition, foreign contractors are alllowed to participate in the construction of only internationally bid and foreign-finance/assisted projects in the Philippines. For this purpose, foreign contractors must apply to the Philippine Contractors Accreditation Board (PCAB) for a special license which is used on a project-by-project basis.

Openness to Foreign Investment

In the investment area, there are continuing restrictions on company and land ownership. The 1991 Foreign Investment Act (FIA) allows foreign equity in Filipino enterprises to exceed 40 percent, provided no investment incentives are sought and provided the company does not engage in an activity which appears on the "negative list" (no activities are currently

> The Philippine government is a large, direct importer of many essentail products, including road building equipment and military and defense equipment. Government agencies pattern their regulations and procedures after those of the U.S.

noted on the negative list). Pending legislation, supported by the government, seeks to abolish this list altogether. In 1994, the law was amended to simplify rules and regulations, permit negotiations on unsolicited proposals (for private sector-initiated projects not necessarily on the government's priority list), and permit projects valued in excess of one billion pesos to apply for government incentives.

Firms engaged in government-preferred activities who wish to take advantage of the investment incentives program are generally required to limit the foreign equity to 40 percent. One hundred percent foreign ownership is, however, permitted in many areas.

Special Considerations

Intellectual Property Rights

In recent years, the Philippines has not consistently and effectively protected intellectual property rights, in part as a result of inadequate laws and regulations and insufficient resources for enforcement. The Philippines was moved from the U.S. Trade Representative's Special 301 "priority watch list" to the regular "watch list" following an agreement signed in April 1993, in which the government committed itself to significantly strengthen protection of intellectual property rights in the Philippines. The Philippine government is currently considering draft legislation on

Leading Sources of Imports/Destination of Exports

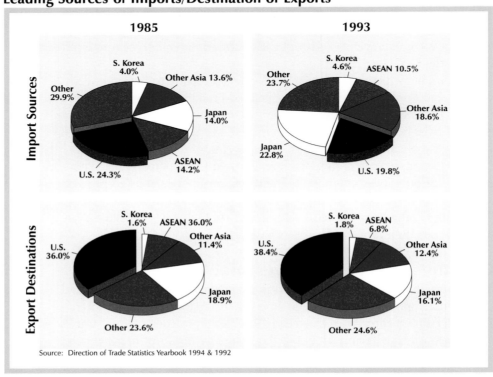

Source: Direction of Trade Statistics Yearbook 1994 & 1992

patents, trademarks and copyrights which it intends to submit to the Philippine Congress in 1995. The Philippines remains on the Special 301 "watch list."

THE COMPETITION

The U.S. is the Philippines' largest trading partner in terms of overall trade turnover, and it has traditionally been the Philippines' top supplier. But in 1993, Philippine imports from Japan totalled $4.1 billion, topping the $3.55 billion from the U.S. Historically the U.S. has been far and away the largest investor in the Philippines. However, in the last several years Japan and the U.S. have vied for the top spot. Key areas of Japanese investment include metalworking and engineering (especially in automotive assembly and parts manufacture), electronic components, consumer electronics, computer software development, and construction materials. Furthermore, through its Overseas Economic Cooperation Fund (OECF), Japan has the largest bilateral donor program, providing soft-loan financing to the Philippines, furnishing over $4 billion in concessionary loan assistance between 1989-93.

Singapore:

Geography
3.5 times the size of
Washington, D.C.
Total Area: 632.6 sq. km.

Population
2.9 Million

Languages
English, Mandarin, Tamil,
various Chinese dialects.
English is the lingua
franca for government,
education and business.

Cultural Mix
76% Chinese
15% Malay
6% Indian
2% Other

GDP
US$ 60.61 Billion

GDP Growth Rate
10.2%

Per Capita GDP
US$ 20,900

Inflation Rate
3.5%

1994. Source: U.S. Embassy, Singapore

Singapore's exotic past has been paved over with skyscrapers and highways, making it a modern city on a par with Hong Kong and New York. In making these improvements, Singapore has strategically positioned itself as a regional hub for ASEAN and a gateway to Asia.

Singapore is overwhelmingly dependent on foreign trade — which totals almost three times the country's GNP. More than a third of its imports are re-exported. To support its role as a regional center, Singapore has developed excellent infrastructure, including world-class air and seaports, an extensive road network, an efficient subway and state-of-the-art telecommunications and public utilities.

Only three-and-one-half times the size of Washington D.C., Singapore has developed an outward-looking, export-oriented economic policy that encourages two-way trade and investment. Boosted by the rapid expansion of its ASEAN neighbors, and supporting an 11 percent growth rate in the first part of 1994, Singapore is a requisite stop for any company interested in Asia. Bechtel, General Motors and Fluor Daniel have established regional headquarters in Singapore that make virtually all corporate decisions about projects in Asia—in one case, the company stationed one of its board members in Singapore to be closer to the action.

Singapore is the U.S.'s 10th largest export market, and because it serves as a gateway to Asia, almost any American product can find an interested buyer. Shipments from the U.S. accounted for 16.2 percent of Singapore's total imports, or $13.8 billion, in 1993. Total imports rose 5.9 percent each year between 1990-1993. Re-exports are growing at a rate of 19 percent. Currently, some 1,000 U.S. companies operate in Singapore, selling in this lucrative market, using the island as a regional base for buying for the U.S. market or for manufacturing. Those selling American products find that 96 percent of their products enter Singapore duty free. An additional 3,600 U.S. companies have representatives in Singapore—many of whom have regional responsibilities. Singapore has relatively few obstacles to trade, maintaining barriers in only a few sectors—legal services, banking, and some telecommunication and tobacco products.

Singapore offers a highly sophisticated "user-friendly" market for a wide range of American products and services and an excellent base from which to explore opportunities elsewhere in the rapidly growing Southeast Asian region. Currently, the Singaporean government is encouraging firms to invest further afield, especially in China. U.S. firms

ASEAN'S Hub

can capitalize on Singapore's efforts to regionalize and globalize by joining forces with Singapore firms that are actively involved in overseas projects. Singaporean partners could provide contacts and U.S. firms could bring the innovative products and technologies.

U.S. firms have successfully utilized joint ventures with Singapore companies to win projects in China. Black & Veatch coordinated with a Singapore partner to undertake significant wastewater and environmental treatment projects in China, and a Black & Veatch subsidiary, The Pritchard Corporation, has done the same in the processed petrochemical industries. The Singapore partner of the Chili's restaurant chain is carrying the purveyor of American-style food into the rest of Southeast Asia and to China.

The U.S. has maintained formal diplomatic relations with Singapore since it became independent in 1965. Singapore's efforts to maintain economic growth and political stability and its support for regional cooperation form a solid basis for amicable relations. The growth of U.S. investment in Singapore and the large number of Americans living there enhance opportunities for contact between Singapore and the U.S.

At the same time, Singapore's political and social institutions have come under fire recently in the U.S., resulting in negative headlines that have at times overshadowed what is generally a close bilateral relationship. Business practices, however, are straightforward and no-nonsense. Corruption is virtually nonexistent. English is widely used and business people are skilled as well as technically knowledgeable. Most agents and distributors have paid numerous visits to the U.S.

Still, long-term structural problems will continue to dog economic policy makers in Singapore. The rapid economic growth and declining birth rate have put increasing pressure on labor resources. Wage growth continues to rise more rapidly than productivity growth. In order to sustain its growth, Singapore is upgrading the skills of its workforce, encouraging firms to automate, and shifting labor-intensive activities offshore, as well as promoting indigenous research and development capabilities.

Singapore has strategically positioned itself as a regional hub for ASEAN and a gateway to Asia.

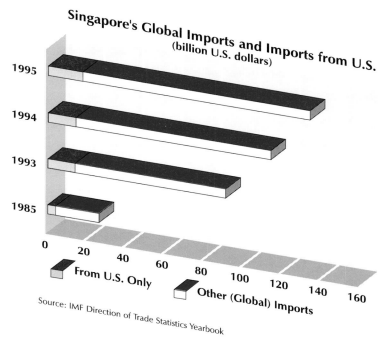

Singapore's Global Imports and Imports from U.S. (billion U.S. dollars)

Source: IMF Direction of Trade Statistics Yearbook

BIG EMERGING SECTORS

Energy

The Singapore market for electrical power systems can be divided into two areas: municipal and private/industrial. The municipal market consists mainly of equipment supplied to Singapore's Public Utilities Board (PUB), such as high-capacity generators and related accessories. PUB projects are conducted on an international competitive bid basis, with preferential treatment given to bids using local manufacturers of ancillary equipment. Japanese and European companies have dominated this market, often because U.S. firms have been too strict on their terms of offer and their prices have not been competitive.

U.S. companies are strong in the lower-capacity generators for the private/industrial market. Some companies are using Singapore as an assembly and distribution center to market their equipment into the much larger regional market. Growth is expected to be at least 10 percent in this sector. Most promising subsectors include high-capacity generators, generating sets, and cables and accessories.

Share of Singapore's Import Market for Energy Technology, 1993

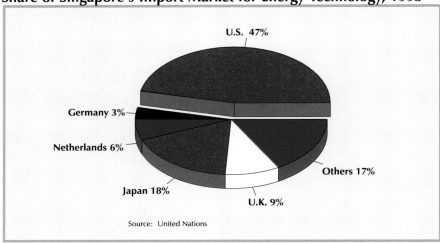

U.S. 47%
Germany 3%
Netherlands 6%
Japan 18%
U.K. 9%
Others 17%

Source: United Nations

Environmental Technology

Singapore has a more developed market for environmental products and services than the rest of ASEAN. It has established itself as a center for the region by taking the lead in banning a range of environmentally unfriendly products, including the importation or manufacture of non-pharmaceutical aerosols and polystyrene sheets and products, most mercury oxides, zinc carbon, and alkaline batteries. Singapore has also introduced unleaded gasoline and phased out the importation of CFCs/halons. To improve air quality, Singapore has strengthened emission standards. By the end of 1995, Singapore will have installed an advanced air monitoring system throughout the island, even though current emissions are well within U.S. EPA standards.

The U.S. competes against Japan, Germany and Australia for Singapore's pollution control market. The U.S. has been losing ground because foreign competitors are making strategic partnerships and agreements for joint ventures or local distributorship.

1995 Best Prospects in Singapore

- Electronic components
- Industrial chemicals
- Aircraft and parts
- Computers and peripherals
- Electronics
- Pumps, valves and compressors
- Laboratory and scientific instruments
- Apparel
- Franchising
- Oil/gas machinery and services

Healthcare Technology

Singapore has the most advanced healthcare system in the region. Much of Singapore's future healthcare needs will focus on caring for its aging population—the number of people over the age of 60 is expected to increase to 12 percent by the year 2000. To ensure that Singapore nationals can afford quality medical care, the Singapore government implemented Medisave, a compulsory medical savings plan. Finally, as Singapore's population becomes more affluent and lives longer, it contracts different diseases. More Singaporeans are becoming afflicted with more chronic degenerative diseases and fewer infectious diseases. The end results of these demographic changes will be the need to maintain a highly sophisticated market for medical equipment.

In 1993, total imports of healthcare products reached $564 million, reflecting an average annual growth rate of 21.6 percent since 1989. Currently, the private sector accounts for 70 percent of total healthcare expenditures, with the government making up the remaining 30 percent.

Singapore re-exports approximately 40 percent of its total imports to other countries, thereby maintaining its role as a regional hub for medical technology. In addition, Singapore operates as a regional medical center. In some private hospitals up to 30 percent of the patients are from foreign countries. Singapore will be able to remain a regional force if it continues to invest in the latest technology and can provide medical expertise and equipment to its ASEAN neighbors.

Transportation

In an effort to control the congestion so common in other ASEAN countries, the Singapore government tightly controls Singapore's vehicle population. Despite the high costs of vehicle ownership, which are the result of a vast array of extremely high duties and taxes—even for access to roads during rush hour—demand exceeds supply. Many Singaporeans have the means to purchase cars, and car ownership is considered a status symbol.

There is no local automotive assembly industry, in line with Singapore's policy of discouraging most heavy industries; all of the automobiles on Singapore roads are imports. But like the rest of ASEAN, Japanese brands dominate, with nine of the top 10 selling automobiles Japanese models. Singapore does, however, encourage its automotive component manufacturing industry, especially for products requiring high-technology equipment. More than 200 companies make auto parts in Singapore, less than 50 of them producing for original equipment manufacturing. Some of the U.S. auto component giants—including GM, Rockwell, Dana, Caterpillar, Allison Transmission, Federal Mogul and Ingersoll-Rand—have a presence in Singapore.

> ### Competing More Effectively
>
> In the future, U.S. companies will have to pay more attention to after-sales servicing and demonstrate a stronger commitment to the region if they want to maintain this position. An American company's ability to compete is often hampered by the belief among Singaporean healthcare providers that when problems arise, the Japanese "send in the cavalry" while the Americans send a fax.

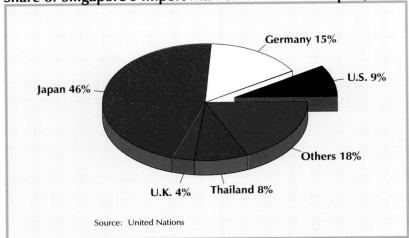

Share of Singapore's Import Market for Auto Transport, 1993

Germany 15%

U.S. 9%

Japan 46%

Others 18%

U.K. 4%   Thailand 8%

Source: United Nations

Companies interested in the Singapore auto components market should note that Singapore focuses on producing high-technology and few labor-intensive parts. In addition, Singapore does not restrict imports of auto parts, making the market extremely accessible and competitive. Singapore has positioned itself as the regional center for the manufacture and design of high-tech auto components for the original equipment manufacturing (OEM) and the replacement parts market.

Because car ownership is so expensive, Singaporeans tend to take excellent care of their vehicles. Continued growth in this sector is expected—especially in vehicle repair, body work and new replacement parts. Car care products and accessories—such as rust protection systems, sealants, lubricants and car mats—are in high demand. Other prospects for auto-related products include mobile phones, car audio systems and security systems.

In addition, Singapore is leading the "greening" of the automobile industry in ASEAN by promoting the use of electrically powered cars, introducing unleaded gas, and encouraging the use of catalytic converters.

Information Technology

Telecommunications Equipment and Services

Shopping and paying for goods or using a computer system to plan the least congested route—all from the comfort of home—could be realities for Singaporeans under their government's national telecommunications plan.

Planning to transform itself into an "intelligent island" by 2005, Singapore is emerging as a first-rate international telecommunications hub. With an economy dependent on trade, Singapore realizes the necessity of maintaining a state-of-the-art telecommunications infrastructure. Toward that end, Singapore was the first country to provide a national broadband Integrated Services Digital Network (ISDN), a system with phone lines that carry music, images, computerized services, voice and data, all at the same time.

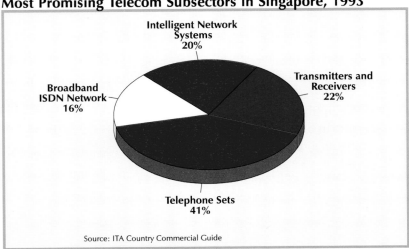

Most Promising Telecom Subsectors in Singapore, 1993

Intelligent Network Systems 20%

Transmitters and Receivers 22%

Broadband ISDN Network 16%

Telephone Sets 41%

Source: ITA Country Commercial Guide

Singapore plans to build a telecommunications network equipped with intelligent networks, broadband ISDN and optical fiber links to all homes and offices. With easy access to a wide range of services and information, Singaporean residents will have advanced, on-line at-home services such as banking, entertainment, information and news. While heavy expenses preclude most small and medium-sized companies from obtaining significant share, opportunities do exist in the market for local area network (LAN) related equipment. Small companies can succeed in the Singapore market by adopting niche strategies, and selling specialized equipment such as data compressors, data encryptors, fiber optic cables and digital termination blocks.

From 1988-92, Singapore spent $1.5 billion to build one of the world's most advanced telecommunications systems. From now until 1997, the government plans to spend another $2.4 billion. U.S. firms are beginning to take advantage of these government tender opportunities. In 1993, the U.S. exported $128 million in telecommunication equipment and services to Singapore, a 156 percent increase from 1989.

Singapore, as a regional hub, also offers opportunities beyond its own market. For example, as the manufacture of high-technology products is phased out in Singapore, the technology can be introduced in other ASEAN markets.

> ## Singapore's IT 2000
>
> - Develop Singapore as a global hub for information, finance and transportation.
> - Boost manufacturing, commerce, construction and tourism with IT.
> - Enhance individual potential through training in IT.
> - Link communities locally and globally through IT networking.
> - Improve quality of life through IT.

Computer Equipment and Software

Singapore's claim to be the IT hub for ASEAN is bolstered by the following factors: strategic geographic location in the center of the region; many system integrators; higher level of intellectual property protection; established financial, telecommunications and transportation infrastructure; the best exhibition and convention centers in ASEAN to support new product introductions; and a tax structure designed to encourage the establishment of regional offices.

Singapore is the most mature of the ASEAN countries in terms of its computer infrastructure, IT knowledge and servicing capability. This maturity, as well as the small size of the Singapore market—a population of only three million—has encouraged Singapore firms to regionalize their operations.

> ## Singapore's Computer Infrastructure
>
> Singapore is the most advanced ASEAN market in terms of its computer infrastructure. A 1992 survey by the National Computer Board (NCB) showed that 84 percent of Singapore firms with 10 or more employees were computerized and 63 percent were networked. One reason for this is that NCB, created in 1981 to promote IT development and networking, subsidizes consultants for network development in small and medium-sized firms and will pay for 70 percent of the cost of a feasibility study and 50 percent of the cost of an implementation study.
>
> In addition, Singapore Network Services (SNS), a company largely owned by the Trade Development Board and the National Computer Board has introduced many useful network systems including Biznet (electronic information on businesses), $ Link (allows all kinds of commercial documents to be exchanged from one computer to another), MailLink (e-mail linking businesses), RealNet (information on property, local and international) and CoinNet (information for the construction industry), LawNet (computerized legal database), TradeNet (paperless trade documentation), and many others.

Share of Singapore's Import Market for Infotech, 1993

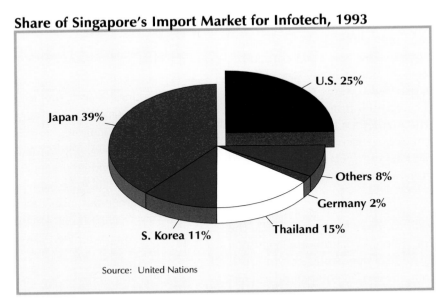

Japan 39%

U.S. 25%

Others 8%

Germany 2%

Thailand 15%

S. Korea 11%

Source: United Nations

IT sales in Singapore are about $2 billion a year, and about 40 percent of this total comes from exports. Individual firms' shipments to other ASEAN countries range from 20 to 90 percent of their total turnover. Neighboring Malaysia is their largest market, followed by Thailand, Indonesia and the Philippines.

Large multinational IT consulting firms and systems integrators have established Singapore offices to provide their services to ASEAN. Major software manufacturers are also using Singapore as a base to localize, customize and duplicate U.S.-developed software for export throughout the ASEAN region.

Although Singapore is a hub, more distributors, manufacturers and system integrators will open offices in countries throughout ASEAN as IT markets develop throughout the region. The local offices of these firms will likely assume responsibility for marketing and sales, systems integration, and technical servicing, while the Singapore office will provide backup.

Software development is a key element in Singapore's IT-2000 strategy to leapfrog into the 21st century. The software industry is relatively small in Singapore, so the main players are foreign suppliers. And more than 70 percent of information technology engineers and executives in Singapore with overseas training graduated from U.S. universities, which can enhance the U.S. market position.

A significant amount of IT hardware is also produced in Singapore. For example, in 1994, Compaq announced a second factory at a cost of about $150 million, and Apple Computer announced a $36 million expansion of its existing facilities. Seagate broke ground in May 1995 for a new disk drive plant on this island that already produces the majority of the world's hard drives.

Aerospace

Singapore's Changi airport is the major Southeast Asian air hub, linking 108 cities through more than 2,100 flights via 58 airlines each week. Singapore plans to become the foremost airport hub in the entire Asia-Pacific region by the year 2000. With two terminals and two runways, Changi is capable of handling 24 million passengers per year. Work has begun on a third terminal; a fourth terminal and a third runway are in the planning stages. More than 50 aircraft component manufacturing, maintenance and aerospace firms operate in Singapore and over 30 international aviation companies have regional marketing offices headquartered there as well.

Singapore Airlines, the country's national carrier, has a fleet of over 55 aircraft, 38 of which are long-haul 747-300 and 400 aircraft. The airline intends to increase its fleet by at least 40 aircraft over the next five years. Silk Air, a subsidiary of Singapore Airlines which serves regional routes, expects to add eight aircraft to its existing fleet of five by 1997.

Demand for ground support equipment will increase as more planes fly to Singapore. Airport cargo facilities will be expanded to cater to a total cargo capacity of 1.3 million tons. Expansion plans present significant opportunities for U.S. suppliers of airport equipment and for consulting engineers.

Also, Singapore is evolving into a world class aero-component manufacturing and overhaul center for the world market. Aerospace is one of the high value-added industries targeted by the Singapore government in its "National Technology Plan" for development. The aircraft component overhaul and manufacturing industry has grown steadily at 10 percent annually over the last five years, and is expected to continue growing at an accelerated pace well into the 21st century. The output of a variety of components manufactured by Singapore's aerospace industry has more than doubled in the last 10 years, reaching $781 million in 1993.

MARKET ACCESS

Tariffs and Import Barriers

Singapore imposes very few tariffs on imports; 96 percent of imports enter duty-free. Singapore currently maintains tariffs on less than one percent of its tariff lines (non-petroleum trade).

As of April 1, 1994 Singapore implemented a three percent Goods and Services Tax. Essentially a form of value-added tax or VAT, the GST applies to all business of at least S$1 million in goods and services in Singapore; all services received from overseas are also taxable. The tax is anticipated to remain in effect for five years. This tax has significant implications for firms doing or anticipating doing business in Singapore. Firms will have to adjust their pricing policies to determine the amount of increase in costs to pass on to the customer. Because of the GST levy system, terms of credit in the retail arena will increasingly favor cash over credit.

Singapore is evolving into a world class aero-component manufacturing and overhaul center for the world market. Aerospace is one of the high value-added industries targeted by the Singapore government in its "National Technology Plan" for development.

Government policies encourage local firms to form strategic partnerships with multinational corporations (MNCs), especially in high technology activities. There are no taxes on capital gains and no restrictions on foreign ownership of businesses.

Government Procurement Practices

Singapore is noted for its largely transparent procurement practices. With few exceptions, virtually all procurements are accomplished through open international tenders. Almost no complaints are heard from American competitors about procurement processes.

Openness to Foreign Investment

Singapore's open investment policy overcomes land, resource and labor limitations by selectively encouraging firms that can build up the country's technological base and bring about improvement in the skills of its labor force. The Singapore Economic Development Board acts as the "business architect," identifying sectors with high potential for contributing to the economy, and drafting tax and fiscal incentives to encourage foreign investment in these targeted sectors. The Board also provides a one-stop service for foreign investors, and helps them to avoid the proverbial red tape. Investors are free to purchase material from any source and are not limited by access to foreign exchange or required local entity ownership in the investment. Every company, however, must have at least two directors—one of which must reside in Singapore.

Government policies encourage local firms to form strategic partnerships with multinational corporations (MNCs), especially in high technology activities. There are no taxes on capital gains and no restrictions on foreign ownership of businesses. Foreign investors are not required to take on private or official joint ventures or cede management control to local interests. The Economic Development Board assists foreign and domestic firms to invest in new technology, automation, training and product development activities through a variety of incentives.

Special Considerations

Intellectual Property Rights

U.S. companies can be somewhat secure in Singapore's intellectual property rights (IPR) protection and prosecution of violators. Singapore enacted a strict, comprehensive copyright legislation in 1987 and strengthened the Trademark Law in 1991. A new patent law entered into force in February 1995, which brings patent registration to Singapore (previously, a patent had to be registered in the U.K. to be recognized in Singapore), and provides for product protection and a 20-year term. However, the provisions of the law concerning compulsory licensing and government use are inconsistent with the WTO TRIPS Agreement, and, in some respects, inferior to the provisions in Singapore's previous patent law. The government of Singapore has begun work to bring its Patent Act and other IPR legislation into compliance with the TRIPS Agreement.

Intellectual property rights are not protected adequately in all cases. The illegal copying, use and distribution of computer software, including on the hard disks of newly purchased personal computers, has

ASEAN

posed problems for the U.S. industry. Private firms are allowed, with the approval of the appropriate authorities, to investigate and prosecute copyright violators. As a result of these efforts, penalties have been imposed in some significant cases of piracy. The Singapore government has also prosecuted major pirates under criminal statutes, initiated a public campaign in favor of IPR protection, and created a special IPR Warrant Unit of the Police Force, charged with executing search warrants for all IPR cases, in February 1995. Singapore is on the USTR's Special 301 "watch list."

Government-Linked Corporations

A major facet of Singapore's economy of which American suppliers should be aware is that many of the country's top companies are actually government-linked corporations (GLCs)—state-owned companies. Some 44 percent of the economy is accounted for by GLCs including such world-class firms as Singapore Airlines, Singapore Technologies, Chartered Industries, the Keppel Group and the Sembawang Group. GLCs typically operate as if they were purely private companies seeking to maximize profits. Although they will respond to official requests to undertake special projects and tasks, they normally behave as private sector companies, and they usually have strong financial backing.

THE COMPETITION

Competition in Singapore is fierce—with many countries vying for position in the market. In addition to the Singaporeans, major competitors include the Japanese, British, French and Germans. The Singapore government tries to keep a "level playing field," so competition is driven by price and quality. After-sale service and maintenance continue to be problematic for U.S. firms, in part because of the distances involved.

There is a lingering perception that American companies put less stress on follow-up support than other countries. This perception is slowly improving, but some buyers still feel that if something goes wrong "the Japanese will send engineers while the Americans send faxes." To combat this negative perception, numerous U.S. companies have opened regional servicing and distribution operations. Among recent additions are Caterpillar's significant expansion in Singapore and the new Boeing and Rockwell avionics maintenance facilities near Singapore's Changi Airport.

Leading Sources of Imports/Destination of Exports

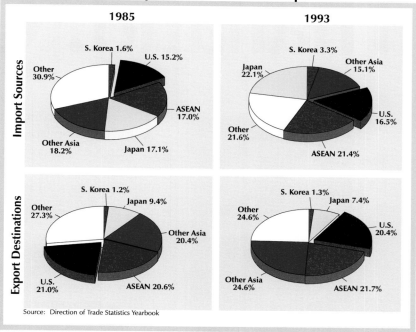

Source: Direction of Trade Statistics Yearbook

The government tries to keep a level playing field, so competition is driven by price and quality.

The Big Emerging Markets

181

Thailand: Outward-

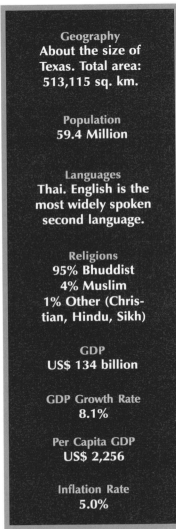

Geography
About the size of Texas. Total area: 513,115 sq. km.

Population
59.4 Million

Languages
Thai. English is the most widely spoken second language.

Religions
95% Bhuddist
4% Muslim
1% Other (Christian, Hindu, Sikh)

GDP
US$ 134 billion

GDP Growth Rate
8.1%

Per Capita GDP
US$ 2,256

Inflation Rate
5.0%

1994. Source: U.S. Embassy, Thailand; IMF

The only country in Southeast Asia never colonized, Thailand prides itself on its independence and balance in its international relations. Thailand has developed an open-market economy based on the free enterprise system. Despite frequent changes in government, Thailand has consistently pursued policies characterized by openness to the outside world and general understanding and support of the strategic objectives of the U.S. and other industrialized democracies. In addition, Thailand has followed conservative fiscal, monetary and private sector-oriented business structure policies, based on close cooperation between the public and private sectors. Political and economic stability are assured by a balance of crown, military, bureaucratic and business interests.

Thailand's outward-looking, market-oriented economic policies encourage foreign direct investment as a means of promoting economic development, employment and technology transfer. Thailand welcomes trade and investment from all countries and seeks to avoid dependence on any one country. As a result of the growing success of these policies, Thailand has enjoyed annual economic growth rates averaging nearly 10 percent between 1983-1993.

Thailand's GDP has doubled in just over five years; per capita income is rising sharply; the country has a balance of payments and a government budget surplus, and foreign exchange reserves reached $29.3 billion in 1994. With this internal stability, Thailand's economic development focus is no longer export promotion, but industrial decentralization—to promote investment outside the Bangkok metropolitan area so as to provide employment to the 66 percent of the labor force that is still involved in the agricultural sector.

Thailand is also a key country in ASEAN, helping it to rival China as a market and an offshore production base. In addition, it is strategically located next to the "northern tier" countries of Burma, Laos, Cambodia and Vietnam.

The second-largest economy in the ASEAN region, Thailand's economy was launched into double-digit growth rates in the second half of the 1980s when the yen doubled in value, forcing many Japanese firms into offshore production. Many of these firms chose Thailand as the strategic center for their manufacturing investment in the ASEAN region. According to Japanese investors, Thailand was their first-choice site for manufacturing investment because of its large internal market, homogenous population and culture, high-quality labor force and pro-business government.

Looking Market

In 1991, however, Thai leaders recognized that their economic development depended too much on Japanese investment in export-driven industries. They proposed to other countries in Southeast Asia a regional free trade area that would be an investment magnet to rival the allure of China. Nomura Securities, the leading Japanese investment house, believes this is a real possibility, and commented not long ago that, "The five major ASEAN countries' GDP in 1991 was $337 billion, about 85 percent of China's in the same year. When ASEAN reduces the barriers to the flow of goods under AFTA, services, funds and human resources, MNCs will find the region more attractive than China, both as a market and as an offshore production base."

Thailand's trade has expanded rapidly. Although agricultural exports are still substantial (rice, tapioca, rubber and sugar), manufactured goods now account for most of Thailand's exports, including textile products, integrated circuits, footwear, furniture, jewelry, and plastic products. In 1994, Thailand exported to the U.S. about $10.3 billion in products including garments, computers and parts, and integrated circuits. Thai imports from the U.S. total roughly $4.8 billion, and include electrical and non-electrical machinery and parts, chemicals, aircraft and ships, and electrical appliances.

Thailand's rapid growth has caused infrastructure bottlenecks, environmental degradation, and shortages of skilled personnel. Thailand will spend more than $100 billion between 1995-2000 on infrastructure, with $30 billion on expanded electrical generating capacity. In addition to building new electric power plants, other major projects in the works include two new oil refineries, a second international airport for Bangkok, six million telephone lines, mass transit systems for Bangkok and regional centers, new rail and highway development and expansions, new ports development and expansions, development of a new central government administrative city, and solid waste and wastewater treatment centers for Bangkok and provincial cities.

Thailand's outward-looking, market-oriented economic policies encourage foreign direct investment as a means of promoting economic development, employment and technology transfer.

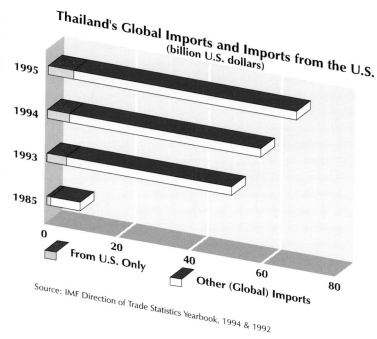

Thailand's Global Imports and Imports from the U.S.
(billion U.S. dollars)

Source: IMF Direction of Trade Statistics Yearbook, 1994 & 1992

Energy

The Electricity Generating Authority of Thailand (EGAT) projects that capacity will increase from 13,075 MW by 1996, to 19,000 MW by 2001 and 25,515 MW by 2006. Capital investment in new power plants will reach $10 billion during 1992-1996 and $22 billion in 1997-2001.

Share of Thailand's Import Market for Energy Technology, 1993

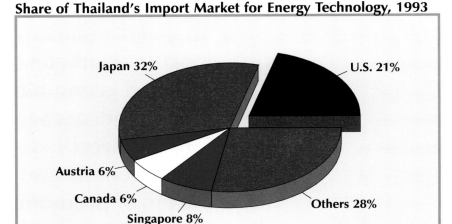

Japan 32%
U.S. 21%
Austria 6%
Canada 6%
Singapore 8%
Others 28%

Source: United Nations

Representative opportunities for U.S. firms in selling to EGAT include a 2,800 megawatt (4 x 700MW) thermal power plant in Ratchaburi province scheduled for commissioning by 1998. Black & Veatch, headquartered in Kansas City, is preparing the terms of reference for the bidding.

Although EGAT will remain the principal customer in Thailand, recent moves to allow increased private sector participation in electric power generation in Thailand also offer opportunities.

New opportunities in the electric power systems sector have also come from "demand side management" and environmental pollution control. On the demand side management front, the Thai National Energy Policy Office requires factories and buildings whose annual energy consumption exceeds 1,000 kw to submit a conservation plan for review/approval and implementation by 1997. To help companies comply with this requirement, the Thai government has allocated $240 million for loans from the Energy Conservation Fund. This should offer a good opportunity to U.S. firms to conduct energy audits and market products and systems such as software applications and computerized control units to perform operation and control of buildings' power usage.

Environmental Technology

Three thousand two-ton garbage trucks are needed to remove the daily waste produced by Bangkok residents. By the year 2000, Bangkok may require 5,500 of such trucks. Sprawling population growth, combined with the Thai government's focus on enforcement of environmental regulations offers U.S. environmental businesses unique opportunities. For example, a couple years ago the provincial authorities of northeast Thailand ordered the closing of the Phoenix Pulp and Paper Company for dumping untreated waste into the Pang River. The subsequent six-week shutdown cost the company $2.5 million in cleanup and lost revenue.

By assessing Thailand's future development needs, taking the time to meet the players and working in conjunction with the U.S. government's efforts, U.S. companies will be able to break into the environmental technology market. Thailand is addressing its environmental problems through legislation. It has also restructured its environmental agency, now the Ministry of Science, Technology and Environment (MOSTE), and has established an environmental fund with a projected annual budget of $80 million through 1996. As in other ASEAN countries, the Thai government is focusing on banning leaded gasoline by the year 1996; limiting emission of hazardous wastes; and encouraging efficient use of energy.

ASEAN's environmental degradation will continue to take an increased toll on the local population unless it is abated. This degradation will also take its toll in dollars as ASEAN's tourism industry suffers and as the retroactive costs of cleaning the environment mount. U.S. firms are in an excellent position to take advantage of the fast-growing ASEAN market if they take a long-term approach needed to assess each country's needs, develop business relationships and adopt new sales approaches that include training and involving the local residents in the technology operation and maintenance, and in cleaner production processes adapted to local environments.

Share of Thailand's Import Market for Healthcare Technology, 1993

U.S. 33%

Japan 27%

Others 19%

Germany 11%

Singapore 10%

Source: United Nations

Healthcare Technology

Thailand is the largest market for healthcare expenditures in Southeast Asia. In 1991, Thailand spent $3.5 billion on health-related expenditures—almost 6 percent of its GDP, more than the total health expenditures of Singapore, Malaysia and the Philippines combined. Thai imports of medical equipment, valued at $64 million in 1989, will grow at an estimated 44 percent over the next five years. Because the industry's needs are so great and the government does not have the resources to meet this demand, private investors are setting up private hospitals.

Thai buyers prefer U.S. products, which have a reputation for durability and superior quality. In addition, many Thai doctors are familiar with U.S. technology and products because many of them were educated in the U.S.

Share of Thailand's Import Market for Auto Transport, 1993

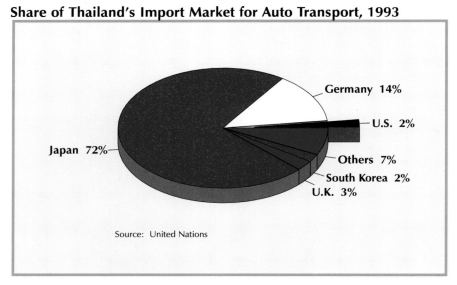

Germany 14%

U.S. 2%

Japan 72%

Others 7%

South Korea 2%

U.K. 3%

Source: United Nations

A dependence on imports inevitably raises the cost of health-care. Thailand is working to lower costs by developing its local production capabilities. The Thai government encourages direct foreign investment, specifically for joint ventures with local Thai companies to enhance efforts to expand local production capabilities.

Transportation

Motor Vehicles and Parts

Bangkok's traffic is notorious, and the streets are packed with Japanese vehicles. Japanese manufacturers dominate both the assembly and components sectors, through direct investments, joint ventures and technical licensing agreements. Five Japanese automakers—led by Toyota, Isuzu and Mitsubishi—control 76 percent of the passenger car market and 99 percent of the commercial vehicle market.

Historically, there have been three key automotive industry drivers: tax policy, local content policy and sustained economic growth. Vigorous real average economic growth of 8.5 percent annually during 1983-1991 led to rising incomes and an increase in demand for automobiles. High import duties and outright bans on certain imports, combined with a local content policy, provided protection to domestic assemblers and an incentive to domestic parts makers.

To date, market entry has been a challenge for U.S. companies in Thailand. Chrysler, for example, spent three years trying to break into the Thai automotive market. Chrysler executives spent long hours negotiating with the Royal Thai Government on customs tariff classification and duty levels on its Jeep Cherokee kits. Their time and energy paid off—Chrysler was permitted to import kits from U.S. parts.

Similar to Indonesia and Malaysia, a new set of policies designed to promote the local components industry was created in Thailand in the 1970s. Also, a schedule of import duties, excise taxes and import bans and local content regulations were established. Local content requirements have increased over time to encourage assemblers to make parts of international quality at a competitive price—reaching their peak in 1991.

In recent years, Thai government policies have shifted from protecting the local assembly industry at any cost to significant liberalization to meet General Agreement on Tariffs and Trade (GATT) requirements and to encourage the local assemblers and component manufacturers to become internationally competitive.

In the components sector, Japanese keiretsu companies are well entrenched in labor intensive auto parts production. Larger volume Japanese assemblers and their keiretsu companies are prospering, taking advantage of the liberalization policies to invest in export oriented assembly and components manufacturing operations. This sector is expected to grow as import duties on raw materials are lowered and demand rises, Japanese manufacturers shift production to Thailand, and U.S. automakers re-enter the ASEAN marketplace.

The Japanese, however, are reluctant to transfer design and engineering expertise to their Thai production partners, many of whom are now planning their own vehicle models with non-Japanese, mainly Italian, assistance. Many Thai components and supporting industry companies would welcome a U.S. partner from whom they could obtain the latest technology, as well as access to international markets.

Information Technology

Telecommunications Equipment and Services

There are 1.2 million reminders—the number of applicants on Bangkok's waiting list for telephone lines—that Thailand has significant telecommunications needs. Opportunities to supply telephone switching equipment, optic fiber cables, mobile telephones, paging systems, private automatic branch exchanges, facsimile machines, cable TV broadcasting network equipment and satellite signal receiving equipment are plentiful. In 1993, Thailand imported $571 million worth of telecommunications equipment, up 94 percent since 1989.

After more than a century of monopoly-based telecommunication service, the Thai Ministry of Transportation and Communication (MOTC) is opening its doors to the private sector. Opportunities exist in a number of areas. Projects currently underway include the installation of six million telephone lines by the year 2001; the creation of a national network management system; the installation of a 3,000 kilometer fiber optic submarine cable connecting Vietnam and Hong Kong with Thailand; the operation of low-orbiting satellites in a venture with Motorola, and working with the Chinese government to operate the APSTAR 1 and APSTAR 2 satellites.

> **The Japanese are reluctant to transfer design and engineering expertise to their Thai production partners. Many Thai companies would welcome a U.S. partner from whom they could obtain the latest technology.**

Share of Thailand's Import Market for Infotech, 1993

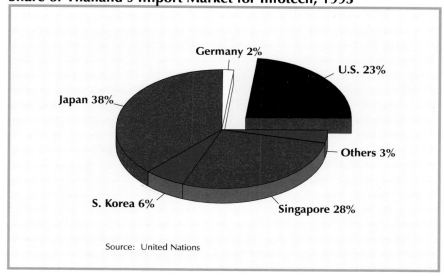

Japan 38%
Germany 2%
U.S. 23%
Others 3%
Singapore 28%
S. Korea 6%

Source: United Nations

Quality and reliability are the most important factors in clinching sales in Thailand's telecommunication market. In addition, costs and financing are often key to closing a deal.

Quality and reliability are the most important factors in clinching deals in Thailand's telecommunication market. In addition, costs and financing are often key to making the sale. Local telecommunications service providers usually receive concessionary loans as well as suppliers' long-term credits. Companies, to be competitive in the long run, should consider seeking strategic partners.

As Thailand works to meet its development plans for the next century, U.S. companies are poised to play a strategic role in providing not only leading-edge technology, but also technical and managerial training. Technical training programs such as those provided by the U.S. Telecommunications Training Institute are often the added incentive needed to win deals in Thailand.

Computer Equipment and Software

Third largest in the ASEAN region, the Thai computer market has been focused on organizational users such as financial institutions, telecommunications, government agencies and state enterprises, and manufacturing and transportation firms. It is on the verge, however, of shifting to focus more on mass consumption. Nearly 200,000 computers were sold in Thailand in 1994, and distribution channels are changing to include not only distributors' stores for business customers but also department stores and other retail outlets that cater to individuals.

Japanese firms' hardware market share of 26 percent slightly edges out U.S. suppliers, who have a 21 percent share. Dominant U.S. suppliers include IBM, Compaq, DEC and Hewlett-Packard. Most manufacturing investment in Thailand is of Japanese origin, and these firms favor Japanese information technology products; retro-fitting existing equipment and facilities is only now becoming attractive for smaller Thai manufacturers, who are more inclined to buy U.S. products.

Offsetting a downward trend in larger systems is the growing demand for personal computers —estimated at 20 percent in 1994. Increasingly, users consider software applications first and then select hardware. Software sales are growing at more than 80 percent per year, driven by increased demand for industry-specific applications, especially networking and multimedia systems. The growth rate could double in 1995, following the 1994 enactment of a new copyright law that protects software. U.S. firms dominate the market with more than 80 percent market share.

Aerospace

Thailand is geographically located in the center of Asia's air traffic. With a projected annual traffic growth of 9 percent, its main airport, Bangkok's Don Muang, will reach its capacity of 16 million passengers by the year 2000. Thailand has become a magnet for tourists — travelling to the beaches of Phuket in the south and the mountains of Chiang Mai and Chiang Rai in the north. Nearby Vietnam, Cambodia and Laos are also being added to the list of holiday destinations.

As a result of this increase in tourism, Bangkok's current airport traffic is expected to increase steadily over the next few years. To relieve this pressure, the Thai government is building a second international airport at Nong Ngu Hao, about 18 miles east of Bangkok, at a cost of about $4 billion. The new facility, which will be designed by a U.S. consortium, is expected to rival Singapore's Changi airport as a regional hub, and will have a passenger handling capacity of 100 million passengers per year by the year 2020.

U.S. firms are the main suppliers for Thailand's inter-continental aircraft. Mid-range and short-haul aircraft are purchased from the U.S., France and the United Kingdom. Thai Airways International Limited (THAI), the only national airline, has signed contracts for another 20 aircraft with Boeing Commercial Aircraft and Airbus.

For aircraft parts, U.S. firms account for 70-80 percent of total imports. Thai Airways International has a yearly budget of approximately $12 million for spare parts, while the Royal Thai Armed Forces has a combined yearly budget of approximately $120 million. The annual growth rate for aircraft parts in the next three years is estimated at about five percent per year.

MARKET ACCESS

Tariffs and Import Barriers

There are trade barriers to overcome in exporting to Thailand, including high import duties, arbitrary customs valuation, and illegal copying and piracy of copyright, patents and trademarks. High import duties have been a major trade barrier for U.S. exporters, with current duty rates in the 30 to 60 percent range for many products. As part of Thailand's investment promotion strategy, duty exemptions are a routine part of incentives offered to investors, and import duties on raw materials are rebated upon export of finished product. In recent years, the Thai government has taken major steps to reduce and simplify import tariffs to open its market to imports. To comply with GATT standards, Thailand is reducing duties on many manufactured goods.

Government Procurement Practices

U.S. exporters have actively pursued government procurement opportunities mostly in the power generation and transmission, petroleum, refining, and petrochemicals, telecommunications, transportation, environment, healthcare and defense equipment sectors. For U.S. firms, the key to successful bidding on Thai government contracts and supply tenders is to have a reputable local representative with good access to the procuring agency and knowledge of specific requirements and practice. Without the assistance of an effective representative, it is very difficult to sell to the government. Local representatives are an accepted,

For U.S. firms, the key to successful bidding on Thai government contracts and supply tenders is to have a reputable local representative. Without the assistance of an effective representative, it is very difficult to sell to the government.

legitimate part of the bidding process. Agents often will alert U.S. firms to attractive tenders, and before tenders are issued, they will work to ensure that the principal's product is specified.

The "Prime Minister's Procurement Regulations" govern public sector procurement. Although the regulations specify non-discriminatory treatment for all potential foreign bidders, they provide preferential treatment for domestic suppliers, who receive an automatic 15 percent advantage over foreign bidders in initial-round bid evaluation.

Openness to Foreign Investment

The most serious investment barriers are complicated specifications regulating foreign ownership and control of companies, including in several sectors in which foreigners are simply prohibited from participation.

The U.S.-Thai *Treaty of Amity and Economic Relations* allows U.S. citizens and businesses incorporated in the U.S. to engage in business on the same basis as Thais. In return, Thais are extended reciprocal rights to invest in the U.S. Notwithstanding their treaty rights, many American firms choose to form joint ventures with Thai partners and allow them to hold majority shares because of their familiarity with the Thai economy and local regulations.

Leading Sources of Imports/Destination of Exports

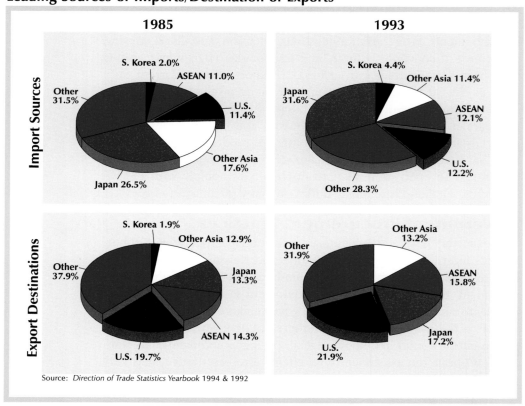

Source: *Direction of Trade Statistics Yearbook* 1994 & 1992

In many cases U.S. exporters will need to consider joint ventures and licensing as market entry strategies to cope with trade barriers and enhance export sales. Often, combining U.S. high-technology components with Thai assembly and finishing may be the only means of overcoming costly freight charges, import restrictions and duties, and competition from cheaper local products. Increasingly, Thai firms are actively seeking U.S. joint venture partners who will bring technical, marketing and management skills to a business relationship. In turn, the Thai firms offer plenty of capital, a strong local presence through valuable on-the-spot contacts with local vendors, customers and government officials, and regional relationships as well.

Special Considerations
Intellectual Property Rights
Inadequate protection is still a serious issue for U.S. copyright, patent and trademark holders in Thailand. U.S. firms should protect their intellectual property rights by registering their patents and trademarks. Lawyers specializing in intellectual property protection can be used to take legal action to suppress piracy, although this can be a lengthy process. Thailand passed a new copyright law in 1994 and, as a result, was removed from the USTR's Special 301 "priority watch list" and placed on the "watch list." The Thai government is now taking legislative and administrative steps to improve enforcement.

THE COMPETITION
Competition in Thailand is strong. U.S. exporters will confront their global competitors from Japan and Europe as well as Thai and ASEAN companies. U.S. firms must do what they do best, namely draw on their products' technical advantages and their own marketing and technical skills. They must choose market niches carefully, localize their products and constantly upgrade and improve their product offerings. Many Thai firms believe that U.S. firms should also offer more styles and designs, new models, new technology and a strong commitment to customer training.

Thai competitors often compete on price and relationships. Japanese and European firms understand the Thai business environment, which is based on strong market experience and a strategic view of the market within the ASEAN region. They use financing, quality and customer service to the maximum, and show great flexibility and a willingness to do things the Thai way. U.S. firms must match all this; they can also use training and human resource development of customer staff as key sales tools.

Increasingly, Thai firms are actively seeking U.S. joint venture partners who will bring technical, marketing and management skills to a business relationship. The Thai firms offer capital, a strong local presence and regional relationships as well.

Vietnam: ASEAN's

Geography
Larger than Virginia,
North Carolina and South
Carolina combined.
Total area: approximately
332,000 sq. km.

Population
73 Million

Languages
Vietnamese (official),
English, Chinese, French

Cultural Mix
Almost 90% Vietnamese,
Hoa (Chinese) at 1.8%,
and 52 ethnic minorities
including Tay, Thai,
Khmer, Muong

GDP
US$ 18 Billion

GDP Growth Rate
8.7%

Per Capita GDP
US$ 250

Inflation
14%

1994. Source: CIA World Factbook

The speed with which Vietnam has found acceptance in the Associa tion of Southeast Asian Nations (ASEAN), the very organization created in part to contain it, is instructive of the changes it has undergone. Since it initiated moves toward a market-driven economy in 1986, Vietnam's economy has been growing at an average of 8 percent annually. This growth rate is in line with its ASEAN neighbors—despite the obstacles presented by an economy in transition.

On July 11, 1995, President Clinton announced the establishment of full diplomatic relations between the United States and Vietnam. As latecomers to the Vietnamese market, U.S. companies are faced with a host of disadvantages in addition to lack of experience in this new environment. Business opportunities have been lost to the competition because of lack of access to competitive financing, a key factor in winning major projects in Vietnam. The establishment of diplomatic relations allows U.S. government agencies to assist U.S. companies on the full range of trade policy issues including financing. The US&FCS will soon establish an office in Hanoi to serve U.S. companies on the ground in Vietnam. The very positive reception American companies and businesspeople currently enjoy in Vietnam should go a long way toward building strong business ties.

Vietnam is widely recognized as a dynamic emerging market with numerous opportunities. These lucrative opportunities are tempered by the many difficulties associated with doing business in an economy in transition. The business climate has improved a great deal since the introduction of extensive economic reform measures, including a liberal foreign investment code, in its efforts to move toward a more market-driven economy. If current trends continue, Vietnam will grow at a healthy clip of 8-10 percent annually until the year 2000. With a large population — 80 million by the year 2000 — and a more open, expanding economy, Vietnam will be able to exert a strong influence on the economies of its regional neighbors.

Yet the lack of infrastructure, a weak commercial legal framework, cumbersome bureaucracy, and inadequate access to financing pose formidable challenges to doing business in Vietnam. The government lacks the financial resources to pay for many of its improvement plans;

Newest Member

its current GDP is estimated at $18 billion, small in comparison to its ASEAN neighbors. Foreign investment — $3.7 billion in 1994 — is a major source of funding for Vietnam's economic expansion plans. It secured nearly $4 billion from international financial institutions — a majority from Japan's ODA program — in only the past two years. Also, Vietnam imported $4.5 billion worth of goods last year, up $600 million from the previous year. Clearly, there are numerous opportunities for foreign companies to get involved in the Vietnamese market.

Since the February 1994 lifting of the U.S. embargo, U.S. companies have for the first time gained equal access to potential commercial opportunities in Vietnam. U.S. investors reportedly had lined up 28 projects worth $270 million as of February 1995. Additionally, long-suppressed demand for consumer goods has surfaced, buoyed by more available disposable income, fewer government restrictions and a greater confidence in the economy. The country is actively pursuing an export-led growth strategy in hope of developing its economy along the lines of its ASEAN neighbors.

BIG EMERGING SECTORS

Greater economic exchange with Vietnam will only increase the U.S.'s market share and opportunities for U.S. companies. Generally, opportunities in Vietnam exist in all sectors. Given the limited financial resources available to the government of Vietnam, certain projects — such as roads, airports, power generation, water treatment, petroleum exploration and improving the tourism industry — have been designated as priorities.

Vietnam is an important market for a wide range of American goods and services, especially telecommunications equipment, power generation, aviation and avionic equipment, hotel and tourism, construction, food processing and packaging, textile machinery, transportation, financial and legal services, and consumer products.

Companies intending to do business in Vietnam should have a presence on the ground in order to benefit from this rapidly expanding market. Being able to offer an attractive financing package is the single most important element to winning contracts in this hard currency-scarce environment. Time, patience and hard work are other key ingredients to success.

Although Vietnam is one of the least developed countries in Asia, economic reforms are beginning to unleash potential that could move it toward rapid growth.

Real GDP Growth through 2010 (billion U.S. dollars)

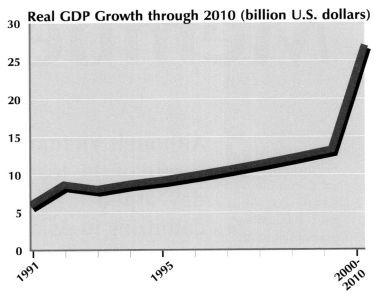

Source: Citibank, Ministry of Trade of the SRV

Modernizing its telecommunications system is a top priority for the Vietnamese government — a goal they hope to accomplish by 2000.

Infrastructure

As Vietnam seeks to meet demands for inputs to build its infrastructure and industrial base, demand will be strongest for goods and services in those sectors. U.S. companies will find many opportunities in Multilateral Development Banks (MDB) and Japanese ODA-funded infrastructure projects, which have the advantage of being priority projects that already have financing. Larger U.S. firms will find opportunities in the multitude of major infrastructure projects, and smaller U.S. firms can participate as subcontractors and equipment vendors.

An estimated annual growth rate of 14 percent over the next five years translates into a strong demand for building and construction materials in Vietnam — an estimated $2 billion per year will be spent on construction materials. Because Vietnam lacks the ability to produce sufficient building materials domestically, builders are forced to import large quantities of high-priced supplies — especially cement, iron and glass. Demand for these products will only grow as Vietnam's plans for infrastructure projects such as roads, ports, bridges, residential and commercial structures are executed.

Vietnam's current seaport infrastructure cannot support its growing economy — the increasing number of goods shipped by sea is taking its toll on the outdated port infrastructure. The potential for sales of port equipment is tremendous — equipment such as cranes and container handling equipment are desperately needed. Also, opportunities exist for companies or consortia that can provide port management communications systems or ship repair facilities. In general, U.S. equipment has a very good reputation; however, some buyers believe that it is expensive and that it is difficult to get spare parts.

Although the government of Vietnam wants to upgrade its seaports, it lacks sufficient capital to execute its goals. Private investment as well as foreign aid will be critical to the successful development of Vietnam's port system.

Information Technology

Telecommunications Equipment and Services

Modernizing its telecommunications system is a top priority for the Vietnamese government—a goal they hope to accomplish by 2000. Currently, there is only one telephone per 220 people, and government plans aim to reduce this number to 33 in the next five years. The recent increase in foreign business travelers and rising incomes among local residents has put added pressure on the telecommunications network, especially in Vietnam's larger cities.

Rather than revitalize existing systems, the government has elected to replace entire telecommunications systems with state-of-the-art imported equipment. Part of Vietnam's telecommunications upgrade plan includes building a national fiber optic line, an upgrade of their satellite stations, and developing research and training centers—at a cost of approximately $2.7 billion.

Since the lifting of the trade embargo, U.S. companies have not yet captured a significant share of this market. As in the rest of the Southeast Asian telecommunications industry, U.S. companies are competing against their rivals from Japan and Germany. The major problem with securing a foothold in the Vietnamese market is financing — most projects must be financed from sources outside the country.

Computer Equipment and Software

The market for computers is in its infancy stage. The market is small, but it is expected to grow 30-40 percent annually for the next five years as the country pursues an information technology policy.

Competition in the market is tough—the U.S. holds only 10 percent of the import market. The markets for computer components and printers are dominated by Taiwan, Japan and Singapore — which sell products at a lower price than U.S. firms. But as the Vietnamese become more familiar with U.S. brands of computers, sales of U.S. computer hardware are expected to increase. Several of the largest American computer manufacturers have offices in Vietnam, but small and medium-sized firms may find it difficult to break into this market due to its extreme price consciousness.

Because the Vietnamese computer industry is relatively unsophisticated, opportunities exist for U.S. firms that can supply older personal computers and dot matrix and laser printers.

Vietnam plans to double electricity production in the next five years and supply the entire country with power by 2010. The government expects that interested firms will provide both feasibility studies and a complete financial package in their proposals.

Direct Foreign Investment, 1994

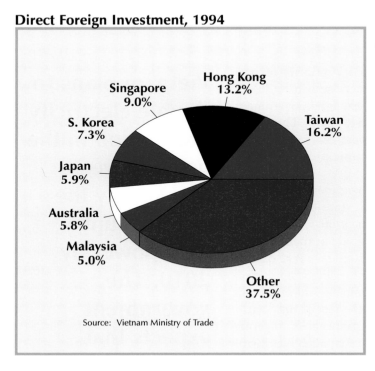

Hong Kong 13.2%
Singapore 9.0%
S. Korea 7.3%
Taiwan 16.2%
Japan 5.9%
Australia 5.8%
Malaysia 5.0%
Other 37.5%

Source: Vietnam Ministry of Trade

Power

Construction of a large number of power plants and renovation of the power transmission and distribution system will be needed to meet Vietnam's goals of doubling electricity production in the next five years and supplying the entire country with power by 2010. The Vietnamese government expects that interested firms will provide their own feasibility studies and a complete financial package as part of their proposal. In general, Vietnam is encouraging build-operate-transfer (BOT) proposals and/or joint ventures with local partners. Open international bidding may be rare, used only when several companies deliver proposals on the same project.

Opportunities exist for sales of a full range of power generation equipment to Vietnam—especially power transmission and distribution equipment. Also, U.S. companies interested in build-operate-transfer and build-own-operate projects—and that can provide financing—stand a good chance of getting a deal done. One problem, however, is that few Vietnamese buyers are familiar with U.S. products—they are uncertain of the quality and concerned about high prices. And most sales are financed through overseas development assistance, which could pose problems for U.S. suppliers, as most of the assistance comes from Japan and is geared to benefit Japanese suppliers.

Transportation

Airports

Air transportation is not a viable mode of transportation in Vietnam, because the country does not have a well-developed airport system. Efforts are being made to upgrade the infrastructure, but much work remains to be done. And, as with other industries in Vietnam, foreign investment and/or aid is needed to make improvements in runways, airport terminals, equipment and air navigation systems.

Motor Vehicles

According to Vietnamese officials, no more than four automotive assembly plants will be built in the country. Vietnam Motors and Mekong Motors already have plants in operation, but they could be merged or bought out by a major foreign manufacturer. So far, Chrysler, Ford, Hyundai, Mitsubishi, Toyota and Renault have all expressed interest in the automobile market. In October 1994, Chrysler announced its commitment to a major investment in Vietnam, a joint-venture plant with the Vietnamese-owned diesel engine manufacturing company Vinapro. Chrysler officials indicated they will build an assembly plant in Dong Nai Prong, near Ho Chi Minh City. Ford is increasing its efforts to break into the Vietnamese auto market and has applied for permission to build a vehicle assembly plant. The firm has exhibited selected models at an auto show in Ho Chi Minh City, and it plans to begin selling cars in Vietnam in the near future.

Healthcare Technology

In order to keep its people healthy, Vietnam will have to invest millions of dollars to upgrade its health care system. Many of Vietnam's hospitals have not been repaired for decades. Most are in desperate need of basic supplies as well as high-tech equipment. The entire country lacks a sufficient supply of medical equipment; even basic equipment such as syringes and x-ray machines are scarce.

Vietnam already imports 99 percent of its medical equipment, and industry improvement plans rely on a steady flow of imports. Officials also hope to attract more foreign investors, specifically those with expertise in healthcare management systems and advanced medical equipment.

Leading Destinations of Exports

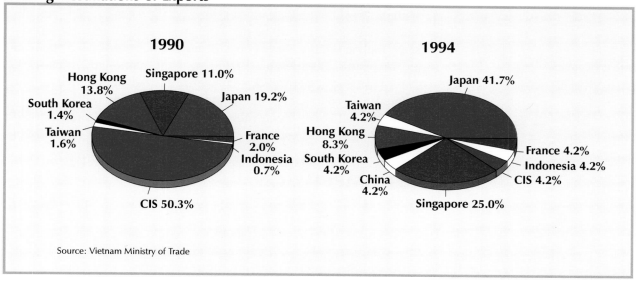

1990

Hong Kong 13.8%
Singapore 11.0%
South Korea 1.4%
Japan 19.2%
Taiwan 1.6%
France 2.0%
Indonesia 0.7%
CIS 50.3%

1994

Japan 41.7%
Taiwan 4.2%
Hong Kong 8.3%
South Korea 4.2%
France 4.2%
Indonesia 4.2%
China 4.2%
CIS 4.2%
Singapore 25.0%

Source: Vietnam Ministry of Trade

Existing Vietnamese preferences for U.S. goods and services, if coupled with competitive pricing and attractive financing terms, should be sufficient to overcome the disadvantages the U.S. faces as a latecomer to this market.

After the trade embargo was lifted, many of the U.S.'s largest medical equipment companies rushed into Vietnam. But to date, they have captured only 2 percent of the market. U.S. exports are expected to grow since U.S. medical products are preferred by many Vietnamese healthcare providers.

As in other industries, Vietnam medical equipment buyers lack sufficient funding to purchase their much-needed equipment. Companies that can offer low-interest loans, installment payment plans, or outright grants will do well in this market.

MARKET ACCESS

Market access is problematic, as the appropriate rules and regulations are in a constant state of flux. The universe of licensed importers is small but growing. Nevertheless, foreign exchange availability may impinge on purchases. Customs can be high, but this is less of a concern than simply finding a legal importer who has an exchange allocation. Domestic distribution is largely restricted to locally-owned companies. Likely customers include large numbers of recently formed state-owned companies that are still figuring out what a free market is all about. There are growing numbers, too, of private firms, some of which show remarkable entrepreneurship.

While obtaining Most Favored Nation (MFN) and Generalized System of Preferences (GSP) treatment for Vietnam are the highest priority of the business community, these agreements take a considerable amount of time to negotiate and will be the latter steps in the normalization process. In the meantime, trade policy issues will be addressed in the near future are taxation treaties, bilateral investment treaties and intellectual property rights agreements. One competitive disadvantage that will be eliminated as a result of the normalization of relations will be Section 901(j) of the tax code, which subjects earnings arising in foreign countries that have no diplomatic relations with the U.S. to double and immediate taxation.

THE COMPETITION

Since the lifting of the trade embargo, the American share of trade and investment, $223 million and $270 million respectively, is still a tiny fraction of the market. As Vietnam fulfills its plans to develop its infrastructure and basic industries, U.S. companies that participate in these projects will be the long-term players in Vietnam's future economic development. Commercial relations are expected to improve further when new opportunities arise as the economy develops. Existing Vietnamese preferences for U.S.

goods and services, if coupled with competitive pricing and attractive financing terms, should be sufficient to overcome the disadvantages which the U.S. faces as a latecomer to this important emerging market.

The French and the Japanese, as well as other countries, have been doing business in Vietnam for many years. Australia is well represented in the market, as are the Taiwanese, Singaporeans and South Koreans.

CEA: The

Economies
People's Republic of China, Hong Kong, Taiwan

Population
1.2 Billion

Population Growth Rate
1.2%

Gross Domestic Product
US$ 783.7 Billion

GDP Growth Rate
9.91%

Per Capita GDP
US$ 702

Inflation Rate
15.3%

Industrial Production, % Change
13.2%

1994. Source: U.S. Dept. of Commerce, ITA
Some numbers are aggregated and derived from
DRI/McGraw Hill, World Markets Executive
Overview, second quarter 1995

The Chinese Economic Area (CEA)—China, Hong Kong and Taiwan combined —is by far the biggest of the Big Emerging Markets worldwide. The usage of the term CEA is meant to highlight the commercial interaction among the three vibrant economies of China, Hong Kong and Taiwan. This characterization in no way represents a change in U.S. policy towards each of these entities.

By the end of 1995, the nation of China alone may surpass the U.S. as the globe's number one destination for foreign investment. The seventh largest economy in the world, with a combined GDP of $783.7 billion in 1994, the CEA offers the largest potential market for infrastructure spending worldwide. Between 1993 and 2000, over $500 billion in proposed expenditures in the fields of transportation, telecommunications and energy, among others, will be required to bring the CEA in line with its modernization goals.

The CEA is the world's fourth largest trading entity, with foreign trade totaling about $724 billion in 1994, of which exports were valued at over $362 billion. This accounts for 8.2 percent of the world's exports, ranking fourth worldwide behind the U.S., Japan and Germany. Imports also added up to $362 billion, 7.7 percent of the world's imports, third, behind the U.S. and Germany. These figures will only be increasing in the future.

In the past five to six years, China, Hong Kong and Taiwan have enjoyed unprecedented growth in trade, financial, personal and even political exchanges, as the world has watched, enthralled. Before 1987, for a resident of Taiwan to travel to China was a criminal offense. Taiwan residents now make 1.5 million trips a year to China. And Hong Kong's role as intermediary in this exchange of funds, goods, passengers — every manner of business enterprise technique and method — has correspondingly grown tremendously in the last few years.

Exports from Taiwan and Hong Kong to China have boomed, partly as a result of the increasingly large volume of direct investment in China. Hong Kong's re-exports have risen at a 20 percent average annual rate in volume terms since 1988, with nearly 90 percent involving China, either as a source or a destination. Taiwan has also seen a sharp boost in its two-way trade with China from $3.5 billion in 1989 to an estimated $14 billion for 1994—and that's with the prohibition of direct trade links with the mainland.

Biggest BEM

The growing economic links among the CEA economies in recent years have stimulated their growth further, especially in China. Fueled by the progress in market-oriented economic reforms, China, with a population of 1.2 billion, has attained a 13 percent growth rate for two years in a row. It is well worth noting that China has grown at an average of 6 percent a year in the last 30. By some measures, China is already the third largest economy in the world and could become the second, or even the largest economy in the early 21st century.

These three economies, taken together, constitute the U.S.'s third largest trading partner, third largest supplier and fourth largest export market. Approximately 7.5 percent of U.S. exports, or $37.7 billion, went to the CEA in 1994, up from 5 percent in 1985. In China alone, U.S. investment grew by $2.6 billion in 1992 and another $3.7 billion in 1993. In 1994, the U.S. was the second largest foreign investor in China (behind Hong Kong) and also the third largest investor in the CEA.

As the triangular relationship among the CEA deepens, these dynamic economies are likely to maintain high growth rates in the years to come, creating a bounty of opportunities for U.S. exporters and investors.

By the end of 1995, China may surpass the U.S. as the globe's number one destination for foreign investment.

BIG EMERGING SECTORS

Keeping the economic expansion in the CEA booming depends significantly on overcoming severe infrastructure weaknesses— transportation bottlenecks, dated telecommunications facilities, and energy shortages. Approximately $340 billion will be spent in the CEA on imports of infrastructure-related equipment and technology alone.

Although foreign involvement will vary by sector, preliminary estimates based on past sales trends and domestic manufacturing and design skills suggest that the area will look to overseas firms to supply 30 to 35 percent of China's needs, 25 to 30 percent of Taiwan's needs, and 70 to 80 percent of Hong Kong's needs for equipment, technology and expertise for infrastructure- related projects in the energy, telecommunications,

Origin of the Term "Chinese Economic Area"

The term "Chinese Economic Area" (CEA) was originally developed in 1993 by the World Bank to describe the intensive economic interaction occuring among the Chinese populations of China, Hong Kong and Taiwan. A broader definition of CEA would include Macau, Singapore and the overseas Chinese community and a narrower definition would only include Hong Kong, Taiwan and the provinces of Guangdong and Fujian in China. In this book we use the World Bank meaning of CEA.

The term CEA has earlier roots in the name "Greater China," which was used during the Qing dynasty to describe the Chinese empire, which included the 18 provinces populated by Han Chinese, "Inner China," and other surrounding areas primarily populated by ethnic minorities, "Outer China." The first contemporary use of the term Greater China appeared in the mid to late 1980s. Similar to the term CEA, Greater China reflects the area's interlocking and reenforcing economic vibrance.

The usage of the term CEA is meant to highlight the commercial interaction among the three vibrant economies of China, Hong Kong, and Taiwan. This characterization in no way represents a change in U.S. policy toward any of these entities.

The CEA offers the largest potential market — over $500 billion's worth — for infrastructure spending in the world.

transportation and environmental technology sectors. There is no reason U.S. firms shouldn't perform especially well in areas such as power generation, advanced telecommunications equipment, engineering and design services, pollution control equipment and services, automobiles, heavy construction equipment, offshore and onshore drilling and commercial aircraft—all sectors in which U.S. companies are recognized as global leaders.

Beijing, Taipei and, to a lesser extent, Hong Kong also want technology and expertise to enable them to improve indigenous production capabilities. They are relying on joint ventures and coproduction arrangements with Japanese and Western — particularly U.S. — firms to meet that goal. Sales of technology and equipment associated with the production of electronic components, steel, chemicals, pharmaceuticals, medical equipment and consumer goods will reflect this.

The fits and starts of China's economic reform effort will tend to slow the decision-making process on purchases of big-ticket infrastructure and other import priorities. Disagreements between the People's Republic of China and Hong Kong on Hong Kong's transition in 1997 have, for example, slowed the pace of development of Hong Kong's Chek Lap Kok Airport, perhaps the largest airport project in the world. Political disagreements between the mainland and the colony are likely to continue to affect the pace and character of infrastructure development in Hong Kong. Recently, because of more conservative growth estimates, Taiwan also pared back its infrastructure ambitions originally envisioned under its Six-Year Development Plan, from expenditures of $305 billion to between $100-200 billion.

But despite the nature of the region's politics, infrastructure needs will remain vast. They will be broadest in China, which has farthest to go. For Hong Kong and Taiwan, with vastly smaller populations, much higher per capita incomes, much greater openness to the outside world, and a different focus on economic development, infrastructure needs often translate into refinements of existing infrastructure rather than laying the foundation for it.

MARKET ACCESS

While the economic exchange and interaction among CEA economies is intense, it is also important to recognize their differences. China is essentially a continental economy with a large domestic market, while both Taiwan and Hong Kong are island economies depending heavily on foreign trade for economic development. China is only now appreciating the importance of developing a sound regulatory environment for commerce which can serve to retain and attract additional investment.

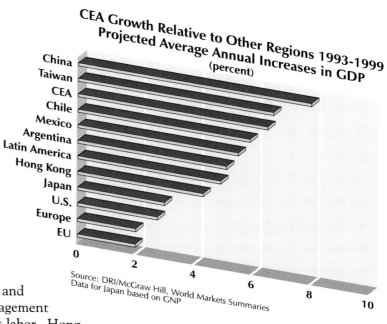

CEA Growth Relative to Other Regions 1993-1999
Projected Average Annual Increases in GDP
(percent)

Source: DRI/McGraw Hill, World Markets Summaries
Data for Japan based on GNP

These economic differences among CEA economies have led to a well-defined division of labor marked by the transfer of labor-intensive manufacturing operations from Taiwan and Hong Kong to the Chinese mainland. Taiwan and Hong Kong provide capital, technology and management expertise, while China supplies cheap, abundant labor. Hong Kong also acts as financier, investor, supplier and provider of technology for southern China, not to mention as an entrepot for China as a whole. Keeping this division of labor in mind should help facilitate market penetration of the CEA by U.S. goods and service providers.

While individually each of these markets has its own distinctive characteristics and contains significant commercial opportunities apart from the others, the sum of the opportunities are best seen together as the focus for American trade and investment strategies. It is often logical for U.S. firms to consider approaching the three as a cohesive unit when developing long-term marketing plans. By taking advantage of some combination of Hong Kong's excellent financial and services companies, Taiwan's modernizing infrastructure, management expertise and technical know- how, and China's low labor costs and network of Hong Kong-based trading companies, U.S. firms can use the CEA as a springboard for developing business relationships throughout Asia. Without this perspective, U.S. businesses may miss a fantastic opportunity to expand their involvement in one of the key emerging markets—of today and tomorrow.

The Periphery

In ancient as well as modern times, most forces for change originated from the "periphery." Whether through Mongol or Manchu dynasty conquests from the north, the entry of Buddhism or far-flung trade via the Silk Road to the west, or Western and Japanese coastal concessions and, more recently, aggressive investment by overseas Chinese to the south and east, the periphery has traditionally provided the catalyst for both welcome and unwelcome changes that challenged the inertia of the "center."

A Chinese proverb expresses the essence of this center-periphery tension, "Tian gao, huang di yuan," signifying, "the farther from the emperor, the greater the freedom."

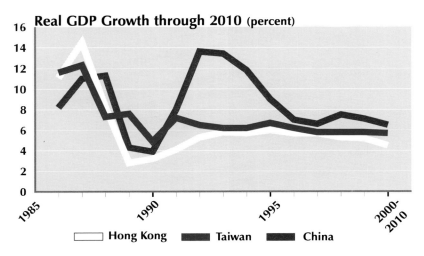

Real GDP Growth through 2010 (percent)

Hong Kong Taiwan China

Source: DRI/McGraw-Hill, *World Markets Executive Overview*, second quarter 1995

THE COMPETITION

Naturally, competition for market share in the CEA will be fierce. Japan continues to dominate and expand its reach, and the European Union and several other Asian countries clearly have targeted the CEA as a top priority for the future. Foreign competition is bolstered significantly by official development assistance from their governments— Japan's overseas development assistance surpasses the lending of the World Bank and Asian Development Bank as the largest source of financing for China.

Interestingly, the Japanese and the Europeans have set their sights on areas where U.S. companies have the most to gain—energy, telecommunications, transportation and other related infrastructure pursuits. The battle to capture a larger share of lucrative infrastructure projects in which initial suppliers have the opportunity to define downstream equipment and technology import requirements will be the most savage—and vital—one of all.

Even the economic integration of the three CEA economies, useful as it is, poses challenges for some U.S. firms in specific industry sectors. With increasing Taiwanese and Hong Kong investment in China, U.S. firms are likely to see greater competition from Taiwan- and Hong Kong-invested firms in the CEA and in third markets. Today that contest can be observed in light manufactures, but U.S. market access may be challenged in other sectors as Hong Kong and Taiwan investment increases in higher technology areas.

— *Contributors: Donald Forest, Cheryl McQueen, Scott Goddin, Sheila Baker, Chris Cerone, Paul Kullman, Laurette Newsom, Laura McCall, Jamie Horsley, Craig Allen, Charles Martin, Zhiqiang Huang, David Katz, Rosemary Gallant, Ira Kasoff, Matt Brady, Olevia Yim, Caroline Yuen, Victor Ho, Elanna Tam, Alan Turley, Bob Chu, Shirley Wang*

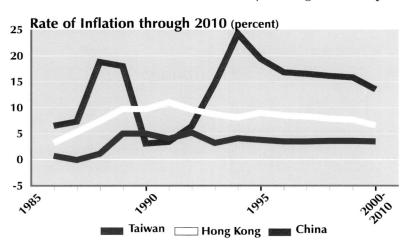

Rate of Inflation through 2010 (percent)

Taiwan Hong Kong China

Source: DRI/McGraw-Hill, *World Markets Executive Overview*, second quarter 1995

China: Leaps

Geography
9.6 million sq. km.

Population
1.2 Billion

Languages
Standard Chinese, also
Cantonese, Shanghaiese,
Minbei, Minnan, Xiang,
Gan and Hakka dialects

Cultural Mix
93% Han Chinese
6.7% Ahuang, Uygur,
Hui, Yi, Tibetan, Miao,
Manchu, Mongol, Buyi,
Korean and others

GDP
US$ 417.6
Billion

GDP Growth Rate
11.5%

Per Capita GDP
US$ 517+

Inflation Rate
24%

1994. Source: Country Commercial Guide

The complexity and pace of China's modernization as well as the vast opportunities emerging from it have lately been captivating the imaginations and the wallets of businesses all over the world. To say that China's economy is transforming from a centrally planned to a more market-oriented one is only to hint at what such a metamorphosis can mean to industry inside and outside its boundaries.

As in past incarnations, China's opening to the outside has favored the southern and eastern coastal provinces; opening to international trade and investment benefits these areas directly and the inland provinces indirectly, although a small portion of foreign investment has actually gone directly inland, particularly in natural resource extraction.

More and more, China is turning into a fragmented market of regions. What used to be a more or less unified national market has now split off into a number of regional markets, each pursuing its own development strategy, each jousting with the others to attract foreign investment and technology.

Local governments and enterprises are gaining greater autonomy every day. Some 8,000 companies now have import and export rights. The national economic plan determines less and less each year, while sales of commodities and imports of equipment and technology flow ever more freely.

As most of the heavy industrial sectors are still controlled by the central government, even if more loosely than in the past, the national economic plan is an important channel for state investment funds into priority industries and projects. Energy, petrochemicals, transportation, communications, electronics, agriculture, water conservation and industrial enterprise renovation remain, and are likely to remain, the key targets.

For the most part, China's top political leaders are strongly supportive of foreign business investment in China, realizing that foreign investment plays an integral part part in supporting China's modernization drive. China welcomed President Clinton's decision to renew most-favored nation status and to delink trade and human rights concerns.

The Chinese government introduced in early 1994 major reforms of its trade regime, foreign exchange and taxation systems, and in 1995 it announced a series of important economic laws, including commercial and central banking laws, an insurance law and a securities law. Of course, some of these reforms were also undertaken with an eye to China's application to join the World Trade Organization (WTO).

and Bounds

According to China's State Statistical Bureau, contracted direct foreign investment, which measures the commitment of private foreign funds to Chinese projects and joint ventures, amounted to $33.8 billion in 1994, an increase of 23 percent over 1993.

From the U.S. alone total contracted investment for 1994 was $6.5 billion. By the end of 1994, over 222,000 foreign-invested enterprises had registered in China. Total contracted foreign investment amounted to $95.7 billion by the end of 1994.

BIG EMERGING SECTORS

China's modernization plans call for imports of equipment and technology of approximately $100 billion per year, with infrastructure expenditures amounting to as much as $250 billion through the remainder of the decade. Under state-guided development plans, priority sectors for development include those in the infrastructure areas, including energy, transportation and telecommunications, and raw materials sectors (steel, coal, building materials, oil and nonferrous metals). Other priority sectors include electronics, machine-building, construction and certain light manufacturing.

For this region, the key inquiry is not "how big is the market" but what can the product and/or technology do for China and how does it correspond to China's economic development scheme. The Chinese generally give priority to acquiring know-how, equipment and assistance in developing domestic manufacturing capability rather than importing final product. They hope to pay for imported technology and equipment by boosting export earnings.

This emphasis on further developing the export sector shifts China's import priorities toward technologies and equipment that will enable it to diversify into production of new, more sophisticated export commodities and improve its manufacture of export goods. The measure of a product's appeal will be judged by the total package — product plus willingness to transfer technology and know-how in producing it.

The most promising prospects and their 1995 import markets are: aircraft and parts ($2.78 billion from the U.S.); electric power systems ($1.19 billion from the U.S.); telecom equipment ($870 million from the U.S.); computers and peripherals ($1.03 billion from the U.S.); agricultural and industrial chemicals ($1.26 billion from the U.S.); and medical equipment ($230 million from the U.S.). U.S. products are highly competitive in both price and quality. (Sales of pirated chemical products

What used to be a more or less unified national market has now split off into a number of regional markets, each pursuing its own development strategy, each jousting with the others to attract foreign investment and technology.

Finally, in 1995 China announced a series of important economic laws, including commercial and central banking laws, an insurance law and a securities law.

and China's own drive for self-sufficiency in basic intermediates may limit growth in chemical exports.)

Energy

One of the major threats to China's ability to sustain its current high-speed growth is the chronic shortage of energy. It is no wonder then that one of the highest priorities of all development planning is the efficient exploitation of China's energy resources and the installation of additional thermal power generating capacity. China is engaging in one of the most ambitious energy development plans any country has ever undertaken. The country may spend as much as $80 billion by the year 2000 on energy and power generating projects, including oil, natural gas and coal development, eight nuclear plants, about 10 large and small hydroelectric facilities, and over 30 thermal power generating plants. Of this amount, 20 percent will be met by foreign investment.

The Chinese are interested in acquiring Western advanced oil recovery technology and specialized drilling equipment to maintain production in their aging fields—Daqing, Shengli and Liaohe—as well as in forming joint ventures to explore and develop geologically and logistically challenging areas. Beijing is also attempting to develop new fields offshore, in 11 southeastern provinces, and in the Junggar and Tarim Basins in northwest China.

China's plans to renovate existing coal mines and develop the Shenfu-Dongsheng mine—which may contain one-third of China's total coal reserves—will present opportunities for U.S. companies to provide coal-washing facilities, continuous miners and safety equipment.

China has the world's fastest growing electric power industry, having added over 20 million kilowatts of generating capacity over the past two years, but that is still not enough. Beijing and local-level officials are planning to add 135 million kilowatts of generating capacity to China's existing 165 million kilowatts by the year 2000.

Most of the capacity increase over the next six years is planned to come from more than 20 large thermal power plants—coal-fired facilities already account for 70 percent of China's electricity production—and some 15 hydroelectric facilities. But Chinese officials recently unveiled long-term plans to have nuclear energy provide 5 percent of electric power by the year

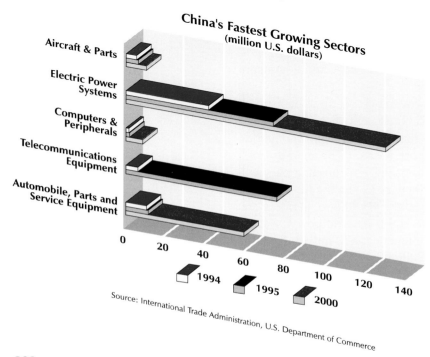

China's Fastest Growing Sectors
(million U.S. dollars)

Aircraft & Parts
Electric Power Systems
Computers & Peripherals
Telecommunications Equipment
Automobile, Parts and Service Equipment

0   20   40   60   80   100   120   140

1994   1995   2000

Source: International Trade Administration, U.S. Department of Commerce

2020—currently nuclear power provides less than half of a percent of the country's electricity supply. A growing number of Chinese provinces, anxious to reduce their dependence on unreliable shipments of coal from northern provinces, are seeking foreign turnkey facilities, and the market for nuclear power reactors and associated technologies is projected to total $6-8 billion by the end of the decade. U.S. firms are precluded from providing nuclear power generating equipment and technology to China, but may, pursuant to a change in policy, provide non-nuclear, balance-of-physical plant equipment and technology for existing or planned nuclear facilities.

Electric Power Plans

Among the best prospects in the energy sector are electric power systems, which analysts estimate range between $6-8 billion per year. The most promising subsectors include steam/gas turbine generators, boilers, and control and communication equipment. Major areas and projects to watch include:

Thermal—The Ministry of Electric Power plans to add 15,000 MW per year, the equivalent of New England's total power capacity, to China's power generation capacity over the next 10 years. Central and provincial expansion plans during this period also include the construction of over 50 power stations.

Hydro—Current plans envision the construction of four huge projects: Three Gorges, to be the largest hydro-power dam in the world (valued at more than $20 billion), in Hubei Province; Xiaolongdi in Henan Province; Longtan in the Guangxi Autonomous Region; and Ertan in Sichuan Province.

Environmental standards are not being ignored, though they are still expensive at this point. However, an experimental incinerator is being built in Guangzhou, and various clean-coal technologies are being included on a trial basis in power projects in several provinces. The Ministry of Environmental Protection is planning to use $200 million from the Asian Development Bank (ADB) to raise the efficiency and environmental protection standards in a large matrix of power plants in the Northeast. Together, the ADB and the World Bank plan to spend approximately $1.5 billion per year on environmental projects in China over the next several years.

Transportation

Beijing needs to modernize its transportation equipment and infrastructure to eliminate the severe bottlenecks that hinder its overall economic performance. China is planning to spend up to $40-50 billion on capital construction and technological renovation through the year 2000. Transportation-related joint ventures and coproduction arrangements with the West are the linchpin of Beijing's strategy, as Chinese officials rely on transfers of foreign advanced technologies to replace

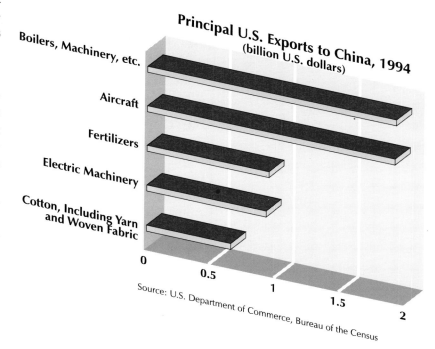

Principal U.S. Exports to China, 1994
(billion U.S. dollars)

Boilers, Machinery, etc.
Aircraft
Fertilizers
Electric Machinery
Cotton, Including Yarn and Woven Fabric

0   0.5   1   1.5   2

Source: U.S. Department of Commerce, Bureau of the Census

The Power of the Periphery

The inordinate strength of the centrifugal forces affecting the CEA is underscored by a comparison of particular attributes of Taiwan and Hong Kong within the CEA context.

Taiwan's land area (slightly smaller than Switzerland) represents less than one half of one percent of the CEA and its population at 21 million (about that of Australia and New Zealand, combined) represents less than two percent of the population of the CEA. However, its GDP, at an estimated $234 billion in 1994, is over one quarter of that of the CEA.

Hong Kong's land area (less than half that of Luxembourg) represents about 1/10,000 percent of the CEA and its population at 6 million (slightly more than Honduras) represents about three-fourths of one percent of the population of the CEA. However, its GDP, at an estimated $132 billion in 1994, equals approximately one sixth of that of the CEA.

Taiwan possesses over $90 billion and Hong Kong over $35 billion in foreign exchange reserves. Taiwan's amount represents roughly double that of the mainland's and Hong Kong's amount represents approximately the same as that of the mainland.

antiquated assembly lines with more modern, automated production equipment.

The automotive and aviation sectors have benefited the most, attracting some 90 percent of the roughly $7 billion worth of joint venture and coproduction deals struck with Western firms to date. The expansion in joint ventures and coproduction projects with the West is not proceeding rapidly enough to meet domestic demand. As a result, analysts expect China will continue to import substantial amounts of transportation equipment through the end of the century—probably $4-6 billion annually.

Motor Vehicles and Parts

China's total vehicle market—cargo and passenger units—will grow by some 10 percent annually through the end of the decade. In 1993, Chinese organizations and individuals owned 1.2 million passenger vehicles (70 percent are imports)—a number that is expected to reach over three million by the year 2000. Auto and auto parts imports in 1994 topped $4 billion, up from $2.5 billion in 1992.

In addition to importing and manufacturing whole units, Beijing encourages joint ventures in components production, hoping to boost the domestic content of its vehicles, and a number of U.S., European and Japanese companies have already begun contract negotiations for parts plants. China's market for auto parts could be worth $5.7 billion by the year 2000. Whole vehicles, however, will be much more difficult to get in.

Aerospace

The near-term prospects for direct sales in the aviation sector are very bright as Beijing takes steps to alleviate the strains on domestic air routes. Chinese airport spending alone will range between $1 billion and $2 billion annually over the next five to 10 years. The Civil Aviation Administration of China (CAAC) — China's air service oversight authority—launched in 1993 a $5.5 billion program to build or renovate 100 airports by 2000, tripling airport capacity to 180 million passengers. Provincial and Hong Kong funding will generate $4-9 billion for these projects. Naturally, all these projects will generate considerable demand for air traffic control equipment, baggage handling equipment, people movers and other equipment associated with air terminals.

CAAC officials estimate the country will need to import some 800 mid- and large-capacity passenger aircraft worth $45 billion. The program will double China's aircraft fleet to 960 by 2010, making China the world's third largest market, after the U.S. and Japan. One example: China, which in 1992 reached an agreement with McDonnell Douglas to co-produce 40 aircraft, re-opened negotiations to expand its procurement to include direct purchase of approximately 20 aircraft and co-manufacture of an additional 20. The $1.6 billion deal was finally inked in late 1994.

Based on China's Air Traffic Control (ATC) upgrade plans, U.S. exports of navigational aids, meteorological equipment, ticketing and service computer systems, runway lighting, flight information displays and ground support vehicles should also increase.

Information Technology

Telecommunications Equipment and Services

Beijing has budgeted $42 billion in investment for the sector through the year 2000. Domestic manufacturing deficiencies will force China to rely heavily on imports and foreign funding to satisfy demand. To upgrade its telecommunications technology by the turn of the century, Beijing will need to focus on fiber optic, satellite, mobile communications, and advanced switching systems.

Among the best prospects in the telecommunications sector are central office switches, private branch exchanges, paging networks (10 million subscribers), cellular networks (1.2 million subscribers), network computer equipment, and CATV equipment. Analysts estimate China's total market for all telecommunications equipment at $7.5 billion for 1995, with imports accounting for $5.3 billion.

Increasingly, China can be expected to turn to U.S. suppliers for digital switching, fiber optics, cellular and radio communications. Burgeoning Chinese demand for pagers, cellular systems, and communications satellites and related technologies appears to offer the most promising opportunities for U.S. firms.

Financing

The greatest competitive challenge U.S. firms face in the CEA, and in China in particular, is from more favorable financing terms offered by competitors. Frequently, competitors from China's other major trading partners, notably Japan, Germany and other countries of the EU, are supported by offers of concessional loans, tied and untied aid, or other forms of official development assistance. China is one of the world's largest recipients of Overseas Development Aid (ODA). Competitor governments use these offers to target projects and sectors of interest to their industries.

The U.S.-Export Import Bank program of loans, guarantees and insurance is the U.S. government's most active financing program for China—the U.S. Trade and Development Agency and the Overseas Private Investment Corporation, while active in Taiwan and Hong Kong, suspended their programs in China in 1989. Eximbank, through its Tied Aid Capital Projects Fund, aggressively employs tied aid to counter trade-distorting foreign tied aid credits.

In China, there are over 150 major laws and regulations which apply to foreign trade and investment, and many of these laws and regulations are fraught with ambiguities.

Computer Equipment and Software

China plans to invest roughly $3 billion from now to the year 2000 to raise its computer industry's output from the current 1 percent to 3-4 percent of GNP. That means acquiring advanced foreign technology through joint ventures to produce greater numbers of high-performance microcomputers and workstations, as well as to create a large-scale software engineering industry. One not being anywhere near enough, China is setting up nine "Silicon Valleys" for high-technology companies to work on computer research and development. China's microelectronics production investment program as well as the loosening of Western export controls will provide excellent opportunities for U.S. firms to form joint ventures and sell production facilities, equipment and expertise.

Metallurgy

China plans to raise steel production to 100 million tons per year by 2000 and to 120 million tons per year by 2005. To help achieve these goals the government has approved the construction of three new steel complexes at Jinan, Jilin Province, Zhanjiang, Guangdong Province, and Ningbo, Zhejiang Province. Three existing plants have been approved for expansion: Baoshan in Shanghai, Anshan in Liaoning Province and Capital Iron and Steel in Beijing.

Factory Renovations

China's traditional state-owned heavy industrial base is in serious need of technological renovation. Central government approval has been granted for the renovation and expansion of hundreds of industrial enterprises in Harbin in Heilongjiang Province, Shenyang in Liaoning Province, Chongqing in Sichuan Province and Shanghai. These enterprises have been authorized either to import new technology and equipment directly or to enter into joint ventures with foreign companies.

MARKET ACCESS

China has a complex system of trade and investment incentives and disincentives—some of which may work for exporters and investors and some of which may work against them—and its services sectors are open only on an experimental basis. One of the most challenging features of gaining access to China's market is that it is an economy in the midst of reforms. Rules and regulations can change, are often ambiguous, are applied inconsistently and are nontransparent.

Major Transportation Projects

Other major transportation development projects and plans of interest to U.S. suppliers include:

Railways — China is receiving loans from the World Bank and the Asian Development Bank to build and expand six rail lines and to import communications networks, intermodal container transportation and loading systems, computer and signaling systems, software and track maintenance equipment.

Municipal Transportation — There are at least four major subway projects now either under way or in the planning stages over the next several years—Beijing, Shanghai, Guangzhou and Tianjin—and twice as many planned in the next eight to 10 years. Although American companies have only a small portion of the Guangzhou Metro, there are other new systems on the way: the Shenyang Light Rail, a new Qingdao Metro, a new subway for Nanjing and an expansion of the Beijing Metro system.

Tariffs and Import Barriers

Of the three CEA markets, tariffs are highest in China. Customs regulations are not uniformly applied in China, making exporting there unpredictable at times. U.S. exporters may also face arbitrary determinations of value by customs officials, and there are frequent reports of being charged different rates for the same product. Most special economic zones, open cities and foreign trade zones offer preferential duty reductions or exemptions.

Import taxes, in the form of a value-added tax (VAT) and other taxes, are also levied in addition to tariffs on items entering China, adding to costs for exporters. China collects a value-added tax, generally equal to 17 percent, on imported items. Certain luxury items are also subject to a consumption tax ranging from 3-45 percent.

China uses non-tariff barriers extensively to regulate trade and investment. This is a subject of intense negotiation in discussions regarding accession to the WTO.

While numerous barriers have been removed since 1992, China continues to administer a complex system of individual quotas, import licensing requirements and a tendering system applied to both quota and non-quota commodities, among others. China currently retains non-tariff measures (quotas, licenses or tenders) for hundreds of individual tariff line items. The absence of transparency is a further barrier to U.S. exports.

Foreign Investment Moves Inland

Traditionally, most foreign investment in China over the past two decades has been based in the coastal commercial areas, such as Shanghai and Guangzhou. The Ministry of Foreign Trade and Economic Cooperation calculated, for instance, that only 4 percent of the total foreign investment in 1992 was based in the interior parts of China, such as Inner Mongolia, Sichuan and Xinjiang. To inject economic growth into these areas and to halt the trend of increasing unemployment of rural workers there, China is seeking to bring investment to interior cities like Changchun, Chengdu, Xian and Zhengzhou through a number of investment incentives. Examples include specialized commercial banks, improved tax incentives similar to those available in the special economic zones, and increased opportunities for foreign investment in the pivotal infrastructure sectors such as oil and gas.

Government Procurement Practices

U.S. firms have been hindered in the bidding on major projects in China by non-transparent bidding procedures. Although open and competitive bidding is increasingly used for both domestic and foreign-funded projects, the great majority of government procurement contracts in China are handled through domestic tenders or direct negotiation with selected suppliers. Projects in certain fields require government approval, usually from several different organizations and levels. Procedures are opaque, and foreign suppliers are routinely discriminated against in areas where domestic suppliers exist.

Guangdong Province

China's leaders have set an ambitious target for Guangdong Province: catch up with Asia's four little dragons (Hong Kong, Taiwan, South Korea and Singapore) by the year 2010. To do this, Guangdong has drawn together the Pearl Delta Economic Zone Plan which aims to build an extensive transport and telecommunications network and transform its light industrial sector from labor- to capital-intensive high-tech production.

The province has unique advantages in its modernization effort. It borders on Hong Kong and Macau and has a long coastline endowed with many natural ports. Guangdong is also the homeland of some 20 million overseas Chinese living in more than 100 countries, of whom some 70 percent still have close relatives in the province.

Openness to Foreign Investment

China's legal and regulatory system is characterized by a general lack of transparency and inconsistent enforcement, creating uncertainty for foreign investors. China has a complex web of national and local laws and regulations which apply to foreign trade and investment and many of these laws and regulations are still fraught with ambiguities. China's leadership is attempting to reform the legal system to rationalize the various sets of regulations governing commercial activity, and, in the past few years, China has made a number of reforms to improve its trade regime. Even if a project meets one of more of the government's investment screening requirements, it may still be rejected if it is determined that the contract is unfair, that the technology is available elsewhere in China, or that China already has sufficient production capacity of the particular product.

Leading Sources of Imports/Destination of Exports

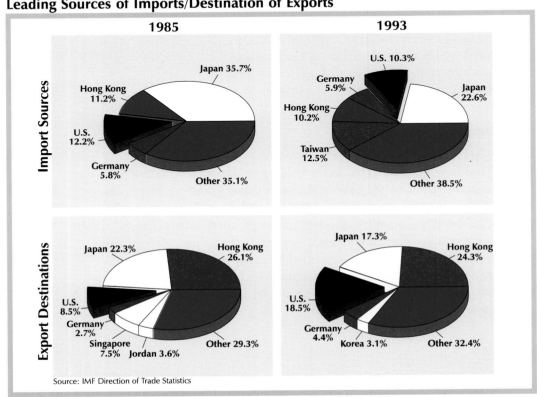

Source: IMF Direction of Trade Statistics

China offers certain investment incentives which have been developed since the late 1970s to channel investment into particular sectors and to encourage the transfer of technology. In China, the special economic zones of Shenzhen, Shantou, Zhuhai, Xiamen and Hainan, 14 open coastal cities, certain inland cities and provinces all promote investment with unique packages of tax exemptions, reductions and incentives. These incentive packages are currently under review at the center.

While China's investment laws and regulations do not require technology transfer, they strongly encourage it, and foreign investors are likely to encounter pressure to agree to it.

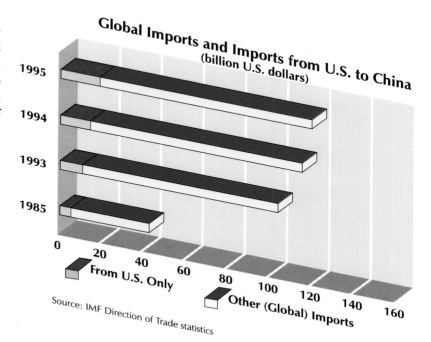

Global Imports and Imports from U.S. to China (billion U.S. dollars)

Source: IMF Direction of Trade statistics

From U.S. Only
Other (Global) Imports

Special Considerations

Intellectual Property Rights

Although each of the three markets protects and enforces intellectual property rights (IPR) independently, problems with protection and enforcement have shifted throughout the markets of the CEA. Although China has significantly improved its legal regime, enforcement has been a problem, particularly of copyrights and trademarks. China has markedly improved its IPR legal regime under the 1992 U.S.-China Memorandum of Understanding on Intellectual Property Rights. A copyright law went into effect in June 1991, a trade secret law was passed and went into effect in October 1993, and the patent law was amended in January 1993. China has also acceded to a number of intellectual property rights conventions. In early 1995, China signed a Memorandum of Understanding with the U.S. on IPR enforcement and market access. The 1995 agreement calls for bilateral quarterly consultations on IPR protection.

THE COMPETITION

U.S. firms face increasingly aggressive competition from major competitors in this exciting region, particularly from Japan, Germany and France. Other participants in the China market include Hong Kong, Taiwan, South Korea and the United Kingdom. Even Russia has made notable gains in some areas.

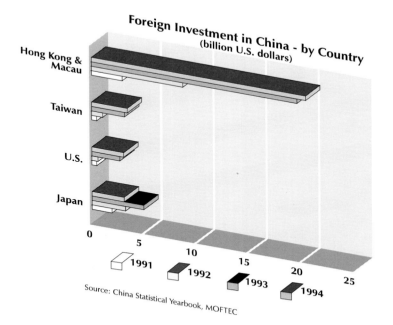

Foreign Investment in China - by Country
(billion U.S. dollars)

Hong Kong & Macau

Taiwan

U.S.

Japan

0   5   10   15   20   25

1991 1992 1993 1994

Source: China Statistical Yearbook, MOFTEC

China's drive to substantially improve its infrastructure will require sources of capital well beyond its current domestic capacity. Japan, Germany, France and South Korea have all expanded their aid and financing programs to win greater market share for their exporters.

Japan
As a result of intensified trade links with Japan, China became Japan's second largest trading partner in 1993 — up from fifth place in 1992. The trade expansion was driven largely by increased sales of Japanese goods to China. Increased Japanese investment in China also played a part in expanded Japanese sales to the mainland.

Germany
Germany saw large gains in its sales to China in 1993 and 1994, with exports rising more than 65 percent. Germany accounted for roughly 40 percent of all EU sales to China. Some German exports were probably helped by Bonn's decision in 1993 to cancel the sale of submarines to Taiwan, which spurred Beijing to increase contracts awarded to German firms.

France
French sales grew 15 percent in 1993 and although sales flattened somewhat in 1994, France was the only country of China's top four trading partners in the EU—France, Germany, Italy and the United Kingdom — to suffer a loss in market share. Although France saw large gains in aircraft sales, French exports of other key commodities dropped by more than 20 percent. French producers may still be paying a price for Paris' decision in late 1992 to sell fighter aircraft to Taiwan.

Other European Union
Sales by the United Kingdom and Italy to China grew more than 65 percent, but they started from much smaller bases.

Hong Kong
Hong Kong saw only modest growth—roughly 2 percent—in overall domestic sales to China but had large gains in some higher

Xia Hai

Historically, the political forces controlling the center have vigorously opposed or attempted to co-opt the more entrepreneurial forces along the periphery. This latter approach provided a source of revenue for the center, but also often served to legitimize economic activity generated from the periphery, thereby assuring the gradual permeation and evolution of the periphery's influence throughout the Chinese system.

This phenomenon is occurring today with Taiwan, Hong Kong, Guangdong and Fujian trailblazing the path of economic growth. Their proven success has led other areas throughout China to "xia hai" or "take the plunge" into the capitalist experiment.

technology areas, which could reflect shifting investment patterns. As Beijing seeks to direct investment into areas requiring technology transfer and as wages in the coastal provinces rise—squeezing profit margins on labor-intensive goods—Hong Kong investors interested in low-cost export processing ventures are beginning to look elsewhere.

Taiwan

Hong Kong trade statistics indicate that Taiwan fared much better, boosting indirect exports to China by 20 percent in 1993 to $7.6 billion. Taiwan's Board of Foreign Trade, however, estimates Taiwan sales—ncluding illegal direct shipment to the mainland—were much higher, closer to $12.7 billion. The island's sales to China continue to be concentrated in inputs for Taiwan factories on the mainland.

South Korea

China has become the largest recipient of South Korean investment, accounting for nearly 60 percent of South Korea's foreign outlays in 1993. These growing business ties helped South Korean sales increase nearly 85 percent last year—to $4.9 billion—expanding South Korea's share of Chinese imports of raw materials and inputs.

Hong Kong:

Geography
1,076 sq. km.

Population
6.15 Million

Languages
English and Cantonese.
Mandarin Chinese
speakers are increasing.

Culural Mix
98% Chinese,
2% Other

GDP
US$ 132
Billion

GDP Growth Rate
5.5%

Per Capita GDP
US$ 21,800

Inflation Rate
8.5%

1994. Source: U.S. Dept. of Commerce, ITA

Hong Kong's famed and fabled economy is the epitome of robust capitalism at its freest. Along with this open economy, its geographic proximity to the mainland, and a highly educated and industrious population, Hong Kong stands out not just in the region but among the world's economies for its relative lack of import barriers (and its total lack of value-added taxes). The foreign investment to be found in such massive quantities in Hong Kong is often used to fuel and profit from the economic growth of China, Hong Kong functions as a gateway to and from the mainland for regional and international traders, investors and tourists. Hong Kong is tailor-made to serve as an entrepot for China's exports to the world and for foreign goods entering China.

For the immediate future, Singapore's distance and Taipei's regulations will likely give Hong Kong the edge in becoming East Asia's financial center after Tokyo. Shanghai, although favored in many ways by Beijing, remains about 15 years behind, and Hong Kong is not standing still.

In 1994, Hong Kong re-exported $123 billion worth of goods made elsewhere, more than three times as much as it produced domestically for export ($29 billion). One-third of all of China's exports flowed through Hong Kong to third countries, and 25 percent of China's imports come via Hong Kong. The development of Guangdong province as a low-cost manufacturing base has encouraged Hong Kong to shift from a manufacturing to a services-based economy; over 75 percent of Hong Kong's GDP now derives from the services sector, much of it connected in one way or another with China.

Hong Kong's economy grew an estimated 5.9 percent in 1993, despite a slowdown in trade with the territory's major export markets in Europe, North America and Japan. GDP increased 5.7 percent in 1994. The unemployment rate was only about 2 percent in 1994, while inflation remained constant at 8.5 percent.

Hong Kong will continue to see strong economic growth, although at a slightly slower pace. Real GDP is expected to be up 4.5 percent in 1995. The unemployment and inflation rates will remain basically unchanged. While employment in manufacturing will continue its downward trend, the burgeoning and well-developed services sector is where the new job action is. An estimated two-thirds of the workforce is employed in services. That accounts for 76 percent of GDP. This sector is slated to become ever more important in the economy. That means computers, telecommunications and consumer goods, among others, will be in great demand.

Regional Gateway

The transition on July 1, 1997, from British to Chinese sovereignty overshadows every other issue in shaping Hong Kong's current and future political and economic agenda. Business and investor confidence has stayed strong in the face of increased Sino-British tensions over proposed electoral reforms. And Hong Kong continues as a major destination for U.S. and international investments. Chinese investment in Hong Kong is also growing rapidly. The port is vital to China's interests and supplies much needed infrastructure support to the growth of South China. China would have to be under severe pressure to threaten this golden goose.

The Hong Kong government is an investor's dream as it continues to pursue economic policies of noninterference in commercial decisions, low and predictable taxation, government spending increases within the bounds of real economic growth, and competition subject to transparent and consistent application of the rule of law.

The port's economic integration with China will keep accelerating. Its geographic proximity, cultural and linguistic ties (particularly with prosperous Guangdong province), and excellent infrastructure and services make that inevitable.

Chinese companies increasingly use Hong Kong's highly developed financial, transportation, communications and marketing capabilities, while the territory's manufacturers continue to shift production to lower-cost facilities in southern China.

BIG EMERGING SECTORS

Hong Kong, with the third-highest per capita income in East Asia and its economic window to China, offers bountiful opportunities for U.S. business. Hong Kong's bright economic prospects, its open economy, focus on infrastructure development and its educated and sophisticated bilingual consumer population translate into an excellent environment for selling everything from high-value food products to franchises to airport equipment. The demand for capital goods and consumer goods is expanding.

Some of the best prospects include computers and telecommunications equipment for the information technology needs of Hong Kong's booming trading and financial offices; construction machinery for major infrastructure projects—notably the $21 billion Chek Lap Kok Airport—as well as the private office and housing markets; and medical and diagnostic equipment. The outlook for pollution abatement equipment, technology and engineering services is also particularly good. On the services side, insurance, financial and engineering services are a mainstay of Hong Kong and sub-sectors in which U.S. firms have long had a presence.

The foreign investment to be found in such massive quantities in Hong Kong is often used to fuel and profit from the economic growth of China.

Hong Kong also eats up U.S. companies' food and other agricultural items. U.S. agricultural exports to Hong Kong reached $1.7 billion in 1994. They're projected to keep growing at about 10 percent annually through 1996.

Technical expertise, supplies and equipment are vital to Hong Kong firms developing projects in China. Hong Kong developers, who are generally highly flexible through their diverse operations, have cash to support projects in China and the connections to make them happen, but often lack the technical expertise. That is where American firms come into the picture.

Hong Kong's Future Status

Hong Kong is designated to become a "Special Administrative Region" (HKSAR) of the People's Republic of China in 1997. While the 1989 Tiananmen Square incident caused sufficient political and economic uncertainty to result in the emigration of large numbers of Hongkongers in its aftermath, the "brain drain" problem has abated over the last two years. The Sino-British Joint Declaration, signed in 1984, and the Basic Law, promulgated by China in 1990, will form the basis for China's "One Country, Two Systems" guarantees for Hong Kong. The Basic Law guarantees the rights and freedoms that Hong Kong residents now enjoy, the continued rule of law, and the maintenance of Hong Kong's capitalist system for 50 years. In addition, the HKSAR shall retain the status of a free port and continue a trade policy of free movement of goods and capital.

Other features of the transition are intended to retain Hong Kong's status as an international financial center. It will, on its own, formulate monetary and financial policies and safeguard the free operation of business and financial markets. The HKSAR will have independent finances, using revenues exclusively for its own purposes. The Hong Kong dollar will continue to be freely convertible and foreign exchange, gold and securities markets will continue to operate. Systems currently in place, including Hong Kong's regulatory and supervisory framework, will remain unchanged. Hong Kong's legal system, including the independence of the judiciary and obligation of the executive authorities to abide by the law, are slated to continue.

Transportation and Infrastructure

Regional economic expansion in East Asia is placing great strains on Hong Kong's transportation infrastructure. As a result, Hong Kong authorities are planning to spend roughly $26 billion on transportation projects through 2000 to upgrade the colony's airport, ports and highways. Topping the list of projects is the new Chek Lap Kok airport and peripheral facilities, which is estimated to cost more than $21 billion. Among those participating in this giant project are Bechtel for overall management consultancy, Greiner Engineering for the design of the air terminal and the design of critical bridges linking it to the rest of the territory, and Morgan Stanley as the financial advisor for the new airport.

In addition, Hong Kong authorities are planning to spend more than $4 billion on port and container terminal facilities and an additional $1.15 billion on highway projects to handle increased transportation traffic. Meanwhile, regional economic growth also will fuel increased demand for automobiles, aircraft and cargo vessels through the 1990s. Nearly all this demand for transportation-related equipment will be fulfilled by imports.

Shipping and Port Activities

Hong Kong enjoys perhaps the best natural deep-water port on the Chinese coast. Hong Kong is the principal hub port for south China. It serves as a transit point both for exports and re-exports to China for processing or consumption and for re-exports to North America, Europe and elsewhere. In 1993, Hong Kong's container throughput totaled 9.3 million twenty-foot equivalent units (TEU), up 17 percent over 1992. By 1994, it reached 11.05 million TEU's, making it the busiest container port in the world The majority of Hong Kong's outward-bound container cargo is generated in Guangdong province. In 1992, Hong Kong handled over 100 million tons of cargo, triple the amount of a decade earlier. By 1994, it had risen to 157 million tons.

Hong Kong functions as a gateway to and from the mainland for regional and international traders, investors and tourists. Singapore's distance and Taipei's regulations will likely give Hong Kong the edge in becoming East Asia's financial center after Tokyo.

With continued high economic growth and industrialization in China, the development of deep water ports at Yantian and Gaolan in south China should be complementary to Hong Kong over the medium term. Over the longer term, increased competition should generate greater efficiencies in service. Hong Kong's container throughput will continue to experience double-digit growth through the turn of the century. Hong Kong projects it will require some 20 new container berths by the year 2006, providing new annual terminal capacity for 8 million TEU. There are currently eight terminals with 19 berths. The U.S. firm Sea-Land is involved in developing Container Terminal 9, a project as large as the port of Seattle.

Airports

Hong Kong's Kai Tak Airport is ranked second in the world in terms of cargo handled and fourth in terms of international passengers. In 1993 the single-runway airport handled more than 24 million passengers and 134,000 aircraft movements. Growth in demand over the next four years is projected to average 5 percent annually. Among projects in this realm, Raytheon has won $48 million in contracts for air traffic control equipment.

To meet the increase in passenger and cargo traffic, the Hong Kong Government in late 1989 announced plans to construct a replacement international airport at Chek Lap Kok, offshore north of Lantau Island. Work on transport links and land reclamation for the $21 billion project is proceeding but it is doubtful the airport will be operational by the targeted June 30, 1997, completion date. U.S. suppliers have an interest in lucrative franchises, air cargo, fuel handling, catering and other services, as well as continuing construction and engineering work associated with Chek Lap Kok's Airport Core Program encompassing an expressway, tunnel and other linkages to Hong Kong proper.

Environmental Technology

The Environmental Protection Department of Hong Kong estimates that the total market for pollution control equipment in Hong Kong will be $6-7 billion through the year 2000. In 1989, the Hong Kong government issued a comprehensive 10-year plan to restore the territory's environment. One result of this plan was the commissioning of three strategic landfills, for which U.S. companies won in excess of $1 billion of landfill construction, management and equipment contracts. Another was the award to the U.S. of a $100 million contract to build and operate a centralized chemical waste treatment plant. Refuse transfer station, landfill restoration, low-level radioactive waste storage, indoor air quality study and centralized special waste incinerator projects being awarded in 1995 offer U.S. business $780 million in business opportunities.

The Hong Kong government embarked in September 1993 on a $2 billion plan to clean up Victoria Harbor, called the Strategic Sewage Disposal Scheme (SSDS). Treatment plans for this four-phase project have recently been revised, creating new and substantial opportunities for U.S. business to supply equipment and engineering services required to provide enhanced chemical treatment of 1.5 million cubic meters/day of domestic sewage.

Stringent industrial effluent controls have also been legislated and took effect in May 1995 — they will affect up to 9,000 small and medium-sized factories over the next three years. Key industries needing wastewater treatment include electroplating, bleaching and dyeing, printed circuit boards and food processing. U.S. firms are well placed to meet local demand for low-waste industrial processes, pollution abatement equipment, new chlorofluorocarbon (CFC)-free solvents, recycling and recovery systems, and extensive engineering and design work. Other promising sales opportunities for U.S.

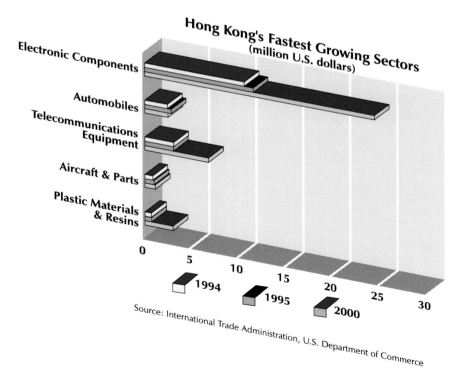

Hong Kong's Fastest Growing Sectors (million U.S. dollars)

Source: International Trade Administration, U.S. Department of Commerce

companies include electric vehicles ($5-10 million market estimated starting in 1996, the result of government tax incentives), diesel particulate control equipment for 2,000 buses, energy-efficiency technology and services ($5-10 million/year), low-noise construction equipment and active noise mitigation technology ($10-20 million/year), and a wide range of environmental monitoring devices ($5-10 million/year).

Information Technology

Telecommunications Equipment and Services

Much of Hong Kong's economic success and growth comes from its modern infrastructure, of which telecommunications is an integral part. Hong Kong's fixed network is completely digitalized, with a penetration rate of 65 telephones per 100 persons. Deregulation of the local telecommunications industry in Hong Kong will open the door to three new telephone service providers. Two U.S. providers have already teamed up with two local consortia to provide technical support and fixed lines local telecommunication service starting from July 1, 1995. On the equipment side, transmission system and networking facilities are the best prospects for U.S. firms for the next few years, with the new fixed network providers expected to invest over $1 billion in equipment infrastructure over the first few years of service.

Hong Kong's mobile network is among the most developed in the world. One in five persons subscribes to public paging services, the highest rate in the world, with high rates of cellular and telepoint (CT-2) usage. Modernization, though, continues unabated. A gradual migration from analog to digital systems by 1997 will allow the Hong Kong mobile network to maintain its technological edge over competing East Asian cities. Further, the Hong Kong Office of Telecommunication Authority is currently soliciting bids for the newest generation of mobile telecommunications services, Personal Communications Service (PCS) and Cordless Access Service (CAS) systems. With estimates placing the cellular market at 1.1 million users within 10 years, the opportunities for American companies to provide service, equipment and technical support are considerable. Several American companies have

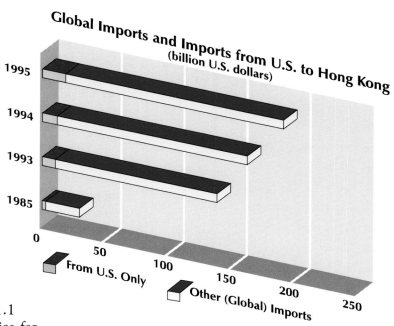

already entered into the fray by teaming up with local companies to bid on the PCS and CAS licenses.

On September 30, 2006, the exclusive franchise granted to Hong Kong Telephone International will expire, thus allowing foreign companies to bid on long distance telephone service.

Deregulation of the local telecommunications industry in Hong Kong opens the door to foreign telephone service providers and equipment manufacturers.

MARKET ACCESS

As one of the most open markets in the world and one of the most successful export processing zones, Hong Kong has a minimum of market access barriers and imposes no incentives or disincentives on trade and foreign investment.

Tariffs and Import Barriers

There are no import duties per se in Hong Kong. Customs regulations are uniformly applied. Domestic consumption taxes (referred to as duties in Hong Kong) are imposed on five items, including tobacco, soft drinks, alcoholic beverages, methyl alcohol and some fuels. These taxes are levied equally on local manufactures and imports.

For Hong Kong, import taxes are negligible. Hong Kong importers are assessed a trade declaration charge of 0.035 percent (35 cents for every $1,000).

Non-tariff barriers to trade are minimal in Hong Kong. However, one barrier for new-to-market firms is the oligopolistic nature of some Hong Kong business. The absence in Hong Kong of any antitrust law or enforcement agency has enabled large conglomerates to dominate certain sectors, and many companies attempting to enter the market for the first time may find channels blocked by existing relationships. The government's policy, however, is to discourage unfair trade practices and is committed to improving competition. This system is not clearly defined as in other Asian countries and can be much more easily overcome. Loyalties are not particularly strong, and keen price competition is often enough to break through any unseen barriers.

Government Procurement Practices

Government procurement practices in Hong Kong pose no problems for U.S. exporters; in fact, U.S. firms are a leading supplier to the Hong Kong government. Government procurement practices in Hong Kong are GATT consistent. The Government Supplies Department (GSD) is responsible for the management of procurement, storage and distribution of suppliers required by the Hong Kong government and related organizations. The

GSD will usually purchase by open tender, with decisions based on price, quality and delivery. The GSD gives no preference to any particular source of supply from any country or organization.

Openness to Foreign Investment

In Hong Kong, the market drives investment. Hong Kong imposes no scheme of incentives or disincentives on foreign investors, and there is no government policy designed to channel their efforts into specified projects or sectors.

With the exception of nondiscriminatory prudential requirements imposed on banks and other financial institutions and restrictions on foreign ownership in television broadcasting and media, Hong Kong imposes no screening requirements on investors. Nor are there more than a very few restrictions, all of which are well-publicized in the port's laws and regulations.

Leading Sources of Imports/Destination of Exports

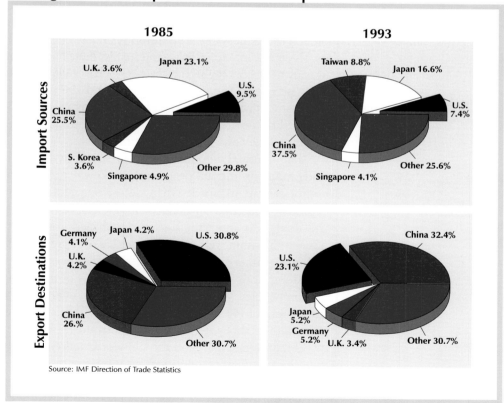

Source: IMF Direction of Trade Statistics

Special Considerations

Intellectual Property Rights

Hong Kong's market is mostly free of infringing products, its laws are solid, and enforcement, for the most part, is effective. While Hong Kong vigorously enforces its intellectual property rights laws, companies selling in this market must be vigilant. Theft of intellectual property still occurs, often in the process of transhipping bonded goods. The best protection for an American company is to have a strong local presence. Good products are most likely to be copied when a firm is not participating in the market.

THE COMPETITION

The nature of activity by competitor trading nations in Hong Kong fits the conventional model for a highly developed and legalistic economy. The local government handles all procurement and project awards through highly monitored tendering boards. Hong Kong, because of its high per capita income level, is not eligible for official development assistance so there is no bilateral tied aid package to offer and promote. The Hong Kong government has always maintained both a laissez-faire approach to business in the community and a policy of reduced government involvement in capital investments. In fact, Hong Kong's infrastructure has always been highly privatized. This includes the telecommunications networks, the port and ferries, and the power plants. These very successful franchisees conduct business via private tender and avoid publicity. The territory's success is based to a large extent on a policy of making money and steering clear of politics.

The minimal amount of high-profile activity (in the form of official trade missions and aid programs) in no way means that the U.S.'s competitor nations are not active in Hong Kong. Hong Kong is the commercial capital of Asia; this is where the financiers, developers and lawyers make the deals. As in other highly developed markets, our competitor nations maintain well-staffed commercial representative offices, most of which are larger than that of the U.S. presence.

Hong Kong has only 400 square miles of territory to support its six million people. With no natural resources, everything needed to support the people of Hong Kong must be imported. The industries which do exist here— shoes, textiles and electronics—are highly competitive in world markets. Japan and the United Kingdom, along with China, provide the principal competition for infrastructure inputs.

U.S. firms, while likely to be competitive suppliers of infrastructure-related expertise, probably will see the majority of transportation equipment sales in Hong Kong go to Japanese and European firms. Tokyo holds a 50 percent share of the transportation import market, with a sizeable majority share in automobiles. Still, U.S. firms have a significant role to play in exports to Hong Kong of construction equipment for infrastructure projects, and U.S. avionics and ground support equipment are preferred.

Historically, U.K. firms have perhaps the closest and strongest ties to Hong Kong, and they have received the largest share of the contracts awarded to date for the Chek Lap Kok Airport project. U.S. firms can expect to experience keen competition from U.K. and Japanese firms which are eager to secure construction contracts outside their own saturated markets.

Taiwan: Rapidly-

Geography
35,981 sq. km.

Population
21 million

Languages
Mandarin (official)
Principal dialects:
Taiwanese, Hakka

Cultural Mix
98% Chinese
2% Ethnic Taiwanese

GDP
US$ 234 Billion

GDP Growth Rate
6.2%

Per Capita GDP
US$ 11,711

Inflation Rate
3.8%

1994. Source: U.S. Dept. of Commerce, ITA

Three major trends are taking hold of the economic powerhouse that is Taiwan and changing it in complicated and sometimes unpredictable ways. While areas of growth are shifting as a result, it almost goes without saying that its position in the CEA and its internal dynamics will continue to usher the country quite successfully into the 21st century. But liberalization, democratization and consumerization are unquestionably affecting the nature of the island and its future.

The continued liberalization of Taiwan's economy can most recently be observed in the loosening of its closed and highly regulated services sector and financial services markets. Over the past few years the authorities have taken several significant steps to open Taiwan's trade regime, financial and insurance markets to new foreign and domestic competitors. While Taiwan's financial markets are still over-regulated, new insurance firms have been allowed to open their doors. Nonetheless, Ministry of Finance (MOF) approval of new insurance products and services is still slow. Privatization plans for parastatal enterprises are underway but behind schedule. However, the pace of and pressure behind liberalization is likely only to increase as Taiwan moves toward accession to the WTO, while also responding to the competitive pressures from other economies in the region.

Democratization is also reshaping Taiwan. Until the mid-1980s the KMT (Kuomintang Party) maintained single-party authoritarian rule. Beginning in the early 1980s and accelerating through the latter half of the decade, however, the KMT began to loosen its tight grip on power. In late 1994, the first direct elections for the mayors of Taiwan's two largest cities, Taipei and Kaohsiung, and for the governor of Taiwan Province were held. Direct presidential elections are planned for 1996. Yet as a very new democracy, it must be remembered, institutions, coalitions and habits are still in flux.

In addition to their new-found political voice, Taiwan's people also have a high level of purchasing power. In 1993, consumer spending for the first time outstripped industrial production as a contributor to Taiwan's GDP (45.6 percent vs. 40.4 percent). Taiwan's 21 million consumers have money and are willing to spend it. Taiwan has one of the highest concentrations of cellular telephones in the world; 98 percent of all households have color TVs, over 75 percent have VCRs, 35 percent have cable television.

Changing Island

In 1993, Taiwanese took 4.7 million trips overseas; credit card usage grew by 46.8 percent and the number of people with life insurance policies reached 1.8 million. The link between these disparate statistics is the importance of the Taiwan consumer, who now has the cash, the education and the desire to spend earnings on a variety of goods and services. Naturally, exporters of consumer goods can greatly benefit in this environment, along with service providers.

The Center and the Periphery

Not to be forgotten in the focus on these new trends, the dynamics of the "center-periphery" relationship with the mainland continue to shape the competitive environment of Taiwan's economy and also the significance of its role within the CEA. According to Taiwan and People's Republic of China (PRC) data, cumulative contracted investment from Taiwan to the mainland was over $15 billion at the end of 1994. While there are good reasons to be suspicious of this figure, it may still represent a conservative estimate due to the relatively modest size of individual projects (the average size is less than $1 million) and the likelihood of capital investment also being funneled through Hong Kong to avoid restrictive regulations and tax liabilities.

This investment relationship has had important implications for both the Chinese and Taiwan economies. It has enabled Taiwan's industry to remain internationally competitive by moving more labor-intensive production offshore, yet keeping it within the CEA, and contributed to the Chinese export juggernaut. At the same time, Taiwan's exports to China have apparently followed its investment capital as Hong Kong (as an entrepot for the mainland) supplanted the U.S. as Taiwan's major export market in 1994.

Trade with China, primarily via transhipment through Hong Kong, accounted for 21.7 percent of Taiwan's total exports in 1993, up from 18.9 percent in all of 1992, and from 7.7 percent in 1987.

This trade has grown at an annual pace of 30 percent since 1988, compared to growth of only 0.4 percent and 5.9 percent respectively for exports to the U.S. and Japan during this period. The broadening of Taiwan's export markets has in large part contributed to the island economy's continued expansion and diversification.

Taiwan's increasing economic prosperity has been accompanied by a major structural transformation. Appreciation of the New Taiwan Dollar (NTD) and rising labor and land costs have led many manufacturers of

The three trends of liberalization, democratization and consumerization are unquestionably affecting the nature of the island and its future.

Regional Operations Center

The rapid expansion of trade and investment ties within the CEA over the last few years has stood in sharp contrast to progress in the political dialogue. While the commercial relationship has flourished largely as a result of indirect contacts through Hong Kong, Taiwan is considering the establishment of "offshore transhipment centers" which would facilitate the movement of cargo within the CEA. Presently, direct transport of cargo between Taiwan and the mainland is prohibited creating inefficiencies for shippers in the region. As a means of furthering the practical economic integration of the CEA, this "extraterritorial" facility proposed for Kaohsiung and other harbors could be set aside for transhipment of goods to the mainland in ways which would not violate the ban on direct transportation links with the mainland. This measure would particularly strengthen Taiwan's role as a regional operations center.

labor-intensive products like toys, apparel and footwear to move offshore, mainly to Southeast Asia and mainland China. Industrial growth is now concentrated in capital and technology-intensive industries—petrochemicals, computers and electronic components—as well as consumer goods industries such as food processing. Taiwan's economy continues to be export oriented, with exports accounting for 44 percent of GNP. But this restructuring means an accompanying change in what kinds of imports will be most welcome.

BIG EMERGING SECTORS

As the island is undergoing rapid transition to a more mature, competitive economy through the production of more capital intensive goods and the development of an increasingly vibrant services sector, the economy has concomitantly moved from double-digit growth to more moderate growth. To ensure continued economic progress, the authorities have been actively seeking to upgrade Taiwan's industrial structure by signing letters of intent to form strategic alliances with multinational companies.

In the coming years, Taiwan expects to enhance its ability to produce high valued-added products by strengthening technological capacities in the areas of design, manufacturing, management and R&D. Taiwan's transition from making simpler, labor-intensive goods to producing more sophisticated capital- and technology-intensive goods has created a booming market for industrial equipment and industrial and business technology.

The consumer market—from cars and computers to insurance and travel—is not only expanding in overall size, but new niches continually open up as Taiwan's consumers become more discerning and sophisticated. Democratization is sparking a demand for better healthcare facilities, more leisure facilities, improved environmental protection and better public services.

Taiwan still has major infrastructure needs, as do all the BEMs—new highways, expanded airports, improved telecommunications networks, new power generation facilities and pollution control facilities. Taiwan has ambitious plans to upgrade its infrastructure to world standards and raise the standard of living on the island. The rallying cry for these plans is the Regional Operating Center (ROC) concept. By upgrading its telecommunications, transportation, regulatory and recreational infrastructure,

Taiwan hopes to turn itself into a Regional Operations Center for manufacturing, shipping (both air and sea), financial services, telecommunications and media.

To accomplish these goals, the authorities plan to spend over $100 billion upgrading the island's physical infrastructure by building a high-speed railway down the crowded west corridor of the island and a second north-south freeway; improving harbor facilities at all three of Taiwan's major harbors; upgrading both Taipei and Kaoshiung's international airport; spending billions on an all-digital switching network, an improved cellular telephone system and a National Information Infrastructure.

Realizing that the private sector will have to be heavily involved if they are to meet their goal of turning Taiwan into an ROC, the authorities have been steadily liberalizing the telecommunications, power generation and financial services markets, and this trend should accelerate. Taiwan has already pledged to privatize its telecommunications monopoly, increased the amount of direct investment foreign institutional investors are allowed to make in the Taiwan stockmarket and given permission for independent power plants. There is much room for greater liberalization and, thus, greater opportunities for foreign firms in all of these areas.

Transportation and Infrastructure

Taipei is undertaking a substantial number of transportation projects to narrow the increasing gap between its economic growth and the development of its transportation infrastructure. Taipei is also motivated by a desire to become a regional transportation hub, particularly in the aerospace sector. Big-ticket projects likely to fuel demand for both transportation equipment and infrastructure projects include a high-speed railway project valued at $17 billion, expansion of two of Taiwan's airports projected to cost nearly $1.2 billion, and new highway construction that could cost as much as $25 billion through 2003.

Taiwan imported more than $5 billion worth of transportation-related equipment in 1994. U.S. companies will enjoy increased export opportunities in the sale of autos, parts and aircraft.

Information Technology

Telecommunications Equipment and Services

To become a regional communications center will require substantial telecommunications upgrades and expansions of local digital switching and toll systems, construction of optical fiber subscriber loops and the development of an ISDN network. The telecommunications authority is also upgrading mobile communications capabilities and packet switching networks.

> **Industrial growth is now concentrated in capital and technology-intensive industries — petrochemicals, computers and electronic components — as well as consumer goods industries.**

The consumer market—from cars and computers to insurance and travel—is not only expanding in overall size, but new niches continually open up as Taiwan's consumers become more discerning and sophisticated.

Energy

Rising environmentalism and bureaucratic infighting over financing during the past decade delayed construction of several power generation facilities, leaving Taiwan with a power shortage that frequently forces Taipower, the island's state-run utility, to ration electricity to industrial users at peak-use periods. Since this threatens Taiwan's industrial growth and attractiveness as a site for foreign and domestic manufacturers, the authorities have placed a priority on completing projects which include thermal and hydroelectric, combined cycle, liquified natural gas and nuclear facilities.

Taipower has been a significant purchaser of U.S. power generation equipment for many years. U.S. firms have also been a major provider of engineering and design services. Taipower's familiarity with U.S. firms' equipment, services and excellent safety track records leaves them well-positioned to take advantage of significant sales and investment opportunities.

Environmental Technology

Environmental projects are a high priority as residents have become increasingly dissatisfied and vocal about current air and water pollution conditions. The current market size is approximately $700 million, with spending expected to increase 10 to 15 percent a year. Foreign imports, which are expected to grow 20 percent a year through the year 2000, currently account for 70 percent of the market.

U.S. equipment and technology is well regarded in Taiwan's market— Camp Dresser McKee, a large Cambridge, Massachusetts-based engineering firm has performed environmental work for the Taiwan central and provincial authorities related to river clean-up (a $340,000 contract) and an incinerator consulting contract (a $7 million contract). In establishing their "regional" presence, the firm also negotiated a $400,000 arrangement to review a wastewater collection and treatment design contract for the Jiangsu Province in the PRC.

Consumer Goods

Taiwan is fast emerging as a high consumption economy. With average household income approaching $28,000 per year — and the top 20 percent of Taiwan families with over $55,000 in average income — disposable income is available to bring home consumer goods and services that could only be dreamed of 10 years ago. This is a new market, so brand loyalties for the most part are not yet strongly established.

Food and beverages

Taiwan's food distribution and retailing system has transformed in the last five years, and consumers are clamoring for imported food and beverages. With total imports estimated at $1.8 billion in 1994 and 10 percent annual growth, new suppliers and new products are welcome.

Skin Care and Makeup

As Taiwan's living standards have improved consumers are spending more than ever for personal care products. Women are using cosmetics at an earlier age. More women are working and represent a growing market for skin care and makeup products. In 1994, Taiwan will import an estimated $185 million worth of these products. Imports should grow at a rate of 15 percent annually over the next few years.

Insurance Services

The overall market for insurance is growing, but the potential is especially promising for life insurance. Companies which support the industry with analytical and other services could also do well in this market. Taiwan's 1994 imports in this sector should reach a value of about $3.0 billion, with sales growing at an estimated 13 percent from 1994 to 1997.

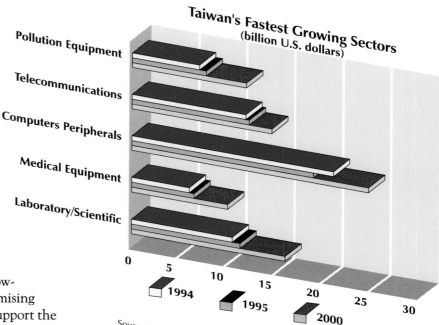

Taiwan's Fastest Growing Sectors
(billion U.S. dollars)

Source: International Trade Administration, U.S. Department of Commerce

Travel and Tourism Services

According to Taiwan statistics, travel to the U.S. grew by 5.0 percent in 1993 (to over 300,000 visitors). Further expansion in the next few years is likely. Taiwan visitors to the U.S. were estimated to have spent approximately $630 million in 1994 on tourism-related services.

MARKET ACCESS

Access to Taiwan's market has improved as a result of gradual market liberalization and, more recently, its drive to become a regional operations center and member of the WTO. Reduced tariffs, a revised customs law and reductions in the number of products requiring import licenses have improved the export climate. Taiwan offers a number of investment incentives to encourage investment, and screening is, as a rule, routine and non-discriminatory

Tariffs and Import Barriers

Tariffs are lower in Taiwan than in China. No systemic problems in customs regulations exist for exporters to Taiwan. In the past five years, Taiwan has made significant progress in reducing tariffs on non-agricultural products of interest to U.S. exporters. Taiwan has also agreed to abide by the WTO customs valuation code. Taiwan also levies import taxes, in the form of a 5 percent value-added tax (also assessed on domestic goods) and a 0.5 percent harbor construction fee, both assessed on the landed cost of the goods. A commodity tax must also be paid if an imported or domestic product falls into one of eight commodity categories. Rates range from 2-60 percent and on a few important products, most notably autos, Taiwan imposes commodity taxes at higher rates for certain types of products not produced locally.

Taiwan uses non-tariff barriers selectively. Taiwan's use of non-tariff barriers is a subject of intense negotiation in discussions regarding accession to the WTO. Taiwan continues to maintain an import licensing system, but the number of items requiring import licenses is being gradually reduced.

Government Procurement Practices

U.S. firms have been hindered in the bidding on major projects in Taiwan by non-transparent bidding procedures. In negotiations regarding its WTO accession, Taiwan has committed to adhering to international practices with regard to government procurement. U.S. firms have a well-established record of success in winning tenders which are administered by Taiwan's Central Trust of China (CTC). However, the bulk of Taiwan authority purchases are administered by the purchasing entities themselves, not the CTC. These tenders may be restricted to firms with a local presence, and it can be difficult for outsiders to obtain advance information on them.

In the course of negotiations on its WTO accession, Taiwan has committed to joining the new WTO Government Procurement Agreement (GPA) scheduled for implementation in January 1996. This should serve to open significant public procurement opportunities to the U.S. and suppliers from other signatories (including Japan, Canada and the EU). The GPA, which requires transparent, uniform and non-discriminatory procurement procedures should help to address a number of concerns which U.S. firms have raised with Taiwan's existing procurement regime.

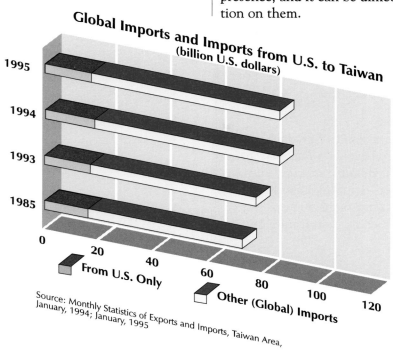

Global Imports and Imports from U.S. to Taiwan
(billion U.S. dollars)

From U.S. Only

Other (Global) Imports

Source: Monthly Statistics of Exports and Imports, Taiwan Area, January, 1994; January, 1995

Openness to Foreign Investment

Taiwan has established three export processing zones in order to encourage investment and to expand the export of products and services. All products imported by enterprises located in these zones for their own use are exempt from customs duties. As a rule, Taiwan relies on investment incentives to encourage the development of particular industries.

U.S. investors will find that Taiwan almost never fails to approve a proposed investment. In Taiwan, applications for investment approval are screened to determine whether the investment project is subject to foreign investment restrictions. Approvals are generally granted in five to 10 working days. Foreign investors are generally afforded national treatment with regard to taxes, access to licenses and procurement.

Meanwhile, restrictions on investment in Taiwan are relatively transparent, and investors can easily determine those sectors which are closed to foreign investment or where it is limited. The "negative list," adopted in July 1990, clearly specifies industries closed to foreign investment, including 54 prohibited industries and 55 industries where foreign ownership is still limited. Most foreign investment applications outside the scope of the negative list are granted approval. In the financial sector, the Taiwan authorities have set a ceiling of $5 billion for all foreign institutional investment in the Taiwan exchange, with each single investor being limited to $100 million dollars.

Special Considerations

Intellectual Property Rights

Taiwan is in the process of developing a comprehensive legal system and is improving protection of intellectual property as well as enforcement. A series of important laws have been passed since 1992, including revised copyright, patent and trademark laws, and a cable television law. Together with new legislation under consideration to protect integrated circuit designs and trade secrets, these laws give Taiwan an IPR legal structure largely consistent with international practices.

Although improved enforcement efforts have reduced the incidence of copyright violations, inconsistencies in the trademark and patent area highlight the need for more standardized examination and registration procedures. In 1994, the U.S. government moved Taiwan from "priority watch" to the "watch list" under the Special 301 provision of the 1988 Trade Act. After the 1995 Special 301 review, Taiwan remains on the "watch list."

THE COMPETITION

The opportunities for U.S. firms in Taiwan's domestic market are excellent. Foreign products are regarded highly by Taiwan's buyers, but competition among U.S., Japanese and European firms is brutal. U.S. products remain competitive, however, assisted by the relative strength of the

The pace of and pressure behind liberalization is likely only to increase as Taiwan moves toward accession to the WTO, while also responding to the competitive pressures from other economies in the region.

Leading Sources of Imports/Destination of Exports

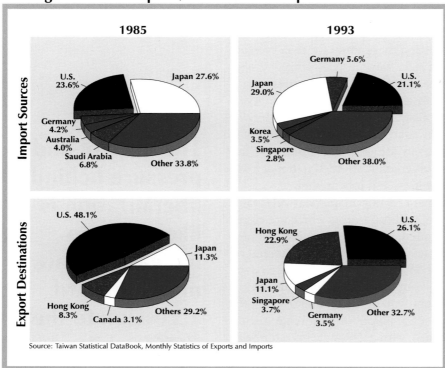

Source: Taiwan Statistical DataBook, Monthly Statistics of Exports and Imports

yen and European currencies versus the dollar.

Several years ago, Taiwan set aside certain tenders exclusively for U.S. bidders, but foreign competitors complained loudly, so Taiwan has gradually phased out the "Buy-America" guidelines. However, Taiwan authorities may still encourage local firms to buy European or American to reduce the significant trade deficit with Japan. Taiwan's sourcing policy can still sometimes help on the margins, but will not help U.S. firms as much as bidding the best technologies and prices will. This "policy" advantage will also be eliminated as Taiwan joins the WTO Procurement Agreement.

Japan

In most areas of the Taiwan domestic market, Japanese firms are the major competitors for U.S. firms. Japan is the primary source of capital equipment goods for Taiwan's industries, and has made strong inroads into Taiwan's booming consumer goods market. The Japanese have the advantages of proximity and a close cultural affinity, but English is the most popular second language on the island and an astounding number of Taiwan representatives and businesspeople have received their higher educations in the U.S.

European Union

European firms have traditionally been strong in only a few, limited sectors—power and transportation among others—but they have made strenuous efforts to cultivate the Taiwan market over the past few years, and those efforts are paying off in greatly increased exports. In recent years, many significant contracts have been awarded to European competitors.

Domestic Taiwan Firms

Within the CEA itself, Taiwan firms are likely to be significant competitors in smaller niche-product markets based on their international competitiveness and, more importantly, on their extensive network of contacts. The insular nature of regional business practices can present a formidable obstacle to third-country suppliers attempting to break into

CEA markets. Two things to bear in mind, however, are the limited capabilities of Taiwan firms based on their (relatively) small size, and the fact that their significant investment presence throughout the region makes them both customer and competitor. Taiwan firms will likely be receptive to cooperative/collaborative commercial relationships with U.S. companies to exploit opportunities in the region.

Still, Taiwan businesspeople are extremely entrepreneurial, and more and more Taiwan firms are becoming world-class competitors in their own right.

India: Charting

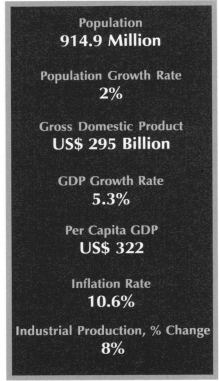

Population
914.9 Million
Population Growth Rate
2%
Gross Domestic Product
US$ 295 Billion
GDP Growth Rate
5.3%
Per Capita GDP
US$ 322
Inflation Rate
10.6%
Industrial Production, % Change
8%

IFY 1993/94. Source: U.S. Dept. of Commerce, ITA

While the 1980s saw India enter the consciousness of emerging market investors and traders, it was only in 1991 that the country's leaders significantly stepped up efforts to loosen the government's substantial hold on the economy — and prompted a significant business response. With the introduction of measures liberalizing this market, India was set solidly on the path to growth.

That's because while India has a growing consumer class, a stable government, budding financial institutions, an able business class, and a highly trained and educated technical work force, it also has an economy hindered by government intervention and public ownership of key industries.

Under Jawaharlal Nehru, India's first prime minister and the socialism-influenced architect of the nation's self reliance and import substitution model, India developed its broad industrial base. Yet as time went on, the shortcomings of an economy dominated by government-owned monopolies and a rigidly controlled private sector became increasingly apparent.

Even with its earlier handicaps, the Indian economy had displayed some remarkable strengths. India has become not only self-sufficient in food production but is a net exporter of food grains. A diversified industrial base produces coal, steel, cement, textiles, heavy machinery and chemicals. India, in conjunction with predominantly U.S. partners, is one of the world's largest exporters of software and has accomplished much in high-technology areas.

However, India's economic development has been less dynamic than that of other Asian countries whose economies were far behind India's when India became independent. India's economic growth averaged 5.6 percent annually during the 1980s, mainly fueled by government borrowing to deal with a financial payments crisis, spurred in part by heavy borrowing during the previous decade. Almost half the population lived below the poverty line. Trade did not play an important role in this largely self-sufficient economy. Monopoly power and a lack of foreign competition in some industrial sectors deprived India of technological advancements, modern methods of production and incentives to improve quality and efficiency.

In 1991, the government of Prime Minister Narasimha Rao launched a major program of economic stabilization and restructuring. The reforms included relaxation of industrial regulations; encouragement of foreign investment and disinvestment in public sector enterprises; liberalization of international trade; devaluation of the rupee and loosening of exchange controls; improvement in the financial sector; and reduction of government spending and subsidies.

A New Course

The Benefits of Reform

The reform program has dramatically altered India's economic landscape. According to the World Bank, "these reforms could enable India to grow at the rates experienced by its successful East Asian neighbors." The economy has bounced back from three years of slow growth, thanks to bountiful agricultural harvests, a strong rise in industrial output and renewed business confidence. GDP increased 5.3 percent in Indian Fiscal Year (IFY) 1994/95 (ending March 31, 1995).

India's balance of payments position is also strong. Foreign exchange reserves totaled $20 billion in March 1995, compared with around $1 billion in July 1991. Exports rose 19.6 percent in IFY 1993/94 and 18.3 percent in 1994/95. And consumer price inflation has slowed from 13.5 percent in IFY 1991/92 to about 10.64 percent in IFY 1994/95.

Much of the momentum for change is generated by the private sector, both foreign and domestic. Company efforts to expand into new business ventures are challenging the bureaucracies and forcing new market openings. The U.S. government also has played a role in encouraging policy reforms in such areas as intellectual property rights and investment.

For many U.S. firms, India's huge and growing population is the primary attraction. India is expected to become the world's most populous nation by about 2060. In addition, twenty-three Indian cities each have more than one million inhabitants.

> "India's road to reform will be neither a German autobahn nor an American interstate. We'll take an Indian road — with potholes, twists and turns, and slowing down at crossings....we will reach our goal."
>
> — P. Chidambaram,
> Minister of Commerce

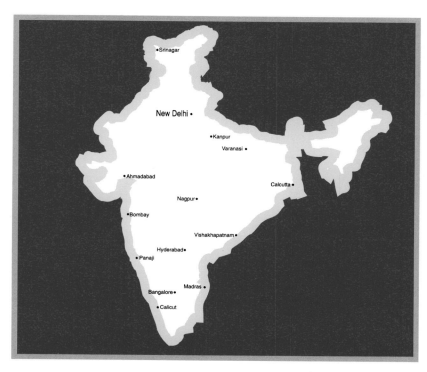

"In our diversity lies our greatest strength, yielding a commercial and intellectual synergy that more homogeneous nations can only envy."

— *Commerce Secretary Ron Brown before the New Delhi Confederation of Indian Industries*

Approximately 3.5 million Indians have scientific, technical, engineering or medical credentials. While per capita consumption is very low, India's growing consumer class—some with money to spend on appliances, others with more limited disposable income for a select array of consumer goods—ranges from 100-300 million people.

Development of India's infrastructure is crucial to its growth strategy. Although its infrastructure is extensive, it is inadequate to meet current demands, let alone rapidly growing future needs. The size of the country, higher economic growth and the need for modernization mean that massive investments will be required for the foreseeable future. India's federal and state governments are turning increasingly to the domestic and foreign private sectors for the funds necessary to implement large infrastructure projects.

U.S. export performance through the remainder of the 1990s will rely heavily on infrastructure development and sales of traditional export items, such as capital equipment. The most attractive prospects are in power, telecommunications, information technology, electronics, hydrocarbons, food processing, transportation and financial services.

According to the World Bank, while imports to India have been projected to increase annually from 6 percent in IFY 1993/94 to 12-13 percent in IFY 1994/95-1996/97 as a result of continued trade liberalization and economic growth of 4.5 to 5.5 percent a year, as it turned out, imports actually increased by almost 22 percent in IFY 1994/95 alone.

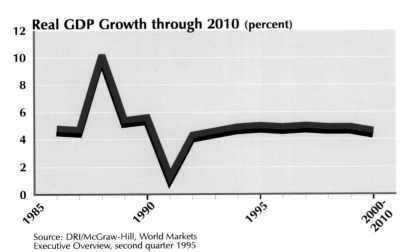

Real GDP Growth through 2010 (percent)

Source: DRI/McGraw-Hill, World Markets Executive Overview, second quarter 1995

An Array of Strengths

India ranks tenth in the world as an industrial nation, although 68 percent of the work force is employed in the agricultural sector. A rich mineral base has helped to build a diverse industrial sector, and large numbers of skilled and educated personnel have contributed in creating a sophisticated high-technology sector. An extensive financial sector, offering a wide range of instruments, is a key part of the Indian economy. Of the 274 commercial banks operating in India, 223 are in the public sector; the remaining banks are privately owned, including at least 25 foreign banks.

Many Indian firms have grown and prospered despite the bewildering maze of licenses, taxes, controls and procedures. As the Indian market opens up, these companies are looking to strategic alliances with U.S. and other foreign firms to take advantage of the reforms at home and export opportunities abroad.

An estimated 200 American firms now have equity investments in India, mostly concentrated in and around Bombay, New Delhi, Bangalore and Madras. Almost half of this investment is in manufacturing, divided equally between industrial and consumer goods. The banking and power sectors comprise the bulk of the remainder. The geographical and sectoral mix of the American presence in India is likely to diversify substantially over the next few years. U.S. firms are looking at less expensive cities in the secondary urban areas and at infrastructure projects in cities and regions that are likely to grow faster than major metropolitan areas.

BIG EMERGING SECTORS

The key sectors experiencing rapid growth are in the infrastructure area, especially power and telecommunications. As India continues to open its economy to domestic and foreign competition, other sectors, such as financial services, especially insurance, and consumer goods will benefit.

Energy

Modernization and expansion of energy facilities is the government's first priority. The demand for electrical power in India exceeds current supply by 8 percent, and peak demand exceeds supply by 20 percent. The chronic shortage of energy, leading to frequent power failures and brownouts, threatens India's economic growth. As a result, the government plans to exploit energy resources more efficiently and install enough generating capacity to double the available power supply in 12 years. By 2007, India

For many U.S. firms, India's huge and growing population is the primary attraction. India's consumer class ranges from 100 – 300 million people.

Composition of U.S. Exports to India

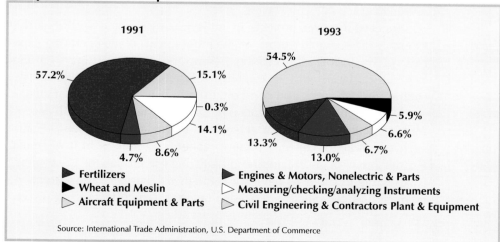

1991

57.2% 15.1%
0.3%
14.1%
4.7% 8.6%

1993

54.5%
5.9%
6.6%
13.3% 6.7%
13.0%

▶ Fertilizers   ▶ Engines & Motors, Nonelectric & Parts
▶ Wheat and Meslin   ▷ Measuring/checking/analyzing Instruments
▷ Aircraft Equipment & Parts   ▷ Civil Engineering & Contractors Plant & Equipment

Source: International Trade Administration, U.S. Department of Commerce

The Emerging Consumer

The consuming class in India is growing rapidly because of a number of factors: the expansion of the manufacturing and service sectors, rising untaxed rural incomes, larger urban populations, two-income families, rising education levels and exposure to ideas and products through travel and television. Television reaches the masses, and U.S. soap operas and MTV, so popular in urban areas, are as effective in promoting U.S. brand loyalty in India as everywhere else.

American companies are engaged in this consumer revolution. In 1987, Whirlpool Corporation entered into a joint venture to manufacture automatic washers in India. With the adoption of a more liberal regime for foreign investment, Whirlpool purchased its Indian partners' stake in the joint venture. In the summer of 1994, Whirlpool purchased the controlling interest in Kelvinator of India, Ltd., India's largest manufacturer and marketer of refrigerators. At that time, Whirlpool Chairman and CEO Dave Whitwan said, "within the next 10 years, one-half or more of the major appliances sold worldwide will go to Asian consumers, and many of those people will be members of India's rapidly growing middle class."

General Electric and the Indian Godrej Group joined together in 1993 to begin developing, manufacturing and marketing household appliances in India.

plans to have increased power generation capacity by 140 gigawatts (GW), at a cost of roughly $160 billion. Although India is likely to fall short of its ambitious plans through a shortage of capital, the potential for U.S. exports is immense for both large and small firms.

Energy imports, a significant drain on foreign exchange, have increased steadily to 40 million tons of oil equivalent (MTOE) in 1993. The Planning Commission projects that commercial energy demand, fueled by growth in industry and transportation use, will increase from 150 MTOE in 1994 to 350 MTOE in 2009. Investments are needed in oil and gas, pipelines and port facilities for liquid natural gas, refineries, coal and coal washeries, power transmission and refurbishment of inefficient plants.

The country's major shift in investment and trade policies is succeeding in attracting investment by foreign firms. Private companies have submitted proposals for 77 power projects, totaling some 32 GW of capacity at an investment cost of about $33 billion. The government has designated eight of the projects to be "fast track," eligible for counter-guarantees of the power purchase obligations of the State Electricity Boards (though the fast-track guarantee is not always a guarantee of rate of return). Seven of these projects, totaling some $5.7 billion, involve U.S. firms as partners.

U.S. exports of energy-related goods to India have increased rapidly, reaching $460 million in 1993. U.S. exports are likely to increase several fold in the next few years because the share of U.S. equipment in the capital cost of huge projects is as high as 35 to 45 percent.

Most, but not all projects and subsectors in petroleum production and refining are currently open to privatization or foreign competition. Where markets have been opened, U.S. firms have been major players as promoters or members of consortia with domestic Indian firms. U.S. developers and equipment suppliers are therefore expected to play an important role in the expansion of India's oil and gas production and refining capacity.

Successful power projects in India usually involve coalitions that assemble large supplier firms, engineering talent, plant-operating experience, in-country knowledge, contacts and excellent financial capabilities. Firms with an established reputation may be able to raise capital through stock and bond offerings in major financial markets.

U.S. suppliers and investors face opportunities in almost all parts of India's energy sector. Power generation is the largest segment because each megawatt of capacity requires about $1.3 million in investment. Partnership with an Indian firm or enlisting the services of a consultant is advisable in order to navigate through the bureaucratic system. As many as 104 clearances are needed before production can begin; contacts at all levels of government are essential.

Non-conventional energy projects in wind and solar energy are smaller in size but enjoy incentives, subsidized financing and less red tape. Investment and foreign joint ventures also are encouraged in co-generation. In the oil and gas sector, the government has invited private sector bids to develop fields with proven reserves and to explore others. Opportunities also exist in oil refining, the supply of lubrication oils and the manufacture of LPG bottles for households.

India's coal reserves are large, and 62 percent of new power will be generated from coal. The private sector is now allowed to own captive mines. Major opportunities include equipment sales, coal gasification, recovering methane from coal mines, and, because of the high ash content of Indian coal, coal washing and vitrification of fly ash to produce building products. Refurbishing older inefficient power plants, investments in peak power generation capacity, reducing transmission losses (estimated at 20 to 48 percent) and improving energy efficiency also are energy priorities.

Energy-service companies, which can design, finance, install and maintain improvements in customers' overall energy consumption levels, can develop a market for their services in India. Services that have the greatest potential are demand-side management, training, safety analysis, project finance, project management and technical support.

India's energy sector expansion will require massive amounts of equipment. U.S. suppliers lead the world in power generation and coal-washing equipment and technology. To participate in future projects, U.S. firms can join development consortia, sell to promoters that have projects and financing in place, and export to the Indian public sector.

Information Technology

India's $9 billion information technologies market registered a 25 percent annual growth rate during the early 1990s, which makes it one of the fastest-growing in the world. U.S. exports of these products and services to India increased in 1994 to $360 million because of the government's economic liberalization policies. Although India imports only a small percentage of information technology products from the U.S., American manufacturers supply a significant portion of India's needs through overseas subsidiary operations and joint ventures with Indian partners.

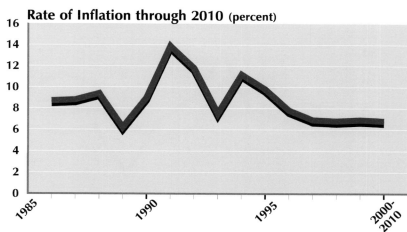

Rate of Inflation through 2010 (percent)

Source: DRI/McGraw-Hill, World Markets
Executive Overview, second quarter 1995

U.S. firms are looking at secondary urban areas and at infrastructure projects in cities and regions that are likely to grow faster than major metropolitan areas.

Comparative Economic Growth in Real GDP (Percent)

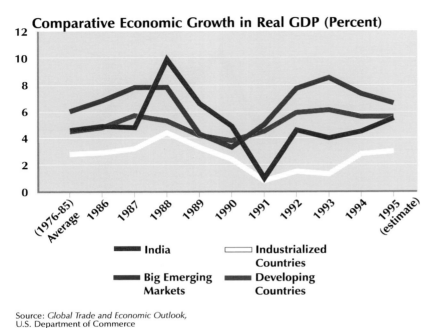

India   **Industrialized Countries**

Big Emerging Markets   **Developing Countries**

Source: *Global Trade and Economic Outlook,*
U.S. Department of Commerce

India's $9 billion infotech market had a 25 percent annual growth rate during the early 1990s — making it one of the fastest growing in the world.

Electronic Components and Test Equipment

Local demand for electronic components is forecast to grow 20 percent annually through 1996. The market for electronic test and semiconductor manufacturing equipment, valued at $110 million in 1993, is rising at a modest 1-3 percent annually.

India's Department of Electronics expects the electronics industry to import at least 25 percent of its electronic components needs for the next few years. The U.S. is India's second-largest supplier with a 20 percent share. This is a result of the perceived quality of U.S. electronic components and the active presence of U.S. companies in the Indian market.

U.S. products dominate imports of semiconductor manufacturing and test instruments, although European and Japanese equipment manufacturers are established in India. U.S. companies are entering into joint ventures with Indian companies in the information technology, industrial electronics, instrumentation, broadcasting and communications sectors. Most of these joint ventures source electronic components from the U.S. to ensure compatibility in the equipment they manufacture. End-users tend to be influenced by price considerations, buying imported equipment only when domestic products do not offer sufficient capabilities.

Computer Equipment and Software

During the 1990s, India's $1.1 billion computer equipment market grew at a much faster pace (31 percent annually) than any other information technology sector. Demand is particularly strong for personal computers, workstations and small scale, multiuser systems. U.S. computer exports to India have risen 6.5 percent annually since 1990, to reach $94 million in 1994. The bulk of U.S. export content has been split almost evenly between computer systems and parts. In general, imports account for about one-third of Indian demand for computer equipment. U.S. firms serve the market from their U.S. facilities and overseas plants, including in-country joint ventures.

Demand for computers and software is fueled by policies encouraging industrialization, exports and the creation of an information infrastructure to link the 70 largest Indian cities. The most promising computer equipment sub-sectors in India include: computer systems, data acquisition systems and peripherals. Best prospects for U.S. software exports to India include data communications software, local and wide area networking software, multimedia products, relational database management systems, CAD/CAM/CAE software, on-line transaction processing software, and object-oriented tools.

Turnkey projects and customized software dominate the Indian software market, but the demand for packaged software is growing quickly. The market for packaged software is estimated to have increased 21 percent annually between 1991 and 1993, reaching $80 million. Moreover, U.S. firms dominate the packaged software market, satisfying 75 percent of Indian demand. Major American software firms that do business in India, through distributors or joint ventures, include Microsoft, WordPerfect, Lotus, Novell, Borland and Intergraph. India's dynamic software industry numbers some 500 firms and 32,000 professionals. Exports are emphasized, but Indian firms supply a growing share of the domestic packaged software market.

India's hardware industry is import-intensive, so the high cost of imported components results in high-priced computers. About 95 percent of domestic Indian hardware manufacturers have expanded into software, systems integration and training to obtain higher profit margins.

Indian suppliers, often in conjunction with foreign hardware manufacturers (many from the U.S.), produce a broad range of personal computers, notebook computers, minicomputers, supermini-computers, large-scale computers and peripheral products. Despite a varied product base, Indian industry continues to import specialized computer systems. However, local manufacturing of components is growing.

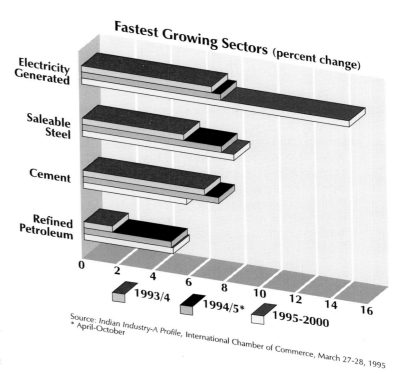

Fastest Growing Sectors (percent change)

Electricity Generated · Saleable Steel · Cement · Refined Petroleum

0　2　4　6　8　10　12　14　16

1993/4　1994/5*　1995-2000

Source: *Indian Industry-A Profile*, International Chamber of Commerce, March 27-28, 1995
* April-October

Megaproject Contenders in Energy

Competition for the megaprojects in India's power sector have drawn some of the biggest names in the industry. U.S. firms such as Enron, General Electric and Westinghouse compete with Germany's Siemens, Switzerland's Asean Brown Boveri (ABB), and the U.K.'s GEC Alsthom, Rolls Royce, National Power and British Gas. The only announced Japanese power venture in India so far is a planned 500MW plant in Maharashtra by a consortium that includes Toshiba and Hitachi. The most ambitious project is a proposal by Hong Kong entrepreneur Gordon Wu to build plants totaling 10,500MW at a cost of $12.7 billion.

U.S. firms also face competition from Danish and German firms in wind power, French and Australian firms in hydro and minihydro, and Canadians and British in solar energy. Britain's Power General has teamed up with the Birlas, a major Indian firm, in a venture to refurbish aging public sector plants.

In the petroleum sector, Hyundai won a $1 billion contract in 1992, C. Itoh is currently seeking financing for a $1.6 billion refinery with an Indian firm and the Oman Oil Co. is studying plans for a $5 billion deepwater gas pipeline from Oman to India. Active U.S. firms include Mobil, Caltex, Enron and Amoco.

Best Sales Prospects in Information Technologies

Printed Circuit Boards • Resistors • Transformers • Capacitors • Digital Signal Processing Chips • Dynamic Random Access Memories (DRAMs) • Easable/Programmable Read Only Memory (EPROM) Chips • Digital/Analog Logic Chips • High-End, Special Application Equipment • High Frequency Oscilloscopes • Oscillographs • Multimeters • Ammeters • Voltmeters • Network and Logic Analyzers • Signal Analyzers • Synthesizers • Oscillators • Automatic Test Equipment.

Telecommunications Equipment and Services

Expenditures for telecommunications products and services should exceed $6.5 billion in 1995, including $3.2 billion for telecommunication services and $3.4 billion for equipment. The annual growth rate in the telecommunications equipment market should average 30 percent over the next few years, while the introduction of cellular services in late 1995 and 1996 will lead to a dramatic growth in service revenues.

In early 1995, the government invited bids for the provision of cellular and basic telephone services throughout the country. Many U.S. firms are responding to this tremendous opportunity. Until recently, only a few U.S. companies were significant players in the Indian telecommunications market. Other U.S. firms are now poised to enter because of the promotion of foreign investment. Government-owned equipment manufacturers and service suppliers have dominated the market with a 90 percent share.

Government policies and practices are in a state of flux. Liberalized policies have been announced, but many details are unclear and the pace of implementation is uncertain. Tariffs for telecommunications equipment are being reduced, but still are well above levels in most other Asian markets. Intellectual property rights have not been a significant issue in the telecommunications markets so far, but that may change as U.S. firms become involved in the provision of services. Investment policies still prevent foreign majority ownership of most telecommunications joint ventures.

Best export prospects include telecommunications switching and transmission equipment, satellite telecommunication systems, cellular phone systems, paging services and pagers.

Information Services

This market is modest but growing—$715 million in 1993. Indian custom software development is the largest sub-sector of the country's information services industry, exporting $330 million in 1993. U.S. exports of information services to India have been small—$6 million in 1993. Nonetheless, U.S. firms are the largest foreign providers of information services in India and supply about 75 percent of the import market.

Global Imports and Imports from the U.S. (billion U.S. dollars)

Source: IMF, Direction of Trade Statistics Yearbook, 1994

From U.S. Only   Other (Global) Imports

India's services market is not as open as those in developed countries. The government agreed to only small market commitments in this sector under the international General Agreement on Trade in Services. India reserved the right to apply foreign equity restrictions, set limits on establishment of branch offices, restrict payment of expenses and remittances, and grant preferential treatment to service providers willing to transfer technology through joint ventures with public sector enterprises.

Still, providers of online services and professional services have opportunities as India modernizes its telecommunications infrastructure and financial sector. Its information superhighway will include data and large file transfer capability, electronic data interchange and video conferencing.

Infrastructure

Indian plans call for spending at least $100 billion for infrastructure development between 1992 and 2000, of which at least $50 billion would be spent in the transportation sector. However, its ability to attract financing will determine the extent and pace of these projects. India must compete with Asian and other rapidly advancing countries to obtain foreign funds for airports, railroads, ports, highways and urban transportation.

Leading Sources of Imports/Destination of Exports

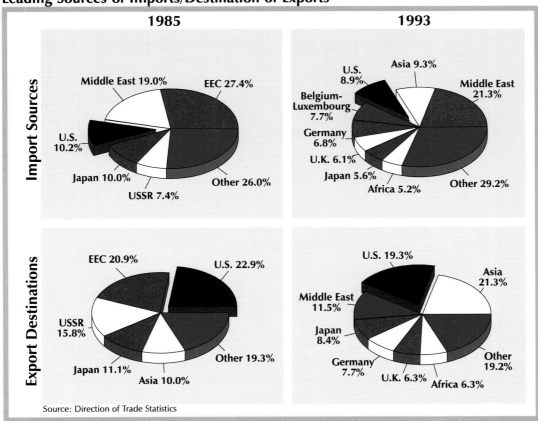

Source: Direction of Trade Statistics

U.S. firms offering high-quality goods with unique features or technology will fare best in the Indian market. There are too many lower-cost products there to compete on price.

With the commercial environment having improved since 1991, India expects to attract the investment capital necessary to achieve higher rates of economic growth. India is exploring the possibilities of infrastructure development through privatization, i.e., BOT (build-own-transfer) or BOO (build-own-operate) arrangements. Major opportunities in this area include:

Airports

Local Indian authorities are moving to develop at least two major airports, Bangalore and Cochin, on a BOT basis.

Ports

National and local governments plan to spend as much as $8 billion on the upgrading of ports in Bombay, Calcutta, Cochin, Haldia, Hazira, Madras, Bangalore, Paradip, Tuticorin and Viakhapatnam.

Railroads

India currently operates the world's largest multigauge rail network. The Indian National Railroad seeks funding for upgrading its locomotive fleet that could offer an export potential in excess of $100 million.

Roads/Highways

Overall requirements are vast. The Indian government is promoting planned BOT schemes to build 11,000 kilometers of toll roads over the next 20 years. The first such road (Bombay to Vadodara) is in the design stage.

Urban Transit

A senior Indian government official recently claimed that "23 Indian cities have the potential to build high-speed tramways [light rail transit systems—modern trolleycars—in U.S. transit jargon] similar to the $952 million system planned for New Delhi."

Goods and Services

Best U.S. export prospects include engineering and construction management services, aviation navigation aids, communications equipment, airport ground services equipment, locomotives for mainline railroads and urban/suburban transportation.

Aerospace

India's aviation sector—a market of $1.2 billion in 1993—is soaring. It is expected to grow 25 percent annually during 1993-95. In March 1994, the government rescinded the Air Corporation Act, which nationalized the airline industry. Since then, private carriers have captured 25 percent of the domestic market. With the increase in traffic, air traffic control systems will be upgraded and expanded to include new instrument landing systems, primary radar and navigation aids. India's two main air carriers, government-owned Indian Airlines and Air India, have announced plans to substantially expand their aircraft fleets, although current difficulties will likely delay the plans. Indian Airlines operates 54 aircraft and plans to buy another 53 planes by 2000. Air India, the country's flagship airline and its only international carrier with 26 planes, plans to purchase 56 aircraft by 2000.

Environmental Technology

India's air and water pollution problems are quickly reaching major proportions. An estimated 30 percent of the population has no access to safe drinking water, and 80 percent (700 million people) do not have proper sanitation facilities. Municipal discharges are the primary contributors of India's water pollutants, but industrial pollutants now contribute one-third of the total. Air pollution is primarily caused by industry, power plants using low-quality coal and vehicles in urban areas. India is presently the second-fastest growing source of greenhouse emissions in the world. The transportation sector is the fastest growing cause of air pollution in the nation, contributing up to 70 percent of the air pollution in urban areas. Of the 10 cities in the world suffering from the highest levels of air pollution, three are in India: Bombay, Calcutta and New Delhi.

The health hazards from environmental degradation are a growing public concern. Pressure will mount on the government to improve the enforcement and implementation of laws, and on companies to use pollution-control equipment and technologies.

The government, recognizing the problem of fly ash from low-quality coal, has made a commitment to increase fly-ash utilization to 50 percent by 2001, by establishing a program of investment incentives and requiring coal users to develop action plans to eliminate ash dumping.

H.J. Heinz's Anticipation

H.J. Heinz & Company's entry into the Indian food business is another success story. The firm applied for a 100 percent equity venture and then set about acquiring an existing food company. Glaxo, the British drug company, was planning to sell its food line and concentrate on its core business in India.

Heinz' decision to buy Glaxo's entire food business gave it an immediate entry into the Indian market, with factories and a well set distribution network. Now Heinz plans to slowly launch several of its products onto the market through this distribution network.

Heinz' strategy of purchasing an existing firm, while expensive, should be considered as a way of reducing the bureaucracy and time delays associated with setting up a new unit.

The deal was finalized only last year, and several new products are expected to be introduced in the next few.

Consumer Goods

Perhaps 75 million Indians can be considered "upper middle class," with household incomes above $1,400 per annum (the equivalent of $4,600 in the U.S.). Another 145 million people could be called "lower middle class," with annual incomes of $700-$1,400 ($2,300-$4,620 in the U.S.). This rapidly growing population, though poor by U.S. standards, is still a huge potential brand name market for U.S. firms.

Most U.S.-made consumer goods cannot be found in the Indian marketplace as a result of high tariffs and nontariff barriers, although significant amounts of brand name goods are brought in by travellers and transshipment/smuggling from the Persian Gulf. Still, official restrictions limit competition for India's consumer goods producers. That means high prices, poor quality and limited selection. However, competing goods are becoming more available because of domestic production by foreign multinationals and limited increases in imports.

The government plans to eliminate the de facto ban on consumer goods imports and reduce maximum customs duties, already cut to 50 percent for most products. So far, U.S. companies interested in marketing consumer goods in India have found it more practical to do so through investments which, in many instances, the Indian government has approved. Multinational firms include Pepsico, Coca-Cola, Kelloggs, McDonald's, General Electric, Whirlpool, RJR, Proctor and Gamble, Levi Strauss and W.D. Lee. The investment is often in joint ventures with Indian firms. European and Japanese multinationals have also invested in consumer goods production.

As trade barriers fall and tariffs come down over the longer term, significant opportunities will emerge in the consumer goods market. Several sectors show promise: recreational equipment; household consumer durables; books and printed materials; jewelry and jeweler's materials; toys and games; processed foods; and alcoholic beverages.

U.S. firms offering high-quality merchandise, with unique features or technology, especially products with well-known and highly regarded brand names, will fare best in the Indian market. Competing on the basis of price alone is difficult because of all the lower-cost products in India and other East and South Asian countries.

Food Processing and Packaging

India is one of the world's largest agricultural producers, but as little as 10 percent of this output is processed. Vast quantities spoil before reaching the consumer. Nevertheless, India is rapidly becoming one of the world's most promising markets for food processing and packaging machinery, equipment and services. Increasing disposable income and exposure to international food choices are causing food tastes to change. In addition, more homemakers working outside the home with less time for meal preparation are attracted to processed and convenience foods. The volume of processed foods is expected to increase from 10 percent of the food market (about $1.9 billion in 1992) to an estimated 25 percent by 1997.

The market for machinery and equipment is turning up because of India's natural resources and government encouragement. In 1993, the combined market for meat and poultry machinery was estimated at $339 million; more than 80 percent was imported. The demand for food processing and packaging machinery is projected to grow about 20 percent annually over the next few years.

U.S.-built machinery enjoys an excellent reputation for quality and performance but suffers from perceptions of high cost. Imports of food processing machinery are supplied mainly by European and American companies. Competitive financing terms and service to smaller customers are important bargaining tools.

A number of U.S. companies, including Kelloggs, Dole Fruits, Coca Cola and Pepsico, have already established Indian operations. Their presence gives U.S. equipment suppliers an entre into the market.

Healthcare Technology

India's health sector accounts for 6 percent of GDP, which is extremely high for a developing country. The primary responsibility for administering public health in India rests with the state governments; the central government sets goals and standards and provides some funding. The latter's "Health for All" plan, calling for full medical care for the whole population by 2000, is an ambitious plan which will require the Ministry of Health and Family Welfare to boost spending in order to reach its goal of improving healthcare facilities and services. The major market for high-end U.S. medical equipment is likely to be the private sector hospitals and teaching hospitals in major cities like Bombay.

Hospitals are the largest end-users of medical device systems. The market for medical devices reached $500 million in 1993 and an estimated $650 million in 1994. Demand is forecast to grow at an average annual rate of 15 to 20 percent through 1997. U.S. exports of medical devices to India were estimated at $48 million in 1994 and are forecast to increase 13 percent, to $54 million, in 1995. U.S. pharmaceutical exports are expected to grow from $157 million in 1994 to $181 million in 1995.

> **Prospects in this sector are promising because healthcare is a centerpiece of social policy and accounts for 6 percent of GDP — high for a developing country.**

During the next three years, India's ultrasonic scanning subsector will grow at an annual rate of over 20 percent, while medical imaging equipment is forecast to grow 10 percent annually. Licensing arrangements offer an attractive vehicle for entering this market.

The prospects in this sector are promising because healthcare is a centerpiece of India's social policy. Economic reforms have created a conducive investment climate for private companies to establish specialty hospitals with an equity ownership of 74 percent. In addition, the government encourages the free flow of foreign technology, management and international finance to stimulate growth, which will lead to a more internationally competitive domestic healthcare industry.

Some major projects ahead are: the All India Institute of Medical Sciences, New Delhi (expansion—estimated cost $17 million); GIL Hospital, Vadodara, Gujarat (a 300-bed hospital—estimated cost

High interest rates and spreads, inefficient domestic firms and the lack of consumer financing are attracting U.S. financial firms to India.

$9.6 million); Somaiya Hospital, Bombay (a 700-bed hospital—estimated cost $40 million); and Wockhardt Pharmaceutical (new hospital—estimated cost $14 million).

Quality consciousness is increasing in both the Indian public and private sectors. U.S. firms producing high-quality goods have excellent potential in the Indian market. The best medical devices and pharmaceutical prospects are: surgical equipment and supplies ($120 million annual market); diagnostic equipment ($190 million); imaging products and equipment ($120 million); and electronic treatment devices ($90 million). The fastest-growing biotechnology sectors are hybrid seeds, tissue culture, waste management, bio-fertilizers and genetic engineering.

Financial Services

India's large financial sector offers a variety of services through the banking system, securities markets, insurance providers and other financial institutions. In IFY 1991/92, Indian authorities initiated a reform program to improve the competitiveness, operational efficiency and transparency of financial institutions. These reforms are likely to provide greater opportunities for U.S. financial firms. High interest rates and spreads, inefficient domestic firms and the lack of consumer financing are attracting major American financial companies to India.

Trends in Selected Stock Market Indicators

	Index	1992 April	1992 December	1993 April	1993 December	1994 April	1994 December
	SENSEX	4131.01	2535.64	2205.37	3301.85	3824.75	3949.78
	National Index	1850.94	1162.92	993.63	1589.25	1855.81	1876.13
Price/Earnings Ratio	**SENSEX**	52.60	31.35	27.19	40.02	46.43	34.50
	National Index	49.13	29.37	4.98	40.28	46.45	38.58
	Average Daily Turnover	672	187	173	438	195	423
	Market Capitalization	278,000	205,000	175,093	305,000	364,868	400,000

Source: Economic Survey 1993-94 and 1994-95, Government of India   *SENSEX = Sensitivity Index of Share Prices*
Monthly average relating to 30 scrips of Bombay Stock Exchange SENSEX.   *Monthly average relating to 100 scrips of Bombay Stock Exchange National Index*
Rs crore. Crore = 10 million

Banking

The commercial banking system includes nationalized and foreign banks. Commercial banks are permitted to provide capital market advisory services through merchant banking subsidiaries. The government has introduced limited liberalization measures into the banking sector. As of March 1994, the Reserve Bank of India (RBI)—the central bank—had approved nine applications for new private sector banks. The government also allows state-owned banks to approach the capital market to sell equity to the public. State ownership in the largest bank in the country has been diluted without a significant change in management. Other nationalized banks are expected to reduce their share of public ownership over the next few years.

Despite these market-oriented reforms, the government remains the dominant force in the banking system. State-owned banks account for about 88 percent of deposits and loans. Deposit and lending rates are regulated, and bank reserve requirements remain quite high. Moreover, a significant percentage of lending must be for government-selected priority sectors.

The more than 25 foreign banks with 150 branches which operate in India account for 7 percent of total banking assets. Citibank, Bank of America and American Express Bank hold nearly 40 percent of the total deposits of foreign banks. Foreign banks enjoy a good reputation for customer satisfaction and have continued to increase their business, despite the limited number of branches.

Capital Markets

Indian capital markets have only recently become significant in size. Twenty-three stock exchanges serve an estimated 25 million investors. Bombay, Calcutta, Madras, New Delhi and Ahmedabad have the largest stock exchanges. There is the Over-the-Counter Exchange of India (OTCEI) for small investors and companies. The stock exchanges also are important sources of financing for Indian companies. The SEBI (Securities and Exchange Board of India) is responsible for investor protection and the development and regulation of Indian capital markets. Indian stock markets remain thinly capitalized and volatile and need reforms in accounting and disclosure regulations. The sizable influx of funds from U.S. mutual funds into India has raised P/E ratios, which are considerably above U.S. levels.

A number of U.S. financial institutions participate in Indian capital markets in various capacities. U.S. and other foreign financial institutions have established joint ventures with their Indian counterparts for erchant/ investment banking, asset management and consumer finance activities. U.S. financial firms have been active in underwriting offshore issues by Indian companies and in managing and marketing mutual funds. The U.S. also accounts for the largest number of foreign institutional investors (FIIs), both active and registered with the SEBI.

While significant progress has been made, the most difficult tasks remain: bureaucratic interference continues to pervade the Indian business climate.

Insurance

India is one of the world's largest untapped markets for U.S. insurance providers. Government proposals to liberalize the insurance sector may soon allow access to a market that is currently reserved for public sector companies (except cargo insurance and reinsurance). Reforms are expected to allow private insurance companies, including those with limited foreign ownership, to be established and operate in competition with existing public sector insurers (who, themselves, would be partially privatized). The policy changes are expected to limit foreign insurance providers to minority ownership. AIG is forming a joint venture in India as is New York Life, but the government monopoly still prevails.

MARKET ACCESS

While significant progress has been made, many difficult tasks remain. Bureaucratic interference continues to pervade the Indian business climate. The easing of government import licensing requirements and investment approval procedures has not eliminated barriers to routine business activity. Unresolved regulatory and operational issues continue to block project implementation. Market liberalization in several sectors, such as telecommunications, has been slowed by political challenges and bureaucratic infighting. The privatization process is slow. Public enterprises remain inefficient because they do not face sufficient competition, receive government assistance and cannot lay off redundant workers. Bureaucratic and labor pressure is strong to keep workers employed while the work force is growing by about six million annually.

Tariffs and Import Barriers

Indian tariffs remain high, especially for goods that can be produced domestically. India has selectively lowered tariffs on some capital goods and semi-manufactured inputs to help Indian manufacturers. The IFY 1995/96 budget lowered the maximum peak tariff from 60 percent to 50 percent. However, many effective duty rates exceed 100 percent.

India's once-comprehensive import licensing regime has been liberalized but still places severe limits on a range of U.S goods which would be competitive in a more open trading environment. In the IFY 1995/96 budget, imports of consumer goods were liberalized to some extent, although many products continue to be effectively banned. Some commodity imports must be channeled ("canalized") through public sector companies, although many canalized goods have been decontrolled recently. The main canalized items are petroleum products, bulk agricultural products such as grains and vegetables, oils and some pharmaceuticals.

Government Procurement Practices

Foreign-sourced procurement for Indian government major projects is derived through internationally advertised tenders. These bid invitations may be either open to suppliers worldwide or limited to select suppliers. Limited tenders are often preceded by a call for bid prequalifications, at which time the tendering organization gathers basic information on the capabilities and prior experience of prospective bidders to assess their technical and financial reliability.

Indian procurement authorities may seek assurances from vendors that they are willing to transfer technology and know-how to India. The policy reflects the government's technology-transfer priorities and attitude that foreign firms make a long-term business commitment to India. Technology-transfer arrangements are subject to economic and financial viability, as well as the availability of an acceptable partner.

India's procurement practices are cumbersome and nontransparent. In the awarding of contracts, government policy favors Indian over foreign suppliers. India is not a signatory to the General Agreement on Tariffs and Trade (GATT) government procurement code, which requires open access to foreign firms on government contracts. When selling to the government, patience, persistence and, in most cases, the assistance of an Indian agent or partner are necessary.

Openness to Foreign Investment

Until recently, external aid and commercial borrowing were India's two main sources of external finance; foreign direct investment played a marginal role. Prior to 1991, foreign firms were allowed to invest only if they met certain requirements, such as contributing technology unavailable in India or promoting exports. Many aspects of production and marketing were tightly controlled — for example, large companies could not increase production or change their product mix without government permission. Some of the foreign companies that came to India eventually abandoned their projects.

Ghosts from the Past

"We are still haunted by the ghost of the East India Company. It is an unfortunate mindset."

— P. Chidambaram,
Minister of Commerce

The British East India Company arrived in the 17th century and laid the foundation for the British Raj. Both that colonial experience and hostility to multinational corporations continue to animate some popular feelings about foreign participation in India's economy. In a recent survey, American executives viewed the Indian bureaucracy as the major obstacle to success in this market. Some with a passion for history will argue that the Indian bureaucracy has picked up its character by imitating the worst traits of both the Moghul rulers and the British Raj. The "license Raj" kept the heavy hand of the government on all commercial activities. As a result, a cynical attitude among Indian corporate executives sometimes developed.

However, the end of the Cold War and the triumph of market economies have given both the U.S. and India a new opportunity to overcome past differences, while economic liberalization has granted freer rein to market forces and generated more positive attitudes toward foreign investors who bring technologies and management skills that contribute to India's economic development and modernization.

The reform program changed these policies, and India now actively seeks foreign investment, although public attitudes toward foreign investment remain ambivalent. Many companies, recognizing the country's potential, are already established in India. The $5.1 billion in foreign investment proposals approved by the government between 1991 and March 1994 were more than the entire amount of foreign investment in India during the 1980s. More than 90 percent of foreign investment is centered in priority industries: power, oil, food processing, chemicals, electrical and electronics equipment, telecommunications, transportation, industrial machinery and tourism.

Despite the rapid expansion of U.S. investment flows, India's investment regime remains cumbersome and overly regulated. Screening of proposed investments, political interference and bureaucratic indecision remain problems. Equity and sectoral limitations, ceilings on royalties and foreign exchange earnings requirements are barriers to some potential investors.

Foreign Investment Approvals—by Country (million U.S. $)

Country	1993	1994	Percent Change
U.S.	1,103.21	1,111.56	0.8
U.K.	198.45	414.01	108.6
Germany	56.06	181.44	223.6
Mauritius	39.59	170.41	330.4
Japan	82.04	127.76	55.7
Italy	37.40	124.58	233.1
Australia	9.42	123.79	1214.1
Singapore	21.27	84.61	297.8
Netherlands	102.50	65.95	-35.7
Hong Kong	28.03	52.51	87.4

Special Considerations

Intellectual Property Rights

Recent legislative and enforcement initiatives have enhanced protection of intellectual property rights (IPR), but problems persist. U.S. government and industry in recent years have made this an important issue in the bilateral relationship. India is on the U.S. Trade Representative's Special 301 "priority watch list."

While Indian statutes give higher priority to the rights of the state than the individual property holder, Indian courts (based on British common law) consistently uphold strong IPR protection. India is not a member of the Paris Convention for the Protection of Industrial Property, nor does it have a bilateral patent agreement with the U.S.

India has agreed to adhere to the Trade Related Intellectual Property Rights (TRIPS) agreement of the Uruguay Round. However, it has signalled its intent to take the 10-year transition period permitted for least-developed countries to implement product patent protection for pharmaceuticals and agrichemicals. As directed under TRIPS, India has established a "mailbox"—by administrative ordinance on December 31, 1994—to preserve patent status until patent protection is provided. The amendments to the copyright law of May 1994 became effective on May 10, 1995, and the expected passage of trademark amendments in 1995 would bring the rest of India's IPR legal regime largely into conformity with the TRIPS agreement.

THE COMPETITION

While the U.S. is India's largest trade and investment partner, U.S. firms face growing international competition in all sectors of the Indian market. Principal trade competitors are Germany, Japan, the United Kingdom and some other members of the Organization for Economic Cooperation and Development (OECD). The European Union nations pose the main challenge to U.S. trade. They furnish roughly 30 percent of India's imports, although no one country exceeds 8.4 percent. In sectors of key importance to U.S. firms (aerospace, power, telecommunications), the Europeans are particularly competitive, aided by official financial support and not constrained by the U.S. Foreign Corrupt Practices Act.

India's Regional Trade Group

The South Asian Association for Regional Cooperation (SAARC) was formed in 1985 to focus on non-contentious issues such as terrorism, narcotics, telecommunications, tourism, rural development and other regional issues. SAARC does not aim at political coordination or economic integration. In April 1993, the members agreed to establish a South Asia Preferential Trade Agreement (SAPTA). During the May 1995 summit, SAARC agreed to inaugurate SAPTA on November 8, 1995.

Although a significant step for regional trade, the tariff reductions apply to only 222 items. The members of SAARC include India, Pakistan, Sri Lanka, Maldives, Bangladesh and Bhutan. The summit also resulted in measures for encouraging regional trade and development, including the creation of a South Asian Free Trade Area, which "cannot be achieved overnight." South Asia accounts for less than 1 percent of global trade, less than 5 percent of India's total exports and under 3 percent of India's total imports.

United Kingdom

The United Kingdom benefits from historic ties with India's trading and manufacturing sectors, backed by longstanding cultural and educational links. Britain pledged $360 million in aid to India in 1993. These funds are devoted principally to power projects, environmental programs and structural adjustment programs. U.K. commercial programs have benefited from regular high-level government visits. In January 1993, Prime Minister Major led a delegation of 17 business executives to India to launch the Indo-British Partnership Initiative. In November 1993, British Foreign Secretary Hurd traveled to India to witness the signing of three power project agreements worth $750 million.

Germany

The German government has been increasingly visible in promoting its commercial interests. When Chancellor Kohl visited India in February 1993, accompanied by 15 prominent German business officials, the two leaders agreed to significantly upgrade trade and investment consultations. German support of commercial programs is channeled primarily though the Indo-German Chamber of Commerce, the largest bilateral chamber in India, with over 5,000 members.

Many executives in India have a global perspective. The government's reform policies were partially the result of lobbying efforts by India's own businesses, which wanted greater autonomy in business and investment decisions.

Japan

Japan's presence in India is relatively modest; its share of imports typically ranges between 6 and 8 percent. Japanese investors, more than others, have been deterred by India's difficult and bureaucratic business climate and the lack of modern infrastructure. During August 1991-April 1993, approved Japanese investment was only 25 percent that of the U.S. However, substantial boosts in Japanese aid levels and heightened official contacts on commercial issues appear to signal a more aggressive Japanese strategy.

Japan will continue to dominate the Indian auto market through a single joint venture between Suzuki and the Indian firm Maruti Udyog. From an initial investment in 1982, Maruti-Suzuki now sells about 75 percent of all cars bought in India. This solid position demonstrates that there are no fundamental reasons why Japan should not become a force in other sectors of the Indian economy.

East Asia

The market penetration of South Korea, Taiwan, Hong Kong and Singapore is modest (6 percent import share in 1992-93) but growing. The South Koreans in particular are making their presence felt in the petroleum sector and in construction. Singapore and Hong Kong are players in the telecommunications sector, particularly paging and cellular services. A delegation of high-level Singaporean business executives visited India in February 1993, followed by the establishment of the Singapore-Indian Chamber of Commerce to promote investment in India.

Domestic Indian Firms

India's economic reforms are a double-edged sword for its private sector. With the elimination of many controls and licensing procedures, Indian private firms have been allowed to expand into new product lines and areas previously reserved for nationalized industries. On the other hand, many Indian companies now must compete with more efficient foreign firms. Consequently, some Indian businesses have argued for time to gear up to meet this competition. Others aggressively seek joint ventures to acquire the technological, financial and marketing edge required to survive in a changing business environment.

The Indian business community is strong and diverse; many executives have a global perspective. The government's reform policies were partially the result of lobbying efforts by India's own businesses, which wanted greater autonomy in business and investment decisions. The major business houses are large and powerful dynasties of family-owned businesses, including Tata, Birla, Ambani, Goenka and Modi. These companies have interests ranging from petrochemicals and power generation to automobiles and electronics. All have formed collaborations with American companies, including some very high-profile joint ventures.

Business organizations and both governments are hoping to increase the involvement of small and medium-sized companies in commerce between the two countries. Given the challenging and increasingly competitive nature of the Indian business climate, the best advice that can be given to most American companies is "pick the right partner." U.S. companies looking for agents, distributors or strategic alliances should not restrict themselves to the major Indian business houses. In Indias's new market-oriented business climate, many well-established medium-sized and small Indian companies are showing dynamic growth. Many of them have impressive technological and management expertise familiar to U.S. firms since they are often run by Indians educated in the U.S. In many sectors, Indian enterprises offer U.S. firms highly skilled professionals, well-trained technicians and deep knowledge and experience in the market.

— *Contributors: Kathleen Keim, John McPhee, Gary Bouck, Jacqueline Rhodes, Art Stern*

South Korea:

Population
44.5 Million

Population Growth Rate
0.9%

Gross Domestic Product
US$ 360 Billion

GDP Growth Rate
8.4%

GDP Per Capita
US$ 8,530

Inflation Rate
6.3%

Industrial Production, % Change
11.1%

1994. Source: IMF International Financial
Statistics Yearbook

South Korea presents a cultural and commercial climate rooted in self-reliance, national pride and the power of its industrial giants. Its unique historic experience of being invaded by virtually all of its neighbors over the past several centuries has contributed to these characteristics. Over the last four decades, Korea has undergone a rapid industrialization based on the manufacture of exports; it now seeks to move to the next level of industrialization through development of its own technology.

South Korea's GDP of roughly $360 billion accounts for approximately 7 percent of total GDP for the Asia-Pacific region. Moreover, its imports of goods and services are projected to grow about 8 percent annually through the year 2000.

Currently, an ambitious transportation infrastructure development program is being implemented that includes major high-speed rail and transit programs, airport development and highway construction. At the same time, South Korea is trying to secure its competitive capabilities in science and technology by launching the Highly Advanced Nation (HAN) Project. The HAN Project is aimed at obtaining core technologies in the strategic areas where South Korea has the capacity to compete with more advanced countries. It will, in many cases, be looking for help from foreign companies and universities in joint projects along these lines.

Still, there is no doubt that parts of the government and media retain strong anti-import sentiments which can significantly impact U.S. exports and sales of consumer, manufactured and agricultural goods. Domestic industry also often puts pressure on the government to impose barriers against foreign companies.

Not so surprising then is the fact that the ratio of foreign investment to South Korea's GNP causes it to be ranked only ninth among Asian economies, behind some of its less developed neighbors. Thirty-one U.S. firms disinvested from South Korea in 1993, though the U.S. is still the country's largest foreign investor, with $3.4 billion invested at year-end 1993, primarily in manufacturing, electronics and banking. New U.S. investment in Korea in 1994 dropped nearly 10 percent to $311 million (according to Korean data).

This nation of 44 million has moved from a stage where its advantage lay in cheap manual labor to one where its advantage now lies in relatively low-cost (but rising) skilled labor and line management. Its exports are no longer dominated by textiles, clothing and footwear, but by automobiles, ships, semiconductors and consumer electronics.

The Next Level

A New Approach

South Korea's rapid advancement has turned the country into one of the most economically powerful in the world. It structured its economic development after the Korean War on the Japanese model: large industrial conglomerates (chaebol, in Korean) focused on exports, with economic and industrial policy set by the government. The chaebol, which receive preferential government loans and other concessions, dominate the economy. This hinders the development of smaller firms, which could react more quickly to market developments but have a difficult time raising capital.

The government's economic policies were oriented toward promoting rapid industrial development, encouraging exports and, in the past, managing its heavy debt burden. Trade policies were designed to facilitate only those imports which fuel its export industries—raw materials, capital equipment, or products embodying significant new technology which cannot be produced in South Korea—and to discourage imports of consumer goods or products which compete with domestic interests.

As a result of these policies, the composition of the economy has changed markedly in the past 30 years. In 1962, for example, the agricultural sector accounted for more than a third of GNP; today, it accounts for less than 8 percent. Conversely, the manufacturing sector's share in GNP grew from about 15 percent to over 27 percent during the same period. Services now account for about 39 percent of total output. Major industrial products include steel, automobiles, petrochemicals, industrial machinery, electronics, ships, textiles, footwear, cement, processed foods, chemical fertilizers, ceramics and glass. These industries also account for the country's principal exports.

Wage levels have risen rapidly over the last decade, heightening international competition for South Korea's labor-intensive industries such as textiles and footwear. A number of factories in such sectors have migrated offshore to lower-wage countries in the region. In a major effort to redefine its economy for the future, the government is placing greater emphasis on high technology industries such as semiconductors and seeks to encourage the growth of innovative small and medium-sized businesses.

South Korea's rapid advancement has turned this nation of 44 million into one of the most economically powerful in the world.

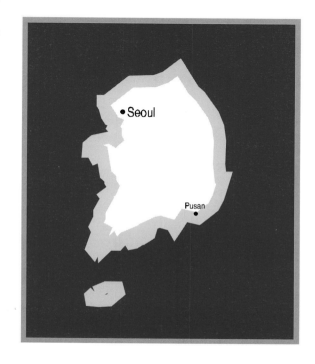

President Kim Young-Sam sees attracting foreign investment and technology as an important means of achieving his goals. His five-year economic plan (1993-97) aims to reduce the government's role in the economy by eliminating "unnecessary" regulations and opening protected industries to foreign competition. The program also includes financial market reforms intended to make capital more affordable for small and medium-sized firms.

Real GDP Growth through 2010 (percent)

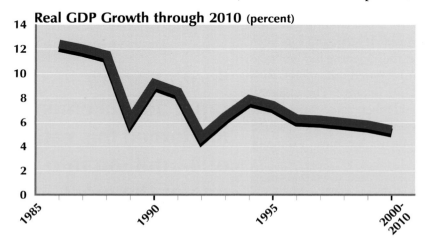

Source: Historic; IMF International Financial Statistics Yearbook, 1994. 1995-2010; DRI/McGraw-Hill.

And the South Korean government is encouraging increased research and development spending, which, at 1.5 percent of GNP, is far below the 4 percent average of most developed countries.

Even so, South Korea's economy has averaged 8.7 percent growth per year over the past two decades. GDP growth was 8.4 percent in 1994, up from 5.8 percent in 1993. The current expansion is investment-led, as the large conglomerates implement ambitious plans to modernize and expand facilities. Consumption spending, which accounts for over half of total GDP, is growing along with optimism about the economy. Recovery in South Korea's export markets assisted as well: exports, aided by the strength of the yen, grew by 15 percent in 1994, ahead of the 7.7 percent rate of 1993. Imports, however, increased more rapidly, so that South Korea's global trade deficit expanded to $3.1 billion.

The Nature of U.S.-Korea Trade

U.S. exports to South Korea are primarily in the area of machinery and transportation equipment — 49 percent in 1994, compared to 36 percent in 1985. The largest items in this category were electronic components ($1.5 billion), aircraft ($1.0 billion), industrial machinery ($577 million), computers ($528 million) and telecommunications equipment ($469 million).

U.S. imports from South Korea are also dominated by the machinery and transport equipment sectors — 60 percent in 1994, compared to only 29 percent in 1985. The largest import items include electronic components ($3.9 billion), computers and parts ($2.5 billion) and automobiles ($1.5 billion).

The U.S. share of both South Korea's imports and exports has lately been shrinking. Our share of South Korea's import market has fallen steadily from its 26 percent peak in 1989 to 22.4 percent in 1992, 21.4 percent in 1993, and 21.1 percent in 1994. Similarly, the U.S. accounted for a third of South Korea's exports in 1989, with this figure steadily decreasing over the past three years from 23.6 percent in 1992, to 22.0 percent in 1993, to 21.4 percent in 1994, with 21.4 percent expected in 1995.

Parts of the government and media retain strong anti-import sentiments which can significantly impact U.S. exports.

BIG EMERGING SECTORS

In the summer of 1994, the National Assembly passed a major new act influencing the manner in which South Korea will in the future undertake its infrastructure development program (Social Overhead Capital or SOC). The new act outlines a structure for the introduction of private capital, from both domestic and foreign sources, for financing these huge projects. It also authorizes the development of public projects by private investors on a concession finance or build-operate-transfer (BOT) basis.

South Korean firms will be seeking strategic alliances with U.S. and other foreign engineering firms to bid on these projects. Total planned expenditures for the next 7-10 years exceeds $140 billion—one of the most ambitious plans in East Asia if implemented as planned.

Of these projects, the sectors holding the most promise for U.S. businesses include energy, telecommunications, environmental technology and transportation.

The South Korean government has traditionally used five-year development plans for guiding its economic expansion program. Under the current five-year plan, the government has identified major infrastructure needs in the following sectors: **(1)** electric power plants; **(2)** new international airports; **(3)** high-speed train; **(4)** regional airport upgrades; **(5)** express highway expansion; **(6)** seaport expansion; **(7)** information superhighway; and **(8)** light electric railway expansion.

Energy

South Korea is struggling to maintain its production of electricity at the levels needed to meet growing demand. Between 1995 and 2001, the South Korean government plans to construct 39 electric power plants ranging in capacity from one to 1,000 megawatts. These will include small hydroelectric and coal-burning power plants, nuclear power plants, solid waste incineration power plants, as well as oil and gas pipelines. This will effectively double South Korea's power generation capacity.

The Korea Electric Power Corporation (KEPCO)—a government-owned company which is the country's primary power generator and sole owner of the nation's power-distribution grid—will build 16 coal-burning facilities: two 500MW plants using domestic anthracite and 14 500MW plants using imported coal. Eight nuclear plants are under construction and six additional ones are in the planning process for the next 10 years. In addition, the South Korean government intends to build 12 liquified natural gas (LNG) plants, 19 hydroelectric plants and one combined-cycle plant. The KEPCO plan requires financing of $3-4 billion per year, and

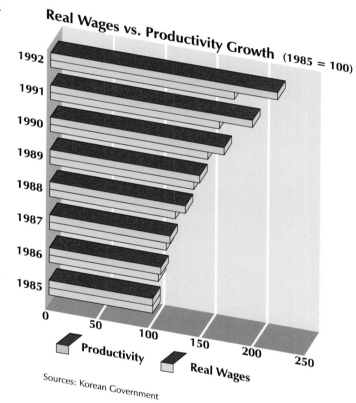

Real Wages vs. Productivity Growth (1985 = 100)

Sources: Korean Government

The Four C's

Companies should know that success in South Korea is eminently achievable. However, as Teledyne, a high technology niche manufacturer, has found, such success is inevitably a function of the 4 C's:

- **Constancy:** The same in-country team has been in place for two decades.

- **Commitment:** Fidelity to obligations and adherence to the sanctity of contracts.

- **Communications:** Both electronic and personal communications are exercised regularly to emphasize the company's dedication to a long-term relationship and partnership with customers and sales representatives.

- **Contacts**: The pool of governmental, industrial and political contacts is maintained, nurtured and replenished at all levels of managment and society.

although much of the equipment is locally manufactured, at least 10-20 percent is from outside sources. Additional demands on KEPCO for the proposed construction of North Korean nuclear plants will further stretch the finances and technical resources available. Several of these projects will, consequently, involve private capital.

Nuclear Power
South Korea currently has 10 operating nuclear power plants which supply 29 percent of the electricity generated in the country. Westinghouse (U.S.) built units 1, 2, 3, 4, 6 and 7. ACEL (Canada) won unit 5, and Framatome (France), units 8 and 9. The American consortium of Sargent & Lundy (design), Asea Brown Boveri-Combustion Engineering (nuclear island), and General Electric (turbine generators) won the contract for units 10 and 11 (the latter should be completed in 1996).ABB-CE and GE were recently awarded Yonggwang units 5 and 6.

Thermal Power
In 1994, Westinghouse signed a contract with KEPCO valued at $250 million for two-combined cycle plants to be built in Ulsan. General Electric was chosen to supply the turbine generators, worth $400 million, for the combined-cycle power station at Seo-Inchon.

Hydroelectric Power
Between 1995 and 1999, South Korea will spend $1.6 billion on five large reservoir restoration projects involving the construction of new or expanded multipurpose dams for power generation, water supply and flood control. While South Korean builders are likely to handle all dam construction, a French manufacturer is likely to supply about 80% of the equipment, including generators, for the hydroelectric facilities.

Oil and Gas
While the South Korean oil and gas sector remains highly regulated and largely closed to foreign investors, the Ministry of Trade, Industry and Energy (MOTIE) has started developing a hydrocarbons liberalization plan. In reaction to a report issued by the International Energy Agency which concluded that extreme oil and gas regulations may be delaying development, MOTIE's Oil and Gas Bureau began discussing a plan that would open up the sector in

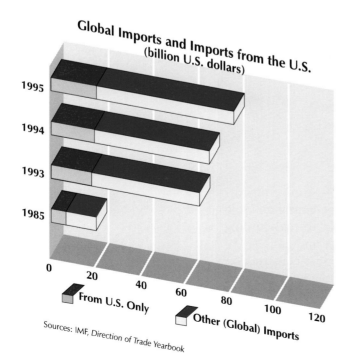

Global Imports and Imports from the U.S. (billion U.S. dollars)

Sources: IMF, Direction of Trade Yearbook

several ways: **(1)** domestic oil and gas prices will be freed; **(2)** restrictions will be removed from imports and exports of oil and oil-related products; **(3)** restrictions on investment in production, refining and distribution will be reduced; **(4)** restrictions on foreign direct investment will be reduced; and **(5)** government regulation will only be permitted in order to police cartels and manage emergency energy supplies.

While the plan is ambitious and would generate substantial interest and opportunities for U.S. firms, previous efforts to liberalize have proceeded very slowly and bogged down. The uncertain time frame of this MOTIE proposal warrants caution.

Like many other developed countries in the Pacific Rim, South Korea is a very promising market for sales of LNG. Major LNG projects, including the massive Exxon project near Natuna Island in Indonesia and the proposed TAGS project in Alaska, are based on hopes of securing long-term guaranteed LNG contracts with South Korea and other Pacific nations.

Private Power Development

In 1993, the government announced plans to open some aspects of power production to the private sector. These areas are limited to production of electricity by coal and LNG. Tenders for construction of private power plants are scheduled to be issued in 1995. Foreign investors would be permitted to hold up to 50 percent equity in such private power projects. Plans were also announced for allowing private companies to supply LNG (currently a public monopoly) and for allowing new entrants into oil refining, currently an oligopoly. Independent power project proposals will be reviewed by MOTIE under the new Electricity Business Act procedures.

Design and Equipment

U.S. design and equipment firms have a good reputation in South Korea; South Korean engineers, especially in the nuclear sector, are very familiar with U.S. standards and procedures. The best opportunities should continue to be in nuclear power, gas turbines and advanced boilers (fluidized bed technology).

South Korean Research and Development

South Korea's total R&D expenditures still lag behind those of most developed countries; just 1/23rd that of the U.S., 1/13th that of Japan and 1/7th that of Germany. South Korea's expenditures in 1993 were approximately $7.8 billion, a 23 percent increase over 1992. The ratio of South Korea's R&D spending to GNP was 2.33 percent, up slightly from the previous year. Outlays from the public sector were $1.3 billion or 17 percent of the total and with the private companies providing the remainder. By the year 2001, South Korea hopes to be spending over 5 percent of GNP on R&D.

The South Korean Ministry of Science and Technology (MOST), responsible for most of the South Korean government's R&D budget, has stated that its core programs for 1995 will emphasize the role of technology in the "First Year of Globalization," i.e., post Uruguay Round. The plan includes four principal programs:

1) The development of an electric car, in order to combat pollution and spur the development of other automotive technologies;

2) investment of $80 million in biotechnology, a high value-added field with large growth potential;

3) $250 million to help in the development of multi-purpose satellites and a twin-engine jet plane; and

4) Studying possible areas of scientific cooperation between North and South Korea.

In 1993, the government announced plans to open some aspects of power production to the private sector. These areas are limited to production of electricity by coal, LNG and water power.

Information Technology

Telecommunications Equipment and Services

South Korea is one of the faster growing telecommunications markets in the world. Opportunities are expected to expand over the next several years for U.S. sales of communications equipment and systems as economic restructuring and deregulation in the telecommunications sector accelerate and the South Korean government loosens its monopoly control on this sector.

The government has already lifted many of the technical barriers to imports of equipment to be attached to the public telecommunications networks. Government procurement procedures and certification requirements can still pose problems, however. A second cellular telephone service provider was licensed in 1994 and is in the process of equipment procurement. South Korea's cable television industry began operating in March 1995, one month ahead of schedule. South Korea is also planning to invest approximately $50 billion to build an integrated "information superhighway" system by 2015.

Leading Sources of Imports/Destination of Exports

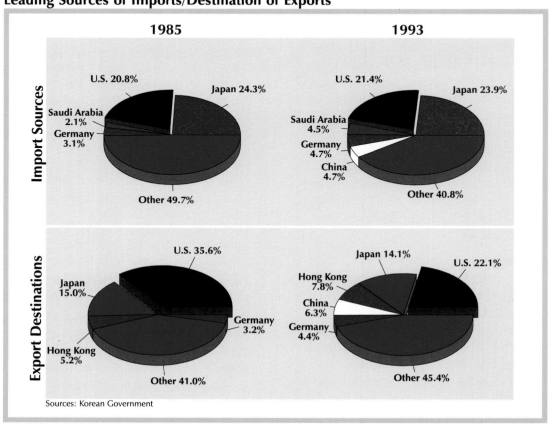

Sources: Korean Government

Local producers have captured the broad middle segment of the market for large volume, commodity-type products, while U.S. suppliers, with their reputation for high quality, maintain a strong competitive position in technologically advanced products.

The total market size in 1995 is estimated to be $3.2 billion. The most promising subsectors, by estimated value, within the telecommunications sector in 1994 were cellular telecom equipment ($118.5 million); broadcast equipment ($205.9 million); and satellite communications equipment ($81.0 million).

Environmental Technology

Forty years of industrial growth have created substantial environmental problems and, consequently, a robust market for pollution control equipment and technologies. Moreover, rising living standards and expectations are fostering a new environmental awareness within the South Korean government, the media, the population and—with a notable lack of enthusiasm—in private industry as well. Continued economic growth should create strong demand for pollution prevention and clean technologies that address waste minimization/process improvements technologies to supplement "end-of-pipe" controls.

The Organization for Economic Cooperation and Development (OECD) reports that in the next five years, the South Korean government is expected to spend $5 billion dollars on environmental improvements. Environmental equipment and services rep-

The Case of Honam Oil

Established in 1967 as one of the priority projects of South Korea's second Five-Year Economic Plan, the Honam Oil Refinery Co., Ltd. a 50/50 joint venture between a U.S. corporation, Caltex Petroleum Corp. of Dallas, Texas, and a South Korean corporation, the Lucky Goldstar Group, is one of the oldest and most successful joint venture companies in the Republic of Korea. With sales in excess of $4 billion making it the 13th largest South Korean corporation, assets in excess of $1 billion, a refinery of 380,000 BPCD, petrochemical facilities, a fleet of five large crude carriers and over 1,700 service stations, Honam Oil is a major industrial company in its own right. Its success was the result of a combination of strong South Korean government support at the outset and the continued dedicated efforts of its two shareholders over the course of almost three decades in which a number of important challenges were met and overcome. At the outset, Caltex contributed capital, technology and management skills – all of which were scarce in the 1970s. The Lucky Goldstar Group contributed knowledge of the local market, human resource management and government contacts. Honam Oil developed a corporate culture that was both separate from, but also derived from the best that each of its shareholders had to offer. The partners shared a vision of Honam Oil's future.

Over the course of its history, Honam Oil confronted two oil crises, the destruction of its records in a fire and other serious threats to its development. What has sustained the joint venture during these periods is the willingness of the partners to talk about the issues, to recognize that circumstances change and matters of importance change, to be flexible in their approach to solutions and to concentrate on the issue of competitive business tactics and strategy rather than on internal disagreements. This has required the dedication of highly skilled and adaptable people on both sides, continuously involved in the process of making the joint venture work.

The Information Superhighway

The South Korean government has formally announced its plan to build an "information superhighway" by 2015. The Prime Minister's office will oversee the $55 billion project. The first phase, 1994 to 1997, will see an initial investment of $2 billion. Phase two will be from 1998 to 2002 and will receive a $5.8 billion injection. Phase three, from 2003 to 2015, will receive the remainder. The plan envisages formation of a broadband integrated services digital network (B-ISDN) connecting public organizations, research institutes and major private business corporations under public funds, and then formation of a super-high-speed public communications network for the general public under private funds, all via a single super-high-speed fiber optic cable network.

resent a new and very rapidly growing market segment in South Korea. According to business sources and the Ministry of Environment (MOE), the market for pollution control equipment and services from 1992 ($3.3 billion) to 1995 ($5 billion expected) increased 34 percent. Both the overall market size and the share held by imports are expected to grow sharply over the next few years as industrial emission standards are tightened and the government attempts to hasten clean-up and prevention projects by applying more efficient technologies and equipment.

Air Pollution Control

South Korea's five-year plan states that the total investment needed to carry out the country's environmental cleanup is $11.4 billion. About 60 percent of that total ($6.3 billion) will be used on air pollution. Environmental research will be targeted for $333.1 million of investment.

The South Korean market for air pollution control equipment, which totalled $557 million in 1992, climbed to an estimated $910 million in 1993. It is estimated to have grown at an average annual rate of 25 percent over the following two years, to reach approximately $1.4 billion in 1995. The single most lucrative area will result from a regulatory clamp-down on sulfur dioxide. The South Korean government will also invest in air quality monitoring equipment. With a price tag of $1.4 billion, 92 air quality monitoring stations are expected to be installed by the end of 1995.

The Market for Telecom Equipment (million U.S. dollars)

	1993	1994 (est.)	1995 (est.)
Total Market Size	2,506.7	2,834.7	3,205.9
Local Production	3,001.9	3,362.2	3,765.6
Exports	1,398.0	1,565.7	1,753.6
Imports	902.8	1,038.2	1,193.9
Imports from the U.S.	424.3	498.3	585.0
US Share ROK Imports	46.9%	48.0%	49.0%
Competitors' Share:			
Japan	15.9%	N/A	N/A
Singapore	10.9%	N/A	N/A

Source: Country Commercial Guide for Korea, 1994

Water Pollution Control

The South Korean market for major water pollution control equipment grew at an annual rate of 25 percent during the past three years, and is likely to more than double from 1991 ($407 million) to 1995 ($1 billion, expected).

The 1991 MOE environmental preservation mid-term comprehensive plan focused on the construction of additional sewage and waste treatment facilities, with $2.8 billion enhancing the sewage treatment ratio from 33 percent to 65 percent in 1995. Another $103 million will be invested in the purification of water supply sources. The South Korean market for water pollution control equipment has grown rapidly over the past years, in part due to public outrage following the discovery of major leaks and dumps of toxic substances into public drinking water sources.

Waste Management

The demand for incineration equipment in South Korea is rising as municipal and industrial wastes continue to increase in large cities and industrial complexes. Incineration is the most economical method to dispose of burnable solid city waste and industrial waste. The South Korean government has an ambitious long-range plan for the construction of incineration systems for local cities and industries from 1993 through 1997. The total amount of investment designated to carry out MOE's plans for incineration from 1994 through 2001 is $10.8 billion.

Kyunggi Province, which surrounds Seoul, is planning to establish 97 waste management facilities over a seven-year period beginning in 1994. Under the plan, a total of $326 million will be invested.

In the next five years, the South Korean government is expected to spend $5 billion on environmental improvements.

The Market for Pollution Control Equipment (million U.S. dollars)

	1993	1994 (est.)	1995 (est.)
Total Market Size	712	968	1,316
Local Production	433	617	874
Exports	49	59	70
Imports	328	410	512
Imports from the U.S.	61	76	94
US Share ROK Imports	18.6%	18.5%	8%
Competitors' Share	81.4%	81.5%	92%

Source: Country Commercial Guide for Korea, 1994.

Infrastructure

South Korea is implementing an ambitious transportation infrastructure development program that includes major high-speed rail and transit programs, airport development and highway construction. However, with the exception of the New Seoul Metropolitan Airport project and other aviation upgradings, only limited opportunities for U.S. firms will be generated.

American firms have had involvement in preliminary technical phases of many South Korean projects in joint ventures with local companies. Examples include the Seoul Metro, the Kimpo and New Seoul Metropolitan Airports, and high-speed rail development.

U.S. industrial competitiveness in the avionics/navaids/communications and airport ground support equipment businesses has also served American firms well. U.S. engineers and construction managers have worldwide experience with and expertise in the design and oversight of major transportation projects.

The new international airport (new Yongjong-do airport) is located on Yongjong-do island west of Seoul near the satellite city of Inchon. It is being built on reclaimed shallow land along the lines of Japan's Kansai airport. Bechtel Corporation assisted with the initial master plan, and terminal design was by the U.S. design firm Fentress. The Korea Airport Construction Authority (KOACA) has been set up to handle contracting and procurement decisions. The cost of the initial phase of the airport, including terminal, navaid system and one runway, is estimated at $4.9 billion. The cost of the total project, including four runways, four concourses, a business center and a linking highway/train, should hit $12- 15 billion.

The Ministry of Construction and Transportation and the Korea Airport Authority (KAA) have plans to improve and modernize the existing regional airport facilities in 14 locations. Most local airports lack modern airport facilities such as air traffic control systems, instrumental landing systems and safety and security systems.

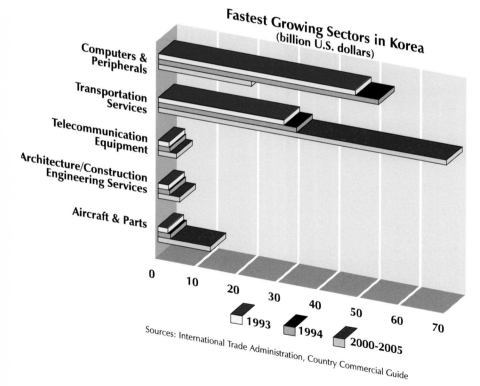

Fastest Growing Sectors in Korea
(billion U.S. dollars)

Computers & Peripherals
Transportation Services
Telecommunication Equipment
Architecture/Construction Engineering Services
Aircraft & Parts

0 10 20 30 40 50 60 70

1993 1994 2000-2005

Sources: International Trade Administration, Country Commercial Guide

The state-run Korea Highway Corporation (KHC) plans to build about $25 billion worth of new express highways. In South Korea, the majority of industrial products are shipped on highways, as rail transportation is scarce. The density of vehicle traffic on existing roads, owing to the rising affluence of South Korean consumers and the growing number of cars on the highways, makes KHC's express highway expansion program of critical importance.

In order to boost exports, South Korea plans to invest approximately $613 million in the construction of major ports like those at Pusan and Inchon, and add new ports at Asan, Kwangyang, Kunjang, Kunsan, Mokpo, Donghae and 27 other spots. South Korea also plans to establish a vessel traffic system for all these ports. In addition, South Korea will construct two inland clearance depot (ICD) terminals for the effective distribution of containers.

Research and Development

South Korea's vision for the 21st century is to join the ranks of the most advanced of the advanced countries. To do so, the country must improve its industrial development capabilities and overcome domestic and overseas hurdles that hinder social and economic progress. However, South Korea, now faced with rising labor costs, is losing its international competitiveness in its traditional light industries. Although South Korea's production and manufacturing technologies have reached nearly the level of advanced countries, key technologies in the field of heavy and high technology industries still lag behind. So South Korea is trying to secure its competitive capabilities in science and technology to move ahead in this realm.

In order to reach this goal, the South Korean Government has launched the Highly Advanced Nation (HAN) Project. With the HAN Project, South Korea is trying not to upgrade its capacity in every field of industry and technology, but rather to sustain its competitiveness and superiority in selected fields through a concentration of its limited R&D resources.

The HAN Project is a large-scale R&D project based on joint investment by the government and private sector, further supported by universities, private industry and government-supported research institutes. In areas where domestic R&D capacity is lacking, international cooperation is actively pursued.

South Korea is implementing an ambitious transportation infrastructure development program that includes major high-speed rail and transit programs, airport development and highway construction.

While South Korea's production and manufacturing technologies have reached nearly the level of advanced countries, in key heavy and high-tech industries they still lag behind.

In 1992, the starting year of the first stage of the HAN Project, total R&D investment was registered at $230 million. In 1993, a total of $309 million was invested in 448 projects, and in 1994 investment was approximately $414 million.

In these projects, foreign participants are slated to include research institutes, universities and private firms. As a condition of joint research projects, the foreign partners are expected to share R&D funding and intellectual property rights.

MARKET ACCESS

South Korea is one of the most difficult markets in Asia in which to invest and to which to export. Its policies remain structured primarily to encourage technology transfer and optimize the use of imports for export industries while discouraging "unnecessary" imports. The problems in the business climate are both systemic and sector-specific. Much of the government-to-government dialogue between the U.S. and South Korea has been aimed at removing these barriers.

Tariffs and Import Barriers

Most South Korean tariffs are assessed on an ad valorem basis. Specific rates apply to a few items, and both ad valorem and specific rates apply on a few others. The dutiable value of imported goods is the normal c.i.f. price at the time of import declaration. Tariffs are payable in won before the goods are permitted to clear customs. In January 1994, South Korea completed a five-year tariff reduction plan which reduced the average tariff rate on imports to 7.9 percent. Duties remain very high (25 percent on average), however, on a large number of high-value agricultural and fisheries products. Pursuant to its Uruguay Round commitments, on January 1, 1995, South Korea lowered duties on some agricultural products and eliminated duties on products in the paper, toys, steel, semiconductor and pharmaceutical sectors. South Korea also bound 90 percent of its tariff lines, which will curtail its ability to raise duties in the face of import surges of low-value goods (e.g., emergency tariffs). Frequently, over the past few years, the government has invoked provisions of its Customs Law to apply special tariff rates under certain adverse economic conditions.

The Han Project

The first category of the HAN Project, the "Products Technology Development Project," calls for the following: **(1)** development of new drugs and agrochemicals ('92-'97); **(2)** development of broadband integrated services and data network (B-ISDN) ('92-2001); **(3)** development of next generation vehicle technology ('92-2001); and **(4)** development of high definition television (HDTV) ('92-'94).

The "Fundamental Technology Development Project," includes: **(1)** development of ultra-large-scale integrated circuits (ULSI) (93-97); **(2)** development of advanced manufacturing systems ('92-2001); **(3)** development of new advanced materials for information, electronics and the energy industry ('92-2001); **(4)** development of environmental technology ('92-2001); **(5)** development of new functional bio-materials ('92-2001); **(6)** development of new energy technology ('92-2001); and **(7)** development of a next generation nuclear reactor ('92-2001).

Since 1977 South Korea's tax system has been composed primarily of a value-added tax (VAT) and special excise tax. At present, a single flat rate of 10 percent is applicable on all imports of items subject to the VAT (applied to the c.i.f. value plus customs duty). The combination of the VAT and tariffs on many agricultural and manufactured products (e.g., autos) are often sufficient to keep imports out of the market or greatly reduce their competitiveness. The special excise tax, ranging from 15 to 100 percent, is levied on certain luxury items (jewelry, fur, golf equipment) and durable consumer goods (air conditioners and refrigerators).

Government Procurement Practices

The Office of Supply, Republic of Korea (OSROK) supervises procurement by government agencies and most of the state-owned firms in which the government holds a majority share. (Korea Telecom and Korea Electric Power Company are the two largest entities not covered by OSROK procurement). OSROK covers roughly one-half of the total of South Korean government non-defense procurement, with total procurement levels at $816 million in 1993, $883 million in 1994 and $925 million (estimated) in 1995.

Government procurement needs are formulated by the ministries and agencies concerned, then screened by the Ministry of Trade and Industry to determine if the needs can be met by local sources. If not, the Ministry of Finance and Economy allocates the necessary foreign exchange. To encourage South Korean firms to develop the needed technologies, OSROK has been releasing three-year forecasts of major requirements in April of each year. The system thus discriminates against all foreign suppliers in cases where goods or services are available domestically. However, foreign-invested companies manufacturing in South Korea can qualify as "domestic sources."

Composition of U.S. Exports to Korea

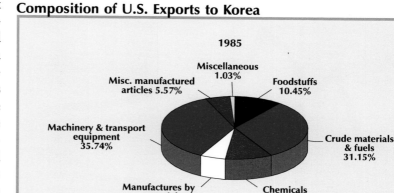

1985

Miscellaneous 1.03%
Misc. manufactured articles 5.57%
Foodstuffs 10.45%
Machinery & transport equipment 35.74%
Crude materials & fuels 31.15%
Manufactures by material 5.58%
Chemicals 10.48%

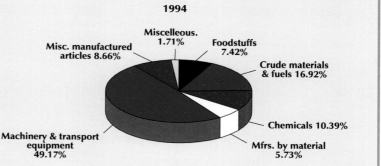

1994

Miscelleous. 1.71%
Misc. manufactured articles 8.66%
Foodstuffs 7.42%
Crude materials & fuels 16.92%
Chemicals 10.39%
Machinery & transport equipment 49.17%
Mfrs. by material 5.73%

Sources: International Trade Administration, U.S. Department of Commerce.

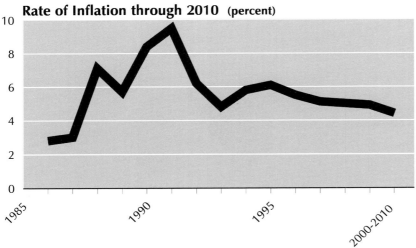

Rate of Inflation through 2010 (percent)

Source: DRI/McGraw-Hill, World Markets Executive Overview, second quarter 1995

South Korea is one of the most difficult markets in Asia in which to invest and to which to export.

Foreign purchases are financed either by government-owned foreign exchange (KFX) or by loan and credit funds from international financial organizations and foreign aid programs. The invitation to bid specifies the source of financing. Worldwide bidding under open, formal procedures is the norm, although occasionally OSROK is obligated to purchase under negotiated contract, as in the case of spare parts for specialized equipment. Specifications are drawn up by the requesting agency, which frequently consults with the South Korean representatives of foreign suppliers. So for American business to participate effectively in the South Korean government market, it helps to have a local representative.

Openness to Foreign Investment

The South Korean regulatory environment, difficult even for South Korean firms, poses a particular challenge to the foreign investor. Laws and regulations are often framed generally. The meaning of the law in practice thus depends on discretionary interpretations by working-level officials, increasing the opportunities for inconsistent application, discrimination and corruption. Working-level officials often rely on unpublished "internal" ministerial guidelines and unwritten "administrative guidance" in interpreting and administering the law.

The reforms that are part of President Kim's five-year economic plan are designed to attract foreign investment and technology. These policy changes, combined with continuing bilateral efforts to improve the business climate for foreign investors, have already eased some of the problems of doing busines, but more needs to be done. There is already some positive effect; foreign investment in South Korea is increasing, probably as a result of the government's measures to improve the investment climate.

South Korea fully recognizes rights of private ownership and has a well-developed body of laws governing the establishment of corporate and other business enterprises. Private entities may generally acquire and dispose of interests in business enterprises in South Korea. However, the Securities and Exchange Act provides that no legal person (individual or firm) may own more than 10 percent of a publicly-listed corporation.

The government announced in mid-June 1994 a new program to attract investment, which offers a one-stop approval service for prospective investors, expanded land availability for factory sites, financing incentives for high technology firms and tax holidays. This program has many promising elements, but the accelerated sectoral liberalizations promised under the program are hedged by joint venture or other stipulations. Also, under the new program foreigners will still be blocked from buying control of existing enterprises.

Special Considerations

Intellectual Property Rights

Intellectual property rights (IPR) protection has remained a top issue on the U.S. trade agenda with South Korea for nearly a decade. The U.S. government has frequently received complaints from U.S. firms about infringement of patents, copyrights, trademarks and trade secrets by South Korean firms, covering a wide range of product areas: film, video and sound recordings; compact discs; computer software; textiles; footwear; pharmaceuticals; high technology; and consumer goods. Since April 1992 South Korea has been cited on the "priority watch list" under the Special 301 provision of U.S. trade law for poor IPR enforcement and delayed improvements to several IPR laws.

In February 1993, the South Korean government began a concerted effort to improve and enforce its IPR laws to satisfy U.S. government and private sector concerns. However, U.S. firms still regularly experience IPR-related difficulties in South Korea. This is because enforcement, while responsive to U.S. complaints, is neither self-initiated

South Korea as a Regional Driver and as a Potential Gateway to China

South Korea's role in the Asian region is fairly limited. It is, however, a regional investor of growing importance. In 1981, its investment in Asia constituted 28 percent of its overseas investment outflow that year, or $9.9 million. Its investment in Latin America was slightly larger, at nearly 30 percent. By 1993, however, Asia was over 38 percent of the total of $1.3 billion, followed by North America (31 percent) and Europe (15 percent). Much of its investment in Asia is in China.

Before South Korea opened up diplomatic relations with China in 1992, South Korean leaders were fond of the idea that South Korea and the U.S. would be excellent partners to work together in business with China. And although South Korea firms were active in China well before the actual beginning of relations, South Korean policy makers also felt that American access and experience in the Chinese market and South Korea's lower level of technology, which is more suitable to Chinese needs, was a natural fit. With extensive and rapidly growing links of its own in China, South Korean officials no longer approach the U.S. with the idea that South Korea would be a good jumping off site for American businesses interested in China. Also, South Korea's nationalist penchant and lack of a more open attitude, especially in the financial services area, have made it impossible for South Korea to compete with Hong Kong, despite geographic proximity.

Some South Koreans see a future role for their country as a hub for transportation and business in Northeast Asia. This is part of the impetus behind constructing the new Yongjong-do International Airport. Also, the opening of air routes into China and across the former Soviet Union has put Europe about as close as the U.S. for business travellers. These developments are having an important, albeit gradual, effect on opening up South Korea as a more important regional center.

The legacy of the Japanese occupation and the fear of being dominated by Japanese imports led South Korea to implement the "Product Diversification" program in 1978.

nor preventive in nature. South Korea needs to accelerate and expand its efforts to heighten awareness in its business community to international norms and standards for the protection of IPR. Therefore, it cannot be emphasized too strongly that all U.S. firms should first register for IPR protection with the appropriate government agency before beginning to do business in South Korea.

Anti-Import Sentiment of South Korean Government and Media

Throughout 1990 and 1991, after the South Korean government had initiated a public campaign to curb "excessive consumption" and promote "austerity," the U.S. government received numerous reports of discriminatory treatment of U.S. consumer products in South Korea. Examples of such activities included removal of imported products from store shelves, limitations on promotional activities and threats of tax audits of South Korean purchasers of imported automobiles. U.S. firms also reported long delays in customs clearance for imported agricultural and consumer goods, and difficulty in receiving product registrations and approvals.

Following U.S. complaints, the South Korean government publicly announced that the intent of the campaign was not to discriminate against imports and reaffirmed its commitment to further trade liberalization. Subsequently, anti-import activities waned and, since 1992, have arisen less frequently (usually at year's end in order to improve South Korea's trade balance). They are usually undertaken by local governments and thus confined to certain regions of the country.

THE COMPETITION

A recent expansion of activity in the South Korean market by third-country governments and firms has been driven by, among other things, South Korea's rising per capita income, the South Korean government's announced massive infrastructure spending plans, and the strong yen causing South Korean manufacturers to rethink their traditional Japanese sources of industrial goods and capital equipment.

For U.S. firms, key determinants of sales are their relationships with major South Korean companies, financing/investment terms, technology transfer, price, quality/technical specifications and government advocacy. U.S. engineers and manufacturers are quite strong in price, quality and technology. Therefore, U.S. firms are and will remain competitive in many sectors of the South Korean market.

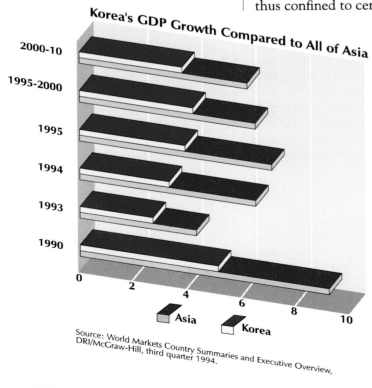

Korea's GDP Growth Compared to All of Asia

Source: World Markets Country Summaries and Executive Overview, DRI/McGraw-Hill, third quarter 1994.

Japan

The legacy of the Japanese occupation and the fear that followed of being dominated by Japanese imports led South Korea to implement the "Product Diversification" program in 1978. This program was enacted to prevent Japanese companies from completely monopolizing the South Korean economy. It has been partly successful in restricting specific product areas, which has been advantageous for U.S. exports. The Japanese are now gearing up to increase their presence in South Korea and negotiating to do away with this plan in exchange for Japanese technology. Japan will be the major foreign competitor for most U.S. firms.

As South Korea's restrictions are eased, the Japanese are expected to concentrate and expand their export efforts in several specific areas: electronic components and parts, power generation equipment, machinery and machine tools, and auto parts and components. The electronics portion will also consist of specialized parts and components for the semiconductor industry (i.e., test equipment and manufacturing components). The year 1994 also saw a major thrust by Japanese auto manufacturers and chemical companies to increase their presence in South Korea.

Japanese companies also have a growing interest in South Korea's lucrative telecommunications industry. The Japanese company KDD has already signed an agreement for joint development of an underwater fiber optic submarine cable linking Russia, Japan and South Korea. In 1994, NEC announced a joint development project for the underwater fiber optic system linking South Korea and China. The Korea Maritime Authority is scheduled to announce a new consortium for the maritime trunked radio system. Initial market analysis indicates a value exceeding $5 billion.

Samsung Electronics Co. and Japan's NEC Corp. agreed in principle on a technical alliance and are proceeding step-by-step toward what most market observers predict will become the strongest partnership ever made between the world's leading semiconductor chip makers. The two companies share interest in the growing need for a strong partnership in order to develop 256-megabyte dynamic random access memory (DRAM) chips. The alliance will open a new horizon in the history of South Korean-Japanese industrial cooperation. South Korea's two other chip makers, Hyundai Electronics and Goldstar Electron, have also formed technical ties with Japanese companies: Hyundai with Fujitsu for the development and production of 64MB DRAMs; and Goldstar with Hitachi for the mass production of 16MB DRAMs.

The Ten Commandments of Business

According to Song-Hyon Jang of S.H. Jang & Associates, Inc.: "My ten commandments for doing business in South Korea are well known. They are:

- Arrange a formal introduction;
- Always have calling cards;
- Ensure your English is completely understood;
- Restrain from pushing your own position;
- Build human relationships;
- Respect your partner;
- Entertain and be entertained;
- Try to know your counterparts;
- Temper the use of Western logic; and,
- Keep fully informed."

There is no getting around the fact that the strongest competition any foreign company faces in South Korea is domestic.

South Korea and Japan have agreed on a joint cooperation program, in which the two nations will try to tie private companies into "strategic partnerships."

The Japanese use an array of personnel to work specific markets. Much is done by the Japanese Embassy's commercial staff, which was increased by 40 percent last year. Also, the Japan External Trade Organization established offices in Seoul and Pusan.

France

The French believe South Korea will be an ideal partner for the 21st century and that South Korea will want to and be able to utilize its high technology in aerospace, genetic engineering, oceanic science, optics, atomic energy and organic chemicals.

South Korea has also been in serious need of an ally in Europe. Its primary goals are to secure high technology and, secondarily, develop a strong partnership to help compete in a world with high barriers on technology transfer.

Starting in late 1993, the French government targeted South Korea to expand its export sales in consumer goods, power plant construction (nuclear and fossil fuel), telecommunications, infrastructure projects, defense equipment and aerospace/aircraft. This initiative started with the visit of then-President Francois Mitterrand, linked with the bidding for a multi-billion dollar high-speed railway system—later won by the French company TGV. The winning of the contract was vital for both countries in setting up high technology transfer and manufacturing in various products. South Korea also gained access to the intellectual property and patent rights for newly developed technologies. The contract, worth $2.1 billion, was financed by a pool of banks led by the French bank, Indosuez.

French enterprises also hope to take part in large infrastructure projects. The French Embassy has added three new commercial affairs officers to be responsible for these projects alone.

Russia

The volume of bilateral trade should increase to over $10 billion by the year 2000. Given Russia's advanced technologies, vast territories and large consumer sector, it is regarded as one of the most suitable economic cooperation partners for South Korea.

South Korea's level of basic science and technology remains low, so it is eager to expand cooperation with Russia, which is known to possess superb technology in various fields including aerospace, new materials and medicine.

Since it was established in December 1990, the South Korea-Russia Committee on Commercial Cooperation has decided to launch 79 joint development items and, of these, 39 are in the research and development stage. South Korea finds it difficult to acquire new technologies from the U.S. and Japan because of the comparative expense. Russia has delivered

24 helicopters to South Korean companies to help offset financial debt to the South Korean government. Also, a research base has already been set up in the aerospace industry with the establishment of more researh bases to follow, especially in the technology transfer area. As a base camp for South Korean companies active in Russia, the Korea Trade Promotion Corp. (KOTRA) built a trade center in Moscow. Korea is also buying land and planning to establish factories for 100 firms representing industries in Nadhoste.

China

China is becoming one of South Korea's largest trading partners: according to the Korea Foreign Trade Association, China-South Korea trade reached an estimated $13 billion for 1994. China is South Korea's third largest trading partner, after the U.S. and Japan. South Korea's exports to China increased by over 90 percent last year: exports of audio systems, videotape recorders and TVs increased 50-60 percent; machinery exports increased 35 percent; petrochemical products 40 percent; oil products 40-50 percent; and paper products 40 percent.

In an example of major industrial cooperation, China and South Korea agreed to a joint national project for developing a mid-sized (100-seat) commercial aircraft. President Kim signed a memorandum of understanding with China in March 1994 on this project. The South Korean side will be 50 percent funded by the government and 50 percent by a private business consortium including Samsung Aerospace, South Korean Air and Daewoo Heavy Industries.

Another major South Korea-China joint project is the intended construction of a Daewoo Motor joint venture producing a car plant in China, at a cost of $1.5 billion.

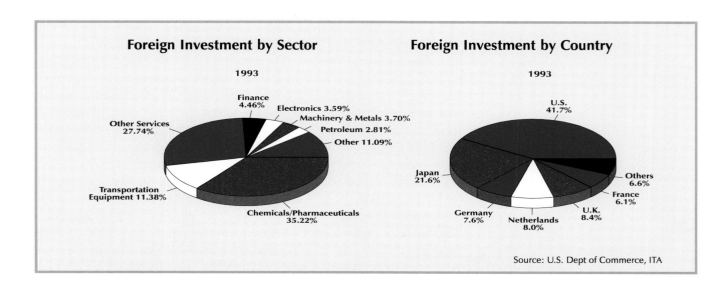

Foreign Investment by Sector

1993

Finance 4.46%
Electronics 3.59%
Machinery & Metals 3.70%
Petroleum 2.81%
Other 11.09%
Other Services 27.74%
Transportation Equipment 11.38%
Chemicals/Pharmaceuticals 35.22%

Foreign Investment by Country

1993

U.S. 41.7%
Others 6.6%
France 6.1%
U.K. 8.4%
Netherlands 8.0%
Germany 7.6%
Japan 21.6%

Source: U.S. Dept of Commerce, ITA

Cheering on the Chaebol

The rapid economic growth of the chaebols into economic global competitors over the past 40 years can be attributed directly to the South Korean government's three major growth policies during that period. First, limiting "excessive" competition in the domestic market; i.e., competition among chaebol, added up to higher profitability for the chaebol in their chosen industrial specializations. Second, explicit import substitution programs meant that a product being imported into South Korea was replaced whenever possible by a similar chaebol-manufactured product regardless of price and quality differences.

Third, offering special low-interest rate "policy loans" to chaebol who obeyed the government's direction allowed these firms to operate at higher margins of profitability than other firms who had to pay market rates for financing, giving the chaebols the ability to cut prices and operate in a predatory, monopolistic fashion to force out potential competitors. The South Korean consumer's interest in low prices and high quality products was subjugated to the government's interest in quickly building up large and integrated industrial conglomerates that could become export platforms to earn much-needed foreign exchange.

South Korea and China signed a Bilateral Industrial Cooperation Agreement on June 6, 1994. The agreement focuses on four industrial sectors; autos, aircraft, digital telephone exchanges and high definition television.

While generally China is not a direct trade competitor of the U.S. in South Korea, the growth of bilateral trade and strengthening technology links between these two countries suggests that many future projects in both South Korea and China will have split sourcing of equipment and technology.

Domestic Korean Firms

Despite the activity of these third-country competitors, there is no getting around the fact that the strongest competition any foreign company faces in South Korea is domestic. South Korea already has a mature and highly competitive engineering and construction industry, which has been exporting its services for more than 20 years.

Certain laws discourage monopolistic practices and unfair competition, but their practical effect is limited by the long-standing economic dominance of a few large business conglomerates, the chaebol. South Korea's Monopoly Regulation and Fair Trade Law was amended in the mid-1980s to specifically address the issue of unwieldy chaebol growth. Cross-equity investments were banned and equity limits set for chaebol holdings in joint venture companies. Only drastic legal change, however, is likely to significantly reduce chaebol economic power.

The term "chaebol" connotes the 30 top South Korean corporations, including Samsung, Hyundai, Daewoo and Lucky-Goldstar, the four largest in South Korea. These companies import whatever technology they require, then manufacture in South Korea to service the domestic market and for export to third countries. These and the other chaebol served as the foundation of South Korea's industrial policy beginning in the 1950s and have enjoyed a long and close relationship with the ruling political elites. As a result, they play a role in virtually every sector of the economy, and typically will be both the main competition and the likeliest partners for U.S. exporters.

Chaebol domination of the South Korean economy causes some practical business problems for foreign investors. Small and medium-sized suppliers, for example, may be reluctant to deal with foreign firms for fear of jeopardizing a prized chaebol relationship. Distribution channels may be blocked by chaebol competitors who own or dominate distribution channels. Seeking credit may be complicated by the privileged relationships competing chaebols enjoy with local banks.

Confronted with this multi-faceted chaebol problem, President Kim launched a "clean government" program which could be used as an instrument of coercion against the powerful chaebol leaders. A second major platform of Kim's reforms was to insist that chaebols pare down their conglomerate mix. This was designed to attract more competition into the economy and greater participation of small and medium-sized businesses.

It is not evident that real decoupling of the government-to-chaebol link has occurred under President Kim, or that this is what he really intended to accomplish under his anti-corruption and specialization programs. What is clear is that relations between the South Korean government and the chaebols are a complex mix of collaboration and confrontation. The net effect is that government and chaebols together are hindering the market liberalization that would enable South Korea to reach the next level of its economic development.

— *Contributors: Linda Droker, Susan Blackman, Jeff Donius, William Golike, Dan Duvall, Robert Connan, Sam Kidder, Helen Lee*

Europe, the Middle East and Africa

Poland: The

Population
38.7 Million

Population Growth Rate
0.35%

Gross Domestic Product
US$ 86.5 Billion

GDP Growth Rate
5.0%

Per Capita GDP
US$ 2,238

Inflation Rate
29.5%

Industrial Production, % Change
13%

1994. Source: U.S. Dept. of Commerce, ITA

Poland, the country that put "shock therapy" on the lips of finance ministers all over Eastern Europe and beyond, has put itself on the map as a Big Emerging Market as a result of its successful course of treatment. As the largest country in Central and Eastern Europe, now with one of the fastest growing economies on the continent, Poland's importance at the crossroads of the New Europe is beyond question.

While some parts of the country continue to suffer as a result of market reforms and shock therapy, Poland has made remarkable strides in turning its economy around as it reaches out to the West. The government of Poland has worked hard to create an attractive business climate for Westerners and remains committed to continuing on the path of economic reform.

The U.S. and other Western countries have responded to the new opportunities available in Poland. The U.S., as the leading foreign investor in Poland, has invested more than $1.7 billion, and bilateral trade with Poland reached almost $1.3 billion in 1994 alone.

Improved economic conditions have given rise to a new consumer class that favors American products. Poland's young, highly-skilled labor force, its attractive investment climate and its market size (over 38 million people) make it a place of great commercial opportunities.

Poland's economy was the first in Eastern Europe to emerge from the post-Communist recession with GDP growth of 2.6 percent in 1992, 3.8 percent in 1993 and 5 percent in 1994. Poland is expected to grow 6.5 percent in 1995 and to continue strong growth through the end of the century. While the privatization of large state-owned enterprises continues to go slowly, the private sector now accounts for 55 percent of GDP and employs over 60 percent of the labor force. The number of private domestic companies jumped from 0.5 million in 1988 to 1.8 million in 1994, and the number of private companies with foreign capital participation exploded from 1,600 to 16,000 over the same period.

In spite of some niggling doubts on the part of domestic companies concerning the rate of economic reform and the stability of Poland's political system, the commercial environment has proven stable.

Changing Times

Over the last several years, U.S. trade with Poland has been on the rise as Polish markets have been opened for almost all goods. The $912 million worth of goods exported by the U.S. in 1993 was 125 percent more than in 1990 when, as markets opened, the very nature of U.S. exports to Poland began to change. Before, the bulk of U.S. exports to Poland were

Big Bang

agricultural products like maize and wheat. Since 1990, when Poland began to develop a market economy, U.S. exports shifted to more standard manufactured goods like machinery, computers, telecommunications equipment, automobiles and large scale sales of U.S. aircraft.

Five years after starting the transition to a free market economy, a period marked initially by contractions in production and employment and by high inflation, the Polish economy is stable and growing. The rate of inflation has continued to decline, although high unemployment remains a major social and political problem. The leftist government elected in September 1993 so far has continued the process of free market economic reform and won support from the international community in recognition of its commitment to disciplined financial policies.

While overall unemployment is high (about 2.6 million jobless), the unemployment rate began to edge down after peaking at almost 17 percent in March 1994. It had fallen to 14.7 percent in May 1995. The annual rate of inflation in Poland, which was almost 600 percent in 1990, has continued to decline to 35 percent in 1993 and 29.5 percent in 1994. Declining inflation has allowed the government, effective as of January 1995, to redenominate the local currency (deleting four zeroes to equal a rate of about two zlotys to one U.S dollar).

In 1994, strong export growth of 18.3 percent far surpassed import growth of 13.2 percent and helped to spur Poland's economic development. While this growth reflects in part surging border trade, much of this trade goes unrecorded and could have contributed at least an extra 1 percent unrecorded GDP growth in 1994. The large surplus in this trade is measured in part by Poland's surging foreign exchange reserves which have been built in large part by revenues from trade along the border. Poland conducts over 60 percent of its total trade with the European Union, of which Germany alone accounts for half.

With one of the fastest growing economies on the continent, Poland's importance at the crossroads of the New Europe is beyond question.

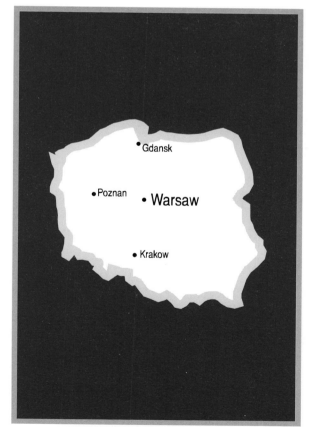

Privatization has begun to accelerate under the new government headed by Prime Minister Josef Oleksy of the Democratic Left Alliance (SLD) since March 1995. Expectations run high for the mass privatization program, which began in late 1994. Under this plan, in July 1995, private management firms took management control of 400 medium-sized companies grouped in 15 national investment funds, shares in which will be sold to the public for a nominal fee. In 1993, 55 companies were sold to private investors, and 199 were leased, usually to company managers and workers. In 1993, proceeds from privatizations totaled around $225 million. Nevertheless over 5,000 state- owned enterprises await privatization. The reorganization of Poland's banking sector also continues, with four of the nine state commercial banks privatized. The fifth bank, Bank Gdanski, will be privatized by the end of 1995.

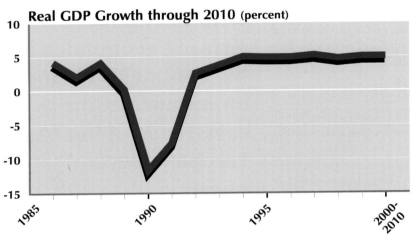

Real GDP Growth through 2010 (percent)

Source: IMF, International Trade Administration estimates

The first country to rebound from the former East Bloc's post-Communist recession, Poland's GDP grew 5 percent in 1994 and should grow at least as fast in 1995 and 1996.

Positive Signals

The Polish government has sent many positive signals to American companies doing business in Poland. The new Polish law on copyrights was a big step toward correcting a major problem for U.S. companies in protecting intellectual property, although Poland still remains on the Special 301 "watch list."

Poland's political leaders have repeatedly given strong public encouragement to Western and specifically U.S. investment: "We need American Generals," President Walesa recently said. "General Electric and General Motors." There are nevertheless domestic political factors at play which impinge on Poland's hospitality to foreign investment. The Polish Peasant Party (PSL) contains fiercely protectionist elements which occasionally prompt hostility toward foreign investors.

Trade union politics are also an element for foreign business to consider. The Polish trade union movement, the engine of Communism's collapse in the 1980s, has occasionally been problematic for foreign investors, particularly when managers of newly-privatized state enterprises have instituted management changes.

U.S. companies doing business in Poland believe their concerns about regulations and the business environment can be addressed. One good sign: many U.S. companies are reinvesting their profits in Poland, even though they could be repatriated.

The prospect of real economic growth and the size of the Polish market are the two top reasons U.S. and other foreign companies do business in Poland. Many believe that Poland is the best market in Central and Eastern Europe for their products and investments. While uncertainty about the regulations on foreign investment in Poland may limit the capital which firms are willing to invest, most multinationals have continued with plans to expand their businesses. Polish officials are doing as much as they can to encourage U.S. business to envision Poland as the "base camp" for the expansion of their activities to the East.

BIG EMERGING SECTORS

Opportunities for trade and investment exist across virtually all industrial and consumer sectors in Poland, and they will continue to emerge as privatization of state industry, which has been slow to date, continues. Major projects will develop in industries with problems related to the environment, including the power and coal sectors.

The number of private domestic companies jumped from half a million in 1988 to 1.8 million in 1994, and the number of private firms with foreign capital participation exploded from 1,600 to 16,000 over the same period.

Aspects of Poland's infrastructure that are beginning the slow process of modernization include roads and bridges, airports, seaports and railways. Opportunities will expand in these areas in all corners of Poland. The aircraft and automotive sectors are currently modernizing; suppliers will quickly be needed for parts and components, including transfers of technology. The Ministry of Industry has highlighted five sectors where major restructuring is planned or underway: defense, metallurgy, petroleum, power generation and ship building.

U.S. firms are currently active in many sectors of the Polish economy. Most are in food, food processing and consumer goods, fields which offer excellent opportunities for trade and investment. Heavy industry, including oil and gas, the coal sector, and heat and power generation are also promising areas for U.S. companies to pursue projects. Radio and television, telecommunications, home and office construction, and the transportation sector will offer significant openings in the future.

Best prospects for U.S. exports to Poland include household consumer goods, medical equipment, air conditioning and refrigeration equipment, building products, apparel, automotive parts, broadcasting equipment and pollution control equipment. Although U.S. exports are generally put in a less favorable position vis-a-vis their EU rivals because of discriminating tariffs, U.S. exports to Poland continue to grow in most sectors.

While manufacturing still dominates the Polish economy, other sectors have been emerging. The communications sector has grown the fastest. Sales of communications services were up by 12 percent in 1993 over 1992, and by over 70 percent in 1994. However, communications accounts for only a fraction of GDP (1.2 percent in 1993). Manufacturing contributed the most to economic growth in 1993, accounting for 40 percent of GDP. Industrial sales in 1993 grew by 7.4 percent, but still lag behind 1989 levels. Industries with the highest real growth rates included electrical engineering, transportation, apparel, food, chemicals, paper and wood. Agriculture remains inefficient and undercapitalized; it accounts for only 7 percent of GDP, while employing almost one quarter of the Polish labor force.

Other areas going through restructuring and/or privatization that offer good opportunities for U.S. manufacturers or service firms include telecommunications, banking, tourism, housing and hotel development.

Energy

Opportunities in Poland will continue to arise in energy conservation and management, oil refinery upgrading and coal mining and preparation. Clean-coal technologies, in particular, may have widespread application in Poland. In addition, the country is investigating bringing in gas supplies from the North Sea and the replacement of some coal-fired power plants with gas-fired combined-cycle ones.

Privatization of Poland's oil and gas sector and the heat and electric power industry offer additional chances for major project involvement.

Now that industrial growth has resumed, there may be opportunities to rebuild some of Poland's heavy industries with better technology, especially U.S. instrumentation and controls. District heating systems that are ineffectual or leaking with stand-alone gas equipment will need to be replaced, though natural gas supplies will need to be augmented if this comes to pass. As elsewhere in the region, wholesale and retail operations involving higher quality energy transformation or conservation devices could find a ready market in small industries and with commercial users. U.S. coal mining, transportation, preparation and combustion equipment should be competitive in Poland.

Information Technology

Telecommunications Equipment and Services

For Poland to achieve a "European level" of telephone density (35 phones per 100 inhabitants) by 2005, broad development targets include the installation of 3.6 million new digital lines by the end of 1995, replacing one million analog lines. Of these, more than two million are to be installed by some 20 local independent operators.

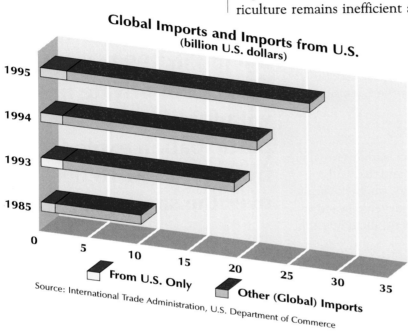

Global Imports and Imports from U.S.
(billion U.S. dollars)

From U.S. Only
Other (Global) Imports

Source: International Trade Administration, U.S. Department of Commerce

The annual rate of inflation in Poland, which was almost 600 percent in 1990, has continued to decline to 35 percent in 1993 and 29.5 percent in 1994.

By the end of 1995, overall network digitalization rates should reach nearly 60 percent, up from 9 percent. An overall telecommunications plan for Poland still needs to be defined. However, Polish operators are making a whole-hearted effort to develop Polish telecommunications, and it is entirely feasible that market demand will push Polish telecommunications to the European level before the end of the century.

Electronic Components and Test Equipment

According to forecasts, the total market for consumer electronics equipment will rise consistently during the next few years. The reshaping of a viable electronics industry, mostly through foreign investment, is one of the top priorities of the Polish government. It is all the more foreseeable now as COCOM restrictions on transfers of technology and know-how are being gradually lifted for the least sensitive components and products.

Rate of Inflation through 2010 (percent)

Source: IMF, International Trade Administration estimates

The best strategy for American companies seeking to enter the Polish consumer electronics market is through direct investment in this sector. Poland possesses two key assets to attract investors to develop local design, assembly and manufacturing in electronics: (1) its market is close to the EU's, and (2) the universally recognized competence of its engineers. As a result of recent trends in the industry, engineering skills are available at competitive costs. Another viable strategy is to develop a strong distribution network.

Healthcare Technology

Although the public health sector is burdened by severe budgetary restrictions, funds for purchasing medical equipment are available through international financial institutions such as the World Bank and the European Bank for Reconstruction and Development (EBRD). The private medical sector is booming with small private clinics opening throughout the country at a rapid rate. A revised social security program might be introduced in 1995 which would allow patients (or clinics) to be reimbursed for medical services.

Additionally, Poland is considered the largest market for laboratory and scientific equipment in Central Europe, anticipated to grow steadily by 10 percent a year. Equipment bought for scientific purposes is exempt from customs duties and taxes.

Major Transportation Projects

Baltic Grain Terminal at the Port of Gdynia: This project is a sub-component of the development of Gdynia port on the southwest coast of the Gulf of Gdansk. The project entails the expansion and operation of existing grain terminal facilities. As of 1992, the port handled over 85 percent of Poland's seaborne container traffic and approximately 45 percent of Poland's general cargo and cereal business. In 1991, the port saw a total of 7.3 million tons of traffic, including 3.3 million tons of general cargo, 784,000 tons of grain and 1.5 million tons of coal.

The terminal's operator, Baltic Grain Terminal, is looking to identify joint venture partners who would play an active role in project development and implementation, assisting not only with the expansion of the grain silo, but also with marketing and operations within the port. It is anticipated that a U.S. investor and joint venture partner will bring capital to the project and will participate actively in the implementation of the three-phase development project, as well as promoting the use of the terminal by North American grain exporters.

Modernization of Polish Civil Aviation Infrastructure: The Polish Ministry of Transport and Maritime Economy is modernizing Poland's civil aviation air traffic control and airport system. The Master Plan describes investments totalling $91.4 million for the Polish Air Traffic Agency, $66.4 million for the Warsaw (Okecie) Airport, and $33.5 million for Polish regional airports. These figures include almost $80 million worth of imported equipment, including radar air traffic control displays, airport navigational lighting equipment, meteorology equipment, telecommunications and emergency equipment.

American companies should note that the U.S. Trade and Development Agency financed the original Master Plan that is being implemented. In the current international market, it is common for equipment suppliers to provide a financial package and training to clinch the sales.

Polish Toll Motorways: As part of Poland's integration into Western Europe, Polish government policy includes the modernization of existing transportation networks and the creation of new ones, allowing the flow of people and goods across the country. Over the next fifteen years the cost of this program could exceed $8 billion, as Poland constructs over 2,600 km of major north-south and east-west motorways. Because financing for these projects will be challenging, the Polish government has approved development of a number of toll motorways.

American engineering and construction work are well-known, particularly as regarding overpasses, by-passes, tunnels and bridges. While it is likely that any financing coming from multilateral lending organizations will include a high "local content" requirement, U.S. companies can leverage their high-value added strengths by teaming with lower cost local construction companies, thereby competitively offering the full range of goods and equipment required for project implementation.

Environmental Technology

Poland has recently begun to put pressure on industry through the collection of environmental fees and fines. This has resulted in demonstrable efforts by polluters to reduce emissions, in addition to putting significant capital into governmental coffers to be used for environmental projects. Thus the market for goods and services in this sector has grown steadily over the last two years.

Increasing environmental awareness and the introduction of significant changes in environmental legislation in Poland have resulted in increased demand for capital equipment to reduce pollution across all sectors of heavy industry in Poland. Air pollution, water and wastewater treatment are the major areas of focus.

Transportation and Infrastructure

Roads top the list of Polish infrastructure needs in the coming decade. Major institutional lenders are already involved in motorway, road, toll road and bridge development projects. Poland has received a $150 million loan from the World Bank to finance the modernization of Poland's main network of roads and bridges. The EBRD has approved a loan of $35 million for upgrades and improvements of specific sections of roads and toll roads. Poland has developed a program for the construction and financing of new motorways, at a total cost of about $8 billion. This program extends through the year 2007 and includes major north-south and east-west highways.

Airports and railways are also being modernized and refurbished across Poland. This includes track maintenance equipment, telecommunication and power supplies, and platform and bridge repairs. Poland's current airport network consists of eight major airports. Development plans through the year 2000 include: installation of navigation lighting systems and meteorological equipment at almost all of the airports; modernization or repavement of runways and aprons for many of the airports; and modernization of emergency equipment and winter maintenance equipment throughout the airport system. All of these projects offer excellent opportunities for U.S. companies.

In general, the most promising areas for U.S. exports in the transport sector are for engineering and design services, specialized and high-technology equipment, and computer software, as well as in air transport, highways and road transport, railroads and ports.

Motor Vehicles and Parts

The automotive sector has exploded in Poland over the past four years. Automotive parts and components are in hot demand as a result. Forecasts estimate that in 1995, 250,000 vehicles of all types will be sold; 300,000 in 1997 and a peak of 350,000 in 2000.

Tourism

Numerous activities in the area of product development have resulted in the enhancement of tourist destinations. In January 1994, an international team of experts began working on a "National Tourism Product Development Plan 1995-2004" for Poland.

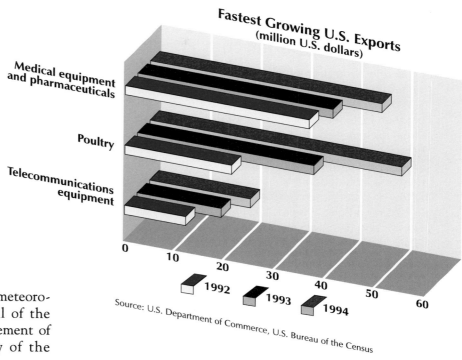

Fastest Growing U.S. Exports (million U.S. dollars)

Medical equipment and pharmaceuticals

Poultry

Telecommunications equipment

0   10   20   30   40   50   60

1992   1993   1994

Source: U.S. Department of Commerce, U.S. Bureau of the Census

Privatization Opens the Door

The Polish government sees the privatization process as central to the move to a market economy and to luring in foreign business interests. The pace of privatization is expected to increase in 1995. And the privatization ministry has selected a number of industrial sectors to be included in a sectoral privatization program. The privatization strategy entails offering shares in privatized companies to foreign investors.

Simultaneously, the government prepared a Mass Privatization Program (MPP) to privatize around 400 state-owned companies. The companies were transferred to investment funds staffed by Western managers in July 1995. Vouchers to purchase shares in each of the funds will be distributed to Poles. The funds will eventually be traded on the Warsaw Stock Exchange.

Major Telecom Projects

The modernization of the Polish telecommunications network will require investments of up to $15-20 billion, with an estimated $10 billion to be spent this decade. A broad telecommunications program includes installation of 49 digital long-distance and international exchanges by the end of 1996. Major tenders are expected between 1995-7 for several components of the expansion. Projects include: expansion of local capacity by 739,000 lines on the networks included in the major urban centers of Warsaw, Krakow, Katowice and Poznan; further development of land mobile services (including cellular, wireless local loop telephony and paging networks); and data transmission (X.25, VSAT) and the introduction of ISDN and frame relay technologies.

Financing for some of Poland's telecommunications projects is being provided by the European Bank for Reconstruction and Development (EBRD), the European Investment Bank (EIB) and the World Bank.

While tariff preferences are extended to some EU telecommunications imports as a result of Poland's association agreement with the EU, the reputation of the high-quality U.S. products and advanced features not available in competitors' systems make for a strong competitive position of American companies. As software becomes increasingly important in the telecommunications area, network integration and management expertise should provide U.S. companies with additional advantages.

Tourism activity accounts for approximately 40 percent of foreign credits made available to Poland. The U.S. & Foreign Commercial Service affirms that Poland has great potential for growth in tourism services, with a base of outstanding but relatively underdeveloped resort areas.

MARKET ACCESS
Tariffs and Import Barriers

In January 1990, a new Customs Law came into force in Poland. This law defined and implemented the Harmonized Tariff System which reclassified products and ultimately formed the basis for new duty rates on imports. Tariff rates have changed several times since (and are still subject to change), and have proved to be a major frustration to U.S. companies actively involved in exports to Poland. A 5 percent import tax is added to the equation on all imports into Poland. Turnover taxes were replaced in 1993 with a general 22 percent value-added tax (VAT). Significant excise taxes apply to certain products as well.

The March 1, 1992, enactment of the trade provisions within Poland's association agreement with the EU lowered or eliminated tariffs on many EU products imported into Poland, while tariffs on U.S. products remained the same. This immediately placed U.S. products in a less competitive and officially less preferential position than their EU competitors.

As a result of U.S. government negotiations, duty-free quotas, or zero duty quotas, have been applied within certain industries including the automotive, computer and pharmaceutical sectors in Poland. U.S. and foreign firms have benefited from these quotas. In some instances the quotas are targeted

Foreign Exchange Reserves (billion U.S. dollars)

Source: IMF

to products originating from specific export regions (e.g. cars from the EU), and in others they have been assessed to help protect local industry (e.g. pharmaceuticals), or to help develop industries (e.g. computer parts and components).

Poland will have implemented its code on product safety by the end of 1995. Currently, all products entering Poland must register to be certified in Poland before the end of the year. Beginning January 1, 1996 all products will have to be pre-certified before entering the market. While the list of products which require certification is being pared down, most products will still need to be separately certified for the Polish market.

In addition to official barriers, U.S. businesses currently have to deal with communications, banking, accounting and distribution systems that are still developing in Poland. Office space, labor, transportation, currency, language and bureaucracy are also problematic.

Government Procurement Practices

Legislation governing bid tendering procedures and government procurement is currently being drafted. There is evidence that the Polish government is striving to tender bids fairly and transparently, but the lack of clear legislation and resulting delays continue to frustrate U.S. business. Allegations of unfair play occasionally surface.

The Polish government approved a public procurement law in 1994. This law will apply in all cases where public money is used to procure commodities, services and construction works. The law's procurement procedures need not be followed in the case of purchases of less than $25,000.

Under the new law, the purchasing agency can request that the commodity to be purchased contains at least 50 percent Polish content. In the case of services, the use of Polish labor can be required. A public purchases office will oversee these activities and publish a bulletin listing public procurement opportunities. An open tender procedure will be used as the standard.

Implementation of this new law on public procurement should help U.S. companies gain easier access and increase opportunities to sell to the Polish government and bid on major government projects. Introduction of transparent procedures for open bid processes in large-scale projects will lay additional groundwork for fair competition.

The most promising areas for U.S. exports in the transport sector include: engineering and design services, high-tech equipment and software.

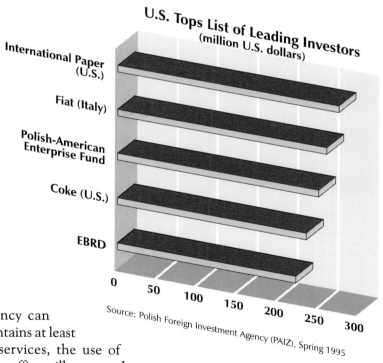

U.S. Tops List of Leading Investors
(million U.S. dollars)

International Paper (U.S.)
Fiat (Italy)
Polish-American Enterprise Fund
Coke (U.S.)
EBRD

0   50   100   150   200   250   300

Source: Polish Foreign Investment Agency (PAIZ), Spring 1995

Poland's association agreement with the EU lowered or eliminated tariffs on many EU products imported into Poland, placing U.S. products in a less competitive position.

In the past, major governmental projects and contracts in Poland have been reopened for examination and expanded bids. Governmental and quasi-governmental committees and consultants were set up to analyze and review major projects and consider bidders and their proposals. Revisions to proposals were requested. This often caused considerable questions and delays.

Openness to Foreign Investment

The government of Poland has often voiced its belief that foreign investment plays an important role in the modernization of the Polish economy and the rationalization of economic activity in accordance with market forces. Although Poland is not yet a member of the EU, an association agreement was signed in December 1991, and trade provisions of that agreement came into force in March 1992, with additional reductions in some tariff rates effective January 1995. The agreement is a step towards the ultimate goal of membership in the EU for Poland. It will build an industrial free-trade zone, harmonize legislation and develop economic cooperation on a wider basis. The EU provides Poland with models on which to base its legislative and regulatory reforms, and the agreement should improve the business climate for foreign investors.

Foreign investment in Poland is governed by the Foreign Investment Act of 1991, and subsequent amendments to the Act, which was intended to open the Polish economy to foreign investment and establish a level playing field between foreign and domestic investors. Incentives are still available for new investments and large-scale investments in regions of high unemployment. Under the law, any level of foreign ownership—up to 100 percent—is allowed.

Under the foreign investment law, an investor must obtain a permit from the Ministry of Privatization to invest in certain areas. Foreign investors must also comply with domestic laws. For example, investment in banking requires the approval of the Central Bank and the Ministry of Finance. Other requirements apply in specific sectors.

Polish privatization programs are open to foreign investors and most of the largest transactions have involved sales to foreign firms. These have accounted for a substantial portion of foreign investment in Poland. In addition to 48 U.S. firms which have each invested more than $1 million in Poland, U.S. companies top the list of largest investors. The U.S. also remains the single largest investor with almost a third of total investment.

Special Considerations

Intellectual Property Rights

Protection of intellectual property has been and continues to be a major concern for U.S. companies. It can be an obstacle to increased foreign investment in Poland. An amended law on trademarks and new copyright laws exists and will help, but enforcement of these laws will remain a key issue.

Poland's trademark law of 1985 was recently amended to impose punishments on those who illegally use registered trademarks in Poland. According to estimates, approximately 80 percent of clothing and 50 percent of coffee on the Polish market is sold under "pirated" trademarks. The former trademark law prohibited the placing of counterfeit trademarks on goods, but did not prevent people or companies from selling or distributing products with pirated trademarks. The law now provides for up to a year imprisonment or penalty for those

Foreign Investment in Poland — by Country, 1995

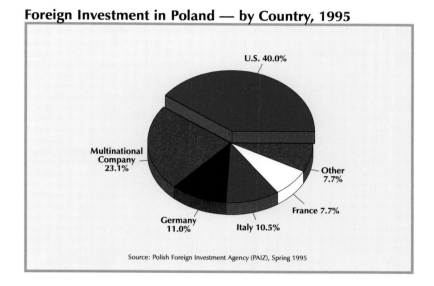

Source: Polish Foreign Investment Agency (PAIZ), Spring 1995

who sell goods with counterfeit trademarks or place such trademarks on goods, and is expected to be an important step toward fighting trademark piracy.

A new copyright law came into force in June 1994. It is in line with international standards and is considered the first significant step towards the protection of intellectual property rights in Poland. The new copyright law introduces protection of not only literary, musical and graphic works, but also of computer software, audio-visual works and industrial patterns. It extends copyright protection from 25 to 50 years to comply with international standards, and protects not only authors, but also producers, artists and performers.

Estimates show that the State Treasury in Poland lost a minimum of $25 million in 1993, and Polish producers and artists lost about $50 million to audio and videocassette piracy alone. The new copyright legislation will allow legal battles to begin, and it provides for the confiscation of products, return of the profits attained and up to a year imprisonment or penalty. It is strongly believed that both the new copyright law and the trademark law will effectively help fight existing piracy, while the quality of protected products legally manufactured will attract new customers.

The U.S. government has placed Poland on the "watch list" under the Special 301 provision of the 1988 Trade Act.

THE COMPETITION

Since 1990, the U.S. has ranked between 6th and 15th on the list of Poland's largest import suppliers, about 4 percent of Poland's total import market. In 1994, 28 percent of Polish imports originated in Germany. Italy and Russia were the next largest import suppliers with 8.4 percent and 6.8 percent of the Polish market respectively. U.S. agricultural exports account for about 11 percent of the total Polish agricultural import market, a jump from 2 percent in 1991. Meanwhile, services account for more than 20 percent of total Polish imports, though Poland is running a trade surplus in services (mostly to Central and Eastern Europe).

Leading Sources of Imports/Destination of Exports

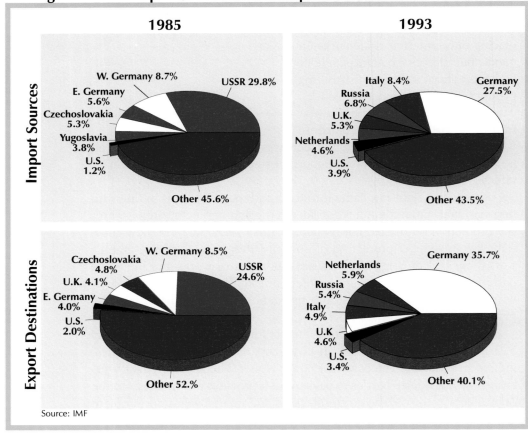

Source: IMF

There is tremendous unrealized demand for Western goods in Poland which creates ample opportunity for a broad range of exports by large, medium-sized and small American producers. Local production in most best prospect export categories is generally low, though more firms start up new manufacturing operations each year. However, U.S. exporters across-the-board face strong competition from European producers. In certain sectors, such as computers and consumer electronics, competition from companies in Asia and Southeast Asia is also a factor.

Given the competition offered by the EU, U.S. exporters must be aggressive, flexible and prepared to waive short-term profits for long-term gains to establish their presence in Poland.

Poland's domestic industry is developing slowly and is still at a stage where U.S. companies can assist with its development. For the foreseeable future, Poland will be a net importer of manufactured goods, particularly those that will help it develop and generate exports.

European governments eagerly aid their industries. Britain's export credit guarantee agency raised Poland from its riskiest country rating in 1994, thus providing coverage at more favorable rates. The Dutch export agency increased its short-term cover for Poland; and France, like Britain, raised Poland's rating. As a result, financing EU exports to Poland is now easier, as in the U.S., where ExIm Bank provides financing.

Given Poland's geographic location, its association and trade agreements and financing options available to EU exporters, U.S. exporters must be aggressive, flexible and prepared to waive short-term profits for long-term gains to establish their presence in Poland.

European Union

Geography is one natural reason there are currently more EU products on the Polish market than American. Locating, purchasing and importing European products is quicker and easier for Polish firms. European companies also travel more and spend more time, at less cost, promoting their products in Poland than U.S. firms. European satellite broadcasts in Poland breed familiarity with European products.

Poland's movement toward EU membership is natural and welcome to many U.S. companies looking to expand from Poland into the EU. Unfortunately, under Poland's current tariff structure with the EU, U.S. imports are discriminated against by significantly higher customs duties. Tariff discrimination affects U.S. investments as well, as customs duties add unnecessary costs to imported capital goods used in production.

The Central European Free Trade Area

CEFTA, the Central European Free Trade Area, encompassing Poland, the Czech Republic, Slovakia and Hungary (Slovenia is expected to be admitted shortly) is emerging as the key regional trading bloc leading the emerging market democracies of the region towards stronger economic alliance and preparing the way for eventual membership in the European Union. Concluded in 1993, the CEFTA Agreement provides for the eventual creation of a free trade area among its member countries by 1997. The agreement mandates a series of gradual tariff reductions that will include almost all product areas. Discussions have begun over the eventual inclusion of Romania, Bulgaria and the Baltic countries.

Central and Eastern Europe (CEE) is now a market worth over $500 billion; it is poised for solid growth that many observers believe will average 5-6 percent a year or better annually -- substantially better for leading sectors.

The CEE region is importing about $50 billion annually -- up one-third in just two years. U.S. firms, though, are not matching their competitors in exporting to this growing market -- and have only 5 percent of the CEE import market.

Over the last few years, the CEE countries have achieved visible successes in reorienting their trade from traditional Eastern markets towards the West. The share of Western industrialized countries in these countries' imports and exports rose from 55 percent in 1990 to 70 percent in 1993. At the same time, the share of their Eastern European trade partners dropped by nearly half from 35 percent to 18 percent on the export side and from 37 pecent to 22 percent on the import side.

Trade liberalization, the end of state monopolies, and the rise of private trading companies all contributed to this transformation in trade. CEFTA countries improved their trade performance in 1994, as exports soared by 18 percent, while imports increased 12 percent. Exports will rise as countries take advantage of phased-in trade concessions from CEFTA, the EU, the European Free Trade Association (EFTA) and continued international economic recovery.

Western firms have invested around $15 billion in CEE countries. The U.S. is the top investor in the region, followed by Germany, Austria and Italy. The region offers a market of 100 million consumers, potential access to another 290 million in the former Soviet Union, and backdoor access to the EU market for non-EU investors.

The U.S. government has successfully negotiated downward many of the tariff barriers stemming from the association agreement. However, the difference between tariffs on similar U.S. and EU goods have become greater in some product categories because, as part of the agreement, further tariff reductions became effective January 1995 for Polish imports of EU products. Poland will continue to annually reduce custom duties on almost all industrial imports from the EU, including machinery, until duties are eliminated in 1999.

— *Contributors: Lian Von Wantoch, Monika Michejda-Goodrich, Pamela Green, Jay A. Burgess, Susanne Lotarski, Franklin J. Vargo*

South Africa:

Population
41 Million

Population Growth Rate
2.3%

Gross Domestic Product
US$ 121.9 Billion

GDP Growth Rate
2.3%

Per Capita GDP
US$ 2,973

Inflation Rate
9.0%

Industrial Production, % Change
4.6%

1994. Source: U.S. Dept. of Commerce, ITA

Already the most advanced, broadly-based and productive economy in Africa, with a GDP that is 45 percent of all Africa's, South Africa's transformation to a democracy will finally enable it to harness and unleash all of its potential, thrusting the nation into true BEM status. Surprising even his supporters with his pro-market attitude, President Nelson Mandela's ascendance has meant that not only is the country open for business, it's expanding its hours of operation.

South Africa represents one of the last major markets not yet thoroughly explored, particularly by many American exporters and investors who for two decades stayed away because of apartheid policies and sanctions. It possesses a modern infrastructure supporting an efficient distribution of goods to major urban centers throughout the region, and well-developed financial, legal, communications, energy and transport sectors. South Africa boasts a global trade surplus of nearly $1 billion and a stock exchange which ranks among the top 10 in the world. Significant growth potential, access to other markets in Africa and the availability of inexpensive electrical power and raw materials add to its economic promise.

President Clinton has called upon all Americans who have been so active in breaking down the pillars of apartheid to help build the non-racial market democracy that comes in its wake. In support of South Africa's democratic transition, the U.S. has undertaken numerous measures to encourage positive bilateral trade and investment relations, including enactment of the South African Transition to Democracy Support Act, formation of the United States-South Africa Binational Commission, and President Clinton's commitment to engage the U.S. private sector in the rebuilding process.

South Africa clearly represents a potential which could translate into significant sales for competitive U.S. firms. The U.S. was once South Africa's largest trading partner, and has rebounded to the number two position among South Africa's suppliers today.

South Africa is the largest export market for U.S. goods and services in sub-Saharan Africa. U.S. exports to South Africa totaled $2.2 billion in 1994, 25 percent more than the level in 1990 and representing roughly 14 percent of South Africa's total import market. As the South African government commences an ambitious socio-economic rebuilding agenda, local business confidence improves and American companies continue to enter or return to the market, U.S.-South African commercial opportunities should expand and reverberate regionally.

Forward Together

South Africa offers excellent potential in the long-term reconstruction and development efforts required to distribute economic benefits, traditionally enjoyed by only five or six million South Africans, to the 35 million people disenfranchised by apartheid. In order to fund and deliver on the new Government of National Unity's promises, substantial investment is needed in areas such as electrification, construction, housing, telecommunications and health care. The most promising sectors for U.S. export growth also include traditional sectors: aircraft and parts, chemicals, agricultural and industrial machinery, computers and electronics, industrial process control, medical equipment, sporting goods and other consumer goods, and franchising.

The Return of American Business

Since Mandela's landmark speech to the United Nations in September 1993, more than a hundred U.S. companies have acquired subsidiaries or affiliates, opened a branch office or placed employees in South Africa. They followed firms that entered the market after President Bush lifted the Comprehensive Anti-Apartheid Act's (CAAA) prohibition on new U.S. investment in South Africa in July 1991. Further illustrating the return of American companies, the membership of the American Chamber of Commerce in South Africa grew from 163 to 223 firms over the three-year period. Today, nearly 700 U.S. firms have investment, employees or non-equity links in South Africa, according to the Investor Responsibility Research Center (IRRC) in Washington, D.C.

The return of American business to South Africa began with U.S. companies re-entering the market they had left during the sanctions era or entering the market for the first time and setting up branch marketing and sales and service offices. In addition, several U.S. firms

In his September 1993 address to the UN, when Nelson Mandela called for the lifting of U.S. sanctions, he said: "We have, together, walked a very long road. We have traveled together to reach a common destination."

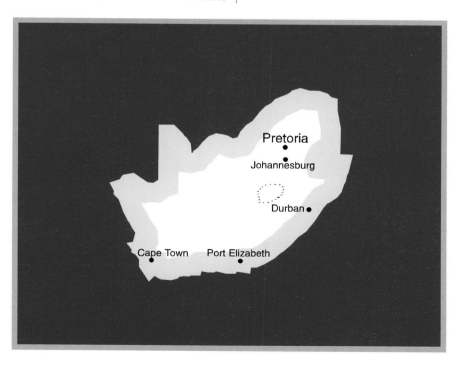

The United States was once South Africa's largest trading partner. It has rebounded to the number two position among South Africa's suppliers today.

that remained in South Africa during the sanctions period have embarked on plans to expand their operations and presence. In less than a year's time since President Mandela's inauguration, a virtual Who's Who of American business opened offices in South Africa, including American Express, AT&T, American International Group, Apple Computer, Chrysler, Compaq, Cray Research, Ford, General Motors, IBM, Kodak, Lotus, Microsoft, Motorola, Nike, Pepsi, Polaroid, Reebok, Tandem Computers and Wordperfect.

On the domestic side, although South Africa's sophisticated local business community has proven itself capable of providing for much of the local demand, it is questionable whether it has the capacity to meet the extreme needs that now exist. There are tremendous political imperatives to address the socio-economic legacies of apartheid as quickly as possible, especially in housing, electification and telecommunication. American companies can make important contributions to this process by providing appropriate, cost-effective technologies.

Another important part of South Africa's economic expansion will be the development of competitive export industries, and minerals and primary product beneficiation for export markets. Such growth will require significant imports of new capital equipment and technologies.

At the same time, change is beginning to come to some of the country's largest corporate conglomerates which traditionally wield much commercial power in South Africa. South Africa's largest firms are examining unbundling in anticipation of the possible adoption of some form of anti-monopoly/antitrust law by the new government. Other initiatives, such as the abolishment of the dual exchange rate system, the goverment's commitment to the removal of the remaining exchange controls, and the elimination of the import surcharge, are designed to open up the South African market and attract foreign investment.

Africa's Springboard

The lifting of trade sanctions by other African countries has finally positioned South Africa as a strong regional force for growth and the gateway to other African markets. In this regard, South Africa has stepped up its regional trade promotion effort in countries which had traditionally scorned the nation for its apartheid

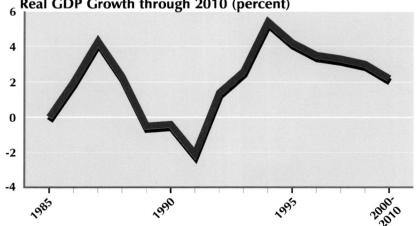

Real GDP Growth through 2010 (percent)

Source: DRI/McGraw Hill, *World Markets Executive Overview,* second quarter 1995

policies. In Uganda, Malawi, Zimbabwe and Mozambique, South Africa is seeking investment and trade opportunities and vying for large Western-funded infrastructure projects. The South African government has opened trade missions in 22 African nations to date.

It is commonly believed that South Africa's political transition and economic rebuilding will catalyze growth for the entire southern Africa region. South Africa has acceded to full membership in the Southern African Development Community (SADC), a regional organization comprising eleven countries in southern Africa: Angola, Botswana, Lesotho, Malawi, Mozambique, Namibia, South Africa, Swaziland, Tanzania, Zambia and Zimbabwe.

The SADC region, a market of approximately 120 million people, offers the strong potential for U.S. export growth in sub-Saharan Africa. The combined markets of SADC, therefore, can and should be viewed as part of South Africa s Big Emerging Market. Many U.S. firms consider South Africa a natural platform from which to expand their operations into Africa. Several U.S. firms have relocated their Africa marketing offices from Europe to Johannesburg. Moreover, U.S. firms that get involved in South Africa's reconstruction and development programs will both contribute to the country's economic revitalization process and gain a strong commercial foothold in the new South Africa and beyond.

BIG EMERGING SECTORS

The South African government's Reconstruction and Development Program (RDP) serves as the blueprint for social development and economic growth in the new South Africa. The RDP's goals can be grouped into three major policy areas, all interdependent: meeting basic needs; developing human resources; and democratizing the state and society. The RDP seeks to provide the recently enfranchised black majority with jobs, land, housing, water, electricity, telecommunications, transport, a clean and healthy environment, nutrition and health care.

The Government of National Unity's goals over the next five years include programs to redistribute a substantial amount of land, build over one million homes, provide clean water and sanitation for all South Africans, electrify 2.5 million new homes and provide access for all to affordable health care and telecommunications. The RDP recommends revamping the educational system, boosting economic productivity and redistributing resources. A road map for financing the program is unclear, although proposals confirm the importance of foreign investment.

As a key part of this transition, the government, facing an economy in which the state generates more than 30 percent of all economic activity, must make some critical choices regarding its army of parastatals. The Minister of Public Enterprises is preparing an inventory of all state assets and state-owned corporations with the objective of privatizing those that are not considered crucial to the objectives of the RDP.

> "There is no question that South Africa is the key to the economic success of southern Africa — indeed, the key to the renewal of the rest of the continent."
>
> — *U.S. Secretary of Commerce Ronald H. Brown*

In 1993, South Africa registered positive growth for the first time, emerging from a four-year recession caused by drought, uncertainty pending the outcome of political negotiations, a sluggish international economy and depressed world commodity prices. Most of the growth experienced in 1993 resulted from recovery from drought in the agricultural sector. Inflation in 1994, at 9.1 percent for consumers and 5.5 percent for producers, had decreased to levels not seen since the early 1970s. 1994's annualized growth rate of 2.3 percent indicates that the economy is responding positively to the economic policies of the new government.

South Africa's economy, with its confluence of both first and third worlds, founded on gold and diamonds, has diversified over the past 50 years and is now very broadly-based. The country offers extensive demand for some of the U.S.'s most competitive and state-of-the-art products. Telecommunications, aircraft, chemicals, computers, medical equipment, franchising and information services are key and important sectors for U.S. involvement.

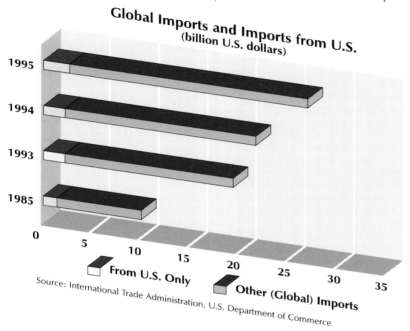

Global Imports and Imports from U.S.
(billion U.S. dollars)

1995
1994
1993
1985

0 5 10 15 20 25 30 35

☐ From U.S. Only   ■ Other (Global) Imports

Source: International Trade Administration, U.S. Department of Commerce

Information Technology

The South African information technology industry has evolved considerably despite international sanctions, trade embargos and four years of recession.

Telecommunications Equipment and Services

South Africans have a high regard for American telecommunications equipment and services, but because of the combined effect of past sanctions and local closed procurement practices, U.S. companies were not able to participate in this market. Interest in U.S. telecommunications equipment is growing as a result of the lifting of trade restrictions.

Telecommunications services in South Africa are provided mainly by Telkom SA Limited, a state-owned corporation. Germany, France and the United Kingdom are the largest suppliers to the South African market. Most telecommunications equipment is free of import restrictions, although certain key items, e.g. telephones and two-way radios, require an import permit to protect domestic assemblers. Cellular services, launched in 1994, are provided by two private consortia. The Department of Posts and Telecommunications is planning to use the new cellular infrastructure to connect heretofore unserviced black communities.

Computer Equipment and Software

South Africa's computer market, valued at close to $1 billion in 1994, is changing its focus from mainframes to personal computers and PC-based networks. This transition, further stimulated by the continually increasing processing power and decreasing prices of personal computers, is also boosting demand for laptop and notebook computers, and peripheral equipment including printers, storage devices and other add-on hardware. Present demand is almost totally for PC-based local area networks (LANs), and 70 percent of South Africa's PCs are forecast to be linked to some form of network by 1996.

Opportunities exist for sales, and growth opportunities are limited only by the shortage of trained people to manage the complex and interconnected networks proliferating everywhere. The introduction of direct sales marketing to South Africa's personal computer end-users in 1993 has allowed at least four American companies to sell LAN hardware directly to them. U.S. firms are bringing established computer brand name products into the market at competitive prices and are regaining market share lost during the sanctions period. Local manufacture of personal computers is negligible because of the large production runs required to achieve economies of scale.

Approximately 85 percent of demand for network operating systems (NOS) is met through imports. Novell is the market leader in networking systems. Other popular networking operating systems are marketed by Digital Networking, LAN/IX Computer Systems, LAN Design, Lasernet, M&PD, Microsoft, Softsource and WorkGroup Systems. The market for LAN operating utilities and application software word processing, value-added processors, spreadsheets, E-mail, LAN basic development platforms, file/record managers and applications software for accounting, banking, factory environments and office automation is estimated to be $4.5 million. Most of these software packages are U.S. designed.

Opportunities to provide information services in South Africa will increase as South African manufacturing and service companies seek to become more competitive with foreign companies entering the South African market. South African companies will also need to become more aggressive in the global marketplace. Information services are essential in improving quality, controlling costs, marketing and providing customer services. Currently, the information services market in South Africa is estimated at $500 million and is growing by about 16 percent annually. In 1993, U.S. exports of information services to South Africa amounted to $16 million. U.S. companies which provide outsourcing services, computer professional services and online information services will benefit from the expanding opportunities in this sector.

> **As a key part of this transition, the government must make some critical choices regarding its army of parastatals.**

South Africa's political transition and economic rebuilding will catalyze growth for the entire southern Africa region.

Aerospace

The U.S. has been a prominant supplier to the South African aircraft market for more than 30 years. U.S. exports of aerospace products to South Africa rose 17 percent in 1993 to $345 million from $295 million in 1992. Similarly, U.S. exports of aerospace products were $431 million in 1991, compared to $138 million in 1989. American aircraft products enjoy an extremely high reputation in South Africa. South Africa imports approximately 60 percent of its aircraft and parts from the U.S. Light aircraft are used extensively to reach outlying areas of South Africa, i.e., ranches, mining sites and neighboring countries. With South African air routes opening up, more large aircraft are needed to cater to the increase in passengers.

Healthcare Technology

The South African government's focus for this sector is on providing primary health care and related infrastructure to black communities. Currently, South Africa's health infrastructure is comprised of 693 hospitals, 158,567 hospital beds, 2,218 health centers and clinics, and 25,375 doctors.

The medical equipment and product market has a size of more than $250 million per year and an annual growth rate of approximately 5 percent—it is ripe for U.S. involvement. With up to 15 major suppliers offering medical equipment and products and well over 60 agents and distributors, this market is sophisticated and extensive. There are more than 500 (mostly foreign) trade names to choose from and no import restrictions in this sector. While South Africa does import the latest in medical technology, practitioners complain of the lack of back-up services from suppliers, presenting opportunities for U.S. companies to fill this need.

In another area of intense market competition, of the some 45 foreign-owned pharmaceutical companies in South Africa, 12 are American. Plenty of local production is taking place in the country. South African consumer

Composition of Merchandise Trade, 1993

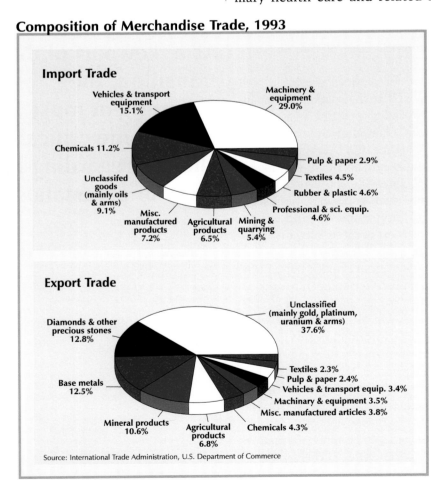

Import Trade

- Machinery & equipment 29.0%
- Vehicles & transport equipment 15.1%
- Chemicals 11.2%
- Unclassifed goods (mainly oils & arms) 9.1%
- Misc. manufactured products 7.2%
- Agricultural products 6.5%
- Mining & quarrying 5.4%
- Professional & sci. equip. 4.6%
- Rubber & plastic 4.6%
- Textiles 4.5%
- Pulp & paper 2.9%

Export Trade

- Unclassified (mainly gold, platinum, uranium & arms) 37.6%
- Diamonds & other precious stones 12.8%
- Base metals 12.5%
- Mineral products 10.6%
- Agricultural products 6.8%
- Chemicals 4.3%
- Misc. manufactured articles 3.8%
- Machinary & equipment 3.5%
- Vehicles & transport equip. 3.4%
- Pulp & paper 2.4%
- Textiles 2.3%

Source: International Trade Administration, U.S. Department of Commerce

resistance to the high cost of brand-name drugs, however, is growing. Generic substitutes are not readily available, except for selected government tenders. The most promising subsector is that of anti-tuberculosis drugs.

Franchising

Franchising is one of the most promising sectors for business growth in South Africa today. There are currently some 90 franchisors in South Africa, 60 of whom are members of the Franchise Association of Southern Africa (FASA). By far the largest franchise sector in South Africa is the fast food industry, followed by other service sectors such as automobile servicing, educational training, hair care salons and industrial cleaning services.

Sectoral Contributions to GDP, 1993

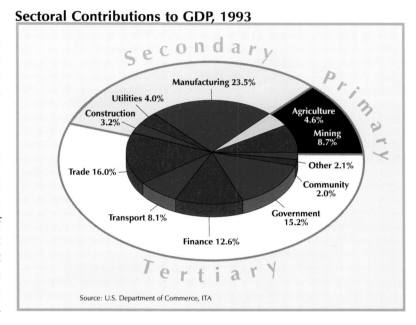

Source: U.S. Department of Commerce, ITA

MARKET ACCESS

The South African government, along with leading bankers and economists, is endeavoring to transform the economy from an isolated import substitution regime into an outward-oriented one based on export production. The South African economy achieved some measure of diversification and self-sufficiency through policies of import substitution, protection of infant industries through high tariffs and the establishment of parastatal industries. The regime reflects a strong reluctance on the part of the local established business community to have to compete against new entrants into the market.

The reduction of tariffs, elimination of import permits and removal of import surcharges are of paramount importance to achieving greater market access for American companies, not to mention the key role that such actions would play in enhancing South Africa's international competitiveness.

U.S. firms involved in South Africa's reconstruction and development programs will contribute to the country's revitalization process while gaining a strong commercial foothold in the new South Africa and beyond.

Tariffs and Import Barriers

South Africa's Minister of Trade and Industry, Trevor Manuel, has already moved forward to implement tariff reductions in selected industries (textiles and autos, for example) and pledged to terminate past protective policies of increasing tariffs whenever a local company or industry perceives a threat of foreign competition. The import surcharge on capital goods was eliminated last year and the import surcharge will

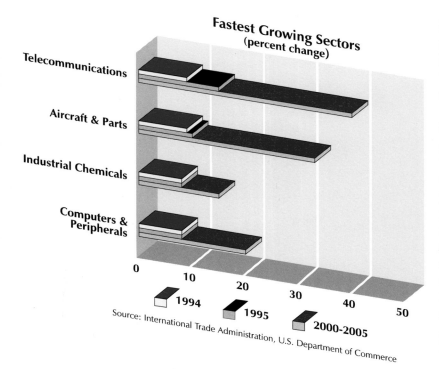

Fastest Growing Sectors
(percent change)

Telecommunications

Aircraft & Parts

Industrial Chemicals

Computers & Peripherals

0   10   20   30   40   50

1994   1995   2000-2005

Source: International Trade Administration, U.S. Department of Commerce

be eliminated on October 1, 1995. The government has stated its intention to honor its General Agreement on Tariffs and Trade (GATT) commitments. South Africa was a founding member of the GATT.

South Africa follows the Harmonized System (HS) of import classification. Many goods enter duty free, while those subject to duty generally pay at a rate between 5 and 25 percent. South Africa imposes high protective tariffs and import surcharges on products that are manufactured locally and on luxury goods. Import permits are only required for selected products. Importers are subject to exchange control approval, administered by the South African Reserve Bank — often just a formality. However, advance payment for imports is limited and generally not allowed under the Reserve Bank's exchange control regulations.

A value-added tax (VAT) of 14 percent is payable on nearly all imports. Goods imported for use in manufacturing or resale by registered traders may be exempt from the VAT. Also various rebates and relief of duties exist for cases in which the imported commodity will be used in a subsequent domestic production process.

Government Procurement Practices

Government purchasing is a significant factor in the South African economy. Nearly all such purchasing is done through competitive bidding on invitations for tenders, which are published in an official state publication. The purchasing procedures of the central government and parastatal institutions favor products of local manufacture and local content. Foreign firms must bid through local agents. As part of the government's policy to encourage local industry, a price preference schedule, based on the percent of local content in relation to the tendered price, is employed to compare tenders.

The government is currently reviewing the procurement process with a view toward enhancing the participation of

---

Trevor Manuel on the Private Sector

"The democratization of South Africa is something much deeper than our elections and the wonderful inauguration of our president...[It] is about our economy. ...it is about ensuring that we can become more competitive, that we can enlarge [our economy's] strengths...[the] role of government is defined and limited in [this] respect. We have some role to play in shaping the vision and bringing parties together, but at the end of the day it is firms that will compete with firms."

— *Trevor Manuel, South African Minister of Trade and Industry, Co-Chair, U.S.-South Africa Business Development Committee*

---

small and medium-sized companies in contracting. Provincial government purchases are increasingly significant and follow similar procedures. With the establishment of nine new provincial governments in South Africa, the prospects for additional government procurement below the central government level are noteworthy.

Openness to Foreign Investment

The government treats foreign investment essentially the same as domestic enterprise. Foreign investors are permitted 100 percent ownership. Screening of foreign investment does not normally occur. No performance requirements are levied in order to obtain permission for foreign investment. There are, however, local content requirements in the automotive, telecommunication equipment, and television assembly sectors. Foreign insurance and banking firms are required to incorporate locally.

The only significant difference for the foreign investor is a limitation on access to local borrowing. Companies that are 25 percent or more owned or controlled by non-residents face limits on local borrowing. The primary purpose of these restrictions, according to the South Africans, is to ensure the adequate capitalization of foreign investments and to prevent excessive gearing, i.e., a company borrowing against its share capital. The definition of local borrowing includes overdrafts, financial leasing of capital equipment, mortgage bonds and local shareholders' loans in excess of foreign shareholders' loans.

It is estimated that a foreign investor' potential tax liability in South Africa is 48 percent. Although no bilateral tax agreement is in force between South Africa and the U.S., the two governments have begun the process of negotiating a new bilateral tax treaty to replace the 1947 one terminated by the Comprehensive Anti-Apartheid Act of 1986. South Africa has bilateral investment agreements with several governments,

President Mandela's Pledge

Addressing a February 13, 1995, investment conference in Johannesburg, President Mandela pledged a positive climate in South Africa for foreign investment and economic growth, based on fiscal discipline, frugal use of resources, respect for GATT obligations, diminished protectionism and eased foreign exchange controls. He commented that the new South Africa had achieved a degree of national reconciliation, unity and stability that many would have thought impossible. Consultation among all parties would remain the order of the day; South Africa was a nation united in pursuit of common goals. He said that South Africa's strategy for growth and development would be developed in joint partnership between government, business and labor. Mandela's remarks were warmly received by the audience of 400 South African business leaders, foreign investors and government officials.

Foreign Investment in South Africa—by Region

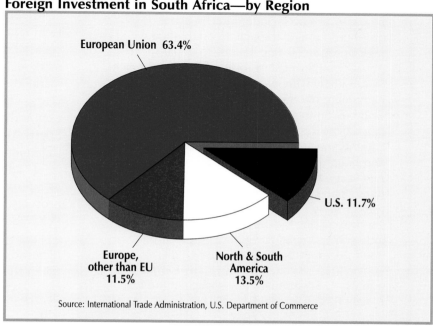

European Union 63.4%

U.S. 11.7%

Europe, other than EU 11.5%

North & South America 13.5%

Source: International Trade Administration, U.S. Department of Commerce

including Paraguay and Taiwan. The U.S. and South Africa are hopeful to negotiate a bilateral investment treaty in the near future. The country became a member of the Multilateral Investment Guarantee Agency (MIGA) in 1993.

Special Considerations

Intellectual Property Rights

South Africa's intellectual property laws and practices are generally in conformity with those of the industrialized nations, including the U.S. South Africa, like the U.S., is a member of the two major multilateral conventions pertaining to intellectual property: the Paris Convention for the Protection of Industrial Property and the Berne Convention for the Protection of Literary and Artistic Works. In addition, South Africa is a signatory to the World Trade Organization (WTO) Agreement on Trade Related Aspects of Intellectual Property Rights (TRIPS).

The basic objective of South African government policy with respect to foreign intellectual property rights holders is to secure access to foreign technology and information. Copyright legislation enacted in 1992 provides further protection for computer software. The Trademarks Act of 1993 and implementing regulations came into effect in May 1995 and, for the most part, bring South Africa into compliance with its international obligations.

Recently, a number of U.S. companies have complained about facing problems in establishing and defending their trademarks. Some companies which had registered trademarks in South Africa but refrained from conducting business during the anti-apartheid sanctions period are being challenged by local companies and risk losing their trademarks because of non-use. Both the old and new trademark legislation permit expungement of registered marks that have not been used for more than five years, unless there are special circumstances to excuse the non-use. It is not yet clear whether the South African courts will consider non-use during the sanctions period a valid special circumstance.

In addition, South Africa's 1963 trademark law, as interpreted by the courts, provided inadequate protection to well-known international marks. While South Africa's new trademark law provides adequate protection prospectively, it does not protect those companies whose marks were pirated under the old law.

Representation in the Market

South Africa offers foreign exporters a wide variety of methods to distribute and sell their products. These include using an agent or distributor; selling through an established wholesaler or dealer; selling directly to department stores or other retailers; or establishing a branch or subsidiary with its own sales force. Capital equipment often is best handled by distributors who buy on their own account and carry a wide range of spares. Distributors frequently handle commodities such as chemicals, pharmaceuticals and brand name products on an exclusive basis. Agents are often used for the distribution of durable and nondurable consumer goods, as well as some industrial raw materials. Consumer goods requiring maintenance of stocks and industrial raw materials often are exported to South Africa through established wholesalers. South Africa does not maintain any formal import quotas. U.S. nationals may engage in the full range of trade activities.

For these reasons, the U.S. Trade Representative placed South Africa on the "watch list" after the 1995 Special 301 review.

Future Political Risks

Another major factor which will potentially affect the business climate in South Africa is the extent of politically and criminally motivated violence in certain areas of the country. Although the elections proceeded peacefully throughout the country, the threat of political violence is nonetheless still present in KwaZulu/Natal, the only province where the Inkatha Freedom Party won the election and where the results were bitterly disputed by the African National Congress (ANC). Throughout the rest of the country, however, political violence is expected to remain at a low ebb.

The makeup of any future government, which will operate under a new constitution yet to be written, could have a direct affect on the stability for investment. In his opening address to the ANC conference, Mandela acknowledged that the vast majority of black South Africans have yet to see tangible benefits from the defeat of white-minority rule. He admitted that his government has been slow in implementing social programs for the so-long disenfranchised. Yet delegates confirmed South Africa's black majority is willing to give the new government time to deliver on the promises of jobs, houses, health care and education.

THE COMPETITION

With the ready acceptance and good reputation American products enjoy in South Africa, the U.S. can edge foreign competition, even though many of our rivals did not impose or enforce sanctions as vigorously. The contest for a piece of the South African market, however, will be intense and results-oriented. South Africa's emerging market will require U.S. private sector innovation, productivity, market savvy and determination.

In the Commerce Department's effort to aid U.S. business, the department has both raised the profile and expanded the staff of its Foreign Commercial Service (FCS) office in Johannesburg. The Secretary assigned to South Africa his one personal political appointment as Minister Counselor. This official is responsible for developing a road map to increase the U.S. commercial presence in South Africa and throughout the southern Africa region.

The regional program developed by the minister counselor is designed to assist American firms in participating in the economic rebuilding of South Africa and gaining enhanced competitive access to markets throughout the region. In addition to this appointment, the commercial staff presence in the country has been augmented. Meanwhile, all of South Africa's major trading partners have stepped up their trade promotion activities and announced trade and investment finance and insurance programs to promote stronger commercial ties. Some 400 foreign business delegations have visited South Africa since the country's political transition.

1994's annualized growth rate of 2.3 percent indicates that the economy is responding positively to the economic policies of the new government.

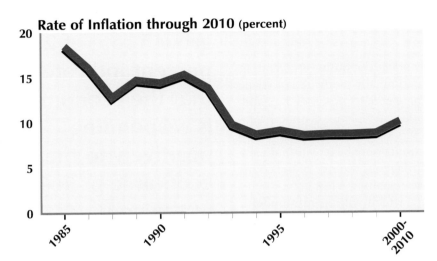

Rate of Inflation through 2010 (percent)

Source: DRI/McGraw Hill, *World Markets Executive Overview,* second quarter 1995

Germany

Germany is South Africa's leading supplier, with the U.S. a close second. Germany's interests overall are represented by about 350 companies. German companies—most of which remained in South Africa during the sanctions era—started consolidating investments in 1993. Siemens, the electronics/instrumentation company, is planning a major manufacturing plant in South Africa. German-based giants—including BMW, Mercedes-Benz and Volkswagen—also are investigating the possibilities of broadening their investments in the country. South Africa is in discussions with Germany for a reciprocal investment protection agreement.

United Kingdom

Projects in telecommunications, construction, security and water purification sectors have been identified for British companies and for the EU program for Reconstruction and Development in South Africa. About 50 percent of the U.K.'s overseas development aid budget has been allocated to developing South Africa into a thriving business partner. The U.K. announced a series of trade and business measures aimed at fostering bilateral relations with South Africa this year, including nine trade missions of leading British industrialists to South Africa. The campaign—called Britain Means Business and initiated by Prime Minister Major—began with "Opportunity Cape Town" in March 1995. "Opportunity Johannesburg" begins in September and will include a U.K. Industrial and Technological exhibition, with an "Opportunity Durban" to take place next year. Britain has about 1,500 companies in South Africa at this time.

France

Foreign investment also is on the rise. The French government has set impressive goals for an increased share of the market, stating its desire to double private sector investment stock in South Africa to $1 billion by mid-1996. Even before the South African elections and their peaceful outcome, French investment had increased from about 60 companies. New investment includes a French development funding institution, Caisse Francaise de Development, which started this year. Since the lifting of sanctions, the number of French companies in South Africa has almost doubled.

Asia

South Africa's main Asian market is Japan, supplying 10 percent of South African imports. South Africa's exports to Pacific Rim nations—most notably Taiwan, Hong Kong, South Korea, Singapore, Malaysia, Thailand, Indonesia and the Philippines—grew in 1994 following a 15 percent increase in 1993.

South Africa's second leading Asian market is Taiwan, followed by Hong Kong, South Korea, Singapore and Thailand. Export growth to Malaysia and Indonesia has been dramatic, clearly in response to the end of apartheid. Most of South Africa's exports to the Asian region are coal, minerals, base metals, chemicals, and pulp and paper. South Africa is in discussions with Taiwan over possible investment in the petrochemical industry and the development of state-owned fuel-from-gas producer Mossgas. An informal joint task force is considering a Taiwanese proposal to invest in a refinery, an olefins plant, an aromatics plant and downstream plastics fiber and textile production facilities.

> — *Contributors: Emily Solomon, Katie Moore,*
> *Dennis Goldenson, Sally Miller*

Leading Sources of Imports/Destination of Exports

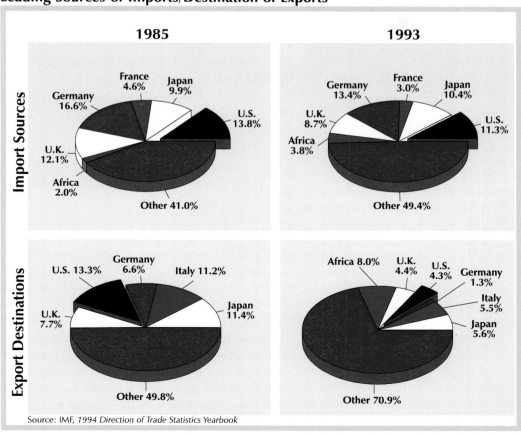

Source: IMF, *1994 Direction of Trade Statistics Yearbook*

Turkey: At

The Turkish economy is a study in contrasts. Dynamic industries coexist with pockets of subsistence agriculture. Hubs of major, cosmopolitan cities with financial and trading centers in western Anatolia exist alongside the barely developed east. There are even great disparities among Turkey's main agricultural regions: the Mediterranean coast, with its large export-oriented commercial farms; the central plateau, with its traditional grain farmers; and eastern Anatolia, where subsistence farmers and nomadic shepherds predominate.

But with a young and rapidly growing population of 61.2 million and a land mass larger than any country in Western Europe (roughly the size of Texas), Turkey possesses a small, very wealthy, Western-oriented upper class and a sizeable and growing middle class of salaried workers and small business owners who are becoming major consumers of imports. As per capita income continues to grow, both disposable income and domestic consumption levels will fuel demand for more imports.

In addition, one of Turkey's most salient characteristics is its location, standing at the crossroads where Europe meets Asia, an added attraction for businesses interested in building relationships in both the West and the East. Turkey's historic trading links with the neighboring Arab countries, the Near East and Europe are growing. Turkey is serving as a launching site for doing business with the republics of the former Soviet Union, with Istanbul becoming an airline transportation hub for the region and a commercial gateway for the general area.

Turkey's economy is one of the largest outside of the industrialized world with a GDP of $131 billion. U.S. exports to Turkey were a record $3.4 billion in 1993, rising almost 26 percent over 1992 levels. During the 1981-93 period, Turkey grew at an average annual rate of 5 percent, ranking it at the top of the Organization of Economic Cooperation and Development (OECD) markets. As a result of a brief and sharp downturn, Turkey's GDP fell by 5.4 percent in 1994 (U.S. exports to Turkey also dropped 20 percent in 1994 to about $2.8 billion), it is projected that Turkey's economy will rebound in 1995 and 1996, with growth rates of 3 and 5 percent respectively.

Turkish industry is divided among public enterprises dominated by heavy industry and raw materials processing (many of which are on the privatization block); diversified, large family-owned holding companies which account for 20 percent of the nation's GDP; and generally smaller private sector firms concentrating on producing consumer goods. The services sector is perhaps the most diverse, ranging from large marketing

Population	**61 Million**
Population Growth Rate	**2.2%**
Gross Domestic Product	**US$ 131 Billion**
GDP Growth Rate	**– 5.4%**
Per Capita GDP	**US$ 2,139**
Inflation Rate	**130%**
Industrial Production, % Change	**– 5.7%**

1994. Source: U.S. Dept. of Commerce, ITA
Note: 1994 figures for GDP growth rate and industrial production are atypical. GDP growth for 1996-2000 is projected at 5+% annually. Industrial growth is projected to resume high-level increases over the next decade.

the Crossroads

groups that dominate exporting to small shops. Services, including construction, trade, tourism, transport and communications, account for roughly 60 percent of Turkey's GDP; industry accounts for 25 percent; and agriculture accounts for 15 percent.

At the present time, the U.S., with a 10.4 percent share of Turkey's imports in 1994, is the second largest supplier to the Turkish market after Germany. With appropriate marketing and effective local representation, U.S. exporters should be able to increase their presence during the current economic expansion. The U.S. share of the Turkish market already is higher than the U.S. share of the European Union market.

An Almost Smooth Transition

From the 1930s until 1980, Turkey maintained a protected economy, with large state enterprises and high tariff barriers. That began to change in 1980 when the country embarked on an economic development program that included the liberalization of import restrictions, fostering greater domestic competition, privatization of state enterprises and the reduction of taxes. The rapid growth policy initiated by the government promoted extensive industrialization and construction of major projects at the national and local level. Real gross national product growth averaged 5 percent annually from 1981 to 1993— a much higher growth level than the other western OECD countries. This high growth rate meant substantial and broadly-based improvements in the standard of living.

Then in 1994, Turkey experienced an abrupt interruption in its development. After a decade of rapid growth and expanding output, Turkey suffered a financial crisis brought on by chronic public sector deficits, galloping inflation, lack of

Turkey's economy is one of the largest outside of the industrialized world, with a GDP of $131 billion.

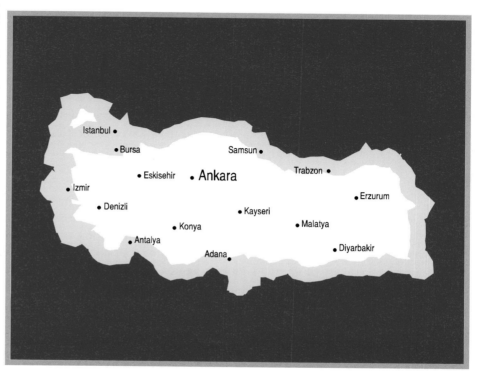

Ataturk's Legacy

No discussion of Turkey, no matter how brief, would ever be complete without mentioning the contribution of Mustafa Kemal Atatürk. He alone was the key person who united Turkey, gained its independence, and then as the first president, introduced numerous reforms to propel the new nation from the Ottoman days into the modern era.

Mustafa Kemal was born in 1881 in Salonika, at that time part of the Ottoman Empire. He received military training and became a distinguished Commander in World War I when he defeated the British at Gallipoli. When Turkey was partitioned by the occupying Allied powers after World War I, Kemal established Ankara as his base and drove the occupying forces out of Anatolia. On October 29, 1923, Turkey became a republic, Ankara the capital city, and Kemal the president.

Mustafa Kemal then embarked on a series of revolutionary reforms that transformed the way of life in Turkey. While respecting religious traditions, he promoted the secular laws for equal treatment regardless of religion, introduced a modified Latin alphabet enabling the Turkish language to be written phonetically, and women were given equal status to men--polygamy became illegal. When the Surname Act was adopted in 1934, requiring a family name to be taken, Kemal was given the surname Atatürk - "Father of all Turks" by Parliament.

confidence by international financial institutions in making loans and the government's slow response to resolving these problems. With the onset of the crisis, a government austerity program was imposed in April 1994, bringing cutbacks in government procurement and a freeze on major projects. The Turkish lira was devalued.

The economy now appears to be responding to the austerity measures, and other corrective steps are being considered, among them, reduction of public sector employment, reform of the social security system, tax reform and accelerated privatization of state enterprises. Before these programs can be implemented, however, the present government must gain the support of its coalition partners and pass needed legislation in the Parliament. With some decisive government action, Turkey could quickly return to rapid industrial expansion and major project development, which would again provide an extensive range of opportunities for U.S. export sales.

After 1995, Turkey should be in a good position to resume growth rates which could average 5 percent annually for the next decade. Import and export levels should also resume a more normal growth pattern after 1995. Again, if past is prologue, Turkish imports should grow by some 15 percent annually until the year 2000.

Major infrastructure projects top the list of opportunities for exporters. Over the next several years, emphasis will be placed on new power generation projects undertaken on a build-operate-transfer (BOT) basis, as well as the upgrading of existing power generation facilities. The telecommunications sector is also expected to offer exciting opportunities for U.S. suppliers through licensing of value-added services and privatization. A rapidly growing consumer market also offers U.S. firms a wide array of sales opportunities at the retail level. Environmental concerns and industrialization are creating a mounting need for pollution control equipment and waste disposal plants as well as consulting services in this sector. Turkey should enjoy additional stimulus to its economy as trade opens up with the EU and other countries in Europe. Conclusion of a customs union with the EU will spur investment spending.

In addition, the government has been pursuing a privatization program for many years and has sold off several state economic enterprises (SEEs). But overall, the program has proceeded slowly. Ultimately, firms from paper plants to the national airline are slated to be sold. The Turkish government's plan to privatize its many state-owned enterprises has been stalled due to the lack of political will needed to deal with the large lay-offs that would result and court decisions which have dealt setbacks to the wide-ranging temporary powers given the Privatization Administration. However, Turkey's economic crisis and the need to reduce public-sector deficits may have provided the impetus to move forward.

Sectoral Components of GDP, 1993

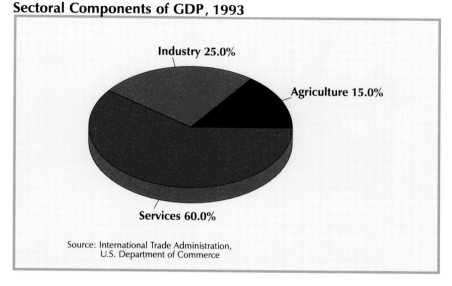

Industry 25.0%

Agriculture 15.0%

Services 60.0%

Source: International Trade Administration, U.S. Department of Commerce

The major outstanding trade issues for the U.S. in its relations with Turkey include the lack of effective intellectual property rights in Turkey, lengthy, convoluted bidding procedures for large Turkish government contracts, and Turkey's approaching customs union with the EU.

The other notable question mark in Turkey is the Kurdistan Workers' Party (PKK), a terrorist group active primarily in southeastern Turkey, although it also has planted several bombs in the urbanized west and Aegean resorts to harm the Turkish tourism industry. This activity—which distracts and worries Turkey's trading partners—and the human rights criticism accompanying Turkey's battle with terrorists are dark spots on an otherwise bright picture. Yet even before these problems are resolved, Turkey's economic reforms and accession to the EU customs area will move it forward in the eyes of Western businesspeople on the alert for vast potential export markets.

BIG EMERGING SECTORS

Turkey is seeking rapid economic and industrial growth. It has established numerous national and regional projects to propel the nation onto a self-sustaining high growth path, creating more jobs and a better way of life for its citizens. In addition to the capital investment made by the private sector and the purchases of consumer goods by a growing middle class, Turkish government authorities are seeking to construct a vast range of major infrastructure projects.

Turkey possesses a small, Western-oriented upper class and a sizeable and growing middle class. Both are major consumers of imports.

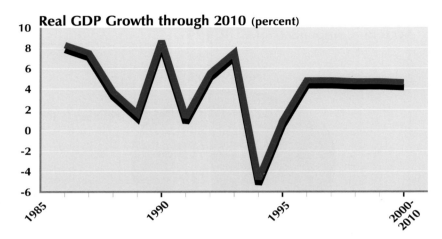

Real GDP Growth through 2010 (percent)

Source: DRI/McGraw Hill, *World Markets Executive Overview,* second quarter 1995

Local municipalities, cities such as Istanbul and Izmir, are planning major water and sanitation facilities to cope with a growing population and demands for improved services. Roadways, schools, hospitals and power plants must be built or upgraded and expanded. The central authorities are undertaking infrastructure projects of unusually massive scale to prepare the country for global competition and greater productivity. One of the most ambitious projects in the world is Turkey's Southeast Anatolia Regional Development Project (GAP).

Infrastructure

Over the past dozen years, Turkey has provided a key market for major infrastructure projects. U.S. firms are currently involved with projects ranging from the construction of highways to the provision of satellite data transmission services. The government continues to emphasize megaprojects as the way to develop Turkey's infrastructure: power plants, water and sewage systems, new ports and airports, urban transportation projects and continuation of the Southeast Anatolia Regional Development Project.

The Turkish government is attempting to carry out these projects mostly on a build-operate-transfer (BOT) basis or through the revenue-sharing model; transferring much of the financial and operating risk to the foreign supplier.

Turkey's 1994 economic crisis has frozen action and/or decisions on many projects and has slowed "non-essential" work on ongoing projects. That said, Turkey's infrastructure needs are tremendous, and Turkey will continue to offer an excellent market for U.S. goods and services. The following is a run-down of projects currently underway.

Southeast Anatolia Regional Development Project

The largest ongoing project in Turkey (and one of the largest in the world) is the Southeast Anatolia Regional Development Project (GAP) worth an estimated $30 billion. To date more than $10 billion already has been spent on the GAP, primarily to build dams for irrigation and power generation. This integrated regional development project envisages the construction of a complete infrastructure including power, irrigation systems, roads, airports, agro-industry, schools, training centers and hospitals.

Motorways

Motorway construction includes the Trans-European Motorway from Istanbul to the Syrian border. The section between Istanbul and Ankara is largely finished, while most of the work from Ankara to the Syrian border, with the exception of a patch already completed near Adana in the south, is in the design stage and has not yet been tendered. Motorways are planned and underway in other parts of the country but have not received the same priority. Bridge and tunnel crossings, which lend themselves to revenue-sharing, are in the planning stage for Izmit Bay (bridge) and the Bosphorous (tunnel).

Airports

The contractor selection process is near completion for modernization and expansion of the Istanbul and Antalya Airports on a BOT basis. A new international airport terminal is scheduled to be tendered for Ankara Esenboga Airport. For this terminal, project drawings and planning are complete. The U.S. Trade and Development Agency (TDA) has provided a $720,000 grant for design engineering work and project analysis associated with the development of a new international airport near Sanliurfa in the GAP region of Turkey. GAP administration has evaluated the bids and selected a consortium. This project is expected to be realized in the medium- to long-term, depending on the availability of financing and development of the region where large agricultural and agro-industry projects are underway.

Ports

Plans are underway for the Izmir Port Dredging Project, the Izmir Port Expansion Project, Candarli Port Project (construction of a new port near Izmir) and the Filyos Port Project (near Zonguldak on the Black Sea Coast). The government hopes that these major works can be done with private investors on a BOT basis.

A Customs Union With Europe

Turkey has been seeking to establish a customs union relationship with the EU which could lead, in time, to eventual full EU membership. The customs union relationship would permit duty-free trade between Turkey and the EU members for most industrial products. Agricultural products would not be included.

EU and European Free Trade Agreement (EFTA) countries currently receive a lower duty rate from Turkey than other countries do under Turkey's association agreement with the EU and its free-trade agreement with EFTA countries. If Turkey reaches a complete customs union with the EU, then most industrial goods imported from the EU will then enter Turkey duty free.

The customs union arrangement, while currently agreed upon, has not been finalized by the European Parliament because of concerns over human rights developments in Turkey. The Parliament is expected to review Turkey's overall human rights record in the fall of 1995 and vote on customs union status then.

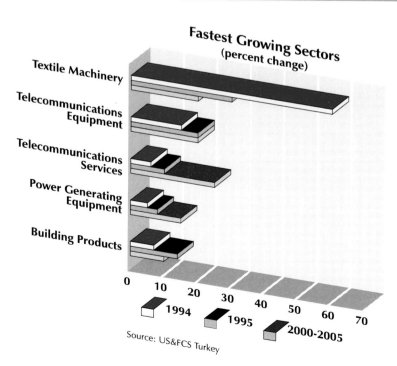

Fastest Growing Sectors
(percent change)

Textile Machinery
Telecommunications Equipment
Telecommunications Services
Power Generating Equipment
Building Products

0   10   20   30   40   50   60   70

1994   1995   2000-2005

Source: US&FCS Turkey

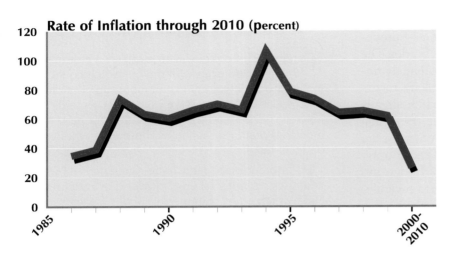

Rate of Inflation through 2010 (percent)

Source: DRI/McGraw Hill, *World Markets Executive Overview,* second quarter 1995

Newly Independent Central Asian Republics

Several of the newly independent republics which formed after the collapse of the Soviet Union have a common ethnic and religious background with Turkey. Many speak the Turkic language and look to Turkey as a rapidly growing and developing nation for commercial ties. The new republics of Azerbaijan, Kazakhstan, Kyrgyzstan, Tajikistan, Turkmenistan and Uzbekistan are Muslim states having natural ties to Turkey. These six states have a combined population of about 58 million and abundant natural resources—but little hard currency.

Energy

Turkey will require an average of 2500 MW additional power capacity each year through the year 2010 to meet increased demand. Turkey's 1993 electricity demand was 73.7 billion KW and is expected to increase to 95 billion KW in 1996, 130 billion KW in 2000, 190 billion KW in 2005 and 271 billion KW by the year 2010. Such an increase in capacity will require outlays of $31.5 billion over the next 15 years. Additionally, $8.5 billion will be required for the construction of transmission and distribution lines.

U.S. technology is well-known in Turkey for its quality and, increasingly, for its competitive price. The best sales prospects for American exporters include: co-generation equipment, boilers and heat exchangers, steam turbines, gas turbines, transformers, switches, switchgear and switchboard apparatus, as well as insulated electric conductors.

A recent long-term demand projection study conducted by the Turkish Electricity Generation Transmission Company (TEAS) indicates that Turkey's current 20,500 MW installed power generation capacity needs to be increased to 60,000 MW by the year 2010. To accomplish that, 26,500 MW additional thermal and 13,000 MW additional hydroelectric power plants must be built. Thermal power plant projects currently include: 33 fossil-fuel (lignite) power plant units; 14 natural gas combined-cycle power plant units; 12 fossil fuel (imported hard coal) power plant units; and two nuclear power plants.

In 1994, the thermal and hydroelectric power generating equipment market was approximately $225 million. Some 90 percent of total market demand was met by imported equipment. Imports of thermal and hydro power generating equipment were $230 million in 1993. After falling back to $225 million in 1994, they are expected to total $250 million in 1995. An average annual growth rate of 8 percent is anticipated over the next three years for this market.

The 1995 market demand for electrical generating equipment (90 percent of which is imported) is estimated at $275 million. During the next three years, an annual growth rate of 8 percent is expected in this sector, as well. New thermal and hydro power plant construction will keep this trend going. Cogeneration plant demand for large industrial plants and housing complexes will also continue growing for a supply of more reliable and cheaper electricity. The greatest demand will be for combined-cycle and small hydro power generation equipment.

Since natural gas was introduced to Turkey, public awareness of clean technologies has increased and therefore combined-cycle type power generation and clean-coal technologies will be used more to reduce air pollution, especially near Istanbul.

Privatization of thermal power plants and the regional distribution companies of the Turkish Electricity Distribution Company (TEDAS), the other division of the Turkish Electricity Authority, is planned and should create additional opportunities for U.S. companies

Aerospace

U.S. products in this sector enjoy a superb reputation. A significant number of the small airplanes used in Turkey are Cessnas. American-made planes also dominate the market for large-capacity aircraft. U.S. aircraft parts also enjoy a high reputation in Turkey.

In 1993, Turkey imported $1.4 billion worth of aircraft and aircraft parts. Turkey has imported $40 million worth of aircraft parts annually for the last several years. Such imports are expected to show steady growth (3 percent annually) in future years. There is little local production in Turkey, and American firms will be competing mainly with Western European suppliers to satisfy the increased demand, although their market share is significantly lower than that of U.S. suppliers, which has averaged 80 percent.

The state-owned Turkish airline, THY, will continue to offer a good market for aircraft and parts as it implements plans to modernize its fleet of approximately 450 aircraft to compete with Europe's major carriers. Imports of aircraft parts also are expected to increase because THY is now receiving requests from the Turkic republics of the former Soviet Union to perform maintenance and overhaul on their aircraft at its FAA-authorized facility at Istanbul Airport. At present, mostly THY aircraft are being serviced at this facility. Turkey, through THY, has established Istanbul as a hub for its increasing service to the newly independent republics and is hoping that other airlines will also use its maintenance/service facility in Istanbul.

Information Technology

Telecommunications Equipment and Service

With appropriate project financing and advanced technology and management techniques, American firms can significantly expand their market presence in Turkey, at the same time, allowing Turkey to leapfrog into the next millennium with the most advanced systems in the world. Imports of American products in 1993 accounted for approximately 13 percent of the total telecommunications import market. For 1993, Turkish imports of U.S. telecommunications equipment were over $43 million. U.S. imports are expected to grow at an average rate of almost 12 percent annually over the next three years.

> In 1993, Turkey imported $1.4 billion worth of aircraft and aircraft parts. American-made planes dominate the market for large-capacity aircraft.

Hanging On In The Telecom Business

A U.S. corporation, one of the world's leading providers of wireless communications equipment and services, finally succeeded in entering the Turkish cellular market. But it wasn't easy.

The firm first approached Turkish PTT (TPTT), now Turk Telecom, in 1990 and proposed establishing a total access cellular system (TACS) on a revenue-sharing basis. TPTT would provide the physical plant, the contractor providing equipment at its cost, and TPTT would operate the system with the technical support and marketing of the contractor. TPTT would collect the revenue from subscribers and share with the contractor. The revenue-sharing concept put forward by the U.S. firm was built into a tender by TPTT

TPTT made a tender on a revenue-sharing basis for an analog type cellular system in 1991. There were three bidders: the U.S. firm and two European companies. Then the Turks cancelled the tender. In 1992, TPTT made a new one and the same firms bid again. The U.S. firm made the best revenue-sharing offer.

It was the end of 1992 when TPTT decided to go with two firms, the U.S. company was one of them. The winners were given a month to prepare a draft contract and to come to TPTT to negotiate. But the U.S. firm had no office in Turkey. By the time it came to negotiate, almost a month had passed. TPTT cancelled the project and switched its goal to a different kind of cell system. The U.S. firm kept on bidding in the next stage; while it eventually lost out to two other providers, it refused to despair. It set up an office in Istanbul. Thanks to excellent marketing and relentless day-to-day contact, the company won a large contract worth $25 million from one of the winning service providers (along with the prospect of future similar deals).

The Turks generally consider U.S. telecommunications products to be of high quality and reliability. Best sales prospects for U.S. exporters include: fiber optic cable and related equipment, VSAT systems, IBS earth stations, mobile earth stations and mobile satellite services, synthesized hand-held radio systems, trunked radio systems, GSM-type pocket phones, data transmission equipment, chipcard-type public phones, CATV equipment and lightweight portable satcom terminals.

For 1993, the telecommunications equipment market in Turkey was valued at an estimated $750 million. Although a significant amount of telecommunications equipment is produced domestically, imports account for some 45 percent ($338 million) of the total market, which is expected to approach $1.3 billion by the year 2000 and to surpass $1.5 billion by 2005.

The modernization of Turkey's telephone network began in earnest in 1984, when total exchange capacity was at 1.9 million lines. Today, that number has increased to approximately 13.7 million lines (or a teledensity of 20 lines per 100), with 89 percent of the trunk network and 73 percent of the local exchange network served by digital exchanges. Of existing lines, 55 percent are residential and 45 percent are for business, with the residential market increasing. Since 1984, telephone service has increased from approximately 28 percent of the rural villages to virtually 100 percent coverage today.

Turk Telecom's cellular telephone system covers all of the urban centers, most provinces of western, central and southern Anatolia and the highways linking these areas. Geographic coverage is extensive and there are currently around 90,000 subscribers. The cellular system has capacity constraints in the cities and the quality of portable phones varies. Paging is presently available in 40 provinces and is being extended to achieve nationwide coverage.

CATV service, provided by Turk Telecom, is available in nine regions of Turkey with 202,000 subscribers and a basic package offering 20 television channels and 20 radio stations, later expandable to 35 TV and 40 radio channels. By the end of 1995, the number of CATV subscribers in Turkey is expected to increase to somewhere between 300,000 and 400,000.

Packet-switched data services (TURKPAK), videotext, electronic mail and ISDN services are all in their developmental stages in Turkey, with significant long-term growth potential predicted. Turk Telecom is also exploring possibilities for radio local loop systems as a potential quick fix for the lack of facilities in certain areas. International telephone traffic, which has grown at an annual rate of 20 percent, will continue to expand rapidly.

According to a ten-year master plan prepared by Turk Telecom, approximately $12 billion will be spent for telecommunications infrastructure investments during the period 1993-2002. Privatization is the most significant development in this market. Currently, Turk Telecom is wholly-owned by the Turkish state, which retains the concession for domestic and international telecommunications services and is the major purchaser of telecommunications equipment in Turkey.

At present, Turk Telecom is almost completely closed to foreign suppliers of network equipment—the only major private vendors being three major switching ventures with two European firms and one Canadian firm. In 1994, the Turkish government called for Turk Telecom to be privatized regionally with new services to be established, and permitting private sector companies, foreign or domestic, to obtain licenses on a fee basis.

Transportation

Motor Vehicles and Parts

For many years the U.S. was the only supplier to the Turkish market, but gradually, European vehicles using European parts took over with the introduction of locally produced Renault and Fiat vehicles. Today, as the primary producers in the Turkish market, Europeans dominate the market with imported parts, joint venture partnerships and licensed production. However, for certain parts such as catalytic converters (mandatory in 1996), engine bearings, radiators, mufflers, exhaust pipes and service equipment including die cabinets and gas analyzers and diagnostic equipment, American products retain a sizeable market share.

Imports account for some 45 percent ($338 million) of the total telecom equipment market, which is expected to grow from $750 million in 1993 to more than $1.3 billion in 2000.

The Turkish automotive market is expected to enjoy significant growth over the next decade. While the number of vehicles per 1,000 persons is only 37 — the worldwide average is 86 and in the EU it is 350-400 — Turkey is poised to catch up.

The Turkish automotive market is expected to enjoy significant growth over the next decade. While the number of vehicles per 1,000 persons is only 37—the worldwide average is 86 and in the EU it is 350-400—Turkey is poised to catch up. The current automobile market stands at 2.7 million vehicles. Demand for automotive parts and service equipment in 1994 was estimated at $3.6 billion, some 20 percent of which was imported. Imports increased by 24 percent in 1993, but a similar increase is not expected until 1996. Expanded automobile service facilities will provide an additional market for service equipment totalling $60-70 million.

The main drag on consumer demand is the high taxes paid on vehicle purchases. Taxes total nearly 50 percent of the cost of the vehicle, while in the EU taxes average only 16 percent. The automotive sector is very sensitive to changes in the economy and thus demand dropped in 1994 as a result of the economic crisis. Demand had climbed to a record level in 1993. The reason, in part, was the availability of attractive consumer credits provided for vehicle purchasers and the expectation of both a rise in automobile taxes and hyperinflation. This buying spree created a new vehicle fleet, limiting the need for major aftermarket products for a while. After 1996, the market should resume its rapid growth rate.

For automotive parts, Turkey's expanded vehicle fleet will continue to require additional spare parts for maintenance and repair. All parts in the automotive sector except carburetors and spark plugs are produced in Turkey, some with foreign partners, some under foreign license agreements, and some with no foreign contribution. Most service equipment is imported; there is no significant local production in this field.

Environmental Technology

Although the reputation of U.S. products is generally good in the Turkish market, price and financing, as well as the design of a given project also affect receptivity. European engineering and contracting firms in Turkey are more active in specifying their own products than are U.S. counterparts, and this affects the origin of equipment used in a project. When a specific country finances a particular project, it ends up supplying most of the equipment and supplies required in that project. European suppliers also enjoy favorable customs duty rates for their products, charged in accordance with the EU-Turkey association agreement. U.S. market share has fluctuated between 9-12 percent over the last few years.

Market Share of Envirotech Sector, 1994

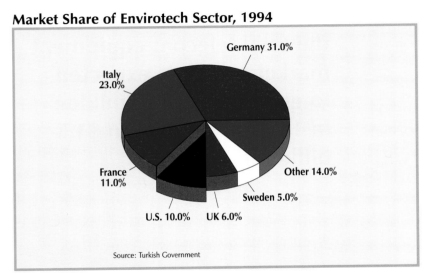

Germany 31.0%
Italy 23.0%
France 11.0%
U.S. 10.0% UK 6.0%
Sweden 5.0%
Other 14.0%

Source: Turkish Government

With the establishment of the Ministry of Environment in 1991, environmental issues have gained increased prominence. An Environmental Impact Assessment (EIA) regulation issued in 1993 requires each new industrial investor to prepare an EIA report and to include pollution control and treatment facilities. New regulations regarding sewage, medical waste and power plant emissions, among others, will add to the growth of this sector.

Moreover, past Turkish industrialization and continuing urbanization have created significant environmental challenges. Urban air pollution and water pollution in the Sea of Marmara and along the Aegean coast are of serious concern. Existing lignite-fired power generation plants need pollution control equipment retrofitting, while Turkish government plans for 20 new lignite plants will generate significant demand for clean-coal technology, particularly flue gas desulphurization systems. Other significant end-users of air pollution control equipment are the petrochemical, chemical, fertilizer, cement, automotive and metal-working industries. Turkish municipal governments are the most important buyers of water pollution/treatment equipment and systems.

Solid waste disposal is also a major problem and source of environmental pollution. Approximately 60 percent of Turkey's population lives in cities and towns with the disposal of waste made at unsupervised landfill areas. These locations may be within catchment basins of water reservoirs, close to residential areas, agricultural fields or forests.

The key market in Turkey for this sector is the local municipalities contracting for facilities and projects that are procured by competitive bidding procedures. The market is spurred even further by the need for municipalities to comply with regulations on solid and medical waste control regulations recently issued by Turkey's Ministry of Environment. Public and private organizations which generate solid wastes constitute the main group to adopt recycling technologies.

The total market demand exceeded $100 million in 1993, a 30 percent increase over 1992. A large market increase is expected in future years as the implementation of new projects proceeds.

Major Environmental Projects

The following ongoing and planned projects on disposal and recycling of solid wastes present export opportunities for U.S. firms over the next few years:

- Construction of new landfill sites and bio-gas facilities at Kemerburgaz and Sile, and six transfer stations, including procurement of 178 transfer containers;
- Rehabilitation of the Halkali, Kemerburgaz, and Umraniye landfill sites, and construction of an incinerator and a compost plant;
- Rehabilitation of a major landfill site at Mamak by the Ankara Metropolitan Municipality (AMM), currently serving three million people. The project has an estimated cost of $8.5 million;
- Construction of a new landfill site at Sincan and three transfer stations. Procurement of 30 transfer trucks and 84 transfer containers; and
- Construction of a new disposal site, and new transfer stations to serve the Izmir metropolitan area (with a population of approximately 2 million with projections of waste disposal needs of approximately 2,370 tons per day).

When a specific country finances a particular project, it ends up supplying most of the equipment and supplies required in that project.

Local production is limited to construction of containers and trucks, small-sized street sweepers, and screening and separating machines; the percentage of imports in the Turkish market is high. Turkey imports all equipment and apparatus for incineration plants, landfill compactors, transfer trucks and containers, large-size street sweepers, plastic geomembranes and laboratory measurement and analysis equipment. Imports reached $50 million in 1993, a 30 percent increase over 1992. An annual 30 percent increase in demand is expected to continue from 1994 on. This shows that imports will continue to play a major part in meeting total market demand in forthcoming years.

Several cities throughout Turkey are in need of project evaluation, design and construction to contain waste disposal in the context of a rapidly growing population and rapidly growing industrial development.

MARKET ACCESS

Tariffs and Import Barriers

Turkey is a member of the General Agreement on Tariffs and Trade (GATT) and regulates its customs practices in line with GATT requirements. In 1989, Turkey, along with the U.S., converted to the new Harmonized System (HS) of product classification for statistical and tariff purposes.

Turkey signed the final texts of the GATT Uruguay Round Agreement, thereby accepting the establishment of the World Trade Organization (WTO), the successor to the GATT, which formally came into being on January 1, 1995. Turkey ratified the WTO agreement in March 1995, but its obligations became effective on January 1, 1995. Turkey undertook few significant reductions on industrial tariffs in the Uruguay Round, choosing instead to cut rates from GATT bound levels on only a small percentage (28 percent) of its industrial tariff lines. Reductions on these items were generally within the range of a one-third cut, staged in over a five-year period. Consequently, tariffs on many items will remain high.

Trade with the U.S. is based on the Treaty of Commerce and Navigation of 1929. It provides for most-favored-nation (MFN) treatment in the application of all import and export duties and restrictions.

Foreign Investment in Turkey — by Country, 1994

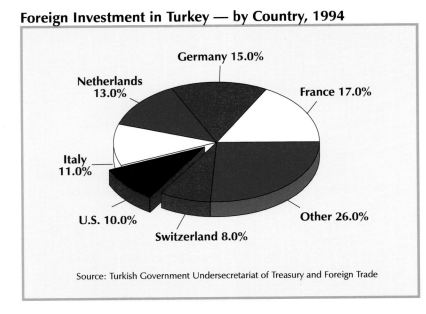

Germany 15.0%
Netherlands 13.0%
France 17.0%
Italy 11.0%
U.S. 10.0%
Switzerland 8.0%
Other 26.0%

Source: Turkish Government Undersecretariat of Treasury and Foreign Trade

Government Procurement Practices

Turkey normally follows competitive bidding procedures for domestic, international and multilateral development bank-assisted tenders. Turkey's procedures do not generally discriminate against U.S. suppliers, who succeed in winning a number of tenders. What frustrates U.S. companies, however, is the lengthy and often complicated bidding/negotiating process. Tenders for large projects are frequently opened, closed, revised and opened again. Repeated "best and final offers" are sometimes requested. In several cases, years have passed without a contractor being selected.

Furthermore, signing a contract does not mean that a firm can relax--contractual disputes and payment delays are common for large government projects. The government expects firms to be flexible when it changes contract terms or delays the implementation schedule (without price adjustments), but firms are strictly held to their commitments. Program changes are sometimes thought to be used to delay payments.

Also, as a consequence of Turkey's financial problems, supplier financing dramatically improves an exporter's chances of landing a major project tender; financing should be considered an important competitive aspect of the bid.

How To Begin Exporting to Turkey

1) Get on the Supplier List

As a general rule, government agencies procure through tenders and competitive bidding. Sometimes they buy directly from one specific company without calling tenders. Private companies can buy directly from the supplier of their choice. U.S. suppliers should contact the buyer for the government agency or the private firm directly to introduce their company and products and seek to get on the supplier list for future purchases.

2) Get an Agent or Distributor in Turkey

In Turkey, agency and distributor agreements are private contracts between the principals and the foreign firm. There are no unusual regulations which govern commission rates or termination rights. Advertising, and market promotion, as well as sales training, are essential tools in selling in Turkey. American companies are encouraged to identify aggressive agents who could provide these services. U.S. exporters can take advantage of U.S. Department of Commerce services to find an appropriate Agent/Distributor (ADS Service) or to find out more about a particular Turkish firm (WTDR Service) by applying to the U.S. Department of Commerce's local district office.

U.S. companies should be aware that, in addition to Turkey's main law which administers government procurement and which applies to agencies which have budgets allocated to them from the central budget, state-owned corporations (the SEEs) maintain their own procurement rules and regulations. These regulations are much more flexible since the SEEs operate as quasi-private sector companies.

BOT investments currently are the preferred procurement method by the Turkish government, especially in power, airport and port projects. In BOT projects, usually a consortium of companies arranges financing without government guarantees. The length of the agreement is determined by a feasibility study and must be agreed to by the Turkish government in negotiations. The U.S. Eximbank's new non-recourse project finance facility and Overseas Private Investment Corporation (OPIC) financing are excellent tools for American companies pursuing Turkish BOT projects.

The Turkish government encourages foreign investment and has made great strides in the last decade to enhance its investment climate. Turkey grants all rights, incentives, exemptions and privileges that are available to domestic firms to foreign investors.

BOT legislation effective as of June 1994 allows foreign firms to participate in some of the state investment projects which require advanced technology and/or large amounts of financing on a BOT basis.

Openness to Foreign Investment

The Turkish government encourages foreign investment and has made great strides in the last decade to enhance its investment climate. In principle, there is no discrimination against foreign investors at any stage of investment. Turkey grants all rights, incentives, exemptions and privileges that are available to domestic firms to foreign investors. In the aviation, maritime transportation, insurance, broadcasting and telecommunications areas, the equity participation ratio of foreign shareholders is limited to 49 percent. In no other major sectors do foreign investors not receive national treatment.

While Turkey recently has simplified investment procedures by establishing the General Directorate of Foreign Investment (GDFI) as a one-stop shop to deal with processing investment applications, granting investment incentives and locating joint venture partners, it continues to screen foreign investment. While Turkey's screening mechanism is routine and non-discriminatory, it can also be an impediment to the free flow of capital. Criteria for rejecting an investment are not restricted to national security concerns. Turkey also may impose performance requirements for completing an investment if the prospective investor is slated to benefit from government tax or investment incentives.

Prospective investors should also be aware that in some cases American investors have been forced to submit to protracted negotiations with the government of Turkey, whose position in these negotiations can be ill-defined, leading to the sense that the decision process is non-transparent.

A bilateral investment treaty (BIT) between the U.S. and Turkey entered into force on May 18, 1990. The BIT provides that American investors in Turkey will receive national treatment, except in certain sectors listed in the Annex. The BIT also provides for the right to repatriate capital, profits and dividends, and it guarantees access to binding international arbitration of disputes.

Special Considerations

Intellectual Property Rights

Turkey lacks adequate, modern laws concerning intellectual property protection, and even in cases of clear infringement, enforcement is lax and penalties are not severe enough to act as a deterrent. In order for action to be taken, a company must present authorities with an iron-clad case. In this legal climate, protecting products becomes a creative challenge for vulnerable companies.

As a result of its inadequate protection of intellectual property, since 1992 the U.S. has kept Turkey on the "priority watch list" under the Special 301 provisions of the 1988 Trade Act. In the course of customs union negotiations, Turkey has given assurances to the EU that it will modernize its intellectual property laws to conform with EU standards, but progress has been slow.

Under Turkish law, when the WTO/GATT Uruguay Round agreements come into force for Turkey in 1995, its Trade Related Intellectual Property Rights (TRIPs) provisions will take precedence over Turkish domestic legislation.

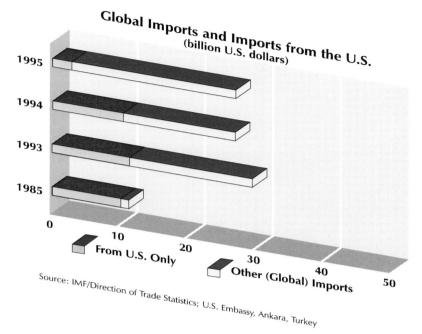

Global Imports and Imports from the U.S. (billion U.S. dollars)

Source: IMF/Direction of Trade Statistics; U.S. Embassy, Ankara, Turkey

THE COMPETITION

Although the U.S., with a 10.4 percent market share, is second only to Germany (16 percent share) as a supplier to the Turkish market, trade competition is fierce in both the market for government contracts and for opportunities within the private sector. Italy, France, the United Kingdom and Japan round out the list of the top foreign competitors.

Financing is key and some competitors combine project development financing with project financing for goods and services—and then together with the Turkish government decide annually on a list of priority projects to pursue. For example, for the Gaziantep Wastewater Treatment Plant Project, the U.S. Trade and Development Agency offered funding for a feasibility study, but the French offered that plus concessional financing for the project. Complete financing packages offer the best way to beat the competition out of the starting gate and across the finish line.

U.S. firms are well reminded that there will be no import duty rates applied by Turkey on products of European suppliers once their customs union is in place at the end of 1995.

Germany

Germany is Turkey's largest supplier, with a 16 percent share of the market. Approximately two million Turks now live in Germany, and many Turks were trained in Germany, providing Germany with a natural base from which to work.

The German finance agency, Kreditanstalt fuer Wiederaufbau (KfW), is very active in Turkey. KfW provides an average of $100-130 million in project finance credit availability per year to the Turkish government. KfW also provides grants for feasibility studies and full grants for projects in certain sectors such as environment, education and health or for particular geographic regions. KfW grants can be used for equipment procurement. Every year KfW signs a finance agreement with the Treasury. In addition, KfW provides export and commercial credits, which are generally more competitive than private bank credits, with lower interest rates and up to 100 percent financing. KfW's annual new exposure in Turkey exceeds $200 million.

Germany's Investment and Development Corporation (DEG) helps finance private German investment in Turkey. DEG has provided financing for approximately 15 projects totalling more than $35 million in Turkey. DEG's Istanbul office acts as a liaison to the Union of German Chambers of Trade and Industry and provides services to German business executives at cost or on a no-cost basis. Turkish firms can use the DEG to locate German trade and investment partners. In addition, the Germans established a Turkish-German Chamber of Commerce and Industry in 1994.

German firms are well represented in Turkey. Siemens, MAN, Hoechst, and Mercedes-Benz are some of the largest investors.

Leading Sources of Imports/Destination of Exports

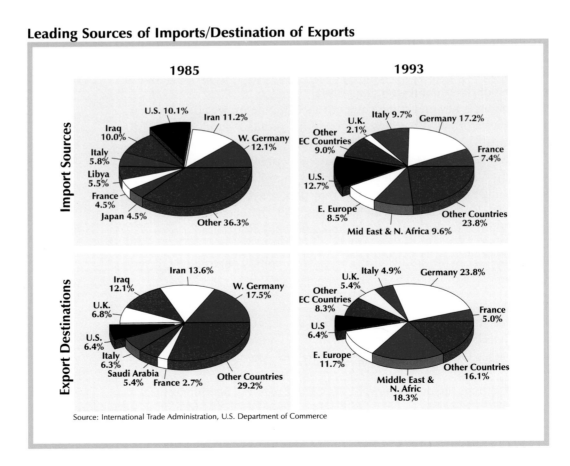

Source: International Trade Administration, U.S. Department of Commerce

Italy

Italy is Turkey's number three trading partner, with total exports exceeding $2.5 billion in 1993. This figure represents a 30 percent increase over 1992. Italy's export drive to Turkey started in 1990—its exports went up over 60 percent in one year from $1 billion to $1.7 billion.

The two leading organizations responsible for promotion of Italy's trade in Turkey are the Italian Foreign Trade Institute (ICE), a government agency operating under the Ministry of Foreign Trade, and the Italian Chamber of Commerce in Turkey. Both offices are located in Istanbul. ICE appears to be the most active in promoting Italian industry, providing commercial information and matchmaking between Italian and Turkish companies. Recently, ICE formed a special department to provide Italian firms with market information and joint venture opportunities in conjunction with Turkish firms in Central Asia.

Italian investments in Turkey increased in 1993 by a record $419 million. The main fields of Italian investment and Italian firms' involvement are: automotive and agricultural tractors (Fiat), trucks (Iveco), tires (Pirelli), automotive parts (Marelli), iron and steel (Ilva), durable household goods (Merloni), apparel (Benetton), insurance (Generali), computers (Olivetti), pharmaceuticals (Carlo Erba), bicycles (Bianchi), diesel engines (Lombardini, Ruggerini), ceramic tiles (Marazzi), and food processing (Barilla, Perfetti, Venezia). Italian firms also are intensively involved in the contracting business.

France

France is one of the major OECD countries extending financial assistance to Turkey under bilateral agreements. French firms are increasingly involved in international tenders in Turkey, particularly in the fields of construction, communications, electronics and defense. France ranks as Turkey's fourth largest trading partner and has recently become one of its largest foreign investors.

Selected key imports from France include: electrical machinery and equipment; iron and steel; land vehicles and parts; helicopters; airplanes; and organic/inorganic chemicals.

Turkey, NATO and the Defense Industry

Turkey, a key member of the North Atlantic Treaty Organization (NATO), continues to benefit from this association, and so do U.S. companies. Lockheed is building the F-16 in a Turkish joint venture using FMS and national funds; Loral is making the electronic countermeasures system for the F-16, and GE the engines; FMC has a contract to manufacture 1,698 armored infantry vehicles (AIV); Texas Instruments has a contract through ASELSAN to produce the optical sights for the AIV; Alison Transmission and Detroit Diesel are building the power plant; Cadillac Gage the cupola; and GIAT (French) the turret and gun. Other projects include C-3, light transport aircraft and utility helicopters.

Meanwhile, U.S. exporters, including engineering and technical consulting services firms, should also note that Turkey is a major beneficiary of the NATO infrastructure development program. Spending on NATO projects, which runs the gamut from harbor development projects to satellite communications networks, is expected to continue at the recent level of about $350 million/year. U.S. firms wishing to compete for these projects must possess a NATO security clearance and must be certified by the Office of International Major Projects of the U.S. Department of Commerce as financially and technically qualified.

Business and the EU

Should the EU agree in October 1995 to extend customs union status to Turkey, both Turkish and American firms would see some improvements and difficulties in the business environment that would result. Benefits for Turkish firms would include cheaper sources of supplies and easier access to the world's largest and most affluent market. However, Turkish firms would also be faced with stronger competition from the EU firms that have advanced products, production techniques and larger production runs. American firms would be faced with a tariff differential and increased competition from EU suppliers to the Turkish market.

EU customs accession will impose a small tariff penalty on U.S. suppliers vis-a-vis European competition. However, the economic boost that Turkey will derive from accession will be highly trade creating. This will affect the tariff penalty and lead to higher levels of U.S. exports. Accession will also render Turkey a low-cost base for manufacturing products destined for EU markets.

By acting now, American firms can establish the needed distribution ties and commercial alliances to meet the competition ahead. Joint ventures, licensing or coproduction arrangements between American and Turkish firms can provide the needed blend of resources to not only expand sales in Turkey but also in the EU and adjoining countries. Turkey is a natural regional distribution hub.

United Kingdom

Over most of the 1980s, the U.K. was Turkey's third largest trading partner in the EU, after Germany and Italy. In 1990, it moved to fourth position, replaced by France. Mechanical and electrical machinery accounts for about 40 percent, and iron and steel products 10-12 percent of total imports from the U.K. Britain also is one of the main investors in Turkey.

The U.K. has played a large part in Turkey's economic development. The Turkish motor industry has its roots in the British motor industry. The U.K. assisted in the construction of the first Bosphorus bridge which opened in 1973 and has helped build up Turkey's defense industries in recent years. It is currently one of Turkey's largest suppliers of defense equipment.

Japan

Japan is Turkey's eighth largest trading partner. Its exports to Turkey consist mainly of vehicles, electrical and electronic equipment, organic chemicals, petrochemicals, and iron and steel. Japan's eximbank, the Overseas Economic Cooperation Fund (OECF), Japan International Cooperation Agency (JICA), and private Japanese banks like Sumitomo Bank, Mitsubishi and Mitsui provide finance for trade with Turkey. JICA's programs are in the form of grants. In 1993, Japanese Eximbank provided a $200 million credit to finance projects and exports of investment goods. This was the first time a credit had not been tied to a specific project.

Russia

Russia is the largest exporter to Turkey outside of the OECD countries. Total exports to Turkey were over $1.5 billion in 1993, a 50 percent increase from the previous year. Although oil and gas shipments account for nearly one-third of the total, diversification of export items is under way and includes iron and steel, fertilizers, land vehicles, cotton, paper and paper products, and inorganic chemicals. Russian investment in Turkey is very small; there are only 39 Russian firms operating there. Turkish-Russian commercial relations are expected to further expand under the Black Sea Economic Cooperation Treaty signed in 1992, which allows regional cooperation not only in trade and services, but also in infrastructure investments, healthcare, and science and technology.

> — *Contributers: Eileen Hill, Boyce Fitzpatrick, James Wilson, Charles Ludolph*

Directory of Resources

In the following Resource Directory, we have put together a set of basic contact information for each economy covered in this book. While we have done our best to include the very latest and most complete information, we cannot guarantee that some details will not have changed by or after publication.

As a starting place for exporting information, we offer the following lists of U.S. and local government contacts; trade associations and chambers of commerce; local market research firms and commercial banks; U.S. embassy trade personnel; Washington-based U.S. government contacts; and other organizations supporting trade with these economies.

We also provide a listing of available market research data, a schedule of various industry and trade events, and a bibliography of helpful reading material (and where to find it).

This listing is intended to be as extensive as possible but we make no representation that it is comprehensive. Furthermore, listings of foreign, private or non-governmental organizations in this directory should not suggest the endorsement of or any special relationship with the United States government. Readers undertake interaction with listed organizations at their own risk.

We hope you find the following information useful as a jumping off point for your activities in these Big Emerging Markets.

Resources: General

Country Commercial Guides (CCGs): Country Commercial Guides (CCGs) provide, in one report, a comprehensive picture of the commercial environment in more than 100 foreign markets, including Mexico. Key information includes market conditions, the economic and political situation, trade and investment regulations, best export sectors, financing, and U.S. and country contacts. CCGs are available on the National Trade Data Bank (NTDB), the government's complete source of international business information (see below). CCGs are also available through the National Technincal Information Service (NTIS) electronically and in hard copy. Call 1-800-553-NTIS to order or to request information.

NAFTA Facts Flashfax: NAFTA Facts is the automated information service of the Office of the North American Free Trade Agreement. It is designed to provide convenient access to current trade-related documents concerning NAFTA and doing business in Mexico and Canada. Documents from the NAFTA Facts Flashfax can be ordered by phone and sent to you by fax by dialing 202-482-4464.

National Technical Information Service (NTIS): The Department's most basic marketing documents, including numerous Industry Sector Analyses (ISAs) and special reports can be ordered for a fee from NTIS, the U.S. Government's central source for scientific, technical, and business related information. To place an order, contact NTIS at (703) 487-4650. For rush service, call (800) 553-6847. To receive by fax a list of documents available through NTIS, call 703-487-4099.

National Trade Data Bank (NTDB): The NTDB is a data base, published monthly on CD-ROM, of more than 100,000 documents containing the most up-to-date information on foreign trade and export promotion from the collections of 17 government agencies, including our embassies abroad. Most of the documents available from NTIS, in addition to many others, are available free of charge from the NTDB. The NTDB is available at over 700 federal depository libraries throughout the U.S. For the library nearest you with access to NTDB, contact your local Department of Commerce District Office or the Trade Information Center at 1-800-USA-TRADE, 1-800-872-8723. The NTDB is also accessible via Internet on the following locations: 1) FTP: ftp.stat-usa.gov 2) Gopher: gopher.stat-usa.gov 3) Mosaic: www.stat-usa.gov To order the NTDB or to learn more about the service, call 202-482-1986.

The Trade Information Center: The Trade Information Center's mission is to guide businesses through the export process and through the myriad of exporter assistance programs available from the 19 federal agencies which have a role in trade promotion. As the contact point for information on federal export programs, the Center provides export counseling covering a wide range of questions including how to begin exporting, export financing, documentation, seminars and conferences, and overseas trade events. The Center also maintains state files which include information on export assistance offered by local economic development agencies, world trade centers, chamber of commerce, and small business development agencies. For assistance, contact the Center at (800) USA-TRADE, 1-800-872-8723.

THE HONORABLE J. BRIAN ATWOOD
Administrator, Agency for International Development
320 21st Street N.W.
Washington, DC 20523
Tel: 202-647-9620
Fax: 202-647-0148

THE HONORABLE DAN R. GLICKMAN
Secretary of Agriculture
14th and Independence N.W.
Washington, DC 20250
Tel: 202-720-3631
Fax: 202-720-5437

THE HONORABLE WILLIAM PERRY
Secretary, Department of Defense
The Pentagon, Room 3E-880
Washington, DC 20301
Tel: 703-695-5261
Fax: 703-697-9080

THE HONORABLE HAZEL O'LEARY
Secretary, Department of Energy
1000 Independence Avenue, S.W.
Washington, DC 20585
Tel: 202-586-6210
Fax: 202-586-4403

THE HONORABLE BRUCE E. BABBITT
Secretary, Department of the Interior
1849 C Street N.W.
Washington, DC 20240
Tel: 202-208-4123
Fax: 202-219-1220

THE HONORABLE ROBERT REICH
Secretary, Department of Labor
200 Constitution Avenue, N.W.
Washington, DC 20210
Tel: 202-219-8271
Fax: 202-219-8820

**THE HONORABLE
WARREN CHRISTOPHER**
Secretary, Department of State
2201 C Street, N.W.
Washington, DC 20520
Tel: 202-647-5291
Fax: 202-647-6434

THE HONORABLE FEDERICO PENA
Secretary, Department of Transportation
400 Seventh Street, S.W., Room 10-200
Washington, DC 20590
Tel: 202-366-1111
Fax: 202-366-7202

THE HONORABLE ROBERT RUBIN
Secretary, Department of the Treasury
15th and Pennsylvania, N.W.
Washington, DC 20220
Tel: 622-1100
Fax: 622-0073

THE HONORABLE CAROL BROWNER
Administrator, Environmental Protection
Agency
401 M Street, S.W.
Washington, DC 20460 ·
Tel: 202-260-4700
Fax: 202-260-0279

**THE HONORABLE LAURA D'ANDREA
TYSON**
Chair, Council of Economic Advisors
Old Executive Office Building
17th & Penn. Ave., N.W.
Washington, DC 20500
Tel: 202-395-5042
Fax: 202-395-6947

**THE HONORABLE
KENNETH D. BRODY**
Chairman, Export-Import Bank
811 Vermont Avenue, N.W.
Washington, DC 20571
Tel: 202-565-3500
Fax: 202-565-3505

THE HONORABLE ANTHONY LAKE
Assistant to the President for
National Security Affairs
National Security Council
The White House
Washington, DC 20500
Tel: 202-456-2255
Fax: 202-395-3380

**THE HONORABLE
ALICE M. RIVLIN**
Director, Office of Management and Budget
Old Executive Office Building
17th & Penn. Ave., N.W.
Washington, DC 20503
Tel: 202-395-4840
Fax: 202-395-3888

MS. RUTH R. HARKIN
President and Chief Executive Officer
Overseas Private Investment Corporation
1100 New York Ave., N.W. (12th Floor)
Washington, DC 20527
Tel: 202-336-8404
Fax: 202-408-5133

MR. PHILIP LADER
Administrator, Small Business Administration
409 Third Street, S.W.
Washington, DC 20416
Tel: 202-205-6605
Fax: 202-205-6802

DR. JOSEPH DUFFEY
Director, U.S. Information Agency
301 Fourth Street, S.W.
Washington, DC 20547
Tel: 202-619-4742
Fax: 202-619-6705

MR. J. JOSEPH GRANDMAISON
1621 N. Kent St.
Director, U.S. Trade and Development Agency
Rm 309, Rosslyn Plaza Room 309,
State Annex 16
Arlington, VA
Washington, DC 20523-1602
Tel: 703-875-4357
Fax: 703-875-4009

THE HONORABLE MICKEY KANTOR
Ambassador,
United States Trade Representative
600 Seventeenth Street, N.W.
Washington, DC 20506
Tel: 202-395-3204
Fax: 202-395-3390

U.S. DEPARTMENT OF COMMERCE INTERNATIONAL TRADE ADMINISTRATION, U.S. AND FOREIGN COMMERCIAL SERVICE DISTRICT OFFICE DIRECTORY

ALABAMA
BIRMINGHAM - Patrick T. Wall, Director
Medical Forum Building, 7th Floor
950 22nd Street North, ZIP: 35203
Tel: (205) 731-1331, Fax: (205) 731-0076

ALASKA
ANCHORAGE - Charles Becker, Director
World Trade Center, 421 W. First St.; ZIP: 99501
4201 Tudor Centre Drive, ZIP: 99508
Tel: (907) 271-6237, Fax: (907) 271-6242

ARIZONA
PHOENIX - Frank Woods, Director
Tower One, Suite 970
2901 N. Central Avenue, ZIP: 85012
Tel: (602) 640-2513, Fax: (602) 640-2518

ARKANSAS
LITTLE ROCK - Lon J. Hardin, Director
TCBY Tower Building, Suite 700
425 West Capitol Avenue, ZIP: 72201
Tel: (501) 324-5794, Fax: (501) 324-7380

CALIFORNIA
LOS ANGELES - Steve Morrison, Director
11000 Wilshire Blvd., Room 9200, ZIP: 90024
Tel: (310) 235-7104, Fax: (310) 235-7220

General

(*) NEWPORT BEACH
3300 Irvine Avenue, Suite 305, ZIP: 92660
Tel: (714) 660-1688, Fax: (714) 660-8039

(**) LONG BEACH USEAC
Joe Sachs, Director
US&FCS Manager - Maria Solomon
One World Trade Center, Ste. 1670,
ZIP: 90831
Tel: (310) 980-4551, Fax: (310) 980-4561

(**) ONTARIO USEAC
Fred Latuperissa, Dir.
3281 E. Gausti Road, Ste. 100; ZIP 91761
Tel: (909) 390-5650, Fax: (909) 390-5759

SAN DIEGO
Mary Delmege, Director
6363 Greenwich Drive, Suite 230, ZIP: 92122
Tel: (619) 557-5395, Fax: (619) 557-6176

SAN FRANCISCO
James S. Kennedy, Act. Dir.
250 Montgomery St., 14th Floor, ZIP: 94104
Tel: (415) 705-2300, Fax: (415) 705-2297

(*) SANTA CLARA
5201 Great American Pkwy., #456, ZIP: 95054
Tel: (408) 970-4610, Fax: (408) 970-4618

COLORADO
DENVER - Neil Hesse, Director
1625 Broadway, Suite 680, ZIP: 80202
Tel: (303) 844-6622, Fax: (303) 844-5651

CONNECTICUT
HARTFORD - Carl Jacobsen, Director
Room 610B, 450 Main Street, ZIP: 06103
Tel: (203) 240-3530, Fax: (203) 240-3473

DELAWARE
Served by the Philadelphia District Office

DISTRICT OF COLUMBIA
Served by the Baltimore USEAC

FLORIDA
(**) MIAMI USEAC - Peter B. Alois, Director
P.O. Box 590570, ZIP: 33159
5600 Northwest 36th St., Ste. 617, ZIP: 33166
Tel: (305) 526-7425, Fax: (305) 526-7434

(*) CLEARWATER
128 North Osceola Avenue, ZIP: 34615
Tel: (813) 461-0011, Fax: (813) 449-2889

(*) ORLANDO
Eola Park Centre, Suite 1270
200 E. Robinson Street, ZIP: 32801
Tel: (407) 648-6235, Fax: (407) 648-6756

(*) TALLAHASSEE
107 West Gaines Street, Room 366G, ZIP: 32399
Tel: (904) 488-6469, Fax: (904) 487-1407

GEORGIA
ATLANTA - George T. Norton, Jr., Director
Plaza Square North, Suite 310
4360 Chamblee Dunwoody Road, ZIP: 30341
Tel: (404) 452-9101, Fax: (404) 452-9105

SAVANNAH - Barbara Prieto, Director
120 Barnard Street, Room A-107, ZIP: 31401
Tel: (912) 652-4204, Fax: (912) 652-4241

HAWAII
HONOLULU - George B. Dolan, Director
P.O. Box 50026
300 Ala Moana Blvd., Room 4106, ZIP: 96850
Tel: (808) 541-1782, Fax: (808) 541-3435

IDAHO
(*) BOISE - Portland District Office
700 West State Street, 2nd Floor, ZIP: 83720
Tel: (208) 334-3857, Fax: (208) 334-2783

ILLINOIS
(**) CHICAGO USEAC - Brad Dunderman,
Director
Stanley Bokota, US&FCS Director
Xerox Center
55 West Monroe Street, Suite 2440, ZIP: 60603
Tel: (312) 353-8040, Fax: (312) 353-8098

(*) WHEATON
c/o Illinois Institute of Technology
201 East Loop Road, ZIP: 60187
Tel: (312) 353-4332, Fax: (312) 353-4336

(*) ROCKFORD
P.O. Box 1747
515 North Court Street, ZIP: 61110
Tel: (815) 987-8123, Fax: (815) 963-7943

INDIANA
INDIANAPOLIS - Andrew Thress, Director
Penwood One, Suite 106
11405 N. Pennsylvania Street
Carmel, IN. 46032
Tel: (317) 582-2300, Fax: (317) 582-2301

IOWA
DES MOINES - Randall J. LaBounty, Director
Room 817, Federal Building
210 Walnut Street, ZIP: 50309
Tel: (515) 284-4222, Fax: (515) 284-4021

KANSAS
(*) WICHITA
Kansas City District Office
151 N. Volutsia, ZIP: 67214
Tel: (316) 269-6160, Fax: (316) 683-7326

KENTUCKY
LOUISVILLE - John Autin, Director
601 W. Broadway, Room 634B, ZIP: 40202
Tel: (502) 582-5066, Fax: (502) 582-6573

LOUISIANA
NEW ORLEANS
Paul K. Rees, Acting Director
Hale Boggs Federal Building
501 Magazine Street, Room 1043, ZIP: 70130
Tel: (504) 589-6546, Fax: (504) 589-2337

MAINE
(*) AUGUSTA
Vacant
40 Western Ave. Ste 506A. ZIP: 04333
Tel: (207) 622-8249, Fax: (207) 626-9156

MARYLAND
(**) BALTIMORE USEAC
Roger Fortner, Director
World Trade Center, Suite 2432
401 East Pratt Street, ZIP: 21202
Tel: (410) 962-4539 Fax: (410) 962-4529

MASSACHUSETTS
BOSTON
Frank J. O'Connor, Director
164 Northern Avenue
World Trade Center, Suite 307, ZIP: 02210
Tel: (617) 424-5990, Fax: (617) 424-5992

MICHIGAN
DETROIT
Dean Peterson, Director
1140 McNamara Building
477 Michigan Avenue, ZIP: 48226
Tel: (313) 226-3650, Fax: (313) 226-3657

(*) GRAND RAPIDS
300 Monroe N.W., Room 406, ZIP: 49503
Tel: (616) 456-2411, Fax: (616) 456-2695

MINNESOTA
MINNEAPOLIS
Ronald E. Kramer, Director
108 Federal Building
110 South 4th Street, ZIP: 55401
Tel: (612) 348-1638, Fax: (612) 348-1650

MISSISSIPPI
JACKSON - Mark E. Spinney, Director
201 W. Capitol Street, Suite 310, ZIP: 39201
Tel: (601) 965-4388, Fax: (601) 965-5386

MISSOURI
ST. LOUIS - Sandra Gerley, Director
8182 Maryland Avenue, Suite 303, ZIP: 63105
Tel: (314) 425-3302, Fax: (314) 425-3381

KANSAS CITY
Rick Villalobos, Director
601 East 12th Street, Room 635, ZIP: 64106
Tel: (816) 426-3141, Fax: (816) 426-3140

MONTANA
Served by the Boise Branch Office

NEBRASKA
(*) OMAHA
Des Moines District Office
11135 "O" Street, ZIP: 68137
Tel: (402) 221-3664, Fax: (402) 221-3668

NEVADA
RENO
James K. Hellwig, Director
1755 East Plumb Lane, Suite 152, ZIP: 89502
Tel: (702) 784-5203, Fax: (702) 784-5343

NEW HAMPSHIRE
(*) NASHUA - Susan S. Berry, Mgr.
547 Amherst Street, 2nd floor, ZIP: 03063
Phone: (603)-598-4315, Fax: (603) 598-4323

(*) PORTSMOUTH
Boston District Office
601 Spaulding Turnpike, Suite 29, ZIP: 03801
Tel: (603) 334-6074, Fax: (603) 334-6110

NEW JERSEY
TRENTON
Rod Stuart, Director
3131 Princeton Pike, Bldg. #6,
Suite 100, ZIP: 08648
Tel: (609) 989-2100, Fax: (609) 989-2395

NEW MEXICO
(*) SANTA FE
Denver District Office
c/o New Mexico Dept. of Economic Development
1100 St. Francis Drive, ZIP: 87503
Tel: (505) 827-0350, Fax: (505) 827-0263

NEW YORK
BUFFALO
George Buchanan, Director
1304 Federal Building
111 West Huron Street, ZIP: 14202
Tel: (716) 846-4191, Fax: (716) 846-5290

(**) ROCHESTER USEAC
James C. Mariano
111 East Avenue, Suite 220, ZIP: 14604
Tel: (716) 263-6480, Fax: (716) 325-6505

NEW YORK
Joel W. Barkan, Director
26 Federal Plaza, Room 3718, ZIP: 10278
Tel: (212) 264-0634, Fax: (212) 264-1356

NORTH CAROLINA
GREENSBORO
Samuel P. Troy, Director
400 West Market Street, Suite 400, ZIP: 27401
Tel: (910) 333-5345, Fax: (910) 333-5158

NORTH DAKOTA
Served by the Minneapolis District Office

OHIO
CINCINNATI
John M. McCaslin, Director
550 Main Street, Room 9504, ZIP: 45202
Tel: (513) 684-2944, Fax: (513) 684-3200

CLEVELAND
Toby T. Zettler, Director
Bank One Center
600 Superior Avenue, East, Ste 700, ZIP: 44114
Tel: (216) 522-4750, Fax: (216) 522-2235

OKLAHOMA
OKLAHOMA CITY - Ronald L. Wilson, Director
6601 Broadway Extension, Rm. 200, ZIP: 73116
Tel: (405) 231-5302, Fax: (405) 231-4211

(*) TULSA
440 South Houston Street, Rm 505, ZIP: 74127
Tel: (918) 581-7650, Fax: (918) 581-2844

OREGON
PORTLAND - Denny Barnes, Director
One World Trade Center, Suite 242
121 SW Salmon Street, ZIP: 97204
Tel: (503) 326-3001, Fax: (503) 326-6351

PENNSYLVANIA
PHILADELPHIA - Robert E. Kistler, Director
660 American Avenue, Suite 201
King of Prussia, PA ZIP: 19406
Tel: (610) 962-4980, Fax: (610) 962-4989

PITTSBURGH - John A. McCartney, Director
2002 Federal Building
1000 Liberty Avenue, ZIP: 15222
Tel: (412) 644-2850, Fax: (412) 644-4875

PUERTO RICO
SAN JUAN (Hato Rey) - J. Enrique Vilella, Director
Room G-55, Federal Building
Chardon Avenue, ZIP: 00918
Tel: (809) 766-5555, Fax: (809) 766-5692

RHODE ISLAND
(*) PROVIDENCE - Raimond Meerbach, Mgr.
7 Jackson Walkway, ZIP: 02903
Tel: (401) 528-5104, Fax: (401) 528-5067

SOUTH CAROLINA
COLUMBIA - Ann H. Watts, Director
Strom Thurmond Federal Bldg., Suite 172
1835 Assembly Street, ZIP: 29201
Tel: (803) 765-5345, Fax: (803) 253-3614

(*) CHARLESTON
P.O. Box 975, ZIP: 29402
81 Mary Street, ZIP: 29403
Tel: (803) 727-4051, Fax: (803) 727-4052

SOUTH DAKOTA
(*) SIOUX FALLS
Des Moines District Office
200 N. Phillips Avenue, Commerce Center
Suite 302, ZIP: 57102
Tel: (605) 330-4264, Fax: (605) 330-4266

TENNESSEE
NASHVILLE
Jim Charlet, Director
Parkway Towers, Suite 114
404 James Robertson Parkway, ZIP: 37219
Tel: (615) 736-5161, Fax: (615) 736-2454

(*) MEMPHIS
22 North Front Street, Suite 200, ZIP: 38103
Tel: (901) 544-4137, Fax: (901) 575-3510

(*) KNOXVILLE
301 East Church Avenue, ZIP: 37915
Tel: (615) 545-4637, Fax: (615) 545-4435

TEXAS
DALLAS
vacant, Director
P.O. Box 58130
2050 N. Stemmons Fwy., Suite 170, ZIP: 75258
Tel: (214) 767-0542, Fax: (214) 767-8240

(*) AUSTIN
P.O. Box 12728
1700 Congress, 2nd floor, ZIP: 78701
Tel: (512) 482-5939, Fax: (512) 482-5940

HOUSTON
James D. Cook, Director
#1 Allen Center, Suite 1160
500 Dallas, ZIP: 77002
Tel: (713) 229-2578, Fax: (713) 229-2203

UTAH
SALT LAKE CITY
Stephen P. Smoot, Director
324 S. State Street, Suite 105, ZIP: 84111
Tel: (801) 524-5116, Fax: (801) 524-5886

VERMONT
(*) MONTPELIER
James Cox - Branch Manager
109 State Street, 4th Floor, ZIP: 05609
Tel: (802) 828-4508, Fax: (802) 828-3258

VIRGINIA
RICHMOND
Philip A. Ouzts, Director
700 Centre
704 East Franklin Street, Suite 550, ZIP:
23219
Tel: (804) 771-2246, Fax: (804) 771-2390

WASHINGTON
SEATTLE
Lisa Kjaer-Schade, Director
3131 Elliott Avenue, Suite 290, ZIP: 98121
Tel: (206) 553-5615, Fax: (206) 553-7253

(*) TRI-CITIES
320 North Johnson Street, Suite 350
Kennewick, WA. 99336
Tel: (509) 735-2751, Fax: (509)783-9385

WEST VIRGINIA
CHARLESTON
W. Davis Coale, Jr., Director
405 Capitol Street, Suite 807, ZIP: 25301
Tel: (304) 347-5123, Fax: (304) 347-5408

WISCONSIN
MILWAUKEE
Paul D. Churchill, Director
517 E. Wisconsin Avenue, Room 596, ZIP:
53202
Tel: (414) 297-3473, Fax: (414) 297-3470

WYOMING
Served by the Denver District Office

REGIONAL OFFICES:

(***) REGION I, PHILADELPHIA
Paul Walters, Regional Director
660 American Avenue, Suite 202
King of Prussia, PA. 19406
Tel: (610) 962-4990, Fax: (610) 962-1326

(***) REGION II, ATLANTA
LoRee Silloway, Regional Director
Plaza Square North, Suite 405
4360 Chamblee Dunwoody Road, 30341
Tel: (404) 455-7860, Fax: (404) 455-7865

(***) REGION III, CINCINNATI
Gordon Thomas, Regional Director
9504 Federal Building
550 Main Street, ZIP: 45202
Tel: (513) 684-2947, Fax: (513) 684-3200

(***) REGION IV, ST. LOUIS
Donald R. Loso, Regional Director
8182 Maryland Avenue, Suite 305, ZIP:
63105
Tel: (314) 425-3300, Fax: (314) 425-3375

(***) REGION V, SAN FRANCISCO
Michael Liikala, Regional Director
250 Montgomery St., 14th Floor, ZIP: 94104
Tel: (415) 705-2310, Fax: (415) 705-2299

*(*) - DENOTES TRADE SPECIALIST AT
A BRANCH OFFICE*

*(**) - DENOTES A U.S. EXPORT
ASSISTANCE CENTER*

*(***) - OFFICE WITH MANAGERIAL
AND ADMINISTRATIVE OVERSIGHT
RESPONSIBILITIES (OFFERS NO
DIRECT BUSINESS COUNSELING)*

General

Resources: Argentina

U.S. AND COUNTRY CONTACTS

COUNTRY GOVERNMENT AGENCIES

ADMINISTRACION NACIONAL DE ADUANAS
(Customs Adminstration)
Contact: Lic. Gustavo A. Parino, National
Adminstrator
Azopardo 350
(1328) Buenos Aires
Tel: 54-1-331-7606/35
Fax: 54-1-331-9881; 345-1778

MINISTERIO DE ECONOMIA
(Ministry of Economy)
Contact: Dr. Domingo F. Cavallo (Minister)
Hipolito Yrigoyen 250
(1310) Buenos Aires
Tel: 54-1-342-6411; 342-6421/29
Fax: 54-1-331-0292

SECRETARIA DE COMERCIO E INVERSIONES
(Secretariat of Trade and Investments)
Contact: Dr. Carlos Sanchez
Hipolito Yrigoyen 250
1310 Buenos Aires
Tel: 54-1-331-2208
Fax: 54-1-349-5422

SECRETARIA DE HACIENDA
(Secretariat of Finance)
Contact: Mr. Ricardo Angel Gutierrez
Hipolito Yrigoyen 250
(1310) Buenos Aires
Tel: 54-1-331-0731; 342-2937
Fax: 54-1-349-6116

SECRETARIA DE INDUSTRIA
(Secretariat of Industry)
Contact: Lic. Carlos A. Magarinos
Av. J.A. Roca 651
1322 Buenos Aires
Tel: 54-1-349-3406/07/08
Fax: 54-1-331-3218

SECRETARIA DE MINERIA
(Secretariat of Mining)
Contact: Mr. Angel Eduardo Maza
Av. J. A. Roca 651
1322 Buenos Aires
Tel: 54-1-331-9954, 343-6314

SECRETARIA DE ENERGIA E HIDROCARBUROS
(Secretariat of Energy and Hydrocarbons)
Contact: Ing. Carlos Manuel Bastos
Av. J. A. Roca 651
1322 Buenos Aires
Tel: 54-1-334-5138; 343-0890; 343-7118/7138
Fax: 54-1-343-6404

SECRETARIA DE AGRICULTURA, GANADERIA Y PESCA
(Secretariat of Agriculture, Livestock and Fisheries)
Contact: Ing. Felipe Sola
Av. Paseo Colon 982
1063 Buenos Aires
Tel: 54-1-362-2365, 362-5091
Fax: 54-1-349-2504

SECRETARIA DE OBRAS PUBLICAS Y COMUNICACIONES
(Secretariat of Public Works and Communications)
Contact: Dr. Wylian Rolando Otrera
Sarmiento 151
1041 Buenos Aires
Tel: 54-1-49-9481, 312-1283

DIRECCION NACIONAL DE RECURSOS HIDRICOS
(National Bureau of Water Resources)
Contact: Ing. Eduardo Davila
Paseo Colon 171
1063 Buenos Aires
Tel: 54-1-383-1152/5250

SECRETARIA DE TRANSPORTE
(Secretariat of Transportation)
Contact: Lic. Edmundo Del Valle Soria
Av. 9 De Julio 1925
1332 Buenos Aires
Tel: 54-1-381-1435/4007

MINISTERIO DE RELACIONES EXTERIORES
(Ministry of Foreign Affairs)
Contact: Ing. Guido Mario Di Tella (Minister)
Reconquista 1088
1003 Buenos Aires
Tel: 54-1-331-0071/9
Fax: 54-1-312-3593/3423

SECRETARIA DE RELACIONES ECONOMICAS INTERNACIONALES
(Secretariat of International Economic Relations)
Contact: Ing. Jorge Campbell
Reconquista 1088
1003 Buenos Aires
Tel: 54-1-331-7281/4073
Fax: 54-1-312-0965

MINISTERIO DE DEFENSA
(Ministry of Defense)
Contact: Dr. Oscar H. Camilion
Paseo Colon 255
1063 Buenos Aires
Tel: 54-1-343-1561/9

MINISTERIO DE SALUD PUBLICA Y ACCION SOCIAL
(Ministry of Public Health and Social Action)
Contact: Dr. Alberto Jose Mazza (Minister)
Defensa 120
1345 Buenos Aires
Tel: 54-1-34-0048
Fax: 54-1-953-3223

MINISTERIO DE CULTURA Y EDUCACION
(Ministry of Culture and Education)
Contact: Ing. Agr. Jorge A. Rodriguez
Pizzurno 935
1020 Buenos Aires
Tel: 54-1-42-4551/9

MINISTERIO DE JUSTICIA
(Ministry of Justice)
Contact: Dr. Jorge Luis Maiorano
Gelly Obes 2289
1425 Buenos Aires
Tel: 54-1-803-4051/2/3
Fax: 54-1-803-3955

MINISTERIO DEL INTERIOR
(Ministry of the Interior)
Contact:Dr. Carlos V. Corach (Minister)
Balcarce 24
1064 Buenos Aires
Tel: 54-1-46-9841/9

**MINISTERIO DE TRABAJO Y
SEGURIDAD SOCIAL**
(Ministry of Labor and Social Security)
Contact:Dr. Jose Armando Caro Figueroa
Av. L.N. Alem 650
1001 Buenos Aires
Tel: 54-1-311-3303/2945

LAW FIRMS IN ARGENTINA

BRONS AND SALAS
Contact: Dr. Thomas Boywitt, Partner
Marcelo T. de Alvear 624, Piso 1
(1058) Buenos Aires, Argentina
Tel: 54-1-311-9271/79
Fax: 54-1-311-7025

COUNTRY TRADE ASSOCIATIONS/ CHAMBERS OF COMMERCE

CAMARA ARGENTINA DE COMERCIO
(Argentine Chamber of Commerce)
Mr. Jorge Luis Di Fiori, President
Av. L.N. Alem 36, P.B.
1003 Buenos Aires
Tel: 54-1-311-8051/5
Fax: 54-1-342-6371

**CAMARA DE COMERCIO DE LOS
ESTADOS UNIDOS EN ARGENTINA**
(American Chamber of
Commerce in Argentina)
Mr. Félix Zumelzu, ExecutiveDirector
Av. L. N. Alem 1110, Piso 13
1001 Buenos Aires
Tel: 54-1-311-5420/5126
Fax: 54-1-311-9076

UNION INDUSTRIAL ARGENTINA
(Argentine Industry Association)
Mr. Jorge Blanco Villegas, President
Av. Leandro N. Alem 1067
Pisos 10 y 11
1001 Buenos Aires
Tel: 54-1-313-2561/2611, 311-6188/8429

**CAMARA ARGENTINA DE
SUPERMERCADOS**
(Association of Super Markets)
Dr. Ovidio Vicente Bolo, President
Paraguay 577, Piso 3
1057 Buenos Aires
Tel: 54-1-312-3790/5419
Fax: 54-1-312-5846

**ASOCIACION DE IMPORTADORES Y
EXPORTADORES DE LA REP.
ARGENTINA**
(Association of Argentine Importers
and Exporters)
Lic. Fernando A. Raimondo, President
Belgrano 124, Piso 1
1092 Buenos Aires
Tel: 54-1-342-0010/0018/0019
Fax: 54-1-342-1312

**CAMARA DE IMPORTADORES DE LA
REPUBLICA ARGENTINA**
(Chamber of Importers)
Mr.Diego Pérez Santisteban, President
Av. Belgrano 427, Piso 7
1092 Buenos Aires
Tel: 54-1-342-1101/0523
Fax: 54-1-331- 9342

**CAMARA DE COMERCIO
EXTERIORDEL CENTRO DE LA
REPUBLICA**
(Chamber of Foreign Trade of Central
Argentina)
Eng. Víctor Mucaria, President
Av. Callao 332, P.B.
1022 Buenos Aires
Tel: 54-1-46-6912

SOCIEDAD RURAL ARGENTINA
(Argentine Agricultural Association)
Mr. Eduardo A. C. De Zavalía, President
Florida 460
1005 Buenos Aires
Tel: 54-1-322-3431/2030

**CAMARA DE COMERCIO,
INDUSTRIA Y PRODUCCION DE LA
REP. ARG.**
(Chamber of Commerce, Industry and
Production of the Arg. Republic)
Dra. María Arsenia Tula, President
Florida 1, Piso 4
1005 Buenos Aires
Tel: 54-1-342-8252; 343-5638; 331-0813
Fax: 54-1-331-9116

**BOLSA DE COMERCIO DE
BUENOS AIRES**
(Buenos Aires Stock Exchange)
Dr. Jullio A Maccki, President
Sarmiento 299, Piso 1
1353 Buenos Aires
Tel: 54-1-311-5231/33/1174; 313-4812/4544
Fax: 54-1-312-9332

**CAMARA DE COMERCIO EXTERIOR
DE CORDOBA**
(Chamber of Foreign Trade of Cordoba)
Mr. Héctor Linares, President
Av. Callao 332, P.B.
1022 Buenos Aires
Tel: 54-1-374-6912

COUNTRY MARKET RESEARCH FIRMS

R.G. ASOCIADOS
Defensa 649, P. 5 "A"
1265 Buenos Aires
Tel: 54-1-342-9355

A&C
Salta 1007
1074 Buenos Aires
Contact:Dr. Carlos Kaplan
Tel: 54-1-27-9007; 304-6309/8213
Fax: 54-1-27-8800

GUILLERMO BRAVO Y ASOCIADOS
Av. De Mayo 1480 E.P.
Buenos Aires
Contact:Dr. Guillermo Bravo
Tel/Fax: 54-1-381-7892/2540/5625

MERCADOS DIRECTOS
Lavalle 1515, Piso 1
1048 Buenos Aires
Tel: 54-1-375-0772/73
Fax: 54-1-375-2012

COUNTRY COMMERCIAL BANKS

BANCO DE LA NACION ARGENTINA
(Bank of the Argentine Nation)
Bartolome Mitre 326
Contact:Dr. Aldo Antonio Dadone-President
1036 Buenos Aires
Tel: 54-1-343-1011/21
Fax: 54-1-331-8745

BANCO DE LA PROVINCIA DE BUENOS AIRES
San Martin 137
1004 Buenos Aires
Contact: Lic. Rodolfo Frigeri-President
Tel: 54-1-331-2561/9/4011/3584

CITIBANK N.A.
Bme. Mitre 530
1036 Buenos Aires
Contact: Sr. Jorge Bermudez-President
Tel: 54-1-329-1000; 331-8281/4031
Fax: 54-1-331-8180

THE FIRST NATIONAL BANK OF BOSTON
Florida 99
1005 Buenos Aires
Contact: Ing. Manuel R. Sacerdote-President
Tel: 54-1-342-3051/8801/8861
Fax: 54-1-343-7303

BANCO RIO DE LA PLATA S.A.
Bme. Mitre 480
1036 Buenos Aires
Contact: Sr. J. Gregorio Perez Companc-President
Tel: 54-1-331-0555/7551/8361

BANCO DE GALICIA Y BUENOS AIRES
Tte. Gral. J.D. Peron 407
1038 Buenos Aires
Contact: Lic. Eduardo J. Escasany-President
Tel: 54-1-394-7080/7291/8151
Fax: 54-1-325-8886

BANCO CREDITO ARGENTINO S.A.
Reconquista 40
1002 Buenos Aires
Contact:Dr. Fernando De Santibanes-President
Tel: 54-1-334-5241/4421/6561
Fax: 54-1-334-8089

U.S. EMBASSY TRADE PERSONNEL

AMERICAN EMBASSY
Av. Colombia 4300
1425 Buenos Aires
Argentina
Tel: 54-1-777-4533/4534
Fax: 54-1-777-0673
Mr. Albert Alexander, Commercial Counselor
Mr. Robert M. Shipley, Commercial Attache
Mr. Thomas Martin, Economic Counselor

WASHINGTON-BASED USG COUNTRY CONTACTS

COUNTRY SPECIALIST/ARGENTINA
Ms. Carrie Clark
ITA/IEP/WH/OLA/SC, Rm. 3025
U.S. Department of Commerce
Washington, D.C. 20230
Tel: 202-482-0447
Fax: 202-482-4157

ARGENTINA DESK OFFICER
Mr. Jack Deasy
AR/SC 5911
U.S. Department of State
Washington, D.C. 20520
Tel: 202-647-3402
Fax: 202-736-4475

REGIONAL SPECIALIST/MERCOSUR
Mr. Randolph Mye
ITA/IEP/WH/OlA/OSC, Room 3025
U.S. Department of Commerce
Washington, D.C. 20230
Tel: 202-482-1744
Fax: 202-482-4157

U.S. DEPARTMENT OF TREASURY
Mr. Jeff Neil, Argentina Desk
Office of the Assistant Secretary for International Affairs
Office of Latin America and Caribbean
Room 5413
15th & Pennsylvania Avenue, N.W.
Washington, D.C. 20220
Tel: 202-622-1268
Fax: 202-622-1273

LATIN AMERICA REGIONAL DIRECTOR
Mr. Al Angulo
U.S. Trade and Development Agency
Room 309, S.A. - 16
Department of State
Washington, D.C. 20523-1602
Tel: 703-875-4357
Fax: 703-875-4009

U.S.-BASED MULTIPLIERS RELEVANT FOR COUNTRY

MIAMI FOREIGN TRADE ASSOCIATION
Mr. Lorenzo J. Lopez, President
3555 NW 74th. Avenue
Miami, Florida 33122
Tel: 305-592-4893
Fax: 305-594-7862

FLORIDA DEPARTMENT OF COMMERCE
Mr. John Macho, Director for
Latin American Trade
2701 Le Jeune Road, Suite 330
Coral Gables, Florida 33134
Tel: 305-442-6921
Fax: 305-442-6931

ARGENTINE AMERICAN CHAMBER OF COMMERCE, INC
10 Rockefeller PL, Suite 1014
New York, New York 10020
Tel: 212-245-2512
Fax: 212-489-7317

ARGENTINE AMERICAN CHAMBER OF COMMERCE IN FLORIDA
One World Trade Plaza Suite 1800
80 SW 8th St.
Miami, FL 33139
Tel: 305-371-6644

COUNTRY CONSULATES AND TRADE OFFICES IN THE U.S.

THE EMBASSY OF ARGENTINA
Ambassador Raul Granillo Ocampo
1600 New Hampshire Ave. NW.
Washington, D.C. 20009
Tel: 202-939-6400/6422/6424/6425
Fax: 202-332-3171

Trade Office:
1600 New Hampshire Ave
NW., Washington, D.C. 20009
Tel: 202-939-6419/6414/6413
Fax: 202-775-4388

THE OFFICE OF THE ARGENTINE FINANCIAL REPRESENTATIVE

Hilia de Greca
1901 L St., NW, Suite 606
Washington, D.C. 20036
Tel: 202-466-3021
Fax: 202-463-8793

ECONOMIC AND COMMERCIAL REPRESENTATIVE

Contact: Marcelo Regunaga, Economic and Commercial Representative
1901 L Street, N.W., Suite 640
Washington, D.C. 20036
Tel: 202-331-3723
Fax: 202-857-5211

CONSULATE AND TRADE OFFICE

Chicago
Richard Gauthier, Counsul General
205 N. Michigan Ave. Suite 4209
Chicago, Illinois 60601
Tel: 312-819-2620\2606/2608/2022
Fax: 312-819-2626

New York
Juan Garibaldi, Consul General
12 West 56th Street
New York, NY 10019
Tel: 212-603-0400
Fax: 212-397-3523

Los Angeles
Claudio Gell, Consul General
5055 Wilshire Blvd. Suite 210
Los Angeles, California 90036
Tel: 213-954-9155/9235/937-3873/954-9233
Fax: 213-934-9076/937-3841

Houston
Facyndo Vila, Consul General
1990 Post Oak Blvd. Suite 770
Houston, Texas 77056
Tel: 713-871-8935/6
Fax: 713-871-0639

Atlanta
Ruben Patto, Consul General
Cain Tower 229 Peachtree St. Suite 1401
Atlanta G.A. 30303
Tel: 404-880-0805
Fax: 404-880-0806

CONSULATE AND TOURIST OFFICE

Juan Carlos Krechler, Consul General
800 Brickell Avenue
Penthouse 1
Miami, Florida 33131
Tel: 305-373-7794/1889/4705
Fax: 305-371-7108

U.S. DEPARTMENT OF COMMERCE MARKET RESEARCH AVAILABLE

INDUSTRY SUBSECTOR ANALYSES

— Local area and wide area networks (4/30/95)
— Environmental impact assessments (10/31/94)
— Industrial waste treatment equipment (10/31/94)
— Privatization and Infrastructure-Provinces (11/30/94)
— Women's casual apparel (12/31/94)
— Packaging machinery: non-food (12/31/94)
— Skin care and makeup products (3/31/95)
— Education in the United States (4/30/95)
— Laboratory and Scientific Instruments (4/30/95)
— Automotive aftermarket products (4/30/95)
— Defense commercial support program (6/30/95)
— Telecommunications: market niches (6/30/95)
— Medical Diagnostic kits (6/30/95)
— Franchising: Non-Food (7/31/95)
— Mining: Current Developments (5/31/95)

TRADE EVENTS SCHEDULE

SEPTEMBER 21-22, 1995
Conference on "Latin American Health Care Opportunities". Institute of the Americas, San Diego, California. Contact: Lee Tablewski, Director of Programs, Tel: 619-453-5560

OCTOBER 1995
Doing Business With the Biggest Emerging Market. Meeting with Columbia Business School. New York, USA

OCTOBER 1995
Congressional Elections for one-third of the Chamber of Deputies and one-third of the Senate. Argentina

OCTOBER 1995
State of Michigan Trade Mission. Buenos Aires, Argentina

OCTOBER 11-14, 1995
Commonwealth of Massachusetts Trade Mission. Buenos Aires, Argentina. Contact: Elizabeth Ozon, Director, Massachusetts Office of International Trade and Investment. Contact: Whitley, Tel: 202-482-2107

OCTOBER 25-27, 1995
EMEA/APAA/ASIA Show Automotive Aftermarket Show Sands Expo Center, Las Vegas, Nevada. Contact: William T. Glasgow, Inc. Tel: 708-333-9292

OCTOBER 26, 1995
The U.S.A. Today Tourism Trade Show. Buenos Aires

OCTOBER 21-25, 1995
Commonwealth of Pennsylvania Trade Mission. Buenos Aires, Argentina

OCTOBER 30, 1995
U.S. - Argentina Business Development Council Infrastructure and Business Promotion Working Group Meeting. Institute of the Americas, La Jolla, California. Contact: Carrie Clark, Tel: 202-482-0477

OCTOBER 30-NOV 1, 1995
Jacksonville, Fl Chamber of Commerce Trade Missions. Buenos Aires, Argentina.

OCTOBER 31, 1995
U.S. - Argentina Business Development Council. Agribusiness Seminar and Matchmaker. Nebraska Contact: Carrie Clark, Tel: 202-482-0477

NOVEMBER 1995
CLAA Conference on the Americas. Miami, Florida Contact: 202-466-7464

NOVEMBER 1-3, 1995
Multi-State Regional Catalog Show. Buenos Aires, Argentina

NOVEMBER 2-3, 1995
Conference on Telecommunications Opportunities in the Americas. Santa Clara, California. Contact: Institute of the Americas, Tel: 619-453-5560

NOVEMBER 5, 1995
Congressman Amo Houghton (NY) Trade Mission. Buenos Aires, Argentina

NOVEMBER 14, 1995
Electrical Transmission Trade Mission. Buenos Aires, Argentina. Contact: Wondermuhll, Tel: 202-482-2390

NOVEMBER 13-14, 1995
Infrastructure Opportunities and Policy Reform in Latin America. San Diego, California. Contact: Institute of the Americas, Tel: 619-453-5560

NOVEMBER 15, 1995
Columbia Journal of World Business Big Emerging Markets Issue. Contact: Daniel London, Tel: 212-854-4750

LATE NOVEMBER
OTEXA Industrial Fabric Trade Mission. Buenos Aires, Argentina

DECEMBER 1, 1995
Computer Software Trade Mission. Buenos Aires, Argentina. Contact Person: Heidi Hijikata, Tel: 202-482-0569

DECEMBER 4, 1995
U.S. - Argentina Business Development Council Standards Working Group Meeting. Buenos Aires, Argentina, Rio de Janiero, Brazil. Contact: Stanley Warshaw, Tel: 202-482-5853

DECEMBER 4-5, 1995
Latin America Mining Conference. Denver, Colorado. Contact: Institute of the Americas, Tel: 619-453-5560

1996 TBD
State of Arkansas Trade Mission. Buenos Aires, La Plata

MARCH 1996
Power Expo '96. Buenos Aires, Argentina

MARCH 1996
2nd Hemispheric Trade and Commerce Forum. Cartagena, Colombia. Contact: Stephen Jacobs, Tel: 202-482-2314

MARCH 1, 1996
Minority Business Matchmaker. Argentina. Contact: Molly Costa, Tel: 202-482-0692

MARCH 1, 1996
Minority Business Matchmaker. São Paulo, Brazil. Contact: Molly Costa, Tel: 202-482-0692

MARCH 1 - AUGUST 1, 1996
Medical and Healthcare USA. Catalog Show. Buenos Aires, Argentina. Contact: Brenda Coleman, Tel: 202-482-3973

MARCH 9-12, 1996
Energy Trade Mission. Buenos Aires, Argentina. Contact: Julia Rauner, Tel: 202-482-2736

MARCH 28 - 29, 1995
Destino USA 96. Solo Fair Overseas Recruited. Buenos Aires. Contact: Karen Ware, Tel: 202-482-2736

APRIL 1996
Penetrating Latin America: Strategies for Mid-size Companies. Texas A&M University. Contact: Dr. Julian Gaspar, Tel: 409-847-8754

April 1, 1996
Medical Matchmaker. Buenos Aires, Argentina. Contact: Molly Costa, Tel: 202-482-0692

MAY 1, 1996
Training Services. Business Facilitation Event. Buenos Aires, Argentina. Contact: Achamma Chandersekara, Tel: 202-482-1316

MAY 1, 1996
Microelectronics Trade Mission. Buenos Aires. Contact: Marlene Ruffin, Tel: 202-482-0507

JUNE 1996
State of Rhode Island Trade Mission. Buenos Aires, Argentina

JULY 1996
Computer Software Trade Mission. Buenos Aires, Argentina

AUGUST 1, 1996
Telecom Mission. Buenos Aires. Contact: Don Edwards, Tel: 202-482-4331

SEPTEMBER 1996
Food-a-World. Food and Food Processing. Contact: CNR International Fair Organizations & Trade, Inc. Tel: 212-663-0881, Fax: 212-663-0975

SEPTEMBER 1996
Ipack '96. Packing Industry. Contact: CNR International Fair Organizations & Trade, Inc. Tel: 212-663-0881, Fax: 212-663-0975

SEPTEMBER 1996
Medical, Hospital & Dental. Contact: CNR International Fair Organizations & Trade, Inc. Tel: 212-663-0881, Fax: 212-663-0975

INFORMATION CHECKLIST & BIBLIOGRAPHY

BUSINESS GUIDES

Guia Practica del Exportador e Importador, (monthly), Lavalle 1125; piso 3, of 8; 1048 Buenos Aires, Argentina

Nomenclador, Arancelario, Aduanero, (weekly), Editorial I.A.R.A. SRL; Castillo 362; 1414 Buenos Aires, Argentina

Doing Business in Argentina, Price Waterhouse & Co., Distribution Center; P.O. Box 30004, Tampa, Florida 33630; Tel: 813-876-9000

Taxation in Argentina, Deloitte and Touche, 1114 Avenue of the Americas, New York, New York 10036

Argentina, International Series, Ernst & Young, International Operations, 153 East 53rd Street, New York, New York 10022; Tel: 212-888-9100

Tax and Trade Profiles: South and Central America (Section on Argentina), Touche Ross & Co., Publications Department, 1635 Broadway, New York, New York 10019; Tel: 212-839-6620

Summary of Business Conditions in Argentina, Harteneck, Lopez y Cia (Representatives of Coopers & Lybrand) Montevideo 496; 1019 Buenos Aires, Argentina

Business Corporations in Argentina: An Updated Handbook of Legislation and Statistics; Foreign Investment in Argentina, Latin American Linguistic Service; Av. Caseros 796-Piso 5; Casilla de Correo 3699; 1000 Buenos Aires, Argentina

Investing, Licensing and Trade Conditions Abroad; Argentina, Business International Corp., One Dag Hammerskjold Plaza; New York, New York 10019; Tel: 212-750-6326

Tax & Trade Guide, Arthur Andersen & Co., International Tax Departament, 1345 Avenue of the Americas, New York, New York 10105; Tel: 212-708-4000

Investment Laws of the World: Argentina, International Center for Settlement of Investment Disputes, Oceanus Publications, Inc. Dobbs Ferry, New York, New York 10522

Laws of Argentina in Matters Affecting Business, General Secretariat, Organization of American States (OAS), Department of Publications, Washington, D.C. 20006, Tel: 202-941-1617

ECONOMIC/BUSINESS PERIODICALS

El Cronista Comercial, (weekdays), Honduras 5665, 1414 Capital Federal, Argentina Tel: 54-1-777-1717

Ambito Financiero, (weekdays), Pasaje Carabelas 241 - Piso 3; 1009 Buenos Aires, Argentina Tel: 54-1-331-5528 Fax: 54-1-331-1404

Mercado, (weekly), Alsina 547; 1087 Buenos Aires, Argentina

Business Trends: A Weekly Report to Management on the Argentine Economy, Consejo Tecnico de Inversiones S.A.; Esmeralda 320 - Piso 6; 1342 Buenos Aires, Argentina

Review of the River Plate, (3/month), Casilla de Correo 294 (Suc. 13-B); 1431 Buenos Aires, Argentina

AMCHAM Weekly News, American Chamber of Commerce in Argentina, Av. Leandro N. Alem 1110 - Piso 13; 1001 Buenos Aires, Argentina

Business Latin America, (weekly), Business International Corp., One Dag Hammerskjold Plaza, New York, New York 10017

La Nacior: Bouchard 557, 1106 Capital Federal, Argentina, Tel: 54-1-313-1003/1453 Fax: 54-1-313-1277

Clargin: Tacuari 1842, 1139 Capital Federal Tel: 54-1-307-0330 Fax: 54-1-307-0311

GENERAL REFERENCE

Guia de la Industria, Rivadavia 819; 1002 Buenos Aires, Argentina

Produccion y Consumo, Avenida Boedo 822; 1218 Buenos Aires, Argentina

List As, Ensenada 37; 1407 Buenos Aires, Argentina

Reference Book: Argentina, Dun & Bradstreet, Florida 234, piso 4, Buenos Aires, Argentina; in U.S.: One World Trade Center, Suite 9069; New York, N.Y. 10048; Tel: 212-938-8400

Directory of Argentine Exporters & Importers, Editorial Scott S.A., Guemes 3440 P.B. "A"; 1425 Buenos Aires, Argentina

American Business in Argentina, American Chamber of Commerce in Argentina; Av. Pte. Roque Saenz Pena 567, Piso 6; 1352 Buenos Aires; Argentina

U.S. Firms, Subsidiaries and Affiliates in Argentina, World Trade Academy Press, Inc., 50 East 42nd Street, Suite 805; New York, New York 10017; Tel: 212-697-4999

OFFICE OF LATIN AMERICA AND THE CARIBBEAN
Automated Fascimile System
Tel: 202-482-4464

STATISTICAL SOURCES

Comercio Exterior; Indicadores Industriales; Boletin Estadistico Trimestral, INDEC - Instituto Nacional de Estadistica y Censos; Hipolito Yrigoyen 250; 1086 Buenos Aires, Argentina

Memoria Anual; Boletin Estadistico, Banco Central de la Republica Argentina, Reconquista 266, Buenos Aires, Argentina

Informe Economico: Resena Estadistico, Ministerio de Economia; Area de Coyuntura, Hipolito 250, Piso 8, Of. 829; 1086 Buenos Aires, Argentina

Boletin de Comercio Exterior Argentino, Secretaria de Industria y Comercio Exterior, Direccion Nacional de Investicaciones Sectoriales, Julio Roca 651; 1322 Buenos Aires, Argentina

Anuario de la Economia Argentina/Annual Report of the Argentine Economy; Consejo Tecnico de Inversiones S.A., Esmeralda 320, Piso 6; 1343 Buenos Aires, Argentina
Anuario de Comercio Exterior: Analisis Estadistico, Central de Estadisticas Nacionales de la Republica Argentina, Av. de Mayo 953, Piso 10; 1084 Buenos Aires, Argentina

World Fact Book
Superintendent of Documents
P.O. Box 371954
Pittsburgh, PA 15250
Tel: 202-512-1800
Fax: 202-512-2250

World Bank Atlas
The World Bank
Publication Department, 1818 H Street, N.W.
Washington, D.C. 20433
Tel: 202-473-2209
Fax: 202-676-0581

U.N. Statistical Yearbook, 39th Ediition
United Nations Publications
Two UN Plaza, Room DC2-853
New York, New York 10017
Tel: 212-963-8302; 1-800-253-9646

International Trade Statistics Yearbook
United Nations Publications
Two UN Plaza, Room DC2-853
New York, New York 10017
Tel: 212-963-8302

LATINFINANCE
2121 Ponce de Leon Boulevard
Suite 1020
Coral Gables, Florida 33134
Tel: 305-448-6593
Fax: 305-448-0718

U.S./LATIN TRADE
P.O. Box 11640
Miami, Florida 33111
Fax: 305-358-9166

Resources: ASEAN (General)

U.S GOVERNMENT COUNTRY CONTACTS

Trade/Economy

DIRECTOR, OFFICE OF EAST ASIA AND THE PACIFIC
Mr. Herbert Cochran
U.S. Department of Commerce
Room 1229 Herbert Hoover Building
14th Street & Constitution Ave, NW
Washinton, DC 20230
Tel: 202-482-2422
Fax: 202-482-3159

DESK OFFICER, ASEAN
Mr. Kevin Boyd
U.S. Department of Commerce, Room 2036
14th and Constitution Ave, NW
Washington, DC 20230
Tel: 202-482-3894
Fax: 202-482-4453

ASSISTANT UNITED STATES TRADE REPRESENTATIVE FOR ASIA AND THE PACIFIC
Mr. Robert Cassidy
Office of the U.S. Trade Representative
Room 309A Winder Building
600 17th Street, NW
Washington, DC 20506
Tel: 202-395-3430
Fax: 202-395-3512

DIRECTOR, OFFICE FOR PHILIPPINES, MALAYSIA, BRUNEI AND SINGAPORE
W. Scott Butcher
U.S. Department of State
Room 5206
2201 C Street, NW
Washington, DC 20520
Tel: 202-647-3276
Fax: 202-647-3996

Defense

COUNTRY DIRECTOR FOR PHILIPPINES, INDONESIA, SINGAPORE, MALAYSIA AND BRUNEI
Ms. Mary Tighe
U.S. Department of Defense
Room 4C840
2400 Defense Pentagon
Washington, DC 20301-2400
Tel: 703-697-0555

Communications

UNITED STATES INFORMATION AGENCY
Ms. Meg Gilroy
Room 766
301 4th Street, SW
Washington, DC 20547
Tel: 202-619-5836

Transportation

U.S. DEPARTMENT OF TRANSPORTATION
Mr. Kevin Sample
Room 10300 Nassif Building
400 7th Street, SW
Washington, DC 20590
Tel: 202-366-9526
Fax: 202-366-7414

Agriculture and Rural Affairs

DIRECTOR, ASIA, AFRICA AND EASTERN EUROPE DIVISION
Ms. Patricia Sheikh
Foreign Agricultural Service
U.S. Department of Agriculture
Room 5509 South Building
14th Street and Independence Ave, SW
Washington, DC 20250
Tel: 202-720-1289

MARKET PROMOTION PROGRAM
Contact: Sharon McClure
Marketing Operations Staff
Tel: 202-720-4327

Energy & Natural Resources

DEPUTY ASSISTANT SECRETARY FOR INTERNATIONAL ENERGY
Mr. John Brodman
U.S. Department of Energy
Room 7C-034 Forrestal Building
1000 Independence Ave, SW
Washington, DC 20585
Tel: 202-586-5915

Mining

U.S. BUREAU OF MINES
Mr. John Wu
810 7th Street, NW
Washington, DC 20241
Tel: 202-501-9697
Fax: 202-219-2489

Health

ASSOCIATE DIRECTOR FOR ASIA AND THE PACIFIC
Miss Julia Ho
International Affairs Staff
Food and Drug Administration
Room 15A30
5600 Fishers Lane
Rockville, MD 20857
Tel: 301-443-4480
Fax: 301-443-0235

Environment

OFFICE OF INTERNATIONAL ACTIVITIES
Environmental Protection Agency
401 M Street, SW
Washington, DC 20460
Tel: 202-260-4870

Education

SOUTHEAST ASIAN STUDIES CENTER FOR INTERNATIONAL EDUCATION
Ms. Sarah West
U.S. Department of Education
Washington, DC 20202-5331
Tel: 202-401-9782
Fax: 202-205-9489

U.S. EXPORT-IMPORT BANK

811 Vermont Avenue, N.W.
Washington, D.C. 20571
Contact: Roy Shrobe
Loan Officer - Asia Division
Tel: 202-566-8949
Fax: 202-566-7524
Frank Wilson, Loan Officer for Asia
Tel: 202 566-8877
Hotline:1-800-424-5201
Telex:(TRT) 197681 EXIM UT
TDD: 202-535-3913

SMALL BUSINESS ADMINISTRATION
OFFICE OF INTERNATIONAL TRADE

409 3rd St, 8th Floor, SW
Washington, DC 20416
Tel: 202-205-6720
Fax: 202-205-6722

U.S. TRADE AND DEVELOPMENT
AGENCY (TDA)

Fred Eberhart, Regional Director Asia
Tel: 703-875-4357
John Herrman, Country Manager, Malaysia
Tel: 703-875-4357
Room 309, SA-16
Washington, D.C. 20523-1602
Tel:703-875-4357
Fax: 703-875-4009

OVERSEAS PRIVATE INVESTMENT
CORPORATION (OPIC)

1615 M Street, N.W.
Washington, D.C. 20527
Contact: Maurice A. Johnson
Regional Manager Asia, Africa & Middle East
Tel: 202-336-8574; 800-424-6742
Fax: 202-408-5142
Victoria Peters, Finance Officer
Tel: 202-457-7182
InfoLine: 202-336-8799
FactsLine: 202-336-8700

WORLD BANK/INTERNATIONAL
FINANCE CORPORATION

Capital Markets (Southeast Asia)
Rashad Kaldany, Manager
Tel: 202-473-6787

OTHER CONTACTS

AXCAP

The Banker's Association for Foreign Trade (BAFT) is an association of banking institutions dedicated to fostering and promoting American exports, international trade, finance and investment between the U.S. and its trading partners. As the oldest international banking trade association in the U.S., BAFT plays a unique role in bringing together financial institutions worldwide which have an interest in business, commerce and finance in the U.S.

BAFT's Access to Export Capital (AXCAP) program serves as an essential resource for assisting exporters seeking trade finance and banks that provide trade finance services. In essence, AXCAP serves as a national catalogue listing the trade finance services of banks, over 200 financiers and other companies. In addition, the database includes information on funding of environmental projects in Asia. Thirdly, AXCAP contains a national inventory of the services offered by government export credit agencies, including Eximbank, OPIC and SBA.

The AXCAP service is free of charge and can be reached by calling 1-800-49AXCAP. The exporter or inquirer is connected to a trade specialist who then matches the caller's specific needs with the appropriate information in the database.

ASIAN DEVELOPMENT BANK

6 ADB Ave
Mandaluyong, Metro Manila
PO BOX: 789
APO AP 96440
Tel: 632-632-6050
Fax: 632-632-4003

US&FCS OFFICER AT ADB

Janet Thomas
395 Buemida Ave
Ext. Makati, Metro Manila
Tel: 632-813-3248
Fax: 632-632-4003

INFORMATION CHECKLIST
AND BIBLIOGRAPHY

BOOKS

A History of Southeast Asia, D.G.E. Hall

An Eye for the Dragon: Southeast Asia Observed 1954-1970, Dennis Bloodworth

Culture of Southeast Asia, Reginald Le May

ASEAN

Resources: Brazil

COUNTRY GOVERNMENT AGENCIES

SECRETARIAT OF AGRICULTURE & LIVESTOCK DEFENSE
Ministry of Agriculture
MAARA-SDA Esplanada dos Ministerios,
Bloco D, Anexo B, 4o.andar
70043-900 Brasilia, DF
Tel: 55-61-226-9771
Fax: 55-61-224-3995

BANCO CENTRAL DO BRASIL
Brazilian Central Bank
SBS - Edifício Sede do Banco Central do Brasil
70074-900 Brasília, DF
Tel: 55-61-214-1020-214-1000
Fax: 55-61-224-4119

BANCO DO BRASIL S-A - BB
Bank of Brazil
SBS, Qd.4, Lote 32, Bloco C,
Ed. Sede III, 20 andar
70073-900 Brasília, DF
Tel: 55-61-212-2211
Fax: 55-61-2230156

BANCO NACIONAL DE DESENVOLVIMENTO ECONOMICO SOCIAL - BNDES
National Bank of Economic Social
Development
Av. República do Chile 100
20139-900 Rio de Janeiro, RJ
Tel: 55-21-277-7447
Fax: 55-21-262-8513

MINISTÉRIO DA CIÊNCIA E TECNOLOGIA - MCT
Ministry of Science and Technology
Esplanada dos Ministérios
Bloco E, 4 andar
70062-900 Brasília, DF
Tel: 55-61-321-8886
Fax: 55-61-225-1141

EMPRESA BRASILEIRA DE AERONÁUTICA - EMBRAER
Brazilian Aeronautic Company
Av. Brig. Faria Lima 2170
12227-901 São José dos Campos, SP
Tel: 55-123-25-1000
Fax: 55-123-21-8466

EMPRESA BRASILEIRA DE TELECOMUNICAÇÕES - EMBRATEL
Brazilian Long Distance Telephone Company
Av. Presidente Vargas 1012
Edifício Sede, 15 andar
20179-900 Rio de Janeiro, RJ
Tel: 55-21-216-8182
Fax: 55-21-224-1175

INSTITUTO NACIONAL DA PROPRIEDADE INDUSTRIAL - INPI
Brazilian Industrial Property Institute
Praça Mauá 7, 18 andar - Centro
20081-240 Rio de Janeiro, RJ
Tel: 55-21-291-1224
Fax: 55-21-263-2539

MINISTÉRIO DA AERONÁUTICA - MAER
Ministry of Aeronautics
Esplanada dos Ministérios - Bloco M
70045-900 Brasília, DF
Tel: 55-61-313-2345; Fax: 55-61-313-2110

SECRETARIAT FOR HEALTH SURVEILANCE
Romero Claus
Tel: 55-61-226-9169

MINISTÉRIO DA INDÚSTRIA E COMÉRCIO - MIC
Ministry of Industry and Commerce
Esplanada dos Ministérios, Bloco J, 6 andar
70056-900 Brasília, DF
Tel: 55-61-225-8105

SECRETARIA DE COMERCIO EXTERIOR
Secretariat of Foreign Trade
Esplanada Dos Ministerios
Bloco J, 8 andar
70056-900 Brasília, DF
Tel: 55-61-224-0639
Fax: 55-61-225-7230

MINISTÉRIO DA FAZENDA - MF
Ministry of Finance
Esplanada dos Ministérios - Bloco P
70048-900 Brasília, DF
Tel: 55-61-314-2000
Fax: 55-61-223-5239

PETRÓLEO BRASILEIRO S.A. - PETROBRÁS
Brazilian Petroleum Company
Av. República do Chile 65, 24 andar
20031-900 Rio de Janeiro, RJ
Tel: 55-21-534-4477 Fax: 55-21-240-9394

DEPARTAMENTO DE AERONAUTICA CIVIL - DAC
Department of Civil Aviation
Aeroporto Santos Dumont, 4 andar
20021-000 Rio de Janeiro, RJ
Tel: 55-21-220-6927; Fax: 55-21-220-5177

Automotive Components Manufacturers
SINDPEÇAS
Rua Abilio Soares 1487
04005-005 São Paulo, SP
Tel: 55-11-884-4599 Fax: 55-11-884-0584

Dental, Medical and Hospital Equipment
SINDICATO DA INDÚSTRIA DE ARTIGOS E EQUIPAMENTOS ODONTOLÓGICOS, MÉDICOS E HOSPITALARES E DE LABORATÓRIOS
Av. Paulista 1313, 8 andar, cj.806
01311-923 São Paulo, SP
Tel: 55-11-285-0155; Fax: 55-11-285-0018

Electric and Electronics Industry
**ASSOCIAÇÃO BRASILEIRA DA
INDÚSTRIA ELETRICA E ELETRONICA
- ABINEE**
Av. Paulista 1313, 7 andar
01311-923 São Paulo, SP
Tel: 55-11-251-1577
Fax: 55-11-285-0607

Electric Conductors
**SINDICATO DE CONDUTORES
ELETRICOS - SINDCEL**
Rua Mariana Correa 52
01444-000 São Paulo, SP
Tel: 55-11-883-2622
Fax: 55-11-883-2814

Electrical Energy
**SINDICATO DA INDÚSTRIA DE
ENERGIA ELÉTRICA**
Alameda Campinas 433, 10 andar
01404-901 São Paulo, SP
Tel: 55-11-288-1166
Fax: 55-11-288-8524

Food Processing—Dairy Products
**SINDICATO DA INDÚSTRIA DE
LATICÍNIOS E PRODUTOS
DERIVADOS**
Praça Dom José Gaspar 30, 10 andar
01047-901 São Paulo, SP
Tel: 55-11-259-3251
Fax: 55-11-259-8482

**WHEAT MILLERS ASSOCIATION -
ABITRIGO**
Rua Benedito Otoni, No. 24, Sao Cristovao
20940-180 Rio de Janeiro, RJ
Tel: 55-21-589-4522
Fax: 55-21-589-3384

Franchising
**ASSOCIAÇÃO BRASILEIRA DE
FRANCHISING - ABF**
Travessa Meruipe 18
04012-000 São Paulo, SP
Tel: 55-11-571-1393
Fax: 55-11-575-5590

Food
**ASSOCIAÇÃO BRASILEIRA DAS
INDÚSTRIAS DA ALIMENTAÇÃO -
ABIA**
Av. Brig. Faria Lima 2003,
11 andar, cjs. 1104-1116
01451-001 São Paulo, SP
Tel: 55-11-816-5733
Fax: 55-11-814-6688

Foundries
**ASSOCIAÇÃO BRASILEIRA DE
FUNDIÇÃO - ABIFA**
Av. Eng. Billings 526
05321-010 São Paulo, SP
Tel: 55-11-819-2515
Fax: 55-11-819-3783

Machines Manufacturers
**ASSOCIAÇÃO BRASILEIRA DE
MÁQUINAS - ABIMAQ**
Av. Jabaquara 2925, 3 andar
04045-902 São Paulo, SP
Tel: 55-11-579-5044
Fax: 55-11-579-3498

Material Handling and Storage
**INSTITUTO DE MOVIMENTAÇÃO E
ARMAZENAGEM DE MATERIAIS -
IMAM**
Rua Topázio 243
04105-904 São Paulo, SP
Tel: 55-11-277-9188
Fax: 55-11-277-9144

Metal Structure Constructors
**ASSOCIAÇÃO MINEIRA DOS
CONSTRUTORES DE
ESTRUTURAS METÁLICAS - AMICEM**
Av. do Contorno 4520, 3 andar
30110-090 Belo Horizonte, MG
Tel: 55-31-227-8540

Mining
**INSTITUTO BRASILEIRO DE
MINERAÇÃO**
SCS 1, Bloco F, 5 andar,
Edifício Camargo Correa
70302-000 Brasília, DF
Tel: 55-61-226-9367
Fax: 55-61-226-9580

Motor-Vehicles: Importers
**ASSOCIAÇÃO BRASILEIRA DOS
IMPORTADORES DE VEÍCULOS
AUTOMOTORES — ABEIVA**
Rua Bento da Andrade 103
04503-010 São Paulo, SP
TeleFax: 55-11-884-1622

Motor-Vehicles: Independent Importers
**ASSOCIAÇÃO BRASILEIRA DOS
IMPORTADORES
INDEPENDENTES DE VEÍCULOS
AUTOMOTORES — ABRASIVA**
Av. Brigadeiro Faria Lima 1885, 4 andar, cj.420
01451-001 São Paulo, SP
TeleFax: 55-11-211-9447

Pharmaceuticals
**ASSOCIAÇÃO BRASILEIRA DE
INDÚSTRIA FARMACEUTICA —
ABIFARMA**
Rua Beira Rio 57, 7 andar
04548-050 São Paulo, SP
Tel: 55-11-820-3775; Fax: 55-11-822-6628

Plastics
**SINDICATO DA INDÚSTRIA DE
MATERIAL PLÁSTICO**
Av. Paulista 2439, 8 andar, cjs.81-82
01311-936 São Paulo, SP
Tel: 55-11-282-8288; Fax: 55-11-282-8042

Printing
**ASSOCIAÇÃO BRASILEIRA DA
INDÚSTRIA GRÁFICA — ABIGRAF**
Rua Marquês de Itú 70, 12 andar
01270-900 São Paulo, SP
Tel: 55-11-231-4733
Fax: 55-11-231-4743

Railway and Highway Equipment
**SINDICATO INTERESTADUAL DA
INDÚSTRIA DE MATERIAIS E
EQUIPAMENTOS FERROVIÁRIOS
E RODOVIÁRIOS—SIMEFRE**
Av. Paulista 1313, 8 andar, cj.811
01311-923 São Paulo, SP
Tel: 55-11-289-9166
Fax: 55-11-289-5823

Brazil

Road Transportation
ASSOCIAÇÃO NACIONAL DAS EMPRESAS DE TRANSPORTES RODOVIÁRIOS DE CARGA - NTC
Rua da Gávea 1390
02121-020 São Paulo, SP
Tel: 55-11-954-1400
Fax: 55-11-954-1127

Software
ASSOCIAÇÃO BRASILEIRA DAS EMPRESAS DE SOFTWARE
Av. Brig. Faria Lima 1857, 3 andar, cj.307
01451-001 São Paulo, SP
Tel: 55-11-813-2057-9511-9704
Fax: 55-11-815-0359

Toiletries
SINDICATO DA INDÚSTRIA DE PERFUMARIAS E ARTIGOS DE TOUCADOR
Av. Paulista 1313, 9 andar, cj.901
01311-923 São Paulo, SP
Tel: 55-11-251-1999
Fax: 55-11-287-9207

SINDICATO DA INDÚSTRIA DE INSTRUMENTOS MUSICAIS E DE BRINQUEDOS
Av. Pedroso de Morais 2219
05419-001 São Paulo, SP
Tel: 55-11-816-3644
Fax: 55-11-211-0226

FEDERAÇÃO DAS INDÚSTRIAS DO ESTADO DE SÃO PAULO - FIESP
(State of São Paulo Federation of Industries)
Av. Paulista 1313
01311-923 São Paulo, SP
Tel: 55-11-251-3522
Fax: 55-11-284-3971

FEDERAÇÃO DAS INDÚSTRIAS DO ESTADO DO RIO DE JANEIRO
(State of Rio de Janeiro Federation of Industries)
Av. Calogeras 15, 9 andar
20030-070 Rio de Janeiro, RJ
Tel: 55-21-292-3939
Fax: 55-21-262-6705

AMERICAN CHAMBER OF COMMERCE SÃO PAULO
Rua Alexandre Dumas 1976
04717-004 São Paulo, SP
Tel: 55-11-246-9199
Fax: 55-11-246-9080

AMERICAN CHAMBER OF COMMERCE RIO DE JANEIRO
Praça Pio X 15, 5 andar
20040-020 Rio de Janeiro, RJ
Tel: 55-21-203-2477
Fax: 55-21-263-4477

COUNTRY MARKET RESEARCH FIRMS

A.C. NIELSEN S-C LTDA.
Av. Bernardino de Campos, 98, 9o. andar
04004-040 São Paulo, SP
Tel: 55-11-889-7077
Fax: 55-11-889-8220

BOOZ, ALLEN & HAMILTON DO BRASIL CONSULTORES LTDA.
Rua Gomes de Carvalho 1765, 5 andar
04547-901 São Paulo, SP
Tel: 55-11-820-1900
Fax: 55-11-820-6750

M & L MAGNUS LANDMANN CONSULTORES EMPRESARIAIS
Av. Brig. Faria Lima 1544, 4 andar, cj.41
01452-001 São Paulo, SP
Tel: 55-11-816-3144;
Fax: 55-11-816-7864

BICHUETTI CONSULTORIA EMPRESARIAL S-C LTDA.
Av. Brig. Faria Lima 1541 - 6B
01451-000 São Paulo, SP
Tel: 55-11-813-9744
Fax: 55-11-816-0908

DATAMARK CONSULTORES S-C LTDA.
Av. Brig. Faria Lima 1238, 3 andar, cj.31
01452-000 São Paulo, SP
Tel: 55-11-814-7355
Fax: 55-11-814-8890

BARROS RIBEIRO PLANEJAMENTO, CONSULTORIA E REPRESENTAÇÕES LTDA.
Rua Dr. João Climaco Pereira 46
04532-070 São Paulo, SP
Tel: 55-11-820-7422
Fax: 55-11-820-0720

ADELA EMPREENDIMENTOS E CONSULTORIA LTDA.
Av. Brig. Faria Lima 1541, 7 andar, cj.7D
01451-000 São Paulo, SP
Tel: 55-11-813-7111
Fax: 55-11-212-7675

ARTHUR D. LITTLE S-C LTDA.
Av. Brig. Faria Lima 2003,
19-20 andares, cj.1901-2015
01451-001 São Paulo, SP
Tel: 55-11-814-8144
Fax: 55-11-815-7540

SCHLOCHAUER & ASSOCIADOS CONSULTORIA E REPRESENTAÇÃO LTDA.
Caixa Postal 21151
04698-970 São Paulo, SP
Tel: 55-11-247-6631
Fax: 55-11-247-6631-829-7556

S. BEKIN & CONSULTORES S-C LTDA.
Rua Estela 265, casa 11
04011-001 São Paulo, SP
TeleFax: 55-11-572-3112

LINDSEY CONSULTORES S-C LTDA.
Rua Bela Cintra 1932
01415-002 São Paulo, SP
Tel: 55-11-280-8122
Fax: 55-11-853-7787

SIMONSEN ASSOCIADOS S-C LTDA.
Av. 9 de Julho 5017, 12 andar
01407-200 São Paulo, SP
Tel: 55-11-853-4733
Fax: 55-11-883-4958

COUNTRY COMMERCIAL BANKS

NOTE: Most banks in Brazil operate as multiple banks, accumulating the functions of commercial and investment banks and are also active in the capital market. These are the ten largest Brazilian-owned private multiple banks according to deposit values.

Banco Brasileiro de Descontos - BRADESCO - São Paulo;
Banco Itau - São Paulo;
Banco Nacional - Minas Gerais;
Banco Bamerindus - Parana;
União de Bancos Brasileiros - UNIBANCO - São Paulo;
Banco Safra - São Paulo;
Banco Economico - Bahia;
Banco de Crédito Nacional - BCN - São Paulo;
Banco Bozano Simonsen - Rio de Janeiro;
Banco Mercantil de São Paulo - São Paulo.

U.S. EMBASSY TRADE PERSONNEL

U.S. MISSION IN BRAZIL
Brasília:
Ambassador: Melvyn Levitsky
Economic Counselor: Paul Wackerbarth
Commercial Attaché (FCS): Larry Farris
Tel: 55-61-321-7272

Agricultural Counselor: Shackford Pitcher
Tel: 55-61-226-3159

São Paulo:
Senior Commercial Officer (FCS):
Migual Pardo de Zela (acting)
Events Director (FCS):Willaim Vigneault
Tel: 55-11-853-2011

Cansul-General: Melissa Wells
Consul-Economic Affairs: Gilbert Donahue
Agricultural Officer: Robert Hoff
Tel: 55-11-881-6511

Rio de Janeiro:
Consul-General: Robert Durham
Principal Commercial Officer (FCS): Dar Pribyl
FAA Representative: Santiago Garcia
Tel: 55-21-292-7117

WASHINGTON-BASED USG COUNTRY CONTACTS

DEPARTMENT OF AGRICULTURE (FAS)
Chad Russell
Latin America - Policy
Tel: 202-720-1335

Susan Hale
Trade Promotion
Tel: 202-720-6343

AID
Babette Prevot
Brazil
Tel: 202-647-4359

BXA
Bob Dunn
Tel: 202-482-3984
Fax: 202-482-5650

CENSUS-POPULATION
John Reed
Demographer - L.A. Countries
Tel: 301-763-4221

COMMERCE (ITA)
Jay Dowling
Dir., Southern Cone Div.
Tel: 202-482-1648

Brazil Desk
Paulo Mendes
Laura Zeiger-Hatfield
Tel: 202-482-3872

CUSTOMS
Dina Henry
International Affairs
Tel: 202-927-0440

DEFENSE
Lt. Col. Harris
Int. Sec. Affairs; Brazil Desk
Tel: 703-697-9301

ENERGY
Moustafa Soliman
Latin America
Tel: 202-586-5904

EPA
Carmeryl Hill-Macon
Latin America Programs
Tel: 202-260-6009

EXIMBANK
Marion Hichman
Loan Officer--Brazil
Tel: 202-565-3410

Leon White
Promotion--Brazil
Tel: 202-565-3923

Carl Leik
VP Latin America
Tel: 202-565-3401

FAA
Santiago Garcia
FAA Representative
Tel: 55- 21- 292-7117
Fax: 55- 21-240-9853

HHS-FDA
Marilyn Veek
Intl. Affairs-Americas
Tel: 301-443-4480

INTERIOR (MINERALS)
Alfredo Gu-mendi
Latin America
Tel: 202-632-5062

INTERNET
202-387-5445

LABOR
Harold Davey
Officer; Foreign Affairs BILA
Tel: 202-219-6257

MARINE FISHERIES
Dennis Weidner
Latin America
Tel: 301-713-2286

NIST
Joanne Overman
NCSCI-NIST
Tel: 301-975-4037

Mary Saunders
Brazil
Tel: 301-975-2396;
Fax: 301-963-2871

NTDB
202-482-1986

NTIA
Nancy Eskenazi
Brazil
Tel: 202-482-1864;
Fax: 202-482-1865

OPIC
Britt Doughtie
Insurance
Tel: 202-336-8652

Richard Greenberg
Investment
Tel: 202-336-8616

Manoel Fernandez
Finance
Tel: 202-336-8489

PTO
Kathy Dussault
Brazil
Tel: 703-305-9300;
Fax: 703-305-8885

STATE-ARA
Donald Planty
Director, Braz. & Southern Cone
Tel: 202-647-6541

Eric Luftman
Economic Officer
Tel: 202-647-6538;
Fax: 202-736-7481

Brazil

TELECOM-TRADE DEV.
Clay Mowry
Industry Specialist
Tel: 202-482-2872

TRADE & DEV. AGENCY
Albert Angulo
Reg Dir., Lat. Am.
Gisele Saralegui
Tel: 703-875-4357;
Fax: 703-875-4009

TRANSPORTATION
Gwen Baker
Latin America
Tel: 202-366-9521;
Fax: 202-366-7417

TREASURY
Anthony Marcus
Brazil Desk
Tel: 202-622-1218

USIA
Michael Korff
Brazil Desk
Tel: 202-619-6835;
Fax: 202-619-5093

Lesley Vossem
Senior Program Officer
Tel: 202-619-5245;
Fax: 202-619-5172

USTR (WHITE HOUSE)
Karen Chopra
Director, Southern Common Market
Tel: 202-395-5190;
Fax: 202-395-3911

USTTA
Jon Arthur
Regional Director LA
Tel: 305-526-2912;
Fax: 305-526-2915

Wanda Burquin
Brazil
Tel: 202-501-8105;
Fax: 202-482-2887

Helen Marano
Brazil
Tel: 202-501-8105;
Fax: 202-482-2887

COUNTRY CONSULATES AND TRADE OFFICES IN THE U.S.

BRAZILIAN EMBASSY
3006 Mass. Ave., NW
Washington, D.C. 20008
Ambassador Paulo Taurso Flecha de Lima
Tel: 202-745-2700;
Fax: 202-945-2827

Minister Counselor &
Deputy Chief of Mission
Frederico Cezar de Araújo
Tel: 202-745-2700

Economic Minister Maria Stella P.B. Frota
Tel: 202-745-2722

Financial Minister Fernando Coimbra
Tel: 202-745-2749

Commercial Counselor (Promo) Sergio Taam
Tel: 202-745-2766

Commercial Counselor (Policy)
Paulo Fontoura
Tel: 202-745-2780
Consular Section Roberto Ardenghy
Tel: 202-745-2737

Science and Technology Attache
Jose Manoel Montenegro
Tel: 202-745-2750

Environment & Human Rights
Marcia Donner
Tel: 202-745-2776

Banco do Brasil
New York
Espirito Santo
Tel: 212-626-7100

Washington
Paulo de Tarso Medeiros
Tel: 202-857-0320

BRAZILIAN GOVERNMENT TRADE BUREAU
Tel: 212-916-3200
Maria Andrade
Tel: 212-916-3247

CVRD (RIO DOCE AMERICAS)
Tel: 212-626-9800

PETROBRAS
Gerson Braune, General Manager
Tel: 212-974-0777
Petrobras America, Inc.
Antonio Eraldo Porto, Commercial Manager
Tel: 212-397-3650

INTERNATIONAL FINANCIAL INSTITUTIONS, WASHINGTON, D.C.

WORLD BANK (IBRD)
Dir. Brazil Department
Gobind Nankami
Tel: 202-473-7726

Agriculture & Environment
Mark Wilson
Tel: 202-473-9200

Energy & Industry
Steve Ettenger
Tel: 202-473-9320

Country Operations
Paul Meo
Tel: 202-473-8452

Jim Stevens
Tel: 202-473-1869

Infrastructure Div.
Afonso Sanchez
Tel: 202-473-0001

INTER-AMERICAN DEVELOPMENT BANK
Chief for Brazil & Suriname Division
Manuel Rappaport
Tel: 202-623-1470

Coordinator for Brazil
Branimir Lobo
Tel: 202-623-1641

INT'L MONETARY FUND (IMF)
Division Chief, Brazil
Jose Fajgenbaum
Tel: 202-623-8637

OAS
Director for SICE
Cynthia Miller
Tel: 202-458-3725
Foreign Trade Information

PRIVATE ORGANIZATIONS IN U.S.

AACCLA (AMERICAN CHAMBERS OF COMMERCE IN LATIN AMERICA)
U.S.-Brazil Business Council
David Hirschmann
Executive VP, U.S. section
Tel: 202-463-5485

BRAZILIAN-AMERICAN CHAMBER OF COMMERCE (NEW YORK)
Sueli Bonaparte
General Manager
Tel: 212-575-9030

COUNCIL OF THE AMERICAS
Ludlow (Kim) Flower
Tel: 202-659-1547
Lowell Fleischer

New York Office
Alice Lentz
Tel: 212-628-3200

CENTER OF BRAZILIAN STUDIES - JOHNS HOPKINS UNIVERSITY (SAIS)
Riordan Roett
Tel: 202-663-5733

INSTITUTE OF BRAZILIAN BUSINESS AND PUBLIC MANAGEMENT ISSUES - IBI
George Washington University
James Ferrer
Tel: 202-994-5205

THE BRAZIL SOCIETY OF NORTHERN CALIFORNIA
Synthia Elliott
Tel: 415-989-2884

PARTNERS OF THE AMERICAS
Regional Director Brazil
Stuart Beecher
Tel: 202-628-3300

U.S. DEPARTMENT OF COMMERCE MARKET RESEARCH AVAILABLE

INDUSTRY SUBSECTOR ANALYSES

— Active Electronic Components (ELC) (5-93)
— Agricultural Storage Facilities (12-92)
— Air Conditioning and Refrigeration Equipment, Parts and Components (8-93)
— Cellular Mobile Equipment (12-92)
— Chromatographic and Spectroscopical Equipment (5-93)
— Compressors and Parts Thereof (4-93)
— Discretionary Pleasure Travel To The U.S.A. (4-93)
— Disposable Medical Products (8-93)
— Electric Power Distribution & Transmission Equip. (10-93)
— Engine Emission Control Instrumentation (7-93)
— Fast Food and Restaurant Equipment (4-93)
— Fine Chemicals (5-93)
— Fitness Equipment (12-93)
— Franchised Fast Food Stores (5-93)
— High-Tech Forestry Equipment (2-94)
— Information Services (4-93)
— Laser Cutting Machine-Tool (4-93)
— Lumber Mill Equipment (7-93)
— Non Prescription Drugs-Vitamins-Provitamins (4-93)
— Nonwovens - (7-93)
— Oil and Gas Pipeline Installation Equipment (2-93)
— PCB Production Equipment (2-94)
— Paper Recycling Machinery (7-93)
— Plastics Extrusion Machinery (1-93)
— Programmable Logic Controllers (4-93)
— Public Telephone Network System (5-94)
— Pumps and Parts (4-94)
— Security Equipment (7-93)
— Sludge Treatment and Management (4-93)
— Value Added Services (4-93)
— Bicycles (SPG) (4-94)
— Broadcasting Equipment (TEL) (6-95)
— Building Products (BLD) (9-95)
— Cardiological and Cardiovascular Equipment (MED) (7-95)
— Electrical Power Distribution Equipment (ELP) (12-94)
— Environmental Consulting Services (GSV) (4-95)
— Executive General Aviation Aircraft (AIR) (9-95)
— Fine Chemicals (ICH) (6-94)
— Graphics Software (CSF) (7-95)
— Home Furnishing Textiles (TXP) (3-95)
— Household Consumer Goods (HCG) (5-95)
— Materials Handling Equipment (MHM) (4-95)
— Metal Cutting Machine Tools (MTL) (6-95)
— Oil & Gas: Offshore Platforms (OGM) (4-95)
— Plastics materials and resins (PMR) (3-95)
— Poultry Equipment (ACG) (12-94)
— Process Controls for the Chemical Industry (PCI) (12-94)
— Railroad Services (TRN) (9-95)
— Telephone Switching Equipment (TEL) (5-95)

FCS reports available on the National Trade Data Bank (NTDB)

USDA-FAS-Commodity Reports and Market Briefs

FAS reports available from Reports Office-USDA-FAS, Washington, D.C. 20250. These reports are expected to become available later in the National Trade Data Bank.

TRADE EVENTS SCHEDULE

SEP 26-29-95
Compugrafic '95
TFW
São Paulo

SEP 14-20-95
Study USA '95
(Continuing Education Courses)
SFO
Rio de Janeiro
São Paulo

SEP 18-19/95
Gov. Wisconsin Trade Mission
TM
São Paulo

OCT 2-4/95
Michigan Environmental Delegation
TM
São Paulo

OCT 9-11/95
Massachusetts Trade Mission
TM
São Paulo

OCT 16-18/95
New York Rep-Com
TME
São Paulo

NOV 6-7/95
Defense Diversification MKR
MKR
São Paulo
Rio de Janeiro

NOVEMBER
New York Congressional Mission
TM
São Paulo

DEC 4-5/95
OTEXA Trade Mission
TM
São Paulo

1996
MARCH 1996
Minority Matchmaker
MKR
São Paulo

MARCH 1996
Visit USA '96
SFO
São Paulo

MAR 26-29/96
U.S. Pavilion at TELEXPO '96
BFC
São Paulo

APRIL 1996
Hardware Matchmaker
(to be confirmed)
MKR
São Paulo

APRIL 1996
Medical Matchmaker
(to be confirmed)
MKR
São Paulo

APR 23-26/96
Comdex/Rio '96
BFC
Rio de Janeiro

MAR 18-23/96
U.S. Pavilion at the 14th FIEPAG
TFO
São Paulo

MAY 1996
*Electrical Distribution, Transmission and Control
Trade Mission*
(to be confirmed)
TM
São Paulo
Rio de Janeiro

MAY 1996
Microeletronics Trade Mission
(to be confirmed)
TM
São Paulo

JUN 11-14/96
U.S. Pavilion at the 12th FISPAL
TFO
São Paulo

JUN 18-21/96
U.S. Pavilion at HOSPITALAR '96
TFO
São Paulo

JUN 25-28/96
U.S. Pavilion at FENIT '96
BFC
São Paulo

JULY 1996
Computer Software Trade Mission
(to be confirmed)
TM
São Paulo

JUL 17-21/96
U.S. Pavilion at FENASOFT '96
BFC
São Paulo

AUG 13-16/96
Productivity/ Instrumentation USA '96
SFO/SFW
São Paulo

AUG 12-15/96
U.S. Pavilion at COSMÉTICA '96
TFW
São Paulo

AUGUST 1996
Telecom Trade Mission
TM
São Paulo

SEP 1996
Comdex/Sucesu South America '96
BFC
São Paulo

SEP 1996
Study USA '96 (Continuing Education Courses)
SFO
Rio de Janeiro
São Paulo

SEP 9-12/96
Autoparts Matchmaker
MKR
São Paulo
Porto Alegre

SEP 30-OCT 2/96
Plastics Industries Trade Mission
TM
São Paulo

OCT 1-5/96
U.S. Pavilion at EQUIPOTEL '96
BFC
São Paulo

SFO: Solo Fair-Local Recruitment
TFO :   Trade Fair-International Exhibition-
        Local Recruitment
TFW: Trade Fair-Intl. Exhibition-
        Washington Recruitment
TM: Trade Mission

INFORMATION CHECKLIST AND BIBLIOGRAPHY

BUSINESS GUIDES (IN ENGLISH)

American Firms Operating in Brazil. A list of firms compiled by World Trade Academy Press, Inc., 50 East 42nd Street, New York, NY 10017; Tel: 212- 697-4999.

Brazilian-American Who's Who. Includes companies in the United States and their subsidiaries and affiliates in Brazil. Available from the Brazilian-American Chamber of Commerce, Inc., 22 West 48th Street, New York, NY 10036-1886; Tel: 212-575-9030.

Brazil Company Handbook. Contains data and information on major listed companies in Brazil. Also, *Brazilian Privatization Program.* Provides the international financial and investment community with information and data on privatization in Brazil. Order from the International Company Handbook, Gateway Lake Headquarters, 1280 S.W. 36th Ave. Suite 210, Pompano Beach, FL 33069-9826; Tel: 305-978-0553.

Foreign Business in Brazil — A Practical Law Guide. (2nd edition), Thomas Benes Felsberg, 336 pp. Order from IBDT: Livereiros e Editores Ltda., Avenida Paulista, 1471, conj. 919, 01311 São Paulo, SP, Brazil.

Doing Business in Brazil. Pinheiro Neto & Co. Binder of monthly updates. Available for a yearly subscription from Matthew Bender Company, Customer Service Department, 1275 Broadway, Albany, NY 12201; Tel: 1-800-833-3630.

Information Guide: Doing Business in Brazil (January 1991), Price Waterhouse & Company, International. Order from Distribution Center, Price Waterhouse & Company, P.O. Box 30004, Tampa, FL 33630; Tel: 813-287-9000, or order from local branches. Free of charge.

Investment in Brazil (1992). Limited copies available from KPMG-Peat Marwick, Distribution Center, 3 Chestnut Ridge Rd., Montville, NJ, 07645, Tel: 201-307-7931.

International Business Series: Doing Business in Brazil (March 1992), Ernst & Young International. Member firms may obtain copies through Ernst & Young International, 787 Seventh Ave., New York, NY, 10019.

International Tax and Business Guide for Brazil. Available through Deloitte Touche Tohmatsu International. Order from Deloitte & Touche, Suite 350N, 1001 Pennsylvania Ave., NW, Washington, DC, 20004; Tel: 202-879-5600.

Investing, Licensing and Trade Conditions Abroad: Brazil. Available in major libraries or from Business International, Subscriptions Department, One Dag Hammerskjold Plaza, 7th floor, New York, NY 10017; Tel: 212-460-0600.

Summary of Investment Legislation in Brazil. Banco do Brasil, 118 pp. Order from Banco do Brasil, 550 Fifth Avenue, New York, NY 10036; Tel: 212-730-6700. Free of charge.

Commercial & Investment Law: Latin America. Transnational Juris Publications, Inc.; One Bridge St., Irvington, N.Y. 10533; Tel: 914-591-4288 & 1-800-914-8186.

BUSINESS GUIDES
(IN PORTUGUESE)

Anuário das Indústrias. Comprehensive list of Brazilian manufacturers by product area. Order from Editora Pesquisa e Indústrias Ltda., Rua da Consolação 2043; 01031, São Paulo, S.P., Brazil; Tel: 55-11-259-1344.

São Paulo Yearbook. Annual directory of members of São Paulo branch of the American Chamber of Commerce. Order from the American Chamber of Commerce for Brazil; C.P. 12518; 04798, São Paulo, S.P., Brazil; Tel: 55-11-246-9199.

BUSINESS NEWSLETTERS AND MAGAZINES (*ENGLISH*)

Brazilian News Briefs. Summary of important items from the Brazilian press and other sources. American Chamber of Commerce for Brazil; Avenida Rio Branco, 123, 21 andar; C.P. 916; 20000, Rio de Janeiro, R.J. Brazil.

Brazilian Business Trends. A weekly report to management on the Brazilian economy. Order from Análise Editora Ltda., Avenida Pedroso de Morais, 433; 05419 São Paulo, S.P. Brazil; Tel: 55-11-815-0879.

Brazilian-American Business Review-Directory (1991). Brazilian-American Chamber of Commerce, Inc., 22 West 48th Street, New York, NY 10036-1886; Tel: 212-575-9030.

Business Latin America. Weekly newsletter containing business articles on Brazil and other Latin American countries. Published by Business International, Subscriptions Department, 215 Park Avenue South, 18th floor, New York, NY 10003; Tel: 212-460-0600.

Gazeta Mercantil (New York Weekly Edition). English excerpt from the Brazilian daily business newspaper, *Gazeta Mercantil.* Order from Flavio Ebert, 220 East 42nd Street, room 930, New York, NY 10017; Tel: 914-665-9867.

News Bulletin. A monthly review of Brazilian business and financial news. Brazilian-American Chamber of Commerce, Inc., 22 West 48th Street, New York, NY 10036-1886; Tel: 212-575-9030. Free of charge to Chamber members.

Update. A bilingual newsletter on the investment climate and economic conditions in Brazil. Order from the American Chamber of Commerce for Brazil, C.P. 12518, CEP 04798, São Paulo, S.P., Brazil; Tel: 55-11-246-9199.

Brazil File. A monthly English newsletter of current political and economic conditions. Prepared by the Institute of Brazilian Business and Public Management Issues -- IBI, at the George Washington University. Tel: 202-994-5205.

Latin American Law and Business Report. A monthly publication of current commercial and legal issues in Latin American countries. World Trade Executive, Inc., 30 Monument Square, Suite 145, P.O. Box 761, Concord MA 01742. Tel: 508-287-0301.

Brasilinform Newsletter. A biweekly newsletter of political analysis and economic information geared towards the business community. Published by C.V. Brasil Comercio de Boletins Informativos Ltda. C.P. 37584; 22642-970 Rio de Janeiro, RJ Brazil. Tel: 55-21-322-5583.

BUSINESS NEWSLETTERS AND MAGAZINES (*PORTUGUESE*)

Banco Central do Brasil. Informativo Mensal. Available on request from Economics Department, Banco Central do Brasil, Setor de Autarquisas Sul, 70070 Brasília, D.F., Brazil; Tel: 55-61-224-7115.

Banco do Brasil-Monthly letter. Order from International Division (ASPLA), Banco do Brasil, C.P. 1150, 20000 Rio de Janeiro, R.J., Brazil.

Brazilian Business Trends. Order from Rua José de Freitas Guimarães, 65, 01237 - São Paulo - SP, Brazil; Tel: 55-11-263-1295.

Carta Semprel de Brasília. Order from Setor Comercial Sul, quadra 06, Bloco A, No. 157 Edifício Bandeirantes, Salas 301-304, 70300, Brasília, DF, Brasil; Tel: 55-61-321-1324.

Conjuntura Economica. A monthly magazine with in-depth articles on Brazil's economic, commercial, industrial and financial situation, and many statistical tables. Order from: Fundação Getulio Vargas, Praia de Botafogo 190, C.P. 9052, 22253, Rio de Janeiro, R.J., Brazil; Tel: 55-21-551-1542.

Gazeta Mercantil. A Brazilian daily business newspaper. Also, *Balanço Anual.* A yearly business guide magazine with articles and statistical tables on Brazilian companies and industries. Order both publications from: Gazeta Mercantil S.A., Rua Major Quedinho 90, C.P. 6503, 01050 São Paulo, Brasil; Tel: 55-11-256-3133.

Exame. A monthly general business magazine. *Veja.* A weekly general interest news magazine. Order both from Editora Abril, Avenida Otaviano Alves de Lima, 800 São Paulo, S.P., Brazil.

Manchete. A weekly general interest magazine. *Tendencia.* A monthly business magazine. order both from Bloch Editores, Rua do Russel, 766, 22210 Rio de Janeiro, R.J., Brazil.

Brazil

Visão. A weekly, general news magazine. *Quem e Quem na Economia Brasileira.* An annual who's who of the Brazilian economy with sector analyses and financial data on the more important firms within each sector. Subscriptions for both publications available from: Visao Magazine, National Press Building, Room 735, 529 14th Street, N.W., Washington, DC 20045, Tel: 202-347-3810.

Electricidade Moderno (Electrical industry). *Quimica e Derivados* (Chemical industry); Transporte Moderno (Transportation) DeFilippes Company. 420 Lexington Avenue, Room 1760, New York, NY 10170, Tel: 212-697-8185.

Data News (A major computer industry publication in Brazil). *Anuario de Informática CWB* (Yearbook). Order from: C.W.B. Servicos e Pulicações, Rua Alcindo Guanabara 25, 10 andar; 20031 Rio de Janeiro, R.J., Brazil; Tel: 55-21-240-8225.

Panorama do Setor de Informática (Special yearly). Secretaria Especial de Informatica, SAS Lote 6, C.P. 040390, 70070 Brasilia, DF, Brazil, Tel: 55-61-225-7475.

Letter. Setor Comercial Sul, quadra 08, Bloco B-50, Sala 443, 70333 - Brasilia - DF, Tel: 55-61-225-0811.

Brazil Faxletter (daily economic, political, business and social news). Manager Worldwide Corporate. 80 S.W. 8th. St. at Brickell Ave. - Suite 2076 World Trade Center; Miami, FL 33130 Tel: 305-577-4454.

Globo Fax (daily three-page fax send the previous evening with news from the "O Globo" newspaper. Multimedia, Inc. - 7061 Grand National Drive, Suite 127 - Orlando, FL 32819-8377; Tel: 1-800-985-8588

BRAZILIAN STATISTICAL SOURCES (IN PORTUGUESE)

Anuário Estatístico do Brasil. Available from Fundação IBGE (Instituto Brasileiro de Estatística), Avenida Franklin Roosevelt, 166, 20000 Rio de Janeiro, R.J., Brazil.

Comércio Exterior do Brasil (import-export statistics). Centro de Informações Econômico-Fiscais (CIEF), Secretaria de Receita Federal, Ministerio da Fazenda, 70000 Brasilia, D.F., Brazil.

Boletím do Banco Central do Brasil (banking and finance). Banco Central do Brasil, Departamento Econômico, C.P. 04-0170, 70000 Brasilia, D.F., Brazil.

OTHER INFORMATION SOURCES

Annual Report on Exchange Restrictions. International Monetary Fund. Approximately 500 pp. Worldwide survey of exchange regulations with section on Brazil. Available from Publications Office, International Monetary Fund, Washington, DC 20431; Tel: 202-623-7430.

Douanes, International Customs Journal: Brazil, 1986. Available from the International Customs Tariff Bureau, Rue de l'Association 38 - B, 1,000 Brussels, Belgium.

Manual de Atualização da Tarifa Aduaneira do Brasil, (Brazilian tariff book). Editora Agenco, Ltda.; Rua Senador Dantas, 75, 4 andar; 20037 Rio de Janeiro, R.J., Brazil.

Translations. List of translations of official Brazilian Government measures, with prices, available from American Chamber of Commerce for Brazil; Avenida Rio Branco, 123, 21° andar; C.P. 916; 20000 Rio de Janeiro, R.J.; Brazil.

Country Labor Profile: Brazil, Bureau of International Labor Affairs S-5015, U.S. Department of Labor, Washington, DC 20210; Tel: 202-523-7631.

Background Notes: Brazil, Office of Brazilian Affairs, Room 4262, U.S. Department of State, Washington, DC 20520; Tel: 202-647-6541.

BOOKS ON BRAZIL

Brazil: Politics in a Patrimonial Society; Roett, Riordan, Praeger Publishers, 1978

The Brazilian Economy: Its Growth and Development; Baer, Werner; Grid Publishing, 1979.

The Politics of Military Rule in Brazil 1964-85. Skidmore, Thomas E.

Sixty Years of Populism in Brazil; Castro, Paulo Rabello, in Rudiger Dornbush and Sebastian Edwards *The Macroeconomics of Populism in Latin America;* Chicago and London; The University of Chicago Press, 1991.

OTHER ORGANIZATIONS WITH CURRENT INFORMATION ON BRAZIL

U.S. CHAMBER OF COMMERCE
International Division, Room 619
1615 H Street, Washington, DC 20062
Director of Latin American Affairs
Tel: 202-463-5485.

BRAZILIAN AMERICAN CHAMBER OF COMMERCE
22 W. 48th Street,
New York, NY 10036
Tel: 212-575-9030.

COUNCIL OF THE AMERICAS
1625 K Street, N.W., Suite 1200
Washington, DC 20006
Tel: 202-659-1547

BRAZILIAN GOVERNMENT TRADE BUREAU
(Commercial Information)
551 Fifth Ave., Suite 201
New York, NY 10176;
Tel: 212-916-3200

BRAZIL-SOUTHERN CALIFORNIA TRADE ASSOCIATION
World Trade Center, #226
350 South Aqueroa
Los Angeles, CA 90071
Tel: 213-627-0634

EXPORT-IMPORT BANK OF THE UNITED STATES
Annual Report
811 Vermont Avenue, N.W.
Washington, DC 20571
Tel: 202-566-2117

NOTES
The Banco do Brasil has offices in the United States in New York, Miami, and Washington. Their addresses and telephone numbers are: New York — 550 Fifth Avenue, New York, N.Y. 10036, Tel: 212-730-6700; Miami — 1 Biscayne Tower, 38th floor, Suite 3870, 2 South Biscayne Blvd., P.O. Box 010231, Biscayne, FL 33131, Tel: 305-358-3586; Washington, D.C. — 2020 K St., N.W., Washington, D.C. 20006, Tel: 202-857-0320.

Brazil

Resources: Brunei Darussalam

U.S. AND COUNTRY CONTACTS

U.S. EMBASSY TRADE PERSONNEL

ECONOMIC OFFICER
Mr. Anthony M. Kolankiewicz
American Embassy
Third Floor, Teck Guan Plaza
Jalan Sultan
Tel: 673-2-229-670
Fax: 673-2-225-293

APL Postal Address from the U.S.:

AMERICAN EMBASSY BRUNEI
Box B
APO AP 96440

PRIVATE ORGANIZATIONS

U.S.-ASEAN COUNCIL
Ernie Bower, President
1400 L Street, NW, Suite 375
Washington, DC 20005-3509
Tel: 202-289-1911
Fax: 202-289-0159

U.S. CHAMBER OF COMMERCE
Asia-Pacific Affairs/International Division
1615 H Street NW
Washington, D.C. 20062
Tel: 202-463-5668
Fax: 202-463-3114

COUNTRY CONSULATES AND TRADE OFFICES IN THE U.S.

EMBASSY OF THE STATE OF BRUNEI DARUSSALAM
Watergate, Suite 300, 3rd Floor
2600 Virginia Avenue, NW
Washington, DC 20037
Tel: 202-342-0159
Fax: 202-342-0158

Ambassador
His Excellency Haji Jaya bin Abdul Latif

First Secretary
Miss Janeh Sukaimi

Second Secretary
Mr. Abu Bakar bin Haji Donglah

Third Secretary (Consular)
Mr. Abdullah Haji Abu Hanifah

Third Secretary (Administration and Finance)
Mr. Haji Morshidi

Attache (Communications)
Mr. Ahmad Haji Jukin

U.S. DEPARTMENT OF COMMERCE MARKET RESEARCH AVAILABLE

The market research reports listed below are available on the National Trade Data Bank.

Fishing Industry Overview (1995)
Medical Equipment Market Overview (1994)
Fisheries Development Project (1994)
Fishery Support Vessel Purchase (1994)
Health Products Trade Show (1994)

INFORMATION CHECKLIST AND BIBLIOGRAPHY

PERIODICALS

Asian Wall Street Journal
Far Eastern Economic Review
Borneo Bulletin

BOOKS

Borneo People, Malcolm MacDonald

Brunei—The Modern Southeast Asian Islamic State, David Leake, Jr.

By God's Will, Lord Alun Chalfont

The Malay Dilemma, Mahatir bin Mohamad

The Offshore Petroleum Resources of Southeast Asia, Economic Implications of Evolving Property Rights Arrangements, Corazon Morales Siddayao

Rajas and Rebels, Robert Pringle

Brunei Darussalam (ASEAN)

Resources: China

U.S. AND COUNTRY CONTACTS

COUNTRY GOVERNMENT AGENCIES

**MINISTRY OF FOREIGN TRADE
AND ECONOMIC COOPERATION**
2 Dongchangan Avenue, Dongcheng District
Beijing 100731
Tel: 8610-519-8804; Fax: 8610-519-8904
Contact: Sun Zhenyu

MINISTRY OF NATIONAL DEFENSE
25 Huang Si Avenue, Deshengmen Wai
Beijing 100011
Contact: Chi Haotian
Tel: 8610-201-8305; Fax: 8610-201-8356

MINISTRY OF COMMUNICATIONS
10 Fuxing Road, Haidian District
Beijing 100845
Tel: 8610-326-5544
Contact: Meng Guangju

MINISTRY OF POWER INDUSTRY
137 Fuyoujie, Xicheng District
Beijing 100031
Contact: Shi Dazhen
Tel: 8610-602-3816; Fax: 8610-601-6077

MINISTRY OF AGRICULTURE
11 Nongzhanguan Nanli
Beijing 100026
Contact: Liu Jiang
Tel: 8610-5004363; Fax: 8610-5002448

MINISTRY OF PUBLIC HEALTH
44 Hohaibeiyan, Xicheng District
Beijing 100725
Tel: 8610-403-4433; Fax: 8610-401-4331
Contact: Li Shichuo

**ENVIRONMENTAL
PROTECTION AGENCY**
115 Xizhimennei Nanxiaojie, Xicheng District
Beijing 100035
Tel: 8610-601-5642; Fax: 8610-601-5641
Contact: Qu Geping, Director

COUNTRY TRADE ASSOCIATIONS/ CHAMBERS OF COMMERCE

**AMERICAN CHAMBER OF
COMMERCE IN BEIJING**
Room 301, Great Wall Sheraton Hotel
Beijing 100026
Tel: 8610-500-5566, x.2271
Fax: 8610-501-8273
Philip Carmichael, President

AMERICAN SOYBEAN ASSOCIATION
China World Tower, Room 1323
Beijing 100004
Tel: 8610-505-1830/1831/3533
Fax: 8610-505-2201
Don Bushman, Representative

U.S.-CHINA BUSINESS COUNCIL
CITIC Building, Room 22C
Beijing 100004
Tel: 8610-500-2255, x2263 or 2266
Fax: 8610-512-5854
Anne Stevenson-Yang, Chief Representative

U.S. FEED GRAINS COUNCIL
China World Tower, Room 1320
Beijing 100004
Tel: 8610-505-1314/1302; Fax: 8610-505-2201
Jeff Brown, Director

U.S. WHEAT ASSOCIATES
China World Tower, Room 1318
Beijing 100004
Tel: 8610-505-1278/3866; Fax: 8610-505-2201
Matt Weimar, Director

**CHINA COUNCIL FOR
THE PROMOTION OF
INTERNATIONAL TRADE**
1 Fuxingmenwai Street
Beijing 100860
Tel: 8610-851-3344; Fax: 8610-851-1370
Zheng Hongye, Chairman

**CHINA CHAMBER OF
INTERNATIONAL COMMERCE**
1 Fuxingmenwai Street
Beijing 100860
Tel: 8610-851-3344; Fax: 8610-851-1370

**ALL-CHINA FEDERATION OF
INDUSTRY AND COMMERCE**
93 Beiheyan Dajie, Dongcheng
Beijing 100006
Tel: 8610-512-7232/513-6677, ext. 2176
Fax: 8610-513-1769
Jin Shuping, Chairman

COUNTRY MARKET RESEARCH FIRMS

**BEIJING EXPLORER DESIGN
AND COMMUNICATIONS CORP.**
44 A Baishiqiao Road, Beijing 100081
Tel: 8610-831-4488, x 2004
Fax: 8610-823-3164
Contact: Zhao Yi

**CHINA INTERNATIONAL
ECONOMIC CONSULTANTS, INC.**
13/F Capital Mansion
6 Xin Yuan Nan Road
P.O. Box 9412
Beijing 100004
Tel: 8610-466-0088, x1304, 466-3012
Fax: 8610-466-2468
Contact: Zhang Zai

**ALL CHINA MARKETING
RESEARCH COMPANY**
No. 3 Yuetan Beijie, Beijing 100037
Tel: 8610-835-4703; Fax: 8610-835-4718
Contact: David Liu

**CONNECTIONS CONSULTING
COMPANY OF CHINA**
61 A Wan Quan He Lu, Haidian District
Beijing 100080
Tel: 8610-401-5321; Fax: 8610-500-3590
Contact: Zhao Qi

CONSULTEC
B-12 Guanghua Road, Jianguomenwai,
Beijing 100020
Tel: 8610-505-1588/2255, x1201
Fax: 8610-505-1571
Contact: Hao Mei

THE GALLUP ORGANIZATION
G-202 Huiyuan Gongyu International
Asian Games Village, Beijing 100101
Tel: 8610-499-1749
Fax: 8610-499-1749
Contact: Ren Qimin

MTI - MANAGEMENT TECHNOLOGIES INTERNATIONAL, INC.
23 Youyi Road, Room 231
Tianjin 300201
Tel: 8610-835-9918, x481; Fax: 8610-835-9389
Contact: Joe T. Peebles

MESSAGE FACTORS, INC.
Xin Qiao Hotel, Suite 579
Tel: 8610-513-3366, x 1579
Fax: 8610-513-3516, 901-368-0499
Contact: Allen Smith

PINNACLE MANAGEMENT
Room 359 Shangrila Hotel
Beijing 100081
Tel: 8610-841-2211, x 355, or 842-5669
Fax: 8610-842-8271
Contact: Eric Zhang & Martin C. Liu

WKI - WILLIAM KENT INTERNATIONAL, INC.
Room 552, Tianlun Dynasty Hotel
50 Wangfujing Avenue
Beijing, China 100006
Tel: 86-1-513-3888, x 552,or 8152
Fax: 86-1-513-7866
Contact: Sarah Neroni

COUNTRY COMMERCIAL BANKS

CHINESE
PEOPLE'S BANK OF CHINA
32 Chengfang Street
Beijing, China 100800
Tel: 86-1-601-6705/6016707
Fax: 86-1-601-6704
Director of Communication Division:
Mr. Bao Mingyou,

BANK OF CHINA (HEADQUARTERS)
410 Fuchengmennei Dajie
Beijing, China 100034
Tel: 86-1-601-1829
Director of American & Oceanic Division of the Foreign Affairs Bureau: Li Aihua

BANK OF CHINA, BEIJING BRANCH
19 Dong'anmen Dajie
Beijing, China 100006
Tel: 86-1-519-9114; Fax: 86-1-512-2177
Director of Business Affairs Office: Li Hanjie

AGRICULTURE BANK OF CHINA
40 Fucheng Road, Yulong Hotel 3/F #3008
Beijing, China 100046
Tel: 86-1-841-5588 x23007-23009/2301
Fax: 86-1-841-3128
Director of Foreign Affairs Office: Chen Jianjie

INDUSTRIAL & COMMERCIAL BANK OF CHINA
26 Xichangan Street
Beijing, China 100031
Tel: 86-1-603-1062/3262299;
Fax: 86-1-603-1056
Director of Foreign Affairs Office:
Wang Qungyun

PEOPLE'S CONSTRUCTION BANK OF CHINA (HEADQUARTERS)
C 12 Fuxing Road
Beijing, China 100810
Tel: 86-1-851-4488 x 4111/327-2505
Director of Foreign Affairs Office: Tao Li

PEOPLE'S CONSTRUCTION BANK OF CHINA, BEIJING BRANCH
Yanjing Hotel 2/F # 13226
Beijing, China 100046
Tel: 86-1-835-6688 x 13226;
Fax: 86-1-835-7531
General Manager of Foreign Affairs Dept.:
Zhang Xiangqun

INVESTMENT BANK OF CHINA
B11 A Zuo Fuxing Road, Meidiya Hotel Office Bldg. # 4455
Beijing, China 100038
Tel: 86-1-851-5900; Fax: 86-1-851-6088
Deputy Director of Foreign Affairs Office:
Meng Fanjun

COMMUNICATION BANK OF CHINA
12 Tiantan Dongli
Beijing, China 100061
Tel: 86-1-701-2255 x 3206/702-8807/511-4392
Fax: 86-1-701-6524
Director of Foreign Affairs Office:
Wang Jinglan

CITIC INDUSTRIAL BANK
Capital Mansion, 6 Xinyuan Nanli
Beijing, China 100027
Tel: 86-1-466-0344; Fax: 86-1-466-1059
Manager of Foreign Affairs Office:
Liu Weili

STATE DEVELOPMENT BANK
Yulong Hotel, 40 Fucheng Road, Haidian District
Beijing, China 100046
Tel: 86-1-843-7253; Fax: 86-1-843-7254
President: Yao Zhenyou

U.S.
AMERICAN EXPRESS BANK
Beijing Representative Office
Room 2702, China World Trade Centre
Beijing 100004
Tel: 86-1-505-2838/5054626
Fax: 86-1-505-4626
Deputy Representative: Sandy So

GUANGZHOU REPRESENTATIVE OFFICE
International Hotel, 339 Huanshi Dong Lu,
Guangzhou 510060
Tel: 86-20-331-1771; Fax: 86-20-331-3535
CI, G/F., Central Lobby, Guangdong

SHANGHAI REPRESENTATIVE OFFICE
Ruijin Building, Room 205,
205 Mao Ming Nan Road,
Shanghai 200020
Tel: 86-21-472-9390/472-7589
Fax: 86-21-472-8400
Deputy Representative: Lennon Lau

BANK OF AMERICA
Beijing Representative Office
Room 2722-23, China World Trade Centre,
Beijing 100004
Tel: 86-1-505-3546/505-3508/505-3545
Fax: 86-1-505-3509
Chief Representative: Tony Cheng

Guangzhou Branch

China (CEA)

Li Mingwei (Manager)
Room 1325, Dong Fang Hotel, 120 Liuhua Lu,
Guangzhou 510016
Tel: 86-20-667-8063/666-9900-1325
Fax: 86-20-667-8063

Shanghai Branch
James Cheng-Kuang Chiou, Manager
Room 104-107A, Union Building Ground Floor,
100 Yanan Dong Lu, Shanghai 200002
Tel: 86-21-329-2828; Fax: 86-21-320-1297

BANKERS TRUST COMPANY
Beijing Representative Office
Suite 125, Ground Floor, Lufthansa Center
50 Liangmaqiao Road, Chaoyang District
Tel: 86-1-463-8-38; Fax: 86-1-463-8037
Chief Representative: Vincent J.J. Lien

CHASE MANHATTAN BANK, N.A.
Beijing Representative Office
Room 509/512,
China Science & Technology Exchange Centre,
Beijing 100004
Tel: 86-1-512-3457; Fax: 86-1-512-3693
Chief Representative: P.K. Mathur

Shanghai Representative Office
Shanghai Centre, Shanghai 200040
Tel: 86-21-279-7022

Tianjin Branch
14/F., Tianjin International Building,
75 Nanjing Road, Tianjin 300050
Tel: 86-22-339-5111; Fax: 86-22-339-8111
General Manager: Douglas Red

CHEMICAL BANK
Beijing Representative Office
Room 1205/1812,
China Science & Technology Exchange Centre,
Beijing 100004
Tel: 86-1-512-3700; Fax: 86-1-512-3771
Chief Representative: Hua Qingcheng

Shanghai Representative Office
Room 2606, Union Building,
100 Yanan Dong Lu, Shanghai 200002
Tel: 86-21-326-1888/3263888
Fax: 86-21-320-1524

CITIBANK, N.A.
Beijing Representative Office
Room 1801/1811, Citic Building,
Beijing 100004
Tel: 86-1-500-4425
Fax: 86-1-500-4425/5127930
Chief Representative: John Law

Guangzhou Representative Office
Room 1215, Dong Fang Hotel,
Guangzhou 510060
Tel: 86-20-6667150
Manager: Dong Shaowen

Shanghai Branch
Suite 509, Union Building, 100 Yanan Road
Shanghai 200002
Tel: 86-21-328-9661, 328-9662, 320-1988
Fax: 86-21-273-1317
Manager: Zhong Minmin

Shenzhen Branch
38/F., International Financial Building,
23 Jianshe Road,
Shenzhen 528000
Tel: 86-755-231138/232338
Fax: 86-755-231238
General Manager: Abraham Wong

Xiamen Representative Office
8/f., Meilihua Hotel, Xiamen 361006
Tel: 86-592-562-1666-818
Fax: 86-592-621814
Chief Representative: Liang Suiyi

FIRST NATIONAL BANK OF BOSTON
Shanghai Representative Office
6/f., 9 Business Centre, Union Building,
100 Yan An Road East,
Shanghai 200002
Tel: 86-21-329-0808 ext. 55/57
Fax: 86-21-320-0244

FIRST NATIONAL BANK OF CHICAGO
Beijing Representative Office
Room 1605, Citic Building,
Beijing 100004
Tel: 86-1-5003281/5003514; 5002255 x 1640/41/50
Fax: 86-1-5003166
Chief Representative: Robert W. Poole

REPUBLIC NATIONAL BANK OF NEW YORK
Beijing Representative Office
Room 2201, Liang Ma Tower, Chao Yang District,
Beijing 100004
Tel: 86-1-506-6549; fax: 86-1-506-6943
Chief Representative: Henning Kjledmann

SECURITY PACIFIC NATIONAL BANK
Guangzhou Office
Suite 1350-51, Garden Hotel Office Tower,
368 Huanshi Dong Road, Guangzhou
Tel: 86-20-333-8999 ext. 1337-38
Fax: 86-20-335-0706
Secretary: Ms. Chen Wen Shan

CHINA INTERNATIONAL FINANCE CO. LTD. (SECURITY PACIFIC NATIONAL BANK JV)
33/F., International Trade Center
Renmin Nan Road, Shenzhen, Guangdong, PRC
Tel: 86-755-251-510/237567
Fax: 86-755-237566
(General Manager): Shoji Moriguchi

U.S. EMBASSY TRADE PERSONNEL

U.S. EMBASSY BEIJING
No. 3 Xiu Shui Beijie
Beijing, China 100600

Mailing Address from U.S.:
U.S. Embassy Beijing
Department of State
Washington, D.C. 20521-7300

AMBASSADOR'S OFFICE
Ambassador
Tel: 532-3831 X400; Fax: 532-3178
DCM Scott S. Hallford
Tel: 532-3831 x401; Fax: 532-3178

DEFENSE ATTACHE OFFICE
Assistant Air Attache:
Captain Mark Stokes
Tel: 532-3831 x601; Fax: 532-2160

ECONOMIC SECTION
Minister-Counselor for
Economic Affairs: Chris Szymanski
Tel: 532-3831, x423l; Fax: 532-3178
Deputy William Monroe
Tel: 532-3831, x432; Fax: 532-3178

FOREIGN COMMERCIAL SERVICE
Commercial Counselor: Ying Lam
Tel: 532-3831, x480; Fax: 532-3297
Commercial Attache: Jamie P. Horsley
Tel: 532-3831, x483; Fax: 532-3297

FOREIGN AGRICULTURAL SERVICE
Agricultural Counselor: William Brant
Tel: 532-3431, x275; Fax: 532-2962
Agricultural Trade Officer: Scott Reynolds
Tel: 505-4575/6; Fax: 505-4574

POLITICAL SECTION
Minister-Counselor for Political
Affairs: Neil Silver
Tel: 532-3831, x560; Fax: 532-3178
Deputy Joseph Donovan
Tel: 532-3831, x565; Fax: 532-3178

VISA SECTION
Minister-Counselor for Consular
Affairs: Arturo Macias
Tel: 532-3431, x253; Fax: 532-2483
Non-Immigrant Visas - Rick Haynes
Tel: 532-3431, x235; Fax: 532-2483

AMERICAN CITIZEN SERVICES
Consul, Daniel Piccuta
Tel: 532-3431, x252; Fax: 532-2483

AMERICAN CONSULATE CHENGDU
No. 4 Lingshiguan Road, Section 4
Renmin Nanlu
Chengdu 610041
Consul General: Don Camp
Tel: 028-555-3119; Fax: 028-558-3520
Economic Officer: John Ellis
Tel: 028-555-3119; Fax: 028-558-3520

AMERICAN CONSULATE GUANGZHOU
No. 1 South Shamian Street
Guangzhou 510133
Consul General: Eugene G. Martin
Tel: 020-666-9900; Fax: 020-886-2341
Principal Commercial Officer: William Strotman
Tel: 020-667-7842; Fax: 020-666-6409

AMERICAN CONSULATE SHANGHAI
1469 Huaihai Zhong Lu
Shanghai 200031
Consul General: Pamela Slutz
Tel: 021 433-6880; Fax: 021 433-4122
Principal Commercial Officer: David Murphy
Tel: 021-433-2492; Fax: 021-433-1576 X1681

AMERICAN CONSULATE SHENYANG
No. 52, 14th Wei Road
Heping District
Shenyang 110003
Consul General: Gerard Pascua
Tel: 024-282-0068; Fax: 024-282-0074
Commercial Officer: Jennifer Young
Tel: 024-282-0057; Fax: 024-282-0074

WASHINGTON-BASED USG CHINA CONTACTS

U.S. DEPARTMENT OF COMMERCE
Office of the Chinese Economic Area
International Trade Administration
Room 2317, 14th & Constitution Avenue, NW
Washington, D.C. 20230
Tel: 202-482-5527; Fax: 202-482-1576

U.S. DEPARTMENT OF STATE
Office of China and Mongolia
Bureau of East Asia & Pacific Affairs
Room 4318, 2201 C Street, N.W.
Washington, D.C. 20520
Tel: 202-647-6796; Fax: 202-647-6820

U.S. DEPARTMENT OF AGRICULTURE
Foreign Agricultural Service
Foreign Agricultural Affairs: East Asia & Pacific
AG Box 1080
Washington, D.C. 20250-1080
Tel: 202-720-2690; Fax: 202-720-6063

OFFICE OF U.S. TRADE REPRESENTATIVE
China Desk
600 17th Street, NW
Washington, DC 20506
Tel: 202-395-5050; Fax: 202-395-3911

U.S.-BASED MULTIPLIERS RELEVANT TO CHINA

U.S.-CHINA BUSINESS COUNCIL
1818 N Street, N.W., Suite 500
Washington, D.C. 20036-5559
Tel: 202-429-0340; Fax: 202-775-2476
President: Robert Kapp

American Chamber of Commerce, Beijing
Room 301, Great Wall Sheraton Hotel
North Donghuan Avenue
Beijing 100026
Tel: 8610 500-5566 ext. 2271; Fax: 8610 501-8273

U.S.-China Business Council
16th floor, Yue Xiu Building
160-174 Lockhart Rd. Wan Chai
Hong Kong

U.S. DEPARTMENT OF COMMERCE MARKET RESEARCH AVAILABLE

Foreign Commercial Service:
Available Industrial Subsector Analyses (ISAs)
— Agricultural Machinery 08/01/93
— Air Traffic Control 07/14/93
— Annual Oil and Gas Report 12/10/93
— Automotive Industry 01/30/93
— Building Materials 10/04/93
— Clean Coal Technology 05/13/94
— Construction Equipment 06/01/93
— Fast Food 04/25/93

— Food Processing Equipment in Guangdong
— Province 08/31/93
— Foundry Equipment 09/20/91
— Franchise 04/25/94
— Fruit and Vegetable Equipment 02/29/92
— Hydroelectric Power 09/10/93
— Information on M 11 Sanctions 08/10/93
— Insurance 10/21/93
— Investment Climate Statement 07/10/93
— Major Projects List 05/04/94
— Medical 04/26/93
— Metal Working Machine Tool Industry 08/31/91
— Municipal Waste Water Treatment 01/08/94
— Personal Computer Market 01/10/94
— Port Development 09/30/91
— Pharmaceutical 04/14/93
— Printed Circuit Board 03/01/93
— Printing Equipment 05/30/92
— Railroad 07/15/93
— Retail 11/06/93
— Solid Waste Management 02/18/94
— Telecommunications 02/20/92
— Thermal Power Plant 08/16/93
— Wastepaper 12/31/91
— Vietnam 06/20/93

Available Special Topic Reports
— P.C. Software in China
— China's Forging Industry
— Basic Guidelines for Establishment of a Representative Office
— Mechanisms for Dispute Resolution in China
— U.S.-China Market Access Agreement--Benefits for U.S. Business
— Basic Guidelines for Selection of Sales Agents
— Foreign Economic Trends
— Chinese Law on Foreign Trade and Investment
— China, the World's Fastest Growing Market for 1993
— Guidance for China's Licensing System (93) Fourth Quarter Economic Summary for China for 1993
— Guangdong Economic Summary (93)

Fiscal Year 1994 ISAs
— Chemical Production Machinery 09/30/94
— Computer Software (update) 10/30/94
— Aircraft & Parts 07/30/94
— Industrial Chemicals 10/30/94
— Electronics Components 07/22/94
— Paper and Paperboard 08/30/94
— Electronics Ind. Pro/Eq 08/30/94

China (CEA)

— Plastics Materials/Resins 10/30/94
— Petrochemical Equipment 07/10/94
— Hotel/Restaurant Equip. 10/30/94
— Medical Equip. In Guangdong 10/30/94
— Semiconductor Mfg Equipment 08/01/94
— Software, North China 10/01/94
— Data Communications Systems 10/01/94

Fiscal Year 1995 ISAs
— Telecommunications Services 03/01/95
— Medical Equipment in Guangdong
   (update) 06/01/95
— Food Processing Industry 4/01/95
— Environmental Technology/Infrastructure
   10/01/95
— Aviation Services and Equipment 06/01/95
— Hotel and Restaurant Equipment
   (Beijing Version) 10/01/95
— Food Processing Equipment
   (Beijing Version) 10/01/95
— Food Packaging Equipment
   (update) 10/01/95
— Automotive Aftermarket 01/01/96
— Highway Construction 03/01/95
— Mining equipment 03/01/95
— Leasing 03/01/95
— Electricity Transmission Systems 03/01/95

Foreign Agricultural Service
Commodity Reports

Commodity	Annual Due Dates
Livestock Semiannual	February 1
Grain And Feed Annual	February 1
Foreign Buyer List	March 15
Sugar Annual	April 10
Tobacco Annual	May 1
Cotton Annual	June 1
Poultry Annual	June 20
Forest Products Annual	July 15
Livestock Annual	August 1
Tree Nuts Annual	August 20
Honey Annual	August 25
Tobacco Semiannual	November 1
Dairy Annual	November 30
Citrus Annual	December 1

Market Briefs

Market Information Report	July 15
Poultry meat	August, '94
Apples	September '94
Beef	October, '94
South China Guide	January, '95

Note: FCS reports are available on the National Trade Data Bank. FAS reports are available from the Reports Office/USDA/FAS, Washington, D.C. 20250.

TRADE EVENTS SCHEDULE

CHINA'S TRADE FAIRS AND EXHIBITIONS 1995-96 ARRANGED BY SECTOR

Department of Commerce Office of China, Hong Kong and Mongolia
Compiled by Karen Nowicki and Andrew Lavinsky, February, 1995 (Contact Information Follows)

AUTOMOBILES
OCTOBER 3-7, 1995
EVENT: International Automobile Manufacturing Exhibition
PLACE: Wuhan
CONTACT: Oriental-Western Promotions, HK Tel: 852-807-7633

OCTOBER 20-24, 1995
EVENT: Beijing International Auto Parts Show
PLACE: Beijing
CONTACT: CIEC

NOVEMBER 15-18, 1995
EVENT: Motor and Cycle Expo
PLACE: Tianjin
CONTACT: China Promotions Ltd., HK Tel: 852-511-7427

JUNE 18-24, 1996
EVENT: Auto China '96 -Beijing International Automotive Industry Exhibition
PLACE: Beijing
CONTACT: CIEC

OCTOBER 8-11, 1996
EVENT: Motor Parts
PLACE: Shanghai
CONTACT: China Promotions Ltd., HK Tel: 852-511-7427

AVIATION
OCTOBER 10-14, 1995
EVENT: Aviation Expo./China '95
PLACE: Beijing
CONTACT: CIEC

MAY 28-31, 1996
EVENT: Aviation & Airport
PLACE: Shanghai
CONTACT: China Promotion Ltd., HK Tel: 852-511-7427

OCTOBER 1996
EVENT: Airport
PLACE: Beijing
CONTACT: China Promotions, Ltd., HK Tel: 852-511-7427

NOVEMBER 1996
EVENT: Aerospace China
PLACE: Beijing
CONTACT: E.J. Krause & Associates, Inc.

BEAUTY
SEPTEMBER 20-24, 1995
EVENT: International Cosmetic and Beauty Exhibition
PLACE: Shanghai
CONTACT: Shanghai Centre, Mr. XIA Guoliang Tel: 86-21-279-7048

SEPTEMBER 26-29, 1995
EVENT: Shenzhen International Cosmetics, Hair & Beauty
PLACE: Shenzhen
CONTACT: China Promotion Ltd., HK Tel: 852-511-7427

OCTOBER 12-16, 1995
EVENT: China Beauty '95 - Third China International Perfume, Cosmetic and Hair Care Products & Producing Machinery Exhibition
PLACE: Shanghai
CONTACT: SIEC

COMPUTER
SEPTEMBER 25-29, 1995
EVENT: Beijing International Electronic Publishing System Exhibition
PLACE: Beijing
CONTACT: China World Trade Center

OCTOBER 5-16, 1995
EVENT: China Computer World '95
PLACE: Beijing
CONTACT: CIEC

OCTOBER 7-11, 1995
EVENT: ICA '95
PLACE: Shanghai
CONTACT: Shanghai Centre, Mr. Xia Guoliang Tel: 86-21-279-7048

NOVEMBER 12-26, 1995
EVENT: International Surface Finishing & Coating Exhbn. International PC Board Making & Electro Chemicals Exhbn.
PLACE: Beijing
CONTACT: CIEC

JUNE 1, 1996
EVENT: Computer Software
PLACE: Beijing
CONTACT: DOC Heidi Hijikata
Tel: 202-482-0569

JUNE 1, 1996
EVENT: Computer Software
PLACE: Guangzhou
CONTACT: DOC Heidi Hijikata
Tel: 202-482-0569

SEPTEMBER 11-15, 1996
EVENT: China Computer World Exhibition
PLACE: Beijing
CONTACT: CIEC

CONSTRUCTION
SEPTEMBER, 1995
EVENT: Second China International Furnishings, Interior Equipment, Construction and Engineering Products & Materials Exhibition
PLACE: Shanghai
CONTACT: Worldwide Convention & Expositions, HK Tel: 852-2750-2868

OCTOBER 7-11, 1995
EVENT: CTC Construction Technology China '95
PLACE: Shanghai
CONTACT: SIEC

OCTOBER 7-11, 1995
EVENT: Building Shanghai '95 - Shanghai International Exhibition on Building Materials and Services and Interior Decoration
PLACE: Shanghai
CONTACT: ADSALE

OCTOBER 10-14, 1995
EVENT: China Construct '95
PLACE: Shanghai
CONTACT: Oriental-Western Promotions Ltd., HK Tel: 8-52-807-7633

OCTOBER 11-14, 1995
EVENT: Chinabex '95 - China Int'l Building & Construction Expo
PLACE: Beijing
CONTACT: CIEC

OCTOBER 10-14, 1995
EVENT: International Building Materials & Construction Machinery Exhibition
PLACE: Shanghai
CONTACT: Oriental-Western Promotions, HK Tel: 852-807-7633

OCTOBER 16-19, 1995
EVENT: Construction, Building Materials & Products
PLACE: Tianjin
CONTACT: China Promotions Ltd., HK Tel: 852-511-7427

OCTOBER 16-19, 1995
EVENT: Marble, Ceramic & Glass
PLACE: Tianjin
CONTACT: China Promotion Ltd., HK Tel: 852-511-7427

MARCH 1, 1996
EVENT: Building South China
PLACE: Guangzhou
CONTACT: DOC Kristensen Tel:202-482-0384

MAY 28-31, 1996
EVENT: Public Works (Civil, Water, Road)
PLACE: Shanghai
CONTACT: China Promotions Ltd., HK Tel: 852-511-7427

JUNE 30-JULY 16, 1996
EVENT: International Exhibition on Building and Construction
PLACE: Beijing
CONTACT: CIEC

CONSUMER
SEPTEMBER 25-29, 1995
EVENT: Modern Life '95 - International Consumer Goods Exhibition
PLACE: Shanghai
CONTACT: SIEC

SEPTEMBER 26-29, 1995
EVENT: Shenzhen Consumer Electronics & Electrical Expo
PLACE: Shenzhen
CONTACT: China Promotion, Ltd. HK Tel: 852-511-7427

NOVEMBER 1996
EVENT: CIC '96 - Third China International Consumer Electronics Exhibition
PLACE: Shanghai
CONTACT: Top Repute, HK Tel: 852-851-8603

ELECTRONICS
SEPTEMBER 12-15, 1995
EVENT: Electronics China
PLACE: Shenzhen
CONTACT: China Promotion Ltd., HK Tel: 852-511-7427

SEPTEMBER 18-OCTOBER 3, 1995
EVENT: CIEE '95 - China International Electronics Exhibition
PLACE: Beijing
CONTACT: Top Repute

SEPTEMBER 20-30, 1995
EVENT: Fourth China Int'l Electronics Communication Exhibition
PLACE: Beijing
CONTACT: CIEC

SEPTEMBER 23-27, 1995
EVENT: China International Electronics Exhibition
PLACE: Beijing
CONTACT: Top Repute, HK Tel: 852-851-8603

SEPTEMBER 24-28, 1995
EVENT: International High-tech Autoelectronics Exhibition
PLACE: Beijing
CONTACT: East Lake International, Mr. Tang Baolin Tel: 212-868-0340

SEPTEMBER 26-29, 1995
EVENT: Electronics China
PLACE: Shenzhen
CONTACT: China Promotion Ltd., HK Tel: 852-511-7427

OCTOBER 24-27, 1995
EVENT: Fourth International Electonics Material and PCB Equipment and Technology
PLACE: Beijing
CONTACT: East Lake International, Tang Baolin Tel: 212-868-0340

NOVEMBER 13-17, 1995
EVENT: Fourth China International Electronics & Telecommunications Exhibition
PLACE: Beijing
CONTACT: Worldwide Conventions & Expositions, HK Tel: 852-2750-2868

FEBRUARY 1, 1996
EVENT: Microelectronics Mission
PLACE: Beijing
CONTACT: DOC Roark Tel: 202-482-3090

APRIL 23-26, 1996
EVENT: Eighth INTERNEPCON/SEMI-CONDUCTOR BEIJING '96
PLACE: Beijing
CONTACT: CIEC

China (CEA)

ENERGY
OCTOBER 1, 1995
EVENT: Petroleum China '95
PLACE: Tianjin
CONTACT: DOC Wiening Tel:202-482-4708

OCTOBER 27-NOVEMBER 6, 1995
EVENT: North China Power and
         Electricity Exhibition
PLACE: Beijing
CONTACT: CIEC

NOVEMBER 2-5, 1995
EVENT: Gas China '95
PLACE: Shanghai
CONTACT: SIEC

NOVEMBER 6-14, 1995
EVENT: Coal Preparation/Liquefaction/Gas
PLACE: Guangzhou
CONTACT: DOE Litman Tel:202-586-4344

NOVEMBER 7-11, 1995
EVENT: Shanghai International Exhibition on
         Electric-Power Utility & Supply
PLACE: Shanghai
CONTACT: Coastal International,
         HK Tel: 852-827-6766

DECEMBER 13-15, 1995
EVENT: POWER CHINA - International
         Hydrocarbon, Hydroelectric,
         Geothermal, and Nuclear Power
         Generation and Transmission
         Technology and Supplies
PLACE: Shanghai
CONTACT: HK Exhibition Services,
         HK Tel: 852-804-1500

SEPTEMBER, 1996
EVENT: **China Petro**
PLACE: Beijing
CONTACT: E.J. Krause & Associates, Inc.

SEPTEMBER 19-23, 1996
EVENT: International Exhibition on
         Petrochemical Industries
PLACE: Shanghai
CONTACT: Top Repute, Tel: 852-851-8603

NOVEMBER 12-15, 1996
EVENT: Offshore (Oil & Gas)
PLACE: Guangzhou
CONTACT: China Promotions Ltd.,
         HK Tel: 852-511-7427

NOVEMBER 12-15, 1996
EVENT: Electricity
PLACE: Guangzhou
CONTACT: China Promotions Ltd.,
         HK Tel: 852-511-7427

ENVIRONMENT
AUGUST 25-29, 1995
EVENT: International Environmental Control
         Equipment Exhibition
PLACE: Shanghai
CONTACT: Oriental-Western Promotion, Ltd.,
         HK Tel: 852- 807-7633

SEPTEMBER 11-20, 1995
EVENT: China Air Quality/Advanced Coal
PLACE: Beijing
CONTACT: DOC Litman, Tel: 202-586-4344

SEPTEMBER 11-20, 1995
EVENT: China Air Quality/Advanced Coal
PLACE: Shanghai
CONTACT: DOC Litman, Tel: 202-586-4344

SEPTEMBER 11-20, 1995
EVENT: China Air Quality/Advanced Coal
PLACE: Guangzhou
CONTACT: DOE Litman, Tel: 202-586-4344

NOVEMBER 7-11, 1995
EVENT: 4th International Forestry, Wood
         Resources & Technology Exhbn.
PLACE: Beijing
CONTACT: E.J. Krause & Associates,
         Tel: 301-986-7800

NOVEMBER 24-27, 1995
EVENT: Filtration, Water & Waste Water Treat-
         ment Systems China
PLACE: Beijing
CONTACT: HQ Link Pte. Ltd., Singapore Tel:
65-534-3588

APRIL 15-30, 1996
EVENT: Enviro-Pro Expo China '96
PLACE: Beijing
CONTACT: CIEC

DECEMBER 13-16, 1995
EVENT: ENVIRO TECH CHINA - Interna-
         tional Environmental Protection
         Technology, Pollution Control and
         Management Systems and
         Supplies Exhibition
PLACE: Shanghai
CONTACT: HK Exhibition Services,
         HK Tel: 852-804-1500

FEBRUARY 19-28, 1996
EVENT: Nuclear Safety/Waste Management
PLACE: Beijing
CONTACT: DOE Litman, Tel: 202-586-4344

JUNE 30-JULY 16, 1996
EVENT: Environment Protection Exhibition
PLACE: Beijing
CONTACT: CIEC

FASHIONWEAR AND ACCESSORIES
AUGUST 26-30, 1995
EVENT: Shanghai International Jewelry &
         Watch Show
PLACE: Shanghai
CONTACT: HK Exhibition Production,
         HK Tel: 852-833-0186

SEPTEMBER 16-20, 1995
EVENT: Shanghai International
         Fashion Exhibition
PLACE: Shanghai
CONTACT: SIEC

OCTOBER 26-29, 1995
EVENT: Jewel & Time
PLACE: Shanghai
CONTACT: Seacliff Ltd., Shanghai
         Tel: 86-21-279-8600

NOVEMBER 30 - DECEMBER 3, 1995
EVENT: International Jewellery and
         Watch Show '95
PLACE: Shanghai
CONTACT: Shanghai Centre, Mr. Xia Guoliang
         Tel: 86-21-279-7048

FOOD AND FOOD PROCESSING
AUGUST 22-25, 1995
EVENT: MEAT TECH CHINA - Interna-
         tional Meat, Fish & Poultry
         Processing Technology and
         Supplies Exhibition
PLACE: Shanghai
CONTACT: HK Exhibition Services,
         HK Tel: 852-804-1500

AUGUST 22-25, 1995
EVENT: BREW & BEV TECH CHINA -
         International Brewing & Beverage
         Production, Bottling and Packaging
         Technology and Supplies Exhibition
PLACE: Shanghai
CONTACT: HK Exhibition Services,
         HK Tel: 852-804-1500

SEPTEMBER 1-5, 1995
EVENT: Food Expo
PLACE: Shanghai
CONTACT: Seacliff, Ltd. Shanghai
         Tel: 86-21-279-8600

SEPTEMBER 4-8, 1995
EVENT: Foodtech China
PLACE: Shanghai
CONTACT: China Interexpo, Shanghai
Tel: 86-21-472-2559

SEPTEMBER 4-8, 1995
EVENT: PACK/PRINT/FOODTECH
CHINA - International Packaging/
Printing/Food Processing Equipment,
Material & Technology Trade Fair
PLACE: Shanghai
CONTACT: China Promotion Ltd.,
HK Tel: 852-511-7427

SEPTEMBER 5-8, 1995
EVENT: DRINKS CHINA - The International
Spirits, Wines and Beer Exhibition
PLACE: Shanghai
CONTACT: HK Exhibition Services,
HK Tel: 852-804-1500

SEPTEMBER 5-8, 1995
EVENT: International Bakery, Confectionary
and Ice Cream Production
Technology and Supplies Exhibition
PLACE: Shanghai
CONTACT: HK Exhibition Services,
HK Tel: 852-804-1500

SEPTEMBER 5-8, 1995
EVENT: FOOD & HOTEL: CHINA -
International Food, Drink,
Supermarket, Hotel and Catering
Supplies Exhibition
PLACE: Shanghai
CONTACT: HK Exhibition Services,
HK Tel: 852-804-1500

SEPTEMBER 16-20, 1995
EVENT: DRINKTEC SHANGHAI - Interna-
tional Beverage Technology
and Machinery
PLACE: Shanghai
CONTACT: SIEC

SEPTEMBER 20-25, 1995
EVENT: Pack-Print '95 - International Food
Processing Packaging & Printing
Equipment Exhibition
PLACE: Beijing
CONTACT: GOODWILL Exhibition &
Promotion Ltd.

NOVEMBER 2-7, 1995
EVENT: International Food Processing
Machinery Exhibition
PLACE: Beijing
CONTACT: CIEC

DECEMBER 2-6, 1995
EVENT: South China Packprint and Food
Processing Expo
PLACE: Guangzhou
CONTACT: China Promotion Ltd.,
HK Tel: 852-511-7427

DECEMBER 2-6, 1995
EVENT: China Food, Beverages and
Banquet Expo
PLACE: Guangzhou
CONTACT: China Promotion Ltd.,
HK Tel: 852-511-7427

APRIL 1996
EVENT: Agro Expo China
PLACE: Beijing
CONTACT: E.J. Krause & Associates, Inc.

HOTEL
AUGUST 27-SEPTEMBER 9, 1996
EVENT: International Exhibition on
Hotel Facilities
PLACE: Beijing
CONTACT: CIEC

INSTRUMENTATION AND OPTICS
AUGUST 25-29, 1995
EVENT: International Instrumentation and
Technology Exhibition
PLACE: Shanghai
CONTACT: Oriental-Western Promotions,
HK Tel: 852-807-7633

OCTOBER 14-18, 1995
EVENT: International Time &
Optics Exhibition
PLACE: Beijing
CONTACT: China World Trade Center

OCTOBER 15-18, 1995
EVENT: China Vision
PLACE: Shanghai
CONTACT: Seacliff Ltd., Shanghai
Tel: 86-21-279-8600

NOVEMBER 1995
EVENT: International Instrumentation,
Analytical and Environmental
Equipment
PLACE: Wuhan
CONTACT: Goodwill Exhibition & Promotions,
HK Tel: 852-893-4338

INTERIOR DESIGN AND DECORATION
OCTOBER 7-11, 1995
EVENT: Building Shanghai '95 - Shanghai
International Exhibition on Building
Materials and Services and
Interior Decoration
PLACE: Shanghai
CONTACT: ADSALE

OCTOBER 10-14, 1995
EVENT: International Showcase on Interior
Designs, Decorations and Fixtures
PLACE: Shanghai
CONTACT: Oriental-Western Promotions,
HK Tel: 852-807-7633

DECEMBER 9-13, 1995
EVENT: Bathroom, Kitchen Facilities &
Home Appliance
PLACE: Shanghai
CONTACT: Seacliff Ltd., Shanghai
Tel: 86-21-279-8610

MACHINERY
OCTOBER 20-23, 1995
EVENT: CIGME '95 - 4th China Int'l Garment
Machinery Exhibition
PLACE: Beijing
CONTACT: CIEC

MARCH 7-12, 1996
EVENT: China Machine Tool Fair '96
PLACE: Beijing
CONTACT: CIEC

JUNE 30-JULY 16, 1996
EVENT: MACHIMPEX-METALWORK '96 -
International Exhibitiion on
Metalworking Machinery
PLACE: Beijing
CONTACT: CIEC

MANUFACTURING
OCTOBER 10-13, 1995
EVENT: International Exhibition on Shoes &
Leather Industry
PLACE: Shanghai
CONTACT: Top Repute

OCTOBER 12-16, 1995
EVENT: Leather China '95 - 5th International
Exhibition on Leather Industry and
Shoe Making
PLACE: Beijing
CONTACT: ADSALE

OCTOBER 1995
EVENT: First International Exhibition on
Leather Goods and Material
PLACE: Beijing
CONTACT: ADSALE

China (CEA)

NOVEMBER 11-14, 1995
EVENT: International Leather Trade Fair
PLACE: Shenzhen
CONTACT: Coastal International,
          HK Tel: 852-827-6766

JUNE 5-8, 1996
EVENT: Shoes & Leather '96 - International
        Exhibition on Garment & Textile
        Machinery, Accessories & Products
PLACE: Guangzhou
CONTACT: Top Repute, HK Tel: 852-2851-8603

OCTOBER 8-11, 1996
EVENT: Shoes & Leather '96 - Fourth
        International Exhibition on Shoes &
        Leather Industry
PLACE: Shanghai
CONTACT: Top Repute, HK Tel: 852-851-8603

MEDICAL AND PHARMACEUTICAL
OCTOBER, 1995
EVENT: Shanghai Med '95
PLACE: Shanghai
CONTACT: SIEC

JUNE 19-24, 1996
EVENT: Medical '96 - Sixth International
        Medical, Instrument, Equipment &
        Technology Exhibition
PLACE: Shanghai
CONTACT: Top Repute, HK Tel: 852-851-8603

JUNE 19-24, 1996
EVENT: Pharmacy '96 - International
        Exhibition of Equipment and Tech-
        nology for Pharmaceutical Industry
PLACE: Shanghai
CONTACT: Top Repute, HK Tel: 852-851-8603

METALLURGY AND WELDING
OCTOBER 17-31, 1995
EVENT: 4th International Boiler & Pressure
        Vessel Manufacture &
        Welding Exhbn.
PLACE: Beijing
CONTACT: CIEC

JUNE 18-21, 1996
EVENT: Metal
PLACE: Shanghai
CONTACT: China Promotions Ltd.,
          HK Tel: 852-511-7427

DECEMBER, 1996
EVENT: Metal
PLACE: Wuhan
CONTACT: China Promotions Ltd.,
          HK Tel: 852-511-7427

OFFICE AUTOMATION
SEPTEMBER 26-29, 1995
EVENT: Office Equipment and Furniture
PLACE: Shenzhen
CONTACT: China Promotion Ltd.,
          HK Tel: 852-511-7427

PACKAGING
SEPTEMBER 19-23, 1995
EVENT: Guangzhou International Exposition
        on Packaging & Printing Technol-
        ogy Equipment
PLACE: Guangzhou
CONTACT: US-China Information Service
          Tel: 202-338-3888

OCTOBER 11-15, 1995
EVENT: Beijing International Packaging &
        Printing Equipment Exhibition
PLACE: Beijing
CONTACT: Goodwill Exhibition and Promo-
          tion, HK Tel: 852-893-4338

NOVEMBER 14-18, 1995
EVENT: The Second International Printing
        Machinery and Packaging Equip-
        ment Exhibition (PMPE '95)
PLACE: Beijing - China World Trade Center
CONTACT: Ms. Liu Lihua
          Tel: 86-1-505-2288 x8448
          or Mr. George Sun,
          Tel: 86-1-505-2288 x8442
          Fax: 86-1-505-3260

NOVEMBER 23-27, 1995
EVENT: PFP - Plastpack Shanghai '95 -
        International Exhibition on Plastics
        and Packaging Industries
PLACE: Shanghai
CONTACT: ADSALE

SEPTEMBER 18-22, 1996
EVENT: International Packaging
        Technology Exhibition
PLACE: Beijing
CONTACT: CIEC

PLASTICS AND RUBBER
OCTOBER 10-14, 1995
EVENT: SINO-PLAS '95 - China
        Interna-tional Exhibition for Rubber
        & Plastic Industry
PLACE: Nanjing
CONTACT: Worldwide Conventions &
          Expositions, HK Tel: 852-2750-2868

NOVEMBER 23-27, 1995
EVENT: PFP - Plastpack Shanghai '95 -
        International Exhibition on Plastics
        and Packaging Industries
PLACE: Shanghai
CONTACT: ADSALE

MARCH 26-31, 1996
EVENT: Tenth Int'l Exhibition on Plastics and
        Rubber Industries
PLACE: Beijing
CONTACT: CIEC

SEPTEMBER 19-23, 1996
EVENT: Rubber & Plastics '96 - International
        Exhibition on Plastics and
        Rubber Industries
PLACE: Shanghai
CONTACT: Top Repute,
          HK Tel: 852-851-8603

PRINTING
SEPTEMBER 18-OCTOBER 4, 1995
EVENT: CONVERFLEX '95 - International
        Exhibition for the Paper, Paper
        Converting and Package Printing
        Machines and Materials
PLACE: Beijing
CONTACT: CIEC

NOVEMBER
EVENT: Writing & Stationary '95
PLACE: Shanghai
CONTACT: SIEC

NOVEMBER 1-15, 1995
EVENT: 5th International Pulp, Paper &
        Converting Exhbn. and Conference
PLACE: Beijing
CONTACT: CIEC

NOVEMBER 3-6, 1995
EVENT: PaperTex Shanghai '95
PLACE: Shanghai
CONTACT: Shanghai Centre, Mr. Xia Guoliang
          Tel: 86-21-279-7048

NOVEMBER 14-18, 1995
EVENT: The Second International Printing
        Machinery and Packaging Equipment
        Exhibition (PMPE '95)
PLACE: Beijing - China World Trade Center
CONTACT: Ms. Liu Lihua
          Tel: 86-1-505-2288 x8448
          or Mr. George Sun,
          Tel: 86-1-505-2288 x 8442
          Fax: 86-1-505-3260

MAY 30 - JUNE 4, 1996
EVENT: Print Expo '96 - Second International
Printing Equipment & Materials Expo
PLACE: Beijing
CONTACT: CIEC

NOVEMBER 7-11, 1995
EVENT: China Paper/Forest
PLACE: Beijing
CONTACT: DOC B. Smith, Tel: 202-482-0106

NOVEMBER 19-23, 1996
EVENT: China Paper South
PLACE: Guangzhou
CONTACT: E.J. Krause & Associates, Inc.

SERVICES AND BANKING
NOVEMBER 20-24, 1995
EVENT: Inter-Bank
PLACE: Shanghai
CONTACT: Seacliff Ltd., Shanghai
          Tel: 86-21-279-8600

SPORTS
NOVEMBER 24-28, 1995
PEVENT: International Water Expo '95
          (IWEC '95)
LACE: Beijing World Trade Center
CONTACT: Mr. George Sun, Tel:86-1-505-0545
          or Mr. Huang Jinge,
          Tel: 86-1-505-1012
          Fax: 86-1-505-3260

TELECOMMUNICATIONS
SEPTEMBER 18-22, 1995
EVENT: Shanghai International Exhibition on
          Telecommunication
PLACE: Shanghai
CONTACT: Coastal International,
          HK Tel: 852- 827-6766

NOVEMBER 15-17, 1995
EVENT: China InfoTech '95
PLACE: Shanghai
CONTACT: Shanghai Centre, Mr. Xia Guoliang
          Tel: 86-21-279-7048

DECEMBER 5-9, 1995
EVENT: International Telecommunications
          Computer and Office Automation
          Exhibition and Conference for the
          South China Region and Hong Kong
PLACE: Guangzhou
CONTACT: E.J. Krause & Associates,
          Tel: 301-986-7800

APRIL 1, 1996
EVENT: Telecom Mission
PLACE:
CONTACT: DOC Edwards, Tel: 202-482-4331

NOVEMBER 5-9, 1996
EVENT: PT/Expo Comm China
PLACE: Beijing
CONTACT: E.J. Krause & Associates, Inc.

TEXTILES
MAY 3-18, 1996
EVENT: International Exhibition on
          Adhesive-bonded Fabric
PLACE: Beijing
CONTACT: CIEC

JUNE 5-8, 1996
EVENT: Garment & Textile '96
PLACE: Guangzhou
CONTACT: Top Repute, HK Tel: 852-851-8603

TOYS
SEPTEMBER 4-8, 1995
EVENT: Third China International Gifts &
          Toys Exhibition
PLACE: Shanghai
CONTACT: Worldwide Conventions
          & Expositions,
          HK Tel: 852-2750-2868

SEPTEMBER 26-29, 1995
EVENT: Shenzhen Electronic Toys & Games
PLACE: Shenzhen
CONTACT: China Promotion Ltd.,
          HK Tel: 852-511-7427

TRANSPORTATION
SEPTEMBER 14-18, 1995
EVENT: International Modern
          Railways Exhibition
PLACE: Beijing
CONTACT: China World Trade Center

SEPTEMBER 18-30, 1995
EVENT: 2nd International Exhibition
          on Transportation
PLACE: Beijing
CONTACT: CIEC

OCTOBER 3-7, 1995
EVENT: International Traffic, Highway &
          Subway Exhibition
PLACE: Guangzhou
CONTACT: US-China Information,
          Tel: 202-338-3888

NOVEMBER 15-18, 1995
EVENT: Port, Material Handling &
          Truck Expo
PLACE: Tianjin
CONTACT: China Promotions, Ltd.,
          HK Tel: 852-511-7427

OCTOBER 1996
EVENT: Subway & Light Rail
PLACE: Beijing
CONTACT: China Promotions Ltd.,
          HK Tel: 852-511-7427

NOVEMBER 12-15, 1996
EVENT: Port & Marine
PLACE: Guangzhou
CONTACT: China Promotions Ltd.,
          HK Tel: 852-511-7427

OTHER
SEPTEMBER, 1995
EVENT: China Cycle '95
PLACE: Shanghai
CONTACT: SIEC

SEPTEMBER 23-27, 1995
EVENT: International Famous
          Brand Trade Fair
PLACE: Beijing
CONTACT: CIEC

SEPTEMBER 27-30, 1995
EVENT: China Property '95
PLACE: Shanghai
CONTACT: Shanghai Centre, Mr. Xia Guoliang
          Tel: 86-21-279-7048

OCTOBER, 1995
EVENT: INTERSTOFF '95
PLACE: Beijing
CONTACT: CIEC

OCTOBER 1, 1995
EVENT: Insurance
PLACE: Beijing
CONTACT: DOC Muir Tel: 202-482-0349

OCTOBER 15-30, 1995
EVENT: China Export Commodities Fair for
          Enterprises with Foreign Investment
PLACE: Guangzhou
CONTACT: US-China Information,
          Tel: 202-338-3888

OCTOBER 16-19, 1995
EVENT: International Famous Branded
          Products Show
PLACE: Shanghai
CONTACT: Shanghai Centre, Mr. Xia Guoliang
          Tel: 86-21-279-7048

China (CEA)

OCTOBER 24-28, 1995
EVENT: China International Industry Fair
PLACE: Shanghai
CONTACT: China Interexpo, Shanghai
Tel: 86-21-472-2559

NOVEMBER 1-5, 1995
EVENT: International Material Handling &
Storage Equipment Exhibition
PLACE: Beijing
CONTACT: CIEC

NOVEMBER 7-19, 1995
EVENT: International Petroleum Chemical
Industry Technology &
Equipment Expo
PLACE: Beijing
CONTACT: CIEC

NOVEMBER 9-11, 1995
EVENT: International Water Supplying
Technology Exhibition
PLACE: Shanghai
CONTACT: Shanghai Centre, Mr. Xia Guoliang
Tel: 86-21-279-7048

NOVEMBER 17-30, 1995
EVENT: International Chemical Industry
Products Show
PLACE: Beijing
CONTACT: CIEC

NOVEMBER 22-25, 1995
PEVENT: International Bar Code
Technology Exhibition
LACE: Shanghai
CONTACT: Shanghai Centre, Mr. Xia Guoliang
Tel: 86-21-279-7048

DECEMBER 4-6, 1995
EVENT: Sixth Shanghai International
Nonwovens Conference
& Exhibition
PLACE: Shanghai
CONTACT: Miller Freeman Inc.,
Bettina Mesches Tel: 415-905-2707

DECEMBER 5-8, 1995
EVENT: QC China '95 - Quality Control &
Testing Equipment
PLACE: Shanghai
CONTACT: Worldwide Conventions &
Expositions,
HK Tel: 852-2750-2868

DECEMBER 5-8, 1995
EVENT: International Maritime Conference
& Exhibition
PLACE: Shanghai
CONTACT: HK Trade Fair Group
HK Tel: 852-2827-6211

DECEMBER 13-16, 1995
EVENT: Elenex China
PLACE: Shanghai
CONTACT: HK Exhibition Services,
HK Tel: 852-804-1500

MARCH 21-26, 1996
EVENT: China International Woodworking
and Furniture Machinery Show
PLACE: Beijing
CONTACT: CIEC

APRIL 9-14, 1996
EVENT: International Stone Processing
Machinery and Equipment Exhibition
PLACE: Beijing
CONTACT: CIEC

MAY 5-20, 1996
EVENT: ENGINE CHINA '96
PLACE: Beijing
CONTACT: CIEC

MAY 18-24, 1996
EVENT: Ninth Asian International
PhilaTel:ic Exhibition
PLACE: Beijing
CONTACT: CIEC

AUGUST 29-SEPTEMBER 9, 1996
EVENT: Beijing International Clock &
Watch Fair '96
PLACE: Beijing
CONTACT: CIEC

SEPTEMBER 2-9, 1996
EVENT: International Exquisite Products
Exhibition of International Women's
Shopping Festival
PLACE: Beijing
CONTACT: Copro

SEPTEMBER 1-6, 1996
EVENT: BIBF '96 - Sixth Beijing International
Book Fair
PLACE: Beijing
CONTACT: CIEC

SEPTEMBER 11-27, 1996
EVENT: ICIF '96 - International Chemical
Industry Fair
PLACE: Beijing
CONTACT: CIEC

DECEMBER 4-10, 1996
EVENT: International Children's Articles and
Manufacturing Technology Fair
PLACE: Beijing
CONTACT: China World Trade Center

SOME IMPORTANT ADDRESSES AND NUMBERS

ADSALE EXHIBITION SERVICES
Adsale People, Inc.
3080 Olcott Street
Suite 225D
Santa Clara, CA 95054
Tel: 408-986-8384; Fax: 408-986-1580
Manager: Monica Kan

CHINA WORLD TRADE CENTER
1 Jian Guo Men Wai Avenue
Beijing, China 200082
Tel: 861-505-2288; Fax: 861-505-1002

SHANGHAI INTERNATIONAL EXHIBITION CO (SIEC)
817 Dong Da Ming Road
Shanghai, China 200082
Tel: 86-21-546-3810, 545-6707, 541-4780
Fax: 86-21-545-5124 Telex: 33046

CHINA INTERNATIONAL EXHIBITION CENTRE (CIEC)
#6 Beisanhuan East Road
Chaoyang District, Beijing 10028
Tel: (861) 466-4433; Fax: (861) 467-6811
Telex: 210214 CEXHN CN
HK Office Tel: 852-827-5078 Fax: 852-827-5533

REED EXHIBITION CO.
2805 Office Tower
Convention Plaza
1 Harbor Road
Wanchai, HK
Tel: 852-824-0330; Fax: 852-824-0246

SHENZHEN INT'L EXHIBITION CENTER
Shangby Bei Lu
Shenzhen, PRC
Tel: 86755-263-838; Fax: 86755-264-250

HONG KONG EXHIBITION PRODUCTION LTD.
10th floor, Kiu Yin
Commercial Bldg.
361-363 Lockhart Road
Hong Kong
Tel: 852-833-0186; Fax: 852-833-5445

**COASTAL INT'L
EXHIBITION CO. LTD.**
3808 China Resources Bldg.
26 Harbour Road
Hong Kong
Tel: 852-827-6766; Fax: 852-827-5224
Telex: 80295 CIICR HX

**GRAND CHINA
EXHIBITION CO. LTD.**
P.O. Box 44-109
Taipei, Taiwan
Tel: 886-2-784-9623; Fax: 886-2-755-7624

**PANASIA CONVENTIONS
& EXHIBITIONS LTD.**
1101 On Hong Commercial Bldg.
145 Hennessy Road
Hong Kong
Tel: 852-861-3331; Fax: 852-861-3228

E.J. KRAUSE & ASSOCIATES INC.
7315 Wisconsin Ave.
Suite 450
North Bethesda, MD 20814
Tel: 301-986-7800; Fax: 301-986-4538
Telex: 4944 944 EJKEXPO

**HONG KONG
PRODUCTIVITY COUNCIL**
HKPC Building
78 Tat Chee Avenue
Hong Kong
Tel: 852-788-5678; Fax: 852-788-5042
Telex: 32842 HKPCHX

EXPOCONSULT PTE LTD.
46 A Horne Road
0820 Singapore
Tel: 65-299-9273
Fax: 65-299-9782

SHANGHAI CENTRE
1376 Nan Jing
Xi Lu, Suite 568
Shanghai 2000-40
Tel: 86-21-279-8600; Fax: 86-21-279-8600

TOP REPUTE CO., LTD.
Fu Fai Commercial Center
Room 2102
27 Hillier Street
Hong Kong
Tel: 852-851-8603; Fax: 852-851-8637

CCPIT CHINA
Fuxingmenwai Dajie
1000860 Beijing
Tel: 86-10-466-4999; Fax: 86-10-801-1370

**GOODWILL EXHIBITION
& PROMOTION LTD.**
Room 1801, Cameron
Commercial Centre
458-468 Hennessy Rd.
Causeway Bay, HK
Tel: 852-893-4338; Fax: 852-834-3137 or 1388

USA CHINA WORLD TRADE
Rex Evans
111 E. Amelia St.
Orlando, FL 32802
Tel: 407-841-8888; Fax: 407-423-8888

**TIANIJN WORLD ECONOMY TRADE
EXHIBITON CENTRE**
30 Youyi Lu, Hexiqu
Tianjin, PRC 300061
Tel: 8622-342-222; Fax: 8622-349-855

GUANGDONG SUB-COUNCIL
305 Dongfeng Zong Lu
Guangzhou, PRC
Tel: 8620-332-756

**TIANJIN INTERNATIONAL
EXHIBITION CENTRE**
No. 32, You Yi Road
Hexi District
300061 Tianjin
Tel: 022-835-2222; Fax: 022-835-9855
Telex: 234075 TWTC CN

**COPRO INTERNATIONAL
SERVICES**
2003 Hing Yip Commercial Centre
272-284 Des Voeux Rd. C.
Hong Kong
Tel: 852-541-9196; Fax: 852-545-7639

**HONG KONG TRADE
DEVELOPMENT COUNCIL**
36-39th Floor
Office Tower
Convention Plaza
1 Harbor Rd.
Hong Kong
Tel: 852-584-4333; Fax: 852-824-0249
Telex: 73898 CONHK HX

**BUSINESS & INDUSTRIAL
TRADE FAIRS LTD.**
181 F., First Pacific Bank Centre
51 Gloucester Rd.
Hong Kong
Tel: 852-865-2633; Fax: 852-866-1770
Telex: 64 882 ASIEX HX

**ORIENTAL-WESTERN
PROMOTIONS LTD.**
China Harbour Bldg. 6/F
370 King's Rd.
Hong Kong
Tel: 852-807-7633; Fax: 852-570-5917
Telex: 895875 HKIS HX

CHINA PROMOTION LTD.
2801 Tung Wai Commercial Bldg.
109 Gloucester Rd.
Hong Kong
Tel: 852-511-7427; Fax: 852-511-9692
Telex: 76270 CHICH HX

**WORLDWIDE CONVENTIONS
& EXPOSITIONS LTD.**
1431 Star House
3 Salisbury Road
Hong Kong
Tel: 852-375-7721; Fax: 852-375-0686
Telex: 44874 WWXPO HX

INFORMATION CHECKLIST
AND BIBLIOGRAPHY

BUSINESS GUIDES

China Business Guide. Published by the U.S. Department of Commerce, it is available from the U.S. Government Printing Office, Washington, DC 20402-9328

China Business Guide Book, 1994-95, China Intric Ltd.

Doing Business in China, Arne DeKejzier

Doing Business in China's Booming Triangle, Christopher Engholm. Published by Prentice Hall

NEWSLETTERS AND MAGAZINES

Far Eastern Economic Review. Published weekly, it can be obtained from YellowStone International Corporation, 87 Burlews Court, Hackensack, NJ 07601

China (CEA)

Business America. Published monthly by the U.S. Department of Commerce, it can be obtained from the U.S. Government Printing Office, Washington, DC 20402

STATISTICAL SOURCES

China Statistics Abstract, 1994, State Statistical Bureau

Direction of Trade Statistics Quarterly, Dec. 1994, IMF

International Financial Statistics, Jan. 1995, IMF

OTHER INFORMATION SOURCES

China Fax and Telex Directory, 1995, China Phone Book Co., Ltd.

China Phone Book and Business Directory, Jan.-June 1995, China Phone Book Co., Ltd.

Almanac of China's Foreign Economic Relations and Trade, 1994-95, China Resources Advertising, Ltd.

China Tariff Book, 1994, Chinese Customs

Foreign Trade Barriers, 1994, USTR
The Chinese at the Negotiating Table, Alfred Wilhelm, U.S. Government Printing Office, Washington, DC 20402-9328

China in the World Economy, Nicholas Lardy, Institute for International Economics, 11 Dupont Circle, Washington, DC 20036

BOOKS

People's Republic of China Year Book, 1993-94, PRC Year Book, Ltd. and Wah Gar Group (Hong Kong)

China (CEA)

Resources: Hong Kong

U.S. AND COUNTRY CONTACTS

COUNTRY GOVERNMENT AGENCIES

HONG KONG TRADE DEPARTMENT
Trade Department Tower
700 Nathan Road
Kowloon, Hong Kong
Tel: 852-2398-5333; Fax: 852-2789-2491

**HONG KONG OFFICE OF
THE TELECOMMUNICATIONS
AUTHORITY**
29th Floor, Wu Chung House
213 Queen's Road East
Wanchai, Hong Kong
Tel: 852-2961-6333; Fax: 852-2803-5110

**HONG KONG TRANSPORT
DEPARTMENT**
41st Floor, Immigration Tower
7 Gloucester Road
Hong Kong
Tel: 852-2829-5258; Fax: 852-2824-0433

**HONG KONG AGRICULTURE
& FISHERIES DEPARTMENT**
Canton Road Government Offices
393 Canton Road
Kowloon, Hong Kong
Tel: 852-2733-2211; Fax: 852-2311-3731

**HONG KONG DEPARTMENT OF
HEALTH**
17th & 18th Floors, Wu Chung House
213 Queen's Road East
Wanchai, Hong Kong
Tel: 852-2961-8989; Fax: 852-2836-0071

**HONG KONG ENVIRONMENTAL
PROTECTION DEPARTMENT**
24th-28th Floors, Southorn Centre
130 Hennessy Road
Wanchai, Hong Kong
Tel: 852-2835-1018; Fax: 852-2838-3111

**HONG KONG EDUCATION
DEPARTMENT**
9th-16th Floors, Wu Chung House
213 Queen's Road East
Wanchai, Hong Kong
Tel: 852-2891-0088; Fax: 852-2893-0858

**HONG KONG HIGHWAYS
DEPARTMENT**
5th Floor, Ho Man Tin Government Offices
88 Chung Hau Street, Ho Man Tin
Kowloon, Hong Kong
Tel: 852-2762-3333; Fax: 852-2714-5216
Airport Crash (24 hours) 852-2848-1111.

**HONG KONG CUSTOMS
& EXCISE DEPARTMENT**
6th-9th Floors, Harbour Building
38 Pier Road
Central, Hong Kong
Tel: 852-2852-1411; Fax: 852-2542-3334

**HONG KONG TRADE
DEVELOPMENT COUNCIL**
38th Floor, Office Tower, Convention Plaza
1 Harbour Road
Wanchai, Hong Kong
Tel: 852-2584-4333; Fax: 852-2824-0249

**HONG KONG EXPORT CREDIT
INSURANCE CORPORATION**
2nd Floor, Tower I, South Seas Centre
75 Mody Road, Tsim Sha Tsui East
Kowloon, Hong Kong
Tel: 852-2723-3883; Fax: 852-2722-6277

**HONG KONG TOURIST
ASSOCIATION**
35th Floor, Jardine House
1 Connaught Place
Central, Hong Kong
Tel: 852-2805-6789; Fax: 852-28104877

COUNTRY TRADE ASSOCIATIONS/ CHAMBERS OF COMMERCE

**AMERICAN CHAMBER
OF COMMERCE - HONG KONG**
1030 Swire House
Central
Hong Kong
Tel: 85- 2526-0165; Fax: 852-2810-1289
President: Frank G. Martin

COUNTRY MARKET RESEARCH FIRMS

**INTERNATIONAL DATA
CORPORATION
CHINA/HONG KONG LTD.**
Suite 3004 Universal Trade Center
3 Arbuthnot Road
Central
Hong Kong
Tel: 852-2530-3831; Fax: 852-2547-0154

LOU RAUSCHER ASSOCIATES
Block A 1313 Hoi Luen Ind Center
55 Hoi Yuen Road
Kwun Tong
Kowloon, Hong Kong
Tel: 852-2341-6256; Fax: 852-2341-6643

ASIAN STRATEGIES LTD.
4404 China Resources Bldg.
26 Harbour Road
Wanchai, Hong Kong
Tel: 852-2827-4627; Fax: 852-2827-6097

DATAQUEST HONG KONG
2E04 HKPC Building
78 Tat Chee Avenue
Kowloon, Hong Kong
Tel: 852-2788-5432; Fax: 852-2788-5433

**HONG KONG
PRODUCTIVITY COUNCIL
MARKETING GROUP**
HKPC Building
78 Tat Chee Avenue
Yau Yat Chuen, Hong Kong
Tel: 852-2788-5678; Fax: 852-2788-5042

MACNEIL PACIFIC LTD.
10th Floor, Allied Capital Resources Bldg.
32-38 Ice House Street
Central, Hong Kong
Tel: 852-2521-1676; Fax: 852-2845-2950

BOSTON CONSULTING GROUP, THE
Room 1603-6 Times Square
Shell Tower
1 Matheson Street
Causeway Bay, Hong Kong
Tel: 852-2506-2111; Fax: 852-2506-9084

NOMURA RESEARCH INSTITUTE (HK) LTD.
20th Floor, Citibank Tower
3 Garden Road
Central
Hong Kong
Tel: 852-2536-1800; Fax: 852-2536-1818

OGILVY & MATHER (ASIA) PTE. LTD.
8th Floor, Mount Parker House
Taikooshing
Quarry Bay, Hong Kong
Tel: 852-2568-0161; Fax: 852-2567-7240

RESEARCHASIA LTD.
1st Floor, China-Hong Kong Tower
8-12 Hennessy Road
Wanchai, Hong Kong
Tel: 852-2527-7881; Fax: 852-2520-0079

WIN CONCEPT CONSULTING COMPANY
Unit 2911, 29th Floor
Metroplaza, Tower II
Hing Fong Road
Kwai Chung, Hong Kong
Tel: 852-2410-8618; Fax: 852-2426-1233

SURVEY RESEARCH HK LTD. (SRH LTD.)
7th Floor, Warwick House, East Wing
979 King's Road
Quarry Bay, Hong Kong
Tel: 852-2880-3388; Fax: 852-2565-0418

SRG CHINA (SURVEY RESEARCH GROUP)
26th Floor Devon House
979 King's Road
Quarry Bay, Hong Kong
Tel: 852-2856-7333; Fax: 852-2516-6856

COUNTRY COMMERCIAL BANKS

AMERICAN EXPRESS BANK LTD.
35th Floor, One Pacific Place
88 Queensway
Hong Kong
Tel: 852-2844-0688; Fax: 852-2845-3637

BANK OF AMERICA NT & SA
1st Floor, Bank of America Tower
12 Harcourt Road
Hong Kong
Tel: 852-2847-5333; Fax: 852-2847-5410

BANK OF CALIFORNIA
1006-8, 10th Floor, Asia Pacific Finance Tower
Citibank Plaza
3 Garden Road
Hong Kong
Tel: 852-2826-0600; Fax: 852-2877-2666

BANK OF NEW YORK
7th Floor, New Henry House
10 Ice House Street
Hong Kong
Tel: 852-2840-9888; Fax: 852-2810-5279

BANKERS TRUST COMPANY
36th Floor, Two Pacific Place
88 Queensway
Hong Kong
Tel: 852-2533-8000; Fax: 852-2845-1868

CHASE MANHATTAN BANK NA
12th Floor, World Trade Center
280 Gloucester Road
Hong Kong
Tel: 852-2837-5111; Fax: 852-2837-5099

CITIBANK NA
40-50th Floor, Citibank Tower Citibank Plaza
3 Garden Road, Central
Hong Kong
Tel: 852-2868-8888; Fax: 852-2868-8111

FIRST NATIONAL BANK OF BOSTON
Suites 801-809, Jardine House
Connaught Place
Central
Hong Kong
Tel: 852-2526-4361; Fax: 852-2845-9222

FIRST NATIONAL BANK OF CHICAGO
13th Floor, Jardine House
1 Connaught Place
Hong Kong
Tel: 852-2844-9222; Fax: 852-2844-9318

HAWAII FINANCIAL CORP (HONG KONG) LTD.
Suite 501 Shell House
24-28 Queen's Road
Central
Hong Kong
Tel: 852-2521-0107; Fax: 852-2810-4806

NBD BANK, NA
Room 804 Lippo Tower, Lippo Centre
89 Queensway
Hong Kong
Tel: 852-2523-1189; Fax: 852-2810-6582

NORWEST BANK MINNESOTA, NA
4102-3 Central Plaza
18 Harbour Road
Wanchai
Hong Kong
Tel: 852-2519-2500; Fax: 852-2827-8290

Hong Kong (CEA)

U.S. EMBASSY TRADE PERSONNEL

U.S. CONSULATE GENERAL

26 Garden Road
Hong Kong
Tel: 852-2521-1467; Fax: 852-2845-9800
Foreign Commercial Service
Sr. Commercial Officer: David Katz
Commercial Officer: Ira Kasoff
Commercial Officer: Rosemary Gallant
Foreign Agricultural Service - Hong Kong
Tel: 852-2841-2350
Fax: 852-2845-0943
Agricultural Trade Officer: LaVerne E. Brabant
Asst. Agricultural Trade Officer: Emiko M. Purdy

WASHINGTON-BASED USG COUNTRY CONTACTS

DEPARTMENT OF COMMERCE - INTERNATIONAL TRADE ADMINISTRATION

Department of Commerce
Room 2317
Office of the Chinese Economic Area
Herbert C. Hoover Building
14th & Constitution Ave., NW
Washington, DC. 29230, USA
Tel: 202-482-4681; Fax: 202-482-1576
Country Desk Officer: Sheila Baker

U.S. Department of Commerce
East Asia and Pacific
Office of Int'l Operations
Room 1229
Tel: 202-482-2422: Fax: 202-482-5179
US&FCS Director: Herbert Cochran

COUNTRY CONSULATE AND TRADE OFFICES IN THE U.S.

HONG KONG ECONOMIC & TRADE OFFICE

In New York
680 Fifth Avenue, 22nd Floor
New York, NY 10019
Tel: 212-265-8888; Fax: 212-974-3209

In Washington, D.C.
1150 18th Street, N.W., Suite 475
Washington, D.C. 20036
Tel: 202-331-8947; Fax: 202-331-8968

In San Francisco
British Consulate General
222 Kearny Street, 4th Floor, Suite 402
San Francisco, CA 94108
Tel: 415-956-4560; Fax: 415-421-0646

HONG KONG TRADE DEVELOPMENT COUNCIL -

In New York
219 E. 46th Street
New York, NY 10017
Tel: 212-838-8688; Fax: 212-838-8941

In Illinois
333 N. Michigan Ave., #2028
Chicago, IL 60601
Tel: 312-726.4515; Fax: 312-726.2441

In Texas
Suite 120, World Trade Center
2050 Stemmons Freeway
Dallas, TX 75207
Tel: 214-748-8162; Fax: 214-742-6701

In California
Los Angeles World Trade Center
350 S. Figueroa Street, Suite 282
Los Angeles, CA 90071-1386
Tel: 213-622-3194; Fax: 213-613-1490
or c/o Hong Kong Economic & Trade Office
222 Kearny Street, Suite 402
San Francisco, CA 94108
Tel: 415-677-9038; Fax: 415-421-0646

In Florida
Courvoisier Center, Suite 402
501 Brickell Key Drive
Miami, FL 33131
Tel: 305-577-0414; Fax: 305-372-9142

U.S. DEPARTMENT OF COMMERCE MARKET RESEARCH AVAILABLE

INDUSTRY SUBSECTOR ANALYSES (ISAS)

In an effort to expand the available reporting from post, FCS Hong Kong proposes to complete 15 ISA reports on very specific subjects. These reports have been chosen on the basis of the demand expressed by local businesses and by the relative contribution we feel this reporting will make to U.S. industries. In FY 94, Post prepared the following Industry Subsector Analysis reports which are available via the National

Trade Databank:
— (COS) Skin Care Products
— (SPT) Playground and Recreational Equipment
— (POL) Sludge Treatment Equipment
— (POL) Diesel Particulate Trapping Apparatus
— (APP) Children's Wear
— (APG) Baggage Handling Equipment
— (BLD) Structural Steel
— (ELP) Power Generating Turbines
— (ELP) Steam Generation Equipment for Electric Power Plants
— (APS) Automobile Service Equipment
— (CSF) Business and Financial Software
— (PMR) Polymer Resins
— (MED) Medical Diagnostic Equipment
— (INS) Marine Casualty Insurance
— (DRG) Over-the-Counter Drugs

The following reports will be completed by FCS Hong Kong in FY'95:
— (ELC) Electronic Parts and Components March 30, 1995
— (AUT) Electric Vehicles, March 30, 1995
— (AIR) Aircraft Parts, July 30, 1995
— (PMR) Plastic Resins, July 30, 1995
— (POL) Air Pollution Control Equipment and Services, May 30, 1995
— (CPT) PCs and Lap Top Computers April 30, 1995
— (LAB) Measuring, Checking, Analysing/ Controlling Instruments, July 30, 1995
— (ELP) Standby Power Generator July 30, 1995
— (COS) Make Up Preparation April 30, 1995
— (STR) Special Topic Report - Opportunities in Macau, March 30, 1995
— (TRA) Travel and Tourism, March 30, 1995
— (BLD) Curtain Wall Glass, Jan. 30, 1995
— (BLD) Lifts and Escalators, April 30, 1995
— (PKG) Food Packaging Equipment June 30, 1995
— (MCS) Management Consultancy —ISO 9000, March 30, 1995
Reports Prepared by FAS

MARKET OVERVIEWS

The Agricultural Trade Office (ATO) Hong Kong prepares a broad range of market overviews which are available to the public by contacting the Foreign Agricultural Service, PSC 464, Box 30, FPO AP 96522-0002 or fax 852 845-0943. Market overviews are updated as often as possible, and new overviews are added according to market trends. The current list of overviews includes the following subjects:

— Airline Caterers & Ship Suppliers
— Microwave Foods
— Beer Market
— Poultry Market
— Bottled Water
— Pre-packed Food
— Chinese Fruit Products & Trade
— Retailing
— Commodities U.S. Agricultural
— Rice Market
— Convenient Stores
— Sauces, Condiments and Spices
— Dairy Products
— Seafood Industry
— Economic Trends Report
— Snack Foods (Savory & Sweet)
— Eggs
— The Joint Declaration on HK &
— Entering the HK Market
— Basic Law
— FAS/US$A Offices in HK
— Timber & Wood
— Fast Food Market
— U.S. Market Development
— Flowers Cut
— Organizations
— Fresh Food Retailing
— USAPEEC: Member list
— Fruit Fresh
— USAPEEC: Part list of Importers
— Fruit Dried and Nuts
— USSP Members
— Fruit Juice
— Vegetable Oil Market
— Fur Market
— Vegetables
— Ginseng Market
— Wine Market
— Health Food
— Wine & Spirit
— High Value Agricultural Products
— Hong Kong Overview
— Importation of Food to HK
— Importing Meat and Poultry to the U.S
— Indulgent Desserts
— Labeling Laws
— Market for U.S Food & Farm Products
— Meat Packaged, Canned & Frozen
— Meat Market

Commodity Reports

Semi-annual and annual commodity reports are written and sent to the USIA via the Global Economic Development Entry System. Required reports cover livestock, poultry, cotton and tobacco.

Voluntary Reports

Voluntary reports include the Agricultural Trade Office Monthly Report, which highlights the events of the month, including notable contact functions, new market trends, and general market and post issues. Voluntary reports are also written as event-specific reports as a means of informing or alerting FAS Washington of developments in Hong Kong/Macau and the South China region.

TRADE EVENTS SCHEDULE

The FY 1995 trade event plan includes events approved by the U.S. Department of Commerce and scheduled on the export promotion calendar. States-initiated trade missions, including IOGA's and SOGA's, and post initiated events are not always reflected in this schedule, since these often come with very short notice.

FCS Hong Kong is directing special efforts to increasing U.S. Department of Commerce certified trade shows and to promote the Foreign Buyers Program for 1995 to provide additional market entry opportunities for infrequent small to medium-size exporters. FCS Hong Kong will hold additional post initiated promotions as opportunities occur.

FY 95 Events include:

SEPTEMBER 95
Building Materials/Construction Machine Matchmaker
Theme: Building Materials
Type of Event: Matchmaker
ID No.: 95000171
Location: FCS Hong Kong

Trade Events organized by the Foreign Agricultural Service

OCTOBER 95
FMI AsiaMart
Theme: Food Market Institute Food Show
ID No.: N/A
Location: Hong Kong

The following major trade shows are also scheduled for Hong Kong although FCS is not directly involved with them.

SEPTEMBER 17 - 21, 1995
JLR - 16th Hong Kong Jewelry and Watch Fair
Hong Kong Convention and Exhibition Center
Organized by: HTFL
Textile Homefurnishing Trade Mission

NOVEMBER 2 - 3 OR 16 - 17, 1995
Trade Mission
Theme: Textile Homefurnishing Goods
Location: Hong Kong

OCTOBER 29 - NOVEMBER 1, 1995
Sporting Goods Matchmaker
Theme: Sporting Goods
Event: Matchmaker
Location: Hong Kong

DECEMBER 1995
Construction Equipment Trade Mission
Theme: Construction Materials
Event: Trade Mission
Location: Hong Kong

DECEMBER 9-13, 1995
Environmental Equipment and Services Trade Mission
Theme: Pollution Control Equipment
Event: Trade Mission
Location: Hong Kong

FEBRUARY 1996
Education and Career Expo
Theme: Education and Manpower Training
Event: Certified Trade Show (USA Pavilion)
Location: Hong Kong

MARCH OR SUMMER 1996
U.S. Pleasure Boat Trade Mission
Theme: Sporting Goods and Pleasure Boats
Event: Trade Mission
Location: Hong Kong

JULY 3 - 6, 1996
Asia Beauty '96
Theme: Beauty and Cosmetics Goods
Event: Certified Trade Show (USA Pavilion)
Location: Hong Kong

SEPTEMBER 1996
Jewelry Trade Mission
Theme: Jewelry
Event: Trade Mission
Location: Hong Kong

The Following major trade shows are also scheduled for Hong Kong although the Commercial Service Hong Kong is not directly involved with them.

OCTOBER 3 - 6, 1995
FOT - The 11th Hong Kong International Footwear Fair
Hong Kong Convention and Exhibition Center
Organized by: HTFL

Hong Kong (CEA)

OCTOBER 3 - 6, 1995
LFP - The 10th Hong Kong International Handbags
and Leather Goods Fair
Hong Kong Convention and Exhibition Center
Organized by: HTFL

OCTOBER 11 - 14, 1995
ELC - The 15th Hong Kong Electronics Fair
Hong Kong Convention and Exhibition Center
Organized by: HKTDC

OCTOBER 18 - 20, 1995
FOD - Food Marketing Institute (AsiaMart '95)
Hong Kong Convention and Exhibition Center
Organized by: FMI

OCTOBER 18 -20, 1995
TXF - Interstoff Asia '95 (International Fabric
Show)
Hong Kong Convention and Exhibition Center
Organized by: MFHKL

NOVEMBER 1 - 5, 1995
AUV - The 7th International Audio and Visual Show
Hong Kong Convention and Exhibition Center
Organized by: HKTDC

NOVEMBER 2 - 5, 1995
FUR, BLD - The 12th Hong Kong International
Furniture Fair (For Home, Offices and Special
Projects)
Hong Kong Convention and Exhibition Center
Organized by: HTFL

NOVEMBER 7 - 11, 1995
SPT - Hong Kong Golf Conference and Exhibition
Hong Kong Convention and Exhibition Center
Organized by: GMG

DECEMBER 5 - 7, 1995
PGA - Screen Printing Asia '95 (The 9th Interna-
tional Exhibition of Screen Making and Screen Print-
ing Equipment and Services for Asia)
International Trademart, Hong Kong
Organized by: EPL

DECEMBER 15 - 19, 1995
GFT - The 8th Christmas Showcase
Hong Kong Convention and Exhibition Center
Organized by: HKTDC

DECEMBER 15 - 19, 1995
BLD, FUR, HCG - The 6th Ideal Home Expo
Hong Kong Convention and Exhibition Center
Organized by: HKTDC

JANUARY 10 - 13, 1996
TOY - The 22nd Hong Kong Toys and Games Fair
Hong Kong Convention and Exhibition Center
Organized by: HKTDC

JANUARY 19 - 20, 1996
APP - The 27th Hong Kong Fashion Week -
Fall/Winter
Hong Kong Convention and Exhibition Center
Organized by: HKTDC

FEBRUARY 8 - 11, 1996
EDS - The 6th Education and Careers Expo
Hong Kong Convention and Exhibition Center
Organized by: HKTDC

FEBRUARY 28 - MARCH 2, 1996
APP, LFP - 1996 Hong Kong International Fur and
Fashion Fair
Hong Kong Convention and Exhibition Center
Organized by: FFMDHKL

MARCH 11 - 14, 1996
JLR - The 14th Hong Kong International
Jewellery Show
Hong Kong Convention and Exhibition Center
Organized by: HKTDC

MARCH 28 - 31, 1996
MTL - Hong Kong International Machine Tool --
Linkage Industry Exhibition '96
Hong Kong Convention and Exhibition Center
Organized by: PCES

MARCH 28 - 31, 1996
LAB, PKG, PME - Exhibition of Modern Labora-
tory Equipment, Supplies and Services 96, Plastics
and Packaging '96
Hong Kong Convention and Exhibition Center
Organized by: PCES

APRIL 17 - 20, 1996
GFT, HCG - The 11th Hong Kong Gifts and
Houseware Fair
Hong Kong Convention and Exhibition Center
Organized by: HKTDC

APRIL 17 - 20, 1996
GFT - The 6th Hong Kong Premium Show
Hong Kong Convention and Exhibition Center
Organized by: HKTDC

APRIL 22 -25, 1996
APP, LFP - Asia Pacific Leather Fair Part I
Hong Kong Convention and Exhibition Center/
China Resources Exhibition Center
Organized by: HKTFG

APRIL 29 - 1 MAY, 1996
APP, LFP - Asia Pacific Leather Fair Part II
Hong Kong Convention and Exhibition Center
Organized by: HKTFG

APRIL 1996
FUR, HCG - The 7th Electric Home
Appliances Expo
Hong Kong Convention and Exhibition Center
Organized by: HKTDC

MAY 30 - JUNE 2, 1996
TRA - International Travel Expo Hong Kong 1996
TRA - The Annual International Tourism Ex-
position of Asia 1996
Hong Kong Convention and Exhibition Center
Organized by: ITEHKL

MAY 1996
CPT, CSF - COMPUTER '96 (The 12th Interna-
tional Computer Expo)
Hong Kong Convention and Exhibition Center
Organized by: BITFL

MAY 1996
PME, PMR - PLASTIC ASIA '96 (The 13th International Plastics Machinery, Materials, Production Technology and Ancillary Equipment Exhibition
for Asia)
Hong Kong Convention and Exhibition Center
Organized by: BITFL

MAY 1996
PGA, PKG - The 10th International Packaging and
Printing Machinery and Materials Exhibition for Asia
Hong Kong Convention and Exhibition Center
Organized by: BITFL

JUNE 1996
JLR - The 10th Hong Kong International Fashion
Jewelry and Accessories Fair
Hong Kong Convention and Exhibition Center
Organized by: HTFL

JUNE 1996
GCG, GFT, PAP - The 7th Hong Kong Interna-
tional Stationery and Premium Fair
Hong Kong Convention and Exhibition Center
Organized by: HTFL

JUNE 1996
APP - The 10th Hong Kong International Apparel
Fair
Hong Kong Convention and Exhibition Center
Organized by: HTFL

JULY 3 - 6, 1996
COS - The Asia Pacific Beauty Fair '96
Hong Kong Convention and Exhibition Center
Organized by: HKTFG

JULY 25 - 29, 1996
BOK - Hong Kong Book Fair
Hong Kong Convention and Exhibition Center
Organized by: HKTDC

JULY 1996
APP - *The 28th Hong Kong Fashion Week - Spring/Summer*
Hong Kong Convention and Exhibition Center
Organized by: HKTDC

JULY 1996
MHM, MTL - *MEX '96 (The 17th International Machinery and Material Exhibition for Asia -- Machine Tools and Tools Manufacturing Technology)*
Hong Kong Convention and Exhibition Center
Organized by: BITFL

JULY 1996
EIP - *EIE '96 (The 13th International Electronics Industry, Testing Equipment and Instrument Exhibition for Asia)*
Hong Kong Convention and Exhibition Center
Organized by: BITFL

JULY 1996
ELC - *ECA '96 (The 8th International Electronic Component Exhibition for Asia)*
Hong Kong Convention and Exhibition Center
Organized by: BITFL

JULY 1996
MTL - *SMT '96 (The 10th International Surface Mount Technology Exhibition for Asia)*
Hong Kong Convention and Exhibition Center
Organized by: BITFL

AUGUST 21 - 25, 1996
FOD - *The 7th Food Expo*
Hong Kong Convention and Exhibition Center
Organized by: HKTDC

SEPTEMBER 5 - 8, 1996
GCG - *The 15th Hong Kong Watch and Clock Fair*
Hong Kong Convention and Exhibition Center
Organized by: HKTDC

SEPTEMBER 1996
GCG, JLR - *The 18th Hong Kong Jewelry and Watch Fair*
Hong Kong Convention and Exhibition Center
Organized by: HTFL

SEPTEMBER 1996
TXM - *GARMENTEX '96 (The 10th International Garment Machinery, Materials and Accessories Exhibition for Asia)*
Hong Kong Convention and Exhibition Center
Organized by: BITFL

SEPTEMBER 1996
TXM - *TEXTILE MACHINERY EXPO '96 (The 6th International Textile Machinery, Materials and Accessories Exhibition for Asia)*
Hong Kong Convention and Exhibition Center
Organized by: BITFL

Contact Addresses of Organizers:

HEADWAY TRADE FAIRS LTD. (HTFL)
907 Great Eagle Center
23 Harbor Road
Wanchai, Hong Kong
Tel: 852-2827-5121
Fax: 852-2827-7064

HONG KONG TRADE DEVELOPMENT COUNCIL (HKTDC)
36-39 Floors, Office Tower
Convention Plaza, 1 Harbor Road
Wanchai, Hong Kong
Tel: 852-2584-4333
Fax: 852-2824-0249

FOOD MARKETING INSTITUTE (FMI)
800 Connecticut Ave., N.W.
Washington DC, 20006-2701
Tel: 202-452-8444
Fax: 202-429-4519

GOLF MEDIA GROUP (GMG)
Level 1, 36 Kings Park Road
West Perth, Western Australia 6005
Australia
Tel: 619-322-3222
Fax: 619-321-6461

EXPOCONSULT PTE LTD. (EPL)
100 Beach Road
#26-00 Shaw Tower
Singapore 0718
Tel: 65-299 9273
Fax: 65-299-9782

FEDERATION OF FUR MANUFAC-TURERS AND DEALERS (HK) LTD. (FFMDHKL)
Room 603, Chevalier House
45-51 Chatham Road South
Tsimshatsui, Kowloon
Hong Kong
Tel: 852-2367-4646
Fax: 852-2739-0799

PAPER COMMUNICATION EXHIBITION SERVICES
Room 16, 12 Floor, Wah Shing Center
11 Shing Yip Street
Kwun Tong, Kowloon
Hong Kong
Tel: 852-2763-9012
Fax: 852-2341-0379

HONG KONG TRADE FAIR GROUP
44 Floor, China Resources Building
26 Harbor Road
Wanchai, Hong Kong
Tel: 852-2827-6211
Fax: 852-2827-7831

INTERNATIONAL TRAVEL EXPO HK LTD.
Room 1702B, Fortress Tower
250 King's Road
North Point, Hong Kong
Tel: 852-2508-6655
Fax: 852-2510-7016

BUSINESS AND INDUSTRIAL TRADE FAIRS LTD.
18th Floor, First Pacific Bank Center
51 Gloucester Road
Wanchai, Hong Kong
Tel: 852-2865-2633
Fax: 852-2866-1770

KENFAIR INTERNATIONAL LTD. (KIL)
Room 1002, Perfect Commercial Building
20 Austin Avenue
Tsimshatsui, Kowloon
Hong Kong
Tel: 852-2311-8216; Fax: 852-2311-6629

MESSE FRANKFURT (HONG KONG) LTD. (MFL)
1808 Harbour Centre
25 Harbour Road
Wanchai, Hong Kong
Tel: 852-2802-7728; Fax: 852-2511-3466

CHINESE MANUFACTURERS' ASSO-CIATION OF HONG KONG (CMA)
5th Floor, CMA Building
64-66 Connaught Road
Central, Hong Kong
Tel: 852-2524-8600; Fax: 852-2541-4541

ADVANSTAR COMMUNICATIONS ASIA LTD. (ACAL)
23rd Floor, Tai Yau Building
181 Johnston Road
Wanchai, Hong Kong
Tel: 852-2832-4998; Fax: 852-2575-4611

Hong Kong (CEA)

**HONG KONG EXHIBITION
SERVICES LTD. (HKESL)**
Unit 902, 9th Floor, Shiu Lam Building
23 Luard Road
Wanchai, Hong Kong
Tel: 852-2804-1500; Fax: 852-2528-3103

**BUSINESS & INDUSTRIAL
TRADE FAIRS LTD. (B&ITFL)**
18th Floor, First Pacific Bank Centre
51 Gloucester Road
Wanchai, Hong Kong
Tel: 852-2865-2633; Fax: 852-2866-1770

**INTERNATIONAL TRAVEL
EXPO HK LTD. (ITEHKL)**
802 Federal Building
369 Lockhart Road
Wanchai, Hong Kong
Tel: 852-2838-0329; Fax: 852-2838-2013

REED EXHIBITIONS LTD. (REL)
2805 Convention Plaza
1 Harbour Road
Wanchai, Hong Kong
Tel: 852-2824-0330; Fax: 852-2824-0246

INFORMATION CHECKLIST AND BIBLIOGRAPHY

BUSINESS GUIDES

"Hong Kong Country Commercial Guide" - compiled by US&FCS — available on NTDB

"American Food & Beverages in Hong Kong" - Published by the American Chamber of Commerce in Hong Kong (AmCham)

"Doing Business in Today's Hong Kong" - AmCham
"Establishing an Office in Hong Kong" - AmCham

"Hong Kong Electronics Handbook/Directory" - AmCham

"Hong Kong Employment Guide" - AmCham

"Hong Kong's Training Services" - AmCham

"PRC Business Firms in Hong Kong & Macau" - AmCham

"Who's Who in Hong Kong Communications" - AmCham

NEWSLETTERS AND MAGAZINES

"AmCham" - Published by the American Chamber of Commerce in Hong Kong

"Hong Kong Digest" - Published by the Hong Kong Economic & Trade Office (USA)

"Hong Kong Trader" - Published by the Hong Kong Trade Development Council

"Canada and Hong Kong Update" - Published by the Canada and Hong Kong Project Joint Centre for Asia Pacific Studies

STATISTICAL SOURCES

U.S. Department of Commerce, Bureau of the Census
"Hong Kong Annual Digest of Statistics"
"Hong Kong External Trade"
"Hong Kong" (annual)

OTHER INFORMATION SOURCES

"Living in Hong Kong" - AmCham

BOOKS

Hong Kong: A Unique Case of Development, Leung Chuen Chau, World Bank, 1993

Hong Kong Business: The Portable Encyclopedia for Doing Business with Hong Kong, Christine Genzberger et al, World Trade Press, 1994

Hong Kong, China & 1997: Essays in Legal Theory, Ed. by R.I. Wacks, Hong Kong University Press, 1994

Hong Kong Images: On Chinese Customs, Folklore and Traditional Life, Hugh Baker, Hong Kong University Press, 1990

Hong Kong (CEA)

Resources: India

U.S. AND COUNTRY CONTACTS

COUNTRY GOVERNMENT AGENCIES

To receive official duty rates for India or other Indian customs information:
CENTRAL BOARD OF EXCISE AND CUSTOMS
Tel: 91-11-301-2849

DEPARTMENT OF REVENUE
Ministry of Finance
Government of India
156 E, North Block
New Delhi 100 001 India
Fax: 91-11-301-6475

For an overview of the Indian Standards System:
BUREAU OF INDIAN STANDARDS (BIS)
Manah Bhavan
9 Bahadur Shah Zafar Marg
New Delhi 110 002 India
Tel: 91-11-331-0131
Fax: 91-11-331-4062

For information on selling pharmaeuticals to India:
DRUGS CONTROLLER
Director General of Health Services
Nirman Bhavan
New Delhi 110 011, India
Tel: 91-11-30-8438
Fax: 91-11-30-4252

For information on investment approvals:
RESERVE BANK OF INDIA (RBI)
Shaheed Bhagat Singh Road
P.O. Box 1055
Bombay 400 023 India
Tel: 91-22-286-1602
Fax: 91-22-286-5330

DEPARTMENT OF INDUSTRIAL DEVELOPMENT
Secretariat for Industrial Approvals (SIA)
Udyog Bhavan
New Delhi 110 011 India
Tel: 91-11-301-1983
Fax: 91-11-301-1770

COUNTRY TRADE ASSOCIATIONS/ CHAMBERS OF COMMERCE

FEDERATION OF INDIAN CHAMBERS OF COMMERCE & INDUSTRY (FICCI)
Foreign Investment & Trade Promotion Office (FITPO)
Federation House, Tansen Marg.
New Delhi 110 001 India
Tel: 91-11-331-9251
Fax: 91-11-332-0714

CONFEDERATION OF INDIAN INDUSTRY (CII)
23,26 Institutional Area
Lodi Road
New Delhi 110 003 India
Tel: 91-11-462-9994
Fax: 91-11-463-3168

THE ASSOCIATED CHAMBERS OF COMMERCE AND INDUSTRY OF INDIA (ASSOCHAM)
Allahabad Bank Building (2nd Floor)
17 Parliament Street
New Delhi 110 001 India
Tel: 91-11-310704
Fax: 91-11-312193

INDIAN MERCHANTS CHAMBER
Secretary General
Churchgate
Bombay 400 020 India
Tel: 91-22-204-6633
Fax: 91-22-204-8508

For information on how to invest in India:
THE CHAIRMAN
Indian Investment Centre
Jeevan Vihar Bldg.
Sansad Marg
New Delhi 110 001 India
Tel: 91-11-373-3673
Fax: 91-11-373-2245

U.S. EMBASSY TRADE PERSONNEL

U.S. & FOREIGN COMMERCIAL SERVICE
American Embassy - New Delhi
Shanti Path
Chanakyapuri (New Delhi) 110021
Tel: 91-11-600651
Fax: 91-11-6872391

U.S.-BASED MULTIPLIERS RELEVANT TO COUNTRY

INDIA-AMERICA CHAMBER OF COMMERCE
125 West 55th Street, 16th Floor
New York, NY 10019-5389
Tel: 212-424-8256
Fax: 212-424-8500

COUNTRY CONSULATES AND TRADE OFFICES IN THE U.S.

EMBASSY OF INDIA
2536 Massachusetts Ave., NW
Washington, D.C. 20008
Tel: 202-939-9826
Fax: 202-797-4693
For information on government procurement in India:
Commerce Wing
Tel: 202-939-9826

INDIAN CONSULATE
New York
3 East 64th Street
New York, NY 10021
Tel: 212-879-7888
Fax: 212-861-3788; 988-6423

Chicago
150 North Michigan Avenue
Suite 1100
Chicago, IL 60601
Tel: 312-781-6280
Fax: 312-781-6269

San Francisco
540 Arguello Blvd.
San Francisco, CA 94118
Tel: 415-668-0998
Fax: 415-668-2073; 668-7968

WASHINGTON BASED USG AND RELATED COUNTRY CONTACTS

For information on antidumping and countervailing duties:
OFFICE OF INVESTIGATIONS
Import Administration
U.S. Department of Commerce, Rm. 3099
Washington, D.C. 20230
Tel: 202-482-5403
Fax: 202-482-1059

OFFICE OF ANTIDUMPING COMPLIANCE
Import Administration
U.S. Department of Commerce, Rm. 3069A
Washington, D.C. 20230
Tel: 202-482-2104
Fax: 202-482-5105

OFFICE OF COUNTERVAILING COMPLIANCE
Import Administration
U.S. Department of Commerce, Rm. 3069A
Washington, D.C. 20230
Tel: 202-482-2786
Fax: 202-482-4001

For information on importing goods from India:
INDIA TRADE PROMOTION ORGANIZATION
445 Park Avenue
New York, New York 10022
Tel: 212-753-6655
Fax: 212-319-6914

For information on rates of duty assessed by Indian customs on U.S.-origin products being exported to India:
OFFICE OF SOUTH ASIA/OCEANIA "FLASHFACTS"
Use from touchtone phone. When asked to enter document numbers, enter document #4100, the menu for the Indian Tariff Schedule. The Schedule is based on the internationally-used Harmonized System (HS); see below to obtain HS numbers).
Fax: 202-482-1064

ASIA BUSINESS CENTER
Room 2308
U.S. Department of Commerce
14th and Constitution
Washington, D.C. 20230
Tel: 202-482-2954

For help in determining the Harmonized System (HS) classification number. (Indian import tariffs are based on the Harmonized System--sometimes called the "Schedule B" number.)
U.S. CENSUS BUREAU
Suitland, Maryland
Tel: 301-763-5200

For information on environmental issues concerning India:
U.S. ENVIRONMENTAL PROTECTION AGENCY
Office of International Activities
401 M Street, SW
Washington, D.C. 20460
Tel: 202-260-4870
Fax: 202-260-4470

For information on obtaining an export license and/ or determining if one is needed :
BUREAU OF EXPORT ADMINISTRA-TION (BXA)
India Desk
U.S. Department of Commerce, Rm. 2705
Washington, D.C. 20230
Tel: 202-482-4252

For information on how to start an Export Trading Company:
OFFICE OF EXPORT TRADING COMPANY AFFAIRS
U.S. Department of Commerce, Rm. 1800
Washington, D.C. 20230
Tel: 202-482-5131

For information concerning copyright, trademark and patent protection in India :
PATENT AND TRADEMARK OFFICE
U.S. Department of Commerce
Crystal City
Arlington, Virginia
Tel: 703-305-9300

For information on labor issues affecting India:
BUREAU OF INTERNATIONAL LABOR AFFAIRS
Area Advisor Near East and South Asia
U.S Department of Labor
Washington, D.C. 20210
Tel: 202-219-6257
Fax: 202-219-5613

For inquiries for non-agricultural standards, obtain the Indian code number of the desired product from:
THE NATIONAL CENTER FOR STANDARDS AND CERTIFICATION INFORMATION
National Institute of Standards and Technology
TRF Building, Room K-163
Gaithersburg, Maryland 20899
Tel: 301-975-4040

Using the Indian code number, obtain the standard(s) from:
THE AMERICAN NATIONAL STAN-DARDS INSTITUTE
11 West 42nd Street
New York, New York 10036
Tel: 212-642-4900

For information on major projects in India:
OFFICE OF MAJOR PROJECTS
U.S. Department of Commerce, Rm. 2015B
Washington, D.C. 20230
Tel: 202-482-5225

OFFICE OF MULTILATERAL DEVELOP-MENT BANK OPERATIONS
U.S. Department of Commerce, Rm. 1107
Washington, D.C. 20230
Tel: 202-482-3399
Fax: 202-273-0927

THE WORLD BANK
1818 H Street
Washington, D.C.
Tel: 202-477-1234

India

ASIAN DEVELOPMENT BANK
#6 ADB Avenue
P.O. Box 789
Mandaluyong, Metro Manila, Philippines
Tel: 632-632-6050; 632-4003

For advocacy for American firms competing against third-country competitors for major contracts in India contact:
ADVOCACY CENTER
U.S. Department of Commerce, Rm. 3814A
Washington, D.C. 20230
Tel: 202-482-3896

For information on marketing in India :
OFFICE OF SOUTH ASIA/OCEANIA "FLASHFACTS"
The automated fax information system contains much general information on doing business in India and South Asia. Use from any touchtone phone and follow the instructions to have the documents sent to your fax machine. When asked to enter the document numbers, enter Document #4000 (a complete listing of documents on the system). With the menu in hand, call back and order the documents desired.
Fax: 202-482-1064

NATIONAL TRADE DATA BANK (NTDB) HOTLINE
Tel: 202-482-1986

For information on how to begin exporting products:
THE TRADE INFORMATION CENTER
U.S. Department of Commerce, Rm. 7424
Washington, D.C. 20230
Tel: 1-800-USA-TRADE

For information on agricultural exports:
TRADE ASSISTANCE & PROMOTION OFFICE
U.S Department of Agriculture (USDA)
Room 4939, South Building
14th & Independence Ave., S.W.
Washington, D.C. 20250
Tel: 202-720-7420
Fax: 202-690-4374

FOREIGN AGRICULTURAL SERVICE
India Desk
U.S. Department of Agriculture
14th and Independence
Washington, D.C. 20250
Tel: 202-720-0762
Fax: 202-690-1093

For information on selling insurance services to India:
OFFICE OF SERVICE INDUSTRIES
U.S. Department of Commerce
Rm. 1128
Washington, D.C. 20230
Tel: 202-482-5261
Fax: 202-482-4775

For information on providing financial services in India:
INTERNATIONAL AFFAIRS
U.S. Department of the Treasury
15th and Pennsylvania
Washington, D.C. 20220
Tel: 202-622-1986
Fax: 202-622-1956

For information on selling telecommunications services and equipment to India :
OFFICE OF TELECOMMUNICATIONS
U.S. Department of Commerce, Rm. 1009
Washington, D.C. 20230
Tel: 202-482-4466
Fax: 202-482-5834

For information on textiles and apparel relating to India:
OFFICE OF TEXTILES AND APPAREL
India Desk
U.S. Department of Commerce, Rm. 3001A
Washington, D.C. 20230
Tel: 202-482-4212
Fax: 202-482-2331

TRADE EVENTS SCHEDULE

09/28-30/95
Lab USA 95 (SFO)
Hyderabad

10/05-08/95
U.S. Pavilion Life 2000
Bombay

10/05-08/95
U.S. Medical Equipment Catalog Show Life 2000
Bombay

MID-OCTOBER 1995
Fourth Issue of US&FCS India Commercial Newsletter "In USA"
New Delhi

10/25-28/95
U.S. Pavilion at Broadcast, Cable And Satellite India 95 (BIO) (CTF) (U.S. Department of Commerce Certified)
New Delhi

10/28-11/7
U.S. Plastics Industry Trade Mission To India (TM)
Delhi, Calcutta, Madras, Bombay

11/04-07/95
Promote the Megashow (Food & Dairy Expo and IEFP), Chicago, Il. As a U.S.-India commercial Alliance Event.
Chicago

DECEMBER 1995
Santa Clara Trade Mission (TM) (Tentative)

12/12-15/95
U.S. Pavilion at Avia India 95 (TFO) (Tentative)
Bangalore

12/07-10/95
U.S. Pavilion at Communications India 95 (BIO) (CTF)
New Delhi

01/16-19/96
U.S. Pavilion or U.S. Mining Calcutta Equipment Catalog Exhibit at the 4th Intl. Mining Machinery Exhibition (Imme 96) (TFO or RC)
Calcutta

01/18-23/96
U.S. Pavilion at the 18th Asia Dental Congress & Exhibition (TFO)
Bombay

END-JANUARY 1996
Fifth Issue of US&FCS India Commercial Newsletter "In USA"
New Delhi

02/01-07/96
U.S. Pavilion at Wisitex 96 (TFO)
New Delhi

FEBRUARY 1996
U.S. Computer Software Trade Mission to India (TM)
New Delhi, Bombay, Bangalore

MARCH 1996
U.S. Plastics/Paints Technical Seminar Mission to India (SM) (Tentative)
Bombay, New Delhi

MARCH 1996
Food Processing & Packaging Seminar Mission to India (SM) (Tentative)
New Delhi, Bombay

04/02-03/96
Products for Development USA Multi-State/Catalog Exhibition (Combined MSTC/RC)
New Delhi

10/95-03/96
U.S. Food Processing and Packaging Machinery Exhibition (SFO) (Tentative)
New Delhi

10/95-03/96
Ohio State Trade Mission to India Led by Governor Voinovich (TM) (Tentative)

10/95-03/96
New York State Trade Mission to India Led by the Governor (TM) (Tentative)

10/95-03/96
California State Trade Mission to India Led by Lieutenant Governor Gray Davis (TM) (Tentative)
India

10/95-03/96
New Jersey State Trade Mission (TM) (Tentative)
India

10/95-03/96
Medical/Healthcare Trade Mission to India Organized by Grand Rapids D.O. (TM) (Tentative)

MAY 1996
U.S. Insurance Seminar Mission to India (SM) (Tentative)
New Delhi, Bombay

AUGUST 1996
U.S. Aerospace/Aviation Trade Mission To India (TM) (Tentative)
New Delhi, Bangalore, Bombay

AUGUST 1996
U.S. Water Treatment Technical Seminar Mission to India (SM) (Tentative)
Delhi,Bombay

SEPTEMBER 1996
Electronics USA 96 (SFO) (Tentative)
Bangalore

TFO - Trade Fair (Recruited) Overseas
SFO - Solo Fair (Recruited) Overseas
RC - Regular Catalog Show
MSTD - Multi-State Trade Days
TM - Trade Mission
SM - Seminar Mission
CTF -U.S. Dept. of Commerce Certified Trade Event

INFORMATION CHECKLIST AND BIBLIOGRAPHY

The National Trade Data Bank (NTDB) is a CD-ROM available for purchase by subscription or single copy or for use at depository libraries. The NTDB is also available on Internet. The NTDB contains basic export information, country-specific information, industry-specific information, and much more: details on market assessment, the competitive situation, market access, trade promotion opportunities, best sales prospects and statistical data:

Country Commercial Guide. Market information needed to successfully conduct business in foreign markets. Each Country Commercial Guide (CCG) presents a comprehensive look at that country's commercial environment through economic, political and market analyses. In addition, the CCG includes best prospect export sectors, trade regulations, business travel information, and an upcoming trade events schedule.

Foreign Traders Index. FTI is a listing of foreign agents, distributors, and importers who have shown interest in working with U.S. exporters. This list can be searched by product and country of interest. The FTI contains basic information, such as address and product lines, about the foreign firm.

BUSINESS GUIDES (U.S. GOVERNMENT)

Background Notes, India, a periodically-updated country profile available from the U.S. Department of State, Washington, D.C. 20520.

India Commercial Guide, 1995, U.S. Embassy, New Delhi. (Available on the National Trade Data Bank.)

BUSINESS GUIDES (NON-GOVERNMENT)

American Firms in India, a section of the publication *American Firms Operating in Foreign Countries,* 1994, World Trade Academy Press, 50 E. 42nd Street, New York, N.Y. 10017.
Tel: 212- 697-4999.

Cen-Cus Customs Tariff, Cen-Cus Publications, Sujaan Book Agency, C-7 Main Market, Vasant Vihar, New Delhi 110057.

Doing Business in India, 1994, Price Waterhouse, 1301 K St. N.W., Washington, D.C. 20005.
Tel: 202-414-1890.

Kothari s Industrial Directory of India, Kothari Enterprises, Post Box No. 3309 Nangambakkam High Road, Madras.

NEWSLETTERS AND MAGAZINES

Business America, (a monthly magazine on international trade), Superintendent of Documents, U.S. Government Printing Office, Washington, D.C. 20402.

Business India, (a biweekly magazine), Wadia Building, 17/19 Dalal Street, Fort, Bombay 400001.

Business World, (a biweekly magazine), 145 Atlanta, 209 Ceremonial Boulevard, Nariman Point, Bombay 400021.

Commercial Bulletin, Commerce Wing, Embassy of India, 2536 Massachusetts Avenue, N.W., Washington, D.C. 20008. Tel: 202-939-7050.

Economic News, Information Service, Embassy of India, 2107 Massachusetts Avenue, N.W., Washington, D.C. 20008. Tel: 202-939-7050.

India News, Information Service, Embassy of India, 2107 Massachusetts Avenue, N.W., Washington, D.C. 20008. Tel: 202-939-7048.

OTHER INFORMATION SOURCES

International Book Links, 601 Churchgate Chamber, 6 New Marine Lines, Bombay 5000020.

Jain Book Agency, C-9 Prem House, Connaught Place, New Delhi 110001.

Kitab Mahal, State Emporium Building, Kharak Singh Marg, New Delhi 110001.

Publications Division, Government of India, Ministry of Information and Broadcasting, Patiala House, New Deli 110001.

BOOKS ON INDIA (GENERAL)

India, Stanley Wolpert, Berkeley, University of California Press, 1993.

India: Facing the Twenty-First Century, Barbara Crossette, Bloomington, Indiana University Press, 1993.

BOOKS ON INDIA
(ECONOMY)

Economic Development in India, London, International Labour Office, 1993.

Economic Liberalisation and Indian Agriculture, G.S. Bhalla (Ed.), Delhi, Institute for Studies in Industrial Development, 1994.

India in Transition. Freeing the Economy, Jagdish Bhagwati, Oxford, Clarendon Press, 1993.

Industrial Growth and Stagnation, Deepak Nayyar (Ed.), New Delhi, Oxford University Press, 1994.

Selected Economic Writings, Delhi, Oxford University Press, 1993.

State and Development Planning in India, Terence Byres, New Delhi, Oxford University Press, 1994.

Unfinished Agenda, India and the World Economy, A. M. Khusro, New Delhi, Wiley Eastern Ltd. 1994.

India

Resources: Indonesia

U.S. AND COUNTRY CONTACTS

COUNTRY GOVERNMENT AGENCIES

MINISTER, DEPARTMENT OF AGRICULTURE
Prof. Dr. Ir. Sjarifuddin Baharsjah, Msc.
Jl. Harsono R.M. 3
Ragunan, Bldg. A
Pasar Minggu, Jakarta 12550
Indonesia
Tel: 62-21-780-6131-34
Fax: 62-21-780-4237

DEPARTMENT OF DEFENSE AND SECURITY
Gen. Edi Sudradjat
Menhankam
Jl. Merdeka Barat 13
1st Floor
Jakarta, Indonesia
Tel: 62-21-345-6184

MINISTER, DEPARTMENT OF EDUCATION AND CULTURE
Prof. Dr. Ing. Wardiman Djojonegoro
Jl. Jend Dudirman
Jakarta, Indonesia
Tel: 62-21-573-1618

MINISTER, DEPARTMENT OF FOREIGN AFFAIRS
Ali Alatas, SH
Jl. Taman Pejambon 6
Jakarta, Indonesia
Tel: 62-21-345-6014
Fax: 62-21-384-9412

MINISTER, DEPARTMENT OF HEALTH
Prof. Dr. Sujudi
Jl. HR Rasuna Said Blok 25, Kav. 4-9
2nd Floor
Jakarta, Indonesia
Tel: 62-21-520-1587

MINISTER, DEPARTMENT OF INDUSTRY
Ir. Tunky Ariwibano
Jl. Gatot Subroto
Kav 52-53
Jakarta, Indonesia
Tel: 62-21-5200700
Fax: 62-21-520-1606

MINISTER, DEPARTMENT OF MINES AND ENERGY
Lt. Gen. I.B. Sudjana
Jl. Merdeka Selatan 18, 2nd Floor
Jakarta, Indonesia
Tel: 62-21-384-6596
Fax: 62-21-384-7461

MINISTER, STATE MINISTRY FOR INVESTMENT
Lf. Sanyoto Sastrowardoyo
Capital Investment Coordinating Board
Jl. Jend. Gatot Subroto 44.
2nd Floor
Tel: 62-21-525-0023
Fax: 32-21-525-4945

MINISTER, DEPARTMENT OF TOURISM, POST AND TELECOMMUNICATIONS
Joop Ave
Jl. Kebon Sirih 36, 2nd Floor
Jakarta, Indonesia
Tel: 62-21-345-6705
Fax: 62-21-375-409

PRESIDENT, PT TELKOM
Drs. Setyanto P. Santosa, MA
Gedung Graha Citra Caraka
Jl. Jend. Gatot Subroto 52
1st Floor
Jakarta, Indonesia
Tel: 62-21-521-5271
Fax: 62-21-520-3322

MINISTER, DEPARTMENT OF TRADE
Prof. Dr. Satrio Budiarfjo Joedono
Jl. M. I. Ridwwan Rais 5
3rd Floor
Jakarta, Indonesia
Tel: 62-21-384-8667
Fax: 62-21-374-361

MINISTER, DEPARTMENT OF COMMUNICATIONS
Dr. Haryanto Danutirto
Jl. Merdeka Barat 8
9th Floor
Jakarta, Indonesia
Tel: 62-21-345-6332
Fax: 62-21-345-1657

COUNTRY TRADE ASSOCIATIONS/ CHAMBERS OF COMMERCE

AMERICAN INDONESIAN CHAMBER OF COMMERCE
711 Third Ave. 17th Floor
New York, NY 10017
Tel : 212-687-4505
Fax: 212-867-9882

AMERICAN CHAMBER OF COMMERCE
World Trade Center, 11th Floor
Jl. Jend. Sudirman 29-31
Jakarta 12084
Tel: 62-21 526-2860
Fax: 62-21-526-2861

KADIN (INDONESIAN CHAMBER OF COMMERCE)
Jalan M.H. Thamrin 20
Jakarta 10350
Tel: 62-21-315-0242
Fax: 62-21-525-1589

KADIN (KADIN INDONESIA KOMITE AMERIKA SERIKAT)
(Kadin Indonesia - U.S. Committee under its umbrella.)
c/o P.T. Indokor Indonesia
Lippo Life Building
Suite 103
Jalan H.R. Rasuna Said
Kav. B10-11
Jakarta 12910
Tel: 62-21-520-5510
Fax: 62-21-797-2233

**IMPORTERS ASSOCIATION OF
INDONESIA (GINSI)**
CTC Building, 4th Fl.
Jl. Kramat Raya 94-96
PO Box 2744, Jakarta 10027
Tel: 62-21-3901559, 3908480, 3908481
Fax: 62-21-3908479

**INDONESIAN EXPORTERS
ASSOCIATION (GPEI)**
Jalan Kramat Raya 4-6,
Jakarta Pusat
Tel: (62)(21) 356-099

**HIPMI (HIMPUNAN PENGUSAHA
MUDA INDONESIA)**
(Young Businessmen Association of Indonesia)
Jl. Raya Pasar Minggu 1-A
Jakarta 12780
Tel: 62-21-797-2233/2299
Fax: 62-21-797-2233

COUNTRY MARKET
RESEARCH FIRMS

**INKINDO, THE ASSOCIATION OF
INDONESIAN CONSULTANTS**
Jalan Bendungan Hilir Raya,
No. 29. Jakarta Pusat,
Indonesia.
Tel: 62-21- 5738577/78. Fax: 62-21-5733474

**IMPORTERS ASSOCIATION OF
INDONESIA (GINSI),**
CTC Building, 4th Fl.
Jl. Kramat Raya 94-96
P.O. Box 2744, Jakarta 10027
Tel: 62-21-3901559, 3908480, 3908481
Fax: 62-21-3908479

**INDONESIAN EXPORTERS
ASSOCIATION (GPEI)**
Jalan Kramat Raya 4-6
Jakarta Pusat
Tel: 62-21-356-099

**NATIONAL AGENCY FOR EXPORT
DEVELOPMENT**
Jl. Gajah Mada No. 8
Jakarta 10130
Tel: 62-21-362-666, 384-5096, 385-7184
Fax: 62-21-384-4588, 3848380, 3853135

**SGV UTOMO MANAGEMENT
CONSULTANTS**
Chase Plaza
Jalan Jend. Sudirman Kav. 21
Jakarta Pusat, Indonesia
Contact: Budiman Elkana, Managing Partner
Tel: 62-21 5208199; Fax: 62-21-5704347

P.T. SRI INTERNATIONAL
Wisma Bank Dharmala, 15th Fl.
Jl. Jend Sudirman Kav 28
Jakarta 12920, Indonesia
Tel: 62-21-5212200; Fax: 62-21-5212203
Contact: David Sparks

PLANSEARCH ASSOCIATES
Jalan Limau 1/28A
Jakarta Selatan, Indonesia
Contact: Gunter Shwarze, Senior Consultant
Tel: 62-21-739-5017; Fax: 62 -21-739-5018

P.T. DATA CONSULT INC.
Jalan Kramat Raya No. 5- L
Jakarta 10450, Indonesia
Contact: IR. Sulaeman Krisnandhi, President
Tel: 62-21-3904711,4714752
Fax: 62-21-3901878, 4895196

BUSINESS ADVISORY INDONESIA
Kuningan Plaza, Suite 304 North
Jl. H.R. Rasuna Said Cll- 14
Jakarta 12941, Indonesia
Contact: James W. Castle, Technical Advisor
Tel: 62-21-520-7696, 520-7689
Fax: 62-21-5250604, 5202557

HARVEST INTERNATIONAL INC.
Wisma Metropolitan I, 10th Floor
Jalan Jendral Sudirman, KAV 29
Jakarta Pusat, 12920, Indonesia
Contact: Harvey Goldstein, Chairman and CEO
Tel: 62-21-5251641
Fax: 62-21-520-7789

COUNTRY COMMERCIAL BANKS

*Indonesia has one of the most deregulated, market-
based banking systems in the developing world. Since
the 1988 banking deregulation package, the Indonesian banking sector has expanded rapidly, presenting numerous financing options to U.S. exporters.
Four American banks have branch offices in Indonesia:*

CHASE MANHATTAN
Chase Plaza, 5th Floor
Jl. Jend. Sudirman
Jakarta
Tel: 62-21-5780088

CITIBANK
The Landmark Center
Jl. Jend. Sudirman 1
Jakarta
Tel: 62-21-578191

BANK OF AMERICA
Wisma Antara
Jl. Merdeka Selatan 17
Jakarta Pusat
Tel: 62-21-347031

AMERICAN EXPRESS BANK
Arthaloka Building
Jl. Jend. Sudirman
Jakarta
Tel: 62-21-587401

The following seven U.S. banks have representative offices there: Chemical Bank,
J.P. Morgan, Bank of Boston, Bank of California,
Philadelphia National, Republic National,
and Banker's Trust.

In addition, the following Indonesian banks
have correspondent relationships with
American banks:

BANK UMUM NASIONAL
Jl. Prapatan 50
Jakarta
Tel: 62-21-365563

BANK NIAGA
Jl. M.H. Thamrin 55
Jakarta Pusat
Tel: 62-21-333936

BANK BALI
Bank Bali Building, 7th Floor
Jl. Hayam Wuruk No. 84.85
Jakarta
Tel: 62-21-6498006

Bank International Indonesia, Bank Dagang
Nasional Indonesia, Bank Duta, Panin Bank,
Bank Pacific, Bank Buana Indonesia, Bank

Indonesia (ASEAN)

Utama (OEB), Bank Universal, Sejahtera Bank Umum, Bank Asia Pacific, Bank Surya, Tamara Bank, Unibank, Arta Prima Bank, Bank Central Dagang, Prima Express Bank, Bank NISP, Intermodern Bank, Bank Artha Graha, Bank Tiara, Bank Unum Servitia, Subentra Bank, Nusa Bank, Bank Bumi Arta Indonesia, Bank Rama, Bank Dagang Bali, Haga Bank, Bank Bahari, Bank Arta Niago Kencana, Bank Mashill Utama, Bank Ekonomi Raharja, Antardaerah Bank, Bank Pelita.

U.S. EMBASSY TRADE PERSONNEL

AMERICAN EMBASSY
via U.S. Mail
U.S. Embassy Indonesia
Box 1, Unit 8129
A.P.O. AP 96520-0001

via International Mail:
American Embassy Jakarta
Jalan Medan Merdeka Selatan 5
Jakarta 10110, Indonesia

U.S. COMMERCIAL CENTER
Wisma Metropolitan II, 3rd Floor
Jl. Jend Sudirman Kav. 31
Jakarta 12920
Indonesia
Tel: 62-21-526-2850
Fax: 62-21-526-2855

U.S. & FOREIGN COMMERCIAL SERVICE AT U.S. EMBASSY
Merdan Merdeka Selatan 5
Jakarta, Indonesia
Tel: 62-21-360-360
Fax: 62-21-385-1632

Counselor for Commercial Affairs
Michael J. Hand
Ned Quistorff, Commercial Attache
Charles Reese, Ass't Commercial Attache
James McCarthy, Commercial Officer

FOREIGN AGRICULTURAL SERVICE
Counselor for Agricultural Affairs
Michael Humphrey,
Margie Bauer, Agricultural Attache
Tel: 62-21-360-360 ext. 2161
Fax: 62-21-380-1363

AGENCY FOR INTERNATIONAL DEVELOPMENT (US-AID)
William Frej, Chief, Private Sector
Development Office
Tel: 62-21-360-360 ext. 2308
Fax: 62-21-380-6694

AMERICAN CONSULATE GENERAL
Jalan Imam Bonjol #13
Medan, Indonesia
Tel: 62-61-322-200
Fax: 62-61-518-711
Trade Personnel: Wagiman Tandun,
Commercial Specialist

AMERICAN CONSULATE GENERAL
Jalan Raya Dr. Sutomo #33
Surabaya, Indonesia
Tel: 62-31-582-287;
Fax: 62-31-574-492
Trade Personnel: Midji Sumiasih Kwee,
Commercial Specialist

U.S.-BASED MULTIPLIERS FOR INDONESIA

U.S. - ASEAN COUNCIL FOR BUSINESS AND TECHNOLOGY
Robert Driscoll, President
1400 L. St., NW, Suite 375
Washington, D.C. 20005-3509
Tel: 202-289-1911
Fax: 202-289-0519

PACIFIC BASIN ECONOMIC COUNCIL (PBEC)
Ann R. Wise, Director General
PBEC U.S. Member Committee
1100 Connecticut Avenue, NW, Suite 1300
Washington, D.C. 20036
Tel: 202-728-0993
Fax: 202-728-0998

INDONESIAN AMERICAN CHAMBER OF COMMERCE
Wayne Forrest, Director
711 Third Avenue, 17th floor
New York, NY 10017
Tel: 212-687-4505
Fax: 212-867-9882

COUNTRY CONSULATES AND TRADE OFFICES IN THE U.S.

EMBASSY OF THE REPUBLIC OF INDONESIA
2020 Massachusetts Ave. NW
Washington, DC 20036
Tel: 202-775-5200
Fax: 202-775-5365

Commercial Office
Tel: 202-775-5350
Fax: 202-775-5365

Economic Counselor
Benny Permadi Suryawinata
Defense attache: Brig. Gen. Benny Mandalika
Agriculture: Patuan Natigor Siagian
Education: Subekti Dhirdjosaputro

CONSULATES
New York
5 E. 68th St
New York, NY 10021
Tel : 212-879-0600
FAX: 212-570-6206

Chicago
233 N. Michigan Ave.. Suite 1422
Chicago, IL 60601
Tel: 312-938-0101
Fax: 312-938-3148

San Francisco
1111 Columbus Ave
San Francisco, CA 94133
Tel:415-474-9571
Fax: 415-441-4320

TRADE EVENTS SCHEDULE

SEPTEMBER 12 - 19, 1995
Market Place, USA TFO,
Consumer Goods. Surabaya, Indonesia
Contact: Brian Freeters Tel: 6231-582-287

SEPTEMBER 18 - 28, 1995
Environmental Technologies Matchmaker.
Indonesia and Thailand. Contact: Michael
Slater, Dept. of Commerce Tel: 619-557-5395

SEPTEMBER 25-26, 1995
State of California, Environmental Technology Partnership. Jakarta, Indonesia. Contact: Tim Ogburn Tel: 916-322-3670

OCTOBER 9-20, 1995
Small and Medium-Sized Business Mission to Southeast Asia. Manila, Philippines; Bangkok, Thailand; Jakarta, Indonesia; Kuala Lumpur, Malaysia
Contact: Steven Patillo, U.S.-ASEAN Council
Tel: 202-289-1911

OCTOBER 21-25, 1995
State of Maine Trade Mission to Indonesia.
Jakarta, Indonesia. Contact: Keith Kirkham,
Fax: 207-287-5701

OCTOBER 23-24, 1995
West Virginia Trade Mission to Indonesia. Mining
and Equipment
Contact: W. Davis Coale

OCTOBER 30 - NOVEMBER 7, 1995
Sporting Goods /Physical Fitness Matchmaker
Singapore, Indonesia
Contact: Derek Parks, Dept. of Commerce
Tel: 202-482-0287

NOVEMBER 1-5, 1995
BIMP-EAGA
Exposition and Forum. Brunei, Indonesia,
Malaysia, Philippines-East ASEAN Growth
Area. Contact: Steven Patillo, U.S.-ASEAN
Council Tel: 202-289-1911

NOVEMBER 1-10, 1995
Clean Coal Technology
Indonesia. Contact Person: Tom Litman, Dept.
of Energy Tel: 202-586-4344

NOVEMBER 6-7, 1995
State of Nebraska Trade Mission to Indonesia.
Jakarta, Indonesia. Contact: Robert Burns
Tel: 402-471-3770

NOVEMBER 7-11, 1995
Manufacturing Indonesia Trade Show. Jakarta,
Indoneisia. Contact: Charles Reese
Tel: 62-21-526-2850

NOVEMBER 7-11, 1995
*Pollution and Environmental Technology Indonesia
'95.* Jakarta, Indonesia. Contact: Harlow
Russell Tel: 62-21-526-2844

NOVEMBER 22-25, 1995
Mining Indonesia Trade Show. Jakarta,
Indonesia. Contact: George Zanetakos
Tel: 202-482-0552

DECEMBER 6-9, 1995
Oil & Gas Technology Indonesia. Jakarta,
Indonesia. Contact: Mary Wiening, Dept. of
Commerce Tel: 202-482-4708

DECEMBER 12-13, 1995
Telecommunications/Information
Technologies Matchmaker
Thailand, Indonesia, and the Philippines
Contact: Molly Costa Tel: 202-482-0692

FEBRUARY 1996
ACE Matchmaker to Indonesia
Jakarta, Indoneisia. Contact: Molly Costa
Tel: 202-482-0692

FEBRUARY 5 - 6, 1996
Clean Coal Technology Trade Mission. Jakarta,
Indonesia. Contact: Tom Litman
Tel: 202-586-4344

FEBRUARY 5 - 6, 1996
Clean Coal Technology Trade Mission. Jakarta,
Indonesia. Contact: Tom Litman Tel: 202-
586-4344

MARCH 1996
Franchising Matchmaker to Indonesia. Jakarta,
Indonesia. Contact: Molly Costa Tel: 202-
482-0692

APRIL 1, 1996
Electric Power Generation /Transmission. Kuala
Lumpur, Malaysia and Jakarta, Indonesia.
Contact: Molly Costa Tel: 202-482-0692

AUGUST 1, 1996
Growth Industries USA. Jakarta, Indonesia.
Contact: Brenda Coleman, Dept. of
Commerce Tel: 202-482-3973

MAY 1, 1996
Computer Software TM. Jakarta, Indonesia and
Bangkok, Thailand. Contact: Heidi Hijikata,
Dept. of Commerce Tel: 202-482-0569

MAY 14 - 18, 1996
*State of Pennsylvania Trade Mission to Indonesia
and Malaysia.* Contact: Deborah Doherty
Tel: 717-255-3252

JUNE 1996
Growth Industries. Jakarta, Indonesia. Contact:
Brenda Coleman Tel: 202-482-3973

JUNE 22 - JULY 1, 1996
Indonesian Air Show
Jakarta, Indonesia
Contact: Betty Smith Tel: 202-482-0106
or Ludene Capone Tel: 202-482-2835

FALL 1996
*Environmental Equipment and Services Trade
Mission to South East Asia*
Jakarta, Indonesia. Contact: Denise
Carpenter Tel: 202-482-1500

U.S. DEPARTMENT OF COMMERCE MARKET RESEARCH AVAILABLE

Aircraft and Parts: Passenger/Cargo Aircraft
and Engines (Mar. 92) $20

Aircraft and Parts: Civilian Helicopters
(Apr. 92) $20

Analytical and Scientific Instruments
(Nov. 89) $5

Bottling and Container Packaging Equipment
(Sept. 91) $10

Cellular Telephone Equipment
(Dec. 92) $30

Commercial Vessels and Related Equipment:
Floating/Submersible Drilling Production
Platforms: Oil and Gas (Jun. 92) $20

Computers, Mini and Micro
(Oct. 91) $10

Computers and Peripherals
(Nov. 89) $5

Construction Equipment: Public Works
(Feb. 92) $20

Electric Power Distribution Equipment
(Aug. 91) $10

Electric Power Distribution and
Transmission Equipment (July 92) $20

Electric Power Generating Equipment and
Parts (May 92) $20

Electric Power Sector, Narrative Report
(Jan. 92) $20.00

Fiber Optic Cables (Feb. 93) $30

Food Processing and Packaging Machinery
(June 93) $30

Hydro and Geothermal Elecrtic Power Plants
(Sept. 93) $30

Industrial Chemicals Organic and Inorganic
(Sept. 89) $5

Industrial Organic Chemicals (June 92) $20

Industrial Pumps and Parts (Jan. 92) $20

Inorganic Industrial Chemicals (May 91) $10

Iron and Steel Flat-rolled Tube, Pipe, Bar and
Rod Products (May 93) $30

Lifting Apparatus and Materials Handling
Equipment (June 92) $20

Machine Tools and Metalworking Equipment,
Miscellaneous (June 92) $20

Maritime Equipment (Feb. 90) $5

Metalworking Equipment (Nov. 89) $5

Mining Equipment (Feb. 90) $10

Oil and Gas Exploration Equipment
(Mar. 92) $20

Oil and Gas Production Equipment
(Aug. 93) $30

Petroleum Report (Aug. 93) $25.00

Petroleum Report (Aug. 92) $10

Plastic Molding Machinery and Parts
(Dec. 92) $30

Polyethylene and Polypropylene (June 91) $10

Process Control Instruments (July 92) $20

Pulp and Paper Machinery and Parts
(Aug. 93) $30

Pulp, Waste Paper and Paper Products
(Nov. 89) $5

Telecommunications ISDN Equipment
(Jan. 92) $20

Indonesia (ASEAN)

Telecommunications Equipment and Systems
(Sept. 1989) $5

Textile Yarn (June 93) $30

Water Pollution Control Equipment
(Oct. 92) $30

Woodworking Machinery, Miscellaneous
(Oct. 92) $30

Yarn Preparing Machinery and Parts
(Mar. 93) $30

GENERAL REPORTS

Best Prospects - $30

Foreign Economic Trends Report- Free

Major Project Listing - $20

U.S. Businesses in Indonesia (Apr 92) $20

OTHER REPORTS

Printing and Graphic Arts Equipment

Security Equipment

Waste and Scrap Metal

Medical Equipment

Pharmaceutical Products

Hazardous Waste Treatment Equipment

Leather Products

Telecommunications: Broadcast Equipment

Miscellaneous Architectural & Construction
Engineering Services

Miscellaneous Building Materials & Products

Electric Power Generating Equipment

Miscellaneous Mining Equipment

Motor Vehicle for Transport of Goods

Electric Power Transmission and Distribution
Equipment

Franchising: Non Fast-Food

Computer Software: General Business
Application

Computer Software: Multimedia

Telecommunications: Central Office
Switching Equipment

Telecommunications: Keyphone Systems/PBXs

Telecommunications: Test Equipment

Security and Safety Equipment: Airport
Security Equipment

Pollution Control Equipment: Pollution
Control Instrument

Sporting and Recreation Goods: Golf and
Health/Exercise Facilities

INFORMATION CHECKLIST AND BIBLIOGRAPHY

BUSINESS GUIDES

Country Commercial Guide, U.S. Embassy

Indonesia Country Paper, American Chamber of
Commerce (address above)

Indonesia - An Investment Guide, Citibank
(Indonesia)

Indonesia - A Brief Guide for Investors, State
Ministry of Investment/Investment Coordinating Board (BKPM), see address on attached list
of ministries

Doing Business in Indonesia and *United States
Investment in Indonesia*; both Harvest International

Guide to Agency Arrangements in Indonesia,
Accounting Firm of Drs. Hadi Sutanto and
Associates (Price Waterhouse), Ficorinvest
Building; Jl. H.R. Rasuna Said Kav. c-18;
Kuningan, South Jakarta
Tel: 62-21-829-8811
Fax: 62-21-829-8917

NEWSLETTERS AND MAGAZINES

Indonesian Business Trend, P.T. Ekamasni Consult,
Jl. Walter Monginsidi No.
24A; Kebayoran Baru, Jakarta 12170
Tel: 62-21-725-2261
Fax: 62-21-720-6193

Indocommercial, P.T. Capricorn Indonesia Consult;
Jalan Raden Saleh No. 46;
Jakarta 10330
Tel: 62-21-310-1081
Fax: 62-21-310-1505

Economic & Business Review Indonesia,
Dr. Janner Sinaga, Publisher
Jl. Singaraja C4/11; Kuningan, Jakarta 12950
Tel: 62-21-522-1831
Fax: 62-21-525-0781

Warta Cafi Economic Bulletin, Yayasan CAFI;
Jalan Proboliggo No. 5; Jakarta 10350
Tel: 62-21-315-5385
Fax: 62-21-322-2479

Indonesian Commercial Newsletter, P.T. Data
Consult; Maya Indah Building II;
Jl. Kramat Raya No. 5-L; Jakarta 10450
Tel: 62-21-390-4711
Fax: 62-21-390-1878

STATISTICAL SOURCES

See Central Bureau of Statistic (last address on
attached list). Also: P.T. SRI International

Amcham Cost of Living Report (Quarterly)

OTHER INFORMATIONAL SOURCES

*The Directory of American Business in Indonesia
(1955)*, (on sale June 1995 from U.S. Embassy,
Business Advisory International, and Amcham
Indonesia)

BOOKS

A History of Modern Indonesia, 1300 to the Present,
M.C. Rickelfs

A Nation in Waiting--Indonesia in the 1990's, Adam
Schwartz (former correspondent for the Far Eastern Economic Review) Allen & Unwinm 1994.*

Culture and Politics in Indonesia, Claire Holt, ed.

Culture Shock—Indonesia (available in most U.S.
bookstores)

In Search of Southeast Asia, David Joel Steinberg

*Indonesia and the Philippines: American Interests
in Island Southeast Asia*, Robert Pringle

Indonesian Politics Under Soeharto, Michael R.J.
Vatikiotis, Routledge, Loundon and New York,
revised 1994*

Suharto's Indonesia, Hamish McDonald

* These books are mildly controversial in nature
and critical of the current administration.
Nonetheless, they are current and good analyses of
the business and political scene here.

Indonesia (ASEAN)

Resources: Malaysia

U.S. & COUNTRY CONTACTS

COUNTRY GOVERNMENT AGENCIES

MINISTRY OF INTERNATIONAL TRADE AND INDUSTRY (MITI)
YB Dato' Seri Rafidah Aziz, Minister
YB En. Chua Jui Meng, Deputy Minister
Blk. 10, Government Offices Complex
Jalan Duta
50622 Kuala Lumpur
Tel: 60-3-254-0033
Fax: 60-3-255-0827

MINISTRY OF ENERGY, TELECOMMU-NICATIONS AND POSTS
YB Dato' Seri S. Samy Vellu, Minister
1st Floor, Wisma Damansara
Jalan Semantan
59668 Kuala Lumpur
Tel: 60-3-256-2222
Fax: 60-3-255-7901

MINISTRY OF SCIENCE, TECHNOL-OGY & ENVIRONMENT
YB Datuk Law Hieng Ding, Minister
14th Floor, Wisma Sime Darby
Jalan Raja Laut, Kuala Lumpur
Tel: 60-3-293-8955
Fax: 60-3-392-6006

MINISTRY OF WORKS
YB Datuk Leo Moggie Anak Irok, Minister
TJalan Sultan Salahuddin
50580 Kuala Lumpur
Tel: 60-3-291-9011
Fax: 60-3-292-1202

MALAYSIAN INDUSTRIAL DEVELOP-MENT AGENCY (MIDA)
YBhg Tan Sri Datuk Zainal
Abidin Sulong, Chairman
YBhg Dato' N. Sadasivan, Director General
Wisma Damansara, Jalan Semantan
P.O. Box 10618
50720 Kuala Lumpur
Tel: 60-3- 255-3633
Fax: 60-3- 255-7970

COUNTRY TRADE ASSOCIATIONS/ CHAMBERS OF COMMERCE

AMERICAN - MALAYSIAN CHAMBER OF COMMERCE (AMCHAM)
John H. Hawes, Executive Director
11.03 AMODA, 22, Jalan Imbi
Kuala Lumpur
Tel: 60-3-248-2540
Fax: 60-3-242-8540

FEDERATION OF MALAYSIAN MANUFACTURERS (FMM)
Mr. Tan Keok Yin
Chief Executive Officer
17th Floor, Wisma Sime Darby
Jalan Raja Laut, 50359 Kuala Lumpur
Tel: 60-3-293-1244
Fax: 60-3-293-5105

MALAYSIAN INTERNATIONAL CHAMBER OF COMMERCE & INDUSTRY
Peter J. L. Jenkins, Executive Director
Wisma Damansara
P.O. Box 10192
50706 Kuala Lumpur
Tel: 60-3-254-2205
Fax: 60-3-255-4946

PITO MALAYSIA
(Private Investment and Trade Opportunities)
Goon Veiven, Director
Yee Seng Building, 7th floor
15 Jalan Raja Chulan
50200 Kuala Lumpur
Tel: 60-3-238-9491
Fax: 60-3-238-9493

COUNTRY MARKET RESEARCH FIRMS

J. WALTER THOMPSON SDN. BHD.
Jennifer Chan, Managing Director
21st Floor, Wisma Sime Darby
Jalan Raja Laut
50350 Kuala Lumpur
Tel: 60-3-291-7788
Fax: 60-3-293-9363

BURSON-MARSTELLER (M) SDN. BHD.
Monica Voon, Managing Director
11th Floor, Bangunan Getah Asli
148 Jalan Ampang
50450 Kuala Lumpur
Tel: 60-3-261-7900
Fax: 60-3-261-3828

LEO BURNETT ADVERTISING SDN. BHD.
Philip J. Fiebig, Managing Director
10th Floor, MCB Plaza
6 Changkat Raja Chulan
50200 Kuala Lumpur
Tel: 60-3-201-0998
Fax: 60-3-201-0972

LINTAS WORLDWIDE (M) SDN. BHD.
Jim Bell, Managing Director
Wisma Perdana, Jalan Dungun
Damansara Heights
50490 Kuala Lumpur
Tel: 60-3-254-5122
Fax: 60-3-255-9985

BOZELL SDN. BHD.
Robert A. Seymour, Chief Executive Officer
18A Jalan SS 22/25
47400 Petaling Jaya
Tel: 60-3-719-2332
Fax: 60-3-717-1841

OGILVY & MATHER (M) SDN. BHD.
John R. Hoyle, Group Managing Director
8th Floor, Wisma MCIS
Jalan Barat
46200 Petaling Jaya
Tel: 60-3-756-9066
Fax: 60-3-755-4572

MCCANN ERICKSON (M) SDN. BHD.
Ray A. Dempsey, Managing Director
18th floor, Menara Aik Hua
Cangkat Raja Chulan
50200 Kuala Lumpur
Tel: 60-3-230-5677
Fax: 60-3-230-5598

COUNTRY COMMERCIAL BANKS

United States exporters should encourage their Malaysian clients to seek financing assistance from banks and financial institutions in the country. The banking sector is now generally very liquid and flush with cash. Malaysian banks are expected to continue to chalk up high earning performances over the next three years as the economy continues on its strong growth path.

The banking system in Malaysia is dynamic and has developed rapidly. It comprises Bank Negara (the Central Bank), commercial banks, merchant banks, finance companies, the National Savings Bank, the Islamic Bank, development finance institutions and other financial intermediaries such as unit trusts and the provident fund. Currently, Bank of America, Citibank and Chase Manhattan Bank operate Kuala Lumpur branches, and Citibank has a Penang branch as well.

Most Malaysian banks have correspondent relationships with banks in the United States.

CHEMICAL BANK
9th Floor, Bangunan Getah Asli
148 Jalan Ampang
50450 Kuala Lumpur
Tel: 60-3-2617700

MANUFACTURERS HANOVER TRUST CO.
9th Floor, Wisma Getah Asli
148 Jalan Ampang
50450 Kuala Lumpur
Tel: 60-3-2617700

BANK BUMIPUTRA MALAYSIA BERHAD
Menara Bumiputra, Jalan Melaka
50100 Kuala Lumpur
P.O. Box 10407
50913 Kuala Lumpur
Tel: 60-3-2988011

BANK OF AMERICA NT & SA
1st Floor
Kompleks Antarabangsa
Jalan Sultan Ismail
50250 Kuala Lumpur
Tel: 60-3-2422755

BANK OF TOKYO LTD.
No. 1, Leboh Ampang
50100 Kuala Lumpur
Tel: 60-3-2389100

CITIBANK NA
28, Medan Pasar
50050 Kuala Lumpur
Tel: 60-3-2325334

CHASE MANHATTAN BANK NA
Bangunan Pernas Int.l, 2nd Floor
Jalan Sultan Ismail
50250 Kuala Lumpur
Tel: 60-3-2610011

MALAYAN BANKING BHD
Menara Maybank, Bukit Mahkamah
100 Jalan Tun Perak
50050 Kuala Lumpur
Tel: 60-3-2308833

SECURITY PACIFIC ASIAN BANK
Plaza See Hoy Chan
Jalan Raja Chulan
50200 Kuala Lumpur
Tel: 60-3-2387922

UNITED MALAYAN BANKING CORP.
Bangunan UMBC
Jalan Sultan Sulaiman
50935 Kuala Lumpur
Tel: 60-3-2305833

STANDARD CHARTERED BANK
2, Jalan Ampang
50450 Kuala Lumpur
Tel: 60-3-2326555

CITIBANK
Citibank Building
28 Medan Pasar
P.O. Box 10112,
50904 Kuala Lumpur
Tel: 60-3-232-8585
Fax: 60-3-232-8763

BANK OF AMERICA
Kompleks Antarabangsa Kuala Lumpur
P.O. Box 10950
Jalan Sultan Ismail,Kuala Lumpur
Tel: 60-3-242-2755
Fax: 60-3-248-0301

CHASE MANHATTAN BANK
Banganun Pernas International
Kuala Lumpur
Tel: 60-3-262-0011

BANK BUMIPUTRA MALAYSIA BERHAD
Menara Bumiputra,
Jalan Melaka,
50100 Kuala Lumpur
Tel: 60-3-298-8011

New York Office:
BBMB, 900 Third Avenue, 11th Floor
New York, N.Y. 10022
Tel: (212) 644-1280

BANK OF COMMERCE
6 Jalan Tun Perak,
50050 Kuala Lumpur
Tel: 60-3-292-1722
Fax: 60-3-298-6628

MALAYAN BANKING BERHAD (MAYBANK)
Menara Maybank,
Kuala Lumpur
Tel: 60-3-230-8833

UNITED MALAYAN BANKING CORPORATION BERHAD
Bangunan UMBC,
Jalan Sultan Ismail,
Kuala Lumpur
Tel: 60-3-230-5833
Fax: 60-3-232-2627

MBF FINANCE BERHAD
Plaza MBF
P.O. Box 10027,
50901 Kuala Lumpur
Tel: 60-3-261-1177
Fax: 60-3-261-8124

PUBLIC BANK BERHAD
Banganun Public Bank,
6 Jalan Sultan Sulaiman
50000 Kuala Lumpur
Tel: 60-3-274-1788
Fax: 60-3-274-2179

Malaysia (ASEAN)

U.S. EMBASSY TRADE PERSONNEL

FOREIGN COMMERCIAL SERVICE

Paul Scogna, Commercial Counselor
U.S. Embassy, Kuala Lumpur, Malaysia
376 Jalan Tun Razak, Kuala Lumpur

APO Postal Address from the US:
Commercial Section
American Embassy
APO AP 96535-5000
Tel: 60-3-248-9011
Fax: 60-3-242-1866

FOREIGN AGRICULTURE SERVICE

Kent Sisson, Agriculture Attache
U.S. Embassy, Kuala Lumpur, Malaysia
376 Jalan Tun Razak, Kuala Lumpur

APO Postal Address from the US:
Agriculture Attache
American Embassy
APO AP 96535-5000
Tel: 60-3-248-9011
Fax: 60-3-242-1866

Economic Section
Deborah Linde, Economic Counselor
John Wecker, Economic Officer
Daniel Martinez, Economic Officer
Daniel Moore, Economic Officer
U.S. Embassy, Kuala Lumpur, Malaysia
376 Jalan Tun Razak, Kuala Lumpur

APO Postal Address from the US
Economic Counselor
American Embassy
APO AP 96535-5000
Tel: 60-3-248-9011
Fax: 60-3-242-2207

U.S. - ASIA ENVIRONMENTAL PARTNERSHIP PROGRAM (US-AEP)

Cathy Fuselier, Director
Suite 20-02, Menara Tan & Tan
207 Jalan Tun Razak, Kuala Lumpur

COUNTRY CONSULATES AND TRADE OFFICES IN THE U.S.

EMBASSY OF MALAYSIA

2401 Massachusetts Ave, NW
Washington, DC 20008
Tel: 202-797-1007

Ambassador
His Excellency Dato Mohamed Abdul Majid
2701 Albermarle St., NW
Washington, DC 20008
Tel: 202-362-0400

Minister-Counselor (Deputy Chief of Mission)
Dr. Rajmah Hussain

Minister-Counselor
Mr. Zainal Abidin Jamalluddin

First Secretary (Information)
Mr. Jamaluddin Ramli

First Secretary
Mr. Ahmad Lutfi Yusoh

Second Secretary (Financial and Administrative)
Mr. Haroon Mohamed Desa

Third Secretary (Administration)
Mr. Mohamed Nasir Aris

Attache (Education)
Mr. Zainal Abidin Mohamed Yusof

Attache (Science)
Mr. Mohammad Jaaffar Ahmad

Consular Section
2407 California Street, NW
Washington, DC 20008
Tel: 202-328-2742 / 97 / 98

UNITED STATES-BASED MULTIPLIERS FOR MALAYSIA

U.S. - ASEAN COUNCIL

Ernest Z. Bower, President
1400 L. St., NW, Suite 375
Washington, D.C. 20005-3509
Tel: 202-289-1911
Fax: 202-289-0519

PACIFIC BASIN ECONOMIC COUNCIL (PBEC)

Ann R. Wise, Director General
PBEC U.S. Member Committee
1100 Connecticut Avenue, NW, Suite 1300
Washington, D.C. 20036
Tel: 202-728-0993
Fax: 202-728-099

U.S. DEPARTMENT OF COMMERCE MARKET RESEARCH AVAILABLE

Available and Forthcoming USDOC/Foreign Commercial Service (FCS) Industry Sector Analysis (ISA's):

— Air Pollution Control Measurement
  Equipment (6/93-
— Airport Security Equipment (3/94)
— Automobile Emission Control Measurement
  Equipment (12/92)
— Ball Bearings (10/90)
— Books & Magazines (5/94)
— Broadcasting Equipment (3/94)
— Cellular Phones (6/94)
— Central Office Switches: Telecom (8/92)
— Cosmetics (1/92)
— Defense Equipment (6/92)
— Digital Communication Interface
  Equipment (11/93-
— Drilling Equipment (9/92)
— Electronics Industry Production and
  Test Equipment (6/92)
— Engineering Workstations (3/92)
— Ferrous Waste and Scrap (3/92)
— Fiber Optic Transmission Equipment
  (10/92)
— Food Processing and Packaging
  Equipment (4/91)
— Golf Equipment (4/94)
— Herbicides, Plant Regulators (1/93-
— Industrial Waste Treatment Equipment
  (3/94)
— Industrial Wastewater Treatment
  Equipment (5/94)
— Inorganic Industrial Chemicals (5/94)
— Local Area Network Equipment (10/92)
— Mainframes (7/92)
— Medical Laboratory Equipment (4/92)
— Networking Software (4/94)
— Oil & Gas Pipeline Systems/Equipment
  (4/93-
— Petrochemicals (1/92)
— Pharmaceutical Intermediates (3/93-
— Plastic Injection, Extrusion and Blow
  Moulding Machines (1/92)
— Pollution Control Chemicals (3/93-
— Pollution Control Equipment (3/92)

— Provitamins & Vitamins (12/90)
— Semiconductor Production Equipment (5/94)
— Software (9/92)
— Taps, Cocks, and Valves (10/93)
— Telecommunications Cables (8/92)
— Transmission and Distribution Electric Equipment (3/93-
— Value Added Networks (12/92)
— Woodworking (1/93-

Forthcoming ISA's for Fiscal Year 1995:

— Personal Computers and PC Peripherals
— Business and Financial Software
— Industrial Organic Chemicals
— Surgical Appliances/Supplies
— Metal Cutting Machine Tools
— Food Processing and Packaging Equipment
— Cosmetics
— Sewage Treatment Equipment
— Drilling and Boring Machinery and Tools
— Fitness and Gymnasium Equipment
— Oil Spill Recovery Equipment

Available and Forthcoming USDA/Foreign Agricultural Service Commodity Reports and Market Briefs:

— Cocoa report
— Grain and feed report
— Oilseeds and products report
— Sugar report
— Tobacco report
— Forest products report
— General agriculture report
— Malaysia Market Profile for *"High-Value and High-Value-Added Products"* by D. Richmond & Associates.

TRADE EVENT SCHEDULE

U.S. Department of Agriculture, Foreign Agriculture Service:

SEPTEMBER 24 - 27, 1995
Food & Hotel Malaysia (FHM '95)
Kuala Lumpur, Malaysia

SEPTEMBER 21- 24, 1995
Food and Hotel Malaysia Trade Show
Kuala Lumpur, Malaysia
Contact: T. Jones, Tel: 202-690-1182

SEPTEMBER 24, 1995
Malaysia National Productivity Corporation

OCTOBER 3, 1995
Mission to the United States
Milpitas, CA; Memphis, TN; Boston, MA; Schaumburg, IL; Washington, DC
Contact: Yin Lim Star,U.S. ASEAN Council
Tel: 202-289-1911

OCTOBER 9-20, 1995
Small and Medium-Sized Business Mission to Southeast Asia
Manila, Philippines; Bangkok, Thailand; Jakarta, Indonesia; Kuala Lumpur, Malaysia
Contact: Steven Patillo, U.S.-ASEAN Council
Tel: 202-289-1911

NOVEMBER 1-5, 1995
BIMP-EAGA Exposition and Forum
Brunei, Indonesia, Malaysia, Philippines-East ASEAN Growth Area
Contact: Steven Patillo, U.S.-ASEAN Council
Tel: 202-289-1911

DECEMBER 5-10, 1995
Lima '95
Langkawi, Malaysia
Contact: Betty Smith, Dept. of Commerce (202) 482-0106 or Tony Largay, Dept. of Commerce
Tel: 202-482-2835

APRIL 1, 1996
Electric Power Generation /Transmission
Kuala Lumpur, Malaysia and Jakarta, Indonesia
Contact: Molly Costa , Tel: 202-482-0692

MAY 14 - 18, 1996
State of Pennsylvania Trade Mission to Indonesia and Malaysia
Contact: Deborah Doherty, Tel: 717-255-3252

AUGUST 1996
Computer Software Trade Mission
Singapore, Kuala Lumpur, Malaysia
Contact: Heidi Hijikata , Tel: 202-482-0569

AUGUST 20 - 21, 1996
Computer Software Trade Mission
Singapore, Kuala Lumpur, Malaysia
Contact: Heidi Hijikata, Dept. of Commerce
Tel: 202-482-0569

INFORMATION CHECKLIST AND BIBLIOGRAPHY

PERIODICALS

Asian Wall Street Journal
Far Eastern Economic Review

BOOKS

A History of Malaysia, Barbara Watson and Leonard Y. Andaya

Area Handbook for Malaysia, John W. Henderson, et.al.

The Cultural Heritage of Malaysia, N.J. Ryan

Islamic Resurgence in Malaysia, Muzaffar Chandra

The Malay Dilemma, Datuk Seri Mahatir bin Mohammed

Malaysia and Singapore: The Building of New States, Stanley S. Bedlington

Malaysian Customs and Etiquette: A Practical Handbook, Noor Ainu Syed Amin

Malaysian Politics: The Second Generation, Gordon P. Means

Malaysia (ASEAN)

Resources: Mexico

COUNTRY GOVERNMENT AGENCIES

**SECRETARIA DE COMERCIO Y
FOMENTO INDUSTRIAL (SECOFI)**
(Secretariat of Commerce and Industrial
Development)
Dr. Pedro Noyola
Under Secretary of Foreign Trade and Investment
Alfonso Reyes 30, Piso 9
Colonia Hipodromo-Condesa
06140 Mexico, D.F.
Tel: 52-5-729-91-00
Fax: 52-5-729-93-43

Lic. Luis Guillermo Ibarra
Director General of Standards
Puente de Tecamachalco 1
Lomas de Tecamachalco
53950 Naucalpan, Edo. de Mexico
Tel: 52-5-729-93-00/9475/76
Fax: 52-5-729-94-84

**INSTITUTO MEXICANO DE LA
PROPIEDAD INDUSTRIAL Y
DESARROLLO TECNOLOGICO**
(Mexican Institute of Industrial Property and
Technological development)
Lic. Jorge Amigo Castañeda
Director General
Azafran 18, Piso 3
Colonia Granjas Mexico
08400 Mexico, D.F.
Tel: 52-5-650-49-28
Fax: 52-5-654-07-71

**SECRETARIA DE EDUCACION
PUBLICA (SEP)**
(Secretariat of Public Education)
Lic. Carmen Quintanilla Madero
Director General of Copyrights
Mariano Escobedo 438, 4o Piso
Colonia Nueva Anzures
11590 Mexico, D.F.
Tel: 52-5-250-03-80
Fax: 52-5-203-15-84

**SECRETARIA DE ENERGIA, MINAS E
INDUSTRIA PARAESTATAL (SEMIP)**
(Secretariat of Energy, Mines and Parastatal In-
dustry)
Lic. Carlos Perez Garcia
Under Secretary of Mines and Parastatal
Industry
Avenida Insurgentes 552, 3er Piso
Colonia Roma Sur
06769 Mexico, D.F.
Tel: 52-5-564-96-51
Fax: 52-5-564-96-40

Ing. Alfredo Elias Ayub
Under Secretary of Hydrocarbons
Avenida Insurgentes 552, 3er Piso
Colonia Roma Sur
06769 Mexico, D.F.
Tel: 52-5-584-65-33
Fax: 52-5-574-35-94

**SECRETARIA DE MEDIO AMBIENTE,
RECURSOS NATURALES Y PESCO
(SEMARNAP)**
(Secretrait for the Environment, Natural
Resources and Fisheries)
Ing. Gabriel Quadri de la Torré
President National Institue of Ecology
Rio Elba 20, Piso 16
Colonia Cuauhtemoc
06500 Mexico, D.F.
Tel: 52-5-553-95-38
Fax: 52-5-286-66-25

Lic. Antonio Azuela de la Cueva
Federal Attorney for Protection of
the Environment
Insurgentes Sur 1480 Piso 4
Colonia Barrio Acitpan
Delegación Benito Juarez
03230 Mexico, D.F.
Tel: 52-5-524-2124
Fax: 52-5-534-7559

**SECRETARIA DE DESARROLLO
SOCIAL (SEDESOL)**
(Secretariat of Social Development)
Lic. Alfredo Phillips Olmedo
Under Secretary of Housing
Avenida Constituyentes 947,
Edif. C, Planta Alta
Colonia Belen de las Flores
01110 Mexico, D.F.
Tel: 52-5-271-28-44
Fax: 52-5-271-16-59

**SECRETARIA DE COMUNICACIONES
Y TRANSPORTE (SCT)**
(Secretariat of Communications and Transport)
Lic. Andres Massieu Berlanga
Under Secretary of Communications and Tech-
nological Development
Centro Nacional SCT
Edificio "C", 1er Piso
Xola y Avenida Universidad
Colonia Narvarte
03028 Mexico, D.F.
Tel: 52-5-530-30-60/538-0945/519-5201/0680
Fax: 52-5-559-8708

C.P. Gustavo Patiño Guerrero
Under Secretary of Transportation
Centro Nacional SCT
Edificio "C", 1er Piso, Ala Oriente
Xola y Avenida Universidad
Colonia Narvarte
03028 Mexico, D.F.
Tel: 52-5-530-30-60/559-51-65/530-73-90/
519-44-68
Fax: 52-5-519-48-71

Dr. Rogelio Gasca Neri
Under Secretary of Infrastructure
Centro Nacional SCT
Edificio "C", 1er Piso, Ala Oriente
Xola y Avenida Universidad
Colonia Narvarte
03028 Mexico, D.F.

COUNTRY TRADE ASSOCIATIONS/ CHAMBERS OF COMMERCE

AMERICAN CHAMBER OF COMMERCE OF MEXICO, A.C.
Mr. Brendan Hudson
Director of International Trade and Investment
Lucerna 78
Colonia Juarez
06600 Mexico, D.F.
Tel: 52-5-724-38-00
Fax: 52-5-703-29-11

UNITED STATES HISPANIC CHAMBER OF COMMERCE
Mr. Hector X. Porras
Director of International Affairs
CONCANACO-SERVYTUR
Balderas 144, Piso 3
Colonia Centro
06079 Mexico, D.F.
Tel: 52-5-709-03-73
Fax: 52-5-709-11-52

CAMARA NACIONAL DE COMERCIO DE LA CIUDAD DE MEXICO (CANACO)
(National Chamber of Commerce of Mexico City)
Lic. Roman Vidal Tamayo
Director of Foreign Trade
Paseo de la Reforma 42
Colonia Centro
06048 Mexico, D.F.
Tel: 52-5-705-04-24
Fax: 52-5-705-53-10

CONFEDERACION DE CAMARAS NACIONALES DE COMERCIO (CONCANACO)
(Confederation of National Chambers of Commerce)
Lic. Jose de Jesus Castellanos Lopez
Director General
Balderas 144, Piso 3
Colonia Centro
06079 Mexico, D.F.
Tel: 52-5-709-15-59
Fax: 52-5-709-11-52

CAMARA NACIONAL DE LA INDUSTRIA DE LA TRANSFORMACION
(National Manufacturing Industry Chamber)
Lic. Luis Miguel Pando Leyva
Executive Director
Avenida San Antonio 256
Colonia Ampliacion Napoles
03849 Mexico, D.F.
Tel: 52-5-563-34-00
Fax: 52-5-598-94-67

CONFEDERACION DE CAMARAS INDUSTRIALES DE LOS ESTADOS UNIDOS MEXICANOS (CONCAMIN)
(Confederation of Industrial Chambers of Mexico)
Lic. Armando Cobos Perez
Director General
Manuel Ma. Contreras 133, Piso 2
Colonia San Rafael
06570 Mexico, D.F.
Tel: 52-5-566-78-22
Fax: 52-5-535-68-71

ASOCIACION NACIONAL DE IMPORTADORES Y EXPORTADORES DE LA REPUBLICA MEXICANA (ANIERM)
(Association of Importers and Exporters of Mexico)
Ing. Juan Autrique Gomez
Director General
Monterrey 130
Colonia Roma
Tel: 52-5-584-95-22
Fax: 52-5-584-53-17

COUNTRY MARKET RESEARCH FIRMS

A.C. NIELSEN COMPANY
Sr. Roberto O. Pedraza P.
Commercial Manager
Blvd. Manuel Avila Camacho 191-7
Colonia Polanco
11510 Mexico, D.F.
Tel: 52-5-395-03-99
Fax: 52-5-580-1957

ARTHUR D. LITTLE DE MEXICO, S.A.
Lic. Andrew Wigard
General Manager
Sinaloa 149, Piso 10
Colonia Roma Norte
06700 Mexico, D.F.
Tel: 52-5-208-75-64
Fax: 52-5-207-75-92

BIMSA, S.A. DE C.V.
Lic. Cesar Ortega de la Roquette
President and Director General
Ingenieros Militares No. 91
Colonia Lomas de Sotelo
11200 Mexico, D.F.
Tel: 52-5-395-21-81
Fax: 52-5-395-86-48

BURO DE INVESTIGACION DE MERCADO, S.A.
Lic. Cesar Ortega Gomez
President and Director General
Avenida Irrigacion No. 108
Colonia Irrigacion
11500 Mexico, D.F.
Tel: 52-5-557-26-43
Fax: 52-5-557-14-40

IMOP-GALLUP DE MEXICO, S.A. DE C.V.
Lic. Gaston Kerriou
Executive Director
Aspergulas 22
Colonia San Clemente Las Aguilas
01740 Mexico, D.F.
Tel: 52-5-593-49-62
Fax: 52-5-593-49-62

INFOTEC
Dr. Irma de la Torre
Executive Director
Avenida San Fernando 37
Colonia Toriello Guerra-Tlalpan
14050 Mexico, D.F.
Tel: 52-5-606-00-11 Exts. 1021/1025
Fax: 52-5-66-03-86

Mexico

NEWELL, ARANO Y ASOCIADOS, S.A. DE C.V.
Sr. Polux Arano Diaz de la Serna
Director General
Avenida Cuernavaca 43
Colonia Condesa
06140 Mexico, D.F.
Tel: 52-5-211-82-95
Fax: 52-5-211-82-62

MARKETING SERVICES MEXICANA, S.A.
Dr. Fabiola Triguro
Director General
Blvd. Adolfo Lopez Mateos 138, 1er Piso
Colonia Merced Gomez
03930 Mexico, D.F.
Tel: 52-5-651-38-64
Fax: 52-5-660-49-36

ORGANIZACION MEVA, S.A. DE C.V.
Mr. Alfred Pepping
Director General
Nicolas San Juan 26, 3er Piso
Colonia Del Valle
03100 Mexico, D.F.
Tel: 52-5- 639-41-71
Fax: 52-5- 639-41-71

NORRIS & ELLIOTT, S.A. DE C.V.
Ing. Agustin Pesquiera
President
Leibnitz 11, 4o Piso
Colonia Veronica Anzures
11590 Mexico, D.F.
Tel: 52-5-254-64-02
Fax: 52-5-254-64-34

TECHNOMIC DE MEXICO, S.A.
Sr. Roberto Diaz Welsh
Director General
Rio Guadalquivir 50, Piso 3
Colonia Cuauhtemoc
06500 Mexico, D.F.
Tel: 52-5-208-13-25
Fax: 52-5-207-47-38

WILSA, S.A.
Sr. Wilbert Sierra
Director General
Cozumel 60
Colonia Condesa
05140 Mexico, D.F.
Tel: 52-5-286-15-31
Fax: 52-5-286-94-57

SR. GUILLERMO SUAREZ Y FARIAS
Independent Market Research Contractor
Salvador Alvarado 39
Colonia Escandon
Tel: 52-5-516-78-92

LIC. CAROLINE VERUT
Independent Market Research Contractor
Avenida Parque Mexico
Colonia Hipodromo
06100 Mexico, D.F.
Tel: 52-5-584-22-79

LIC. MARIO YANDIOLA/LIC. OMAR GONZALEZ
Independent Market Research Contractors
Prolongacion Division del Norte
Andador 24, Casa 33
Colonia Villa Coapa
14390 Mexico, D.F.
Tel: 52-5-594-72-59
Fax: 52-5-673-06-79

COUNTRY COMMERCIAL BANKS

BANCO NACIONAL DE MEXICO, S.A. (BANAMEX)
Sr. James G. Strachen T.
Executive
Import Financing Division
Palma 43, 3er Piso
Colonia Centro
06089 Mexico, D.F.
Tel: 52-5-225-65-08
Fax: 52-5-225-53-89

BANCOMER
Lic. Dorotea Ortiz Markevics
Deputy Director
Eximbank Financing
Avenida Universidad 1200
Colonia Xoco
03339 Mexico, D.F.
Tel: 52-5-621-34-34 Exts: 3860/1175
Fax: 52-5-621-76-35

BANCA SERFIN
Lic. Jose Manuel Ezeta Gonzalez
Manager of U.S. and Canada
Financial Institutions and International
Negotiations
Avenida Ricardo Margain 380, 1er Piso
Colonia Valle del Campestre
Garza Garcia, NL
Tel: 52-83-18-40-10
Fax: 52-83-18-40-07

BANCO INTERNACIONAL
Lic. Mauricio Alaimo
Special Executive
International Area
Paseo de la Reforma 156, Piso 16
Colonia Juarez
06600 Mexico, D.F.
Tel: 52-5-721-27-33
Fax: 52-5-721-23-93

MULTIBANCO COMERMEX
Lic. Martha Alonso
Manager of International Financing
Lorenzo Boturini 206, 1er Piso
Colonia Transito
06820 Mexico, D.F.
Tel: 52-5-229-16-78
Fax: 52-5-728-17-95

BANCO DEL ATLANTICO
Lic. Gilberto Franquebalme
Deputy Director of International Relations
Avenida Hidalgo 128
Coyoacan
04030 Mexico, D.F.
Tel: 52-5-626-10-55
Fax: 52-5-626-17-47

It should be noted that this is just a partial listing of Mexican commercial banks. There are many more national and regional banks.

U.S. EMBASSY/CONSULATE TRADE PERSONNEL

U.S. EMBASSY, MEXICO CITY
Mr. Kevin C. Brennan
Minister-Counselor
and/or
Mr. John Harris
Commercial Counselor
Paseo de la Reforma 305
Colonia Cuauhtemoc
06500 Mexico, D.F.
Tel: 52-5-211-00-42, Ext. 3730
Fax: 52-5-207-88-37
Mail: P.O. Box No. 3087
Laredo, TX 78044-3087

U.S. TRADE CENTER, MEXICO CITY
Mr. Robert W. Miller
Director
Liverpool 31
Colonia Juarez
06600 Mexico, D.F.
Tel: 52-5-591-01-55
Fax: 52-5-566-11-15
Mail: P.O. Box No. 3087
Laredo, TX 78044-3087

U.S. AGRICULTURAL TRADE OFFICE
Mr. Marvin Lehrer
Director
Edificio Virreyes, PH-2
Monte Pelvoux 220
Lomas de Chapultepec
11000 Mexico, D.F.
Tel: 52-5-202-04-34
Fax: 52-5-202-05-28
Mail: P.O. Box No. 3087
Laredo, TX 78044-3087

U.S. CONSULATE GENERAL, MONTERREY
Mr. Robert Jones
Commercial Officer
Avenida Constitucion 411 PTE
64000 Monterrey, NL
Tel: 52-83-45-21-20
Fax: 52-83-42-51-72
Mail: P.O. Box No. 3098
Laredo, TX 78044-3098

U.S. CONSULATE, GUADALAJARA
Mr. Bryan Smith
Commercial Officer
Progreso 175
44100 Guadalara, Jalisco
Tel: (011-52-3) 625-29-98
Fax: (011-52-3) 625-35-76
Mail: P.O. Box No. 3088
Laredo, TX 78044-3088

U.S. STATE TRADE OFFICES IN MEXICO
Arizona
Sr. Jorge Mejia
Director General
Edificio Plaza Caballito, 7o Piso
Paseo de la Reforma 10
Colonia Centro
06500 Mexico, D.F.
Tel: 011-52-5-566-98-50
Fax: 011-52-5-566-96-42

California
Mr. R.C. Schrader
Director General
Paseo de la Reforma 450, 4o Piso
Colonia Juarez
06600 Mexico, D.F.
Tel: 011-52-5-208-51-61
Fax: 011-52-5-208-57-61

Connecticut
Sr. Noe de la Flor
Director
Havre 67, Desp. 107
Colonia Juarez
06600 Mexico, D.F.
Tel: 011-52-5-525-68-07
Fax: 011-52-5-514-84-49

Florida
Sra. Guadalupe Marks Martinez
Director
Rio Marne 17, Desp. 104
Colonia Cuauhtemoc
06500 Mexico, D.F.
Tel: 011-52-5-592-31-28
Fax: 011-52-5-546-57-87

Georgia
Mr. Stephen Rosenberg
Representative
c/de Planeacion Avanzada, S.A. de C.V.
Tabasco 226, Desp. 201
Colonia Roma
06700 Mexico, D.F.
Tel: 011-52-5-207-80-11
Fax: 011-52-5-208-21-79

Idaho
Ing. Armando M. Orellana Villers
Representative
Avenida Niños Heroes 2905-6
44520 Guadalajara, Jalisco
Tel: 011-52-3-647-13-32
Fax: 011-52-3-647-12-84

Illinois
Mr. Raymundo Flores
Director General
Paseo de la Reforma 450, 4o Piso
Colonia Juarez
06600 Mexico, D.F.
Tel: 011-52-5-208-44-50
Fax: 011-52-5-511-20-84

Indiana
Lic. Alma Lilia Carreon
Director
Cerrada 2 de San Jeronimo No. 27
Colonia San Jeronimo Lidice
Mexico, D.F.
Tel: 011-52-5-595-73-75
Fax: 011-52-5-595-73-75

Louisiana
Sra. Nancy Alicia Paez
Director General
Paseo de la Reforma 107, Piso 12, Desp. 103
Colonia Revolucion
06030 Mexico, D.F.
Tel: 011-52-5-703-18-79
Fax: 011-52-5-703-28-38

Michigan
Sr. Manuel Otalora
Director General
Recreo 109
Colonia Del Valle
03100 Mexico, D.F.
Tel: 011-52-5-524-86-50
Fax: 011-52-5-524-95-00

Missouri
Sr. Oscar Gonzalez
Director General
Mexicaltzingo 2189
44150 Guadalajara, Jalisco
Tel: 011-52-3-616-62-48
Fax: 011-52-5-616-65-54

New Mexico
Mr. Jerry Pacheco
Director General
Florencia 57, 3er Piso
Colonia Juarez
06600 Mexico, D.F.
Tel: 011-52-5-208-15-15
Fax: 011-52-5-207-73-55

Oklahoma
Ms. Antoinette Allegretti
Representative
Insurgentes Sur 813, Desp. 1107
Colonia Napoles
03810 Mexico, D.F.
Tel: 011-52-5-687-39-34
Fax: 011-52-5-523-56-18

Oregon
C.P. Joaquin Frias Maures
Representative
c/de PROCORFI Consultores
Jose Maria Velasco 67
San Jose Insurgentes
03900 Mexico, D.F.
Tel: 011-52-5-687-39-34
Fax: 011-52-5-593-59-82

Mexico

Texas
Lic. Marco Delgado Licon
Director General
Paseo de la Reforma 76, Piso 15
Colonia Juarez
06600 Mexico, D.F.
Tel: 011-52-5-546-81-73
Fax: 011-52-5-546-48-30

Utah
Ms. Guadalupe M. de Escalante
Director
Amberes 33, Desp. 904
Colonia Juarez
06600 Mexico, D.F.
Tel: 011-52-5-514-77-55
Fax: 011-52-5-689-19-69

WASHINGTON-BASED USG COUNTRY CONTACTS

OFFICE OF THE NORTH AMERICAN FREE TRADE AGREEMENT (NAFTA)
Ms. Regina Vargo
Director
U.S. Department of Commerce
International Trade Administration,
14th Street & Constitution Avenue, N.W.
Room No. 3022
Washington, D.C. 20230
Tel: 202-482-0305
Fax: 202-482-5865
Flash Fax: 202-482-4464

EXPORT-IMPORT BANK OF THE UNITED STATES
Ms. Paula Swain Priestly
Loan Officer for the Americas
811 Vermont Avenue, N.W., Rm. 915
Washington, D.C. 20571
Tel: 202-565-3921
Fax: 202-565-3931

U.S. TRADE AND DEVELOPMENT AGENCY
Mr. John Herman
Project Officer
1621 N. Kent Street, Rm. 309
Rosslyn, VA 22209
Tel: (703) 875-4357
Fax: (703) 875-4009

U.S. DEPARTMENT OF STATE BUREAU OF INTER-AMERICAN AFFAIRS
Office of Mexican Affairs
Mr. Robert C. Felder
Director
21st and C Streets, N.W., Rm. 4258
Washington, D.C. 20520
Tel: 202-647-9894
Fax: 202-647-5752

OFFICE OF THE UNITED STATES TRADE REPRESENTATIVE, OFFICE OF NORTH AMERICAN AFFAIRS
Mr. John Melle
Director of Mexican Affairs
600 17th Street, N.W., Rm. 514
Washington, D.C.
Tel: 202-395-3412
Fax: 202-395-3911

U.S.-BASED MULTIPLIERS RELEVANT FOR MEXICO

UNITED STATES CHAMBER OF COMMERCE
Mr. Andrew Howell
Assistant Director, Latin American Affairs
1615 H Street, N.W.
Washington, D.C. 20062-2000
Tel: 202-463-5490
Fax: 202-463-3126

UNITED STATES-MEXICO CHAMBER OF COMMERCE
Mr. Martin Rojas
Communications Director
1730 Rhode Island Avenue, N.W., Suite 1112
Washington, D.C. 20036
Tel:202-296-5198
Fax: 202-728-0768

UNITED STATES HISPANIC CHAMBER OF COMMERCE
Mr. Jose F. Niño
President
1030 15th Street, N.W., Suite 206
Washington, D.C. 20005
Tel: 202-842-1212
Fax: 202-842-3221

COUNTRY CONSULATES AND TRADE OFFICES IN THE U.S.

EMBASSY OF MEXICO
1911 Pennsylvania Ave., N.W.
Washington, D.C. 20006
Tel: 202-728-1600
Fax: 202-728-1793

The Trade Commission of Mexico is the country's primary export promotion sgency. It maintains the following offices in the United States to assist those interested in importing from Mexico:

Chicago
255 North Michigan Avenue
Illinois Centrer, Suite 408
Chicago, IL 60601
Tel: 312-856-0316
Fax: 312-856-1834

Georgia
229 Peachtree Street, NE
Suite #708 Cain Tower Bldg.
Atlanta, GA 30343
Tel: 404-522-5373
Fax: 404-681-3361

Miami
Suite 1622
2777 Stemmons Fwy.
100 N. Biscayne Blvd.
Miami, FL 33132
Fax: 305-374-1238

Dallas
Suite 1601
New World Tower
Dallas, TX 75207
(214) 688-4096
Fax: 214-905-3831 or 305-372-9929

San Antonio
350 South Figueroa St.
Suite 409
San Antonio, TX 78213
Tel: 213-628-1220 Fax:
Fax: 213-628-8466

Los Angeles
1100 N.W. Loop 410
World trade Center
Suite 296
Los Angeles, CA 90071
Tel: 210-525-9748
Fax: 210-525-8355

New York
150 East 58th Street
17th Floor
New York, NY 10155
Tel: 212-826-2916
Fax: 212-826-2979

U.S. DEPARTMENT OF COMMERCE MARKET RESEARCH AVAILABLE

INDUSTRY SUBSECTOR ANALYSES

— Cosmetics and Perfumes (10/03/94)
— Electronics Industry Production and Testing Equipment (10/10/94)
— Agribusiness Equipment and Services (10/10/94)
— Agricultural Machinery and Equipment (10/24/94)
— Fixtures for Homes, Including Plumbing (11/07/94)
— Lighting, and Hardware Theatrical Equipment (11/12/94)
— Exercise Equipment (11/21/94)
— Auto Accessories (11/28/94)
— Food Service Equipment for Restaurants and Institutions (12/05/94)
— Electronic Components (12/09/94)
— Optical Products, Supplies & Equipment (12/16/94)
— Prefabricated Housing (12/19/94)
— Food Packaging Equipment (01/19/95)
— Telecommunications Switching Equipment (01/20/95)
— Direct Marketing (01/25/95)
— Women's Apparel (01/31/95)
— Toys (02/16/95)
— Laptop and Microcomputers (02/17/95)
— Industrial Air Pollution Control Equipment and Services (02/22/95)
— Paints and Painting Supplies (02/28/95)
— Water Sports Equipment (03/07/95)
— Food Processing Equipment for Fruits and Vegetables (03/16/95)
— Business Application Software (03/17/95)
— Business Services Franchising (03/28/95)
— Wood pallets, packaging, boxes, and supplies (04/07/95)
— Insurance for Consumers (04/14/95)
— Toxic and Hazardous Waste Equipment and Services (04/28/95)
— Personal Safety and Security Equipment (05/02/95)
— Electric Medical Equipment and Supplies (05/04/95)

— Consumer Credit (05/12/95)
— Numerically Controlled Machine Tools (05/30/95)
— Medical Disposables (06/02/95)
— Energy Saving Equipment, Systems and Services (06/09/95)
— Food Processing Equipment for Dairy Products (06/27/95)
— Intermodal Transport Equipment (06/30/95)
— Electricity Cogenerating Equipment (07/07/95)
— Sewage Treatment Equipment and Services (07/14/95)
— Kitchen Appliances (07/25/95)
— Costume and Fashion Jewelry (07/28/95)
— Men's Apparel (08/06/95)
— Information Services (08/31/95)

USDA/FAS COMODITY REPORTS AND MARKET BRIEFS

01/31/94	Ato activities & (dec)	mx94268
02/01/94	Fresh deciduous fruit semi-annual	mx94098
02/01/94	Livestock semi-annual	mx94528
03/10/94	Grain & feed annual	mx9411a
03/15/94	Foreign buyer list annual report	**
03/15/94	Strawberry annual	mx9432a
03/31/94	Tobacco annual	mx9421a
04/10/94	Oilseeds & products annual	mx9406a
04/10/94	Sugar annual	mx9419a
05/01/94	Citrus semi-annual	mx94088
05/15/94	Coffee annual	mx9403a
05/15/94	Dairy semi- annual	mx9451b
05/30/94	Tomatoes & products semi-annual	mx9422b
06/15/94	Asparagus annual	mx9424sr
06/20/94	Cotton annual	mx9404a
06/20/94	Poultry annual	mx9453a
07/01/94	Potato annual	mx9424sr
07/15/94	Annual marketing plan information report mx9462a2	
08/01/94	Livestock annual	mx9452a
08/20/94	Tree nuts annual	mx9414a
08/25/94	Honey annual	mx9425a
09/01/94	Fresh deciduous fruit annual	mx9409a
09/15/94	Cocoa annual	mx9402a
09/30/94	Agricultural situation annual	mx9424a
10/01/94	Sugar-semi- annual	mx94198
10/10/94	Tobacco semi- annual	mx94218
10/15/94	Dried fruit annual	mx9410a

10/15/94	Forest products annual	mx9455a
11/15/94	Citrus annual	mx9408a
11/15/94	Coffee semi- annual	mx9403b
11/20/94	Poultry semi- annual	mx9453b
11/30/94	Avocado annual	mx9424sr
12/10/94	Brandy annual	mx9424sr
12/10/94	Dairy annual	mx9451a
12/10/94	Wine marketing annual	mx9424sr
12/15/94	Tomatoes & products annual	mx9422a

VOLUNTARY REPORTS

Mexican frozen & regrigerated food mkt. (8/95)
Mexican mkt. fruit juices & concentrates (8/95)
Mexican mkt. confectionaries & candies (8/95)
Mexican food service distribution system (8/95)
Mexican market for seafood (7/95)
Mexican market for ornamental plants (8/95)
Mexican market for rice (8/95)
Mexican market for planting seeds (8/95)
Mexican market for cotton & wool (8/95)
Healthy foods (8/95)

TRADE EVENTS SCHEDULE

MEDILAB '95
September 19-21, 1995
U.S. Trade Center
Liverpool 31, Colonia Juarez
06600 Mexico, D.F.
Telephone: 011-52-5/591-0155 Fax: 566-1115
Exhibition and seminar on medical, diagnostic, surgical and hospital equipment, instruments, supplies and related laboratory equipment, systems, technology and services.
Cost of Participation:
$2,970 (first booth), $2,700 (aaditional booth).
To participate, contact:
Raquel Polo
U.S. Trade Center
P.O. Box 3087
Laredo, TX 78044-3087
Tel: 011/52-5/591-0155
Fax: 011/52-5/566-1115

INFORMATION CHECKLIST AND BIBLIOGRAPHY

BUSINESS GUIDES AND DIRECTORIES

The Complete Twin Plant Guide
Published by Solunet
4416 North Mesa
El Paso, Texas 79902
Tel: 915-532-1166

Mexico

1993-94 METIS Sourcebook (Formerly Twin Plant News Sourcebook)
Published by Metis International, Inc.
1004 W. Agarita
San Antonio, Tx
Tel: 800-734-8328 / 800-374-7230

The U.S.-Mexico Trade Pages
Published by The Global Source, Inc.
1730 K Street, N.W., Suite 304
Washington, D.C. 20006
Tel: 202-429-5582

American Firms in Foreign Countries and Mexican Firms in the United States
World Trade Academy Press, Inc.
50 East 42nd Street
New York, N.Y. 10017
Tel: 212-697-4999

Latin American Securities and Security Dealers
Continental Inervest, Inc.
630 West 34th Street, Suite 201
Austin, Texas 78705
Tel: 512-458-9171
Fax: 512-323-9231

Access Mexico
Cambridge Data & Development Ltd.
307 N. Bryan Street
Arlington, VA 22201
Tel: 1-800-416-2382

Bancomext Trade Directory of Mexico '93
National Foreign Trade Bank
Periferico Sur #4333
Col. Jardines en la Montana
C.P. 14210 , Mexico, D.F.
Tel: 227-9008 / 227-9009; 1-800-835-7480
Fax: 227-9070

Doing Business in Mexico
Price Waterhouse
1251 Avenue of the Americas
New York, NY 10020
Tel: 212-819-5000

Doing Business in Mexico
Ernst & Young International
787 Seventh Avenue
New York, NY 10019
Copies available to member firms

International Tax and Business Guide - Mexico
Deloitte Touche Tohmatsu International
1633 Broadway
New York, NY 10019-6754
Tel: 212-489-1600

Specialized Telephone Directories in Mexico
Bolles Publishing Co.
5290 McNutt Road, Suite 210; P.O. Box 321
Santa Teresa, NM 88008
Tel: 505-589-2100
Fax: 505-589-2500

MAGAZINES

Business Mexico
Published by American Chamber of Commerce in Mexico
Lucerna 78
Colonia Juarez
Delegacion Cuauhtemoc
06600 Mexico D.F. Mexico
Tel: 525-705-0995

Latin Finance
2121 Ponce de Leon Boulevard, Suite 1020
Coral Gables, Florida 33134
Tel: 305-448-6593

Maquila Newsletter
Published by American Chamber of Commerce of Mexico, S.A.
Camara American de Mexico, S.A.
Lucerna 78, Piso 3 y 4
06040 Mexico D.F.
Mexico
Tel: 525-705-0995

Twin Plant News
Published by Nibbe, Hernandez and Associates, Inc.
4110 Rio Bravo Dr., Suite 108
El Paso, Texas 79902
Tel: 800-880-1123 or 915-532-1567

Maquila Magazine: Voice of Free Trade
Published by Joanne Gwinn Burt
114 S.Oregon St.
El Paso, Texas 79001
Tel: 915-542-0103

El Financiero (Mexican financial newspaper)
(financial daily; available on weekly basis in English)
Circulation
El Financiero Weekly International Edition
2300 S. Broadway
Los Angeles, CA 90007
Tel: 213-747-2489

GENERAL NEWSLETTERS

U.S.-Mexico Free Trade Reporter
Published by Thompson-Lesser Publishing Inc.,
1725 K St. N.W.
Suite 200
Washington, D.C. 20006
Tel: 202-785-8595

Mexico - Business Monthly
Published by Kal Wagenheim
52 Maple Ave.
Maplewood, NJ 07040
Tel: 201-762-1565

Mexico Trade and Law Reporter
945 G Street, N.W.
Suite 203
Washington, D.C. 20001-4531
Tel: 202-783-4100

EnviroMexico
MSI, Inc.
905 Duncan Ln. Suite A
Austin, Texas 778705
Tel: 512-477-1021

NAFTA — Focus on Mexico
DuBach Publications, Inc
P.O. Box 2308
Rancho Mirage, CA 92270-1095
Tel: 619-773-3345
Fax: 619-773-9505

DATABASE SERVICES

Inter-American Trade and Investment Law
National Law Center for Inter-American Free Trade
255 W. Alameda, Seven East
P.O. Box 27210
Tucson, AZ 85726
Tel: 800-529-3463 or 800-LAW-FIND

Diario Oficial Service
Porter International Incorporated
P.O. Box 81488
San Diego, CA 92138
Tel: 619-661-4000

VIDEO

Doing Business in Mexico
Big World Inc.
1350 Pine Street, Suite 5
Boulder, CO 80302
Tel: 800-682-1261

STATISTICAL SOURCES

Review of the Economic Situation of Mexico
Grupo Financiero BANAMEX-ACCIVAL
Av. Madero 21
2nd Floor
Mexico, D.F. 06000
Fax: 52-5-225-0025

Estadisticas del Comercio Exteriour de Mexico (Spanish)
Instituto Nacional de Estadistica, Geografia e Informatica
Av. Heroe de Nacozari Num. 2301 Sur, Acceso 11, P.B.
Fracc. Jardines del Parque, CP 20270
Aguascalientres, Ags.
Mexico

Indicadores Economicos (Spanish)
Banco de Mexico
Direccion General de Investigacion Economica
Oficina de Servicious de Informacion
Av. Juarez No. 90, Col Centro
Delegacion Cuauhtemoc
06059 Mexico, D.F.
Tel: 52-5-761-8588 ext. 4027, 4028

Mexican Bulletin of Statistical Information
Av Heroe de Nacozari Num. 2301 Sur
Puerta 10 Acceso
Fracc. Jardines del Parque, CP 20270
Aguascalientes, Ags. Mexico
Fax: 91-49-18-07 39

Elmercadode Valores (Spanish)
MACRO ASSESORIA ECONOMICA, S.C.
Rio Amazonas No. 3
Col. Cuauhtemoc
Mexico, 06500, D.F.
Tel: 52-5-556-8900
Fax: 52-5-592-8039, 592-8245

Anuario Estadistico de Los Estados Unidos MEXICANOS (Spanish)
Instituto Nacional de Estadistica Geografia e Informatica
Av. Heroe de Nacozari Num. 2301 Sur
Fracc. Jardines del Parque, CP 20270
Aguascalientes, Ags. Mexico

OTHER INFORMATION SOURCES

Background Notes: Mexico
U.S. Department of State
Bureau of Public Affairs
Office of Public Communication
Washington D.C. 20520

Office of Mexican Affairs
Tel: 202-647-9292

Annual Report on Exchange Restrictions
International Monetary Fund
Worldwide survey of exchange regulations with section on Mexico
Publications Office
International Monetary Fund
Washington D.C. 20431
Tel: 202-623-7430

OTHER ORGANIZATIONS

U.S. CHAMBER OF COMMERCE
1615 H. St. N.W.
Washington D.C. 20062-2000
Tel: 202-463-5485
Fax: 202-463-3126

COUNCIL OF THE AMERICAS
1310 G. St. N.W., Suite 690
Washington D.C. 20005
Tel: 202-639-0724
Fax: 202-639-0794

U.S-MEXICO CHAMBER OF COMMERCE
1726 M. N.W. Suite 704
Washington D.C. 20036
Tel: 202-296-5198
Fax: 202-728-0768

AMERICAN CHAMBER OF COMMERCE - MEXICO
Lucerna 78-4
06600 Mexico, D.F. Mexico
or
P.O. Box 60326
APDO 113
Houston, TX 77205-1794
Tel: 011-525-724-3800
Fax: 011-525-703-3908 or 703-2911

Mexico

Resources: Philippines

U.S. DEPARTMENT OF COMMERCE
Ms. Jean Kelly, ASEAN Desk Officer
Herbert Hoover Building, Room 2036
14th Street and Constitution Ave, NW
Washington, DC 20230
Tel: 202-482-3448
Fax: 202-482-4453

UNITED STATES INFORMATION AGENCY
Ms. Bea Camp, Country Officer
Office of East Asian and Pacific Affairs
Room 766
301 4th Street, SW
Washington, DC 20547
Tel: 202-619-5838

U.S. BUREAU OF MINES
Mr. Travis Lyday
810 7th Street, NW
Washington, DC 20241
Tel: 202-501-9695
Fax: 202-219-2489

COUNTRY GOVERNMENT AGENCIES

AIR TRANSPORTATION OFFICE
NAIA Road
Pasay City
Metro Manila
Contact: Capt. Panfilo Villaruel, Assistant
Secretary
Tel: 632-832-3308
Fax: 632-833-0125

BANGKO SENTRAL NG PILIPINAS
(Central Bank of the Philippines)
A. Mabini
Malate
Manila
Contact: Mr. Gabriel C. Singson, Governor
Tel: 632-507-051; 593-380 to 81
Fax: 632-522-3987

BASES CONVERSION DEVELOPMENT AUTHORITY
2nd Floor, Rufino Center
Ayala Avenue corner Herrera Street
Makati City 1200
Contact: Dr. Victor A. Lim, Chairman
Tel: 632-813-5383 to 84
Fax: 632-813-5424; 813-5427

BOARD OF INVESTMENTS
Investment and Marketing Department
385 Sen. Gil J. Puyat Avenue
Makati City
Contact: Mr. Efren Leano, Director
Tel: 632-897-6682; 890-1996; 895-3982
Fax: 632-895-3521

BUREAU OF CUSTOMS
Port Area
Manila
Contact: Mr. Guillermo Parayno, Commissioner
Tel: 632-471-329; 474-421
Fax: 632-530-0966

BUREAU OF EXPORT TRADE PROMOTION
Department of Trade and Industry
357 Sen. Gil Puyat Avenue
Makati
Metro Manila
Contact: Mr. Cesar N. Atienza, Director
Tel: 632-817-5298; 817-5203
Fax: 632-817-4923; 819-1816

BUREAU OF FOOD AND DRUGS
DOH Compound
Alabang
Muntinlupa
Contact: Dr. Quintin Kintanar, Director
Tel: 632-842-4583
Fax: 632-842-4603

BUREAU OF INTERNAL REVENUE
Don Mariano Marcos Avenue
Quezon City
Contact: Ms. Liwayway V. Chato, Commissioner
Tel: 632-977-602
Fax: 632-922-4894

BUREAU OF INTERNATIONAL TRADE RELATIONS
Department of Trade and Industry
361 Sen. Gil J. Puyat Avenue
Contact: Mr. Cesar Bautista, Undersecretary
Tel: 632-817-9695
Fax: 632-818-7846

BUREAU OF PATENTS, TRADEMARKS AND TECHNOLOGY TRANSFER
Department of Trade and Industry
361 Sen. Gil J. Puyat Avenue
Makati City
Contact: Ignacio S. Sapalo, Director
Tel: 632-815-4919; 818-3109
Fax: 632-818-4145

BUREAU OF PLANT INDUSTRY
Department of Agriculture
692 San Andres
Malate
Manila
Contact: Mr. Nerius I. Roperos, Director
Tel: 632-571-726; 571-776; 586-201
Fax: 632-810-9363

BUREAU OF TRADE REGULATION AND CONSUMER PROTECTION
Department of Trade and Industry
2nd Floor, Trade & Industry Bldg.
361 Sen. Gil Puyat Avenue
Makati
Metro Manila
Contact: Ms. Lucia Aquino, Director
Tel: 632-817-5280; 817-5340
Fax: 632-810-9363

CIVIL AERONAUTICS BOARD
Old MIA Road
Pasay City
Metro Manila
Contact: Atty. Silvestre Pascual, Executive
Director
Tel: 632-833-6911; 833-7248
Fax: 632-833-7266

CONSTRUCTION INDUSTRY AU-THORITY OF THE PHILIPPINES

6th Floor, Finman Bldg.
Tordesillas Street
Salcedo Village
Makati City
Contact: Ms. Alicia A. Tiongson,
Executive Director
Tel: 632-817-1230; 815-0710
Fax: 632-818-1573

DEPARTMENT OF AGRICULTURE

Elliptical Road
Diliman
Quezon City
Contact: Mr. Roberto S. Sebastian, Secretary
Tel: 632-998-741 to 65
Fax: 632-978-183

DEPARTMENT OF ENERGY

PNPC Complex
Merritt Road
Fort Bonifacio
Makati City
Contact: Mr. Francisco L. Viray, Secretary
Tel: 632-844-1021 to 29
Fax: 632-817-8603

DEPARTMENT OF ENVIRONMENT AND NATURAL RESOURCES

Visayas Avenue
Diliman
Quezon City
Contact: Mr. Victor O. Ramos, Acting
Secretary
Tel: 632-924-2540; 990-691 to 93
Fax: 632-922-6991

DEPARTMENT OF HEALTH

San Lazaro Compund
Rizal Avenue
Sta. Cruz
Manila
Contact: Dr. Juan M. Flavier, Secretary
Tel: 632-711-6080; 711-9502; 711-9503
Fax: 632-711-9509

DEPARTMENT OF INTERIOR AND LOCAL GOVERNMENT

PNCC Bldg.
EDSA cor. Reliance Street
Mandaluyong City
Contact: Mr. Rafael M. Alunan, Secretary
Tel: 632-633-1865; 631-8829; 634-8718
Fax: 632-631-8830

DEPARTMENT OF LABOR AND EMPLOYMENT

DOLE Executive Bldg.
San Jose Street
Intramuros
Manila
Contact: Mr. Jose S. Brillantes, Acting
Secretary
Tel: 632-527-3466
Fax: 632-527-3568

DEPARTMENT OF NATIONAL DEFENSE

Camp Aguinaldo
EDSA
Quezon City
Contact: Gen. Renato S. de Villa, Secretary
Tel: 632-911-6183; 911-6193
Fax : 632-911-6213

DEPARTMENT OF PUBLIC WORKS AND HIGHWAYS

Bonifacio Drive
Port Area
Manila
Contact: Mr. Gregorio Vigilar, Secretary
Tel: 632-473-308
Fax: 632-401-551

DEPARTMENT OF SCIENCE AND TECHNOLOGY

Gen. Santos Avenue
Bicutan
Taguig
Metro Manila
Contact: Mr. William G. Padolina, Secretary
Tel: 632-837-2071 to 75
Fax: 632-837-2939

DEPARTMENT OF TOURISM

T.M. Kalaw Street
Manila
Contact: Mr. Vicente L. Carlos, Secretary
Tel: 632-599-031
Fax: 632-521-7274; 521-7373

DEPARTMENT OF TRADE AND INDUSTRY

4th Floor, BOI Bldg.
385 Sen. Gil Puyat Avenue
Makati City
Contact: Mr. Rizalino S. Navarro, Secretary
Tel: 632-816-0121; 818-456
Fax: 632-851-166

DEPARTMENT OF TRANSPORTATION AND COMMUNICATIONS

3rd Floor, Philcomcen Bldg.
Ortigas Avenue
Pasig City
Contact: Mr. Jesus Garcia, Secretary
Tel: 632-631-8761 to 63
Fax: 632-631-9985

ENVIRONMENTAL MANAGEMENT BUREAU

Topaz Bldg.
Kamias Road
Quezon City
Contact: Mr. Carlos Tumboc, Director
Tel: 632-924-7540
Fax: 632-924-8553

EXPORT PROCESSING ZONE AUTHORITY

4th Floor, Legaspi Towers 300
Roxas Blvd.
Metro Manila
Contact: Tagumpay Jardiniano, Administrator
Tel: 632-521-9725; 521-0419; 521-0547
Fax: 632-521-8659

GARMENT AND TEXTILES EXPORT BOARD

4th Floor, New Solid Building
357 Puyat Avenue
Makati City
Contact: Ms. Escolatica Segovia,
Executive Director
Tel: 632-817-4321; 817-4323
Fax: 632-817-4339

Philippines (ASEAN)

INSURANCE COMMISSION
1071 UN Avenue
Manila
Contact: Ms. Adelita A. Vergel de Dios,
Commissioner
Tel: 632-583-534; 574-886; 599-221
Fax: 632-522-1434

LAND TRANSPORTATION OFFICE
East Avenue
Quezon City
Contact: Ret. Brig. Gen. Manuel Bruan,
Asst. Secretary
Tel: 632-922-9061 to 65
Fax: 632-921-9072

LIGHT RAIL TRANSIT AUTHORITY
Administrative Building, LRT Compound
Aurora Boulevard
Pasay City
Contact: Mr. Alberto Arevalo,
Jr. Administrator
Tel: 632-832-0423
Fax: 632-831-6449

LOCAL WATER UTILITIES
ADMINISTRATION
MWSS-LWUA Complex
Katipunan Road
Balara
Quezon City
Contact: Mr. Antonio de Vera, Administrator
Tel: 632-976-107; 976-203
Fax: 632-922-3434

METROPOLITAN WATERWORKS
AND SEWERAGE SYSTEM
Katipunan Road
Balara
Quezon City
Contact: Mr. Teofilo I. Asuncion,
Administrator
Tel: 632-922-3757; 922-2969
Fax: 632-921-2887

NATIONAL AGRICULTURE AND
FISHERY COUNCIL
Department of Agriculture
Elliptical Road
Diliman
Quezon City
Contact: Mr. Luis T. Villareal, Jr.,
Executive Director
Tel: 632-962-2706; 978-234
Fax: 632-922-8622

NATIONAL COMPUTER CENTER
Camp Gen. Emilio Aguinaldo
Cubao
Quezon City
Contact: Col. Fermin Javier, Managing
Director
Tel: 632-797-631
Fax: 632-781-172

NATIONAL ECONOMIC AND
DEVELOPMENT AUTHORITY
Amber Avenue
Ortigas Complex
Pasig City
Contact: Mr. Cielito Habito, Director
Tel: 632-631-3716; 631-0945 to 64
Fax: 632-631-3747

NATIONAL ELECTRIFICATION
ADMINISTRATION
3rd Floor, D & E Bldg.
1050 Quezon Ave.
Quezon City
Contact: Mr. Teodorico Sanchez, Administrator
Tel: 632-922-9009; 922-5688
Fax: 632-922-9058

NATIONAL HOUSING AUTHORITY
Quezon Memorial Elliptical Road
Diliman
Quezon City
Contact: Mr. Roberto Balao, General Manager
Tel: 632-921-7828; 978-016
Fax: 632-921-0444

NATIONAL IRRIGATION
ADMINISTRATION
2nd Floor, NIA Building
EDSA
Quezon City
Contact: Mr. Apolonio V. Bautista, Administrator
Tel: 632-922-2795
Fax: 632-962-846

NATIONAL MEAT INSPECTION
COMMISSION (NMIC)
Bureau of Animal Industry
Visayas Avenue
Diliman
Quezon City
Contact: Mr. Manuel D. Rocha, Executive
Director
Tel: 632-921-3119
Fax: 632-924-3118

NATIONAL POWER CORPORATION
BIR Road cor. Quezon Ave. and Agham Road
Diliman
Quezon City
Contact: Mr. Guido Alfredo A. Delgado,
President
Tel: 632-921-2998; 921-3541/80
Fax: 632-922-4339

NATIONAL STATISTICS AND
COORDINATING BOARD
2nd Floor, Midland Buendia Bldg.
Sen. Gil Puyat Avenue, Ext.
Makati City
Contact: Dr. Romulo A. Virola, Secretary-
General
Tel: 632-851-778
Fax: 632-816-6941

NATIONAL TELECOMMUNICATIONS
COMMISSION
856 Vibal Bldg.
EDSA cor. Times Street
Quezon City
Contact: Mr. Simeon L. Kintanar, Commissioner
Tel: 632-924-4008; 924-4042; 921-3251
Fax: 632-921-7128

MANILA INTERNATIONAL AIRPORT
AUTHORITY
Paranaque
Metro Manila
Ninoy Aquino International Airport (NAIA)
Contact: Mr. Francisco Atayde, General
Manager
Tel: 632-832-2938; 831-6205
Fax: 632-831-6276

PHILIPPINE NATIONAL OIL
CORPORATION, ENERGY
DEVELOPMENT CORPORATION
PNOC Building
Makati Avenue
Makati City
Contact: Mr. Monico B. Jacob, President
Tel: 632-817-5395; 859-961
Fax: 632-815-2721

PHILIPPINE PORTS AUTHORITY
Marsman Building
Gate I South Harbor
Manila
Contact: Commodore Carlos Agustin, General
Manager
Tel: 632-530-0875
Fax: 632-530-1199

**PHILIPPINE ECONOMIC
ZONE AUTHORITY**
4th Floor, Legaspi Towers 300
Roxas Boulevard
Metro Manila
Contact: Atty. Lilia de Lima, Director General
Tel: 632-521-0419; 521-0547
Fax: 632-521-8659; 521-0419

**SECURITIES AND EXCHANGE
COMMISSION**
Corporate and Legal Department
7th Floor, SEC Bldg.
EDSA Greenhills
Mandaluyong City
Contact: Ms. Sonia Ballo, Director
Tel: 632-780-931
Fax: 632-722-0990

**SUBIC BAY METROPOLITAN
AUTHORITY**
Bldg. 229
Subic Bay Freeport Port
2200 Olongapo City
Contact: Mr. Richard D. Gordon,
Administrator
Tel: (63-47) 222-5454 to 56, 384-5849
Fax: (63-47) 222-5278

TARIFF COMMISSION
5th Floor, Philippine Heart Center
East Avenue
Quezon City
Contact: Ms. Nilda D. Vasquez, Chairman
Tel: 632-921-7960; 998-419
Fax: 632-921-7960

COUNTRY TRADE ASSOCIATIONS/ CHAMBERS OF COMMERCE

**AIRCRAFT OWNERS & PILOTS
ASSOCIATION OF THE PHILIPPINES
(AOPAP)**
Andrews Avenue
Domestic Airport
Pasay City
Contact: Capt. Geronimo A. Amurao,
President
Tel: 632-833-3892
Fax: 632-833-3891

**AMERICAN CHAMBER OF
COMMERCE OF THE PHILIPPINES,
INC. (AMCHAM)**
2nd Floor, Corinthian Plaza
Paseo de Roxas
Makati City
Contact: Mr. William S. Tiffany, President
Tel: 632-818-7911 to 15
Fax: 632-816-6359

**ASSOCIATION OF CONSTRUCTION
EQUIPMENT LESSORS, INC. (ACEL)**
3rd Floor, Padilla Bldg.
Emerald Ave.
Ortigas Complex
Pasig City
Contact: Mr. Eric A. Cruz, President
Tel: 632-631-3136; 633-4994; 631-2773
Fax: 632-673-3719; 921-1223

**BANKERS ASSOCIATION OF
THE PHILIPPINES**
11th Floor, Sagitarius Bldg.
Dela Costa Street
Salcedo Village
Makati
Metro Manila
Contact: Mr. Leonilo G. Coronel, Executive
Director
Tel: 632-851-711; 810-3858; 810-3859
Fax: 632-812-2870; 810-3860

**CHAMBER OF REAL ESTATE &
BUILDERS ASSOCIATIONS, INC.
(CREBA)**
3rd Floor, CREBA Center
Don Alejandro Roces Avenue
cor. South 'A' Street
Quezon City
Contact: Mr. Charlie Gorayeb, President
Tel: 632-983-511; 983-522
Fax: 632-998-401

**CHEMICAL INDUSTRIES
ASSOCIATION OF THE PHILIPPINES**
c/o Rohm & Haas Phils., Inc.
12th Floor, PCI Tower II Bldg.
Makati Avenue
cor. H. V. dela Costa St.
Makati City
Contact: Mr. Eduardo M. Abacan, President
Tel: 632-891-2140; 815-2088
Fax: 632-891-2140

**COMPUTERS DISTRIBUTORS AND
DEALERS ASSOCIATION OF THE
PHILIPPINES (COMDDAP)**
7th Floor, SEDCCO I Bldg.
Legaspi cor. Rada Streets
Legaspi Village
Makati City
Contact: Mr. Salvador L. Lastrilla, President
Tel: 632-810-3814
Fax: 632-815-6531

**CONFEDERATION OF FILIPINO
CONSULTING ORGANIZATIONS,
INC. (COFILCO)**
95 Maginoo Street
Diliman
Quezon City
Contact: Engr. Antonio A. Mansueto,
President
Tel: 632-922-7505
Fax: 632-922-7505

**COUNCIL OF ENGINEERING
CONSULTANTS OF THE PHILIPPINES**
2283 Manila Memorial Park Bldg.
Pasong Tamo Extension
Makati City
Contact: Mr. Pablo D. Arevalo, Jr., President
Tel: 632-815-2409
Fax: 632-818-09-21

**ENERGY MANAGEMENT
ASSOCIATION OF THE PHILIPPINES**
Suite 6-H
6th Floor, Don Tim Bldg.
5468 South Superhighway
Makati
Metro Manila
Contact: Mr. Greg Gonzales, Chairman of the
Board
Tel: 632-881-753
Fax: 632-867-497

**EUROPEAN CHAMBER OF
COMMERCE OF THE PHILIPPINES**
5th Floor, Kings Court II Bldg
Pasong Tamo
Makati
Metro Manila
Contact: Mr. Henry Schumacher, Director
Tel: 632-854-747; 866-9966; 854-4747
Fax: 632-815-2688

Philippines (ASEAN)

FEDERATION OF AVIATION ORGANIZATIONS OF THE PHILIPPINES INC. (FEDAVOR)
Rm. 207, CCH Bldg.
Alfaro Street
Salcedo Village
Makati City
Contact: Capt. Douglas Macias, President
Tel: 632-818-4260; 815-6912
Fax: 632-819-0439

FEDERATION OF FILIPINO-CHINESE CHAMBERS OF COMMERCE AND INDUSTRY, INC.
6th Floor, Federation Center Bldg.
Muelle de Binondo Street
Manila
Contact: Mr. Jimmy Tang, President
Tel: 632-474-921 to 925
Fax: 632-530-1369

GARMENT BUSINESS ASSOCIATION OF THE PHILIPPINES
Room 608, Dona Narcisa Bldg.
8751 Paseo de Roxas
Makati
Metro Manila
Contact: Veronida J. Flores, President
Tel: 632-813-7418; 883-943; 883-946; 883-939

HOSPITAL, MEDICAL, LABORATORY EQUIPMENT & SUPPLY IMPORTERS ASSOCIATION OF THE PHILIPPINES, INC.
c/o 3-1 Philippines
704 Aurora Blvd.
Quezon City
Contact: Mr. Enrique Lim, President
Tel: 632-721-5211
Fax: 632-721-7012

HOTEL AND RESTAURANT ASSOCIATION OF THE PHILIPPINES
Room 205, Regina Bldg.
Aguirre Street
Legaspi Village
Makati
Metro Manila
Contact: Mr. Lorenzo J. Cruz, President
Tel: 632-815-4659
Fax: 632-815-4663

INTEGRATED TELECOMMUNICA-TIONS SUPPLIERS ASSN. OF THE PHILIPPINES
15th Floor
1501 Robinson's Galleria Corporate Center
EDSA corner Ortigas Avenue
Quezon City
Contact: Mr. Felipe S. Magallon, President
Tel: 632-633-8318 to 19
Fax: 632-633-8320

MAKATI BUSINESS CLUB
2nd Floor, Princess Bldg.
104 Esteban Street
Legaspi Village
Makati
Metro Manila
Contact: Mr. Guillermo Luz, Executive Director
Tel: 632-816-2658; 816-2660; 812-3812; 812-3753
Fax: 632-816-2658; 812-3813

MARKET OPINION AND RESEARCH SOCIETY OF THE PHILIPPINES (MORES)
3rd Floor, #60 Libertad Street
Mandaluyong City
Contact: Ms. Ines Reyes, President
Tel/Fax No.: 632-635-01-30

METALWORKING INDUSTRIES ASSOCIATION OF THE PHILIPPINES
c/o Mabuhay Vinyl Corporation
Contact: Mr. Oscar A. Barrera, President
Tel: 632-815-2088
Fax: 632-816-4785

NATIONAL CONFEDERATION OF CONSTRUCTORS ASSOCIATION OF THE PHILIPPINES
Rm. 213, Eagle Court Cond.
26 Matalino Street
Diliman
Quezon City
Contact: Mr. Wilfredo Castro, President
Tel: 632-922-9094
Fax: 632-922-9702

PACKAGING INSTITUTE OF THE PHILIPPINES
Room 216, Comfoods Bldg.
Sen. Gil Puyat Avenue
Makati
Metro Manila
Contact: Ms. Carmencita D. Abelardo, President
Tel: 632-817-2936; 827-8509
Fax: 632-817-2936

PHARMACEUTICAL AND HEALTHCARE ASSOCIATION OF THE PHILIPPINES
Unit 502, One Corporate Plaza
845 Pasay Road
Makati
Metro Manila
Contact: Mr. Leo Wassmer, Jr., EVP & CEO
Tel: 632-816-7334; 816-0618
Fax: 632-819-2702

PHILIPPINE CHAMBER OF COMMERCE AND INDUSTRY (PCCI)
Ground Floor, East Wing, Secretariat Bldg.
Philippine International Convention Center (PICC)
CCP Complex
Roxas Boulevard
Pasay City
Contact: Mr. Jose Luis Yulo, President
Tel: 632-833-8591; 833-8592
Fax: 632-833-8895

PHILIPPINE CHAMBER OF FOOD MANUFACTURERS, INC.
8th Floor, Liberty Bldg.
Pasay Road
Makati
Metro Manila
Contact: Mr. Vicente H. Lim, Jr., President
Tel: 632-865-011, local 350, 351
Fax: 632-865-011, local 350

PHILIPPINE COMPUTER SOCIETY
6th Floor, Emmanuel House
115 Aguirre Street
Legaspi Village
Makati
Metro Manila
Contact: Mr. Edmundo M. Castaneda, President
Tel: 632-818-4227; 817-1820
Fax: 632-818-0381

PHILIPPINE CONSTRUCTORS ASSOCIATION (PCA)
3rd Floor, Padilla Bldg.
Emerald Avenue
Ortigas Complex
Pasig City
Contact: Mr. Rogelio Murga, President
Tel: 632-631-3135
Fax: 632-631-2788

PHILIPPINE ELECTRONICS & TELECOMMUNICATIONS FEDERATION (PETEF)
6th Floor, Telecoms Plaza
316 Sen. Gil Puyat Avenue
Makati City
Contact: Ms. Marilyn Santiago, President
Tel: 632-815-8921 local 379
Fax: 632-818-6967

PHILIPPINE EXPORTERS CONFEDERATION, INC. (PHILEXPORT)
Philippine International Convention Center (PICC)
G/F, Money Museum, Roxas Boulevard, Manila
Contact: Mr. Sergio Ortiz-Luis, Jr., President
Tel: 632-833-2407; 833-2531
Fax : 632-831-3707

PHILIPPINE FOOD PROCESSORS AND EXPORTERS CONFEDERATION
Philippine International Convention Center (PICC)
CCP Complex
Roxas Blvd.
Pasay City
Contact: Mr. Edward David, President
Tel: 632-891-7772; 832-0309 local 7480; 7512; 7532
Fax: 632-831-3707; 831-0231

PHILIPPINE PLASTICS INDUSTRIAL ASSOCIATION, INC.
317 Rizal Avenue Ext.
Grace Park rear Block
Solidbank Bldg.
Caloocan City
Contact: Mr. Antonio Kiac, President
Tel: 632-361-1160
Fax: 632-361-1168

PHILIPPINE HOTEL OWNERS ASSOCIATION
12th Floor, BA Lepanto Bldg.
Paseo de Roxas St.
Makati City
Contact: Dr. Rebecco Panlilio, President
Tel: 632-818-5160
Fax: 632-818-4143

PHILIPPINE MEDICAL ASSOCIATION
PMA Bldg.
North Avenue
Quezon City
Contact: Dr. Primitivo Chua, President
Tel: 632-992-132; 973-514
Fax: 632-974-974

PHILIPPINE SOFTWARE ASSOCIATION, INC. (PSA)
Mezzanine, Republic Glass Building
196 Salcedo Street
Legaspi Village
Makati City
Contact: Mr. Gil V. Guanio, President
Tel/Fax: 632-810-7391

POLLUTION CONTROL ASSOCIATION OF THE PHILIPPINES (PCAPI)
Rms. 2114-2115, V.V. Soliven Bldg.
EDSA
Greenhills
San Juan
Metro Manila
Contact: Mr. Porfirio Macatangay, President
Tel: 632-701-487
Fax: 632-701-487

RENEWABLE ENERGY ASSOCIATION OF THE PHILIPPINES, INC.
Department of Energy, PNPC Building
Merritt Road
Fort Bonifacio
Makati City
Contact: Mr. Abraham L. Cu, President
Tel: 632-851-021 to 31 local 245
Fax: 632-852-298

RP-U.S. BUSINESS COUNCIL
7th Floor, Phinman Bldg.
166 Salcedo Street
Legaspi Village
Makati City
Contact: Amb. Ramon del Rosario, Sr., Chairman
Tel: 632-818-8205
Fax: 632-817-9807

UNITED ARCHITECTS OF THE PHILIPPINES
Upper Basement, CCP Complex
Roxas Boulevard
Manila
Contact: Arch. Nestor S. Mangio, National President
Tel: 632-832-3711; 783-785
Fax: 632-832-3711

MARKET RESEARCH FIRMS

ANDERSEN CONSULTING
SGV Development Center
105 de la Rosa St.
Legaspi Village
Makati
Metro Manila
Contact: Mr. Baltazar Endriga, President
Tel: 632-817-03-01
Fax: 632-817-23-97

APPLIED MARKETING RESEARCH, INC. (AMAR)
No.11 2nd St. Barrio Kapitolyo, Pasig City
Contact: Mr. Patrico B. Barretto, Jr., President & Gen. Manager. Tel./Fax: 632-635-2419

ASIA PACIFIC CENTRE FOR RESEARCH
Rm. 411, Marbella I Condominium
2223 Roxas Boulevard
Pasay City
Contact: Mr. Aniceto Fontanilla, President
Tel: 632-831-5390
Fax: 632-833-3831

CONSUMER PULSE, INC.
Pulse Research Bldg.
San Miguel Avenue
cor. Shaw Boulevard
Ortigas Center
Pasig City
Contact: Mr. Bienvenido C. Niles, Managing Director
Tel: 632-631-1810
Fax: 632-631-6148

FEEDBACK, INC.
Suite 114, Limketkai Bldg.
Ortigas Avenue
Greenhills
San Juan
Metro Manila
Contact: Ms. Fidela Z. Zaballa, President
Tel: 632-721-4456
Fax: 632-798-727

FSA (PHILS.), INC.
3rd Floor, Philippine Social Science Center
Marcos Avenue
Diliman
Quezon City
Contact: Mr. Mel Gaddi, General Manager
Tel: 632-978-741
Fax: 632-976-846

Philippines (ASEAN)

LEVERAGE INTERNATIONAL (CONSULTANTS), INC.
5th Floor, PS Bank Bldg.
Ayala Avenue
Makati City
Contact: Ms. Cecilia Sanchez, Managing Director
Tel: 632-810-1389
Fax: 632-810-1594

PHILIPPINE SURVEY AND RESEARCH CENTER, INC.
PSRC Bldg.
Calbayog cor. Kanlaon Streets
Mandaluyong City
Contact: Ms. Carmencita Esteban, President
Tel: 632-774-802
Fax: 632-774-805

PULSE RESEARCH GROUP
Pulse Research Bldg.
San Miguel Avenue
Ortigas Center
Pasig City
Contact: Ms. Ma. Beatriz R. Gobencion, Associate Research Director
Tel: 632-631-1810
Fax: 632-631-6148

TOTAL RESEARCH NEEDS - MBL, INC.
149 Panay Ave
Quezon City
Contact: Ms. Mercedes Abad
Tel: 632-961-102
Fax: 632-922-2860

COUNTRY COMMERCIAL BANKS

ALLIED BANKING CORP.
6754 Ayala Avenue
cor. Legaspi Street
Makati City
Contact: Mr. Federico C. Pascual, President
Tel: 632-810-2448
Fax: 632-810-2362

AMERICAN EXPRESS BANK, LTD.
11th Floor, 6750 Ayala Avenue
Makati City
Contact: Mr. Vic L. Chua, President
Tel: 632-818-6731
Fax: 632-817-2589

BANK OF AMERICA
BA Building
Paseo de Roxas
Makati City
Contact: Mr. Anthony G. Travers, VP & Country Manager
Tel: 632-815-4550
Fax: 632-815-5895

BANK OF BOSTON
23rd Floor, 6750 Ayala Avenue
Makati City
Contact: Mr. Benjamin C. Sevilla, Country Manager
Tel: 632-817-0456
Fax: 632-819-1251

BANK OF CALIFORNIA, N.A.
8th Floor, Ace Building
Rada and dela Rosa Sts.
Legaspi Village
Makati City
Contact: Mr. Jose Gerardo A. Cruz, VP & Branch Manager
Tel: 632-892-8741
Fax: 632-892-5056

BANK OF THE PHILIPPINE ISLANDS
BPI Bldg., Ayala Avenue, Makati City
Contact: Mr. Xavier P. Loinaz, President
Tel.: 632-816-96-00
Fax : 632-818-80-92

BANK OF TOKYO, LTD.
5th Floor, 6750 Ayala Avenue
Makati City
Contact: Mr. Susumo Nakaichi, General Manager
Tel: 632-892-1976 to 78
Fax: 632-816-0413

BANKER'S TRUST COMPANY
12th Floor, Pacific Star Bldg.
Sen. Gil J. Puyat Avenue
Makati City
Contact: Mr. Jose Isidro N. Camacho, President
Tel: 632-819-0231
Fax: 632-818-7349

CHASE MANHATTAN BANK, N.A.
15th Floor, Pacific Star Bldg.
Sen. Gil Puyat and Makati Avenues
Makati
Metro Manila
Tel: 632-818-9851

CHEMICAL BANK
4th Floor, Corinthian Plaza
121 Paseo de Roxas
Makati City
Contact: Mr. James R. Boardman, VP & Country Manager
Tel: 632-815-9901
Fax: 632-819-0866

CITIBANK
8741 Paseo de Roxas
Makati City
Contact: Mr. Stephen Long, VP & Country Corp. Officer
Tel: 632-815-7701
Fax: 632-815-7703

CITY TRUST BANKING CORP.
Sen. Gil J. Puyat Avenue
Makati City
Contact: Mr. Jose R. Facundo, President
Tel: 632-818-0411
Fax: 632-895-8223

DEVELOPMENT BANK OF THE PHILIPPINES
Project Management Department II
Makati and Sen. Gil Puyat Avenues
Makati
Metro Manila
Contact: Atty. Leopoldo C. Salvador, First Vice President, Institutional Banking Group
Tel: 632-892-1866; 818-9511
Fax: 632-892-1866

EQUITABLE BANKING CORP.
262 Juan Luna Street
Binondo
Manila
Contact: Mr. Wilfrido V. Vergara, President & CEO
Tel: 632-241-5963
Fax: 632-241-6091

FAR EAST BANK & TRUST COMPANY
Muralla Street
Intramuros
Metro Manila
Contact: Mr. Octavio V. Espiritu, President
Tel: 632-530-0071
Fax: 632-49-2770

HONGKONG & SHANGHAI BANKING CORP.
6780 Ayala Avenue
Makati City
Contact: Mr. David H. Hodgkinson, Chief Executive Officer
Tel: 632-810-1246
Fax: 632-817-1953

KOREA BANK
33rd Floor, Citibank Tower
cor. Valero & Villar Streets
Salcedo Village
Makati City
Contact: Don Young Lee, General Manager
Tel: 632-817-2178 to 80
Fax: 632-818-0074

LAND BANK OF THE PHILIPPINES
319 Sen. Gil J. Puyat Avenue Ext.
Makati City
Contact: Mr. Jesli A. Lapus, President
Tel: 632-843-8824
Fax: 632-817-2536

METROPOLITAN BANK AND TRUST CO.
Metrobank Plaza
Sen. Gil J. Puyat Avenue
Makati City
Contact: Mr. Placido L. Mapa, Jr., Vice Chairman
Tel: 632-814-4187
Fax: 632-818-5354

PHILIPPINE BANKING CORPORATION
Ayala Avenue
Makati City
Contact: Mr. Norberto C. Nazareno, President
Tel: 632-812-9201; 817-0901
Fax: 632-817-0892

PHILIPPINE COMMERCIAL INTERNATIONAL BANK
PCI Bank Tower
Makati Avenue
Makati City
Contact: Mr. Rafael B. Buenaventura, President & CEO
Tel: 632-817-2424
Fax: 632-818-3946

PHILIPPINE NATIONAL BANK
PNB Financial Center
Roxas Blvd.
Manila
Contact: Mr. Peter B. Favila, President & CEO
Tel: 632-891-6258 or 67
Fax: 632-891-6266

PNB-REPUBLIC BANK
Legaspi Tower 300
Roxas Blvd.
corner Vito Cruz
Metro Manila
Contact: Mr. Manuel C. Mendoza, President
Tel: 632-521-6177
Fax: 632-521-8513

PRUDENTIAL BANK
Ayala Avenue
Makati City
Contact: Mr. Jose L. Santos, President
Tel: 632-817-8981
Fax: 632-817-5146

RIZAL COMMERCIAL BANKING CORP.
RCBC Bldg.
333 Sen. Gil J. Puyat Avenue
Makati City
Contact: Mr. Armando M. Medina, President & CEO
Tel: 632-891-0900
Fax: 632-891-0993

SECURITY BANK & TRUST COMPANY
SBTC Building
6778 Ayala Avenue
Makati City
Contact: Mr. Frederick Y. Dy, President & Chairman
Tel: 632-818-7677
Fax: 632-817-4295

STANDARD CHARTERED BANK
7901 Makati Avenue
Makati City
Contact: Mr. Peter H. Harris, Exec. Vice Pres. (for Philippines)
Tel: 632-817-2680
Fax: 632-815-5895

UNITED COCONUT PLANTERS BANK
UCPB Building
Makati Avenue
Makati City
Contact: Mr. Tirso D. Antiporda, Jr., Chairman & CEO
Tel: 632-818-1908
Fax: 632-818-0887

U.S. EMBASSY TRADE PERSONNEL

U.S. EMBASSY MANILA
1201 Roxas Boulevard
Manila
U.S. Mailing Address: American Embassy
Manila

APO AP 96440
Contact: John D. Negroponte, Ambassador
Tel: 632-521-7116 ext. 2276
Contact: Raymond F. Burghardt, Deputy Chief of Mission
Tel: 632-521-7116 ext. 2276

Contact: Donald D. McConville, Economic Counselor
Tel: 632-521-7116 ext.2003
Fax: 632-522-4361

U.S. & FOREIGN COMMERCIAL SERVICE (US&FCS)
2nd Floor, Thomas Jefferson Cultural Center
395 Sen. Gil Puyat Avenue
Makati City
Contact: Carmine D'Aloisio, Commercial Counselor
Contact: David Murphy, Commercial Attache
Tel: 632-890-9717; 895-3002; 890-9362
Fax: 632-895-3028

U.S.-ASIAN ENVIRONMENTAL PARTNERSHIP (US-AEP)
c/o U.S. & Foreign Commercial Service
2nd Floor, Thomas Jefferson Cultural Center
395 Sen. Gil Puyat Avenue
Makati City
Contact: Rene Saludes, Director, Technical Cooperation Office
Tel: 632-896-5128; 896-2877
Fax: 632-890-9361

ASIAN DEVELOPMENT BANK - FCS LIAISON
3rd Floor, Thomas Jefferson Cultural Center
395 Sen. Gil J. Puyat Avenue
Makati City
Contact: Cantwell Walsh, Senior Commercial Officer
Tel: 632-521-9116 ext. 2019; 890-9364; 895-3020
Fax: 632-890-9713

FOREIGN AGRICULTURAL SERVICE (FAS)
4th Floor, Thomas Jefferson Cultural Center
395 Sen. Gil Puyat Avenue
Makati City
Contact: Lawrence E. Hall, Agricultural Attache
Contact: John Wade, Asst. Agricultural Attache
Tel: 632-521-7116 ext. 2270; 895-9536; 893-6146
Fax: 632-890-2728

U.S. AGENCY FOR INTERNATIONAL DEVELOPMENT (USAID)
Ramon Magsaysay Center
1680 Roxas Blvd.
Manila
Contact: Kenneth G. Schofield, Director
Tel: 632-522-4411
Fax: 632-521-5241

Philippines (ASEAN)

JOINT MILITARY ASSISTANCE GROUP (JUSMAG)
Contact: Lt. Col. Al Cosio, Security
Assistance Division Officer
Tel: 632-833-3578/80, ext. 6121
Fax: 632-833-3530

OTHER CONTACTS IN MANILA

BOARD OF INVESTMENTS
American Desk
385 Sen. Gil J. Puyat Avenue
Makati
Metro Manila
Contact: Fernando Macias, Investments
Promotion Manager
Tel: 632-852-315
Fax: 632-852-315

WORLD BANK
Central Bank Complex
A. Mabini Street
Manila
Contact: Resident Representative
Thomas Allen
Tel: 632-521-1661; 521-2726
Fax: 632-521-1317

WASHINGTON-BASED USG COUNTRY CONTACTS

U.S. DEPARTMENT OF COMMERCE
Herbert Hoover Building
14th & Constitution Avenue, N.W.
Washington, D.C. 20230-0001
Contact: Janice Mazur, Liaison to the World
Bank
Tel: 202-482-4332; 458-0118
Fax: 202-477-2967

U.S. DEPARTMENT OF STATE
21st & C Streets, N.W.
Washington, D.C. 20520
Desk Officer for the Philippines
Tel: 202-647-1221
Fax: 202-647-0996

U.S. TRADE AND DEVELOPMENT AGENCY
Room 309, SA-16
Washington, D.C. 20523-1602
Contact: Rebecca Respess,
Project Officer - Philippines
Tel: 703-875-4357
Fax: 703-875-4009

COUNTRY CONSULATES AND TRADE OFFICES IN THE U.S.

EMBASSY OF THE REPUBLIC OF THE PHILIPPINES
Raul C. Rabe
Ambassador
1617 Massachusetts Ave., N.W.
Washington, D.C. 20036
Tel: 202-483-1414; 387-2810
Fax: 202-332-2320

PHILIPPINE CONSULATE GENERAL (NEW YORK)
Consul Robert Garcia
Philippine Center
556 Fifth Avenue
New York, NY 10036
Tel: 212-575-7925
Fax: 212-575-7759

PHILIPPINE CONSULATE GENERAL (LOS ANGELES)
Consul Mike Haresco
Office of the Consul (Commercial)
3660 Wilshire Boulevard, Suite 218
Los Angeles, CA 90010
Tel: 213-383-9675
Fax: 213- 738-127

PRIVATE ORGANIZATIONS SUPPORTING TRADE

U.S.-ASEAN COUNCIL FOR BUSINESS & TECHNOLOGY, INC.
1400 L St. N.W., Suite 375
Washington, D.C. 20005-3509
Tel: 202-289-1911
Fax: 202-289-0519
President: Mr. Robert E. Driscoll

U.S. CHAMBER OF COMMERCE INTERNATIONAL DIVISION
1615 H St. N.W.
Washington, D.C. 20062
Tel: 202-463-5300
President: Mr. Richard L. Lesher

PHILIPPINE AMERICAN CHAMBER OF COMMERCE
711 Third Avenue, Suite 1702
New York, NY 10017-4046
Tel: 212-972-9326
Fax: 212-867-9882

U.S. DEPARTMENT OF COMMERCE MARKET RESEARCH AVAILABLE

INDUSTRY SUBSECTOR ANALYSES

Industrial Reports
— Golf Equipment, 12/94
— Fitness Equiment, 1/95
— Men's Apparel, 2/95
— Aircraft Engines and Parts, 4/95
— Avionics and Ground Support Equipment 4/95
— Automotive Parts Aftermarket, 5/94
— Cellular Telephone Systems, 5/95
— Application Software, 7/95
— Mainframe Computers, 7/95
— Hair, Skin, Body Care Products, 7/95

— Radio Transmitters, Transceivers and Receivers, 8/95
— Satellite Space and Ground Equipment, 8/95
— Dental Equipment and Supplies, 9/95
— Organic Chemicals: Industrial, 9/95

Agricultural Reports
— Sugar Semi-Annual, 10/94
— Tobacco Semi-Annual, 11/94
— Grain and Feed Annual, 2/95
— Sugar Annual, 4/95
— Oilseeds Annual, 5/95
— Tobacco Annual, 5/95
— Coffee Annual, 5/95
— Seeds Annual, 5/95
— Cotton Annual, 6/95
— Forest Products Annual, 6/95
— AMP Market Information Report, 7/95
— Livestock Annual, 8/95
— Agricultural Situation Annual, 9/95

Note: FCS reports available on the National Trade Data Bank and FAS reports available from: Reports Office/USDA/FAS, Washington, DC 20250.

TRADE EVENTS SCHEDULE

The following international trade shows are scheduled during CY-1995.

Participation by U.S. firms is highly encouraged. Interested U.S.suppliers are urged to contact FCS Manila for further details.

Name of Event:	USA Foods Promotion
Sector:	Consumer-ready foods
Date:	August or September, 1995 (to be determined)
Location:	A supermarket chain, to be determined
USG Involvement:	U.S. Foreign Agricultural Service to organize a 30-day in-store promotion of U.S. consumer-ready foods

Name of Event:	HOTELEXPO '95
Sector:	Hotel and restaurant
Date:	September 21-23, 1995
Location:	Philippine International Convention Center, Manila
USG Involvement:	No direct involvement

Name of Event:	First International Supermarket Show
Sector:	Supermarket, Food/beverage
Date:	September 27-30, 1995
Location:	Philippine International Convention Center, Manila
USG Involvement:	No direct involvement

Name of Event:	3rd Welding Show (Third Philippine International) Welding Materials, Supplies, Tools, Equipment, Services, and Technology National Welding Technical Conferenc and Exhibition)
Sector:	Welding
Date:	October 19-21, 1995
Location:	Manila
USG Involvement:	No direct involvement

Name of Event:	5th PHILCONSTRUCT '95 (Philippine International Construction Materials and Equipment Conference and Exhibition)
Sector:	Construction and building materials
Date:	November 8-11, 1995
Location:	Manila
USG Involvement:	No direct involvement

Name of Event:	POWERTRENDS 2000
Sector:	Electrical Power
Date:	November 14-16, 1995
Location:	Philippine International Convention Center, Manila
USG Involvement:	No direct involvement

Also:

September 1, 1995 . *Telecommunications / Information Technologies Matchmaker.* Thailand, Indonesia and the Philippines. Contact: Molly Costa (202) 482-0692

September 25, 1995. *Trading Companies Matchmaker* **October 3, 1995.** Singapore, Philippines, Thailand. Contact: Sepia Thompson, Dept. of Commerce (202) 482-5131

October 9-20, 1995 *Small and Medium-Sized Business Mission to Southeast Asia.* Manila, Philippines; Bangkok, Thailand; Jakarta, Indonesia; Kuala Lumpur, Malaysia Contact: Steven Patillo, U.S.-ASEAN Council (202) 289-1911

October 23, 1995. *Dinner in honor of H.E. Fidel Ramos.* President of the Republic of the Philippines. New York. Contact: U.S.-ASEAN Council (202) 289-1911

November 1-5, 1995 *BIMP-EAGA* Exposition and Forum. Brunei, Indonesia, Malaysia, Philippines-East ASEAN Growth Area . Contact: Steven Patillo, U.S.-ASEAN Council (202) 289-1911

November 13-17, 1995. *"Direct from the USA - Products and Services for the Philippines"* Manila, Philippines. Contact: Victoria Montesinas 632-895-3028

November 15-17, 1995. *Power Trends 2000+* Manila, Philippines. Contact: Stephen Banks, Dept. of Commerce (202) 482-0595

December 12-13, 1995. Telecommunications/Information Technologies Matchmaker. Thailand, Indonesia, and the Philippines. Contact: Molly Costa (202) 482-0692

January 15-19, 1996 *Philippine Electric Power* Manila, Philippines. Contact: George Litman, Dept. Of Energy (202) 586-4344

January 15-19, 1996 *Philippine Electric Power* Manila, Philippines. Contact: George Litman, Dept. Of Energy (202) 586-4344

January 15 - 19, 1996. *Philippine Electric Power.* Manila, Philippines. Contact: George Litman, Dept. Of Energy (202) 586-4344

May 22 -25, 1996. *Telecomex Asia '96* Manila, Philippines. Contact: Amy Benson (202) 482-2422

INFORMATION CHECKLIST AND BIBLIOGRAPHY

PERIODICALS

Far Eastern Economic Review
Asian Wall Street Journal
American Chamber of Commerce Business Journal, a monthly publication of the American Chamber of Commerce in the Philippines

BOOKS

A Nation in the Making: The Philippines and the United States, Harvard University Press: Cambridge, 1974; Stanley, Peter.

A Short History of the Philippines; Angoncillo, Teodore A.

The Chinese in Philippine Life. Yale University Press: New Haven, 1965; Wickberg, Edgar

Faces of Manila. Lyceum Press: Manila, 1985; Von Brevern, Mariles

He Who Rides the Tiger. Praeger, New York, 1967; Taruc, Luis

In Our Image (a classic book on the Philippines-United States relationship); Karnow, Stanley

Indonesia and the Philippines: American Interests in Island Southeast Asia; Pringle, Robert

Living in the Philippines; available from the American Chamber of Commerce in the Philippines

The Manila-Washington Connection: Continuities in the Transnational Political Economy of the Philippine Development. University of Sydney, Sydney, 1983; Stauffer, Robert B.

The Philippine Economy and the United States: Studies in Past and Present Interactions; Owen, Norman G.

Philippines: A Country Study; Bunge, Frederica

The Philippines, A Singular and Plural Place. Boulder, CO: Westview Press, 1982; Steinberg, David J.

Philippines Alert; published by Economist Intelligence Unit, Manila

Sitting in Darkness: Americans in the Philippines; Bain, David H.

Resources: Poland

U.S. AND COUNTRY CONTACTS

COUNTRY GOVERNMENT AGENCIES

**MINISTRY OF LAND USE
AND CONSTRUCTION**
ul. Wspolna 2
00-926 Warsaw
Tel: 48-2-661 8111
Fax: 48-2-628 5887 or 48-22-295 389

**MINISTRY OF TRANSPORTATION
AND MARITIME ECONOMY**
ul Chalubinskiego 4/6
00-928 Warsaw
Tel: 48-22-244 411
Fax: 48-22-300 089

**MINISTRY OF ENVIRONMENTAL
PROTECTION**
ul. Wawelska 52/54
00-922 Warsaw
Tel: 48-22-250 001
Fax: 48-22-253 355

**MINISTRY OF AGRICULTURE AND
FOOD ECONOMY**
ul. Wspolna 30
00-519 Warsaw
Tel: 48-2-628 5745
Fax: 48-22-292 894

MINISTRY OF FINANCE
ul. Swietokrzyska 12
00-490 Warsaw
Tel: 48-2-694 5555
Fax: 48-22-266 352

**MINISTRY OF FOREIGN
ECONOMIC RELATIONS**
Pl. Trzech Krzyzy 5
00-507 Warsaw
Tel: 48-2-693 5000 or 628 6125
Fax: 48-2-628 6808 or 625 4944

MINISTRY OF INDUSTRY
ul. Wspolna 2/4
00-926 Warsaw
Tel: 48-2-628 0694 or 661 8111;
Fax: 48-2-628 1758

MINISTRY OF PRIVATIZATION
ul. Krucza 36
00-049 Warsaw
Tel: 48-2-628 9531
Fax: 48-2-625 1114

**THE STATE FOREIGN INVESTMENT
AGENCY**
Aleja Roz 2
00-559 Warszawa
Tel: 48-22-295 717, 216 261
Fax: 48-2-621 8427

COUNTRY TRADE ASSOCIATIONS/ CHAMBERS OF COMMERCE

**NATIONAL CHAMBER
OF COMMERCE OF POLAND**
ul. Trebacka 4
00-950 Warsaw
Tel: 48-22-260 221; Fax: 48-22-274 673

**AMERICAN CHAMBER OF COM-
MERCE IN POLAND (AMCHAM)**
36 Swietokrayska St.
pok. 6
00-116 Warsaw
Tel: 48-21-209-867 ext. 222, 223;
Fax: 48-21-622-5525

BUSINESS FOUNDATION
ul. Krucza 38/42, Room 117
00-512 Warsaw
Tel: 48-2-628 2148; Fax: 48-2-621 9761

**POLISH DISTRIBUTORS
FEDERATION**
ul. Okrezna 2
00-916 Warszawa
Tel: 48-22-409 154; Fax: 48-22-427 986

SMALL BUSINESS CHAMBER
ul. Smocza 27
01-048 Warszawa
Tel: 48-22-380 172; Fax: 48-22-383 553

BUSINESS CENTER CLUB
Palac Lubomirskich
00-136 Warszawa
Plac Zelaznej Bramy 2
Tel: 48-2-625 3037; Fax: 48-2-621 8420

COUNTRY MARKET RESEARCH FIRMS

ALCAT COMMUNICATIONS
ul Karlowicza 9a
02-501 Warsaw
Tel: 48-22-484 640; Fax: 48-22-486 782

ARTHUR ANDERSEN
ul. Nowy Swiat 6/12, 4th Floor
00-400 Warsaw
Tel: 48-2-625 1164; Fax: 48-2-625 1208

COMPANY ASSISTANCE LTD.
ul. Podwale 13
00-950 Warsaw
Tel: 48-2-635 8650; Fax: 48-22-317 920

COOPERS & LYBRAND
ul. Mokotowska 49
02-950 Warsaw
Tel: 48-2-660 0666; Fax: 48-2-660 0572

DELOITTE & TOUCHE
ul. Grzybowska 80/82
00-844 Warsaw
Tel: 48-2-661 5300; Fax: 48-2-661 5350

ERNST & YOUNG
ul. Wspolna 62
00-844 Warsaw
Tel: 48-22-295 241 or 625 5477
Fax: 48-22-294 263

PRICE WATERHOUSE
ul. Emilii Plater 28
00-688 Warsaw
Tel: 48-2-630 3030; Fax: 48-2-630 3040

COUNTRY COMMERCIAL BANKS

AMERBANK
ul. Marszalkowska 115
00-102 Warsaw
Tel: 48-22-248 505; Fax: 48-22-249 981

CITIBANK
ul Senatorska 12
00-082 Warsaw
Tel: 48-2-635 5527; Fax: 48-2-635 5278

**POLISH-AMERICAN
ENTERPRISE FUND**
ul. Nowy Swiat 6/12
00-950 Warszawa
Tel: 48-2-625 2017 or 625 2069
Fax: 48-2-6257933

ENTERPRISE CREDIT CORPORATION
ul. Towarowa 25
00-869 Warszawa
Tel: 48-22-323 508, 321 332, 321 359
Fax: 48-22-327 542

*The following banks have been approved by
EximBank:*

**BANK HANDLOWY W WARSZAWIE
S.A. (COMMERCIAL BANK SA)**
ul. Chalubinskiego 8
00-950 Warszawa
Tel: 48-22-303 000; Fax: 48-22-300 113

**BANK DEPOZYTOWO-KREDYT
OWY SA**
ul. Chopina 6
20-928 Lublin
Tel: 48-81-217 12; Fax: 48-81-713 153

**BANK POLSKA KASA OPIEKI, SA
(PEKAO, SA)**
ul. Traugutta 7/9
00-950 Warszawa
Tel: 48-2-269 211; Fax: 48-2-275 807

**POWSZECHNY BANK
GOSPODARCZYSA**
Al. J. Pilsudskiego 12
90-950 Lodz
Tel: 48-42-361 470; Fax: 48-42-367 772

**BANK ROZWOJU EKSPORTU, SA
(EXPORT DEVELOPMENT BANK SA)**
Plac Bankowy 2
00-950 Warszawa
Tel: 48-2-635 5926; Fax: 48-2-635 2713

POMORSKI BANK KREDYTOWY SA
Pl. Zolnierza Polskiego 16
70-952 Szczecin
Tel: 48-91-334 769; Fax: 48-91-533 114

**POWSZECHNY BANK
KREDYTOWY SA**
ul. Nowy Swiat 6/12
00-950 Warszawa
Tel: 48-2-661 7777; Fax: 48-22-296 988

**POWSZECHNA KASA
OSZCZEDNOSCI**
Bank Panstwowy
(PKO BP - State Bank)
ul. Nowy Swiat 6/12
Tel: 48-22-263 839; Fax: 48-2-635 5855

BANK ZACHODNI SA
ul. Ofiar Oswiecimskich 41/43
50-950 Wroclaw
Tel: 48-71-446 621; Fax: 48-71-441 982

**BANK GOSPODARKI
ZYWNOSCIOWEJ**
Bank for the Food Economy)
ul. Grzybowska 4
00-131 Warszawa
Tel: 48-22-200 251; Fax: 48-22-257 200

BANK GDANSKI SA
ul. Targ Drzewny 1
80-958 Gdansk
Tel: 48-58-379 222; Fax: 48-58-311 500

BANK SLASKI SA
ul. Warszawska 14
40-950 Katowice
Tel: 48-3-1537 281; Fax: 48-3-1537 734

**WIELKOPOLSKI BANK
KREDYTOWY SA**
Pl. Wolnosci 15
60-967 Poznan
Tel: 48-61-542 900; Fax: 48-61-521 116

U.S. EMBASSY TRADE PERSONNEL

Commercial address in Warsaw:
U.S. Trade Center
Aleje Jerozolimskic 56C
IKEA Building, 2d floor
00-803 Warsaw, Poland
Tel: 48-2-621-4515; Fax: 48-2--621-6327

All others:
AmEmbassy Warsaw
Aleje Ujazdowskie 29/31
Warsaw, Poland
Tel: 48-2-628-3041; Fax: 48-2-628-8298

APO address for all Embassy contacts:
AmEmbassy Warsaw
Unit 1340
APO AE 09213-1340

Commercial
Ms. Maria Andrews, Senior Commercial Officer
Ms. Rebecca Mann, Commercial Officer
Agriculture
Mr. Roger Wentzel, Agricultural Counselor
Economics
Mr. John Cloud, Economic Counselor

WASHINGTON-BASED USG COUNTRY CONTACTS

**CENTRAL AND EAST EUROPE
BUSINESS INFORMATION
CENTER (CEEBIC)**
Department of Commerce, Rm 7412
Washington, DC 20230
Tel: 202-482-2645; Fax: 202-482-4473
Lian VonWantoch, Poland Desk Officer
Monika Michejda-Goodrich, CEEBIC
Poland Specialist

**U.S. & FOREIGN
COMMERCIAL SERVICE**
Department of Commerce, Rm 3130
Washington, DC 20230
Tel: 202-482-1599; Fax: 202-482-3159
George Knowles, US&FCS Regional Director

U.S.-BASED MULTIPLIERS RELEVANT TO COUNTRY

POLISH-U.S. ECONOMIC COUNCIL
U.S. Chamber of Commerce
1615 H Street, NW
Washington, DC 20062-2000
Tel: 202-463-5482

U.S.-POLAND CHAMBER OF COMMERCE

812 North Wood Ave.
Linden, NJ 07036
Tel: 908-486-3534; Fax: 908-486-4084

U.S. DEPARTMENT OF COMMERCE MARKET RESEARCH AVAILABLE

INDUSTRY SUBSECTOR ANALYSES

— Dental Equipment, Materials & Supplies
— Housing Industry
— Restaurant and Catering Equipment
— Sporting Equipment
— Personal Computer Software
— New and Used Passenger Cars
— Office Furniture
— Hand and Power Tools
— Industrial Air Pollution Control Equipment
— Architectural Services
— Household Consumer Appliances
— Office Telecommunication Equipment
— Air Conditioning Equipment
— Emergency Medical Equipment
— Consumer Electronics
— Printing Machinery
— Food and Consumer Product Container
— Waste Water Treatment Plants- Services & Equipment
— Printing Inks and Dyes
— Building Materials
— Franchising
— Paper/Paper Products
— Cosmetics
— Gas Station Equipment
— Computers
— Passenger Cars and Light Trucks

Upcoming
— Underwear
— Fruit and Vegetable Processing Equipment
— Lining Materials for Landfills
— Sporting Goods Update
— TV Broadcasting and Studio Equipment
— Radio Broadcasting Equipment

List of Annual USDA/FAS Agricultural Reports
— Livestock
— Fresh Delicious Fruit
— Agricultural Situation
— Sugar
— Dairy
— Forest Products
— Strawberries
— Grain & Feed
— Tobacco
— Cotton
— Poultry

TRADE EVENTS SCHEDULE

SEPTEMBER 1995

9/95. International Military Technology Exhibition. Fair held in Kielce. Attended by Polish and foreign manufacturers of aviation equipment, tanks and armored vehicles, guns, arms, explosives, communication equipment as well as research and design centers. Organized by Folk Expo Center Ltd., Tel: 48-58-51 48 01 and Fax: 48-58-51 48 22.

9/1-9/3. Nekropolie '95, III- Fair of Necropolis art in Wroclaw. Organized by the Wroclaw Fair Office (Biuro Targow); Tel: 48-71-483-091 ext. 222; Fax: 48-71-32-047.

9/7-9/10. Zdrowy Dom- Ecological house-building fair in Torun. Organized by the Miedzynarodowe Targi Pomorza i Kujaw; Tel: 48-56-27-757; Tel/Fax: 48-56-27-699.

9/7-9/11. 3rd International Defence Industry Salon- defence industry, military equipment, weapons, ammunition, uniforms. Organized by Trade Center Kielce; Tel: 48-41-66-06-05; Fax: 48-41-562-61.

9/13-9/16. Office-Shop - Interior design fair (including office and shop design, furniture and accessories) in Gdansk. Organized by the Gdansk International Fair Company; Tel: 48-58-523-706 or 42-58-524-690; Fax: 48-58-522-168 or 522-243.

9/13-9/16. Protechnika - Security and protection technologies and systems fair held in Gdansk. Organized by the Gdansk International Fair Company; Tel: 48-58-523-706 or 42-58-524-690; Fax: 48-58- 522-168 or 522-243.

9/13-9/16. Marketing 95 - Marketing fair (including marketing strategies, promotion and advertising) held in Gdansk. Organized by the Gdansk International Fair Company; Tel: 48-58-523-706 or 42-58-524-690; Fax: 48-58-522-168 or 522-243.

9/14-9/16. Medica Expo- International exhibition of medical equipment and medicines held in Lodz. Organized by the Interservice Co. Ltd.; Tel/Fax: 48-42-371-215, 48-42-371-359.

9/14-9/17. Agrotarol, V- Pomeranian agriculture industry fair in Bydgoszcz. Organized by the Miedzynarodowe Targi Pomorza i Kujaw; Tel: 48-52-225-424, 48-52-220-141; Fax: 48-52-286-588.

9/21-9/23. Digiton V- International Phono-graphic Fair held in Lodz. Organized by the Interservice Co. Ltd.; Tel/Fax: 48-42-371-215, 48-42-371-359.

9/21-9/24. Home Expo '95. The third international trade fair for interior design and decoration (decoration and finishing materials) held in Krakow. Organized by the Krakow Expo Center; Tel: (USA) 508-897-6356; Fax: 508-897-5320.

9/21-9/24. Electro-Light '95. The second international electric light forum (electric light technology, tools and equipment) held in Krakow. Organized by the Krakow Expo Center; Tel: (USA) 508-897-6356; Fax: 508-897-5320.

9/26-9/29. Softarg. International software fair. Organized by Katowice International Fail Company; Tel: 48-32-59-60-61; Fax: 48-3-154-02-27.

9/27-10/1. Housebuilding. Fair of house building and home equipment. Organized by the Gdansk International Fair Company; Tel: 48-58-523-706 or 42-58-524-690; Fax: 48-58-522-168 or 48-58-522-243.

9/28-10/1. Agroinfoexpo, III. Fair of electronics, computer technology and telecommunications held in Torun. Organized by the Miedzynarodowe Targi Pomorza i Kujaw; Tel: 48-56-27-757; Tel/Fax: 48-56-27-699.

9/28-10/1. Kooperacja Handel '95, IV- Polish-German multibranch fair held in Wroclaw. Organized by the Wroclaw Fair Office (Biuro Targow); Tel: 48-71-483-091 ext. 222; Fax: 48-71-32-047.

9/29-10/1. Med & Care '95- The third international medical forum (pharmaceutical technologies, materials, equipment and drugs) held in Krakow. Organized by the Krakow Expo Center; Tel: (USA) 508- 897-6356; Fax: 508-897-5320.

OCTOBER 1995:

10/6-10/8. Autosalon- International car fair. Organized by Katowice International Fail Company; Tel: 48-32-59-60-61; Fax: 48-3-154-02-27.

10/6-10/11. Polagra- Agro-industrial fair in Poznan. Organized by the Poznan International Fair; Fax: 48-61-66-58-27.

10/12-10/15. Intermedia '95- International music fair held in Wroclaw. Organized by the Wroclaw Fair Office (Biuro Targow); Tel: 48-71-483-091 ext. 222; Fax: 48-71-32-047.

10/10-10/13. Tele-Photo-Video '95- Fair held in the Palace of Culture and Science in Warsaw. Organized by the Biuro Reklamy s.a.; Tel: 48-22-493-071, 48-22-496-044; Fax: 48-22-493-584.

10/12-10/15. Activity- Fair of sports, recreation, and hobbies held in Gdansk. Organized by the Gdansk International Fair Company; Tel: 48-58-523-706 or 42-58-524-690; Fax: 48-58-522-168 or 522-243.

10/12-10/15. Creation- Gdansk fashion fair. Organized by the Gdansk International Fair Company; Tel: (48-58) 523-706 or (42-58) 524-690; Fax: (48-58) 522-168 or 522-243.

10/12-10/15. Krak-Konstruma '95- The second international trade fair for construction materials held in Krakow. Organized by the Krakow Expo Center; Tel: (USA) (508) 897-6356; Fax: (508) 897-5320.

10/12-10/15. Edukacja- International educational fair held in Lodz. Organized by the Interservice Co. Ltd.; Tel/Fax: (48-42) 371-215, 371-359.

10/12-10/15. Juventa- Fair of pharmaceutical and cosmetics held in Gdansk. Organized by the Gdansk International Fair Company; Tel: (48-58) 523-706 or (42-58) 524-690; Fax: (48-58) 522-168 or 522-243.

10/12-10/15. Baltmedica- Fair of medical equipment held in Gdansk. Organized by the Gdansk International Fair Company; Tel: (48-58) 523-706 or (42-58) 524-690; Fax: (48-58) 522-168 or 522-243.

10/19-10/22. Poldrink, V- Alcoholic and non-alcoholic beverages fair held in Bydgoszcz, also featuring machines and equipment used in the industry. Organized by the Miedynarodowe Targi Pomorza I Kujaw; Tel: (48-52) 225-424, 220-141; Fax: (48-52) 286-588.

10/19-10/22. Tech-Drink, II- Technical equipment for softdrinks fair; fair of machinery for the beverage industry in Bydgoszcz. Organized by the Miedynarodowe Targi Pomorza I Kujaw; Tel: (48-52) 225-424, 220-141; Fax: (48-52) 286-588.

10/20-10/22. Foto-Video-Film. Fair of rehabilitation equipment and video cassettes held in Lodz. Organized by the Interservice Co. Ltd.; Tel/Fax: (48-42) 371-215, 371-359.

10/24-10/27. Infoman. Fair of information management held in Gdansk. Organized by the Gdansk International Fair Company; Tel: (48-58) 523-706 or (42-58) 524-690; Fax: (48-58) 522-168 or 522-243.

10/24-10/27. Medica '95. Fair held in Warsaw at the Palace of Culture and Science and the Mokotow Fair Center. Organized by the Biuro Reklamy s.a.; Tel: (48-22) 493-071, 496-044; Fax: (48-22) 493-584.

10/24-10/27. Controla '95. Fair of measurement and control technology equipment for scientific research held in Warsaw at the Palace of Culture and Science and the Mokotow Fair Center. Organized by the Biuro Reklamy s.a.; Tel: (48-22) 493-071, 496-044; Fax: (48-22) 493-584.

10/24-10/27. Farmacja '95- Fair held in Warsaw at the Palace of Culture and Science and the Mokotow Fair Center. Organized by the Biuro Reklamy s.a.; Tel: (48-22) 493-071, 496-044; Fax: (48-22) 493-584.

10/24-10/28. Interwelding- Welding fair. Organized by Katowice International Fail Company; Tel: (48-32) 59-60-61; Fax: (48-3) 154-02-27.

10/26-10/28. Rol-Expo. Agricultural and food industry fair in Bialystok. Organized by PRO-ITO Ltd.; Fax: (48-85) 514-244.

10/26-10/28. Papier '95. The second trade fair for the paper industry (technology, equipment and materials) held in Krakow. Organized by the Krakow Expo Center; Tel: (USA) (508) 897-6356; Fax: (508) 897-5320.

10/26-10/28. Print '95- The second printing and publishing forum (machinery, equipment and supplies for print shops; publishing services and book publication offers) held in Krakow. Organized by the Krakow Expo Center; Tel: (USA) (508) 897-6356; Fax: (508) 897-5320.

10/27-10/29. Cycling-Moto-Expo '95- International bicycle and motorcycle fair held in Bydgoszcz. Organized by the Miedynarodowe Targi Pomorza I Kujaw; Tel: (48-52) 225-424, 220-141; Fax: (48-52) 286-588.

NOVEMBER 1995

11/8-11/10. Rehabilitacja, III- Fair of rehabilitation equipment in Lodz. Organized by the Interservice Co. Ltd.; Tel/Fax: (48-42) 371-215, 371-359.

11/9-11/12. Tarel '95, VI. Fair of electronics and electrotechnics held in Wroclaw. Organized by the Wroclaw Fair Office (Biuro Targow); Tel: (48-71) 483-091 ext. 222; Fax: (48-71) 32-047.

11/9-11/12. Zdrowy Dom. International construction fair held in Bydgoszcz. Organized by the Miedynarodowe Targi Pomorza I Kujaw; Tel: (48-52) 225-424, 220-141; Fax: (48-52) 286-588.

11/9-11/12. Wnetrza '95, IV. Fair of house, kitchen, and bathroom furnishings and lighting held in Bydgoszcz. Organized by the Miedynarodowe Targi Pomorza I Kujaw; Tel: (48-52) 225-424, 220-141; Fax: (48-52) 286-588.

11/9-11/12. Jesienna Gielda Budownictwa. Autumn building market. Organized by Katowice International Fail Company; Tel: (48-32) 59-60-61; Fax: (48-3) 154-02-27.

11/14-11/17. Shop-Expo/Gastronomia/Opakowania/Food Expo- Fair featuring shop and restaurant equipment and packaging machines held in Warsaw. Organized by Biuro Reklamy s.a.; Tel: (48-22) 493-071, 496-044; Fax: (48-22) 493-584.

11/14-11/17. Komtel '95. Fair held in Warsaw at the Palace of Culture and Science. Organized by Biuro Reklamy s.a.; Tel: (48-22) 493-071, 496-044; Fax: (48-22) 493-584.

11/14-11/17. Interbank '95. Fair held in Warsaw at the Palace of Culture and Science. Organized by Biuro Reklamy s.a.; Tel: (48-22) 493-071, 496-044; Fax: (48-22) 493-584.

11/14-11/17. Officetech '95. Fair held in Warsaw at the Palace of Culture and Science. Organized by Biuro Reklamy s.a.; Tel: (48-22) 493-071, 496-044; Fax: (48-22) 493-584.

11/16-11/18. MTPik, II. International consumer goods fair held in Torun. Organized by the Miedynarodowe Targi Pomorz i Kujaw; Tel: (48-56) 27-757; Tel/Fax: (48-56) 27-699.

11/16-11/18. Kontrol-Pomiar. Fair of quality management in the consumer goods industry held in Torun. Organized by the Miedynarodowe Targi Pomorz i Kujaw; Tel: (48-56) 27-757; Tel/Fax: (48-56) 27-699.

11/16-11/18. Polmasz. Fair for machinery for consumer goods industry held in Torun. Organized by the Miedynarodowe Targi Pomorz i Kujaw; Tel: (48-56) 27-757; Tel/Fax: (48-56) 27-699.

Poland

11/16-11/19. Gift Show. Fair of advertisement, gifts and jewelry held in Lodz. Organized by the Interservice Co. Ltd.; Tel/Fax: (48-42) 371-215, 371-359.

11/16-11/19. Interflower. Exhibition presenting flowers held in Lodz. Organized by the Lodz International Fair; Fax: (48-42) 37-29-35.

11/16-11/19. Style '95. The second trade fair for trends and fashions (clothes, cosmetics, shoes and jewelry) held in Krakow. Organized by the Krakow Expo Center; Tel: (508) 897-6356; Fax: (508) 897-5320.

11/16-11/19. Baby Market '95. Clothes, cosmetics and care articles for children held in Krakow. Organized by the Krakow Expo Center; Tel: (508) 897-6356; Fax: (508) 897-5320.

11/21-11/24. Everything For Baby '95. Fair held in Warsaw at the Victoria HoTel: Organized by Biuro Reklamy s.a.; Tel: (48-22) 493-071, 496-044; Fax: (48-22) 493-584.

11/23-11/26. Foodtarg-Fall. Food-processing industry machinery and products fair in Katowice. Organized by the Katowice International Fair; Fax: (48-32) 58-89-19.

11/23-11/26. Tardom '95, III. Fair of home furnishings and installations held in Wroclaw. Organized by the Wroclaw Fair Office (Biuro Targow); Tel: (48-71) 483-091 ext. 222; Fax: (48-71) 32-047.

11/30-12/3. Horecamid-Europe '95. Third international trade fair for equipment and supplies for hotels, restaurants and cafes held in Krakow. Organized by the Krakow Expo Center; Tel: (508) 897-6356; Fax: (508) 897-5320.

11/30-12/3. Itemac '95. The third international tourist market fair in Krakow (travel agencies, tour operators, hotels, recreation and transport services). Organized by the Krakow Expo Center; Tel: (508) 897-6356; Fax: (508) 897-5320.

DECEMBER 1995

12/3-12/10. Polupominek. Christmas stock exchange held in Bydgoszcz. Organized by the Miedzynarodowe Targi Pomorza i Kujaw; Tel: (48-52) 225-424; 220-141; Fax: (48-52) 286-588.

12/14-12/17. Gastronomia '95. Fair held in Wroclaw. Organized by the Wroclaw Fair Office (Biuro Targow); Tel: (48-71) 483-091 ext. 222; Fax: (48-71) 32-047.

INFORMATION CHECKLIST AND BIBLIOGRAPHY

Polish Business and Economic Information Available from the Central and Eastern Europe Business Information Center (CEEBIC):

— Fact Sheet/Background Information
— Country Commercial Guide- Poland
— Trade and Investment in Poland
— Commercial Overview
— Economic Trends and Outlook
— Leading U.S. Total Imports from Poland
— Leading U.S. Total Exports to Poland
— Investment Climate in Poland
— Best Prospect Sectors for U.S. Industry Exports
— Best Prospect Sectors for U.S. Agricultural Exports
— Business Travel in Poland
— Marketing U.S. Products and Services in Poland
— PAIZ - The State Agency for Foreign Investment
— Political Environment in Poland
— Financial Environment in Poland
— Polish Trade Agreements
— Polish-American Enterprise Clubs

Poland Looks for Partners
A monthly newsletter containing policy changes, business tips, trade leads, and various pertinent information on Poland. Published by the U.S. Dept. of Commerce, Central and Eastern Europe Business Information Center (CEEBIC), U.S. Dept. of Commerce, Room 7414, Washington, D.C. 20230. Tel: 202-482-2645; Fax: 202-482-4473.

OTHER BUSINESS PERIODICALS FOR POLAND

AmCham News
Mothly magazine of the American Chamber of Commerce in Poland.
American Chamber of Commerce
36, Swietokrzyska St.
Room No. 6
00-116 Warsaw, Poland
Tel/Fax: (48-2) 622-5525 ext. 222, 223

BNA's Eastern Europe Report
Bi-weekly newsletter covering changes in policies, laws, and regulations, as well as market deals in Eastern Europe.
Bureau of National Affairs, Inc.
1231 25th Street, N.W.
Washington, DC 20037
Tel: (202) 452-4200
Telex:285656 BNAI WSH
Customer Relations: 1-800-372-1033

Business Eastern Europe
Weekly newsletter on market opportunities and business information.
Economic Intelligence Unit Ltd.
Customer Service Department
215 Park Avenue South
New York, NY 10003
Tel: (212) 460-0600; Fax: (212) 995-8837

Business in Czech Republic/Slovakia/Hungary/Poland.
Individual reports on doing business in each of the listed countries with updated quarterly reports highlighting the most recent developments.
Transnational Juris Publications, Inc.
P.O. Box 7282
Ardsley-on-Hudson, NY 10503
Tel: (914) 693-0089; Fax: (914) 693-8776

Business Update Poland, Hungary, and Czech Republic-Slovakia.
Faxed twice weekly, these reports are one page newsletters covering business, political, legal, and statistical issues facing business and investments. This newsletter is published by BroadFax:, S.A., Geneva.
Dean & Lake Consulting, Inc.
2306 Cleburne Ridge, Marietta GA 30064
Tel: (404) 514-9100; Fax: (404) 514-9009

Central and Eastern Europe Commercial Update
Published on business information and opportunities. Eastern Europe Business Information Center, U.S. Department of Commerce, Room 7412, 14th and Constitution Ave. NW, Washington, D.C. 20230. Tel: (202) 482-2645; Fax: (202) 482-4473

Central European
A monthly publication concentrating on East European business practices, joint ventures, secondary markets, accounting and banking updates and summaries of new laws and regulations.
International Information Services, Inc.
P.O. Box 3490
Silver Spring, MD 20918
Tel: (301) 555-2975; Fax: (301) 565-2973

Central European Business Weekly
Weekly paper discussing business news in Central/Eastern Europe and the NIS. Includes industry sector analyses and a calendar of upcoming conferences and trade fairs in the region.
Central European Business Weekly
Subscriptions
Malesická 16a
130 69 Prague 3
Czech Republic

Country Report- Poland
Quarterly publication detailing Poland's economic progress including forcasts.
The Economist Intelligence Unit
15 Regent St.
London, SW1Y 4LR
United Kingdom

Daily Report - Eastern Europe
Daily reports based on foreign radio and television broadcasts and news publications.
Foreign Broadcast Information Service
c/o National Technical Information Service
5285 Port Royal Road
Springfield, VA 22161
Tel: (703) 487-4630; Fax: (703) 321-8547

Directory of U.S. Companies Doing Business in the Soviet Union and Eastern Europe
Lists American companies with established business activities in the region and identifies essential sources of assistance for pursuing trade and investment there.
Trade directory (SS # 354-34-3984)
P.O. Box 5393
Arlington, VA 22205
Tel: (703) 241-0586

Doing Business in Eastern Europe
Monthly newsletter from Commerce Clearing House Europe covering current developments in business law, taxation, accounting, and news of important economic developments and business activities.
Commerce Clearing House, Inc.
P.O. Box 5490
Chicago IL 60680-9882
Tel: (800) TELL-CCH;
Fax: (800) 221-4240

Economic and Legal Information from Poland
Quarterly publication with economic, commercial, financial and legal news on Poland.
Embassy of the Republic of Poland
Commerical Counsellor's Office
100 Park Avenue
New York, NY 10017
Tel: (212) 370-5300; Fax: (212) 818-9623

East European and CIS Legal Update
Monthly publication focusing on legal changes in Eastern Europe and the regions of the former Soviet Union.
Baker & McKenzie
Bolshoi Strochenovsky Perelok 22/25
Attention: John Clough
Moscow, Russia 113054
Tel: (7095) 230-6036; Tel/Fax: (212) 891-3799
Fax: (7095) 230-6047

East-West Executive Guide
Monthly publication covering legal and business developments in Eastern Europe and the CIS
World Trade Executive Inc.
P.O. Box 761
Concord, MA 01742
Tel: (508) 287-0301; Fax: (508) 287-0302

East/West Business and Finance Alert
Monthly newsletter describing financing opportunities, business contacts, and provides early intelligence on business opportunities.
World Trade Executive Inc.
P.O. Box 761
Concord, MA 01742
Tel: (508) 287-0301; Fax: (508) 287-0302

East/West Executive Guide
Publication that contains how to reports from top lawyers and business executives on how to structure deals in Eastern Europe
World Trade Executive Inc
P.O. Box 761
Concord, MA 01742
Tel: (508) 287-0301

East-West Letter
Bi-monthly publication dedicated to analysis of economic and political issues in Eastern Europe and the former Soviet Union.
NovEcon Consulting Group
1217 Olivia Avenue
Ann Arbor MI 48104
Tel: (313) 761 1478

East/West Technology Digest
Monthly digest of new technology from the Soviet Union and Eastern Europe
Welt Publishing Company
1413 K. Street, NW Suite 1400
Washington, DC 20005
Tel: 202-371-0555

Eastern Europe Demographics and Business Opportunities
Quarterly updated set of reports on business opportunities in Eastern Europe, including the telecommunications, computer and energy/environmental sectors.
EDI - Enterprise Development International Inc.
5619 Bradley Blvd.
Bethesda, MD 20814
Tel: (301) 652-0141; Fax: (301) 652-0177

Eastern Europe Finance
Bi-weekly newsletter on sources of financing for Eastern Europe.
DP Publications Co.
Michael Morrison
Box 7188
FairFax: Station, VA 22039
Tel: (703) 425-1322; Fax: (703) 425-7911

Eastern Europe: Heading for Reform
A series of 10 country reports covering Eastern European and NIS countries.
Deutsche Bank Capital
Attn: Jones R Kelly, Director
31 West 52nd Street
New York, NY 10019
Tel: (212) 474-7542; Fax: (212) 474-7379

Eastern Europe Newsletter
Bi-monthly publication on political and economic policy forecasts and assessments on Eastern Europe and the Soviet Union.
Eastern Europe Newsletter Ltd.
87 Duke Road
London W4 2BW, U.K.
Tel: (011)(44)(081) 995-3860
Fax: (011)(44)(081) 747-8802

Eastern European Business Directory
Over 8,000 Eastern European companies and organizations described. This is also available on CD-ROM.
Gale Research Inc.
P.O. Box 33477
Detroit, MI 48232-5477
Tel: 1-800-877-GALE; Fax: (313) 961-6083

Eastern European Energy Report
Monthly newsletter focusing on the energy and environmental markets in Eastern Europe.
Strategic Marketing Inc.
Eastern European Marketing Group
7 Lewis Avenue
Hartsdale NY 10530
Tel: (914) 993-9060; Fax: (914) 993-9003

Eastern European & Former Soviet Telecom Report
Monthly newsletter highlighting country and company profiles in the telecommunications, information processing, and broadcasting sectors.
International Technology Consultants
1724 Kalorama Rd. NW,
Suite 210
Washington, DC 20009
Tel: (202) 234-2138;Fax: (202) 483-7922

Poland

Economic Bulletin for Europe
Yearly summary of economic developments and
policies in European economies. Subscriptions
are not available, but complimentary copies
may be obtained.
United Nations Information
Tel: (202) 289-8670

Finance East Europe
Published by the London Financial Times, this
bi-weekly publication highlights developments
in the areas of privatization, cross-border
mergers, financing and banking.
International Information Services, Inc.
P.O. Box 3490
Silver Spring, MD 20918
Tel: (301) 565-2975; Fax: (301) 565-2973

Foreign Broadcast Information Service
Daily or weekly publication featuring news
accounts, commentaries, and Government
statements from foreign broadcasts, press
agency transmissions, newspapers, and
periodicals published in the previous 48-72
hours.
National Technical Information Service (NTIS)
5285 Port Royal Road
Springfield, VA 22161
Tel: 703-487-4630

*The Gammon Directory for Eastern Europe and
the Newly Independent States*
Over 400 pages of contacts for trade, banking
business, U.S. Federal and State Governments,
International Governments, and more.
Gammon International, Inc.
P.O. Box 14359
Clearwater, FL 34629
Tel: 813-531-7664

General Trade Index & Business Guide
Over 700 pages detailing the intricacies of the
Polish legal and tax systems and listing
potential Polish trade partners.
Business Foundation
Warszawa, ul. Wspolna 1/3
Tel: (0-22) 28-40-71 do 87 wew. 438
Fax: 28-05-49; Telex: 817088

Law in Transition
Newsletter on legal cooperation and training
from the European Bank for Reconstruction
and Development which provides infomration
on legal projects and progams funded by both
private and public organizations.

Office of General Counsel
European Bank for Reconstruction
and Development
One Exchange Square
London EC2A 2EH
Tel: 071 338 6246 or 017 496 6246
Fax: 071 338 6150 or 071 496 6150

PlanEcon Report
Weekly publication on economic situations
in Eastern Europe.
PlanEcon Europe Ltd.
Wimbledon Bridge House
1 Hartfield Rd, Wimbledon
London SW19 3RU
United Kingdom
Tel: (44-81) 545-6248; Fax: (44-81) 545 6236

Plan-Econ Business Report
Bi-weekly newsletter that reports on business
developments in the Soviet Union and Eastern
Europe.
Marketing Department
Plan Europe Econ Ltd
Wimbledon Bridge House
1 Harthouse Road
Wimbledon SW19 3RU, UK
Tel: (44-81) 545-6248; Fax: (44-81) 545 6236

Review of Commerce
A newsletter providing information on opportunities in various sectors in Poland, including information on joint ventures.
The Review of Commerce
60-529 Poznan
ul. Dabrowskiego 77
Tel: 426-26; Fax: 424-55

Tracking Eastern Europe
Weekly newsletter on business and investment
opportunities in Eastern Europe.
A.M.F. International Consultants
812 North Wood Avenue
Linden, NJ 07036
Tel: (908) 486-3534; Fax: (908) 486-4084

Transition
The newsletter of economic reform in the
emerging democracies.
Matyas Vince Room N-11-035
The World Bank
1818 H Street, N.W.
Washington, D.C. 20433
Tel: (202) 473-6982

Warsaw Business Journal
Weekly publication on business and business
opportunities in Poland.
Warsaw Business Journal
ul. Mokotowska 24, III p.
00-561 Warsaw, Poland
Tel: (48-2) 628-5618; ax: (48-2) 628-2548

The Warsaw Voice
Weekly publication in English on the Polish
economy, commercial laws, and opportunities.
The Warsaw Voice
413B Logan Boulevard
Lakemont
Altoona, PA 16602
Tel: (800) 488-2939

Wiadomosci Handlowe
Quarterly magazine highlighting American
business activity in Poland.
U.S. Trade Development Center
ul. Wijeska 20 00-490 Warsaw, Poland
Tel: (48) (22) 21-45-15

Poland

Resources: Singapore

U.S. AND COUNTRY CONTACTS

COUNTRY GOVERNMENT AGENCIES

MINISTRY OF TRADE AND INDUSTRY
8 Shenton Way, #48-01
Treasury Bldg. (0106)
Tel: 65-225-9911; Fax: 65-320-9260

**SINGAPORE TRADE
DEVELOPMENT BOARD**
1 Maritime Sq., #10-40 (Lobby D)
World Trade Center
Telok Blangah Rd. (0409)
Tel: 65-271-9388; Fax: 65-274-0770,
278-2518, 271-0985

**REGISTRY OF COMPANIES
AND BUSINESS**
18 Anson Rd., #05-01/15
International Plaza (0207)
Tel: 65-227-8551; Fax: 65-225-1676

**REGISTRY OF TRADE MARKS
AND PATENTS**
51 Bras Basah Rd., #04-01
Plaza by the Park (0718)
Tel: 65-330-2700; Fax: 65-339-0252

CUSTOMS AND EXCISE DEPARTMENT
1 Maritime Sq., #03-01/#10-01
World Trade Centre (0409)
Tel: 65-272-8222; Fax: 65-277-9090

ECONOMIC DEVELOPMENT BOARD
250 North Bridge Rd.,
#24-00 Raffles City Tower (0617)
Tel: 65-336-2288; Fax: 65-339-6077
Finance (Ministry of)
8 Shenton Way, Treasury Bldg. (0106)
Tel: 65-225-9911; Fax: 65-320-9435

MINISTRY OF LAW
250 North Bridge Rd., #21-00
Raffles City Tower (0617)
Tel: 65-336-1177; Fax: 65-330-5887

MINISTRY OF DEFENSE
Gombak Dr., MINDEF Bldg. (2366)
Tel: 65-760-8188; Fax: 65-762-0112

MINISTRY OF COMMUNICATIONS
460 Alexandra Road
#39-00 PSA Bldg. (0511)
Tel: 65-270-7988; 279-9734

**CIVIL AVIATION AUTHORITY
OF SINGAPORE**
Singapore Changi Airport,
P.O. Box 1 (9181)
Tel: 65-542-1122; Fax: 65-542-1231

**MASS RAPID TRANSIT
(MRT) CORPORATION**
251 North Bridge Rd., (0617)
Tel: 65-336-8900; Fax: 65-339-8816

PORT OF SINGAPORE AUTHORITY
460 Alexandra Rd., PSA Bldg. (0511)
Tel: 65-274-7111; Fax: 65-279-5711

**MINISTRY OF NATIONAL
DEVELOPMENT**
5 Maxwell Rd., #21-00 & 22-00
Tower Block MND Complex (0106)
Tel: 65-222-1211; Fax: 65-322-6254

**URBAN REDEVELOPMENT
AUTHORITY**
45 Maxwell Rd., URA Bldg. (0106)
P.O. Box 1393, Robinson Rd. (0106)
Tel: 65-221-6666; Fax: 65-224-8752

MINISTRY OF LABOR
18 Havelock Rd., #07-01 (0105)
Tel: 65-534-1511; Fax: 65-5334-4840

PUBLIC UTILITIES BOARD
111 Somerset Rd., #16-05
PUB Bldg. (0923)
Tel: 65-235-8888; Fax: 65-731-3020

PUBLIC WORKS DEPARTMENT
5 Maxwell Rd., #19-00 & #20-00
Tower Block
MND Complex (0106)
Tel: 65-322-5833; Fax: 65-322-5585

MINISTRY OF HEALTH
16 College Rd., College of
Medicine Bldg., (0316)
Tel: 65-223-7777; Fax: 65-224-1677

**MINISTRY OF THE
ENVIRONMENT**
Environment Bldg., 40 Scotts Rd (0922)
Tel: 65-732-7733; Fax: 65-731-9456

MINISTRY OF EDUCATION
Kay Stang Rd. (1024)
Tel: 65-473-9111; Fax: 65-475-6128

**SINGAPORE INSTITUTE OF
STANDARDS AND
INDUSTRIAL RESEARCH**
1 Science Pl, Dr. (0511)
Tel: 65-778-7777; Fax: 65-778-0086

MINISTRY OF FINANCE
8 Shenton Way, Treasury Bldg. (0106)
Tel: 65-225-9911; Fax: 65-320-9435

**INLAND REVENUE AUTHORITY
OF SINGAPORE**
Fullerton Bldg. (0104)
Tel: 65-535-4244; Fax: 65-535-5393
Commissioner: Mr. Koh Yong Guan

**NATIONAL SCIENCE AND
TECHNOLOGY BOARD**
16 Science Pk. Dr. #01-03, The Pasteur
Singapore Science Park (0511)
Tel: 65-779-7066; Fax: 65-777-1711
Executive Director: Mr. Vijay Mehta

**SINGAPORE BROADCASTING
CORPORATION**
Caldecott Hill, Andrew Rd. (1129)
Tel: 65-256-0401; Fax: 65-253-8808
Chairman: Dr. Cheong Choong Kong

Singapore (ASEAN)

COUNTRY TRADE ASSOCIATIONS/ CHAMBERS OF COMMERCE

SINGAPORE INTERNATIONAL CHAMBER OF COMMERCE
6 Raffles Quay #10-01
John Hancock Tower (0104)
Tel: 65-224-1255; Fax: 65-224-2785
47 Hill St. #09-00 (0617)
Tel: 65-337-8381; Fax: 65-339-0605
President: Mr. Kwek Leng Joo

SINGAPORE FEDERATION OF CHAMBERS OF COMMERCE AND INDUSTRY
47 Hill St. #03-01 Chinese Chamber of
Commerce Bldg. (0617)
Tel: 65-338-9761/2; Fax: 65-339-5630
President: Mr. Boon Yoon Chiang

SINGAPORE INDIAN CHAMBER OF COMMERCE AND INDUSTRY
101 Cecil St. #23-01 Tong Eng Bldg. (0106)
Tel: 65-222-2855, 222-2505; Fax: 65-223-1707
Chairman: Mr. M.K. Chanrai

SINGAPORE INTERNATIONAL CHAMBER OF COMMERCE
6 Raffles Quay #10-01 John Hancock
Tower (0104)
Tel: 65-224-1255; Fax: 65-224-2785
Chairman: Mr. R. E. Hale

SINGAPORE MALAY CHAMBER OF COMMERCE
10 Anson Rd. #24-07
International Plaza (0207)
Tel: 65-221-1066; Fax: 65-223-5811
President: Mr. Jamil Marican

SINGAPORE MANUFACTURERS ASSOCIATION
(The Singapore Export Centre)
20 Orchard Rd., SMA Hse. (0923)
Tel: 65-338-8787; Fax: 65-336-5385
President: Mr. Robert Chua

ASSOCIATION OF SMALL AND MEDIUM ENTERPRISES
Blk. 139, Kim Tian Rd., #02-00 (0316)
Tel: 65-271-2566; Fax: 65-271-1257
President: Mr. Diong Tai Pew

SINGAPORE RETAILERS ASSOCIATION
2 Bukit Merah Central,
#15-03 NPB Bldg. (0315)
Tel: 65-272-3160; Fax: 65-271-3091
Chairman: Mr. Teh Ban Lian

Aerospace
SINGAPORE AEROSPACE LTD.
540 Airport Rd., Paya Lebar (1953)
Tel: 65-287-1111; Fax: 65-280-9713
Vice President: Mr. Jeremy Chan

Automation
AUTOMATION APPLICATION CENTER
61-A Blk., 1 Science Pk. Dr. (0511)
Tel: 65-779-7311; Fax: 65-779-5129
Director: James Ling
Promotes automation in Singapore.

SINGAPORE INDUSTRIAL AUTOMATION ASSOCIATION
151 Chin Swee Rd.,
#03-13 Manhattan House (0316)
Tel: 65-734-6911; Fax: 65-235-5721
Executive Director: Mr. Stephen Teng
Promote the interests of industrial automation users.

Automotive
SINGAPORE CYCLE & MOTOR TRADERS' ASSOCIATION
Blk. 261 Waterloo Centre,
#03-09 Waterloo St. (0718)
Tel: 65-339-7648; Fax: 65-336-6181
Executive Secretary: Mr. Boo Yeow Phong
Association of vehicle traders.

SINGAPORE MOTOR CYCLE TRADE ASSOCIATION
40 Sam Leong Rd. (0820)
Tel: 65-297-1991/297-1313
Admin. Officer: Mr. J. A. Dawes
Association of motor cycle traders.

Computers
INFORMATION TECHNOLOGY INSTITUTE
NCB Building, 71 Science Park Drive (0511)
Tel: 65-772-0967; Fax: 65-779-5996
Director: Dr. Christopher Chia
The applied R & D arm of the National Computer Board.

INSTITUTE OF SYSTEM SCIENCE
National University of Singapore,
Heng Mui Keng Terrace,
Kent Ridge (0511)
Tel: 65-775-6666; Fax: 65-778-2571
Business Development: Mr. K. T. Goh
Formed primarily as a teaching institute but has evolved to include R & D programs with the broad goal of advancing state-of-the-art information technology.

MICROCOMPUTER TRADE ASSOCIATION OF SINGAPORE
211 Henderson Road, #01-01 Henderson
Industrial Estate (0315)
Tel: 65-278-2855; Fax: 65-270-8128
Chairman: Mr. Tan Chin Ngiap
The association was established in 1987 to promote computer trade.

NATIONAL COMPUTER BOARD
71 Science Park Drive (0511)
Tel: 65-778-2211; Fax: 65-778-9641
General Manager: Mr. Ko Kheng Hwa
Government agency responsible for promoting information technology in Singapore.

SINGAPORE COMPUTER SOCIETY
NCB Building, 71 Science Park Drive (0511)
Tel: 65-778-3901; Fax: 65-778-8221
President: Dr. Juzar Motiwalla
National Information Technology society for IT professionals in Singapore.

SINGAPORE FEDERATION OF COMPUTER INDUSTRY
NCB Building, 71 Science Park Drive (0511)
Tel: 65-775-1927; Fax: 65-778-4968
Chairman: Mr. Alex Chan
Represents more than 100 of the most successful computer firms in Singapore.

Construction/Prperty
CONSTRUCTION INDUSTRY DEVELOPMENT BOARD
9 Maxwell Rd., #03-00 National Development
Bldg., Annexe A (0106)
Tel: 65-225-6711; Fax: 65-225-7301
Chief Executive Officer: Mr. Lam Siew Wah
Promote quality and productivity in the construction industry.

ASSOCIATION OF CONSULTING ENGINEERS, SINGAPORE
50 Jln. Sultan,
#07-08 Jln. Sultan Centre (0719)
Tel: 65-292-4660; Fax: 65-292-4628
President: Mr. Lim Hon Chee
The Association is made up of professionally registered engineers in Singapore. Ensure standards and look after interests of practising consulting engineers.

INSTITUTION OF ENGINEERS SINGAPORE
70 Bukit Tinggi Rd. (1128)
Tel: 65-469-5000; Fax: 65-467-1108
President: Dr. Su Guan Ning
Provide information on new technologies. Promote and advance the science, art and profession of engineering in any or all its branches and facilitate the exchange of information and ideas related to engineering.

REAL ESTATE DEVELOPERS ASSOCIATION OF SINGAPORE
190 Clemenceau Ave., #07-01 Singapore
Shopping Centre (0923)
Tel: 65-336-6655; Fax: 65-337-2217
President: Mr. Daniel Teo
Promote the development of the real estate industry in Singapore.

SINGAPORE CONTRACTORS ASSOCIATION LTD. (SCAL)
Construction House, 1 Bukit Merah
Lane 2 (0315)
Tel: 65-278-9577; Fax: 65-273-3977
President: Mr. Kong Mun Kwong
Offer a venue and focus point for contractors to meet and discuss industrial matters, business cooperation and work toward the betterment of contractors.

SINGAPORE INSTITUTE OF ARCHITECTS
20 Orchard Road., #02-00 SMA Hse. (0923)
Tel: 65-338-8977; Fax: 65-336-8708
President: Mr. Goh Chong Chia
Ensure a high standard of practice among practising architects.

SINGAPORE INSTITUTE OF LANDSCAPE ARCHITECTS (SILA)
617 Bukit Timah (1026)
Tel: 65-466-9211; Fax: 65-467-5915
President: Mr. Peter Scotts
Advance the art of landscape architecture and civic design in the Singapore environment.

SINGAPORE INSTITUTE OF PLANNERS
c/o Peoples' Association, Youth Block, Rm. 12,
Kallang (1439)
Tel: 65-348-2586; Fax: 65-440-9450
President: Mr. Ong Teong Tin
Advance the study of town planning, civic design and related arts and sciences.

SINGAPORE INSTITUTE OF SURVEYORS & VALUERS
20 Maxwell Rd.,
#10-09B Maxwell House (0106)
Tel: 65-222-3030; Fax: 65-225-2453
President: Mr. Steven Loh
Secretariat for quantity surveyors, valuers and land surveyors.

Electronics
GINTIC INSTITUTE OF MANUFACTURING TECHNOLOGY
Nanyang Technological University
Nanyang Avenue (2263)
Tel: 65-791-1744; Fax: 65-791-1859
Director: Dr. Frans M. A. Carpay

INSTITUTE OF MICROELECTRONICS
Block 750E, Chai Chee Rd.,
#07-03/04 Chai Chee Industrial Park (1646)
Tel: 65-442-0881; Fax: 65-449-6158
Director: Dr. Bill Chen

NATIONAL SCIENCE AND TECHNOLOGY BOARD
16 Science Park Drive (0511)
Tel: 65-779-7066; Fax: 65-775-5163
Director, Development Division:
Mrs. Adams-Yau Lee Ying

SINGAPORE ECONOMIC DEVELOPMENT BOARD
#24-00 Raffles City Tower,
North Bridge Rd. (0617)
Tel: 65-336-2288; Fax: 65-339-6077
Senior Industry Officer: Mr. K.K. Cheong

SINGAPORE INDUSTRIAL AUTOMATION ASSOCIATION
151 Chin Swee Rd.,
#03-13 Manhattan House (0316)
Tel: 65-734-6911; Fax: 65-235-5721
Executive Director: Mr. Stephen Teng

SINGAPORE INSTITUTE OF STANDARDS AND INDUSTRIAL RESEARCH
1 Science Park Drive (0511)
Tel: 65-778-7777; Fax: 65-778-0672
Chief Executive Officer: Mr. Khoo Lee Meng

SINGAPORE TRADE DEVELOPMENT BOARD
#10-40 World Trade Centre (0409)
Tel: 65-271-9388; Fax: 65-274-0770
Manager: Mr. Thian Tai Chew

THE ASSOCIATION OF ELECTRONIC INDUSTRIES IN SINGAPORE
6001 Beach Rd.,
#18-01 Golden Mile Towers (0719)
Tel: 65-294-0489; Fax: 65-298-4104
President: Mr. Hwang Koh Chee

Film, Video & Music
MUSIC PUBLISHERS SINGAPORE LTD.
9 Penang Rd., #10-01 Park Mall (0923)
Tel: 65-339-0884; Fax: 65-338-1878
Admin. Officer: Mr. Meric Yeo
An association of music publishers.

REDIFFUSION (SINGAPORE) PTE. LTD.
1 Jalan Selanting (2159)
Tel: 65-467-1144; Fax: 65-466-3888
Managing Director: Mr. Wong Ban Kuan
Only private establishment that runs a cable broadcasting station in Singapore.

SINGAPORE CABLEVISION PTE. LTD.
150 Beach Rd., #30-00 Gateway West
Bldg. (0718)
Tel: 65-299-5788; Fax: 65-299-6313
General Manager: Mr. Chan Long Kiat
Only supplier of pay TV in Singapore.

SINGAPORE FEDERATION OF THE PHONOGRAPHIC INDUSTRY
9 Penang Rd., #10-01 Park Mall (0923)
Tel: 65-339-0884; Fax: 65-338-1878
Regional Director: Mr. J. C. Giouw
Promote the phonographic industry in Singapore.

SINGAPORE FILM SOCIETY

Robinson Rd., P.O. Box 3714 (9057)
Tel: 65-235-2088; Fax: 65-732-2088
Contact: Kenneth Tan
Promote "artistic" movies and films in Singapore.

SINGAPORE PHONOGRAM & VIDEOGRAM ASSOCIATION

9 Penang Rd., #10-01 Park Mall (0923)
Tel: 65-339-0726; Fax: 65-338-1876
Admin. Officer: Mr. Eric Yeo
Promote the interests of the recording and video industry in Singapore.

Food Equipment
SINGAPORE ASSOCIATION OF FOOD EQUIPMENT MANUFACTURERS & SUPPLIERS

c/o Focus Management Pte Ltd
#06-03 Maxwell House
20 Maxwell Road
Singapore 0106
Tel: 65-222-8291; Fax: 65-222-3703

Jewelry
DIAMOND EXCHANGE OF SINGAPORE

95 South Bridge Rd., #06-15 Pidemco Centre
(0105)
Tel: 65-532-6565; Fax: 65-533-2165
President: Mr. F.J. Kahfi
Association of diamond traders. Trade in loose diamonds.

SINGAPORE JEWELERS ASSOCIATION

38C North Canal Rd. (0105)
Tel: 65-535-2989; Fax: 65-533-0867
President: Mr. Wan Shung Ming
Association of jewelry manufacturers.

Medical
ACADEMY OF MEDICINE, SINGAPORE

College of Medicine Bldg., 16 College Rd. #01-00 (0316)
Tel: 65-223-8968; Fax: 65-225-5155, 224-7827
Master of the Academy: Dr. Chao Tzee Cheng

BURN INJURIES, ASSOCIATION OF INFECTIOUS DISEASE (SOCIETY OF)

(address same as Academy of Medicine)
c/o Communications Consultants
336 Smith St. #06-302 (0105)
Tel: 65-227-9811; Fax: 65-227-0257
Director: Ms. Nina Sharma

OBSTETRICS & GYNECOLOGICAL SOCIETY OF SINGAPORE

c/o Department of Obstetrics & Gynecology
Kandang Kerbau Hospital, No. 1 Hampshire
Road (0821)
Tel: 65-295-1383; Fax: 65-299-1969
Honorary Secretary: Dr. Tham Kok Fun

PHARMACEUTICAL INDUSTRY (SINGAPORE ASSOCIATION OF)

151 Chin Swee Rd., #02-13A,
14 Manhattan House (0316)
Tel: 65-738-0966; Fax: 65-738-0977
President: Mr. Tan Chwee Choon

PLASTIC SURGEONS (SINGAPORE ASSOCIATION OF)

(address same as Academy of Medicine)

SINGAPORE MEDICAL ASSOCIATION

(address same as Academy of Medicine)
Singapore Society of Ophthalmology
c/o Singapore National Eye Centre, 11 Third
Hospital Ave. (0316)
Tel: 65-227-7255; Fax: 65-227-7290
Medical Director: Professor Arthur Lim

SINGAPORE SOCIETY OF RADIOGRAPHERS

c/o Department of Diagnostic Imaging
National University Hospital, Lower Kent
Ridge Rd. (0511)
Tel: 65-772-5272; Fax: 65-772-5219

SOCIETY FOR LASER MEDICINE & SURGERY

c/o Conference and Exhibition Management
Services Pte. Ltd.
1 Maritime Sq., #09-43 World Trade
Centre (0409)
Tel: 65-278-8666. Fax: 65-278-4077
Managing Director: Mr. Edward Liu

Packagiong
PACKAGING INDUSTRY COUNCIL OF SINGAPORE

c/o Singapore Manufacturers Association
20 Orchard Rd., SMA House (0923)
Tel: 65-338-8787; Fax: 65-338-3358
Chairman: Mr. C.S. Wong
Objectives include keeping members in the industry abreast of the latest development in packaging methods.

Press
STRAITS TIMES PRESS (1975) LTD.

Times House, 390 Kim Seng Rd. (0923)
Tel: 65-737-0011; Fax: 65-732-0131
Editor: Mr. Leslie Fong
Publishers of the Straits Times, Business Times and The New Paper.

Security And Safety Equipment
CHARTERED INDUSTRIES OF SINGAPORE PTE. LTD.

249 Jalan Boon Lay (2261)
Tel: 65-265-1066; Fax: 65-261-6932
President: Mr. Lye Fei
Singapore Government-linked company involved in manufacturing and trading of armaments.

COMMERCIAL AND INDUSTRIAL SECURITY CORPORATION

CISCO Center, 20 Jalan Afifi (1440)
Tel: 65-747-2888; Fax: 65-747-2275
General Manager/CEO: Mr. Chan Boon Kiong
Established under the Ministry of Home Affairs to provide security services. Represents foreign security products.

DEFENCE MATERIALS ORGANIZATION

50 Leo Bldg., Paya Lebar Airport,
Airport Rd. (1953)
Tel: 65-282-5228; Fax: 65-285-3173
Director: Col. Tan Kim Siew
Defense sourcing agency for the Singapore Armed Forces, particularly interested in high technology defence systems and armaments.

DEFENCE SCIENCE ORGANIZATION

20 Science Pk. Dr. (0511)
Tel: 65-776-2255; Fax: 65-775-9011
Director: Dr. Su Guaning
R & D arm of the Ministry of Defence. Interests encompass technology-based area including hardware and software.

MINISTRY OF DEFENCE, DEFENCE PROCUREMENT DIVISION

1st/3rd Level, Leo Bldg., Paya Lebar Airport,
Blk. 50, Airport Rd. (1953)
Tel: 65-380-2700; Fax: 65-287-3052
Assistant Director: Mr. Eng Poh Tian
Defence procurement agency for the Army, Navy and Air Force.

SYSTEMS AND COMPUTER ORGANIZATION

Blk. 8D Dempsey Rd., Tanglin (1024)
Tel: 65-470-7200; Fax: 65-473-8459
Directors: Mr. Goh Chin Hoe, Mr. Stephen Yeo
A division of the Ministry of Defence to computerize various services of the Armed Forces.

Singapore (ASEAN)

Telecommunications
TELECOMMUNICATION AUTHORITY OF SINGAPORE
31 Exeter Rd., Comcenter #05-00 (0923)
Tel: 65-738-7788; Fax: 65-733-0073
Director-General: Mr. Lim Chuan Poh
President & Chief Executive Officer: Mr. Wong Hung Khim.
Regulate and implement telecommunications policies.

TELECOMMUNICATIONS EQUIPMENT SUPPLIERS (ASSOCIATION OF)
50 East Coast Rd., #02-20 Roxy Square (1542)
Tel: 65-447-4267; Fax: 65-344-3206
President: Mr. Alvin Lim
Promote the interests of telecommunications equipment suppliers in Singapore.

Textiles/Apparels
SINGAPORE MASTER TAILORS' ASSOCIATION
3E Lor 12 Geylang (1438)
Tel: 65-748-3878
President: Mr. Kwan Chun Kiew
Promote the interests of tailors.

SINGAPORE TEXTILES & GENERAL MERCHANTS ASSOCIATION
148 Neil Rd. (0208)
Tel: 65-223-8061; Fax: 65-222-3501
President: Mr. Kwong Chi Khiong
Promote the interests of textile merchants.

TEXTILE AND GARMENT MANUFACTURERS' ASSOCIATION OF SINGAPORE
60 Martin Road #07-16
TradeMart Singapore
Singapore 0923
Tel: 65-735-8390
Fax: 65-735-8409
President: Mr. Chris Koh
Promotes the manufacture of textile and garments in Singapore. Represents and safeguards the interest of manufacturers.

SEWING MACHINE TRADERS ASSOCATION
135 Middle Road #03-02
Bylands Building
Singapore 0718
Tel: 65-338-2256
Fax: 65-339-4976
Secretary: Ms. Molly Teo
Promotes the interests of sewing machine traders.

Timber/Furniture
SINGAPORE TIMBER EXPORTERS ASSOCIATION
2 Finlayson Green, #07-01 (0104)
Tel: 65-224-2437; Fax: 65-225-7987
President: Mr. Najmuddin F. Dohadwala
Association of timber exporters.

SINGAPORE TIMBER MANUFACTURERS ASSOCIATION
341B Beach Rd. (0718)
Tel: 65-298-0709; Fax: 65-291-9844
President: Mr. Chua Seng Chong
Association of timber millers.

SINGAPORE PRECISION ENGINEER-ING AND TOOLING ASSOCIATION
15 Kallang Junction (1233)
Tel: 65-295-1970; Fax: 65-292-4517
President: Mr. Hsu Tung Ming
Promote the interest of tool and die manufacturers.

SINGAPORE FURNITURE INDUSTRIES COUNCIL
2 Jurong East St. 21,
#02-110 IMM Bldg. (2260)
Tel: 65-568-2626; Fax: 65-568-2922
President: Mr. James Koh
Association of furniture manufacturers.

Enviornment
SINGAPORE ENVIRONMENTAL MANAGEMENT & ENGINEERING SERVICES PTE. LTD.
40 Scotts Road, Environment Building
Singapore 0922
Tel: 65-738-9720
Fax: 65-738-9719
General Manager: Mr. Donald Goh
A private company owned by ENV Corporation and Singapore Technologies Industrial Corporation. ENV is set up by the Ministry of Environment.

Marine
ASSOCIATION OF SINGAPORE MARINE INDUSTRES
World Trade Center, 1 Maritime Square
#09-10
Singapore 0409
Tel: 65-270-7883
Fax: 65-273-1867
President: Mr. Tan Mong Seng
Promotes the interests of members including shipyards, classification societies, marine suppliers and services.

COUNTRY MARKET RESEARCH FIRMS

D. RICHMOND ASSOCIATES PTE. LTD.
150 Orchard Road #08-12
Orchard Plaza
Singapore 0923
Contact: Ms. Dee Richmond
Tel: 65-738-7550
Fax: 65-732-9727
Fax: 65-479-7565

APPLIED RESEARCH CORPORATION
Engineering Block E4-04-11
National University of Singapore
Singapore 0511
Contact: Mr. Ng Kwan Kee
Tel: 65-775-5822
Fax: 65-773-0924

MARKET BEHAVIOUR (SINGAPORE) PTE. LTD.
1 Sophia Road #04-01 Peace Center
Singapore 0922
Contact: Ms. Tan Jee Lui
Tel: 65-337-6117
Fax: 65-337-6127

COUNTRY COMMERCIAL BANKS (AND FINANCIAL INSTITUTIONS)

Three types of commercial banks operate in Singapore, depending on the type of license they possess. A listing of U.S. banks operating in Singapore—full license, restricted, and offshore—and their basic functions are described below.

Several large commercial banks offer a variety of banking services to manufacturing firms and other clients. Most banks extend credit for five to ten years at competitive interest rates covering up to 50 percent of plant and machinery costs and up to 65 percent of the value of factory buildings. Higher percentages are available for particularly desirable projects and for expansion loans.

In addition to providing loans, many larger Singapore banks also have subsidiaries which carry out merchant banking, insurance, property development, securities trading as members of the stock exchange, and underwriting issues of government bonds. Seventy-seven merchant banks also provide a wide range of services not covered by some commercial banks, including investment portfolio management, investment advisory services, advice on corporate restructuring, takeovers and mergers, arranging finance, lending or participating in syndicated loans, capital equipment leasing and underwriting and floating bond and stock issues. U.S. banks in Singapore are the following:

AMERICAN EXPRESS BANK LTD.
Shenton Way #01-04/05
Shing Kwan House
Singapore 0106
Tel: 65-220-2311; Fax 225-5341

BANK OF AMERICA NT & SA
78 Shenton Way
Singapore 0207
Tel: 65-223-6688; Fax: 65-320-3068

BANK OF HAWAII
4 Shenton Way #19-01
Shing Kwan House
Singapore 0160
Tel: 65-221-0500; Fax: 65-221-1144

THE BANK OF NEW YORK
10 Collyer Quay #14-02/03
Ocean Building
Singapore 0104
Tel: 65-535-4522; Fax: 65-534-4208

MARINE MIDLAND BANK, N.A.
(representative office only)
21 Collyer Quay
#19-01 Hong Kong Bank Building
Singapore 0104
Tel: 65-225-8144; Fax: 65-225-6987

NATIONSBANK OF TEXAS, NA
5 Shenton Way #11-01
UIC Building
Singapore 0106
Tel: 65-220-5755; Fax: 65-220-7315

NORWEST BANK MINNESOTA NA
100 Cecil Street
14-02 Globe Building
Singapore 0106
Tel: 65-226-0809; Fax 226-0874

BANKERS TRUST COMPANY
50 Raffles Place #26-01/06
Shell Tower
Singapore 0104
Tel: 65-222-9191; Fax: 65-225-0813

THE CHASE MANHATTAN BANK NA
Raffles Place #01-01
Shell Tower
Singapore 0104
Tel: 65-530-4111; Fax: 65-224-7950

CHEMICAL BANK
150 Beach Road #06-00
Gateway West
Singapore 0718
Tel: 65-291-1298; Fax: 65-223-7582

CITIBANK NA
5 Shenton Way #06-00
UIC Building
Singapore 0106
Tel: 65-224-2611; Fax: 65-224-9844

THE FIRST NATIONAL BANK OF BOSTON
150 Beach Road #07-00
Gateway West
Singapore 0718
Tel: 65-296-2366; Fax: 65-296-0998

THE PHILADELPHIA NATIONAL BANK
(representative office only)
15 McCallum Street
#05-01 Natwest Center
Singapore 0106
Tel: 65-224-6177; Fax: 65-224-6170

REPUBLIC NATIONAL BANK OF NEW YORK
143 Cecil Street #01-00
GB Building
Singapore 0106
Tel: 65-224-0077; Fax: 65-225-5769

THE ASSOCIATION OF BANKS IN SINGAPORE
10 Shenton Way #12-08 MAS Bldg. (0207)
Tel: 65-224-4300; Fax: 65-224-1785
Director: Mrs. Ong-Ang Ai Boon
Foster the growth of the banking industry in Singapore.

GENERAL INSURANCE ASSOCIATION OF SINGAPORE
1 Shenton Way, #14-01 Robina House (0106)
Tel: 65-221-8788; Fax: 65-227-2051
President: Mr. David Chan
Promotes and safeguard the interests of the general insurance industry in Singapore.

LIFE INSURANCE ASSOCIATION
1 Selegie Rd., #06-17A (0718)
Tel: 65-338-3340; Fax: 65-336-0654
President: Mr. Andrew Tan
Promote and safeguard the interests of the life insurance industry in Singapore.

MONETARY AUTHORITY OF SINGAPORE
10 Shenton Way, MAS Bldg. (0207)
Tel: 65-225-5577; Fax: 65-229-9491
Managing Director: Mr. Lee Ek Tieng
Act as the central bank of Singapore

STOCK EXCHANGE OF SINGAPORE LTD.
1 Raffles Place, #25-00 OUB Centre (0104)
Tel: 65-535-3788; Fax: 65-535-0769
President: Mr. Lim Choo Peng

U.S. EMBASSY TRADE PERSONNEL

AGRICULTURAL TRADE OFFICE
(ATO)
Robert D. Fondahn
Tel: 65-737-1233; Fax: 65-732-8307

CONSULAR SERVICE
Frank C. Turley, Consul
Tel: 65-338-0251, Ext. 328; Fax: 65-337-2253
Information line: 337-2276

CUSTOMS SERVICE
Donal Shruhan
Tel: 65-338-0251, Ext. 345; Fax: 65-338-7308

DEFENSE ATTACHE OFFICE (DAO)
Captain William Cooper (USN)
Tel: 65-338-0251, Ext. 315/316

ECONOMIC/POLITICAL SECTION
Charles B. Jacobini
Tel: 65-338-0251, Ext. 300/309;
Fax: 65-338-4550

FEDERAL AVIATION ADMINISTRATION (FAA)
M. C. (Craig) Beard
Tel: 65-543-1466; Fax: 65-543-1952

FOREIGN COMMERCIAL SERVICE (FCS)
Stephen K. Craven
Tel: 65-338-9722; Fax: 65-338-5010

INTERNAL REVENUE SERVICE (IRS)
Charles W. Landry
Tel: 65-338-0251, Ext. 247; Fax: 65-338-3205

**NAVY REGIONAL
CONTRACTING CENTER**
Captain Dan Allen
Tel: 65-257-5633; Fax: 65-257-4685

SECURITY ASSISTANCE OFFICE (SAO)
Lt. Col. Dennis B. Fowler
Tel: 65-338-0251, Ext. 323; Fax: 65-338-5789

U.S. INFORMATION SERVICE (USIS)
Michael Anderson
Tel: 65-334-0910; Fax: 65-334-2780

WASHINGTON-BASED USG CONTACTS (NOT LISTED UNDER GENERAL ASEAN)

MINING
Mr. Pui-Kwan Tse
U.S. Bureau of Mines
810 7th Street, N.W.
Washington, DC 20241
Tel: 65-202-501-9696; Fax: 65-202-219-2489

U.S.-BASED MULTIPLIERS FOR SINGAPORE

**U.S.-ASEAN COUNCIL FOR
BUSINESS & TECHNOLOGY, INC.**
1400 L St. N.W., Suite 375,
Washington, D.C. 20005-3509
Tel: 202-289-1911; Fax: 202-289-0519
President: Mr. Ernest Z. Bower

U.S. CHAMBER OF COMMERCE
International Division
1615 H St. N.W., Washington, D.C. 20062
Tel: 202-463-5300
President: Mr. Richard L. Lesher

COUNTRY CONSULATES AND TRADE OFFICES IN THE U.S.

**EMBASSY OF THE REPUBLIC
OF SINGAPORE-WASHINGTON**
1824 R. St. N.W.,
Washington, D.C. 20009-1691
Tel: 202-667-7555; Fax: 202-265-7915

**SINGAPORE ECONOMIC
DEVELOPMENT BOARD-BOSTON**
8th Floor, One International Place,
Boston, MA 02110
Tel: 617-261-9981; Fax: 617-261-9983
Centre Directors: Ms. Loh Wai Kiew

**SINGAPORE ECONOMIC
DEVELOPMENT BOARD-CHICAGO**
Two Prudential Plaza,
180 N. Stetson Ave.,
Suite 970
Chicago, IL 60601
Tel: 312-565-1100; Fax: 312-565-1994
Directors: Mr. Suresh Natarajan, Mr. James Ng

**SINGAPORE ECONOMIC DEVELOP-
MENT BOARD, LOS ANGELES**
2049 Century Park East,
Suite 400, Los Angeles, CA 90067
Tel: 310-553-0199; Fax: 310-557-1044
Director: Mr. Tam Chek Ming

**SINGAPORE ECONOMIC
DEVELOPMENT BOARD-NEW YORK**
55 East 59th St., New York, NY 10022
Tel: 212-421-2200; Fax: 212-421-2206
Regional Director: Mr. Goh Eng Ghee
Centre Director : Mr. Ng Nam Sin

**SINGAPORE ECONOMIC DEVELOP-
MENT BOARD-SAN FRANCISCO**
210 Twin Dolphin Dr.,
Redwood City, CA 94065
Tel: 415-591-9102; Fax: 415-591-1328
Directors: Mr. Chong Lit Cheong, Ms.
Adelaine Lim, Mr. Pang Heng Soon

**SINGAPORE ECONOMIC DEVELOP-
MENT BOARD-WASHINGTON**
1350 Connecticut Ave. N.W., Suite 504,
Washington, D.C. 20036-1701
Tel: 202-223-2570/2571;
Fax: 202-223-2572
Director: Mr. Lee Yee Shyan

U.S. DEPARTMENT OF COMMERCE MARKET RESEARCH AVAILABLE

— Aircraft Maintenance Equipment
— Alarms/Other Detection Equipment
— Antibiotics
— Automated Food Processing Equipment
— Building Automation Equipment
— Carpets and Floor Coverings
— Chemical Analysis Instruments
— Communications Equipment: Airborne
— Cranes
— Data Communication Equipment
— Dental Care and Hygiene Products
— Dental Surgical Instruments
— Diagnostic Equipment

— Earthmoving/Machinery Parts
— Electo-Mechanical Robots
— Electrical Generating Equipment
— Electronic Industry Test Equipment
— Electronics Production/Test Equipment
— Elevators/Escalators
— Fine Jewelry
— Franchising: Food Service/Restaurants
— Franchising: Health and Recreation Services
— Household Kitchen Appliances
— Industrial Air Pollution Control Equipment
— Medical Products: Disposable
— Metal Forming Machine Tools
— Networking Software: LAN/WAN
—Operating Room Equipment
— Packaging Equipment: Stretch Wrap
— Photographic Equipment for Graphics
— Printed Circuit Board Assembly Equipment
— Printed Circuit Boards
— Process Controls: Food Processing
— Product Design and Packaging
— Ready-to-eat and Prepared Ingredients
— Refrigerators and Freezers
— Robotics and Automation Equipment
— Shovel Loaders
— Skin Care Products and Makeup
— Tableware and Kitchenware

*Available from U.S. and Foreign Commercial
Service, Steven K. Craven. 65-338-9722;
Fax 65-338-5010*

U.S. DEPARTMENT OF AGRICULTURE COMMODITY REPORTS AND MARKET BRIEFS

—Overview of the Foodstuffs Market
— Food Processing Industry
— Microwave Foods
— Health Foods
— Western Packaged Meals
— Processed Meats
— Juices
— Beer and Ale
— Fresh Vegetables
— Temperate Fresh Fruit
— Stone Fruits
— Apples
— Berries
— Grapes
— Pears
— Nuts
— Pistachios, Macadamias and Walnuts
— Peanuts
— Almonds

U.S. DEPARTMENT OF STATE ECONOMIC REPORTS

— The Growth Triangle, Singapore-Johor-Riau
— Major Infrastructure Projects In Singapore
— National Trade Estimate Report on Foreign Trade Barriers, Singapore
— Singapore Computer Industry Report
— Singapore Electronics Report
— Singapore Investment Survey Report
— Singapore Labor Report
— Singapore Telecommunications Report
— Singapore Textile Report
— Singapore Trade Act Report
— Singapore's Economic Indicators
— Singapore's Environment Report
— Singapore's Government-Linked Companies Report
— Singapore's Petroleum Industry Report
— Singapore's Productivity Report
— Singapore's Property Report
— Singapore's Shipyards Report

TRADE EVENTS SCHEDULE

SEPTEMBER 24-27, 1995
Baucon Asia '95. Singapore. Contact Person: Steve Banks, Tel: 202-482-0595

SEPTEMBER 25 - OCTOBER 3, 1995
Trading Companies Matchmaker. Singapore, Philippines, Thailand. Contact: Sepia Thompson, Dept. of Commerce, Tel: 202-482-5131

OCTOBER 1-12, 1995
Singapore International Chamber of Commerce. Mission to the U.S. Seattle, WA; Kansas City, MO; Indianapolis, IN; New York, NY

OCTOBER 26 - 28, 1995
Comdex /Asia Trade Show. Singapore. Contact: Betty Smith, Tel: 202-482-0106

October 30 - November 7, 1995
Sporting Goods /Physical Fitness Matchmaker. Singapore, Indonesia. Contact: Derek Parks, Dept. of Commerce, Tel: 202-482-0287

FEBRUARY 6 - 11, 1996
Asian Aerospace '96. Singapore. Contact: Betty Smith, Tel: 202- 482-0106

MARCH 1, 1996
International Spring Fair. Singapore. Contact: Fernec Molnar, Tel: 202-482-2043

MARCH 28 - 31, 1996
Golf Asia '96. Singapore. Contact: Steve Banks, Tel: 202-482-0595

APRIL 1, 1996
Environmental Technologies Matchmakers. Singapore. Contact: Molly Costa, Dept. of Commerce, Tel: 202-482-0692

APRIL 16 - 19, 1996
Food & Hotel Asia Trade Show. Singapore. Contact: Hanson, Dept. of Commerce, Tel: 202-720-9423

MAY 16 - 19, 1996
Food & Hotel Asia. Singapore. Contact: Hanson, Tel: 202-720-9423

JUNE 1, 1996
Royal College of Surgeons. Thailand and Singapore. Contact: George Keen, Tel: 202-482-2010

AUGUST 20 - 21, 1996
Computer Software Trade Mission. Singapore, Kuala Lumpur, Malaysia. Contact: Heidi Hijikata, Dept. of Commerce, Tel: 202-482-0569

INFORMATION CHECKLIST AND BIBLIOGRAPHY

The following publications provide further information on Singapore's economic and commercial climate. They are available from USFCS Singapore at cost, plus a nominal postage and handling fee. To order any of the publications, contact USFCS Singapore, Tel: 65-338-9722; Fax: 65-338-5010.

The American Chamber of Commerce in Singapore, Membership Directory
A listing of all coporate and individual members.

American Products & Services in Singapore Buyer's Guide
Four main sections include: U.S. Trade & General Informaion; Alphabetical List of American Firms and Reps; American Products & Services; American Brand/Trade Names.

ASEAN Trade Directory
Profiles major economic activities within ASEAN, contains information on more than 9,800 companies.

Consumer Price Index
This monthly report is based on a household expenditure survey.

Diplomatic and Consular List
Lists foreign diplomats in Singapore. Provides name designations, addresses, contact numbers and working hours of embassies.

Dun & Bradstreet Key Business Director of Singapore (Third Edition)
Directory has 3,000 entries and essential facts about key Singapore companies.

Dun & Bradstreet, The ASEAN Series – Key Business Directories of Singapore, Malaysia, Indonesia/Thailand
A three volume series listing the top 7,000 ASEAN companies in Singapore, Malaysia, Indonesia/Thailand. The directories are cross-referenced by line of business and geographically for Malaysia and Indonesia/Thailand; the key Business Directory of Singapore is cross-referenced by line of business and directory of directors.

Economic Survey of Singapore
Covers Singapore's economic performance, balance of payments, external trade, tourism, etc.

Expatriate Living Costs in Singapore
Information on food, clothing, housing, transport, education, etc.

Hotel & Restaurant Suppliers' Directory
Information on manufacturers/suppliers from 27 countries most of whom are looking for distributors in ASEAN.

U.S. Investment Survey
Survey of U.S. Investment in Singapore. Prepared by the American Embassy.

Kompass Directory of American Business in Singapore
Assists in locating American products and services.

Singapore (ASEAN)

*Kompass Singapore Company Information –
Volume I*

*Kompass Products & Services Information –
Volume II*
These volumes each contain about 900 pages of
business information on companies in Singapore
including, in Vol.I, addresses, names of
executives, contact numbers, number of
employees, office hours, etc. Vol. II locates
suppliers of products and services.

Living in Singapore: An Expatriate's Guide
A guidebook to assist in getting settled into
Singapore. Includes tips on housing, domestic
help, health/medical, entertainment, etc.

*Singapore Chinese Chamber of Commerce
& Industry Directory*
Comprehensive directory of member companies
and trade associations categorized by product
and services.

Singapore Convention/Exhibition Calendar
Directory of conventions/exhibitions
(1994/1997)

Singapore Country Commercial Guide
Guide to doing business in Singapore

Singapore Economic Trends Report
Report on the Singapore economy prepared by
the U.S. Embassy.

*Singapore Electrical, Electronic, and Engineering
Directory*
Products and services information on more
than 3,000 Singapore based companies.

Singapore Electrical Products & Services
This directory provides information on
manufacturers, agents and distributors.

Singapore Electronics Trade Directory
Comprehensive information including
company's date of establishment, staff strength,
company's main banker and sales turnover.

Singapore Government Directory
The bi-annual directory gives information on
government departments, addresses, phone
numbers, names and designations.

*Singapore Industrial Outlook Report: Electrical
Products and Telecommunication Equipment*
Report on one of the major industries in
Singapore. Prepared by the U.S. Embassy.

*Singapore International Chamber of Commerce
(SICC) Annual Report*
A yearly review of the various sectors of the
Singapore economy.

*Singapore Telephone Directory
Singapore Commercial/Industrial Guide
Singapore Buying Guide*
These two volumes of Singapore's Yellow Pages
can be of instrumental help in locating
products and services in Singapore. Business
Listing and Buying Guide.

Singapore Trade Classification & Customs Duties
Guidelines on customs procedures, units of
quantity used in the Singapore trade classification, etc.

Times Guide to Computers
This listing provides names, addresses and
contact numbers of computer companies in
Singapore.

Trade Show Directories
Limited copies of directories from Singapore
major trade shows, including: Singapore
Informatics, Metal Asia, Offshore Southeast
Asia and Asian Aerospace.

*Trade-Link Singapore Manufacturers
Association Directory*
This directory assists foreign business people
and investors seeking to source their
requirements from Singapore. Lists manufacturers, exporters, trading and service
companies' names, addresses, bankers, and
services and products offered by them.

Yearbook of Statistics, Singapore
Contains statistics on the demographic,
economic and social characteristics of
Singapore.

BOOKS

Economic Restructuring in Singapore, Lim chong
Yah. Federal Publications, Singapore, 1984

The First 150 Years of Singapore, Donald and
Joanna Moore. In association with the
Singapore Chamber of Commerce, Singapore,
1983

Government and Politics of Singapore, Quah, Jon
S.T., Chan Heng-Chee, Seah Chee-Meow,
editors. Singapore University Press: Singapore,
1985

*Malaysia and Singapore: The Building of New
States*, Stanley S. Bedlington

Riot and Revolution in Singapore, R. Clutterbuck.
London, Faber 1973

Singapore Development Policies and Trends, Peter
S.J. Chen, editor. Oxford University Press:
Singapore, 1983

The Singapore Economy: New Directions.
Ministry of Trade and Industry

Singapore Towards the Year 2000, Saw, Swee-
hock and R.S. Bathal, editors. Singapore
University Press for Singapore Association for
the Advancement of Science, Singapore, 1981

*Sinister Twilight: The Fall and Rise Again of
Singapore*, Noel Barber. London, W. Collins,
1968

The Tiger and the Trojan Horse, Dennis
Bloodworth. Times Books International:
Singapore, 1986

Singapore (ASEAN)

Resources: South Africa

U.S. AND COUNTRY CONTACTS

COUNTRY GOVERNMENT AGENCIES

MINISTER OF TRADE AND INDUSTRY
Mr. Trevor A. Manuel
Private Bag x274
Pretoria 0001
Tel: (27 12) 32207677
Fax: (27 12) 322-7851
or,
Private Bag x9047
Cape Town 8000
Tel: (27 21) 461-7191; Fax: (27 21) 45-1291

DIRECTOR-GENERAL DEPARTMENT OF TRADE AND INDUSTRY
Dr. Zav Rustomjee
Private Bag x84
Pretoria 0001
Tel: (27 12) 310-9791;
Fax: (27 12) 322-0298

MINISTER OF WATER AFFAIRS & FORESTRY
Professor Kader Asmal
Private Bag X313
Pretoria 0001
Tel: (27 12) 299-2525; Fax: (012) 328-4254

DIRECTOR GENERAL OF WATER AFFAIRS & FORESTRY
Mr. Marthinuis Erasmus
Private Bag X313
Pretoria O001
Tel: (27 12) 299-2944;
Fax: (27 12) 326-2630

MINISTER OF NATIONAL HOUSING
Mrs. Sankie Nkondo
Private Bag X645
Pretoria 0001
Tel: (27 12) 44-1879; Fax: (27 12) 343-8934

DIRECTOR GENERAL HOUSING DEPARTMENT
Mr. Billy Cobbett
Private Bag X644
Pretoria 0001
Tel: (27 12) 341-1725;
Fax: (27 12) 341-2998

MINISTER OF AGRICULTURE
Dr. A.I. Van Niekerk
Private Bag X116
Pretoria 0001
Tel: (27 12) 21-7670
Fax: (27 12) 21-7219

DIRECTOR GENERAL OF AGRICULTURE
Dr. Frans Van Der Merwe
Private Bag X250
Pretoria 0001
Tel: (27 12) 206-3000
Fax: (27 12) 218-558

MINISTER OF FINANCE
Mr. Chris Liebenberg
Private Bag X115
Pretoria 0001
Tel: (27 12) 323-8911
Fax: (27 12) 323-3262

DIRECTOR GENERAL OF FINANCE
Dr. Estian Calitz
Private Bag X115
Pretoria 0001
Tel: (27 12) 326-6311
Fax: (27 12) 323-3262

MINISTER OF MINERAL & ENERGY AFFAIRS
Mr. Pik Botha
Private Bag X646
Pretoria 0001
Tel: (27 12) 322-8695/6
Fax: (27 12) 322-8699

DIRECTOR GENERAL OF MINERAL & ENERGY AFFAIRS
Dr. Peter Jacobus Hugo
Private Bag X59
Pretoria 0001
Tel: (27 12) 317-9130
Fax: (27 12) 320-2105

MINISTER OF ENVIRONMENT AFFAIRS & TOURISM
Dr. David Jacobus De Villiers
Private Bag X883
Pretoria 0001

DIRECTOR GENERAL OF ENVIRONMENT AFFAIRS & TOURISM
Dr. C.M. Cameron
Private Bag X447
Pretoria 0001
Tel: (27 12) 310-3651
Fax: (27 12) 322-2682

MINISTER OF PUBLIC WORKS
Mr. Jeff Radebe
Private Bag X65
Pretoria 0001
Tel: (27 12) 324-1510
Fax: (27 12) 325-6398

DIRECTOR GENERAL OF PUBLIC WORKS
Mr. T. Van Robbroeck
Private Bag X65
Pretoria 0001
Tel: (27 12) 205-2000
Fax: (27 12) 323-2856

MINISTER OF POST, TELECOMMUNICATIONS & BROADCASTING
Dr. Pallo Jordon
Private Bag X882
Pretoria 0001
Tel: (27 12) 319-8000
Fax: (27 12) 319-8020

POST MASTER GENERAL
Advocate P.J.D. Oosthuizen
Private Bag X860
Pretoria 0001
Tel: (27 12) 319-8012
Fax: (27 12) 319-8020

MINISTER OF TRANSPORT
Mr. Satjandranath Ragunanan Maharaj (MAC)
Private Bag X193, Pretoria 0001
Tel: (27 12) 328-3084/5
Fax: (27 12) 328-3194

DIRECTOR GENERAL OF TRANSPORT
Dr. Conrad Frederick Scheepers
Private Bag X193, Pretoria 0001
Tel: (27 12) 290-9111
Fax: (27 12) 324-3486

South Africa

**MINISTER OF SPORTS
& RECREATION**
Mr. Steve Tshwete
Private Bag X869
Pretoria 0001
Tel: (27 12) 21-1781/2
Fax: (27 12) 21-8493

**DIRECTOR GENERAL OF
NATIONAL EDUCATION (&
SPORTS/RECREATION)**
Dr. J.B.Z. Louw
Private Bag X122
Pretoria 0001
Tel: (27 12) 314-6001
Fax: (27 12) 325-2768

MINISTER OF PUBLIC ENTERPRISES
Mrs. Princess Stella Sigcau
P.O. Box 55711
Pretoria 0001
Tel: (27 12) 44-2369
Fax: (27 12) 44-5848

**CHIEF OF THE DEPARTMENT
OF PUBLIC ENTERPRISES**
Dr. E.P. Van Eeden
P.O. Box 55711
Pretoria 0001
Tel: (27 12) 44-2311
Fax: (27 12) 44-5848

**MINISTER OF WELFARE &
POPULATION DEVELOPMENT**
Mr. Abe William
Private Bag X399
Pretoria 0001
Tel: (27 12) 328-4600
Fax: (27 12) 325-7071

**DIRECTOR GENERAL OF WELFARE
& POPULATION DEVELOPMENT**
Dr. C.F. Slabbert
Private Bag X828
Pretoria 0001
Tel: (27 12) 326-0281
Fax: (27 12) 323-0093

MINISTER OF HEALTH
Dr. Nkosazana D. Zuma
Private Bag X399,   Pretoria 0001
Tel: (27 12) 328-4773
Fax: (27 12) 325-5526

**DIRECTOR GENERAL OF DEPART-
MENT OF NATIONAL HEALTH**
Dr. C. F. Slabber
Private Bag X828
Pretoria 0001
Tel: (27 12) 312-0922
Fax: (27 12) 323-0093

NATIONAL FORUMS

NATIONAL ECONOMIC FORUM
P.O. Box 2352
Johannesburg 2000
Tel: (27 11) 614-2251
Fax: (27 11) 618-2078

**NATIONAL EDUCATION
AND TRAINING FORUM**
Private Bag X727
Pretoria 0001
Tel: (27 12) 324-4096
Fax: (27 12) 324-2687

**NATIONAL ELECTRIFICATION
FORUM**
P.O. Box 5719
Halfway House 1885
Tel: (27 11) 313-3027
Fax: (27 11) 313-3663

NATIONAL HEALTH FORUM
Private Bag X828
Pretoria 0001
Tel: (27 12) 312-0995
Fax: (27 12) 325-5706

NATIONAL HOUSING FORUM
P.O. Box 1115
Johannesburg 2000
Tel: (27 11) 838-2822
Fax: (27 11) 838-1825

COUNTRY TRADE ASSOCIATIONS/ CHAMBERS OF COMMERCE

**AMERICAN CHAMBER OF
COMMERCE IN SOUTHERN AFRICA**
P.O. Box 62280
2107 Marshalltown
Tel: (27 11) 788-0265/6
Fax: (27 11) 880-1632

**SOUTH AFRICAN CHAMBER
OF BUSINESS (SACOB)**
P.O. Box 91267
Auckland Park 2006
Tel: (27 11) 482-2524
Fax: (27 11) 726-1344

**SOUTH AFRICAN FOREIGN TRADE
ORGANIZATION (SAFTO)**
P.O. Box 782706
Sandton 2146
Tel: (27 11) 883-3737
Fax: (27 11) 883-6569

**JOHANNESBURG CHAMBER OF
COMMERCE AND INDUSTRY (JCCI)**
Private Bag 34
Auckland Park 2006
Tel: (27 11) 726-5300
Fax: (27 11) 726-8421

**DURBAN REGIONAL
CHAMBER OF BUSINESS**
P.O. Box 1506
Durban 4000
Tel: (27 31) 301-3699
Fax: (27 31) 301-3699

**CAPE TOWN CHAMBER
OF COMMERCE**
P.O. Box 204
Cape Town 8000
Tel: (27 21) 23-2323
Fax: (27 21) 24-1878

**ASSOCIATION FOR THE
PROMOTION OF THE WESTERN
CAPE (WESGRO)**
P.O. Box 1678
Cape Town 8000
Tel: (27 21) 45-3201
Fax: (27 21) 45-3751

**SOUTHERN AFRICA ASSOCIATION
FOR THE CONFERENCE INDUSTRY**
P.O. Box 36715
Menlo Park 0102
Tel: (27 12) 342-1634

CHAMBER OF MINES
5 Hollard Street
P.O. Box 809
Johannesburg
Tel: (27 11) 838-8211
Fax: (27 11) 834-1884

**COMMERCIAL AVIATION
ASSOCIATION OF SOUTH AFRICA**
RA 29, Comair Centre
P.O. Box 18045
Rand Airport
Tel: (27 11) 827-2516
Fax: (27 11) 824-1823

**AGRICULTURAL AND VETERINARY
CHEMICALS ASSOCIATION**
P.O. Box 1995
Halfway House
Tel: (27 11) 805-2079/2070
Fax: (27 11) 805-2222

**COMPUTER USERS INDUSTRY
COUNCIL OF SOUTH AFRICA**
5 Alexandra Avenue
Halfway House Box
1688 Halfway House
Tel: (27 11) 805-3151

**ELECTRONICS AND
TELECOMMUNICATIONS
INDUSTRY ASSOCIATION**

**FERRO ALLOY PRODUCTION
ASSOCIATION**

**IRON & STEEL PRODUCERS
ASSOCIATION**

**NON-FERROUS METAL
INDUSTRY ASSOCIATION**

**MATERIALS HANDLING
ASSOCIATION**

All found at:
P.O. Box 1338
Johannesburg 2000
Tel: (27 11) 833-6033;
Fax: (27 11) 838-1522

MOTOR INDUSTRIES FEDERATION
P.O. Box 2940
Randburg 2125
Tel: (27 11) 789-2542

**SOUTH AFRICA ASSOCIATION OF
FREIGHT FORWARDERS**
P/Bag 34
Auckland Park, Johannesburg
Tel: (22 11) 726-4019
Fax: (27 11) 726-3415

**MOTION PICTURE ASSOCIATION OF
AMERICA**
P.O. Box 52867
Saxonwold 2132
Tel: (27 11) 880-5885
Fax: (27 11) 880-5493

**S.A. DIRECT MARKETING ASSOCIA-
TION**
P.O. Box 85370
Emmarentia 2029
Tel: (27 11) 482-1419
Fax: (27 11) 726-3807

**THE EXHIBITION ASSOCIATION OF
SOUTH AFRICA**
Private Bag X07
Bertsham 2013
Tel: (27 11) 494-9111
Fax: (27 11) 494-1506

**COMPUTING SERVICES ASSOCIA-
TION (CSA)**
Private Bag 34
Auckland Park 2006
Tel: (27 11) 726-5300
Fax: (27 11) 726-8421

**BUSINESS EQUIPMENT ASSOCIA-
TION (BEA)**
P.O. Box 3277
Randburg 2125
Tel: (27 11) 789-3805
Fax: (27 11) 789-3327

**NATIONAL CLOTHING FEDERATION
OF SOUTH AFRICA**
P.O. Box 75755
Gardenview 2047
Tel: (27 11) 622-8125
Fax (27 11) 622-8316

**COUNCIL OF SOUTHERN AFRICAN
BANKS**
P.O. Box 61380
Marshalltown 2107
Tel: (27 11) 838-5833
Fax: (27 11) 833-1072

**THE S.A. ASSOCIATION OF
CONSULTING ENGINEERS**
P.O. Box 1644
Randburg 2125
Tel: (27 11) 787-5944
Fax (27 11) 789-5264

**ELECTRICAL ENGINEERING & ALLIED
INDUSTRIES ASSOCIATION**
P.O. Box 1338
Johannesburg 2000
Tel: (27 11) 833-6033
Fax (27 11) 838-1522

MOTOR INDUSTRIES FEDERATION
P.O. Box 2940
Randburg 2125
Tel: (27 11) 789-2542
Fax (27 11) 789-4525

**THE GROCERY MANUFACTURERS'
ASSOCIATION OF SOUTH AFRICA**
P.O. Box 34 Randburg 2125
Tel: (27 11) 886-3008
Fax (27 11) 886-5375

SOUTH AFRICAN BLACK BUSINESS ORGANIZATIONS

**BLACK ASSOCIATION OF TRAVEL
AGENTS OF SOUTH AFRICA**
P.O. Box 11435
Marine Parade, 4060 Durban
Tel: (27 31) 37-6433/4
Fax: (27 31) 37-3805

BLACK LAWYERS ASSOCIATION
P.O. Box 5217
Johannesburg 2000
Tel: (27 11) 337-1535/6
Fax: (27 11) 337-1539

**ASSOCIATION OF BLACK
ACCOUNTANTS OF
SOUTHERN AFRICA**
34 McCarthy Centre
P.O. Box 5282
Johannesburg 2001
Tel: (27 11) 331-6923
Fax: (27 11) 331-3912

**BLACK MANAGEMENT
FORUM (BMF)**
P.O. Box 197
Booysens 2061
Tel: (27 11) 337-7661
Fax: (27 11) 337-8744

NATIONAL BLACK BUSINESS CAUCUS (NBBC)
P.O. Box 1507
Gallo Manor 2052
Tel: (27 11) 806-5561
Fax: (27 11) 806-5558

FOUNDATION FOR AFRICAN BUSINESS & CONSUMER ORGANIZATIONS (FABCOS)
P.O. Box 8785
Johannesburg, 2000
Tel: (27 11) 832-1911
Fax: (27 11) 836-5920

NATIONAL AFRICAN FEDERATED CHAMBER OF COMMERCE & INDUSTRY (NAFCOC)
Private Bag X81
Soshanguve 0152
Tel: (27 1214) 3204/6
Fax: (27 1214) 2024

SOUTH AFRICAN BLACK FRANCHISORS ASSOCIATION
P.O. Box 80
Meadowlands 1851
Tel: (27 11) 939-2121
Fax: (27 11) 939-2013

SOUTH AFRICAN IMPORT AND EXPORT ASSOCIATION
P.O. Box 9736
Johannesburg 2000
Tel: (27 11) 839-1385/6
Fax: (27 11) 839-1386

AFRICAN INDUSTRIAL DEVELOPMENT CORPORATION
P.O. Box 1280
Edenvale 1610
Tel: (27 11) 609-4053
Fax: (27 11) 452-6403

BUSINESS OPPORTUNITY CENTRE
P.O. Box 828
Auckland Park 2006
Tel: (27 11) 839-2750/1
Fax: (27 11) 839-1897

COUNTRY MARKET RESEARCH FIRMS

SOUTH AFRICA MARKETING RESEARCH ASSOCIATION (SAMRA)
P.O. Box 91879
Auckland Park 2006
Tel: (27 11) 482-1419
Fax: (27 11) 726-3639

SAMRA will be happy to refer U.S. companies to an appropriate market researcher depending on subject matter and type of study required.

COUNTRY COMMERCIAL BANKS

Commercial banks operating in South Africa can be located through:

REGISTRAR OF FINANCIAL INSTITUTIONS
Private Bag X238
Pretoria 0001
Tel: (27 12) 325-2550

U.S. EMBASSY TRADE PERSONNEL

The United States maintains an embassy in Pretoria and consulates in Johannesburg, Cape Town and Durban. The U.S. Foreign & Commercial Service's offices are located in the American Consulates in Johannesburg and Cape Town.

U.S. & FOREIGN COMMERCIAL SERVICE (USFC&S)
c/o American Consulate General Johannesburg
12th Floor, Kine Center
Commissioner and Kruis Streets
Mailing Address:
Department of State (Johannesburg)
Washington, DC 20521-2500
Tel: (27 11) 331-3937
Fax: (27 11) 331-6178

AMERICAN EMBASSY
Thibault House
877 Pretorius Street
Arcadia 0083
Tel: (27 12) 342-1048
Fax: (27 12) 342-2244

AMERICAN CONSULATE GENERAL - CAPE TOWN
Broadway Industries Center
Heerengracht, Foreshore
Mailing Address:
Department of State (Cape Town)
Washington, DC 20520-2480
Tel: (27 21) 214-280

AMERICAN CONSULATE GENERAL-DURBAN
Durban Bay House, 29th Fl.
333 Smith Street
Mailing Address:
Department of State (Durban)
Washington, DC 20520
Tel: (27 31) 304-4737
Fax: (27 31) 301-8206

U.S. AGENCY FOR INTERNATIONAL DEVELOPMENT (USAID)
Sancardia, 9th Floor
524 Church Street
Arcadia, Pretoria 0007
Tel: (27 12) 323-8869
Fax: (27 12) 323-6443

U.S. FOREIGN AGRICULTURAL SERVICE
877 Pretoria Street
Arcadia, Pretoria 002
Tel: (27-12) 342-1048
Fax: (27-12) 342-2264

WASHINGTON-BASED USG COUNTRY CONTACTS

U.S. DEPARTMENT OF COMMERCE
International Trade Administration
Office of Africa, South Africa Desk, Room 2037
Washington, DC 20230
Tel: (202) 482-5148
Fax: (202) 482-5198

U.S. DEPARTMENT OF STATE
Office of Southern African Affairs, Room 4238
Washington, DC 20250
Tel: (202) 647-8432; Fax: (202) 647-5007

EXPORT-IMPORT BANK OF THE UNITED STATES
Loan Officer, Southern and Eastern Africa
811 Vermont Avenue, NW
Washington, DC 20571
Tel: (202) 565-3933;
Fax: (202) 565-3931

South Africa

U.S. TRADE AND DEVELOPMENT PROGRAM

Regional Director, Africa
Room 309, SA-16
U.S. Department of State
Washington, DC 20523-1602
Tel: (703) 875-4357;
Fax: (703) 875-4009

OVERSEAS PRIVATE INVESTMENT CORPORATION

Investment Development
1100 New York Avenue, NW
Washington, DC 20527
Tel: (202) 336-8616;
Fax: (202) 408-5145

U.S. BUREAU OF MINES

Division of International Minerals - Africa
810 Seventh Street, NW
Mail Stop 5205
Washington, D.C. 20241-0002
Tel: (202) 501-9666;
Fax: (202) 219-2489

U.S.-BASED MULTIPLIERS RELEVANT FOR COUNTRY

U.S.-SOUTH AFRICA BUSINESS COUNCIL

1625 K Street NW
Washington, D.C. 20006
Tel: (202) 887-0278
Fax: (202) 452-8160

INVESTOR RESPONSIBILITY RESEARCH CENTER, INC. (IRRC)

Suite 700
1350 Connecticut Avenue NW
Washington, DC 20036
Tel: (202) 833-0700;
Fax: (202) 833-3555

IRRC publishes a number of information materials about American business activity in South Africa, including:

U.S. Business in South Africa: A Directory of U.S. Corporations with Business Links to South Africa

COUNTRY CONSULATE AND TRADE OFFICES IN THE U.S.

The South African Government maintains an Embassy in Washington, D.C., consulates with trade offices in New York, Chicago, and Los Angeles, and a tourism office in New York.

EMBASSY OF SOUTH AFRICA

Economic/Commercial Section
Suite 300
3201 New Mexico Avenue, NW
Washington, DC 20016
Tel: (202) 966-1650; Fax: (202) 966-5919

SOUTH AFRICAN CONSULATE GENERAL

333 East 38th Street, 9th Floor
New York, NY 10016
Tel: (212) 213-4880; Fax: (212) 213-0102

SOUTH AFRICAN CONSULATE GENERAL

200 South Michigan Avenue, 6th Floor
Chicago, IL 60604
Tel: (312) 939-7929; Fax: (312) 939-7481

SOUTH AFRICAN CONSULATE GENERAL

50 N La Cienga Boulevard, Suite 300
Beverly Hills, CA 90211
Tel: (213) 657-9200; Fax: (213) 657-9215

SOUTH AFRICAN TOURISM BOARD

747 Third Avenue
New York, NY 10017
Tel: (212) 838-8841; Fax: (212) 826-6928

U.S. DEPARTMENT OF COMMERCE MARKET RESEARCH AVAILABLE

Industry Sector Analyses (ISAs) on the National Trade Data Bank
— Automobiles and Trucks (ISA9311)
— Automotive Parts and Service Equipment (ISA9310)
— Local Area Networks (ISA9309)
— Medical Equipment and Products (ISA9309)
— Health Care Services (ISA9309)
— Cosmetics/Hair Care (ISA9304)
— Computer Hardware PCS (ISA9302)
— Mining Technologies (ISA9302)
— Telecommunications Equipment (ISA9302)
— Medical Equipment (ISA9201)
— Aircraft (ISA9112)

The Overseas Business Report: Marketing Guide for South Africa is also available on the NTDB (OBR9209).
— Electric Power Transmission/Distribution
— Environmental Technologies
— Films/Videos/Sound Recordings
— Fishing Equipment
— Franchising
— Garment Production Equipment
— Generic Drugs
— Health Care Services
— Investment/Financial Services
— Low Cost Housing
— Medical Equipment
— Mining Equipment
— South Africa's Black Business Community: Agents, Distributors,and Joint Ventures
— Telecommunications
— Water Sports Equipment
— Water Treatment Chemicals

Reports Available from the U.S. Foreign Agricultural Service
— Fresh Deciduous Fruit Annual
— Grain and Feed Update
— Grain Production
— Grain and Feed Annual
— Corn Crop Estimate
— Canned Deciduous Fruit Annual
— Sugar Annual
— Dried Fruit Annual
— Tobacco Annual
— Oilseeds and Products Annual
— Poultry Annual
— Grain Update
— Livestock Annual
— Agricultural Situation Annual

These and other situation reports about South Africa's agricultural sector are available from the Reports Office/U.S. Department of Agriculture/Foreign Agricultural Service (FAS), Washington, D.C. 20250; Tel: (202) 690-4471.

TRADE EVENTS SCHEDULE

The pace of political change in South Africa focuses increased attention on the importance of U.S. commercial relations with that country. To help meet this challenge, we have added — for this year alone — three trade missions and three interactive satellite link-ups to the trade events previously planned.

TRADE MISSIONS

Trade missions are a major element of the federal government's program of public-private cooperation. Through our network of commercial officers around the globe and staff of industry and country specialists in Washington, the U.S. Department of Commerce identifies foreign market opportunities. For these events, we arrange a full schedule of meetings in South Africa with key local officials and business people, conduct official briefings and arrange receptions hosted by the U.S. Embassy or Consulate. Practical arrangements such as visas and in-country travel are taken care of by the Department's trade events staff.

WORLDNET TELECONFERENCES

The WorldNet Teleconference format allows American business and government representatives to discuss with South African experts issues of importance for U.S. trade and investment. These one-hour programs provide for an exchange of the latest information on sector specific issues. Some programs may be re-broadcast at later dates, not only in South Africa but in nearby countries, as well.

*September Health Care Trade Mission
1995 Event Contact Person
Simon Francis
TEL: (202) 482-4071; Fax: (202) 482-4775*

*South Africa International Trade Exhibition
Oct/Nov 1996*

INFORMATION CHECKLIST AND BIBLIOGRAPHY

MAJOR TRADE/BUSINESS JOURNALS

Computer Week
Systems Publishers Pty Limited
Private Bag X8, Craighall 2196
Tel: (27 11) 789-1808
Fax: (27 11) 789-4725

Computing South Africa
Thomson's Publications
P. O. Box 56182, Pinegowrie 2123
Tel: (27 11) 789-2144
Fax: (27 11) 789-3196

The SA Association of Consulting Engineers Directory
P. O. Box 1644, Randburg 2125
Tel: (27 11) 787-5944
Fax: (27 11) 789-5264

Engineering News
Martin Creamer Publications
P. O. Box 75316, Gardenview 2047
Tel: (27 11) 622-3744
Fax: (27 11) 622-9320

South African Builder
Emdon Publishing
P O Box 1123, Pinegowrie 2123
Tel: (27 11) 886-0208
Fax: (27 11) 789-5223

Financial Mail
Times Media Publications
P O Box 9959, Johannesburg 2000
Tel: (27 11) 497-2711
Fax: (27 11) 834-1686

Finance Week
Finance Week Pty Limited
Private Bag 78816, Sandton 2146
Tel: (27 11) 444-0555
Fax: (27 11) 444-0424

Franchise Digest
Franchise Association of Southern Africa
P.O. Box 31708
Braamfontein, 2017
Tel: (27 11) 403-3468
Fax: (27 11) 403-1279

Enterprise Magazine (Black Business)
P.O. Box 91845
Auckland Park, 2006
Tel: (27 11) 483-3863
Fax: (27 11) 483-3194

Sports Trader
P.O. Box 6199
Roggebaai, 8012
Tel: (27 11) 21-7377;
Fax: (27 11) 21-7379

Chem Data
CSIR
P.O. Box 395
Pretoria, 0001
Tel: (27 12) 841-2911
Fax: (27 12) 86-2869

NEWSLETTERS AND MAGAZINES

South Africa: The Journal of Trade, Industry, & Investment ($10)
100 Avenue of the Americas,
New York, NY, 10013-1699.
Tel: 212-679-7010; Fax: 212-679-6915.

South Africa Business Review
U.S.-South Africa Business Council,
Attn: Timothy Lukens
1625 K Street, NW, Washington, DC 20006
Tel: 202-887-0278; Fax: 202-452-8160.

The African Business Handbook
21st Century Africa, Inc.
1825 I Street NW, Suite 400,
Washington, DC 20006
Tel: 202-429-9574; Fax: 202-429-9574.

Portfolio of Black Business in South Africa
WR Publications Ltd.
P.O. Box 7485, Johannesburg 2000,
South Africa
Tel: (27 11) 886-8002
Fax: (27 11) 886-9933.

Financial Mail
P.O. Box 10493, Johannesburg 2000
Tel: (27 11) 358-2072
Fax: (27 11) 726-8430.

In addition, most major accounting firms have produced booklets about "Doing Business in South Africa."

South Africa

Resources: South Korea

U.S. AND COUNTRY CONTACTS

COUNTRY GOVERNMENT AGENCIES

BOARD OF FINANCE AND ECONOMY
1 Chungang dong, Kwacheon shi,
Kyunggi do, 427 760
Securities Policy Division
Securities Bureau
Tel: 82-2-503-9252

Life Insurance Division
Insurance Bureau
Tel: 82-2-503-9255

Non Life Insurance Division
Insurance Bureau
Tel: 82-2-503-9257

Corporate Tax Division
Tax Bureau
Tel: 82-2-503-9286

International Tax Division
Tax Bureau
Tel: 82-2-504-3676

Foreign Exchange Policy Division
International Finance Bureau
Tel: 82-2-503-9262

International Finance Division
International Finance Bureau
Tel: 82-2-503-9266

Foreign Capital Management Division
Economic Cooperation Bureau
Tel: 82-2-503-9278

Foreign Investment Promotion Division
Economic Cooperation Bureau
Tel: 82-2-503-9276/7

MINISTRY OF TRADE, INDUSTRY AND ENERGY (MOTIE)
1, Chungang dong, Kwacheon shi,
Kyunggi do, 427 760

Trade Cooperation Bureau
Rm. 526
Tel: 82-2-503-9443

U.S. Division
Trade Cooperation Bureau
Rm. 525
Tel: 82-2-500-2581

Korea Industrial Property Office (KIPO)
823 1, Yoksam dong,
Kangnam ku, Seoul 135 785

International Cooperation Division
Tel: 82-2-568-6077; Fax: 82-2-553-9584

Industrial Advancement Administration (IAA)
1, Chungang dong Kwacheon shi,
Kyunggi do 427 760

MINISTRY OF NATIONAL DEFENSE
3 1, Yongsan dong, Yongsan ku,
Seoul 140 23

MINISTRY OF INFORMATION AND COMMUNICATIONS (MIC)
100 Sejong ro, Chongro ku, Seoul
Tel: 82-2-750-2001

Director General
Office of Telecommunications Policy
Tel: 82-2-750-2030; Fax: 82-2-750-2317

Information Communications Bureau
Tel: 82-2-750-2060; Fax: 82-2-750-2675

Korea Telecom (KT)
100 Sejong ro, Chongro ku, Seoul

Executive Vice President
Satellite Business Group
Tel: 82-2-458-6000 ; Fax: 82-2-458-6430

Overseas Cooperation Department
External Cooperation Planning Group
Tel: 82-2-750-3810; Fax: 82-2-750 3830

MINISTRY OF CULTURE AND SPORTS (MOCS)
82 1, Sejong ro, Chongro ku, Seoul

Copyright Division
Responsible for International Affairs
Tel: 82-2-720 3151; Fax: 82-2-733 5089

MINISTRY OF CONSTRUCTION AND TRANSPORTATION
1, Chungang dong, Kwacheon shi,
Kyunggi do

Overseas Cooperation Division
Tel: 82-2-503-7396; Fax: 82-2-503-7409

International Cooperation Division
Tel: 82-2-312-3052 Fax: 82-2-392-9809

MINISTRY OF ENVIRONMENT (MOE)
Choong-Ang 1-dong, Kwacheon,
Kyunggido

Air Quality Management Bureau
Tel: 82-2-421-0245; Fax: 82-2-421-0280

Water Quality Management Bureau
Tel: 82-2-421-0253 Fax: 82-2-421-0280

Solid Waste Management Bureau
Tel: 82-2-421 258; Fax: 82-2-421-0280

Engineering & Technology Bureau
Tel: 82-2-421 267; Fax: 82-2-421-0280

Toxic Substances Management Office
Tel: 82-2-421 259; Fax: 82-2-421-0280

International Cooperation Division
Tel: 82-2-421-0303 Fax: 82-2-421-0280

MINISTRY OF SCIENCE & TECHNOLOGY (MOST)
1 Chungang dong, Kwacheon shi,
Kyunggi do, 427 760

Information Industry & Technology Division
Tel: 82-2-503-7661; Fax: 82-2-503-7673

MINISTRY OF HEALTH AND SOCIAL AFFAIRS (MOHSA)
1, Chungang dong, Kwacheon shi,
Kyunggi do, 427 760

International Cooperation Bureau
Tel: 82-2-503-7524; Fax: 82-2-503-7568

MINISTRY OF HOME AFFAIRS (MOHA)
Unified Gov't Bldg. 77 Sejong ro,
Chongro ku, Seoul

MINISTRY OF AGRICULTURE, FORESTRY AND FISHERIES (MAFF)
1 Chungang dong, Kwacheon shi,
Kyunggi do, 427 760

Agricultural Cooperation & Trade Bureau
Rm. 408
Tel: 82-2-503-7226

Trade Cooperation Division I
Rm. 422
Tel: 82-2-503-7228

COUNTRY TRADE ASSOCIATIONS/ CHAMBERS OF COMMERCE

AMERICAN CHAMBER OF COMMERCE (AMCHAM)
Tami Overby, Executive Director
Room 301, Westin Chosun Hotel
87 Sokong dong, Chung ku
Seoul 100, Korea
Tel:82-2-752-3061,82-2-753-6471
82-2-771-0500
Fax: 82-2-755-6577

KOREAN FOREIGN TRADE ASSOCIATION (KFTA)
Rm. 4720, KOEX Bldg., 159 1, Samsung dong,
Kangnam ku, Seoul

Chairman: Koo, Pyong Hoi

Director : Park, Yang Ki
Int'l Affairs Department:

Chung, Sung Ki
Manager, America's Division
Int'l Affairs Department
Tel: 82-2-551-5301; Fax: 82-2-551-5100

Ms. Choi, Young Hee
Trade Consultant
Trade Inquiry Office
KWTC Bldg., 3rd Floor
Tel: 82-2-551-5267/9

KOREA TRADING INTERNATIONAL INC. (KOTI)
11th Fl. KWTC, 159 1, Samsung dong, Kangnam
ku, Seoul
Chae, Yong Kee
Assistant Manager
Tel: 82-2-551 3012; Fax: 82-2-551 3100

FEDERATION OF KOREAN INDUSTRIES (FKI)
28 1, Yoido dong, Yongdongpo ku,
Seoul 150 756
Chey, Jong Hyon
Chairman
Tel: 82-2-780-0821; Fax: 82-2-782-6425

KOREA CHAMBER OF COMMERCE & INDUSTRY (KCCI
45, Namdaemunro 4 ka, Chung ku,
Seoul 100 743

Kim, Sang Ha
President

Kim, Eyo Dae
Executive Director, International Affairs

KOREA CHAMBER OF COMMERCE AND INDUSTRY
Tel: 82-2-316-3523; Fax: 82-2-757-9475

Cha, Sang pil
Executive Vice President
Tel: 82-2-316-3503/4

Minn, Wan kee
Executive Director, International Department
Tel: 82-2-316-3524

KOREA FEDERATION OF SMALL BUSINESSES (KFSB)
16 2, Yoido dong, Youngdeungpo ku,
Seoul 150 010

Park, Sang Kyu
President

Lee, Byung Kyun
Vice President
Tel: 82-2-785-0892; Fax: 82-2-782-0247

Lim, Choong Kyoo
Director, International Cooperation Department
Tel: 82-2-785-0010, ext. 572; Fax: 82-2-785-0199

ASSOCIATION OF FOREIGN TRADING AGENTS OF KOREA (AFTAK)
AFTAK Bldg., 218 Hangang ro 2ka,
Yongsan ku, Seoul
Moon, Heung Yeol
Chairman

Lee, Chae Mu
Manager, Trade Promotion Dept.
Tel: 82-2-780-3377; Fax: 82-2-785-4373

KOREA PETROCHEMICAL INDUSTRY ASSOCIATION
6 Fl. Yeojun Dohae Kwan Bldg.
1 1 Yeon Ji Dong, Chongro ku, Seoul
Tel: 744-0116; Fax: 743-1887
Kim, Hyun Kwon
Deputy General Manager for General Services

KOREA COAL ASSOCIATION
Coal Center Bldg.
806, Soo Song Dong, Chongro ku, Seoul
Tel: 82-2-734-8891; Fax: 82-2-734-7959
Kim, Jae Koo, Manager, Research

KOREA PLASTIC INDUSTRY COOPERATIVE
146 2, Ssanangnim dong, Chung gu, Seoul
Tel: 82-275-7991; Fax: 82-277-5150
La, Keun Bae, Manager, Trade Promotion
Manufacturers of PE/PVC film,
PP plastic parts, FRP products.

IRON STEEL ASSOCIATION
4th Fl. Keoyang Bldg.
51 8, Soosong Dong Chongro Ku, Seoul
Tel: 82-2-732-9231; Fax: 82-2-739-1090
Kim, Sung Woo, Manager, Int'l. Cooperation

South Korea

KOREA LUMBER INDUSTRY COOPERATIVE

44 35, Yoido Dong,
Yungdeungpo Ku, Seoul 150 010
Tel: 82-2-783-0657/9; Fax: 82-2-782-5738
Chung, In Do, Chairman
Small medium size companies manufacturing/supplying flooring boards, plywood and other wood products. Also imports lumber directly for supply to local end users.

KOREA CONSTRUCTION EQUIPMENT ASSOCIATION

Daeyoung Bldg. 44 1, Yoido, Yungdeungpo ku,
Seoul 150 010
Tel: 82-2-783-4001/3; Fax: 82-2-780-4001
Lee, Sang Dal, President
Lee, Jung Shi, Technical Dept.
Introduces construction equipment technologies to the Korean market. Tests and appraises heavy construction equipment.

THE CONSTRUCTION ASSOCIATION OF KOREA

8th Fl. Kunsul Haekwan Bldg.
71 2, Nonhyun Dong, Kangnam ku,
Seoul 135 010
Tel: 82-2-547-6101/7; Fax: 82-2-542-6264
Park, Kyung Hwa, General Manager, International Cooperation
Association members are construction companies in Korea which are involved in domestic/overseas construction.

NATIONAL CONSTRUCTION RESEARCH INSTITUTE

43 87, Hwikyung Dong,
Dongdaemoon Ku, Seoul 130 090
Tel: 82-2-82-244-0801; Fax: 82-2-82-244-0951
Lee, Sun Ho, Director General
Tests and approves imported and locally manufactured pipes and building materials.

OVERSEAS CONSTRUCTION ASSOCIATION OF KOREA

11th Fl. Kukdong Bldg. 3 Ka,
Choongmu Ro, Seoul
Tel: 82-2-274-1617; Fax: 82-2-274-0742/3
So, Jae Oh, International Affairs Department

KOREA ENGINEERING SERVICES ASSOCIATION

3rd Fl. Choongang Sangho
Shinyong Kumko Bldg
61 5, Non Hyun Dong, Kang Nam Ku, Seoul
Tel: 82-2-541-1737; Fax: 82-2-543-5074
Kil, Sung Do, General Manager,
Business Promotion
Activities include recommendation of qualified members for bids.

KOREA ASSOCIATION OF MACHINERY INDUSTRY (KOAMI)

13 31 Yoido dong, Youngdongpo ku, Seoul
Tel: 82-2-369-7863; Fax: 82-2-369-7897
Chung, Kwang Hoon, General Manager for International Affairs
Covers broad range of machinery and plant, including robotics.

KOREA MACHINE TOOL MANUFACTURERS' ASSOCIATION (KOMMA)

4th Flr., Tower Crystal Building
1008 1, Daechi Dong,
Kangnam Ku, Seoul 135 280
Tel: 82-2-565-2721; Fax: 82-2-564-5639
Jin, Jong Yul, Manager
Primarily metal cutting/forming machine tools and parts, and industrial robots. Organizes biennial Seoul International Machine Tool Show (SIMTOS).

KOREA TOOLS INDUSTRY COOPERATIVE

4th Fl. Chungang Bohoun Bldg.
12 5, Yoido dong,
Yeongdongpo ku, Seoul
Tel: 82-2-780-0731; Fax: 82-2-785-2457
Sung, Bark Il, Managing Director
Focusing on hand and power tool manufacturers.

KOREA REFRIGERATION & AIR CONDITIONING INDUSTRIES ASSOCIATION

13 6, Yoido Dong
Yungdeungpo Ku, Seoul 150 010
Tel: 82-2-369-7500; Fax: 82-2-785-1195
Won, Yoon Hee, Chairman

KOREA AUTOMOBILE MANUFACTURERS ASSOCIATION (KAMA)

8th Fl. Daesang (DLI) 63 Bldg.
60, Yoido dong,
Youngdongpo ku, Seoul
Tel: 82-2-782-0534; Fax: 82-2-782-0464
Huh, Yeong Deok, Manager
Korea's seven automotive assemblers.

KOREA AUTO INDUSTRIES COOPERATIVE ASSOCIATION (KAICA)

1638 3 Seocho dong,
Seocho ku, Seoul
Tel: 82-2-587-3416; Fax: 82-2-583-7340
Kim, Seung Man, Assistant Manager, Export Promotion. *All automotive parts and accessories makers in Korea with a focus on export.*

KOREA DEFENSE INDUSTRY ASSOCIATION (KDIA)

13th Fl. Sung Woo Bldg.
51 1 Tohwa 2 dong, Mapo gu, Seoul 121 042
Tel: 82-2-716-0110; Fax: 82-2-716-1132
Jou, Young Il, Manager

KOREA MILITARY CONTRACTORS ASSOCIATION

538, Tohwa 2 dong, Mapo gu, Seoul
Tel: 82-2-715-3071
Park, Hee Tak, President

FEDERATION OF FURNITURE INDUSTRY COOPERATIVE

2nd Fl. Furniture Center Bldg.
374 2, Jangan Dong,
Tongdaemoon Ku, Seoul
Tel: 82-2-215-8838; Fax: 82-2-215-9729
Lee, Jae Sun, President
Chung, Hea Young, (Ms.) PR Dept.
Purchases raw materials and promotes joint sales of finished products for members. Sponsors the International Furniture Fair.

KOREA PAPER MANUFACTURERS' ASSOCIATION

Rm. 302, Songpa Bldg.
505, Shinsa dong, Kangnam ku, Seoul
Tel: 82-2-549-0981/6 ; Fax: 82-2-549-0980
Suh, Jung Mo, Manager, General Affairs Dept.

KOREA PRINTING CULTURAL ASSOCIATION

352 26, Sogyo Dong,
Mapo Ku, Seoul 121 210
Tel: 82-2-335-5881; Fax: 82-2-338-9801
Park, Choong Il, President
Lee Sang Jae

SPINNERS & WEAVERS ASSOCIATION OF KOREA

43 8, Kwanchol dong,
Chongno Ku, Seoul
Tel: 82-2-735-5741 Fax: 82-2-735-5748/9
Oh, Ja Bok, President

KOREA APPAREL INDUSTRIES ASSOCIATION

Rm. 801, KWTC Bldg.
159, Samsung Dong, Kangnam Ku, Seoul
Tel: 82-2-551-1456; Fax: 82-2-551-1519
Kim, Sam Sok, President
Recommends garments and knitwear for export and lobbies MOTIE on the operation of the textile quota system. Sponsors exhibitions.

KOREA BEDDING GOODS INDUSTRY COOPERATIVE
Room 1903, 159 1, Samsung Dong,
Kangnam ku, Seoul
Tel: 82-2-551-1913/7; Fax: 82-2-551-1918
Kim, Young Jun, President
Lee, Chang Joon, Manager
Manufacturers of bedding goods under the aegis of Korean Federation of Small Business (KFSB). Executes selective tenders.

KOREA SEMICONDUCTOR INDUSTRY ASSOCIATION (KSIA)
2nd Fl. Dong Il Bldg.
107, Yangjae dong, Seocho ku, Seoul
Tel: 82-2-576-3472; Fax: 82-2-577-1719
Choi, Hye Bum, General Manager. *Int'l Trade and Relations Manufacturers of Semiconductors.*

ELECTRONIC INDUSTRIES ASSOCIATION OF KOREA (EIAK)
648, Yeoksam dong, Kangnam ku, Seoul
Tel: 82-2-553-0941/7; Fax: 82-2-555-6195
Koo, Ja Hak, Chairman
Choi, Young Bum
General Manager, International
Trade & Relations
Manufacturers and traders of consumer and industrial electronics.

THE KOREA PHONOGRAM & VIDEO ASSOCIATION
Rm. 201 Wooil Bldg.
255 56, Yongdu dong, Dongdaemun ku, Seoul
Tel: 82-2-922-6612; Fax: 82-2-927-6615
Nam, Young Jin, Manager
Local sound and video recording manufacturers. Recording imports are subject to their clearance.

TELECOMMUNICATIONS TECHNOLOGY ASSOCIATION OF KOREA (TTAK)
9th Fl. Seoul Post Office Annex Bldg.
21, 1 ka, Chungmu ro, Chung ku, Seoul
Tel: 82-2-775-9101; Fax: 82-2-775-5544
Moon, Young Hwan, Chairman
Establish standards and protocols of telecom equipment, and network interfaces, int'l exchange of technical information.

KOREA TELECOMMUNICATION INDUSTRY COOPERATIVE (KTIC)
8th Fl. KCE Bldg. 16 60, 3 ka, Kankang ro,
Yongsan ku, Seoul
Tel: 82-2-711-2266; Fax: 82-2-711-2272
Kim, Chang Ju, Chairman
Producers of equipment such as PBXs, telephone sets, handsets.

KOREA TELECOMMUNICATION CONTRACTORS ASSOCIATION (KTCA)
60 Doryum dong, Chongro ku, Seoul
Tel: 82-2-739-4452; Fax: 82-2-739-4456
Shin, Hwa Soon, Chairman
Contractors for installation of telecommunications facilities.

COMPUTER AND COMMUNICATIONS PROMOTION ASSOCIATION (CCPA)
65 228, 3 ka, Hangang ro, Yongsan ku, Seoul
Tel: 82-2-796-6444; Fax: 82-2-796-6510
Chung, Jang Ho, Chairman
Information communications industry.

KOREA SOFTWARE INDUSTRY ASSOCIATION (KSIA)
Room No. 905, Local Administration Bldg.
234 2, Mapo ku, Kongduk dong, Seoul
Tel: 82-2-713-7513;   Fax: 82-2-704-3415
Kim, Young Tae, Chairman
Software developers and distributors.

THE FEDERATION OF KOREAN INFORMATION INDUSTRY
13th Fl. 28 1, Yoido dong,
Youngdongpo ku, Seoul
Tel: 82-2-780-0206; Fax: 82-2-780-1266
Kang, Hoo Don
Works in cooperation with MOST to register computer software.

THE KOREA PHARMACEUTICAL EXPORT/IMPORT ASSOCIATION
KWTC Bldg.
159 1, Samsung dong, Kangnam ku, Seoul
Tel: 82-2-551-1842; Fax: 82-2-551-1850
Park, Hoon, Manager
Traders of pharmaceutical products. Drug imports and exports are subject to their clearance.

THE KOREA PHARMACEUTICAL MANUFACTURERS ASSOCIATION
990 2, Bangbae dong, Seocho ku, Seoul
Tel: 82-2-581-2101, 82-2-581-2104
Fax: 82-2-581-2106
Kim, Jung Ho
Local pharmaceutical manufacturers.

THE KOREA MEDICAL INSTRUMENTS INDUSTRIAL COOPERATIVE
Rm. 504, Nakwon Bldg.
284 6, Nakwon dong, Chongro ku, Seoul
Tel: 82-2-764-3815, 82-2-762-3814
Fax: 82-2-744-6567
Kim, Choong Ho, Manager
Local manufacturers of medical devices. Imports and exports of medical devices require notification to this organization.

THE KOREA DENTAL ASSOCIATION
94 114, Youngdungpo dong,
Youngdungpo ku, Seoul
Tel: 82-2-635-3351; Fax: 82-2-671-3624
Choi, Dong Chul, General Manager

THE KOREA COSMETIC INDUSTRY ASSOCIATION
Keum San Bldg. 17 1, Yoido dong,
Youngdungpo ku, Seoul
Tel: 82-2-782-0948, 82-2-785-7984/85
Fax: 82-2-784-7639
Ok, Chi Kwang, Manager

KOREA SPORTING GOODS INDUSTRY COOPERATIVE
Ste. 814, Life Officetel,
61 3, Yoido Dong, Yungdeungpo Ku, Seoul
Tel: 82-2-786-7762/4; Fax: 82-2-786-7764
Shim, Young Kyu, President
Lee, Kang Hoon
Contracts to provide sporting goods, equipment and facilities to school playgrounds and gymnasiums. Co sponsor of International Sports, Leisure and Boat Show.

KOREA DEEP SEA FISHERIES ASSOCIATION
A dong, 6th Fl,
275 1, Yangjae dong, Seocho ku, Seoul
Tel: 82-2-589-1623/33; Fax: 82-2-589-1630/1
Park, Joon Hyung, President

KOREA FOODS INDUSTRY ASSOCIATION
1002 6, Bangbae dong, Seocho ku, Seoul
Tel: 82-2-585-5052/3; Fax: 82-2-586-4906
Chun, Myung Kee, President
Shin, Sung Pil, Manager
Large food manufacturing/processing companies. Research, standards making, inspection of food and additives. Affiliated with Korea Food. Est. 1969

South Korea

KOREA ALCOHOL & LIQUOR INDUSTRY ASSOCIATION

10, Yoido Dong, Yungdeungpo Ku, Seoul
Tel: 82-2-780-6663 Fax: 82-2-783-8787
Chang, Byung Soon, President
37 alcoholic beverage manufacturers holding 68 liquor licenses. Actively lobbies ONTA on tax issues of member interest. Purchases raw mateirals for manufacturers.

AIR CARGO ASSOCIATION OF KOREA

25 4, Yoido dong, Yongdungpo gu, Seoul
Tel: 82-2-784-7902 Fax: 82-2-780-7808
Kim, Tae Hong, President

KOREA SHIPPING AGENCIES ASSOCIATION

80 6, Chokson dong, Chongro gu, Seoul
Tel: 82-2-734-1531/3 Fax: 82-2-734-6200
Cha, Sung Ung, President

KOREA CUSTOMS ASSOCIATION

16 1, Hangangro 3ga, Yongsan gu, Seoul
Tel: 82-2-701-1456/9 Fax: 82-2-701-1459
Shim, Myung Koo, President

KOREA TOURIST ASSOCIATION

11Fl. Sam An Bldg. Daechi dong,
Kangnam ku, Seoul
Tel: 82-2-556-2456 Fax: 82-2-556-3818/9

Chang, Chul Hi, President
Est. 1963 as inbound/outbound industry promotion counterpart to Korea National Tourism Corpora-tion (KNTC) under MOT. 3,000 members including hotels, travel agencies, attractions, restaurants, shopping outlets. Maintain network of tourist information centers.

KOREA ASSOCIATION OF GENERAL TRAVEL AGENCY (KATA)

4th Fl. Hanil Bldg. 132 4, 1ga, Bongrae dong,
Chung gu, Seoul
Tel: 82-2-752-8692 Fax: 82-2-752-8694
Han, Myung Suk, President
Est. 1992 / 280 members

KOREA MANAGEMENT ASSOCIATION (KMA)

4th Fl. Koryo Bldg. 544, Tohwa dong,
Mapo gu, Seoul
Tel: 82-2-719-8225
Fax: 82-2-719-8978/3796/3768
Kim, Chung Yul, Vice Chairman
Est. 1962. Active in training and international exchange, also has an affiliated Consulting practice, KMAC. Agricultural Cooperatives

NATIONAL AGRICULTURAL COOPERATIVE FEDERATION (NACF)

Seodaemoon PO Box 50, Seoul
75, Choongjung ro 1 ka, Chung ku, Seoul
Tel: 82-2-737-0021/9 Fax: 82-2-737-7815
Han, Ho Sun, President

AGRICULTURAL TECHNOLOGY COOP. CO., LTD.

y15 19, Hangangro 2 ka, Yongsan ku, Seoul
Tel: 82-2-712-8121 Fax: 82-2-719-2521
Kim, Byoung Doo, President

NATIONAL FEDERATION OF FISHERIES COOPERATIVES

88, Kyungwoon dong, Chongro ku, Seoul
Tel: 82-2-730-8021 Fax: 82-2-730-8025
Lee, Bang Ho, Chairman

NATIONAL LIVESTOCK COOPERATIVE FEDERATION (NLCF)

451, Seongnai dong, Kangdong ku, Seoul
Tel: 485-3141 Fax: 475-8129
Myuing, Ui Sik, Chairman

COUNTRY MARKET RESEARCH FIRMS

ALLIANCE & RESEARCH CONSULTANTS

Dr. Kim, Chang Hwan, President
5th Floor, Genoa Bldg.
839 13, Yoksam dong, Kangnam Ku, Seoul
Tel: 82-2-558-1240 Fax: 82-2 558-5888

PACIFIC CONSULTANTS

Dr. Park, Hyun Doo, President
Room No. 5, 33rd Floor
Korea World Trade Center Bldg.
159, Samsung Dong, Kangnam Ku, Seoul
Tel: 82-2-551-3352 Fax: 82-2-551-3360

KOREA AMERICAN BUSINESS INSTITUTE

Mr. Chang, Woo Joo, President
Room No. 808, Paiknam Bldg.
188 3, Ulchi Ro 1 Ka, Chung Ku, Seoul
Tel: 82-2-753-7750 Fax: 82-2-752-6921

S. H. JANG & ASSOCIATES, INC.

Mr. Jang, Song Hyon, President
Room No. 1409, the Korea Herald Bldg.
1 12, Hoehyun Dong 3 Ka, Chung Ku, Seoul
Tel: 82-2-753 4531 Fax: 82-2-756 3635

KOREA RESEARCH CENTER LTD.

Mr. Park, Young Joon, President
4th Floor, Seo Hyun Bldg.
Seocho Dong, Seocho Ku, Seoul
Tel: 82-2-535-3130 Fax: 82-2-535-3488

ASIA MARKET INTELLIGENCE KOREA

Mr. Clive R. Boddy, President
Room No.1001, Poong Lim Bldg.
823, Yoksam dong, Kangnam Ku, Seoul
Tel: 82-2-566-3979 Fax: 82-2-566-4684

COUNTRY COMMERCIAL BANKS

CHO HUNG BANK

CPO Box 2997
Seoul 100 629
Tel: 82-2-733-2000 Fax: 82-2-732-0835

THE CITIZENS NATIONAL BANK

CPO Box 815
Seoul100 608
Tel: 82-2-754-1211 Fax: 82-2-757-3679

THE COMMERCIAL BANK OF KOREA

CPO Box 126
Seoul 100 601
Tel: 82-2-775-0050 Fax: 82-2-754-7773

HANIL BANK

CPO Box 1033
Seoul 100 610
Tel: 82-2-771-2000 Fax: 82-2-775-5628

KOREA FIRST BANK

CPO Box 2242
Seoul 100 622
Tel: 82-2-733-0070 Fax: 82-2-720-1301

U.S. EMBASSY TRADE PERSONNEL

FOREIGN COMMERCIAL SERVICE (FCS)

Jerry Mitchell, Minister Counselor for
Commercial Affairs
American Embassy
Unit #15550
APO AP 96205 0001
Tel: 82-2-397-4208 Fax: 82-2-739-1628

U.S. ASIA ENVIRONMENTAL PARTNERSHIP (USAEP)
Lee, Chi Sun, Director
Business Representative Office
Leema Building, Suite #424
146 1, Soodong dong, Chongro ku,
Seoul 110 140
Tel: 82-2-734-6558, 82-2-737-5492
Fax: 82-2-734-6559

AGRICULTURAL AFFAIRS OFFICE (AGAFF)
David Schoonover, Minister Counselor
for Agricultural Affairs
American Embassy
Unit #15550
APO AP 96205 0001
Tel: 82-2-397-4297   Fax: 82-2-738-7147

AGRICULTURAL TRADE OFFICE (ATO)
Charles Alexander, Director of U.S. Agricultural
Trade Office
Rm. 303, Leema Bldg.
146 1, Soosong dong, Chongro ku, Seoul 110 140
Tel: 82-2-397-4188   Fax: 82-2-752-5626

ECONOMIC SECTION (ECON)
Barbara Griffiths, Minister Counselor
for Economic Affairs
American Embassy
Unit #15550
APO AP 96205 0001
Tel: 82-2-397-4400 Fax: 82-2-722-1429

COUNTRY CONSULATES AND TRADE OFFICES IN THE U.S.

ALABAMA:
Kim, Eui Hoon
Rm. 714, Life Officetel Bldg.,
61 3, Yoido dong,
Youngdeungpo ku, Seoul 150 010
Tel: 82-2-780-1241/2 Fax: 82-2-780-1243

ALASKA:
Yang, Kyung Sun
Suite 2112, Kyobo Bldg.,
1, Chongro 1 ka,
Chongro ku, Seoul 110 121
Tel: 82-2-734-3381 Fax: 82-2-734-3382

COLORADO:
Jon F. Saddoris
2nd Fl., Nam Chang Bldg.,
748 16, Yeoksam dong,
Kangnam ku, Seoul 135 080
Tel: 82-2-569-7388 Fax: 82-2-553-2170

FLORIDA:
Choe, In Soo
Rm. 3206, KOEX Bldg.,
159, Samsung dong,
Kangnam ku, Seoul 135 090
Tel: 82-2-551-6543 Fax: 82-2-551-6530

FLORIDA DEPT. OF CITRUS:
Park, Jong Kook
Rm. 402, Union Bldg.,
961 3, Daechi 3 dong,
Kangnam ku, Seoul 135 283
Tel: 82-2-561-2321   Fax: 82-2-561-2322

GEORGIA:
Peter E. Bartholomew
I.R.C. Ltd.
5 23, Hyochang dong,
Yongsan ku, Seoul 140 120
Tel: 82-2-701-3222 Fax: 82-2-701-9858

IDAHO:
Chang, Woo Joo
Rm. 808, Paik Nam Bldg.,
188 3, Ulchiro 1 ka,
Chung ku, Seoul 100 641
Tel: 82-2-778-7916 Fax: 82-2-752-6921

INDIANA:
Noh, Hung Kwon
Rm. 602, Choong Moo Bldg.,
44 15, Yoido dong,
Youngdeungpo ku, Seoul 150 010
Tel: 82-2-780-0865 Fax: 82-2-786-3283

LOUISIANA:
Kim, Hyung Koo
Rm. 405, Namsong Bldg.,
260 199, Itaewon dong,
Yongsan ku, Seoul 140 200
Tel: 82-2-796 4296/8 Fax: 82-2-795 0181

MISSISSIPPI:
Choi, Seung Bong
Rm. 615, New Seoul Bldg.,
618 3, Sinsa dong,
Kangnam ku, Seoul 135 120
Tel: 82-2-548 3284/5 Fax: 82-2-548 3286

MISSOURI:
Park, Chun Hai
Rm. 4201, KOEX Bldg.,
159 1, Samsung dong,
Kangnam ku, Seoul 135 090
Tel: 82-2-551 3991 Fax: 82-2-551 3993

NEW YORK:
Dr. Kwak, Soo Il
10th Fl., Korea Federation Small Business Bldg.,
16 2, Yoidoding,
Youngdeungpo ku, Seoul 150 010
Tel: 82-2-784-2421 Fax: 82-2-784-3180

OKLAHOMA:
Kim, Jin Sook
Rm. 802, San Jung Bldg.,
15 16, Yoido dong,
Youngdeungpo ku, Seoul 150 010
Tel: 82-2-784-2225/6   Fax: 82-2-784-2256

OKLAHOMA
Song, Kil Hong
Dept. of Agriculture:
6th Fl., Samwoo Bldg.,
732 24, Yeoksam dong,
Kangnam ku, Seoul 135 080
Tel: 82-2-565-6721/5 Fax: 82-2-565-6870

OREGON:
Kim, Jin Won
Rm. 1301, Samkoo Bldg.,
70, Sokong dong,
Chung ku, Seoul 100 070
Tel: 82-2-755-1439 Fax: 82-2-753-5154

UTAH:
Lee, Jai Kap
2nd Fl., Seoyang Bldg.,
1460 1, Seocho dong,
Seocho ku, Seoul 137 070
Tel: 82-2-522-1101 Fax: 82-2-586-7900

UTAH (INVESTMENT):
Kim, In Kil
Suite 1201, Sungjee Heights
Bldg., 702 13, Yeoksam dong,
Kangnam ku, Seoul 135 080
Tel: 82-2-553-6829 Fax: 82-2-555-5230

VIRGINIA PORT AUTHORITY:
Woo, Sang Min
Rm. 1512, Kyobo Bldg.,
1, Chongro 1 ka,
Chongro ku, Seoul 110 121
Tel: 82-2-739-6248/9 Fax: 82-2-739-6538

WISCONSIN:
Dr. Kay, Bong Hyuk
Rm. 1301, Jindo Bldg.,
168 5, Dohwa dong,
Mapo ku, Seoul 121 040
Tel: 82-2-702-6222 Fax: 82-2-702-6036

DELAWARE RIVER PORT AUTHORITY:
Jack A. Dodds
Suite 706, Shinhwa Bldg.,
14 33, Yoido dong,
Youngdeungpo ku, Seoul 150 010
Tel: 82-2-783-6100/6101 Fax: 82-2-784-8545

South Korea

SEATTLE PORT AUTHORITY:
Song, Kang Hyuk
Rm. 801, Sam Song Bldg.,
184 1, Cheongjin dong,
Chongro ku, Seoul
Tel: 82-2-739-6656   Fax: 82-2-739-1703

PORT OF LOS ANGELES
T.E. Wang
Hyopsung Shipping Corp.
Rm. 905, Baek Nam Bldg.,
188 3, Ulchiro 1 ka,
Chung ku, Seoul 100 191
Tel: 82-2-752-2445   Fax: 82-2-755-0587

PORT AUTHORITY OF NY & NJ
Young K. Hah
Suite 1404, Hyoryung Bldg.,
1, Mukyo dong,
Chung ku, Seou 100 170
Tel: 82-2-775-6277   Fax: 82-2-775-6279

GUAM (GUAM VISITORS BUREAU)
Isabelle Yoon (Ms.)
5th Fl., Baeksok Bldg.,
432 3, Shindang dong,
Chung ku, Seoul 100 450
Tel: 82-2-253-0020   Fax: 82-2-253-1185

HAWAII (HAWAII VISITORS BUREAU)
Sho, Jae Phil
10th Fl., Samwon Bldg.,
112 5, Sokong dong,
Chung ku, Seoul 100 070
Tel: 82-2-757-6781/2   Fax: 82-2-757-6783

ORLANDO TOURISM OFFICE
(c/o C.J's World)
Choi, Nancy C.J. (Ms.)
Suite 902, The President Hotel,
188 3 Eulchiro 1 ka,
Chung ku, Seoul
Tel: 82-2-773-6422   Fax: 82-2-773-6442

MARKET RESEARCH AVAILABLE

INDUSTRY SUBSECTOR ANALYSES

Title	Code	Date
Dental Equipment & Supplies	DNT	12/31/94
Education in the U.S.	EDS	"
Plastic Kitchenware	HCG	"
Injection Molding Machines	PME	"
Building Machines	MTL	"
Supercomputers	CPT	"
Leather Handlings & Purses	LFP	3/31/95
Catheters	MED	"
Beer	FOD	"
Icineration Equipment	PUL	"
Pre fabricated House	BLD	"
CATV Equipment	TEL	"
Automobile & Light Truck/Van	AUT	"
Orthopedic Joint Implant	MED	6/30/95
Greeting & Postcards	GFT	"
Stock Market	FNS	"
Packaged Software	CSF	"
Hotel & Restaurant	HTL	"
Construction Service	ACE	"
Outbound Tourism	TRA	9/30/95
Artificial Interocular Lense	MED	"
Upholstery Fabric & Goods	TXF	"
Multimedia Equipment	CPT	"
Engineering Services	ACE	"
Architectural Services	ACE	"
Catering Services	GSV	"

TRADE EVENTS SCHEDULE

Trade events are held at the U.S. Trade Center, American Embassy Seoul, Fax: 822-739-1628

Date	Event
Sep. 15-19, 1995	Seoul Toy Fair
Sep. 15-19, 1995	Korea Automotive Parts and Accessories Show
Sep. 15-19, 1995	Seoul Instrument Certified Trade Fair
Oct. 1, 1995	Travel Trade Fair
Mar. 1, 1996	Study USA
Mar. 1, 1996	International Medical Equipment Show
Mar. 1, 1996	Great American Food Show
April 1, 1996	INPOCO (Environmental) Certified Trade Fair and Matchmaker Mission
April 1, 1996	Computer Software Trade Mission

Contact Heidi Hijikata, (202) 482-0569

April 1, 1996	Computers, Software and Communications Trade Fair

INFORMATION CHECKLIST AND BIBLIOGRAPHY

Bibliography of relevant country private sector and government publications

KOREAN GOVERNMENT PUBLICATIONS

The following publications are all serviceable to the non-Korean reader, if not entirely in English. See note at end of section regarding availability.

A Handbook of Korea. An encyclopedic cultural, political and economic overview. Korean Overseas Information Service, published by Seoul International Publishing House and Hollym.

Banking Supervision in Korea, Monthly, The Bank of Korea.

Classification of Foreign Trade Commodities in the Harmonized Commodity Description and Coding System (Alphabetical index to the HS), 1993, Korea Customs Research Institute.

Regulations Concerning Country of Origin and Their Explanations, 1992

Tariff Schedules of Korea (Annual)

Korean Customs In Brief, 1993, Office of Customs Administration.

Statistical Yearbook of Foreign Trade, 1993, Office of Customs Administration.

Consolidated Foreign Procurement Plan, 1993, (Annual) Office of Supply of the Republic of Korea.

Current Laws of the Republic of Korea, 1992, Korea Legislative Research Institute.

Economic Bulletin, Monthly, Economic Planning Board.

Export & Import Notice. Unofficial translation of MOTIE's trade restricted items. Occasional, Korea Foreign Trade Association.

Foreign Exchange System in Korea, May, 1993, The Bank of Korea.

IBK Trade Directory of Korean Small & Medium Enterprises. Extension Services Dept., Industrial Bank of Korea. (formerly Korea Development Bank) (No. 91 53 6 80, Not for Sale)

Investment Guide to Korea, June 1992, Occasional, policy, guidance and background. Ministry of Finance.

Foreign Capital Inducement Act Enforcement Decree and Working Rules, March, 1993

The Foreign Investment System in Korea, March, 1993, Korean economy & foreign investment climate

Regulations on Foreign Investment, March 1993 Notification No. 93 3.

Regulations on Technology Inducement, March, 1993, Notification 93 4.

Korea Economic Indicators, Quarterly, Economic Planning Board.

Korea Statistical Handbook, 1993, National Statistical Office.

Korea Statistical Yearbook, 1993, Economic Planning Board.

Korea's Policy for Trade, Industry and Energy, October 1993 Ministry of Trade, Industry and Energy (MOTIE).

Korea's Trade and Industry, 1992, Ministry of Trade, Industry and Energy (MOTIE).

Korean Potential Partners for Industrial Cooperation (Annual) Center for Foreign Investment Services. Small & Medium Industry Promotion Corporation.

Korean Taxation (Annual) Ministry of Finance.

Major Statistics of Korean Economy Comprehensive coverage of Korean official statistics. (Annual) National Statistical Office.

Monthly Statistics of Korea Economic Planning Board.

MOTIE Newsletter, Monthly, Trade Policy Division., MOTIE.

New Environment Foreign Investment in Korea, October, 1993, MOTIE.

OSROK Invitation for Bid Forms and General Contract Provisions, July, 1992, Office of Supply, Government of the Republic of Korea.

Providing a Better Environment for Doing Business in Korea, July, 1993, Economic Planning Board.

Report on Mining and Manufacturing, 1992, Annual, Economic Planning Board.

Statistical Yearbook of National Tax, 1993, Office of National Tax Administration.

Statistical Yearbook of Telecommunications, 1993, Korea Telecom.

Yearbook of Agriculture and Forestry, 1993, Ministry of Agriculture and Forestry.

Yearbook of Fisheries Statistics Office of Fisheries Administration.

Korean government publications are available from at least three sources: (1) Korean agencies will often provide a complimentary copy to visitors of those publications for which they are responsible; (2) many major book stores maintain sections where government publications can be purchased; and (3) the Korean government maintains a publications sales center near City Hall. While an English language listing of publications and prices is not available from the center, those overseas can order through the mail by writing:

Attn: Mr. Lee, Sang Keun
(Make checks payable to:)
Government Publication Center
Press Center Arcade
Citizens National Bank
25, 1 ka, Taepyung ro
Acct. #832 01 0064 412
Chung ku, Seoul 100 101
Tel: 82-2-734-6818 Fax: 82-2-734-6819

Resources: Taiwan

U.S. AND TAIWAN CONTACTS

TAIWAN AUTHORITY AGENCIES

MINISTRY OF FOREIGN AFFAIRS
2 Chiehshou Rd., Taipei
Tel: 886-2-311-9292

MINISTRY OF FINANCE
2 Aiko W. Rd., Taipei
Tel: 886-2-322-8000

MINISTRY OF ECONOMIC AFFAIRS
15 Foochow St., Taipei
Tel: 886-2-321-2200

MINISTRY OF NATIONAL DEFENSE
Chiehshou Hall Chungking S. Rd., Taipei
Tel: 886-2-311-6117

MINISTRY OF TRANSPORTATION AND COMMUNICATION
Changsha St., Sec. 1, Taipei
Tel: 886-2-349-29002

COUNCIL OF AGRICULTURE
Tel: 886-2-381-2991

MINISTRY OF THE INTERIOR
5 Hsuchow Rd. Taipei
Tel: 886-2-356-5000

TAIWAN PROVINCIAL BUREAU OF MINES
2 Chenkaiang St., Taipei
Tel: 886-2-391-7341

DEPARTMENT OF HEALTH
100 Aikuo E. Rd., Taipei
Tel: 886-2-321-0151

ENVIRONMENTAL PROTECTION ADMINISTRATION
41 Chunghwa Rd., Sec. 1, Taipei
Tel: 886-2-311-7722

MINISTRY OF EDUCATION
5 Chungshan S. Rd., Taipei
Tel: 886-2-351-3111

U.S. TRADE OFFICIALS IN TAIWAN

AMERICAN INSTITUTE IN TAIWAN, TAIPEI
#7 Lane 134, Hsin Yi Road
Section 3 Taipei, Taiwan;
Tel: 886-2-709-2000,
886-2-709-2013 (Phone, after hours)
Fax: 886-2-702-7675
Contacts: Lynn Pascoe (Director)
Lauren Moriarty (Chief, Economic Section)
William Brekke (Chief, Commercial Section)

AMERICAN TRADE CENTER, TAIPEI
Room 3207, International Trade Building,
Taipei World Trade Center,
333 Keelung Road Section 1,
Taipei 10548, Taiwan
Tel: 886-2-720-1550; Fax: 886-2-757-7162
Contact: William Brekke

AMERICAN INSTITUTE IN TAIWAN, KAOHSIUNG
5th fl., #2 Chung Cheng 3d Rd.
Kaohsiung, Taiwan
Tel: 886-7-224-0154/7; Fax: 886-7-223-8237
Contacts: Jeffrey J. Buczacki, Chief
Amy Chang, Commercial Affairs

WASHINGTON-BASED U.S. - TAIWAN CONTACTS

AMERICAN INSTITUTE IN TAIWAN, WASHINGTON, D.C.
1700 N. Moore St., Suite 1700,
Arlington, VA 22209-1996
Tel: 703-525-8474; Fax: 703-841-1385
Contacts: Natale H. Bellocchi
(Chairman and Director)
Raymond Sander
(Director of Trade and Commercial Programs)

U.S. DEPARTMENT OF COMMERCE, OFFICE OF THE CHINESE ECONOMIC AREA
14th St. and Constitution Ave., N.W.
Washington, D.C. 20230
Tel: 202-482-4681; Fax: 202-482-1576/4453
Contacts: Donald Forest (Director)
Scott Goddin (Taiwan Team Leader)
Laurette Newsom (Taiwan Officer)

TAIWAN REPRESENTATIVE AND TRADE OFFICES IN THE U.S.

TAIPEI ECONOMIC AND CULTURAL REPRESENTATIVE OFFICE (TECRO)
4301 Connecticut Ave., N.W., Suite 420
Washington, D.C. 20008
Tel: 202-686-6400; Fax: 202-363-6294
Contact: Chia-Sheng Pan
(Director, Economic Section)

CHINA EXTERNAL TRADE DEVELOPMENT COUNCIL (CETRA)
420 5th Ave.
New York, NY 10018
Tel: 212-730-4466; Fax: 212-730-4370
Contact: John Liu (Executive Director)

TRADE EVENTS SCHEDULE

Unless otherwise noted, events will be held at the American Trade Center in Taipei. For further information call:

AMERICAN TRADE CENTER
American Institute in Taiwan (AIT)
Room 3207, Taipei World Trade Center
333 Keelung Road, Section 1
Taipei, Taiwan
Tel: (886) 2-757-1550
Fax: (886) 2-757-7162

Taiwan Sponsored Trade Shows are organized by the China External Trade Development Council and held at the Taipei World Trade Center.

For further information contact:
CHINA EXTERNAL TRADE DEVELOPMENT COUNCIL
14th Floor, New York Merchandise Mart
41 Madison Avenue
New York, NY 10010

SEPTEMBER 26 - 30, 1995
TIDEX '95 (Taipei Int'l Design Exhibition)
OCTOBER, 1995
Taipei International Electronics Show
OCTOBER, 24 - 27, 1995
Taipei International Toy Show
NOVEMBER 1 - 4, 1995
Taipei International Gift
& Stationary Autumn Show
NOVEMBER 10 - 12, 1995
Taipei International Medical Equipment
& Pharmaceuticals Show
NOVEMBER 18 - 22, 1995
TAIPEI PACE ' 95 (Taipei Int'l Packaging Machinery & Materials Show)

INFORMATION CHECKLIST AND BIBLIOGRAPHY

PRIVATE SECTOR ORGANIZATIONS

AMERICAN CHAMBER OF COMMERCE IN TAIPEI
R. N. 1012, Chia Hsin Bldg. Anx
96 Chung Shan N. Rd., Sec. 2,
Taipei 104
Tel: 886-2-551-2515; Fax: 886-2-542-3376
Contact: Ms. Lynn Murry Lien

USA/ROC ECONOMIC COUNCIL
Suite 601
1726 17th Street NW
Washington, D.C. 20036
Tel: 202-331-8966; Fax: 202-331-8985
Contact: Mr. David Laux, President

PERIODICALS/NEWSPAPERS

The Commercial Times
Mr. K. H. Yung, Deputy General Manager
Business Service Department
6F, 49 Chunghwa Rd., Sec. 1, Taipei
Tel: 886-2-381-8720; Fax: 886-2-381-0659

The Economic Daily News
Business Services Department
8F, 557 Chunghsiao E. Rd., Sec. 4, Taipei
Tel: 886-2-763-7274; Fax: 886-2-764-5344
Deputy Manager: Mr. Y. L. Tsiang

Business Weekly
Advertisement Department
27F, 99 Tunhwa S. Rd., Sec. 2, Taipei
Tel: 886-2-701-8088; Fax: 886-2-708-8023
AE: Ms. Carol Cheng

Commonwealth
Advertisement Department
4F, 87 Sungkiang Rd., Taipei
Tel: 886-2-507-8627: Fax: 886-2-507-9011
Senior Sales Supervisor: Ms. Freda Wei

Excellence
Advertisement Department
5F, 531 Chungcheng Rd., Hsintien, Taipei Hsien
Tel: 886-2-218-6988; Fax: 886-2-218-6494
Manager: Ms. Sonia Chou

BOOKS

Taiwan: Beyond the Economic Miracle, Ed. by Denis F. Simon & Michael Y. Kau, M.E. Sharpe Publishers, 1992

Taiwan Business Forecaster, Ed. by Lewis B. Sckolnick, Rector Press, 1994

Taiwan Enterprises in Global Perspective, Ed. by N.T. Wang, M.E. Sharpe Publishers, 1992

Taiwan, Hong Kong and the United States, Nancy B. Tucker, Macmillan Press, 1994

Taiwan Tales: Thirteen Short Stories from Contemporary Taiwan, Ed. by Chiu-kuei wang & Chinghsi Peng, Oxford University Press, 1994

DIRECTORIES

Directory of Taiwan - Guide to Visiting, Living and Working in Taiwan. Written and published by The China News, 1993

Taiwan Business Guidebook. Ed. by Lewis B. Sckolnick, Rector Press, 1994

Taiwan Business: The Portable Encyclopedia for Doing Business with Taiwan. Christine Genzberger et al, World Trade Press, 1994

Taiwan Yellow Pages. Written and published by the Taipei World Trade Center, 1994

Trade Yellow Pages. Written and published by the Taiwan Trade Pages Corp., World Phone Limited, 1994

Taiwan (CEA)

Resources: Thailand

U.S AND COUNTRY CONTACTS

COUNTRY GOVERNMENT AGENCIES

Trade/Economy
OFFICE OF THE PERMANENT SECRETARY
Ministry of Commerce
Sanam Chai Road
Bangkok 10200
Tel: 662-221-1890;Fax: 662-226-3319
Permanent Secretary: Mr. Charae Chutharatkul

OFFICE OF THE PERMANENT SECRETARY
Ministry of Finance
Rama VI Road
Bangkok 10400
Tel: 662-273-9202; Fax: 662-273-9402
Permanent Secretary for Finance:
Dr. Aran Thammano

OFFICE OF THE NATIONAL ECONOMIC AND SOCIAL DEVELOPMENT BOARD
962 Krung Kasem Road
Bangkok 10100
Tel: 662-281-0947; Fax: 662-282-4192
Secretary-General: Dr. Sumet Tantivejkul

OFFICE OF THE BOARD OF INVESTMENT
555 Vipavadee Rangsit
Bangkhen, Bangkok 10900
Tel: 662-537-8555; Fax: 662-537-8130
Secretary-General: Mr. Staporn Kavitanon

Defense
OFFICE OF THE PERMANENT SECRETARY
Ministry of Defence
Sanamchai Road
Bangkok 10200
Tel: 662-226-3118; Fax: 662-225-5118
Permanent Secretary: General Prasert Sararithi

SECRETARIAT OF THE NATIONAL SECURITY COUNCIL (NSC)
Government House
Phitsanulok Road
Bangkok 10300
Tel: 662-281-2300; Fax: 662-280-1681
Secretary-General:
General Charan Kullavanijaya

Communications/Transportation
OFFICE OF THE PERMANENT SECRETARY
Ministry of Transport and Communications
Ratchadamnoen Nok Road
Bangkok 10100
Tel: 662-281-3111; Fax: 662-281-5666
Permanent Secretary:
Mr. Mahidol Chantrangkurn

Agriculture/Rural Affairs
OFFICE OF THE PERMANENT SECRETARY
Ministry of Interior
Atsadang Road
Bangkok 10200
Tel: 662-222-3882; Fax: 662-226-1966
Permanent Secretary for Interior:
Mr. Aree Wongsearaya

OFFICE OF THE PERMANENT SECRETARY
Ministry of Agriculture and Cooperatives
Ratchadamnoen Nok Road
Bangkok 10200
Tel: 662-281-0858; Fax: 662-281-3513
Permanent Secretary: Mr. Sommai Surakul

Energy/Natural Resources/Mining/Environment
OFFICE OF THE PERMANENT SECRETARY FOR INDUSTRY
Ministry of Industry
Rama VI Road
Bangkok 10400
Tel: 662-245-9913; Fax: 662-202-3048
Permanent Secretary: Mr. Sivavong Changkasiri

OFFICE OF THE PERMANENT SECRETARY
Ministry of Science, Technology and Environment
Rama VI Road
Phaya Thai, Bangkok 10400
Tel: 662-245-9592; Fax: 662-246-1999
Permanent Secretary: Mr. Kasem Snidvongs

NATIONAL ENERGY POLICY OFFICE (NEPO)
Office of the Prime Minister
78 Ratchadamnoen Nok Road
Dusit, Bangkok 10300
Tel: 662-282-9027; Fax: 662-280-0292
Secretary-General:
Dr. Piyasavasti Amranand

THE ELECTRICITY GENERATING AUTHORITY OF THAILAND (EGAT)
53 Charan Sanit Wong Road
Bang Kruai, Nonthaburi 11000
Tel: 662-436-3000
General Manager: Mr. Somboon Manenava

Education
MINISTRY OF EDUCATION
Wang Chan Kasem
Ratchadamnoen Nok Road
Bangkok 10300
Tel: 662-281-6350; Fax: 662-282-8566
Permanent Secretary:
Mr. Taveesak Senanarong

Health
OFFICE OF THE PERMANENT SECRETARY
Ministry of Public Health
Tivanond Road
Nonthaburi 11000
Tel: 662-591-8504; Fax: 662-591-8525
Permanent Secretary: Dr. Vitura Sangsingkeo

TRADE ASSOCIATIONS/ CHAMBERS OF COMMERCE

AMERICAN CHAMBER OF COMMERCE IN THAILAND
7th Fl., Kian Gwan Bldg.
140 Wireless Road
Bangkok 10330
Tel: 662-251-9266; Fax: 662-255-2454
Executive Director: Mr. Thomas A. Seale

BOARD OF TRADE OF THAILAND
150 Rajbopit Road
Bangkok 10200
Tel: 662-221-0555; Fax: 662-225-3995
Chairman: Mr. Photipong Lamsum

THAI CHAMBER OF COMMERCE
150 Rajbopit Road
Bangkok 10200
Tel: 662-225-0086; Fax: 662-225-3372
Chairman: Mr. Photipong Lamsum

FEDERATION OF THAI INDUSTRIES
394/14 Samsen Road
Dusit, Bangkok 10330
Tel: 662-280-0951/8; Fax: 662-280-0959
Executive Director: Dr. Chockchai Angsornnai

Trade/Economy
BOARD OF TRADE OF THAILAND (BOT)
150 Rajbopit Rd.
Bangkok 10200, Thailand
Tel: 662-221-0555, 221-1827, 222-9031, 223-2069, 221-1827; Fax: 662-225-3995, 226-5563
Telex: 84309 BOT TH
Contact: Mr. Photipong Lamsum (Chairman)

FEDERATION OF THAI INDUSTRIES
394/14 Samsen Road
Dusit, Bangkok 10330, Thailand
Tel: 662-280-0951/8; Fax: 662-280-0959
Telex: 72202 INDUSTI TH

OFFICE OF THE BOARD OF INVESTMENT (BOI)
555 Vipavadee Rungsit Rd.
Bangkok 10300, Thailand
Tel: 662-537-8111,537-8155;
Fax: 662-537-8177;
Telex: 72435 BINVEST TH
Contact: Mr. Staporn Kavitanon
(Secretary-General)

THAI CHAMBER OF COMMERCE (THE)
150 Rajbopit Rd.
Bangkok 10200, Thailand
Tel: 662-225-0086; Fax: 662-225-3372
Telex: 72093 TCCTH
Contact: Mr. Photipong Lamsum (Chairman)

For information on investing in Thailand
OFFICE OF THE ECONOMIC COUNSELOR (INVESTMENT)
Royal Thai Embassy
Five World Trade Center, Suite 3443
New York, NY 10048
Tel: 212-466-1745; Fax: 212-466-9548

For information on importing from Thailand
THAI TRADE CENTER
5 World Trade Center, Suite 3443
New York, NY 10048
Tel: 212-466-1777; Fax: 212-524-0972

THAI TRADE CENTER
245 Peachtree Center Ave., N.E.
Suite 2104, Marquis One Tower
Altanta, GA 30303
Tel: 404-659-0178; Fax: 404-577-6937

THAI TRADE CENTER
3440 Wilshire Blvd., Suite 1101
Los Angeles, CA 90010
Tel: 213-380-5943; Fax: 213-380-6476

ROYAL THAI CONSULATE-GENERAL
35 East Wacker Drive, Suite 1834
Chicago, IL 60601
Tel: 312-236-2447; Fax: 312-236-1906

ROYAL THAI CONSULATE-GENERAL
801 N. LaBrea Avenue
Los Angeles, CA 90038
Tel: 213-937-1894; Fax: 213-937-5987

ROYAL THAI CONSULATE-GENERAL
351 E. 52nd Street
New York, NY 10028
Tel: 212-754-1770; Fax: 212-754-1907

AMERICAN CHAMBER OF COMMERCE IN THAILAND (AMCHAM)
7th Floor, Kian Gwan Bldg.
140 Wireless Rd., Bangkok 10330, Thailand
Tel: 662-251-9266-7, 251-1605
Fax: 662-255-2454
Telex: 82778 KGCOM TH,
82827 TROCOT TH
Contact: Mr. Thomas A. Seale
(Executive Director)

COUNTRY MARKET RESEARCH FIRMS

AGRISOURCE
36/11-12 #21, Soi Lang Suan
Ploenchit Road, Bangkok 10330
Tel: 662-253-5858; Fax: 662-253-5858
Managing Director: Mr. Tim Welsh

THE BROOKER GROUP LTD
2nd floor, Zone D, Room 201/2
Queen Sirikit National Convention Center
60 New Rachadapisek Road
Klongtoey, Bangkok 10110, Thailand
Tel: 662-229-3111; Fax: 662-229-3127
Managing Director, Mr. George Hooker

BUSINESS ADVISORY THAILAND
2nd floor, SMC Building
285 Sukhumvit Road (near Asoke)
Bangkok 10110, Thailand
Tel: 662-253-6291-2, -6295;
Fax: 662-254-4576
President: Mr. Jon Selby

BUSINESS INTERNATIONAL DATACONSULT
Orient Research Ltd.
54 Soi Santipharp, Nares Road
Bangkok 10500
Tel: 662-236-2780, 233-5606;
Fax: 662-236-8143
Director for Indochina & Thailand:
Mr. Christopher Bruton

COOPERS & LYBRAND
8th floor, Sathorn Thani Building
90/14-16 N. Sathorn Road, Bangkok 10500
Tel: 662-236-5227-9, 236-7814;
Fax: 662-237-1201
Managing Director: Mr. A.C. Bekenn

DEEMAR CO LTD
29/5 Soi Saladaeng 1, Saladaeng Road
Bangkok 10500
Tel: 662-234-4520-1, 234-4721;
Fax: 662-236-7747
Contact: Mr. Chris Andrews

DEVELOPMENT SERVICES LTD
130/13 Soi Orapin (Soi 12)
Rama VI Road
Bangkok 10400 Thailand
Tel: 662-279-9500, 279-2913;
Fax: 662-278-3722
Managing Director: Mr. Peter E. Beal

JP ROONEY & ASSOCIATES GROUP
4th floor, Panunee Building
518/3 Ploenchit Road
PO Box 11-1238
Bangkok 10330
Tel: 662-252-0177, 251-9832
Fax: 662-251-2323, 254-7343
Contacts: James P. Rooney, Bill Dawkins

KPMG PEAT MARWICK SUTHEE
9th floor, Sathorn Thani Bldg II
92 North Sathorn Road
Bangkok 10500
Tel: 662-236-6161-4, 236-7877-8
Fax: 662-236-6165
Management Consulting Partner:
 Mr. Sa-nguan Pongswan

MIDAS AGRONOMICS CO LTD
Mekong International Development Associates
Technic Building, Room 403
48 Soi Lertbanya
Sri Ayudthaya Road, Bangkok 10400
PO Box 2-245, Bangkok 10200
Tel: 662-246-1714; Fax: 662-246-5785
President: Mr. Anthony M. Zola

**PRICE WATERHOUSE
MANAGEMENT CONSULTANTS**
4th floor, Chongkolness Building
56 Surawong Road, Bangkok 10500
Tel: 662-233-1470-5, 236-8913
Fax: 662-236-0264, 236-8913, 236-9493
General Manager: Mr. John Kelly

**SGVN-ANDERSEN
CONSULTING CO LTD**
Na Thaland Building, 514/1 Lamluang Road
Dusit, Bangkok 10300
Tel: 662-280-0900; Fax: 662-280-0855
Managing Director: Mr. M.C. Samaniego

**SPHEREX SE ASIA &
MANUFACTURING SERVICES**
P.O. Box 754, Prakanong
Bangkok 10110
Tel: 9662-322-1578; Fax: 662-322-1593
CMfgE: Mr. Ron Hensley

TARA SIAM
21st floor, CP Tower, 313 Silom Road
Bangkok 10500
Tel: 662-231-0463-4, 231-0538-40
Fax: 662-213-0465
Managing Director: Mr. John Johnstone

COUNTRY COMMERCIAL BANKS

U.S. banks with a presence in Bangkok include American Express Bank, Bank of America, Bank of New York, Bankers Trust, Chase Manhattan Bank, Chemical Bank, Citibank, Continental Bank, First Interstate Bank of California, Philadelphia National Bank, and Security Pacific Asian Bank.

All major Thai banks have correspondent relationships with U.S. banks. Thai commercial banks include: Bangkok Bank, Thai Farmers Bank, Krung Thai Bank, Siam Commercial Bank, Bank of Ayudhya, Thai Military Bank, First Bangkok City Bank, Bangkok Metropolitan Bank, Bank of Asia, Thai Danu Bank, Bangkok Bank of Commerce, Union Bank, Nakornthon Bank, Laem Thong Bank.

On March 2, 1993, the Ministry of Finance announced the granting of new offshore banking unit licenses under its Bangkok International Banking Facility (BIBF). Although promoted as a means to develop Bangkok into a regional financial center, the new facility will initially serve largely to lower the cost of foreign source lending into Thailand and to formalize the entry of many foreign banks which have been expanding their operations in recent years.

Forty-seven of 52 applicants received BIBF licenses. All four U.S. banks with existing branch licenses (Chase Manhattan, Citibank, Security Pacific Asian Bank, and Bank of America) received new BIBF licenses. Bankers Trust, American Express Bank and the Bank of New York were among those foreign banks without branches obtaining BIBF licenses. Eight Japanese banks also received licenses as did the 15 Thai domestic banks.

**BANK OF AMERICA
BANGKOK BRANCH**
2/2 Wireless Road
Bangkok 10330, Thailand
Tel: 662-251-6333; Fax: 662-253-1905
Country Manager: Mr. James McCabe

**BANK OF ASIA PUBLIC
COMPANY LTD**
191 South Sathorn Road
Khet Sathorn, Bangkok 10120
Tel: 662-287-2211/3;
Fax: 662-213-2652, 287-2973/4
President and CEO: Mr. Chulakorn Singhakowin

CHASE MANHATTAN BANK
20 North Sathorn Road, Silom
965 Rama I Road, Bangrak, Bangkok 10500
Tel: 662-234-5992/5; Fax: 662-234-8386
Country Manager: Mr. Julian Cole

CITIBANK NA
6th floor, 127 South Sathorn Road
Bangkok 10120, Thailand
Tel: 662-213-2000-7, 213-2441/2
Fax: 662-213-2527, 213-2530
Telex: 82429 CITIBK TH
General Manager: Mr. David Hendrix

KRUNG THAI BANK LTD
35 Sukhumvit Road
Bangkok 10110
Tel: 662-255-2222, 250-0861;
Fax: 662-255-9391/7
VP International: Mr. Vinai Tantramongkol

SIAM CITY BANK LTD
1101 New Petchburi Road
GPO Box 488, Bangkok 10400
Tel: 662-253-0200/9, 208-5000
Fax: 662-253-7061, 253-1240
President: Dr. Som Jatusipitak

SIAM COMMERCIAL BANK LTD
1060 New Petchburi Road
GPO Box 1644, Bangkok 10400
Tel: 662-256-1234;
Fax: 662-253-6697, 254-3359
President: Mr. Olarn Chaipravat

THAI FARMERS BANK LTD
400 Phaholyothin Road
Bangkok 10400
Tel: 662-273-1199, 270-1122
Fax: 662-270-1144, 270-1145
1st Senior Vice-President:
Mr. Thap Rungthanapirom

Banks with BIBF licenses will use Bangkok as a booking center for both "out-out" and "out-in" funding. Under out-out transactions, the banks will bring foreign currencies into Bangkok for funding in neighboring countries. In out-in transactions, the banks will bring foreign currencies into Thailand for domestic lending.

For more information about the recently established Ex-Im Bank/NationsBank bundling facility, the contact points are as follows:

BANK OF ASIA PUBLIC COMPANY LTD.
Mrs. Chitraporn Tangsuwan, Senior V.P. Corporate Banking, Bangkok
Tel: 66-2-287-2956   Fax: 66-2-213-2624

NATIONSBANK
Eileen Riach, V.P. International Trade Banking, NationsBank, Charlotte, NC
Tel: 704-386-8779   Fax: 704-386-6447

NATIONSBANK
Gregory J. Brusberg, Senior V.P. & General Manager, NationsBank, Singapore
Tel: 66-220-5755   Fax: 66-225-7513

U.S. EMBASSY TRADE PERSONNEL

U.S. AND FOREIGN COMMERCIAL SERVICE OFFICE
U.S. & F.C.S. Box 51
U.S. Embassy Bangkok
APO AP 96546
Tel: (662) 255-4365; Fax: (662) 255-2915
Commercial Counsellor: Mrs. Carol Kim
Thailand Desk Officer: Ms. Jean Kelly

Room 2034
U.S. Department of Commerce
Washington, D.C. 20230
Tel: (202) 482-3875; Fax: (202) 482-4453

FOREIGN AGRICULTURAL OFFICE
Agricultural Attache: Mr. Richard Felger
U.S. Embassy Bangkok, Box 41
APO AP 96546
Tel: (662) 252-5040
Fax: (662) 255-2907

FOREIGN AGRICULTURAL OFFICE
USDA
Washington, D.C. 20250
Tel: (202) 720-2690; Fax: (202) 720-6063
East Asian and Pacific Area Officer: Mr. Weyland Beeghly

WASHINGTON-BASED USG COUNTRY CONTACTS (NOT LISTED IN GENERAL ASEAN)

OFFICE OF THAI/BURMA AFFAIRS
Bureau of East Asia and Pacific Affairs
Room 4312
U.S. Department of State
Washington, D.C. 20520-6310
Tel: (202) 647-7108; Fax: (202) 647-6820
Assistant Director (EAP/TB):
Mr. Robert Godec

Trade/Economy
U.S. DEPARTMENT OF COMMERCE
Room 2036 Herbert Hoover Building
14th Street and Constitution Ave, NW
Washington, DC 20230
Tel: 202-482-3448; Fax: 202-482-4453
Ms. Jean Kelly

U.S. DEPARTMENT OF COMMERCE
Liaison to the World Bank
Tel: (202) 482-4332; 458-0118
Fax: (202) 477-2967
Janice Mazur

Defense
U.S. DEPARTMENT OF DEFENSE
Room 4C840
2400 Defense Pentagon
Washington, DC 20301-2400
Tel: 703-697-0555; Fax: 703-695-8222
Country Director for Thailand, Burma, Vietnam, Laos and Cambodia: Mr. Lou Stern

Communications
UNITED STATES INFORMATION AGENCY
Room 766
301 4th Street, SW
Washington, DC 20547
Tel: 202-619-5837
Contact: Ms. Bea Camp

Mining
U.S. BUREAU OF MINES
810 7th Street, NW
Washington, DC 20241
Tel: 202-501-9696; Fax: 202-219-2489
Contact: Mr. Pui-Kwan Tse

Education
U.S. DEPARTMENT OF EDUCATION
Center for International Education
Southeast Asian Studies
Washington, DC 20202-5331
202-401-9782 phone; 202-205-9489 fax
Ms. Sarah West

U.S.-BASED MULTIPLIERS RELEVANT FOR THAILAND

THE THAILAND-U.S. BUSINESS COUNCIL
3000 K Street, N.W., Suite 630
Washington, D.C. 20007
Tel: (202) 337-5973; Fax: (202) 337-0039

THE THAI-AMERICAN CHAMBER OF COMMERCE (TACC)
15 East 26th Street
New York, NY 10010-1579
Tel: (212) 532-3409; Fax: (212) 532-3384

THE U.S.-ASEAN COUNCIL
1400 L Street, N.W., Suite 375
Washington, D.C. 20005
Tel: (202) 289-1911; Fax: (202) 289-0519

THE CALIFORNIA-SOUTHEAST ASIA BUSINESS COUNCIL (CAL-SEA)
1946 Embarcadero, Suite 200
Oakland, CA 94606
Tel: (510) 536-1967; Fax: (510) 261-9598

U.S. DEPARTMENT OF COMMERCE MARKET RESEARCH AVAILABLE

Industry Subsector Analyses
Our summaries of statistics and market insights on industry subsectors. Includes key industry sector contacts, major trade associations, events, publications. $40

1993
— CNC Metal Cutting Machine Tools - Sept.
— Clean Coal Burning - February
— Coal - March
— Medical Equipments - September
— Plastic Materials & Resins - April
— Pumps - June
— Woodworking Machinery - August

1994
— Satellite Signal Receiving - January
— Cim Manufacturing - March
— Non-food Franchising - March
— Automotive Service & Diagnostic Equipment - May

— Telecommunications Equipment &
  Service - May
— Precious Jewelry Manufacturing - May
— Electro-Medial Equipment - August
— Heavy Construction Equipment - August
— Private Electric Power Production - August
— Frozen Seafood Processing - August
— Disposable Medical Products & Medical
  Supplies - September
— Motor Vehicles and Automotive
  Component Part - September 1995
— Mobile Telephones - March

TRADE EVENTS SCHEDULE

SEPTEMBER 1, 1995
*Telecommunications /Information
Technologies Matchmaker*
Thailand, Indonesia and the Philippines
Contact: Molly Costa (202) 482-0692

SEPTEMBER 18 - 28, 1995
Environmental Technologies Matchmaker
Indonesia and Thailand
Contact: Michael Slater, Dept. of Commerce
(619)557-5395

SEPTEMBER 25 -OCTOBER 3, 1995
Trading Companies Matchmaker
Singapore, Philippines, Thailand
Contact: Sepia Thompson, Dept. of Commerce
(202) 482-5131

OCTOBER 9-20, 1995
*Small and Medium-Sized Business Mission to South-
east Asia*
Manila, Philippines; Bangkok, Thailand; Jakarta,
Indonesia; Kuala Lumpur, Malaysia
Contact: Steven Patillo, U.S.-ASEAN Council
(202) 289-1911

OCTOBER 19-22, 1995
THAIBEX '95, (Building and Construction Ma-
terials, Products and Services; Queen Sirikit
National Convention Center)
 Bangkok.
Contact: Reed Tradex Co., Ltd
           Tel: 66/2/260-7103/8
           Fax: 66/2/260-7109

OCTOBER 26 - 30, 1995
Thai Metalex '95
Bangkok, Thailand
Contact: Amy Benson (202) 482-2422

OCTOBER 27-31, 1995
Thai METALEX '95, (Machine Tools; Queen
Sirikit Convention Center)
Bangkok
Contact: Reed Tradex Co., Ltd
           Tel: 66/2/260-7103/8
           Fax: 66/2/260-7109

NOVEMBER 15-18, 1995
World Didac '95
Thailand
Contact: William Corfitzen, Dept. of Commerce
(202) 482-0584

DECEMBER 12-13, 1995
*Telecommunications/Information Technologies
Matchmaker*
Thailand, Indonesia, and the Philippines
Contact: Molly Costa (202) 482-0692

FEBRUARY 1, 1996
Visit USA Travel Fair
Bangkok, Thailand
Contact: Amy Benson, Dept. of Commerce (202)
482-2422

MAY 1, 1996
Computer Software TM
Jakarta, Indonesia and Bangkok, Thailand
Contact: Heidi Hijikata, Dept. of Commerce
(202) 482-0569

JUNE 1, 1996
Royal College of Surgeons
Thailand and Singapore
Contact: George Keen (202) 482-2010

INFORMATION CHECKLIST
AND BIBLIOGRAPHY

*US&FCS Country Commercial Guide Contacts in
Thailand* Contacts to get you off to a fast start in
Thailand: business consulting, market research,
legal, accounting, financial, advertising, trade finance, temporary office, real estate, executive recruitment, venture capital firms, and more. Lists
firm, address, fax, tel, contact name & title. $15

OPERATING BUSINESS IN THAILAND

Business Location Guide Thailand Directory of
Commercial Buildings, transportation routes, and
other key aspects of business location in Bangkok.

Information Profiles on Thai Companies Prepared
by a Tara Siam Business International Ltd., sector market research firm on a "group" or "family"
basis, as looking only at an individual company
in the Thai environment may provide an incom-
plete, and potentially misleading, understanding.
Information Profiles contain details of history/
background, major share holders and decision-
makers, business activities, related/affiliated companies, recent financial institutions and firms
conducting business in Thailand. Many profiles
available, including

- Sahaviriya Group,60pp,7/90
- Siam Cement Group, 178pp, 10/91
- Siam Steel Group, 117pp, 11/91
- Metro Group, est 100pp, 12/91
- and also, CP Group, Dusit Thani Group, Hiang
Seng Fibre, Ital Thai, Loxley (Bangkok), Saha
Union, Samart Telecoms, Shinawatra Computer,
Siam City Cement, Siam Motors, Sino-Thai En-
gineering.

Thai Business Groups, 1994/95. Copyright by Tara
Siam Business International Ltd. Definitive reference work on local business families which
through their groups control much of the Thai
economy. Individual profile of 100 conglomerates in Thailand. Analysis of basic features and
characteristics of Thai business groups, role of
Overseas Chinese, military. $550

Setting up in Thailand - A Guide for Investors 1988
- $32

Thailand Business Basics, 1994. 500 plus page user-
friendly guide, prepared by Tilleke & Gibbins (law
firm) and Standard Chartered Bank. Provides
basic information to ease the investor through
the initial stages of business development in Thailand. Offers a working knowledge of major and
minor issues which could influence the future of
your business. Covers General Business Relationships, Thailand's Trade Agreements, Alien Business Permit, Land Ownership, Identification of
Suppliers, Labor Law, Corporate Taxation, Thai
Courts, Trademarks, Environmental Laws, Financial Deregulation Status, Credit Checking, Thai
Government Administration (Ministries, Departments, and State Enterprises), Special Treaties,
Looseleaf format allows easy updating - $160

Doing Business in Thailand, 1991. ed Revised and
up to date basic information on the laws and
regulations relevant to anyone doing business in
Thailand. Contains general information on Thailand, laws and regulations about work permits,
immigration, taxation, labor laws, protection of
intellectual property, etc.

Starting & Operating a Business in Thailand (1994). Copyright by McGraw-Hill Book Co. Summary of laws affecting business, and practical advice on how to comply and establish a successful business. Chapters cover general situation in Thailand, legal considerations, hiring Thai staff, starting and operating a factory, starting and operating an import/export company, getting things in and out of Thailand, starting and operating other businesses, investing in real estate, taxation, latest trends and developments. $35

Thailand Business Legal Handbook, 8th ed. (1991). Guide to Thai business laws and practices. Introduction to considerations in making investment decisions and in doing business in Thailand. Includes chapters on Institutional Background, Investment Promotion Privileges, Choice of Business Organization, Limited Companies, Partnerships, Commercial and Tax Registrations, Factories, Labor Controls on Alien Business, Immigration, Work Permits, Taxation, Banking, Financing, Securities, Exchange Controls, Stock Exchange of Thailand, Land and Condominiums, Customs, Import and Export Controls, Mining and Petroleum, Patents, Trademarks, and Copyrights, Consumer Protection and Related Legislation, Arbitration. Prepared for the Board of Investment and the Chase Manhattan Bank, revised and updated by International Legal Counsellors Thailand. Price: NA

DIRECTORIES FOR GENERAL PURPOSES

Million Baht Business Information Thailand, 1994 Leading Companies in Thailand, 1995 Published by International Business Research Thailand Co., Ltd. Ranks 274 firms with sales over 1 billion baht (about $40 million). Details on the companies (with address, tel, fax, telex, etc.) Interview with the CEO of the top firm in each sector. $120

American Chamber of Commerce in Thailand Directory, 1995 Profiles member firms - address, tel/fax, activities, background, company ownership, board of directors, senior management, affiliates, and associations. Indexed by company name, business activity, individual member. Business in Thailand section includes trends in economy, mechanics of investment, business regulations, taxation, incentives for investors. Indispensable for U.S. firms considering business in Thailand. $120

The Siam Directory 1994/95 29th ed. Published by Tawanna Publishing Group Ltd. List of firms and organizations in business, finance, health care, education, advertising, media, marketing, trade and professional associations, etc. One of the most complete Thai directories. $200

The Companies Handbook, 1995 Firms listed on the Securities Exchange of Thailand (SET), classified according to international system and types of business- banking, finance & securities, insurance, mutual funds, commerce, services (warehouse & silo firms, hotels), industrial (package, construction material & interior furnishings, automotive, textiles & clothing, mining, food & beverage, electrical equipment, others). Brief profile of listed and authorized firms, nature of shareholders, top five shareholders, executives, subsidiary and/or associated companies, auditor, share registrar, board lot, other significant detail from the fiscal financial statement and other SET statistics. $35

Thailand Investment 1994-95 - Directory of BOI Promoted Companies Published by the Board of Investment (BOI), complete guide to investing in Thailand. Explains BOI structure and role, objectives and policies, new criteria for promotional privileges, how to apply for promotional privileges, industrial parks and estates (name, titles, address, fax and tel) 2vol. $68

Thai Industrial Directory 1994-95 Copyright by Oriental Advertising & Media Co., Ltd. Manufacturers & company profiles, Guide of equipment, chemicals, materials used in industry. Industrial products and services listed under 2,090 classified headings in convenient alphabetical order (from accelerators and acetate polyvinyl to zinc oxide, zinc sulphate and zippers). 5,846 company listings include address, factory address(es), tel, factory tel, telex/fax and products and services for the firm. $40

Thailand Industrial Buyer's Guide 1994 Published by Louis Printing Co., Ltd. $110

Thailand Company Information: 1994-95 Copyright by Advance Research Group Co., Ltd. Corporate and financial information on the top 2,000 companies in Thailand. Shows latest balance sheets, liabilities and shareholders equity, statement for income and retained earnings. Also includes major shareholders, board of directors, type of business, banker(s), No. of employees, year established, address, tel, fax, telex. $80

Thailand Exporters Selected List 1994-95. Published by Royal Thai Government, Department of Export Promotion. Lists 1,462 firms by sector - agriculture; food; rubber & plastics; construction materials; furniture; leather & footwear; textile & garments; chemicals; cosmetics; medical supplies & hygiene products; machinery; tool & equipment; flowers; gift & decorative items; toys; gems & jewelry; household & kitchenware; automotive parts; accessories & other vehicles; electronics; electrical appliances & parts; printing; other products; trading companies; trade associations; commercial banks; hotels; more. $70

Thailand Import Monitor, 1991-92 Copyright by Alpha Research Co., Ltd. Detailed import statistics for years 1989-1991, by country and commodity. Includes section on exporting to Thailand, directory of importers, import service information. $60

Thailand Export Monitor, 1992-3. Copyright by Alpha Research Co., Ltd. Convenient directory of Thai exporters and details of export statistical performance. Exporters' section provides product information, directory of exporters, export service information. Export statistics section provides the year's highlights, 1988-90 statistics by product and by country. $60

Telephone Directories in English, published by Shinawatra Directories, in affiliation with AT&T) $25
Bangkok White Pages, 1995 ed. includes government office, state enterprise.
Bangkok Yellow pages, 1995 ed.

Thailand's Executives Who's Who Published by Tawanna Publishing Group Ltd. $160

Thai Chamber of Commerce Directory, 1994 Includes directory of members and associates (name, address, tel/fax); classified buyers guide; associations and information sources; conducting business in Thailand; economic and business profile of Thailand; organization and operations of Thai Chamber of Commerce. $120

Thailand in Figures, 1994-95. Published by Alpha Research Co., Ltd. Introduction, Thailand in perspective, economy, provincial statistical information. $15

DIRECTORIES FOR SPECIFIC PURPOSES

Thai Telecommunications Directory 1995 Published by Bangkok Post Publishing $40

Who's Who in the Petroleum and Petrochemical Industries of Thailand 1994-95 (with 1992 Supplement). Published by The Petroleum Institute of Thailand. Lists key contacts in Thailand's growing petroleum and petrochemical sector-p.oration companies, petroleum refineries, gas processing plants, oil & gas companies, consultants, construction, drilling firms, concessionaires, state enterprises and government agencies. Firm, address, fax and tel number, etc. If you're in the petroleum business, you need this directory. $80

Who's Who in Construction Published by A-team Advertising Co., Ltd. $55

Construction Machinery & Equipment Directory Published by A-team Advertising Co., Ltd. - $55

The Advertising Book 1994 - Thailand's advertising, marketing and media guide. Published by Thailand Advertising Marketing Media's Guide. The guide to advertising in Thailand. Covers advertising agencies; graphic art, design & photography; TV commercial product; marketing specialists and premium promotion; printing; media (publications, overseas media representatives, TV media, radio media, outdoor, cinema, transportation advertising); who's who in advertising, media, marketing; major marketers & advertisers. $30

Thailand Computer Directory, 1994/95 Published by Bangkok Post Publishing Complete reference guide to Thailand's computer industry. Includes listing for over 400 companies, over 2,000 separate listings. Also, a market overview and trends in industry developments. Published in conjunction with the 8th International Microcomputer and Telecommunications Trade Fair by the Bangkok Post. $50

Thai Automotive Industry 1994/1995 Published by Tara Siam International Business Ltd. It provides the current market structure, current perspective and assessment of future trends in this industry. Full examination of all government regulations including local parts content requirement, assembly plant control import duties, VAT and excise taxes of each vehicle are also included. Profile of top automotive business groups are embodied. $1,500

Thailand Automotive Industry Directory 1994 Published by Federation of Thai Industry. Part I is a overview of the Thai industry, with statistical data on production, imports/exports, government policy, institutions, and associations. Part II is a directory of over 300 factories assembling cars and manufacturing auto parts, lists company name, head office address, tel, fax, representative contact, nature of business, main products. Published by the Thai Auto-parts Manufacturers Association, Automotive Industry Association, Auto-parts Industry Club, and Automotive Industry Club of the Federation of Thai Industries, supported by the Thai Ministry of Industry. $85

Directory of Supporting Industries in Thailand, 1994 Published by SEAMICO Business Information & Research Co., Ltd. An invaluable resource for firms seeking subcontractors in Thailand. Contains detailed information over 1,200 companies and agencies producing parts, components, and inputs, or providing supporting services, ranging from metal-working products to electronic components and technical services. $50

MISCELLANEOUS

Vietnam Business Handbook, 1994. Over 400 pages of business information, includes chapters on: political and administrative structure, economy, agriculture and food industries, active industries (mining, oil & gas), manufacturing, travel and tourism, transport and infrastructure, foreign trade, marketing and media, money and banking, business environment, foreign investment, useful contacts. Price:NA

The Economist Guide - Southeast Asia Encyclopedia for business & travel information for Thailand, Hong Kong, Indonesia, Malaysia, Philippines, Singapore, South Korea, Taiwan. Information for each country on business practice, etiquette, professional advisors, banking and finance, importing and exporting, business framework, industry profiles, political & economic briefings. $46

Visiting & Living in Bangkok / Bangkok Guide:. A Comprehensive Guide to Living in Bangkok, Covers Thailand in Brief, Moving to Bangkok, Getting Settled, General Services and Information, Education, Health, Household, Leisure Activities, Exploring Bangkok, Excursions beyond Bangkok, Reading list. $40

Successful Living in Bangkok Written by wives of expatriate executives in Bangkok, explains how to deal with the real issues and problems of living in a culture so different. Everyday living problems of shopping, schools, getting around, support organizations, health & exercise, more. $30

Bangkok - Insight City Guide to Bangkok Conveys the true flavor of Bangkok with text and photos to recreate the city's atmosphere. History & culture, places to see, canals, markets & parks, dining out, hotels, travel tips. $27

Baedeker's Bangkok Principal sights at facts & figures, population, religion, transport; culture, commerce & industry, Thai system of government, notable personalities, history, Bangkok from A to Z, practical info, useful tel number. $38

The Balancing Act - A History of Modern Thailand Continuity versus change in Thai policies. Thailand is unique in Southeast Asia in that it "never endured direct colonial rule by Europeans." Political struggles have either had "effects too subtle to be seen, or produced abrupt and dramatic events without any lasting consequence." Examines the changing style of leadership in Thailand and the delicate equilibrium for which Thai elites strove as they tried to adapt Western political institutions to suit traditional Thai concepts of leadership and governance. $38

Catalyst for Change - Uprising in May. Bangkok Post's in-depth study of the events of May 17-20, 1992. Chronological look at the political confrontation in the streets of Bangkok, from all angles, military, government, and opposition forces. Helps you understand exactly what happened and the impact on your business. $25

U.S.-Thai Economic Relations in the 1990s; View of some members of Thailand's Economic Elite. prepared by Congressional Research Service. Surveys perceptions of a selected group of prominent Thais. Main conclusions; U.S. trade pressures are not weakening the foundation of the relationship; Japan has replaced the U.S. as Thailand's most important partner, and there is growing admiration for Japan and the teamwork, flexibility, and political savvy of its businessmen; a larger U.S. economic role would be welcomed by Thais, who hope that more U.S. companies will export to and invest in Thailand.

A Guide to Phuket In the turquoise waters of the Andaman Sea, Phuket is Thailand's most popular beach resort. Virtually unknown a few years ago, now served by an international airport and hosting some of the finest resort accommodations in the world, including Club Med. Beaches, hotels restaurants, how to get there. $35

Culture Shock! Thailand. Did you know the Thai word *ngan* means both 'work' and 'party'? This book will help you deal with culture shock in Thailand. Covers religion, Thai way of seeing, the life cycle, absorbing culture shock, do's and taboos, 1988 rev. ed. $35

Thais Mean Business - The Foreign Businessman's Guide to Doing Business in Thailand. Covers human relations aspects of business culture: customers, suppliers, employees; points out where Thais at work differ from non-Thais; helps you survive, profit from and enjoy Thai business. $40

The Best of Thailand, Gualt Millau. Famous French food writers give more than 600 reviews of restaurants, hotels, nightspots and shops. May be the best restaurant guide available about Thailand. $40

A Simple Guide to Etiquette in Thailand Pithy guide to the most important etiquette pointers in Thailand. $25

The Restaurant Guide of Thailand. Selection of some of Thailand's best restaurants in different price ranges. Covers Bangkok, Chiang Mai, Chiang Rai, Hat Yai, Hua Hin, Pattaya, Phuket. $25

BOOKS

Buddhism and Society in Southeast Asia, Donald K. Swearer

The Hinduized States of Southeast Asia, George Coedes

Readings in Thailand's Political Economy, Vichitwong Na Pombhejara

Reflections on Thai Culture, William J. Klausner

Siamese White, Maurice Collis

The Thai Peoples, Erik Seidenfaden

Thai Ways, Dennis Segaller

Thailand: Buddhist Kingdom as Modern Nation State, Charles F. Keyes

Thailand: Its People, Society and Culture, Blanchard, Wendell, et. al.

Thailand: A Short History, David K. Wyatt

Thailand and the Struggle for Southeast Asia, Newchterlein, Donald Edwin

Thailand: Society and Politics, J. Girling

VIDEOS (VHS FOR AMERICAN TV)

Thailand Asia's most exotic country in beautiful color video. Bangkok, Chiang Mai, Chinatow, Phuket, Pattaya, Kanchanaburi (Bridge over the river Kwai), floating markets, ancient cities, and more. The only way to ever rally share the experience of exotic Thailand. 60 minutes Price:NA

Bangkok Truly one of the world's most exciting cities, an amazingly complex blend of ancient and modern. Outwardly a 20th century city, with frantic life and traffic, Bangkok palaces, temples and gardens, which are uncharged from olden times. 40 minutes. Price:NA

Chiang Mai & the North

Phuket & the South

Mail order. *Simply complete order form, include your American Express credit card number, expiration date, and signature or send your US$ check on a U.S. bank made payable to American Embassy, Bangkok*

Fax Order. *You can also fax your order to us at 662-225-2915 anytime day or night. Be sure to fill out the order form completely and include your American Express credit card number, expiration date, telephone and fax number, and your signature.*

We ship orders via U.S. Mail within 24 hours of receipt. You can expect to receive your mail order in about three weeks, or your fax order in about a week to ten days.

Urgent? Give us your Federal Express Account number for faster delivery.
Price and availability of items are subject to change without notice. Prices charged will be those in effect on receipt of order.

NEWSLETTERS AND MAGAZINES

The Bangkok Post (English Language)
Published by: The Post Publishing Co., Ltd.
Bangkok Post Building
136 Na Ranong Rd.
Klong Toey, Bangkok 10100
Tel: 662-240-3700-79
662-240-3800-19 (Classified Section)
Fax: 662-240-3790-1
622-249-3830-31 (Classified Section)

The Nation (English Language)
Published by: The Nation Publishing Group Co., Ltd.
44 Moo 10 Bangna-Trat Rd.(K.M. 4.5)
Prakanong, Bangkok 10260
Tel: 662-317-0052, 317-1486
Fax: 662-317-2057

Matilchon Daily (Thai Language)
Published by: Matichon Co.
12 Thesban-maruman Road
Prachanivej 1
Bangkok 10900, Thailand
Tel: 662-589-0020; Fax: 662-589-5674

Thai Rath Daily News (Thai Language)
Published by: Thai Rath Daily
1 Vibhavadi Rangsit
Bangkok 10900, Thailand
Tel: 662-272-1030; Fax: 662-272-1342

Business in Thailand
(English Language, monthly)
Published by: Business (Thailand) Co., Ltd.
185 Sol Putta-O-Soty (Opp. GPO)New Road
Bangkok 10500, Thailand
Tel: 662-235-6046, 235-6049
Fax: 662-237-1517; Tlx: 20932 BIT TH

Business Review (English Language, bi-weekly)
Published by: B.R. Publication House Co., Ltd.
59 Sol Saengchan, Sukhumvit 42
Bangkok 10110, Thailand
Tel: 662-392-0597, 392-3002
Fax: 662-391-1486; Tlx: 20326 NATION TH

Thansettakij (Thai Language, weekly newspaper)
Published by: Thansettakij Co.
14 Thansettakij Bldg.,
Sol Kor Toey Pradipat Road,
Sapan Kwai,Bangkok 10400, Thailand
Tel: 662-270-0260/9; Fax: 662-270-1929

Resources: Turkey

U.S. AND COUNTRY CONTACTS

COUNTRY GOVERNMENT AGENCIES

Trade/Economy

DEVLET PLANLAMA TESKILATI
(State Planning Organization)
(SPO)
Iktisadi Planlama Genel Mudurlugu
(Public Sector Investments Planning Dept.)
Necatibey Caddesi No. 108
06100 Bakanliklar, Ankara, Turkey
Tel: 90-312230 8-720; Fax: 90-312-231-3498
* (Develops and administers the state's investment programs and priorities.)

HAZINE MUSTESARLIGI
Yabanci Sermaye Genel Mudurlugu
(Undersecretariat of Treasury
General Directorate of Foreign Investment)
Eskisehir Yolu, Inonu Bulvari
06510 Emek, Ankara, Turkey
Tel: 90-312-212-8800; Fax: 90-312-212-8778
* (Information on foreign investment opportunities, procedures and incentives.)

DIS TICARET MUSTESARLIGI
Ithalat Genel Mudurlugu
(Undersecretariat of Foreign Trade,
General Directorate of Imports)
Eskisehir Karayolu, Inonu Bulvari
06510 Emek, Ankara, Turkey
Tel: 90-312-212-8724; Fax: 90-312-212-8765
* (Information on Turkish import regulations and sets customs duties and surcharges on imported products)

HAZINE MUSTESARLIGI
Banka ve Kambiyo Genel Mudurlugu
(Undersecretariat of Treasury,
General Directorate of Banking and
Foreign Exchange General Directorate)
Eskisehir Karayolu, Inonu Bulvari
06510 Emek, Ankara, Turkey
Tel: 90-312-212-8871; Fax: 90-312-212-8775
* (Primary source of information on Turkey's banking regulations)

BASBAKANLIK OZELLESTIRME IDARESI BASKANLIGI
(Prime Ministry, Privatization Administration)
Huseyin Rahmi Gurpinar Cad, No 2
06680 Cankaya, Ankara, Turkey
Tel: 90-312-439-9916; Fax: 90-312-439-8477
* (Privatization of state economic enterprises.)

DEVLET ISTATISTIK ENSTITUSU
(State Institute of Statistics)
Necatibey Caddesi No. 114
06100 Ankara, Turkey
Tel: 90-312-417-6440; Fax: 90-312-418-5027
* (Responsible for all types of statistics)

TURK STANDARTLARI ENSTITUSU (TSE)
Standart Hazirlama Baskanligi
(Turkish Institute of Standards, Standards
Preparation Department)
Necatibey Caddesi No. 112
06100 Bakanliklar, Ankara, Turkey
Tel: 90-312-417-0020; Fax: 90-312-425-4399
* (Sets standards for all types of materials, products and services in Turkey)

TUBITAK TURKIYE BILIMSEL VE TEKNIK
Arastirma Kurumu (The Scientific and
Technical Research Council of Turkey)
Ataturk Bulvari No. 221
06100 Kavaklidere, Ankara, Turkey
Tel: 90-312-468-5300; Fax: 90-312-427-7489
* (Carries out research and development in positive sciences in line with the development plans)

IGEME IHRACATI GELISTIRME MERKEZI
(Export Promotion Center)
Mithatpasa Caddesi No. 60
Kizilay, Ankara, Turkey
Tel: 90-312-417-2223; Fax: 90-312-417-2233
* (Promotes Turkish exports)

Defense

MILLI SAVUNMA BAKANLIGI (MND)
Dis Tedarik Dairesi Baskanligi
(Ministry of National Defense
Foreign Procurement Department)
Mudafaa Caddesi, Bakanliklar
Ankara, Turkey
Tel: 90-312-418-9616; Fax: 90-312-417-7342

MILLI SAVUNMA BAKANLIGI
NATO Enf. Daire Baskanligi
(Ministry of National Defense
NATO Infrastructure Department)
Bakanliklar, Ankara, Turkey
Tel: 90-312-417-1466; Fax: 90-312-418-3384

SAVUNMA SANAYII MUSTESARLIGI (SSM)
(Undersecretariat for Defense Industries)
Inonu Bulvari, Kirazlidere Mevkii
Ankara, Turkey
Tel: 90-312-417-2326; Fax: 90-312-417-3266

JANDARMA GENEL KOMUTANLIGI
Ikmal Sube Mudurlugu
(Turkish Gendarmerie Command
Procurement Department)
Ankara, Turkey
Tel: 90-312-418-2371; Fax: 90-312-418-9208

EMNIYET GENEL MUDURLUGU
Tedarik Sube Mudurlugu
(General Directorate of Security Affairs,
Procurement Department)
Dikmen Yolu No. 89
Yukari Ayranci, Ankara, Turkey
Tel: 90-312-425-4832; Fax: 90-312-418-2152

PUBLIC WORKS AND HOUSING
Bayindirlik ve Iskan Bakanligi
(Ministry of Public Works and
Settlement)
Vekaletler Caddesi No. 1
Bakanliklar, Ankara, Turkey
Tel: 90-312-417-9260; Fax: 90-312-418-0406

ILLER BANKASI GENEL MUDURLUGU
(Municipalities Bank)
Ataturk Bulvari No. 21
Opera, Ulus, Ankara, Turkey
Tel: 90-312-310-3141; Fax: 90-312-312-2989
* (Financing of Municipalities' projects)

T.C. BASBAKANLIK
Guneydogu Anadolu Projesi (GAP)
(Prime Ministry Southeastern Anatolia Project)
Regional Development Administration
Ugur Mumcu Sokak 59
06700 G.O.P. Ankara, Turkey
Tel: 90-312-446-9722; Fax: 90-312-437-6777
* *(Carries out major projects for development of Southeastern Anatolia)*

**DEVLET SU ISLERI
GENEL MUDURLUGU**
(General Directorate of State Water Works)
Inonu Bulvari, 06100 Yucetepe
Ankara, Turkey
Tel: 90-312-418-3409; Fax: 90-312-418-2498
(In charge of construction of dams and hydro electric power plants.)

DEMIRYOLLARI, LIMANLAR VE HAVA
Meydanlari
(DLH) (General Directorate of
Railways,
Harbors and Airports Construction)
Ulastirma Bakanligi
Ankara, Turkey
Tel: 90-312-212-9550; Fax: 90-312-212-3847
(In charge of construction of new railways, harbors and airports.)

Communications
ULASTIRMA BAKANLIGI
(Ministry of Communications
and Transportation)
Bahcelievler Son Durak
Emek, Ankara, Turkey
Tel: 90-312-212-4632; Fax: 90-312-212-4187

**TURKIYE RADYO VE
TELEVIZYON KURUMU**
Genel Mudurlugu (TRT)
(General Directorate of Turkish Radio and
Television)
Ataturk Bulvari No. 108
06100 Kavaklidere, Ankara, Turkey
Tel: 90-312-490-4300; Fax: 90-312-490-1109

**POSTA TELGRAF TELEFON GENEL
MUDURLUGU (PTT)**
(PTT General Directorate)
Samsun Yolu
06101 Aydinliklar, Ankara, Turkey
Tel: 90-312-313-1130; Fax: 90-312-313-1153

TELSIZ GENEL MUDURLUGU
(General Directorate of Radio
Communications)
Ulastirma Bakanligi Sitesi
91 Sokak, No 5, L Blok
06510 Emek, Ankara, Turkey
Tel: 90-312-212-3800; Fax: 90-312-221-3226

Transportation
KARAYOLLARI GENEL MUDURLUGU
(General Directorate of State Highways)
06350 Yucetepe Mahallesi, Ankara, Turkey
Tel: 90-312-425-2343; Fax: 90-312-418-6996

**TURK HAVA YOLLARI GENEL
MUDURLUGU (THY)**
(General Directorate of Turkish Airlines)
Ataturk Havalimani, Yesilkoy
Istanbul, Turkey
Tel:90-212-574-7601; Fax:90-212-574-7444

**DEVLET HAVA MEYDANLARI
ISLETMESI (DHMI)**
(State Airports Administration)
Bahcelerarasi Caddesi
06330 Etiler, Ankara, Turkey
Tel: 90-312-212-2568
Fax: 90-312-222-3754
(*In charge of construction and operation of state airports)

**DEVLET DEMIRYOLLARI
GENEL MUDURLUGU (TCDD)**
(General Directorate of State Railways
Administration)
Istasyon, Ankara, Turkey
Tel: 90-312-309-0515; Fax: 90-312-312-3215

Agriculture and Rural Affairs
**TARIM, ORMAN VE
KOYISLERI BAKANLIGI**
(Ministry of Agriculture, Forestry
and Rural Affairs)
Tarimsal Uretim Gelistirme Genel Mudurlugu
(General Directorate of Agricultural
Production Development)
Milli Mudafaa Caddesi No. 20
Kizilay, Ankara, Turkey
Tel: 90-312-417-8400; Fax: 90-312-425-2016

ORMAN BAKANLIGI
(Ministry of Forestry)
Ataturk Bulvari No. 153
Bakanliklar, Ankara, Turkey
Tel: 90-312-417-6000; Fax: 90-312-418-7354

TOPRAK MAHSULLERI OFISI (TMO)
(Soil Products Office)
Milli Mudafaa Caddesi No. 18
06100 Kizilay, Ankara, Turkey
Tel: 90-312-418-4267; Fax: 90-312-417-5934

**KOY HIZMETLERI GENEL
MUDURLUGU**
(General Directorate of Rural Services)
Eskisehir Yolu 9. Km,
Ankara, Turkey
Tel: 90-312-287-3360; Fax: 90-312-287-7213

**TURKIYE ZIRAI DONATIM
KURUMU (TZDK)**
(Turkish Agricultural Supply
Department)
Fatih Caddesi No. 33
Diskapi, Ankara, Turkey
Tel: 90-312-317-0220; Fax: 90-312-347-0319

Energy and Natural Resources
ENERJI VE TABII KAYNAKLAR
Bakanligi
(Ministry of Energy and Natural
Resources)
Konya Yolu, 06100 Bestepe
Ankara, Turkey
Tel: 90-312- 213-6601; Fax: 90-312- 223-6984

Turkey

TEDAS TURKIYE ELEKTRIK DAGITIM A.S.
(30 lines)
Genel Mudurlugu)
(Turkish Electricity Distribution Co., Inc.)
Inonu Bulvari No. 27
06440 Bahcelievler
Ankara, Turkey
Tel: 90-312-212-6915; Fax: 90-312-222-9890

TEAS TURKIYE ELEKTRIK ILETIM URETIM A.S.
(30 lines)
Genel Mudurlugu
(Turkish Electricity Generation and
Transmission Co. Inc.)
Inonu Bulvari No. 27
06440 Bahcelievler
Ankara, Turkey
Tel: 90-312-212-6915; Fax: 90-312-222-9890

TURKIYE PETROLLERI ANONIM ORTAKLIGI (TPAO)
(Gen. Directorate of Turkish Petroleum Corp.)
Mustafa Kemal Mahallesi 2. Cadde No. 86
06520 Esentepe, Ankara, Turkey
Tel: 90-312- 286 9100; Fax: 90-312- 286 9000
* *(The principal activities of TPAO are exploration, drilling and production of oil, natural gas and geothermal energy)*

BOTAS BORU HATLARI ILE PETROL
Tasima
(Petroleum Pipeline Corporation)
Gunes Sokak No. 11
06690 Guvenevler
Ankara, Turkey
Tel: 90-312-427-8060; Fax: 90-312-427-6659

PETKIM PETROKIMYA HOLDING A.S.
Genel Mudurlugu (General Directorate
of Petrochemical Industries)
P.O. Box 12, 35801 Aliaga
Izmir, Turkey
Tel:90-232-616-1240; Fax:90-232-616-1248

Mining
ETIBANK GENEL MUDURLUGU
Cihan Sokak No. 2
Sihhiye, Ankara, Turkey
Tel: 90-312-229-2955; Fax: 90-312-231-0755
* *(The largest non-ferrous mining, metallurgy and banking enterprise in Turkey)*

TURKIYE DEMIR VE CELIK ISLETMELERI
Genel Mudurlugu (TDCI)
Yatirim ve Planlama Dairesi
(Turkish Iron and Steel Works, Investment
and Planning Department)
Ziya Gokalp Caddesi, Kurtulus, Ankara, Turkey
Tel: 90-312-432-3601; Fax: 90-312-434-4705

TURKIYE KOMUR ISLETMELERI KURUMU GENEL MUDURLUGU (TKI)
(General Directorate of the Turkish
Coal Enterprises)
Hipodrom Caddesi, Ulus, Ankara, Turkey
Tel: 90-312-384-1720; Fax: 90-312-384-1635
* *(Operates lignite, bituminous schist and asphaltite mines in Turkey)*

TURKIYE TASKOMURU KURUMU GENEL MUDURLUGU (TTK)
(General Directorate of the Turkish
Hard Coal Enterprises)
Zonguldak, Turkey
Tel:90-372-252-4048; Fax:90-372-251-1900
* *(Hard coal mining)*

KARADENIZ BAKIR ISLETMELERI A.S. (KBI)
(Black Sea Copper Works Co.)
Ziya Gokalp Caddesi No. 17
06100 Ankara, Turkey
Tel: 90-312-435-5400; Fax: 90-312-432-2013
* *(Mining of copper ore and copper production)*

MADEN TETKIK VE ARAMA ENSTITUSU MTA)
(Mineral Research and Exploration Institute)
Eskisehir Yolu, Balgat
Ankara, Turkey
Tel: 90-312-287-3430; Fax: 90-312-287-9188
* *(Mineral research organization)*

Health
SAGLIK BAKANLIGI (MOH)
(Ministry of Health)
Refik Saydam Institute of Health
Directorate of Environmental Health Research
06410 Sihhiye, Ankara, Turkey
Tel: 90-312-435-5680; Fax: 90-312-435-0546
* *(The directorate operates a central laboratory in environmental pollution measurement, monitoring, control and analysis in Ankara, and has a dozen smaller laboratories in other cities)*

MINISTRY OF HEALTH (MOH)
General Directorate of Basic Health Services
Environmental Health and Health Units Dept.
Mithatpasa Caddesi
06410 Sihhiye, Ankara, Turkey
Tel: 90-312-435-6440; Fax: 90-312-434-4449
* *(The department has 76 provincial directorates operating under provincial Governorates. They are responsible for issuing permits, measurement, monitoring, control and analysis of environmental pollution control)*

Environment
CEVRE BAKANLIGI (MOE)
(Ministry of Environment)
General Directorate of Environmental Impact
Assessment and Planning
and Control Air Management Department
Eskisehir Yolu 8. Km., Ankara, Turkey
Tel: 90-312-285-3283; Fax: 90-312-286-2271
* *(MOE is the regulatory agency in the environmental pollution control field)*

Education
MILLI EGITIM BAKANLIGI
(Ministry of National Education)
Bakanliklar, Ankara, Turkey
Tel: 90-312-425-5330; Fax: 90-312-417-7027

YUKSEK OGRETIM KURULU (YOK)
(Higher Education Council)
Bilkent Universitesi
Ankara, Turkey
Tel: 90-312-266-4700; Fax: 90-312-266-4759

COUNTRY TRADE ASSOCIATIONS/ CHAMBERS OF COMMERCE

DEIK DIS EKONOMIK ILISKILER KURULU
(Foreign Economic Relations Board)
Odakule, Beyoglu, Istanbul, Turkey
Tel:90 212) 243 4180; Fax:90 212) 243 4184
* *(Its mandate is to promote improved external economic relations. DEIK is an excellent source of commercial information and contacts. To this end, DEIK has promoted the establishment of bilateral business councils in addition to the Turkish American Business Council.)*

**TABA TURK AMERIKAN
ISADAMLARI DERNEGI**
(Turkish American Businessmen's Association)
Fahri Gizden Sokak No. 22/5
80280 Gayrettepe, Istanbul, Turkey
Tel:90-212-274-2824; Fax: 90-212-275-9316
* *(Its objective is to increase commercial activity between the United States and Turkey and to promote the exchange of information and joint activities. TABA has been particularly active in promoting U.S. Turkish trade with the Newly Independent States (NIS) in Central Asia, sponsoring several joint trade missions to the region.)*

TABA IZMIR
Sair Esref Bulvari No. 18/505
Altay Is Merkezi
35230 Izmir, Turkey
Tel:90-232-441-4068; Fax:90-232-441-4069
* *(Turkish American Business Association Izmir is a separate organization, independent from the TABA in Istanbul.)*

**TUSIAD TURK SANAYICILERI VE
ISADAMLARI DERNEGI**
(Turkish Industrialists' and Businessmen's Association)
Mesrutiyet Caddesi No. 74
80050 Tepebasi, Istanbul, Turkey
Tel:90-212-249-1929; Fax:90-212-249-1350
90-212-249-0913
* *(Maintains research facilities and publishes an authoritative annual report on the Turkish economy. It counts the largest industrialists in Turkey among its members.)*

**UNION OF CHANBERS OF COM-
MERCE, INDUSTRY, MARITIME
COMMERCE AND COMMODITY
EXCHANGES OF TURKEY (TOBB)**
Ataturk Bulvari No. 149
06640 Bakanliklar, Ankara, Turkey
TOBB Investment Promotion Department
same address as above
Tel: 90-312-4178667; Fax: 90-312-417-9711
Contact: Mr. Mehmet Urcu, Executive Director
(TOBB and the United States Agency for International Development (USAID) have established a new investment promotion program to assist Turkish companies seeking to form joint ventures with U.S. firms)

**ESIAD AEGEAN INDUSTRIALISTS'
AND BUSINESSMEN'S ASSOCIATION**
(TUSIAD's Izmir extension)
Cumhuriyet Meydani No. 12, Kat 6, D. 601
35210 Izmir, Turkey
Tel:90-232-463-7827; Fax: 90-232-463-7693

**YASED YABANCI SERMAYE
KOORDINASYON DERNEGI**
(Assn. for Foreign Capital Coordination)
Barbaros Bulvari, Morbasan Sokak
Koza Is Merkezi B Blok/Kat 1
80700 Besiktas, Istanbul, Turkey
Tel:90-212-272-5094; Fax:90-212-274-6664
* *(YASED works to maintain a dialogue between foreign investors and the Turkish Government on the investment environment and acts as a public relations firm advertising the positive effects of foreign investment.)*

EGE GENC ISADAMLARI DERNEGI
(Aegean Young Businessmen's Association)
Mustafa Kemal Sahil Bulvari
Levent Marina, Cakalburnu
Izmir, Turkey
Tel:90-232-278-3030; Fax: same number
* *(The association is designed to attract both foreign business to the Izmir region and to act as a clearing-house for opportunities)*

Agriculture
**TOHUMCULAR ENDUSTRISI
BIRLIGI DERNEGI**
(Seed Industry Association)
Tunali Hilmi Caddesi No. 60/11
06662 Kucukesat, Ankara, Turkey
Tel: 90-312-427-2978

YEM SANAYICILERI DERNEGI
(Food Industrialists Association)
Tuna Caddesi, Halk Sokak 20/7
Yenisehir, Ankara, Turkey
Tel: 90-312-431-1685; Fax: 90-312-431-2704

Automotive
**OTOMOBIL ITHALATCILARI
DERNEGI**
(Automobile Importers' Association)
Yenitarlabasi Caddesi
Guzel Izmir Apt. 20/3
Taksim, Istanbul, Turkey
Tel:90-212-288-6184; Fax:90-212-275-7069

OTOMOTIV SANAYII DERNEGI
(Automotive Manufacturers' Association)
Atilla Sokak No. 6
81190 Altunizade, Istanbul, Turkey
Tel:90-216-318-2994; Fax:90-216-321-9497

Advertising
REKLAMCILAR DERNEGI
(Advertising Firms' Association)
Yildiz Cicegi Sokak No. 19
80630 Etiler, Istanbul, Turkey
Tel:90-212-257-8873; Fax:90-212-257-8870

Chemicals
KIMYA SANAYICILERI DERNEGI
(Chemical Manufacturers' Association)
Yildiz Posta Caddesi
Ayyildiz Sitesi No. 28/5, 55. Blok
Esentepe, Istanbul, Turkey
Tel:90-212-266-0830; Fax:90-212-273-0898

Computers
TURKIYE BILISIM DERNEGI
(Informatics Association of Turkey)
Selanik Caddesi No. 17/4
06650 Kizilay, Ankara, Turkey
Tel: 90-312-418-4755; Fax: 90-312-425-4817

**TUBISAD BILGI ISLEM HIZMETLERI
SAN. DERNEGI**
(Informatic Services Association)
Nispetiye Mahallesi, Baslik Sokak
Mehap Apt. No. 16/4
80600 Levent, Istanbul, Turkey
Tel:90-212-268-6615; Fax:90-212-282-3998

**CONTRACTING AND
CONSTRUCTION TURKIYE
MUTEAHHITLER BIRLIGI**
(Contractors Association of Turkey)
Ahmet Mithat Efendi Sokak No. 21
96550 Cankaya, Ankara, Turkey
Tel: 90-312-439-1712; Fax: 90-312-439-4621

**TURKIYE INSAAT VE TESISAT
MUTEAHHITLERI BIRLIGI**
(Assn. of Construction Contractors of Turkey)
Ahmet Mithat Efendi Sokak 21/2
96550 Cankaya, Ankara, Turkey
Tel: 90-312-439-1712; Fax: 90-312-439-4621

**TURKIYE PREFABRIKE BETONARME
YAPI URETEN KURULUS
MENSUPLARI BIRLIGI**
(Prefabricated Concrete Construction)
Mesrutiyet Caddesi, Alibey Apt. 29/18
06420 Kizilay, Ankara, Turkey
Tel: 90-312-418-4035; Fax: 90-312-417-1970

**TOPLU KONUT
YAPIMCILARI DERNEGI**
(Mass Housing Association)
Gazeteciler Sitesi, Yazarlar Sokak 28/3
80630 Esentepe, Istanbul, Turkey
Tel:90-212-275-6695; Fax:90-212-275-6696

Turkey

Defense Industry
SASAD SAVUNMA SANAYII IMALATCILARI DERNEGI
(Defense Industries Manufacturers' Assn.)
Cankaya Caddesi 16/3
06680 Cankaya, Ankara, Turkey
Tel: 90-312-440-5566; Fax: 90-312-440-5567

Electronics
ELEKTRONIK CIHAZ IMALATCILARI DERNEGI
(Electronic Equipment Manufacturers' Assn.)
Yildiz, Barbaros Bulvari
Sahir Kesebir Sokak 34
80700 Besiktas, Istanbul, Turkey
Tel:90-212-266-0290; Fax:90-212-272-4711

ELEKTRONIK SANAYICILERI DERNEGI
(Electronic Industrialists Association)
Bagdat Caddesi No. 477/4
81070 Suadiye, Istanbul, Turkey
Tel:90-216-386-0909; Fax:90-216-386-0910

Environment and Pollution Control
CEVRE TEKNOLOJISI UYGULAYICILARI DERNEGI
(Association of Practitioners of Environmental Technology)
Irfan Bastug Caddesi, Yuva Apt. 3/10
80280 Gayrettepe, Istanbul, Ankara
Tel:90-212-272-2904; Fax:90-212-272-2904

TURKIYE'NIN TABIATINI KORUMA DERNEGI
(Association for Preservation of Turkey's Nature)
Kemeralti Caddesi, Vekilharc Sokak No. 16
Kadikoy, Istanbul, Turkey
Tel:90-216-349-6602; Fax:90-216-336-5212

Insurance
TURKIYE SIGORTA SIRKETLERI BIRLIGI
(Turkish Insurance Firms' Association)
Balmumcu, Morbasan Sokak
Koza Is Merkezi, B Blok, Kat 3
Besiktas, Istanbul, Turkey
Tel:90-212-275-8976; Fax:90-212-275-9855

MEDICAL AND HEALTH CARE TABIBLER ODASI
(Chamber of Medical Doctors)
Turkocagi Caddesi 17, Kat 3
Cagaloglu, Istanbul, Turkey
Tel:90-212-522-1911; Fax:90-212-522-7374

DIS HEKIMLERI BIRLIGI
(Turkish Dental Association)
Mesrutiyet Caddesi 32/8
Yenisehir, Ankara, Turkey
Tel: 90-312-417-7492; Fax: 90-312-417-1922

Mining and Minerals
TURKIYE MADENCILER DERNEGI
(Turkish Miners' Association)
Istiklal Caddesi No. 471/1
Beyoglu, Istanbul, Turkey
Tel:90-212-245-1503; Fax:90-212-244-8335

GENC MADENCILER DERNEGI
(Young Miners Association)
4. Levent, Cinar Sokak No. 19
80620 Besiktas, Istanbul, Turkey
Tel:90-212-264-6922; Fax:90 212-264-2996

Packaging and Packing
AMBALAJ SANAYICILERI DERNEGI
(Packaging Industrialists' Association)
Kozyatagi, Inonu Caddesi
STFA Bloklari Blok 3, Kat 8, Daire 35
81090 Kadikoy, Istanbul, Turkey
Tel:90-212-362-8155; Fax:90-212-352-8156

KARTON, AMBALAJ SANAYICILERI DERNEGI
(Carton/Paper Packaging Industrialists' Assn)
23 Temmuz Meydani No. 1, Kat 2
80300 Esentepe, Istanbul, Turkey
Tel:90-212-267-4933; Fax:90-212-267-1207

Paper and Pulp
SELULOZ VE KAGIT SANAYICILERI VAKFI
(Paper and Paper Pulp Industrialists' Foundation)
Buyukdere Caddesi No. 81
Kurgu Is Hani Kat 8, Daire 15
80300 Mecidiyekoy, Istanbul, Turkey
Tel:90-212-266-9524; Fax:90-212-266-9524

Textiles
TURKIYE GIYIM SANAYICILERI DERNEGI
(Turkish Clothing Manufacturers' Assn.)
Yildiz Posta Caddesi
Dedeman Is Hani 48/8
80700 Gayrettepe, Istanbul, Turkey
Tel:90-212-274-2525; Fax:90-212-272-4060

Travel and Tourism
TURKIYE SEYAHAT ACENTALARI DERNEGI
(Travel Agents Association of Turkey)
Cumhuriyet Caddesi No. 3
80230 Elmadag, Istanbul, Turkey
Tel:90-212-245-8950; Fax:90-212-252-3183

TURIZM YATIRIMCILARI DERNEGI
(Tourism Investors Association)
Inonu Caddesi 48, Isik Apt. Kat 3
Gumussuyu, Istanbul, Turkey
Tel:90-212-245-5545; Fax:90-212-245-6031

CHAMBERS OF COMMERCE IN THE THREE LARGEST CITIES IN TURKEY

MARITIME COMMERCE AND COMMODITY EXCHANGES OF TURKEY (TOBB)
Ataturk Bulvari No. 149
06640 Bakanliklar, Ankara, Turkey
Tel: 90-312-418-3360; Fax: 90-312-418-3268
* (TOBB acts as the main office for various chambers located in different cities.)

ANKARA CHAMBER OF COMMERCE
Sehit Tegmen Kalmaz Caddesi No. 30
06050 Ulus, Ankara, Turkey
Tel: 90-312-310-4810; Fax: 90-312-310-8436

ANKARA CHAMBER OF INDUSTRY
Ataturk Bulvari 193/4
Kavaklidere, Ankara, Turkey
Tel: 90-312-417-1200; Fax: 90-312-417-2060

ISTANBUL CHAMBER OF COMMERCE
Ragip Gumuspala Caddesi No. 84
34378 Eminonu, Istanbul, Turkey
Tel:90-212-511-4150; Fax:90-212-526-2197

ISTANBUL CHAMBER OF INDUSTRY
Mesrutiyet Caddesi 118
80050 Tepebasi, Istanbul, Turkey
Tel:90-212-252-2900; Fax:90-212-249-3963

DENIZ TICARET ODASI
(Chamber of Maritime Commerce)
Meclisi Mevusan Caddesi No. 22
80154 Sali Pazari
Istanbul, Turkey
Tel:90-212-252-0130; Fax:90-212-293-7935

IZMIR CHAMBER OF COMMERCE
Ataturk Caddesi No. 126
35210 Pasaport, Izmir, Turkey
Tel:90-232-441-7777; Fax:90-232-483-7853

AEGEAN CHAMBER OF INDUSTRY
Cumhuriyet Bulvari No. 63
Izmir, Turkey
Tel:90-232-484-4330; Fax: 90-312-483-9937

COUNTRY MARKET RESEARCH FIRMS

BS INTERNATIONAL BUSINESS SERVICES A.S.
Abdi Ipekci Caddesi, Kizilkaya Apt. 59/4
80200 Macka, Istanbul, Turkey
Tel:90-212-231-0481; Fax:90-212-231-6614

ARTHUR ANDERSEN & CO. (YALIM A.S.)
Arjantin Caddesi No. 17/6
06700 Kavaklidere, Ankara, Turkey
Tel: 90-312-468-4081; Fax: 90-312-468-4291

DENET TOUCHE ROSS BUYUKDERE CADDESI NO. 121
Ercan Han, Kat 4 6
80300 Gayrettepe, Istanbul, Turkey
Tel:90-212-275-9690; Fax:90-212-272-3323

COUNTRY COMMERCIAL BANKS

CITIBANK, N.A.
Ataturk Bulvari No. 177
06680 Kavaklidere, Ankara, Turkey
Tel: 90-312-417-5060; Fax:90-312-418-4549

KOC AMERIKAN BANK
Ataturk Bulvari, Zafer Ishani 58/1
Kizilay, Ankara, Turkey
Tel: 90-312-418-1804; Fax: 90-312-425-3237

TURKIYE IS BANKASI A.S.
Ataturk Bulvari No. 191
06680 Kavaklidere, Ankara, Turkey
Tel: 90-312-428-1140; Fax: 90-312-425-0750

YAPI VE KREDI BANKASI A.S.
Yapi Kredi Plaza A Blok
Buyukdere Caddesi
80620 Levent, Istanbul, Turkey
Tel:90-212-280-1111; Fax:90-212-280-1670

AKBANK T.A.S.
Sabanci Center, 4. Levent
80745 Istanbul, Turkey
Tel:90-212-270-3355; Fax:90-212-269-7383

T.C. ZIRAAT BANKASI
Gazi Mustafa Kemal Bulvari
Sihhiye, Ankara, Turkey
Tel: 90-312-310-3747

TURKIYE GARANTI BANKASI A.S.
Buyukdere Caddesi No. 63
80670 Maslak, Istanbul, Turkey
Tel:90-212-285-4040; Fax:90-212-286-0135

IKTISAT BANKASI T.A.S.
Buyukdere Caddesi No. 165
80496 Zincirlikuyu, Istanbul, Turkey
Tel:90-212-274-1111; Fax:90-212-274-7028

TURK TICARET BANKASI A.S.
Yildiz Posta Caddesi No. 2
80280 Gayrettepe, Istanbul, Turkey
Tel:90-212-288-5900; Fax:90-212-288-6113

TURKIYE IMAR BANKASI T.A.S.
Buyukdere Caddesi, Dogus Han No. 42 46
80290 Mecidiyekoy, Istanbul, Turkey
Tel:90-212-275-1190; Fax:90-212-272-4720

U.S. EMBASSY TRADE PERSONNEL

AMERICAN EMBASSY
Foreign Commercial Service (FCS)
Ataturk Bulvari 110
06100 Kavaklidere, Ankara, Turkey
Tel: 90-312-4670949; Fax: 90-312-467-1366
Mr. James Wilson
Commercial Counselor

Tel: 90-312-468-6110, ext. 252
Fax: 90-312-468-6138
Mr. Eugene Dorris
Economic Counselor

Tel: 90-312-468-6110, ext. 300
Fax: 90-312-467-4468
Mr. Ron Anthony
Defense Attache

AMERICAN CONSULATE
General Foreign Commercial Service (FCS)
Mesrutiyet Caddesi No. 104 108
80050 Tepebasi, Istanbul, Turkey
Tel:90-212-251-1651; Fax:90-212-2522417
Mr. John Muehlke
Commercial Consul

FOREIGN COMMERCIAL SERVICE
Izmir Office
Izmir Chamber of Commerce
Ataturk Caddesi No. 126, 5th Fl.
35210 Pasaport, Izmir, Turkey
Tel:90-232-441-2446; Fax:90-232-489-0267
Ms. Berrin Erturk
Commercial Assistant

CHIEF ODC (FORMERLY JUSMMAT)
ODC Office of Defense Cooperation, Turkey
Ismet Inonu Bulvari No. 94
Ankara, Turkey
Tel: 90-312-418 -5296; Fax: 90-312-287-9978
Major General Philip W. Nuber,
USAF

WASHINGTON-BASED USG COUNTRY CONTACTS

U.S. DEPARTMENT OF COMMERCE
Office of Western Europe, Room 3042
U.S. Department of Commerce
Washington, D.C. 20230
Tel:202-482-3945; Fax:202-482-2897
Ms. Ann Corro
Turkey Desk Officer

DEPARTMENT OF STATE
Office of Southern Europe
Desk Officer for Turkey
Room 5511
U.S. Department of State
2201 C Street NW
Washington, DC 20520
Tel:202-647-6114; Fax:202-647-5087

U.S. TRADE AND DEVELOPMENT AGENCY (TDA)
Eastern and Southern Europe
Room 309. SA 16
Washington, D.C. 20523 1602
Tel:703-875-4357; Fax:703-875-4009
Geoffrey R. Jackson
Regional Director for Central,

DEPARTMENT OF AGRICULTURE
Washington, D.C. 20250 1000
Area Officer
Tel:202-720-3080; Fax:202-720-6063

EXPORT IMPORT BANK OF THE UNITED STATES
811 Vermont Avenue, NW
Washington, D.C. 29571
Tel: 202-535-4761; Fax: 202-566-7524

Turkey

OVERSEAS PRIVATE INVESTMENT CORPORATION
1100 New York Avenue, NW
Washington, D.C. 50527
Tel:202-336-8476; Fax:202-408-9866

U.S. BASED MULTIPLIERS RELEVANT FOR COUNTRY

AMERICAN TURKISH COUNCIL (ATC)
1010 Vermont Avenue, N.W., Suite 1020
Washington, D.C. 20005 4905
Tel:202-783-0483; Fax:202-783-0511

U.S. DEPARTMENT OF COMMERCE MARKET RESEARCH AVAILABLE

INDUSTRY SUBSECTOR ANALYSES

Title	Date
— Lifting Eq.	01/92
— Mobile Communications	01/92
— Satellite Communications	03/92
— Thermal Insulation Materials	03/92
— Airport Ground Support Eq.	03/92
— Radiology Eq.	05/92
— Coking Coal	05/92
— Railway Eq.	06/92
— Textile Weaving and Knitting Machinery	07/92
— Thermal and Hydro Power Statitions	07/92
— Heavy Construction Eq.	07/92
— Computer Peripherals	08/92
— Packaging and Labelling Eq.	09/92
— Personal Computer	09/92
— Prefabricated Construction	11/92
— Fertilizers	12/92
— Mini and Mainframe Computers	12/92
— Cad/Cam Eq.	01/93
— Computerized Systems	01/93
— Fiber Optic Cable/Transmission Eq.	03/93
— Food Processing Eq.	03/93
— Oil and Gas Exploration Eq.	04/93
— Flat Steel Products	04/93
— Petrochemicals	04/93
— Water Pollution Control Eq.	06/93
— Organic Chemicals Industrial	06/93
— Commercial Kitchen Eq.	06/93
— Irrigation Eq.	07/93
— Defense Projects	08/93
— Flooring, window frames and doors	11/93
— Electro Medical Apparatus	02/94
— Air Pollution Control Eq.	02/94
— Electrical Generating Eq.	02/94
— Civil Engineering and Consulting Services	03/94
— Health/Exercise Facilities; Fitness Equipment	04/94
— Automotive Parts and Service Equipment	05/94
— Data Communications Equipment	06/94
— Defense Projects	06/94
— Chemical and Physical Analysis Equipment	07/94
— Aircraft Parts	08/94
— Sports/Leisure/Casual Apparel	09/94

ISA'S PLANNED FOR FY95

Subsector
Sector Analyst

Solid Waste Treatment Eq.
POL   Ayhan Acar

Optical Instruments
LAB   Berrin Erturk

Personal Computers
CPT   Erol Omer

Thermal and Hydro Power
Generating Equipment
ELP   Serdar Cetinkaya

Defense Projects
DFN   Meral Ishakbeyoglu

Local Area Network Equip.
CPT   Ayhan Acar

Application Software
CSF   Gulsun Bilgen / Konuray

Value Added Networks
TES   Serdar Cetinkaya

Construction Management Services
ACE   Erol Omer

Port Development
ACE   Meral Ishakbeyoglu

Electronics Industry Production/Test Eq.
EIP   Berrin Erturk

Women's Apparel
APP   Gulsun Bilgen / Konuray

FY95 FAS COMMODITY REPORTS AND MARKET BRIEFS

— Agricultural Situation
— Grain and Feed
— Oil seeds and Products
— Livestock
— Poultry
— Tree Nuts
— Dried Fruit
— Sugar
— Tobacco
— Tomatoes and Tomato Paste
— Fresh Deciduous Fruits
— Citrus

Addtional FCS reports including International Market Insights (IMI's) are available on the National Trade Data Bank or from the Turkey Desk Officer, Department of Commerce. FAS reports are available from Reports Office/USDA/FAS, Washington, DC. 20250.

TRADE EVENTS SCHEDULE

Key Trade Fair Organizers
CNR INTERNATIONAL FAIR ORGANIZATIONS & TRADE, INC.
World Trade Center
Cobancosme Kavsagi
Havaalani Karsisi
Yeslikoy 34830 Istanbul TURKEY
Tel: 90-212-663-0881
Fax: 90-212-663-0975

INTERTEKS
Mim Kemal Oke Caddesi 10
Nisantasi 80200 Istanbul TURKEY
Tel: 90-212-225-0920
Fax: 90-212-225-0933

TUYAP
Gazeteciler Mah.
Saglam Fikir Sokak 19
Esentepe 80300 Istanbul TURKEY
Tel: 90-212-211-6704
Fax: 90-212-212-3098

JANUARY
CONSTRUCTION'96
Building and construction materials, pools, paints.
INTERTEKS

ISSOS '96
Heating, air conditioning, sanitation, natural gas
and installation systems.
CNR

CS & RUBBER,
RTEKS PRO/PAK'96
aging, food processing, print technology.
TERTEKS

FEBRUARY
FOOD & BEVERAGE
INTERTEKS

HOBBY AND SPORTS FAIR
TUYAP

IMF'96-1
Fashion fair
CNR

MUSICAVISION 1996
Music, video, and television
TUYAP

SECURITY TECHNOLOGY
AND SERVICES FAIR
TUYAP

TEXTILE, KNITTING, EMBROIDERY,
AND ACCESSORIES
TUYAP

MARCH
ADVANCED MANUFACTURING
INTERTEKS

BICYCLE/MOTORCYCLE'96
INTERTEKS

BOAT SHOW'96
INTERTEKS

CHEMISTRY'96
Chemical and processing engineering
INTERTEKS

EXPODENTAL'96
TUYAP

EXPOMED'96
TUYAP

FLORIST'96
Horicultural fair
CNR

INSTRUMENTATION'96
Measurement, control, test, and automation
INTERTEKS

KITCHEN, BATH, WHITE GOODS'96
CNR

OFFICETECH/SOFTEX'96
TUYAP

TEXMAK'96
Textile machines and accessories
CNR

APRIL
BEAUTY & CARE'96
Cosmetics, perfumery and beauty care
INTERTEKS

BUKOMA'96
Office technology, automation, furniture,
and data processing
INTERTEKS

CERAMIC, KITCHEN, BATHROOM
TUYAP

HEALTHCARE'96
Hospital and medical instruments,
and apparatus
INTERTEKS

MAY
EDEXIM'96
CNR

HOUSEHOLD APPLIANCES'96
INTERTEKS

IDEAL HOME FAIR
TUYAP

JEWELERY'96
CNR

OPTICS'96
CNR

WOODWORKING MACHINERY FAIR'96
CNR

JUNE
HABITAT II
CNR

PRINT & PAPER
CNR

AUGUST
AGRO-GAP'96
Agriculltural fair
CNR

IMF'96-2
Fashion fair
CNR

KNITWEAR FASHION
TUYAP

SEPTEMBER
ESANTIYON'96
Premiums, promotional items and business gifts
CNR

FOODAWORLD
Food and food processing
CNR

IPACK'96
Packing industry
CNR

MEDICAL & HOSPITAL & DENTAL'96
CNR

PRINTING FAIR
TUYAP

OCTOBER
AUTOMOTIVE'96
Automotive components, accesories and
service equipment
CNR

BOOK FAIR
TUYAP

CLOTHING MACHINERY
AND ACCESSORIES
TUYAP

ELENEX'96
Electrical engineering and electronics
INTERTEKS

HOME TEXTILE
TUYAP

KITCHEN/BATHROOM'96
Kitchen, bathroom, and accessories
INTERTEKS

Konfek'96
Clothing Machinery
CNNR

MODEHA'96
Interior design
INTERTEKS

PROMEX'96
Incentives, gifts, and promotional products,
INTERTEKS

TATEF'96
Machine tools
CNR

Turkey

NOVEMBER

AUTO SHOW'96
Auto, motorcycle and accessories
CNR

COMMUNICATIONS'96
Communications, network, and broadcast
INTERTEKS

ENVIRONMENTAL TECHNOLOGY
INTERTEKS

HEVAC'96
Heating and air conditioning, sanitation
INTERTEKS

HOGASCO'96
Canteen, kitchens and servicing,equipment
CNR

INTELCOM'96,
Communication technology
CNR

INTERYAPI'96
Construction technology
CNR

MOTOR-SHOW'96
INTERTEKS

OFFICE DESIGN
TUYAP

WOOD MACHINERY
TUYAP

DECEMBER

BOAT SHOW'96
CNR

FAST FOOD'96
INTERTEKS

GIFT FAIR
TUYAP

*HOTEL RESTAURANT SUPPLIES
AND CATERING*
TUYAP

PLAST & PACK 1996
Packaging technology, machinery, and materials
TUYAP

INFORMATION CHECKLIST AND BIBLIOGRAPHY

Country Commercial Guide, U.S. Department of Commerce, National Technical Information Service, Springfield, VA 22151, Tel: 703-487-4726 ($27.00)

Doing Business in Turkey, Price Waterhouse & Company, P.O. Box 30004, Tampa, FL 33630, Tel: 813-287-9000 (free)

NEWSLETTERS AND MAGAZINES

DEIK Bulletin, DEIK (Foreign Economic Relations Board), Odakule Is Merkezi, Istiklal Caddesi 286, Beyoglu, Istanbul, Tel: 90-212 243-4180

Middle East Business Intelligence, International Executive Reports, 717 D street, N.W., Suite 300, Washington, DC 20004, Tel: 202-628-6900 (subscription)

Turkish Daily News, Tunus Caddesi 50-A/7, K'dere, Tel: 90-312-428-2956

STATISTICAL SOURCES

U.S. Bureau of the Census, U.S. Department of Commerce, Suitland, MD 20233, Tel: 301-763-7754

Devlet Istatistik Enstitusu (State Institute of Statistics) Barbaros Bulvari 45, Besiktas, Istanbul, Tel: 90-212 258-6626

International Financial Statistics, International Monetary Fund, 700 19th Street, N.W., Washington, DC 20036, Tel: 202-623-7430

Turkey, an International Comparison, DEIK (Foreign Economic Relations Board), Odakule Is Merkezi, Istiklal Caddesi 286, Beyoglu, Istanbul, Tel: 90-212 243-4180

OTHER INFORMATION SOURCES

American-Turkish Council, 1010 Vermont Avenue, N.W., Washington, DC 20005-4902, Tel: 202-783-0483 (extensive services for members)

Customs Duties and Taxes, U.S. Department of Commerce, Business Information Staff, 14th Street and Constitution Avenue, Washington, DC 20230, Tel: 202-482-2920

Joint-Venture Opportunities, International Executive Service Corps, P.O. Box 10005, Stamford, 06904, Tel: 203-967-6309

Turkish-American Business Association (TABA), Fahri Gizden Sokak, Gayrettepe, Istanbul, Tel: 90-212 274-2824

U.S. Firms, Subsidiaries, and Affiliates in Turkey, World Trade Academy Press, 50 East 42 Street, New York, NY 10017, Tel: 212-697-4999

National Trade Data Bank, U.S. Department of Commerce, 14th Street and Constution Avenue, N.W., Washington, DC 20230, Tel: 202-482-1986

BOOKS

Exporters' Encyclopaedia, Dun & Bradstreet, 899 Eaton Avenue, Bethlehem, PA 18025-0001, Tel: 1-800-526-0651

OECD Economic Survey, Organization for Economic Cooperation and Development, 2001 L Street, N.W., Washington, DC 20036, Tel: 202-785-6323

World Traveler Books and Maps, 400 South Elliott Road, Chapel Hill, NC 27514, Tel: 919-933-5111 (wide selection of political, tourist, and historical books and maps)